Inside the back cover:
Detailed Contents
Editing Symbols

Why do you need this new edition?

This edition of *The Little, Brown Compact Handbook with Exercises* differs from the previous edition in countless ways. Here are six that make the book indispensable:

1 More help with college reading and writing ▪ A chapter on **academic writing** explains the key academic skill of synthesizing your own and others' views as you write in response to texts and images. ▪ A chapter on **academic skills** emphasizes the habits you need to succeed in college.

2 More help with research writing ▪ Material on **finding and evaluating sources** covers all kinds of print and electronic resources and shows how to distinguish reliable and unreliable sources. ▪ A **research-paper-in-progress** on the environment follows one student's research and writing process, making it easy to see what's expected of you.

3 Up-to-date, more accessible help with citing sources ▪ Detailed explanations and highlighted examples present

the **most recent revisions of MLA, APA, and CSE documentation styles** and show how to document a wide range of print and electronic sources. A fourth style, **Chicago,** includes models for citing new media. ▪ **Annotated sample sources** show you how to find and format bibliographic information in articles, books, and Web sites.

4 New help with the writing process ▪ A **student work-in-progress** on globalization and jobs illustrates how the writing process can serve you in college work.

5 Current, more accessible help with grammar and usage ▪ Material on **text-message and e-mail shortcuts** gives tips for editing them in your academic writing. ▪ **Checklist and summary boxes** with **color highlighting** offer quick-reference help with crafting clear and correct sentences.

6 Access to *MyCompLab* ▪ *The Little, Brown Compact Handbook with Exercises* is even more useful when you combine it with *MyCompLab,* a Web gateway to resources on grammar, writing, and research developed specifically for writers.

PEARSON

PEARSON
mycomplab®

Become a better writer and researcher—and get better grades in all your courses—with *MyCompLab*!

Writing, grammar, and research help are at your fingertips as you draft and revise.

Composing. This dynamic space for composing, revising, and editing is easy to use and built to function like the most popular word-processing programs.

• Use the Writer's Toolkit to search for answers to your writing questions.
• View instructor, peer, and tutor comments on your work in one place.
• Store and manage all your work in one place.
• Access paper review help from experienced tutors through Pearson Tutor Services.

Access instruction, multimedia tutorials, and exercises in the Resources area to help you master skills and get a better grade.

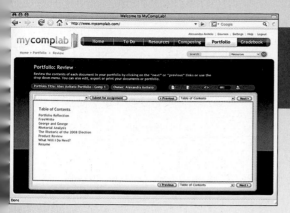

Share e-portfolios of your work with instructors, classmates, and friends.

Portfolio. With this tool, it's easy to create, publish, manage, and share your portfolio. Continue adding material through your college career and beyond!

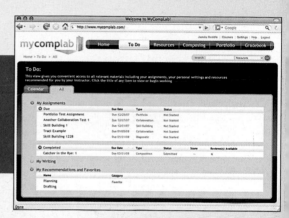

Manage all your written work and assignments online, in one easy-to-use place.

To Do. This area captures assignments and due dates from your instructor along with the personal writing you've done in *MyCompLab*.

Gradebook. This area shows writing and exercise scores. You can see how you are progressing toward a better grade!

Access an e-book version of your handbook
E-book. Access a searchable electronic version of your handbook anywhere you have an Internet connection.

Register for *MyCompLab* today!
Questions? Go to www.mycomplab.com/help.html and click "Student Support."

If this book did not come packaged with an access code to *MyCompLab*, you can purchase access online at **www.mycomplab.com/buy-access.html** or ask your bookstore to order an access card for you.

SEVENTH EDITION

The Little, Brown
Compact Handbook
WITH EXERCISES

Jane E. Aaron

Longman

New York   San Francisco   Boston
London   Toronto   Sydney   Tokyo   Singapore   Madrid
Mexico City   Munich   Paris   Cape Town   Hong Kong   Montreal

Publisher: Joseph Opiela
Senior Development Editor: Anne Brunell Ehrenworth
Senior Supplements Editor: Donna Campion
Senior Media Producer: Stefanie Liebman
Senior Marketing Manager: Susan Stoudt
Production Manager: Bob Ginsberg
Project Coordination, Text Design, and Electronic Page Makeup:
   Nesbitt Graphics, Inc.
Cover Design Manager: John Callahan
Cover Designer: Kay Petronio
Cover Photos: *(clockwise from top):* Anderson Ross/Blend Images/Getty
   Images, Inc.; Stone/Getty; David Fischer/Digital Vision/Getty Images,
   Inc.; Jamie Grill/Iconica/Getty Images, Inc.; Image Source/Getty
Photo Researcher: Rebecca Karamehmedovic
Senior Manufacturing Buyer: Roy L. Pickering, Jr.
Printer and Binder: RR Donnelley & Sons Company/Crawfordsville
Cover Printer: Lehigh-Phoenix Color Corporation

For permission to use copyrighted material, grateful acknowledgment is
made to the copyright holders on pp. 583–84, which are hereby made part of
this copyright page.

Library of Congress Cataloging-in-Publication Data

Aaron, Jane E.
   The Little, Brown compact handbook with exercises / Jane E. Aaron.—7th ed.
      p. cm.
   Includes index.
   ISBN-13: 978-0-205-65170-2
   ISBN-10: 0-205-65170-4
   1. English language—Grammar—Handbooks, manuals, etc. 2. English
language—Rhetoric—Handbooks, manuals, etc. I. Title. II. Title: Compact
handbook.
   PE1112.A23 2009
   428.2--dc22
                                    2008053730

Longman
is an imprint of

1 2 3 4 5 6 7 8 9 10—DOC—12 11 10 09
ISBN-13: 978-0-205-65170-2
ISBN-10:   0-205-65170-4
www.pearsonhighered.com

Preface for Students

The Little, Brown Compact Handbook with Exercises contains the basic information you'll need for writing in and out of school. Here you can find how to get ideas, use commas, search the Internet, cite sources, craft an argument, and write a résumé—all in a convenient, accessible package.

This book is mainly a reference for you to dip into as needs arise. You probably won't read the book all the way through, nor will you use everything it contains: you already know much of the content anyway, whether consciously or not. The trick is to figure out what you *don't* know—taking cues from your own writing experiences and the comments of others—and then to find the answers to your questions in these pages. On most topics, you'll find exercises for practice as well.

Using this book will not by itself make you a good writer; for that, you need to care about your work at every level, from finding a subject to spelling words. But learning how to use the handbook and the information in it can give you the means to write *what* you want in the *way* you want.

Reference aids

You have many ways to find what you need in the handbook:

■ **Use a directory.** The brief contents inside the front cover displays all the book's parts and chapters. The more detailed contents inside the back cover provides each chapter's subheadings as well.

■ **Use a tabbed divider.** At each tab, a detailed outline directs you to the material covered in that part of the book.

■ **Use the glossary.** The Glossary of Usage (**Gl** pp. 569–82) clarifies more than 275 words that are commonly confused and misused.

■ **Use the index.** On the book's last pages, the extensive index includes every term, concept, and problem word or expression mentioned in the book.

■ **Use a list.** Two helpful aids fall at the back of the book. First, the ⟨CULTURE LANGUAGE⟩ Guide (just before the Contents) pulls together all the material for students using standard American English as a second language or a second dialect. And the list of editing symbols (inside the back cover) explains abbreviations often used to mark papers.

■ **Use the elements of the page.** As shown in the following illustrations, each page of the handbook tells you where you are and what you can find there.

x Preface for students

The handbook's page elements

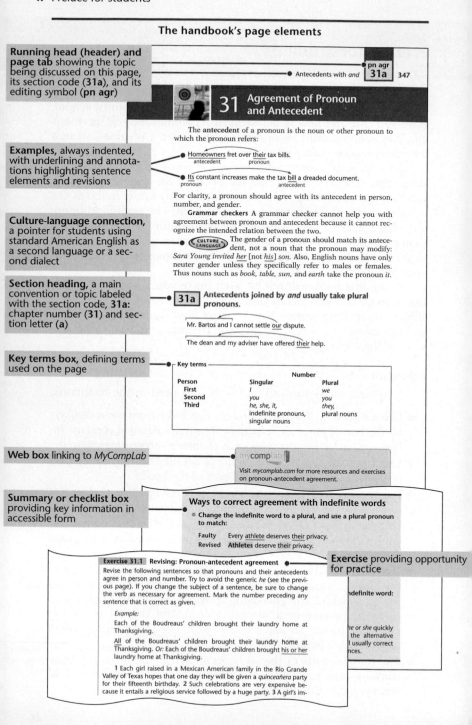

Running head (header) and page tab showing the topic being discussed on this page, its section code (**31a**), and its editing symbol (**pn agr**)

Antecedents with *and* pn agr **31a** 347

31 Agreement of Pronoun and Antecedent

The **antecedent** of a pronoun is the noun or other pronoun to which the pronoun refers:

Examples, always indented, with underlining and annotations highlighting sentence elements and revisions

Homeowners fret over their tax bills.
antecedent   pronoun

Its constant increases make the tax bill a dreaded document.
pronoun   antecedent

For clarity, a pronoun should agree with its antecedent in person, number, and gender.

Grammar checkers A grammar checker cannot help you with agreement between pronoun and antecedent because it cannot recognize the intended relation between the two.

Culture-language connection, a pointer for students using standard American English as a second language or a second dialect

CULTURE LANGUAGE The gender of a pronoun should match its antecedent, not a noun that the pronoun may modify: *Sara Young invited her* [not *his*] *son.* Also, English nouns have only neuter gender unless they specifically refer to males or females. Thus nouns such as *book, table, sun,* and *earth* take the pronoun *it*.

Section heading, a main convention or topic labeled with the section code, **31a:** chapter number (**31**) and section letter (**a**)

31a Antecedents joined by *and* usually take plural pronouns.

Mr. Bartos and I cannot settle our dispute.

The dean and my adviser have offered their help.

Key terms box, defining terms used on the page

Key terms

	Number	
Person	Singular	Plural
First	*I*	*we*
Second	*you*	*you*
Third	*he, she, it,*	*they,*
	indefinite pronouns,	plural nouns
	singular nouns	

Web box linking to *MyCompLab*

mycomplab

Visit *mycomplab.com* for more resources and exercises on pronoun-antecedent agreement.

Summary or checklist box providing key information in accessible form

Ways to correct agreement with indefinite words

■ Change the indefinite word to a plural, and use a plural pronoun to match:

Faulty   Every **athlete** deserves their privacy.
Revised **Athletes** deserve their privacy.

Exercise providing opportunity for practice

Exercise 31.1 Revising: Pronoun-antecedent agreement

Revise the following sentences so that pronouns and their antecedents agree in person and number. Try to avoid the generic *he* (see the previous page). If you change the subject of a sentence, be sure to change the verb as necessary for agreement. Mark the number preceding any sentence that is correct as given.

Example:

Each of the Boudreaus' children brought their laundry home at Thanksgiving.

All of the Boudreaus' children brought their laundry home at Thanksgiving. *Or:* Each of the Boudreaus' children brought his or her laundry home at Thanksgiving.

1 Each girl raised in a Mexican American family in the Rio Grande Valley of Texas hopes that one day they will be given a *quinceañera* party for their fifteenth birthday. 2 Such celebrations are very expensive because it entails a religious service followed by a huge party. 3 A girl's im-

Preface for Instructors

The Little, Brown Compact Handbook with Exercises provides writers with an accessible reference, one that helps them find what they need and then use what they find. Combining the authority of its parent, *The Little, Brown Handbook*, with a briefer and more convenient format, the *Compact Handbook* addresses writers of varying experience, in varying fields, answering common questions about the writing process, grammar and style, research writing, and more.

This new edition improves on the handbook's strengths as a clear, concise, and accessible reference, while keeping pace with rapid changes in writing and its teaching. In the context of the handbook's many reference functions, the following pages highlight as **New** the most significant additions and changes.

A reference for academic writing

The handbook gives students a solid foundation in the goals and requirements of college writing.

- **New** A reorganized Part 2 ("Writing in and out of College") proceeds through a chapter each on academic skills in general, critical thinking and reading, academic writing, argument, online writing, oral presentations, and public writing.
- **New** The revised chapter on academic skills emphasizes taking notes, reading for comprehension, the basics of academic writing, and preparing for exams.
- **New** The reconceived chapter on academic writing shows students how to write in response to texts.
- **New** Synthesis receives special emphasis wherever students might need help balancing their own and others' views, such as in responding to texts.
- **New** Expanded advice on avoiding plagiarism shows students at every turn how to acknowledge borrowed material.
- **New** A greater stress on opposing views in argument includes discussion of Rogerian approaches.
- Parts 7 and 8 give students a solid foundation in research writing, writing about literature, and writing in other humanities, the social sciences, and the natural and applied sciences. Extensive, specially tabbed sections cover documentation and format in MLA, APA, Chicago, and CSE styles.

A reference for research writing

With detailed advice and a sample MLA paper, the handbook always attends closely to research writing. The discussion stresses using the library as Web gateway, managing information, evaluating and synthesizing sources, integrating source material, and avoiding plagiarism.

- **New** A research-paper-in-progress on green consumerism follows a student through the research process and culminates in an annotated paper documented in MLA style.
- **New** An expanded discussion of evaluating sources illustrates critical criteria with sample articles and Web documents.
- **New** Many kinds of electronic resources—including blogs, wikis, and multimedia as well as Web documents—receive attention as possible sources that require careful evaluation and documentation.
- **New** The advice for generating primary sources now covers conducting observations and surveys.
- **New** Updated source lists in Part 8 provide reliable starting points for research in every discipline.

A reference for documenting sources

The extensive coverage of documentation in four styles—MLA, APA, Chicago, and CSE—reflects each style's latest version and includes many examples of electronic sources.

- **New** MLA style is expanded and completely updated to reflect the 2008 *MLA Style Manual and Guide to Scholarly Publishing,* Third Edition.
- **New** APA style is updated to reflect the 2007 supplement *APA Style Guide to Electronic References*.
- **New** CSE style is updated to reflect the 2006 *Scientific Style and Format: The CSE Manual for Authors, Editors, and Publishers,* Seventh Edition.
- **New** Annotated samples of key source types accompany MLA and APA documentation, showing students how to find the bibliographical information needed to cite each type.
- **New** For all styles, color highlighting makes authors, titles, dates, and other citation elements easy to grasp.

A reference for the writing process

The handbook takes a practical approach to assessing the writing situation, generating ideas, developing the thesis statement, revising, and other elements of the writing process.

- **New** A student's work-in-progress on globalization and out-sourcing illustrates the stages of the writing process.
- **New** Coverage of thesis development now includes discussion and examples of explanatory and argumentative thesis statements.
- An extensive chapter on paragraphs provides twenty-five examples.
- An extensive chapter on document design includes help with using illustrations and a section on designing for readers with vision loss.

A reference on usage, grammar, and punctuation

The handbook's core reference material reliably and concisely explains basic concepts and common errors, provides hundreds of annotated examples from across the curriculum, and offers frequent exercises in connected discourse.

- **New** Five added boxes cover coordination, subordination, helping verbs, sentence patterns, and sentence fragments.
- **New** Color highlighting in boxes stresses and distinguishes sentence elements for quick reference.
- **New** Advice on avoiding the informalities common to online communication targets nonstandard grammar, punctuation, abbreviations, and spelling.
- More than 150 built-in exercises give students practice with usage, grammar, punctuation, and mechanics as well as with rhetorical concerns such as thesis statements and paraphrasing. The exercises are in connected discourse, and their subjects come from across the academic curriculum. (The handbook is also available without exercises.)

A guide for culturally and linguistically diverse writers

At notes and sections labeled ⟨CULTURE LANGUAGE⟩, the handbook provides extensive rhetorical and grammatical help for writers whose first language or dialect is not standard American English.

- Fully integrated coverage, instead of a separate section, means that students can find what they need without having to know which problems they do and don't share with native SAE speakers.
- The ⟨CULTURE LANGUAGE⟩ Guide, just before the back endpapers, orients students with advice on mastering SAE and pulls all the integrated coverage together in one place.

A guide to visual literacy

The handbook helps students process visual information and use it effectively in their writing.

- **New** The discussion of viewing images critically uses fresh and diverse examples to demonstrate identifying and analyzing visual elements.
- **New** A student's work illustrates the process of analyzing an advertisement.
- **New** The discussion of reading and using visual arguments includes a new graph, a new photograph, and new advertisements for analysis.
- Detailed help with preparing or finding illustrations appears in the discussions of document design, research writing, and Web composition.
- Illustrations in several of the handbook's student papers show various ways to support written ideas with visual information.

An accessible reference guide

The handbook is an open book for students, with a convenient lay-flat binding, tabbed dividers, and many internal features that help students navigate and use the content.

- **New** A clean, uncluttered page design uses color and type to distinguish parts of the book and elements of the pages.
- **New** A brief table of contents inside the front cover provides an at-a-glance overview of the book. As before, a detailed table of contents appears inside the back cover.
- **New** Color highlighting in boxes and on documentation models distinguishes important elements.
- A unique approach to terminology facilitates reference and reading. Headings in the text and tables of contents avoid or explain terms. And "Key terms" boxes in the text provide essential definitions, dramatically reducing cross-references and page flipping.
- An unusually accessible organization groups related problems so that students can easily find what they need.
- Cross-references give divider numbers in addition to page numbers, sending students directly to the appropriate tabbed section—for instance, "See **3** pp. 143–45."
- Annotations on both visual and verbal examples connect principles and illustrations.
- Dictionary-style headers in the index make it easy to find entries.

■ A preface just for students details reference aids and explains the page layout.

Supplements

Pearson offers a variety of support materials to make teaching easier and to help students improve as writers. The following are geared specifically to *The Little, Brown Compact Handbook with Exercises*. Visit *pearsonhighered.com* or contact your local Pearson sales representative for more information on these and scores of additional supplements.

■ **New** mycomplab The Web site *MyCompLab* (*mycomplab.com*) integrates instruction, multimedia tutorials, and exercises for writing, grammar, and research with an online composing space and assessment tools. This seamless, flexible environment comes from extensive research in partnership with composition faculty and students across the country. It provides help for writers in the context of their writing, with functions for instructors' and peers' commentary. Special features include an e-portfolio, a bibliography tool, tutoring services, an assignment builder, and a gradebook and course-management organization created specifically for writing classes. In addition, an e-book version of *The Little, Brown Compact Handbook with Exercises* integrates the many resources of *MyCompLab* into the text.

■ **New** Students can subscribe to *The Little, Brown Compact Handbook with Exercises* as a *CourseSmart* e-textbook. The site includes all of the handbook's content in a format that enables students to search the text, bookmark passages, integrate their notes, and print reading assignments that incorporate lecture notes. For more information, or to subscribe to the *CourseSmart* e-textbook, visit *coursesmart.com*.

■ The answer key to *The Little, Brown Compact Handbook with Exercises* includes answers to all of the book's exercises.

■ *Developmental Exercises to Accompany The Little, Brown Compact Handbook* provides activities in workbook format for developmental writers. An answer key is available.

■ vango *VangoNotes* are study guides in MP3 format that enable students to download handbook information into their own players and then listen to it whenever and wherever they wish. The notes include "need to know" tips for each handbook chapter, practice tests, audio flash cards for learning key concepts and terms, and a rapid review for exams. For more information, visit *VangoNotes.com*.

■ *Diagnostic and Editing Tests and Exercises* are cross-referenced to *The Little, Brown Compact Handbook with Exercises* and are available both in print and online.

Acknowledgments

The Little, Brown Compact Handbook with Exercises stays fresh and useful because instructors talk with the publisher's sales representatives and editors, answer questionnaires, write detailed reviews, and send me personal notes.

For the seventh edition, the following instructors earn special thanks for detailed reviews in which they drew on their rich experience to offer insights into the handbook and suggestions for its improvement: Martha Bachman, Camden County College; Debbie Bush, Copiah-Lincoln Community College; Lucia Cherciu, Dutchess Community College; Barbara Goldstein, Hillsborough Community College; Ann Jagoe, North Central Texas College; Michael Lueker, Our Lady of the Lakes University; Marilee Motto, Owens Community College; and Nanette Tamer, Villa Julie College.

In responding to the ideas of these thoughtful critics, I had the help of several creative people. Caroline Crouse, George Washington University, guided me through the labyrinth of the contemporary library. Nanette Tamer, Villa Julie College, provided helpful suggestions to improve many exercises. Sylvan Barnet, Tufts University, continued to lend his expertise in the chapter "Reading and Writing About Literature," which is adapted from his *Short Guide to Writing About Literature* and *Introduction to Literature* (with William Burto and William E. Cain). Ellen Kuhl provided creative, meticulous, and invaluable help with the material on research writing. And Carol Hollar-Zwick, sine qua non, served brilliantly as originator, sounding board, critic, coordinator, researcher, producer, and friend.

A superb publishing team helped to make this book. At Longman, editors Joe Opiela and Anne Brunell Ehrenworth offered perceptive insights into instructors' and students' needs, while production editor Bob Ginsberg helped resolve sometimes competing production goals in favor of quality and accuracy. At Nesbitt Graphics, Jerilyn Bockorick created the striking new design, and Susan McIntyre performed her usual calm (and calming) miracles of scheduling and management to produce the book. I am grateful to all these collaborators.

PART 1

The Writing Process

The Writing Process

1 The Writing Situation

Like most writers (even very experienced ones), you may find writing sometimes easy but more often challenging, sometimes smooth but more often halting. Writing involves creation, and creation requires freedom, experimentation, and even missteps. Instead of proceeding in a straight line on a clear path, you might start writing without knowing what you have to say, circle back to explore a new idea, or keep going even though you're sure you'll have to rewrite later.

As uncertain as the writing process may be, you can bring some control to it by assessing your writing situation, particularly your subject, audience, and purpose.

1a   Assessing the writing situation

Any writing you do for others occurs in a context that both limits and clarifies your choices. You are communicating something about a particular subject to a particular audience of readers for a specific reason. You may need to conduct research. You'll probably be up against a length requirement and a deadline. And you may be expected to present your work in a certain format.

These are the elements of the **writing situation**, and analyzing them at the very start of a project can tell you much about how to proceed.

Context

- **What is your writing for?** A course in school? Work? Something else? What do you know of the requirements for writing in this context?
- **Will you present your writing on paper, online, or orally?** What does the presentation method require in preparation time, special skills, and use of technology?
- **How much leeway do you have for this writing?** What does the stated or implied assignment tell you?

Subject (pp. 5–6)

- **What does your writing assignment require you to write about?** If you don't have a specific assignment, what subjects might be appropriate for this situation?

Visit *mycomplab.com* for more resources as well as exercises on the writing situation.

- **What interests you about the subject?** What do you already know about it? What questions do you have about it?
- What does the assignment require you to do with the subject?

Purpose (pp. 6–7)

- **What aim does your assignment specify?** For instance, does it ask you to explain something or argue a point?
- **Why are you writing?**
- **What do you want your work to accomplish?** What effect do you intend it to have on readers?
- How can you best achieve your purpose?

Audience (pp. 7–8)

- **Who will read your writing?**
- **What do your readers already know and think about your subject?** Do they have any characteristics—such as educational background, experience in your field, or political views—that could influence their reception of your writing?
- **How should you project yourself in your writing?** What role should you play in relation to readers, and what information should you give? How informal or formal should your writing be?
- **What do you want readers to do or think after they read your writing?**

Research (7 pp. 371–431)

- **What kinds of evidence will best suit your subject, purpose, and audience?** What combination of facts, examples, and expert opinions will support your ideas?
- **Does your assignment require research?** Will you need to consult sources of information or conduct other research, such as interviews, surveys, or experiments?
- **Even if research is not required, what additional information do you need to develop your subject?** How will you obtain it?
- **What style should you use to cite your sources?** (See 7 pp. 430–31 on source documentation in the academic disciplines.)

Deadline and length

- **When is the assignment due?** How will you apportion the work you have to do in the available time?
- How long should your writing be? If no length is assigned, what seems appropriate for your subject, purpose, and audience?

Document design

- **What organization and format does the assignment require?** (See p. 54 on format in the academic disciplines and 2 pp. 129–40 on format in public writing.)

- How might you use margins, headings, and other elements to achieve your purpose? (See pp. 55–61.)
- How might you use graphs, photographs, or other illustrations to support ideas and interest readers? (See pp. 61–65 and **2** pp. 106–12 on using illustrations in writing.)

1b Finding your subject

A subject for writing has several basic requirements:

- It should be suitable for the assignment.
- It should be neither too general nor too limited for the assigned deadline and paper length.
- It should be something you are willing to learn more about, even something you care about.

When you receive an assignment, study its wording and its implications about your writing situation to guide your choice of subject:

- **What's wanted from you?** Many writing assignments contain words such as *discuss, describe, analyze, report, interpret, explain, define, argue,* or *evaluate.* These words specify the way you are to approach your subject, what kind of thinking is expected of you, and what your general purpose is. (See pp. 6–7.)
- **For whom are you writing?** Many assignments will specify or imply your readers, but sometimes you will have to figure out for yourself who your audience is and what it expects of you. (For more on analyzing your audience, see pp. 7–8.)
- **What kind of research is required?** An assignment may specify the kinds of sources you are expected to consult, and you can use such information to choose your subject. (If you are unsure whether research is required, check with your instructor.)
- **Does the subject need to be narrowed?** To do the subject justice in the length and time required, you'll often need to limit it. (See below.)

Answering questions about your assignment will help set some boundaries for your choice of subject. Then you can explore your own interests and experiences to narrow the subject so that you can cover it adequately within the space and time assigned. Federal aid to college students could be the subject of a book; the kinds of aid available or why the government should increase aid would be a more appropriate subject for a four-page paper due in a week. Here are some guidelines for narrowing broad subjects:

- **Break your broad subject into as many specific subjects as you can think of.** Make a list.

- **For each specific subject that interests you and fits the assignment, roughly sketch out the main ideas.** Consider how many paragraphs or pages of specific facts, examples, and other details you would need to pin those ideas down. This thinking should give you at least a vague idea of how much work you'd have to do and how long the resulting paper might be.
- **Break a too-broad subject down further,** repeating the previous steps.

The Internet can also help you limit a general subject. On the Web, browse a directory such as *BUBL LINK* (*bubl.ac.uk/link*). As you pursue increasingly narrow categories, you may find a suitably limited topic.

1c Defining your purpose

Your **purpose** in writing is your chief reason for communicating something about your subject to a particular audience of readers. It is your answer to a potential reader's question, "So what?"

Most writing you do will have one of four main purposes:

- **To entertain readers.**
- **To express your feelings or ideas.**
- **To explain something to readers (exposition).**
- **To persuade readers to accept or act on your opinion (argument).**

These purposes often overlap in a single essay, but usually one predominates. And the dominant purpose will influence your slant on your subject, the details you choose, and even the words you use.

Many writing assignments narrow the purpose by using a signal word, such as the following:

- **Report:** Survey, organize, and objectively present the available evidence on the subject.
- **Summarize:** Concisely state the main points in a text, argument, theory, or other work.
- **Discuss:** Examine the main points, competing views, or implications of the subject.
- **Compare and contrast:** Explain the similarities and differences between two subjects. (See also pp. 48–49.)
- **Define:** Specify the meaning of a term or a concept—distinctive characteristics, boundaries, and so on. (See also pp. 47–48.)
- **Analyze:** Identify the elements of the subject, and discuss how they work together. (See also p. 48 and **2** p. 81.)
- **Interpret:** Infer the subject's meaning or implications.

■ **Evaluate:** Judge the quality or significance of the subject, considering pros and cons. (See also **2** p. 83.)

■ **Argue:** Take a position on the subject, and support your position with evidence. (See also **2** pp. 97–106.)

You can conceive of your purpose more specifically, too, in a way that incorporates your particular subject and the outcome you intend:

To explain how Annie Dillard's "Total Eclipse" builds to its climax so that readers appreciate the author's skill

To explain the methods of an engineering study so that readers understand and accept your conclusions

To explain the steps in a new office procedure so that staffers will be able to follow it without difficulty

To argue against additional regulation of health-maintenance organizations so that readers will perceive the disadvantages for themselves

1d Considering your audience

The readers likely to see your work—your **audience**—may influence your choice of subject and your definition of purpose. Your audience certainly will influence what you say about your subject and how you say it—for instance, how much background information you give and whether you adopt a serious or a friendly tone.

For much academic and public writing, readers have specific needs and expectations. You still have many choices to make based on audience, but the options are somewhat defined. (See **2** pp. 90–96 and **8** pp. 437–59 on academic writing and **2** pp. 129–40 on public writing.) In other writing situations, the conventions are vaguer and the choices are more open. The following box contains questions that can help you define and make these choices.

Questions about audience

Identity and expectations

■ **Who _are_ my readers?**

■ **What are my readers' expectations for the kind of writing I'm doing?** Do they expect features such as a particular organization and format, distinctive kinds of evidence, or a certain style of documenting sources?

■ **What do I want readers to know or do after reading my work?** How should I make that clear to them?

■ **How should I project myself to my readers?** How formal or informal will they expect me to be? What role and tone should I assume?

(continued)

Questions about audience
(continued)

Characteristics, knowledge, and attitudes

- **What characteristics of readers are relevant for my subject and purpose?** For instance:

  Age and sex
  Occupation: students, professional colleagues, etc.
  Social or economic role: subject-matter experts, voters, car buyers, potential employers, etc.
  Economic or educational background
  Ethnic background
  Political, religious, or moral beliefs and values
  Hobbies or activities

- **How will the characteristics of readers influence their attitudes toward my subject?**
- **What do readers already know and *not* know about my subject?** How much do I have to tell them?
- **How should I handle any specialized terms?** Will readers know them? If not, should I define them?
- **What ideas, arguments, or information might surprise, excite, or offend readers?** How should I handle these points?
- **What misconceptions might readers have of my subject and/or my approach to it?** How can I dispel these misconceptions?

Uses and format

- **What will readers do with my writing?** Should I expect them to read every word from the top, to scan for information, or to look for conclusions? Can I help by providing a summary, headings, illustrations, or other aids? (See pp. 53–66 on document design.)

2   Invention

Writers use a host of techniques to help invent or discover ideas and information about their subjects. **Whichever of the following techniques you use, do your work in writing, not just in your head.** Your ideas will then be retrievable, and the very act of writing will lead you to fresh insights.

Visit *mycomplab.com* for more resources as well as exercises on invention.

CULTURE LANGUAGE The discovery process encouraged here rewards rapid writing without a lot of thinking beforehand about what you will write or how. If your first language is not standard American English, you may find it helpful initially to do this exploratory writing in your native language or dialect and then to translate the worthwhile material for use in your drafts. This process can be productive, but it is extra work. You may want to try it at first and gradually move to composing in standard American English.

2a | Keeping a journal

A **journal** is a diary of ideas kept on paper or on a computer. It gives you a place to record your responses, thoughts, and observations about what you read, see, hear, or experience. It can also provide ideas for writing. Because you write for yourself, you can work out your ideas without the pressure of an audience "out there" who will evaluate logic or organization or correctness. If you write every day, even just for a few minutes, the routine will loosen your writing muscles and improve your confidence.

You can use a journal for varied purposes: perhaps to confide your feelings, explore your responses to movies and other media, practice certain kinds of writing (such as poems or news stories), pursue ideas from your course, or think critically about what you read. One student, Katy Moreno, used her journal for the last purpose. Her composition instructor had distributed "It's a Flat World, After All," an essay by Thomas L. Friedman about globalization and the job market. The instructor then gave the following assignment, calling for a response to reading:

> In "It's a Flat World, After All," Thomas L. Friedman describes today's global job market, focusing not on manufacturing jobs that have been "outsourced" to overseas workers but on jobs that require a college degree and are no longer immune to outsourcing. Friedman argues that keeping jobs in the United States requires that US students, parents, and educators improve math and science education. As a college student, how do you respond to this analysis of the global market for jobs? Does anything Friedman says cause you to rethink how you will spend your college years or what your major will be?

On first reading the essay, Moreno had found it convincing because Friedman's description of the job market matched her family's experience: her mother had lost her job when it was outsourced to India. After rereading the essay, however, Moreno was not persuaded that more math and science would necessarily improve students' opportunities and preserve their future jobs. She compared Friedman's advice with details she recalled from her mother's experience, and she began to develop a response by writing in her journal:

> Friedman is certainly right that more jobs than we realize are going overseas—that's what happened to Mom's job and we were shocked! But he gives only one way for students like me to compete—take more math and science. At first I thought he's totally right. But then I thought that what he said didn't really explain what happened to Mom—she had lots of math + science + tons of experience, but it was her salary, not better training, that caused her job to be outsourced. An overseas worker would do her job for less money. So she lost her job because of money + because she wasn't a manager. Caught in the middle. I want to major in computer science, but I don't think it's smart to try for the kind of job Mom had—at least not as long as it's so much cheaper for companies to hire workers overseas.

(Further examples of Moreno's writing appear in the next three chapters.)

CULTURE LANGUAGE A journal can be especially helpful if your first language is not standard American English. You can practice writing to improve your fluency, try out sentence patterns, and experiment with vocabulary words. Equally important, you can experiment with applying what you know from experience to what you read and observe.

2b Observing your surroundings

Sometimes you can find a good subject or good ideas by looking around you, not in the half-conscious way most of us move from place to place in our daily lives but deliberately, all senses alert. On a bus, for instance, are there certain types of passengers? What seems to be on the driver's mind? To get the most from observation, you should have a notepad and pen or a handheld computer available for taking notes and making sketches. Back at your desk, study your notes and sketches for oddities or patterns that you'd like to explore further.

2c Freewriting

Writing into a subject

Many writers find subjects or discover ideas by **freewriting**: writing without stopping for a certain amount of time (say, ten minutes) or to a certain length (say, one page). The goal of freewriting is to generate ideas and information from *within* yourself by going around the part of your mind that doesn't want to write or can't think of anything to write. You let words themselves suggest other words. *What* you write is not important; that you *keep* writing is. Don't stop, even if that means repeating the same words until new words come. Don't go back to reread, don't censor ideas that seem dumb or repetitious, and above all don't stop to edit: grammar, punctuation, spelling, and the like are irrelevant at this stage.

If you write on a computer, try this technique for moving forward while freewriting: turn off your computer's monitor, or turn its brightness control all the way down so that the screen is dark. The computer will record what you type but keep it from you and thus prevent you from tinkering with your prose. This **invisible writing** may feel uncomfortable at first, but it can free the mind for very creative results.

⟨CULTURE LANGUAGE⟩ Invisible writing can be especially helpful if you are uneasy writing in standard American English and you tend to worry about errors while writing. The blank computer screen leaves you no choice but to explore ideas without regard for their expression. If you choose to write with the monitor on, concentrate on *what* you want to say, not *how* you're saying it.

Focused freewriting

Focused freewriting is more concentrated: you start with your subject and write about it without stopping for, say, fifteen minutes or one full page. As in all freewriting, you push to bypass mental blocks and self-consciousness, not debating what to say or editing what you've written. With focused freewriting, though, you let the physical act of writing take you into and around your subject.

An example of focused freewriting can be found in Katy Moreno's journal response to Thomas L. Friedman's "It's a Flat World, After All" on the previous page. Since she already had an idea about Friedman's essay, Moreno was able to start there and expand on the idea.

2d Brainstorming

A method similar to freewriting is **brainstorming**—focusing intently on a subject for a fixed period (say, fifteen minutes), pushing yourself to list every idea and detail that comes to mind. Like freewriting, brainstorming requires turning off your internal editor so that you keep moving ahead. (The technique of invisible writing on a computer, described above, can help you move forward.)

Here is an example of brainstorming by a student, Johanna Abrams, on what a summer job can teach:

summer work teaches—
    how to look busy while doing nothing
    how to avoid the sun in summer
    seriously: discipline, budgeting money, value of money

which job? Burger King cashier? baby sitter? mail-room clerk?
mail room: how to sort mail into boxes: this is learning??
how to survive getting fired—humiliation, outrage
Mrs. King! the mail-room queen as learning experience
the shock of getting fired: what to tell parents, friends?
Mrs. K was so rigid—dumb procedures
initials instead of names on the mail boxes—confusion!
Mrs. K's anger, resentment: the disadvantages of being smarter than your boss
The odd thing about working in an office: a world with its own rules for how to act
what Mr. D said about the pecking order—big chick (Mrs. K) pecks on little
    chick (me)
a job can beat you down—make you be mean to other people

2e Clustering

Like freewriting and brainstorming, **clustering** also draws on
free association and rapid, unedited work. But it emphasizes the relations between ideas by combining writing and nonlinear drawing.
When clustering, you radiate outward from a center point—your
subject. When an idea occurs, you pursue related ideas in a branching structure until they seem exhausted. Then you do the same with
other ideas, continuously branching out or drawing arrows.

The example below shows how a student used clustering for ten
minutes to expand on a subject he arrived at through freewriting:
writing as a means of disguise.

Clustering

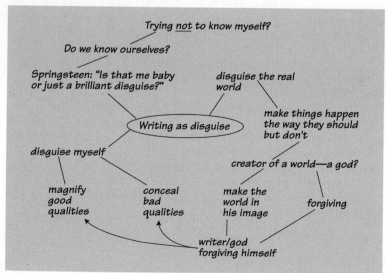

2f   Asking questions

Asking yourself a set of questions about your subject—and writing out the answers—can help you look at the subject objectively and see fresh possibilities in it.

1 Journalist's questions

A journalist with a story to report poses a set of questions:

- **Who was involved?**
- **What happened, and what were the results?**
- **When did it happen?**
- **Where did it happen?**
- **Why did it happen?**
- **How did it happen?**

These questions can also be useful in probing an essay subject, especially when you are telling a story or examining causes and effects.

2 Questions about patterns

We think about and understand a vast range of subjects through patterns such as narration, classification, and comparison and contrast. Asking questions based on the patterns can help you view your subject from many angles. Sometimes you may want to develop an entire essay using just one pattern.

- **How did it happen?** (Narration)
- **How does it look, sound, feel, smell, taste?** (Description)
- **What are examples of it or reasons for it?** (Illustration or support)
- **What is it? What does it encompass, and what does it exclude?** (Definition)
- **What are its parts or characteristics?** (Division or analysis)
- **What groups or categories can it be sorted into?** (Classification)
- **How is it like, or different from, other things?** (Comparison and contrast)
- **Why did it happen? What results did or could it have?** (Cause-and-effect analysis)
- **How do you do it, or how does it work?** (Process analysis)

For more on these patterns, including paragraph-length examples, see pp. 46–50.

3 Thesis and Organization

Shaping your raw material helps you clear away unneeded ideas, spot possible gaps, and energize your subject. The two main operations in shaping material are focusing on a thesis (below) and organizing ideas (p. 17).

3a Conceiving a thesis statement

Your readers will expect your essay to be focused on and controlled by a main idea, or **thesis.** In your final draft you may express this idea in a **thesis statement,** often at the end of your introduction.

1 Functions of the thesis statement

As an expression of the thesis, the thesis statement serves three crucial functions and one optional one:

The thesis statement

- The thesis statement **narrows your subject** to a single, central idea that you want readers to gain from your essay.
- It **claims something specific and significant** about your subject, a claim that requires support.
- It **conveys your purpose**—often explanatory or argumentative in college writing.
- It often concisely **previews the arrangement of ideas,** in which case it can also help you organize your essay.

All of the following thesis statements fulfill the first three functions listed in the box (the nature of the claim is highlighted in brackets). Examples 2 and 5 also fulfill the fourth function, previewing organization. Notice the purposes of the statements. Statements 1 and 2 are **explanatory:** the writers mainly want to explain something to readers. Statements 3–5 are **argumentative:** the authors mainly want to convince readers of something.

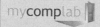

Visit *mycomplab.com* for more resources and exercises on thesis and organization.

Subject	Explanatory thesis statement
1. Abraham Lincoln's delay in emancipating the slaves	Lincoln delayed emancipating any slaves until 1863 because his primary goal was to restore and preserve the Union, with or without slavery. [**Topic:** Lincoln's delay. **Claim:** was caused by his goal of preserving the Union.]
2. Preventing juvenile crime	Juveniles can be diverted from crime by active learning programs, full-time sports, and intervention by mentors and role models. [**Topic:** juveniles. **Claim:** can be diverted from crime in three ways.]

Subject	Argumentative thesis statement
3. Drivers' use of cell phones	Drivers' use of cell phones should be outlawed because people who talk and drive at the same time cause accidents. [**Topic:** drivers' use of cell phones. **Claim:** should be outlawed because it causes accidents.]
4. Federal aid to college students	As an investment in its own economy, the federal government should provide a tuition grant to any college student who qualifies academically. [**Topic:** federal government. **Claim:** should provide a tuition grant to any college student who qualifies academically.]
5. The effects of strip-mining	Strip-mining should be tightly controlled in this region to reduce its pollution of water resources, its destruction of the land, and its devastating effects on people's lives. [**Topic:** strip-mining. **Claim:** should be tightly controlled for three reasons.]

(CULTURE LANGUAGE) In some cultures it is considered rude or unnecessary for a writer to state his or her main idea outright. When writing in standard American English for school or work, you can assume that readers expect a clear and early idea of what you think.

2 Development of the thesis statement

A thesis will not usually leap fully formed into your head: you will have to develop and shape the idea as you develop and shape your essay. Still, trying to draft a thesis statement early can give you a point of reference when changes inevitably occur.

While you are developing your thesis statement, ask the following questions about each attempt:

Checklist for revising the thesis statement

- How well does the **subject** of your statement capture the subject of your paper?
- What **claim** does your statement make about your subject?
- What is the **significance** of the claim? How does it answer "So what?" and convey your purpose?
- How can the claim be **limited** or made more **specific?** Does it state a single idea and clarify the boundaries of the idea?
- How **unified** is the statement? How does each word and phrase contribute to a single idea?

Here are examples of thesis statements revised to meet these requirements:

Original	Revised
This new product brought in over $300,000 last year. [A statement of fact, not a claim about the product: what is significant about the product's success?]	This new product succeeded because of its innovative marketing campaign, including widespread press coverage, instore entertainment, and a consumer newsletter.
People should not go on fad diets. [A vague statement that needs limiting with one or more reasons: what's wrong with fad diets?]	Fad diets can be dangerous when they deprive the body of essential nutrients or rely excessively on potentially harmful foods.
Televised sports are different from live sports. [A general statement that needs to be made more specific: how are they different, and why is the difference significant?]	Although television cannot transmit all the excitement of a live game, its close-ups and slow-motion replays reveal much about the players and the strategy of the game.
Seat belts can save lives, but now carmakers are installing air bags. [Not unified: how do the two parts of the sentence relate to each other?]	If drivers had used lifesaving seat belts more often, carmakers might not have needed to install air bags.

Exercise 3.1 Evaluating thesis statements

Evaluate the following thesis statements, considering whether each one is sufficiently limited, specific, and unified. Rewrite the statements as necessary to meet these goals.

1 Aggression usually leads to violence, injury, and even death, and we should use it constructively.
2 The region of Islam is widely misunderstood in the United States.
3 One evening of a radio talk show amply illustrates both the appeal of such shows and their silliness.
4 Good manners make our society work.
5 The poem is about motherhood.

6 Television is useful for children and a mindless escape for adults who do not want to think about their problems.
7 I disliked American history in high school, but I like it in college.
8 Drunken drivers, whose perception and coordination are impaired, should receive mandatory suspensions of their licenses.
9 Business is a good major for many students.
10 The state's lenient divorce laws undermine the institution of marriage, which is fundamental to our culture, and they should certainly be made stricter for couples who have children.

3b Organizing your ideas

Most essays share a basic pattern of introduction (states the subject), body (develops the subject), and conclusion (pulls the essay's ideas together). Introductions and conclusions are discussed on pp. 50–53. Within the body, every paragraph develops some aspect of the essay's main idea, or thesis. See pp. 34–36 for Katy Moreno's essay, with annotations highlighting the body's pattern of support for the thesis statement.

CULTURE LANGUAGE If you are not used to reading and writing American academic prose, its pattern of introduction-body-conclusion and the particular schemes discussed on the next page may seem unfamiliar. For instance, instead of introductions that focus quickly on the topic and thesis, you may be used to openings that establish personal connections with readers. And instead of body paragraphs that stress general points and support those points with evidence, you may be used to general statements without support (because writers can assume that readers will supply the evidence themselves) or to evidence without explanation (because writers can assume that readers will infer the general points). When writing American academic prose, you need to take into account readers' expectations for directness and for the statement and support of general points.

1 The general and the specific

To organize material for an essay, you need to distinguish general and specific ideas and see the relations between ideas. General and specific refer to the number of instances or objects included in a group signified by a word. The following "ladder" illustrates a general-to-specific hierarchy:

Most general
↑ life form
   plant
   rose
↓ Uncle Dan's prize-winning American Beauty rose
Most specific

As you arrange your material, pick out the general ideas and then the specific points that support them. Set aside points that seem irrelevant to your key ideas. On a computer you can easily experiment with various arrangements of general ideas and supporting information: save your master list of ideas, duplicate it, and then use the Cut and Paste functions to move material around or (a little quicker) drag selected text to where you want it.

2 Schemes for organizing essays

An essay's body paragraphs may be arranged in many ways that are familiar to readers. The choice depends on your subject, purpose, and audience.

- **Spatial:** In describing a person, place, or thing, move through space systematically from a starting point to other features—for instance, top to bottom, near to far, left to right.
- **Chronological:** In recounting a sequence of events, arrange the events as they actually occurred in time, first to last.
- **General to specific:** Begin with an overall discussion of the subject; then fill in details, facts, examples, and other support.
- **Specific to general:** First provide the support; then draw a conclusion from it.
- **Climactic:** Arrange ideas in order of increasing importance to your thesis or increasing interest to the reader.
- **Problem-solution:** First outline a problem that needs solving; then propose a solution.

3 Outlines

It's not essential to craft a detailed outline before you begin drafting an essay; in fact, too detailed a plan could prevent you from discovering ideas while you draft. Still, even a rough scheme can show you patterns of general and specific, suggest proportions, and highlight gaps or overlaps in coverage.

There are several kinds of outlines, some more flexible than others.

Scratch or informal outline

A scratch or informal outline includes key general points in the order they will be covered. It may also list evidence for the points.

Here is Katy Moreno's scratch outline for her essay on the global job market:

Thesis statement

My mother's experience of having her job outsourced taught a lesson that Thomas L. Friedman overlooks: technical training by itself can be too narrow to produce the communicators and problem solvers needed by contemporary businesses.

Scratch outline

Mom's outsourcing experience
    Excellent tech skills
    Salary too high compared to overseas tech workers
    Lack of planning + communication skills, unlike managers who kept jobs
Well-rounded education to protect vs. outsourcing
    Tech training, as Friedman says
    Also, experience in communication, problem solving, other management
      skills

Tree diagram

In a tree diagram, ideas and details branch out in increasing specificity. Unlike more linear outlines, this diagram can be supplemented and extended indefinitely, so it is easy to alter. Johanna Abrams developed the following example from her brainstorming about a summer job (pp. 11–12):

Thesis statement

Two months working in a large agency taught me that an office's pecking order should be respected.

Tree diagram

A tree diagram or other visual map can be especially useful for planning a project for the Web. The diagram can help you lay out the organization of your project and its links and then later can serve as a site map for your readers. (For more on writing for the Web, see **2** pp. 120–25.)

Formal outline

A formal outline not only lays out main ideas and their support but also shows the relative importance of all the essay's elements. On the basis of her scratch outline (previous page), Katy Moreno prepared this formal outline for her essay on the global job market:

Thesis statement

My mother's experience of having her job outsourced taught a lesson that Thomas L. Friedman overlooks: technical training by itself can be too narrow to produce the communicators and problem solvers needed by contemporary businesses.

Formal outline

I. Summary of Friedman's article
   A. Reasons for outsourcing
      1. Improved technology and access
      2. Well-educated workers
      3. Productive workers
      4. Lower wages
   B. Need for improved technical training in US
II. Mother's experience
   A. Outsourcing of job
      1. Mother's education, experience, performance
      2. Employer's cost savings
   B. Retention of managers' jobs
      1. Planning skills
      2. Communication skills
III. Conclusions about ideal education
   A. Needs of US businesses
      1. Technical skills
      2. Management skills
         a. Communication
         b. Problem solving
         c. Versatility
   B. Personal goals
      1. Technical training
      2. English and history courses for management skills

This example illustrates several principles of outlining that can ensure completeness, balance, and clear relationships:

- **All parts are systematically indented and labeled:** Roman numerals (I, II) for primary divisions; indented capital letters (A, B) for secondary divisions; further indented Arabic numerals (1, 2) for supporting examples. The next level down is indented further still and labeled with small letters: a, b.
- **The outline divides the material into several groups.** A long list of points at the same level should be broken up into groups.
- **Topics of equal generality appear in parallel headings,** with the same indention and numbering or lettering.

- **All subdivided headings break into at least two parts.** A topic cannot logically be divided into only one part.
- **All headings are expressed in parallel grammatical form**—in the example, as phrases using a noun plus modifiers. This is a topic outline; in a sentence outline all headings are expressed as full sentences (see **8** p. 509).

Note Because of its structure, a formal outline can be an excellent tool for analyzing a draft before revising it. See p. 26.

4 Unity and coherence

Two qualities of effective writing relate to organization; unity and coherence. When you perceive that someone's writing "flows well," you are probably appreciating these qualities.

To check an outline or draft for **unity**, ask these questions:

- **Is each section relevant to the main idea (thesis) of the essay?**
- **Within main sections, does each example or detail support the principal idea of that section?**

To check your outline or draft for **coherence**, ask the following questions:

- **Do the ideas follow a clear sequence?**
- **Are the parts of the essay logically connected?**
- **Are the connections clear and smooth?**

See also pp. 40–45 on unity and coherence in paragraphs.

Exercise 3.2 **Organizing ideas**

The following list of ideas was extracted by a student from freewriting he did for a brief paper on soccer in the United States. Using his thesis statement as a guide, pick out the general ideas and arrange the relevant specific points under them. In some cases you may have to infer general ideas to cover specific points in the list.

Thesis statement
Although its growth in the United States has been slow and halting, professional soccer may finally be poised to become a major American sport.

List of ideas
In countries of South and Latin America, soccer is the favorite sport.
In the United States the success of a sport depends largely on its ability to attract huge TV audiences.
Soccer was not often presented on US television.
In 2007 soccer's World Cup final was broadcast on ABC and on Spanish-language Univision.
In the past, professional soccer could not get a foothold in the United States because of poor TV coverage and lack of financial backing.

The growing Hispanic population in the United States could help soccer grow as well.

Investors have poured hundreds of millions of dollars into Major league Soccer, the top US professional league.

Potential fans did not have a chance to see soccer games.

Failures like that of the start-up North American Soccer League made potential backers wary of new ventures.

Recently, the outlook for professional soccer has changed dramatically.

Isolated events such as the US's hosting of the World Cup in 1994 greatly increased American interest in soccer.

The US television audience for soccer's 2007 World Cup final was larger than the average US television audience for baseball's World Series the same year.

Past American interest in soccer quickly died down.

Many of Major League Soccer's games are well attended, and some of its teams are making a profit.

4 Drafting

Drafting is an occasion for exploration. Don't expect to transcribe solid thoughts into polished prose: solidity and polish will come with revision and editing. Instead, while drafting let the very act of writing help you find and form your meaning.

4a Starting to draft

Beginning a draft sometimes takes courage, even for seasoned professionals. Procrastination may actually help if you let ideas for writing simmer at the same time. At some point, though, you'll have to face the blank paper or computer screen. The following techniques can help you begin:

■ **Read over what you've already written**—notes, outlines, and so on—and immediately start your draft with whatever comes to mind.

■ **Freewrite** (see p. 10).

Visit *mycomplab.com* for more resources as well as exercises on drafting.

- **Skip the opening and start in the middle.** Or write the conclusion.
- **Write a paragraph.** Explain what you think your essay will be about when you finish it.
- **Start writing the part that you understand best.** Using your outline, divide your essay into chunks—say, one for the introduction, another for the first point, and so on. One of these chunks may call out to be written.

4b Maintaining momentum

Drafting requires momentum: the forward movement opens you to fresh ideas and connections. To keep moving while drafting, try one or more of these techniques.

- **Set aside enough time for yourself.** For a brief essay, a first draft is likely to take at least an hour or two.
- **Work in a quiet place.**
- **If you must stop working, write down what you expect to do next.** Then you can pick up where you stopped with minimal disruption.
- **Be as fluid as possible.** Spontaneity will allow your attitudes toward your subject to surface naturally in your sentences.
- **Keep going.** Skip over sticky spots; leave a blank if you can't find the right word; put alternative ideas or phrasings in brackets so that you can consider them later. If an idea pops out of nowhere but doesn't seem to fit in, quickly jot it down, or write it into the draft and bracket or boldface it for later attention.
- **Resist self-criticism.** Don't worry about your style, grammar, spelling, punctuation, and the like. Don't worry about what your readers will think. These are very important matters, but save them for revision.
- **Use your thesis statement and outline.** They can remind you of your planned purpose, organization, and content. However, if your writing leads you in a more interesting direction, follow.

If you write on a computer, frequently save the text you're drafting—at least every five or ten minutes and every time you leave the computer.

4c Examining a sample first draft

Katy Moreno's first-draft response to Thomas L. Friedman's "It's a Flat World, After All" appears on the next two pages. As part of her assignment, Moreno showed the draft to four classmates whose suggestions for revision appear in the margin of this draft. They used the Comment function of *Microsoft Word*, which allows users to add comments without inserting words into the document's text. (Notice that the classmates ignore errors in grammar and punctuation, concentrating instead on larger issues such as thesis, clarity of ideas, and unity.)

Title?

In "It's a Flat World, After All," Thomas L. Friedman argues that, most US students are not preparing themselves as well as they should to compete in today's economy. Not like students in India, China, and other countries are. The outsourcing of my mother's job proves that Thomas L. Friedman's advice to improve students' technical training is too narrow.

Comment [Jared]: Your mother's job being outsourced is interesting, but your introduction seems rushed.

Comment [Rabia]: The end of your thesis statement is a little unclear—too narrow for what?

Friedman describes a "flat" world where recent technology like the Internet and wireless communication make it possible for college graduates all over the globe, in particular in India and China, to get jobs that once were gotten by graduates of US colleges and universities. He argues that US students need more math and science in order to compete.

Comment [Erin]: Can you include the reasons Friedman gives for overseas students' success?

I came to college with first-hand knowledge of globalization and outsourcing. My mother, who worked for sixteen years in the field of information technology (IT), was laid off six months ago when the company she worked for decided to outsource much of its IT work to a company based in India. My mother majored in computer science, had sixteen years of experience, and her bosses always gave her good reviews. She never expected to be laid off and was surprised when she was. She wasn't laid off because of her background and performance. In fact, my mother had a very strong background in math and science and years of training and job experience. The reason was because her salary and benefits cost the company more than outsourcing her job did. Which hurt my family financially, as you can imagine.

Comment [Nathaniel]: Tighten this paragraph to avoid repetition? Also, how does your mother's experience relate to Friedman and your thesis?

A number of well-paid people in the IT department where my mother worked, namely IT managers, were not laid off. As my mother explained at the time, they kept their jobs because they were better at planning and they communicated

Comment [Erin]: What were the managers better at planning for?

better, they were better writers and speakers than my
mother.

Like my mother, I am more comfortable in front of a
computer than I am in front of a group of people. I planned
to major in computer science. Since my mother lost her job,
though, I have decided to take courses in English and history
too, where the classes will require me to do different kinds of
work. When I enter the job market, my well-rounded education will make me a more attractive job candidate, and, will
help me to be a versatile, productive employee.

> **Comment [Nathaniel]:** Can you be more specific about the kinds of work you'll need to do?

> **Comment [Rabia]:** Can you work this point into your thesis?

We know from our history that Americans have been innovative, hard-working people. We students have educational
opportunities to compete in the global economy, but we must
use our time in college wisely. As Thomas L. Friedman says,
my classmates and I need to be ready for a rapidly changing
future. We will have to work hard each day, which means being prepared for class, getting the best grades we can, and
making the most of each class. Our futures depend on the decisions we make today.

> **Comment [Jared]:** Conclusion seems to go off in a new direction. Friedman mentions hard work, but it hasn't been your focus before.

> **Comment [Rabia]:** Don't forget your works cited.

5 Revising and Editing

During revision—literally "re-seeing"—you shift your focus outward from yourself and your subject toward your readers, concentrating on what will help them respond as you want. It's wise to
revise in at least two stages, one devoted to fundamental meaning
and structure (here called **revising**) and one devoted to word choice,
grammar, punctuation, and other surface features (here called
editing). Knowing that you will edit later gives you the freedom at
first to look beyond the confines of the page or screen to the whole
paper.

mycomplab

Visit *mycomplab.com* for more resources as well as
exercises on revising and editing.

5a Revising the whole essay

To revise your writing, you have to read it critically, and that means you have to create some distance between your draft and yourself. One of the following techniques may help you to see your work objectively.

- **Take a break after finishing the draft.** A few hours may be enough; a whole night or day is preferable.
- **Ask someone to read and react to your draft.** If your instructor encourages collaboration among students, by all means take advantage of the opportunity to hear the responses of others. (See pp. 36–38 for more on collaboration.)
- **Type a handwritten draft.** The act of transcription can reveal gaps in content or problems in structure.
- **Outline your draft.** Highlight the main points supporting the thesis, and convert these sentences to outline form. Then examine the outline you've made for logical order, gaps, and digressions. A formal outline can be especially illuminating because of its careful structure (see pp. 20–21).
- **Listen to your draft.** Read the draft out loud to yourself or a friend or classmate, record and listen to it, or have someone read the draft to you.
- **Ease the pressure.** Don't try to re-see everything in your draft at once. Use the checklist on the facing page, making a separate pass through the draft for each item.

1 Revising on a word processor

When you revise on a computer, take a few precautions to avoid losing your work and to keep track of your drafts:

- **Save your work every five to ten minutes.**
- **After doing any major work on a project, create a backup version of the file.**
- **Work on a duplicate of your latest draft.** Then the original will remain intact until you're truly finished with it. On the duplicate you can use your word processor's Track Changes function, which shows changes alongside the original text and allows you to accept or reject alterations later.
- **Save each draft under its own file name.** You may need to consult previous drafts for ideas or phrasings.

2 Titling your essay

The revision stage is a good time to consider a title because attempting to sum up your essay in a phrase can focus your attention

Checklist for revision

Purpose

What is the essay's purpose? Does it conform to the assignment? Is it consistent throughout the paper? (See pp. 6–7.)

Thesis

What is the thesis of the essay? Where does it become clear? How well do thesis and paper match: Does the paper stray from the thesis? Does it fulfill the commitment of the thesis? (See pp. 14–16.)

Structure

What are the main points of the paper? (List them.) How well does each support the thesis? How effective is their arrangement for the paper's purpose? (See pp. 17–21.)

Development

How well do details, examples, and other evidence support each main point? Where, if at all, might readers find support skimpy or have trouble understanding the content? (See pp. 6–7, 46–50.)

Tone

What is the tone of the paper? How do particular words and sentence structures create the tone? How appropriate is it for the purpose, topic, and intended readers? Where is it most and least successful?

Unity

What does each sentence and paragraph contribute to the thesis? Where, if at all, do digressions occur? Should these be cut, or can they be rewritten to support the thesis? (See pp. 21, 39–40.)

Coherence

How clearly and smoothly does the paper flow? Where does it seem rough or awkward? Can any transitions be improved? (See pp. 21, 45.)

Title, introduction, conclusion

How accurately and interestingly does the title reflect the essay's content? (See opposite.) How well does the introduction engage and focus readers' attention? (See pp. 50–52.) How effective is the conclusion in providing a sense of completion? (See pp. 52–53.)

sharply on your topic, purpose, and audience. The title should tell the reader what your paper is about, but it should not restate the assignment or the thesis statement. Most titles fall into one of these categories:

- A *descriptive title* announces the subject clearly and accurately. Such a title is almost always appropriate and is usually expected for academic writing. Katy Moreno's final title—"Can We Compete? College Education for the Global Economy"—is an example.

- A *suggestive title* hints at the subject to arouse curiosity. Such a title is common in popular magazines and may be appropriate for writing that is somewhat informal. Moreno might have chosen a suggestive title such as "Training for the New World" or "Education for a Flat World" (echoing Thomas L. Friedman's title).

For more information on essay titles, see **MLA** p. 507 (MLA format), **APA** p. 539 (APA format), and **6** p. 358 (capitalizing words in a title).

5b Examining a sample revision

Katy Moreno was satisfied with her first draft: she had her ideas down, and the arrangement seemed logical. Still, from the revision checklist she knew the draft needed work, and her classmates' comments (pp. 24–25) highlighted what she needed to focus on. Following is the first half of her revised draft with marginal annotations highlighting the changes. Moreno used the Track Changes function on her word processor, so that deletions are crossed out and additions are in blue.

Descriptive title names topic and forecasts approach.	Can We Compete? College Education for the Global Economy ~~Title?~~
Expanded introduction draws readers into Moreno's topic, clarifies her point of agreement with Friedman, and states her revised thesis.	Today's students cannot miss news stories about globalization of the economy and outsourcing of jobs, but are students aware of how these trends are affecting the job market? In "It's a Flat World, After All," Thomas L. Friedman argues that most US students are not preparing themselves as well as ~~they should to compete in today's economy. Not like~~ students in India, China, and other countries ~~are.~~ to compete in today's economy, which requires hard-working, productive scientists and engineers. Friedman's argument speaks to me because my mother recently lost her job when it was outsourced to India. But her experience taught a lesson that Friedman overlooks: technical training by itself can be too narrow to produce the communicators and problem solvers needed by contemporary businesses. ~~The outsourcing of my mother's job proves that Thomas L. Friedman's advice to improve students' technical training is too narrow.~~

Friedman describes a "flat" world where recent technology like the Internet and wireless communication makes it possible for college graduates all over the globe, ~~in particular~~ to compete for high paying jobs that once belonged to graduates of US colleges and universities. He focuses on workers in India and China, who graduate from college with excellent educations in math and science, who are eager for new opportunities, and who are willing to work exceptionally hard, often harder than their American counterparts and, for less money. ~~to get jobs that once were gotten by graduates of US colleges and universities.~~ ~~He~~ Friedman argues that US students must be better prepared academically, especially in ~~need more~~ math and science, so that they can get and keep jobs that will otherwise go overseas. ~~in order to compete.~~

> Expanded summary of Friedman's article specifies qualities of overseas workers.

~~I came to college with first hand knowledge of globalization and outsourcing. My mother, who worked for sixteen years in the field of information technology (IT), was laid off six months ago when the company she worked for decided to outsource much of its IT work to a company based in India. My mother~~ At first glance, my mother's experience of losing her job might seem to support the argument of Friedman that better training in math and science is the key to competing in the global job market. Her experience, however, adds dimensions to the globalization story, which Friedman misses. First my mother had the kind of strong background in math and science that Friedman says, today's workers need. She majored in computer science, rose within the information technology (IT) department of a large company, ~~had sixteen years of experience,~~ and her bosses always gave her good performance reviews. Still, when her employer decided to outsource most of its IT work, my mother lost her job. ~~She never expected to be laid off and was surprised when she was. She wasn't laid off because of her background and performance. In fact, my mother had a very strong background in math and science and years of training and job experience.~~ The reason wasn't because her technical skills were inadequate. Instead, her salary and benefits cost the company more than outsourcing her job did. Until wages rise around the globe, jobs like my mother's will be vulnerable. No matter how well you are trained. ~~Which hurt my family financially, as you can imagine.~~

> New opening sentences connect to introduction and thesis statement, restating points of agreement and disagreement with Friedman.

> Revisions condense long example of mother's experience.

> Concluding sentences reinforce the point of the paragraph and connect to thesis statement.

5c **Editing the revised draft**

After you've revised your essay so that all the content is in place, then turn to the important work of removing any surface problems that could interfere with a reader's understanding or enjoyment of your ideas.

1 Strategies for editing

Try these approaches to discover what needs editing:

- **Take a break.** Even fifteen minutes can clear your head.
- **Read the draft slowly, and read what you actually see.** Otherwise, you're likely to read what you intended to write but didn't. (If you have trouble slowing down, try reading your draft from back to front, sentence by sentence.)
- **Read as if you are encountering the draft for the first time.** Put yourself in the reader's place.
- **Have a classmate, friend, or relative read your work.** Make sure you understand and consider the reader's suggestions, even if eventually you decide not to take them.
- **Read the draft aloud or, even better, record it.** Listen for awkward rhythms, repetitive sentence patterns, and missing or clumsy transitions.
- **Learn from your own experience.** Keep a record of the problems that others have pointed out in your writing. When editing, check your work against this record.

In your editing, work first for clear and effective sentences that flow smoothly from one to the next. Then check your sentences for correctness. Use the questions in the checklist opposite to guide your editing, referring to the page numbers in parentheses as needed.

2 A sample edited paragraph

The third paragraph of Katy Moreno's edited draft appears below. Among other changes, she tightened wording, improved parallelism (with *consistently received*), corrected several comma errors, and repaired the final sentence fragment.

At first glance, my mother's experience of losing her job might seem to support ~~the~~ Friedman's argument ~~of Friedman~~ that better training in math and science is the key to competing in the global job market. However, ~~H~~her experience~~,~~ ~~however,~~ adds dimensions to the globalization story~~, which~~ that Friedman misses. First, my mother had the kind of strong background in math and science that Friedman says~~,~~ today's workers need. She majored in computer science, rose within the information technology (IT) department of a large company, and consistently received ~~her bosses always gave her~~ good performance reviews. Still, when her employer decided to outsource most of its IT work, my mother lost her job. The reason wasn't ~~because~~that her technical skills were inadequate. Instead, her salary and benefits cost the company more than outsourcing her job did. Until wages rise around the globe, jobs like my mother's will be vulnerable~~,~~ ~~N~~no matter how well ~~you are~~ a person is trained.

Checklist for editing

Are my sentences clear?

Do my words and sentences mean what I Intend them to mean? Is anything confusing? Check especially for these:

Exact language (**3** pp. 170–77)
Parallelism (**3** pp. 154–56)
Clear modifiers (**4** pp. 273–79)
Clear reference of pronouns (**4** pp. 257–59)
Complete sentences (**4** pp. 280–83)
Sentences separated correctly (**4** pp. 285–89)

Are my sentences effective?

How well do words and sentences engage and hold readers' attention? Where does the writing seem wordy, choppy, or dull? Check especially for these:

Emphasis of main ideas (**3** pp. 143–52)
Smooth and informative transitions (pp. 44–45)
Variety in sentence length and structure (**3** pp. 158–61)
Appropriate language (**3** pp. 162–69)
Concise sentences (**3** pp. 180–85)

Do my sentences contain errors?

Where do surface errors interfere with the clarity and effectiveness of my sentences? Check especially for these:

- **Spelling errors (6** pp. 347–52)
- **Sentence fragments (4** pp. 280–83)
- **Comma splices (4** pp. 285–89)
- **Verb errors**
  Verb forms, especially *-s* and *-ed* endings, correct forms of irregular verbs, and appropriate helping verbs (**4** pp. 213–27)
  Verb tenses, especially consistency (**4** pp. 227–33)
  Agreement between subjects and verbs, especially when words come between them or the subject is *each, everyone,* or a similar word (**4** pp. 239–44)

- **Pronoun errors**
  Pronoun forms, especially subjective (*he, she, they, who*) vs. objective (*him, her, them, whom*) (**4** pp. 246–52)
  Agreement between pronouns and antecedents, especially when the antecedent contains *or* or the antecedent is *each, everyone, person,* or a similar word (**4** pp. 253–56)

- **Punctuation errors**
  Commas, especially with comma splices (**4** pp. 287–88) and with *and* or *but,* with introductory elements, with nonessential elements, and with series (**5** pp. 300–14)
  Apostrophes in possessives but not plural nouns (*Dave's/witches*) and in contractions but not possessive personal pronouns (*it's/its*) (**5** pp. 325–31)

3 Editing on a computer

When you write on a word processor, consider these additional approaches to editing:

- **Don't rely on a spelling or grammar/style checker to find what needs editing.** See the discussion of these checkers below.
- **If possible, work on a double-spaced paper copy.** Most people find it much harder to spot errors on a computer screen than on paper.
- **Use the Find command to locate and correct your common problems**—certain misspellings, overuse of *there is*, wordy phrases such as *the fact that*, and so on.
- **Resist overediting.** The ease of editing on a computer can lead to rewriting sentences over and over, stealing the life from your prose. If your grammar/style checker contributes to the temptation, consider turning it off.
- **Take special care with additions and omissions.** Make sure you haven't omitted needed words or left in unneeded words.

4 Working with spelling and grammar/style checkers

A spelling checker and grammar/style checker can be helpful *if* you work within their limitations. The programs miss many problems and may even flag items that are actually correct. Further, they know nothing of your purpose and your audience, so they cannot make important decisions about your writing. Always use these tools critically:

- **Read your work yourself to ensure that it's clear and error-free.**
- **Consider a checker's suggestions carefully, weighing each one against your intentions.** If you aren't sure whether to accept a checker's suggestion, consult a dictionary, writing handbook, or other source. Your version may be fine.

Using a spelling checker

Your word processor's spelling checker can be a great ally: it will flag words that are spelled incorrectly and will usually suggest alternative spellings that resemble what you've typed. However, this ally can also undermine you because of its limitations:

- **The checker may flag a word that you've spelled correctly** just because the word does not appear in its dictionary.
- **The checker may suggest incorrect alternatives.** In providing a list of alternative spellings for your word, the checker may

highlight the one it considers most likely to be correct. For example, if you misspell *definitely* by typing *definately*, your checker may highlight *defiantly* as the correct option. You need to verify that the alternative suggested by the checker is actually what you intend before selecting it. Consult an online or printed dictionary when you aren't sure about the checker's recommendations.

- **Most important, a spelling checker will not flag words that appear in its dictionary but you have misused.** The jingle in the following screen shot has circulated widely as a warning about spelling checkers.

Spelling checker

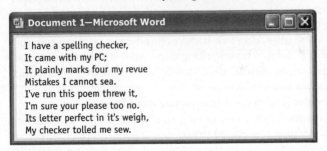

Document 1—Microsoft Word

I have a spelling checker,
It came with my PC;
It plainly marks four my revue
Mistakes I cannot sea.
I've run this poem threw it,
I'm sure your please too no.
Its letter perfect in it's weigh,
My checker tolled me sew.

A spelling checker failed to catch any of the thirteen errors in this jingle. Can you spot them?

Using a grammar/style checker

Grammar/style checkers can flag incorrect grammar or punctuation and wordy or awkward sentences. However, these programs can call your attention only to passages that *may* be faulty. They miss many errors because they are not yet capable of analyzing language in all its complexity. (For instance, they can't accurately distinguish a word's part of speech when there are different possibilities, as *light* can be a noun, a verb, or an adjective.) And they often question passages that don't need editing, such as an appropriate passive verb or a deliberate and emphatic use of repetition.

You can customize a grammar/style checker to suit your needs and habits as a writer. (Select Options under the Tools menu.) Most checkers allow you to specify whether to check grammar only or grammar and style. Some style checkers can be set to the level of writing you intend, such as formal, standard, and informal. (For academic writing choose formal.) You can also instruct the checker to flag specific grammar and style problems that tend to occur in your writing, such as mismatched subjects and verbs, apostrophes in plural nouns, overused passive voice, or a confusion between *its* and *it's*.

5d | Formatting and proofreading the final draft

After editing your essay, retype or print it one last time. Follow the wishes of your instructor in formatting your document. Two common formats are discussed and illustrated in this book: MLA (**MLA** pp. 506–08) and APA (**APA** pp. 539–42). In addition, pp. 53–66 treat principles and elements of document design.

Be sure to proofread the final essay several times to spot and correct errors. To increase the accuracy of your proofreading, you may need to experiment with ways to keep yourself from relaxing into the rhythm and the content of your prose. Here are a few tricks, including some used by professional proofreaders:

- **Read printed copy,** even if you will eventually submit the paper electronically. Most people proofread more accurately when reading type on paper than when reading it on a computer screen. (At the same time, don't view the printed copy as error-free just because it's clean. Clean-looking copy may still harbor errors.)
- **Read the paper aloud,** very slowly, and distinctly pronounce exactly what you see.
- **Place a ruler under each line as you read it.**
- **Read "against copy,"** comparing your final draft one sentence at a time against the edited draft.
- **Ignore content.** To keep the content of your writing from distracting you, read the essay backward sentence by sentence. Or use your word processor to isolate each paragraph from its context by printing it on a separate page. (Of course, reassemble the paragraphs before submitting the paper.)

5e | Examining a sample final draft

Katy Moreno's final essay appears on these pages, typed in MLA format except for page numbers. Comments in the margins point out key features of the essay's content.

Katy Moreno

Professor Lacourse

English 110

14 Nov. 2008

Descriptive title

Can We Compete?

College Education for the Global Economy

Introduction

Today's students cannot miss news stories about globalization of the economy and outsourcing of jobs, but are students aware of how these trends are affecting the job market? In "It's a Flat World, After All,"

Thomas L. Friedman argues that most US students are not preparing themselves as well as students in India, China, and other countries to compete in today's economy, which requires hard-working, productive scientists and engineers. Friedman's argument speaks to me because my mother lost her job when it was outsourced to India. But her experience taught a lesson that Friedman overlooks: technical training by itself can be too narrow to produce the communicators and problem solvers needed by contemporary businesses.

> Thesis statement: basic disagreement with Friedman

Friedman describes a "flat" world where recent technology like the Internet and wireless communication makes it possible for college graduates all over the globe to compete for high-paying jobs that once belonged to graduates of US colleges and universities. He focuses on workers in India and China who graduate from college with excellent educations in math and science, who are eager for new opportunities, and who are willing to work exceptionally hard, often harder than their American counterparts, and for less money. Friedman argues that US students must be better prepared academically, especially in math and science, so that they can get and keep jobs that will otherwise go overseas.

> Summary of Friedman's article

> No source citation for Friedman because paragraph summarizes entire article and mentions Friedman's name

At first glance, my mother's experience of losing her job might seem to support Friedman's argument that better training in math and science is the key to competing in the global job market. However, her experience adds dimensions to the globalization story that Friedman misses. First, my mother had the kind of strong background in math and science that Friedman says today's workers need. She majored in computer science, rose within the information technology (IT) department of a large company, and consistently received good performance reviews. Still, when her employer decided to outsource most of its IT work, my mother lost her job. The reason wasn't that her technical skills were inadequate; instead, her salary and benefits cost the company more than outsourcing her job did. Until wages rise around the globe, jobs like my mother's will be vulnerable, no matter how well a person is trained.

> Transition to disagreements with Friedman

> First disagreement with Friedman

> Examples to support first disagreement

> Example to qualify first disagreement

> Clarification of first disagreement

The second dimension that Friedman misses is that a number of well-paid people in my mother's IT department, namely IT managers, were not laid off. As my mother explained at the time, they kept their jobs because they were experienced at figuring out the company's IT needs, planning for changes, researching and proposing solutions, and communicating in writing and speech—skills that her more narrow training and experience had missed. Friedman misses these skills by focusing only on technical training. Without the ability to solve problems creatively and to communicate,

> Second disagreement with Friedman

> Explanation of second disagreement

> Conclusion summarizing both disagreements with Friedman

people with technical expertise alone may not have enough to save their jobs, as my mother learned.

Like my mother, I am more comfortable in front of a computer than I am in front of a group of people, and I had planned to major in computer science. Since my mother lost her job, however, I have decided to take courses in English and history as well. Classes in these subjects will require me to read broadly, think critically, research, and communicate ideas in writing—in short, to develop skills that make managers. When I enter the job market, my well-rounded education will make me a more attractive job candidate and will help me to become the kind of forward-thinking manager that US companies will always need to employ here in the US.

Many jobs that require a college degree are indeed going overseas, as Thomas L. Friedman says, and my classmates and I need to be ready for a rapidly changing future. But rather than focus only on math and science, we need to broaden our academic experiences so that the skills we develop make us not only employable but also indispensable.

Final point: business needs and author's personal goals

Explanation of final point

Conclusion recapping points of agreement and disagreement with Friedman and summarizing essay

Work Cited

Work cited in MLA style (see MLA p. 473)

Friedman, Thomas L. "It's a Flat World, After All." *New York Times Magazine* 3 Apr. 2005: 32–37. Print.

5f | Revising collaboratively

In many writing courses students work together on writing, most often commenting on each other's work to help with revision. This collaborative writing gives experience in reading written work critically and in reaching others through writing. Collaboration may occur face to face in small groups, via drafts and comments on paper, or on computers.

Whether you collaborate in person, on paper, or on a computer, you will be more comfortable and helpful and will benefit more from others' comments if you follow a few guidelines.

Commenting on others' writing

- **Be sure you know what the writer is saying.** If necessary, summarize the paper to understand its content. (See **2** pp. 72–74.)
- **Address only your most significant concerns with the work.** Use the revision checklist on p. 27 as a guide to what is significant. Unless you have other instructions, ignore mistakes in grammar, punctuation, and the like. (The temptation to focus on such errors may be especially strong if the writer is less experienced than you are with standard American English.) Emphasizing mistakes will contribute little to the writer's revision.

- **Remember that you are the reader, not the writer.** Don't edit sentences, add details, or otherwise assume responsibility for the paper.
- **Phrase your comments carefully.** Avoid misunderstandings by making sure comments are both clear and respectful. If you are responding on paper or online, not face to face with the writer, remember that the writer has nothing but your written words to go on. He or she can't ask you for immediate clarification and can't infer your attitudes from gestures, facial expressions, and tone of voice.
- **Be specific.** If something confuses you, say *why*. If you disagree with a conclusion, say *why*.
- **Be supportive as well as honest.** Tell the writer what you like about the paper. Word comments positively: instead of *This paragraph doesn't interest me,* say *You have an interesting detail here that I almost missed.* Question the writer in a way that emphasizes the effect of the work on you, the reader: *This paragraph confuses me because. . . .* And avoid measuring the work against a set of external standards: *This essay is poorly organized. Your thesis statement is inadequate.*
- **While reading, make your comments in writing.** Even if you will be delivering your comments in person later on, the written record will help you recall what you thought.
- **Link comments to specific parts of a paper.** Especially if you are reading the paper on a computer, be clear about what in the paper each comment relates to. You can embed your comments directly into the paper, distinguishing them with highlighting or color, or you can use a word processor's Comment function.

Benefiting from comments on your writing

- **Think of your readers as counselors or coaches.** They can help you see the virtues and flaws in your work and sharpen your awareness of readers' needs.
- **Read or listen to comments closely.**
- **Know what the critic is saying.** If you need more information, ask for it, or consult the appropriate section of this handbook.
- **Don't become defensive.** Letting comments offend you will only erect a barrier to improvement in your writing. As one writing teacher advises, "Leave your ego at the door."
- **Revise your work in response to appropriate comments,** even if you are not required to do so. You will learn more from actually revising than from just thinking about it.
- **Remember that you are the final authority on your work.** You should be open to suggestions, but you are free to decline advice when you think it is inappropriate.

■ **Keep track of both the strengths and weaknesses others identify.** Then in later assignments you can build on your successes
and give special attention to problem areas.

CULTURE LANGUAGE In some cultures writers do not expect criticism
from readers, or readers do not expect to think and
speak critically about what they read. If critical responses are uncommon in your native culture, collaboration may at first be uncomfortable for you. As a writer, think of a draft or even a final paper as
more an exploration of ideas than the last word on your subject;
then you may be more receptive to readers' suggestions. As a reader,
allow yourself to approach a text skeptically, and know that your
tactful questions and suggestions will usually be considered appropriate.

5g Preparing a writing portfolio

Your writing instructor may ask you to assemble samples of
your writing into a portfolio, or folder, once or more during the
course. Such a portfolio gives you a chance to consider all your
writing over a period and to showcase your best work.

Although the requirements for portfolios vary, most instructors
are looking for a range of writing that demonstrates your progress
and strengths as a writer. You, in turn, see how you have advanced
from one assignment to the next, as you've had time for new knowledge to sink in and time for practice. Instructors often allow students to revise papers before placing them in the portfolio, even if
the papers were submitted earlier. In that case, every paper in the
portfolio can benefit from all your learning.

An assignment to assemble a writing portfolio will probably also
provide guidelines for what to include, how the portfolio will be
evaluated, and how (or whether) it will be weighted for a grade. Be
sure you understand the purpose of the portfolio and who will read
it. For instance, if your composition instructor will be the only
reader and his or her guidelines encourage you to show evidence of
progress, you might include a paper that took big risks but never entirely succeeded. In contrast, if a committee of instructors will read
your work and the guidelines urge you to demonstrate your competence as a writer, you might include only papers that did succeed.

Unless the guidelines specify otherwise, provide error-free
copies of your final drafts, label all your samples with your name,
and assemble them all in a folder. Add a cover letter or memo that
lists the samples, explains why you've included each one, and evaluates your progress as a writer. The self-evaluation involved should
be a learning experience for you and will help your readers assess
your development as a writer.

6 Paragraphs

A **paragraph** is a group of related sentences set off by a beginning indention or, sometimes, by extra space. Paragraphs give you and your readers a breather from long stretches of text, and they indicate key steps in the development of your thesis.

This chapter discusses the three qualities of an effective body paragraph: unity (below), coherence (next page), and development (p. 46). In addition, the chapter discusses two special kinds of paragraphs: introductions and conclusions (pp. 50 and 52).

CULTURE LANGUAGE Not all cultures share the paragraphing conventions of American academic writing. In some other languages, writing moves differently from English—not from left to right, but from right to left or down rows from top to bottom. Even in languages that move as English does, writers may not use paragraphs at all. Or they may use paragraphs but not state the central ideas or provide transitional expressions to show readers how sentences relate. If your native language is not English and you have difficulty with paragraphs, don't worry about paragraphing during drafting. Instead, during a separate step of revision, divide your text into parts that develop your main points. Mark those parts with indentions.

6a   Maintaining paragraph unity

An effective paragraph develops one central idea—in other words, it is **unified.** Here is an example:

> Some people really like chili, apparently, but nobody can agree how the stuff should be made. C. V. Wood, twice winner at Terlingua, uses flank steak, pork chops, chicken, and green chilis. My friend Hughes Rudd of CBS News, who imported five hundred pounds of chili powder into Russia as a condition of accepting employment as Moscow correspondent, favors coarse-ground beef. Isadore Bleckman, the cameraman I must live with on the road, insists upon one-inch cubes of stew beef and puts garlic in his chili, an Illinois affectation. An Indian of my acquaintance, Mr. Fulton Batisse, who eats chili for breakfast when he can, uses buffalo meat and plays an Indian drum while it's cooking. I ask you.
> —Charles Kuralt, *Dateline America*

Checklist for revising paragraphs

- **Is the paragraph unified?** Does it adhere to one general idea that is either stated in a topic sentence or otherwise apparent? (See previous page and below.)
- **Is the paragraph coherent?** Do the sentences follow a clear sequence? Are the sentences linked as needed by parallelism, repetition or restatement, pronouns, consistency, and transitional expressions? (See below.)
- **Is the paragraph developed?** Is the general idea of the paragraph well supported with specific evidence such as details, facts, examples, and reasons? (See p. 46.)

Kuralt's paragraph works because it follows through on its central idea, which is stated in the first sentence, the **topic sentence.** After the topic sentence, each of the next four sentences offers an example of a chili concoction. (In the final sentence Kuralt comments on the examples.)

What if instead Kuralt had written his paragraph as follows? Here the topic of chili preparation is forgotten mid-paragraph, as the sentences digress to describe life in Moscow:

> Some people really like chili, apparently, but nobody can agree how the stuff should be made. C. V. Wood, twice winner at Terlingua, uses flank steak, pork chops, chicken, and green chilis. My friend Hughes Rudd, who imported five hundred pounds of chili powder into Russia as a condition of accepting employment as Moscow correspondent, favors coarse-ground beef. He had some trouble finding the beef in Moscow, though. He sometimes had to scour all the markets and wait in long lines. For any American used to overstocked supermarkets and department stores, Russia can be quite a shock.

Instead of following through on its topic sentence, the paragraph loses its way. It is not unified.

A topic sentence need not always come first in the paragraph. For instance, it may come last, presenting your idea only after you have provided the evidence for it. Or it may not be stated at all, especially in narrative or descriptive writing in which the point becomes clear in the details. But always the idea should govern the paragraph's content as if it were standing guard at the opening.

6b Achieving paragraph coherence

When a paragraph is **coherent,** readers can see how it holds together: the sentences seem to flow logically and smoothly into one another. Exactly the opposite happens with this paragraph:

> The ancient Egyptians were masters of preserving dead people's bodies by making mummies of them. Mummies several thousand years old have been discovered nearly intact. The skin, hair, teeth, finger- and toenails, and facial features of the mummies were evident. One can diagnose the diseases they suffered in life, such as smallpox, arthritis, and nutritional deficiencies. The process was remarkably effective. Sometimes apparent were the fatal afflictions of the dead people: a middle-aged king died from a blow on the head, and polio killed a child king. Mummification consisted of removing the internal organs, applying natural preservatives inside and out, and then wrapping the body in layers of bandages.

The paragraph is hard to read. The sentences lurch instead of gliding from point to point.

The paragraph as it was actually written appears below. It is much clearer because the writer arranged information differently and also built links into his sentences so that they would flow smoothly:

- After stating the central idea in a topic sentence, the writer moves to two more specific explanations and illustrates the second with four sentences of examples.
- (Circled words) repeat or restate key terms or concepts.
- Boxed words link sentences and clarify relationships.
- Underlined phrases are in parallel grammatical form to reflect their parallel content.

Central idea
The ancient Egyptians were masters of preserving dead people's bodies by making mummies of them. Basically, mummification consisted of removing the internal organs, applying natural preservatives inside and out, and then wrapping the body in layers of bandages. And the process was remarkably effective. Indeed, mummies several thousand years old have been discovered nearly intact. Their skin, hair, teeth, finger- and toenails, and facial features are still evident. Their diseases in life, such as smallpox, arthritis, and nutritional deficiencies, are still diagnosable. Even their fatal afflictions are still apparent: a middle-aged king died from a blow on the head; a child king died from polio.

—Mitchell Rosenbaum (student), "Lost Arts of the Egyptians"

1 Paragraph organization

A coherent paragraph organizes information so that readers can easily follow along. These are common paragraph schemes:

- **General to specific:** Sentences downshift from more general statements to more specific ones. (See the paragraph by Rosenbaum on the previous page.)
- **Climactic:** Sentences increase in drama or interest, ending in a climax. (See the paragraph below about sleep.)
- **Spatial:** Sentences scan a person, place, or object from top to bottom, from side to side, or in some other way that approximates the way people actually look at things. (See the paragraph by Woolf on p. 46.)
- **Chronological:** Sentences present events as they occurred in time, earlier to later. (See the paragraph by LaFrank on p. 44.)

2 Parallelism

Parallelism helps tie sentences together. In the following paragraph the underlined parallel structures of *She* and a verb link all sentences to the first one. Parallelism also appears *within* many of the sentences. Aphra Behn (1640–89) was the first Englishwoman to write professionally.

> In addition to her busy career as a writer, Aphra Behn also found time to briefly marry and spend a little while in debtor's prison. She found time to take up a career as a spy for the English in their war against the Dutch. She made the long and difficult voyage to Suriname [in South America] and became involved in a slave rebellion there. She plunged into political debate at Will's Coffee House and defended her position from the stage of the Drury Lane Theater. She actively argued for women's rights to be educated and to marry whom they pleased, or not at all. She defied the seventeenth-century dictum that ladies must be "modest" and wrote freely about sex.
>
> —Angeline Goreau, "Aphra Behn"

3 Repetition and restatement

Repeating or restating key words helps make a paragraph coherent and also reminds readers what the topic is. In the following paragraph note the underlined repetition of *sleep* and the restatement of *adults*.

> Perhaps the simplest fact about sleep is that individual needs for it vary widely. Most adults sleep between seven and nine hours, but occasionally people turn up who need twelve hours or so, while some rare types can get by on three or four. Rarest of all are those legendary types

---

Key term

parallelism The use of similar grammatical structures for similar elements of meaning within or among sentences: *The book caused a stir in the media and aroused debate in Congress.* (See also **3** pp. 154–56.)

who require almost no sleep at all; respected researchers have studied three such people. One of them—a healthy, happy woma her seventies—sleeps about an hour every two or three days. The othe two are men in early middle age, who get by on a few minutes a night. One of them complains about the daily fifteen minutes or so he's forced to "waste" in sleeping.

—Lawrence A. Mayer, "The Confounding Enemy of Sleep"

4 Pronouns

Because pronouns refer to nouns, they can help relate sentences to each other. In the paragraph opposite by Angeline Goreau, *she* works just this way by substituting for *Aphra Behn* in every sentence after the first.

5 Consistency

Consistency (or the lack of it) occurs primarily in the person and number of nouns and pronouns and in the tense of verbs. Any inconsistencies not required by meaning will interfere with a reader's ability to follow the development of ideas.

Note the underlined inconsistencies in the next paragraphs:

Shifts in tense

In the Hopi religion, water is the driving force. Since the Hopi lived in the Arizona desert, they needed water urgently for drinking, cooking, and irrigating crops. Their complex beliefs are focused in part on gaining the assistance of supernatural forces in obtaining water. Many of the Hopi kachinas, or spirit essences, were directly concerned with clouds, rain, and snow.

Shifts in number

Kachinas represent the things and events of the real world, such as clouds, mischief, cornmeal, and even death. A kachina is not worshiped as a god but regarded as an interested friend. They visit the Hopi from December through July in the form of men who dress in kachina costumes and perform dances and other rituals.

Shifts in person

Unlike the man, the Hopi woman does not keep contact with kachinas through costumes and dancing. Instead, one receives a small

---

Key terms

pronoun A word that refers to and functions as a noun, such as *I, you, he, she, it, we, they: The bush had a beehive in it.* (See **4** p. 191.)

tense The form of a verb that indicates the time of its action, such as present (*I run*), past (*I ran*), or future (*I will run*). (See **4** p. 227.)

number The form of a noun, pronoun, or verb that indicates whether it is singular (one) or plural (more than one): *boy is, boys are.*

nina, called a *tihu*, from the man impersonating the
more likely to receive a tihu as a girl approaching mar-
child or older woman may receive one, too.

ckers A grammar checker cannot help you locate
mber, or person among sentences. Shifts are some-
(as when tenses change to reflect actual differences
rmore, a passage with needless shifts may still consist oɪ ͻ‿ s that are grammatically correct, as all the sentences
are in the preceding examples.

6 Transitional expressions

Transitional expressions such as *therefore, in contrast,* or *meanwhile* can forge specific connections between sentences, as do the
underlined expressions in this paragraph:

> Medical science has <u>thus</u> succeeded in identifying the hundreds of
> viruses that can cause the common cold. It has <u>also</u> discovered the most
> effective means of prevention. One person transmits the cold viruses to
> another most often by hand. <u>For instance</u>, an infected person covers his
> mouth to cough. He <u>then</u> picks up the telephone. <u>Half an hour later</u>, his
> daughter picks up the <u>same</u> telephone. <u>Immediately afterward</u>, she rubs
> her eyes. <u>Within a few days</u>, she, <u>too</u>, has a cold. <u>And thus</u> it spreads. To
> avoid colds, <u>therefore</u>, people should wash their hands often and keep
> their hands away from their faces.
> —Kathleen LaFrank (student), "Colds: Myth and Science"

Note that you can use transitional expressions to link paragraphs as
well as sentences. In the first sentence of LaFrank's paragraph, the
word *thus* signals that the sentence refers to an effect discussed in
the preceding paragraph.

The following box lists many transitional expressions by the
functions they perform.

Transitional expressions

To add or show sequence

again, also, and, and then, besides, equally important, finally, first, further, furthermore, in addition, in the first place, last, moreover, next, second, still, too

To compare

also, in the same way, likewise, similarly

Key term

person The form of a pronoun that indicates whether the subject is
speaking (first person: *I, we*), spoken to (second person: *you*), or spoken
about (third person: *he, she, it, they*). All nouns are in the third person.

To contrast

although, and yet, but, but at the same time, despite, even so, even though, for all that, however, in contrast, in spite of, nevertheless, notwithstanding, on the contrary, on the other hand, regardless, still, though, yet

To give examples or intensify

after all, an illustration of, even, for example, for instance, indeed, in fact, it is true, of course, specifically, that is, to illustrate, truly

To indicate place

above, adjacent to, below, elsewhere, farther on, here, near, nearby, on the other side, opposite to, there, to the east, to the left

To indicate time

after a while, afterward, as long as, as soon as, at last, at length, at that time, before, earlier, eventually, formerly, immediately, in the meantime, in the past, lately, later, meanwhile, now, presently, shortly, simultaneously, since, so far, soon, subsequently, suddenly, then, thereafter, until, until now, when

To repeat, summarize, or conclude

all in all, altogether, as has been said, in brief, in conclusion, in other words, in particular, in short, in simpler terms, in summary, on the whole, that is, therefore, to put it differently, to summarize

To show cause or effect

accordingly, as a result, because, consequently, for this purpose, hence, otherwise, since, then, therefore, thereupon, thus, to this end, with this object

Note Draw carefully on this list of transitional expressions because the ones in each group are not interchangeable. For instance, *besides*, *finally*, and *second* may all be used to add information, but each has its own distinct meaning.

CULTURE LANGUAGE If transitional expressions are not common in your native language, you may be tempted to compensate when writing in English by adding them to the beginnings of most sentences. But such explicit transitions aren't needed everywhere, and in fact too many can be intrusive and awkward. When inserting transitional expressions, consider the reader's need for a signal: often the connection from sentence to sentence is already clear from the context or can be made clear by relating the content of sentences more closely (see **3** pp. 146–47). When you do need transitional expressions, try varying their positions in your sentences, as illustrated in the sample paragraph on the facing page.

6c Developing paragraphs

An effective, well-developed paragraph always provides the specific information that readers need and expect in order to understand you and to stay interested in what you say. Paragraph length can be a rough gauge of development: anything much shorter than 100 to 150 words may leave readers with a sense of incompleteness.

To develop or shape an idea in a paragraph, one or more of the following patterns may help. (These patterns may also be used to develop entire essays. See p. 13.)

1 Narration

Narration retells a significant sequence of events, usually in the order of their occurrence (that is, chronologically). A narrator is concerned not just with the sequence of events but also with their consequence, their importance to the whole.

> Jill's story is typical for "recruits" to religious cults. She was very lonely in college and appreciated the attention of the nice young men and women who lived in a house near campus. They persuaded her to share their meals and then to move in with them. Between intense bombardments of "love," they deprived her of sleep and sometimes threatened to throw her out. Jill became increasingly confused and dependent, losing touch with any reality besides the one in the group. She dropped out of school and refused to see or communicate with her family. Before long she, too, was preying on lonely college students.
> —Hillary Begas (student), "The Love Bombers"

2 Description

Description details the sensory qualities of a person, scene, thing, or feeling, using concrete and specific words to convey a dominant mood, illustrate an idea, or achieve some other purpose.

> The sun struck straight upon the house, making the white walls glare between the dark windows. Their panes, woven thickly with green branches, held circles of impenetrable darkness. Sharp-edged wedges of light lay upon the window-sill and showed inside the room plates with blue rings, cups with curved handles, the bulge of a great bowl, the criss-cross pattern in the rug, and the formidable corners and lines of cabinets and bookcases. Behind their conglomeration hung a zone of shadow in which might be a further shape to be disencumbered of shadow or still denser depths of darkness. —Virginia Woolf, *The Waves*

3 Illustration or support

An idea may be developed with several specific examples, like those used by Charles Kuralt on p. 40, or with a single extended example, as in the next paragraph:

The language problem that I was attacking loomed larger and larger as I began to learn more. When I would describe in English certain concepts and objects enmeshed in Korean emotion and imagination, I became slowly aware of nuances, of differences between two languages even in simple expression. The remark "Kim entered the house" seems to be simple enough, yet, unless a reader has a clear visual image of a Korean house, his understanding of the sentence is not complete. When a Korean says he is "in the house," he may be in his courtyard, or on his porch, or in his small room! If I wanted to give a specific picture of entering the house in the Western sense, I had to say "room" instead of house—sometimes. I say "sometimes" because many Koreans entertain their guests on their porches and still are considered to be hospitable, and in the Korean sense, going into the "room" may be a more intimate act than it would be in the English sense. Such problems!

—Kim Yong Ik, "A Book-Writing Venture"

Sometimes you can develop a paragraph by providing your reasons for stating a general idea. For instance:

There are three reasons, quite apart from scientific considerations, that mankind needs to travel in space. The first reason is the need for garbage disposal: we need to transfer industrial processes into space, so that the earth may remain a green and pleasant place for our grandchildren to live in. The second reason is the need to escape material impoverishment: the resources of this planet are finite, and we shall not forgo forever the abundant solar energy and minerals and living space that are spread out all around us. The third reason is our spiritual need for an open frontier: the ultimate purpose of space travel is to bring to humanity not only scientific discoveries and an occasional spectacular show on television but a real expansion of our spirit.

—Freeman Dyson, "Disturbing the Universe"

4 Definition

Defining a complicated, abstract, or controversial term often requires extended explanation. The following definition comes from an essay asserting that "quality in product and effort has become a vanishing element of current civilization." Notice how the writer pins down meaning with examples and contrasts.

In the hope of possibly reducing the hail of censure which is certain to greet this essay (I am thinking of going to Alaska or possibly Patagonia in the week it is published), let me say that quality, as I understand it, means investment of the best skill and effort possible to produce the finest and most admirable result possible. Its presence or absence in some degree characterizes every manmade object, service, skilled or unskilled labor—laying bricks, painting a picture, ironing shirts, practicing medicine, shoemaking, scholarship, writing a book. You do it well or you do it half-well. Materials are sound and durable or they are sleazy; method is painstaking or whatever is easiest. Quality is achieving or reaching for the highest standard as against being satisfied with the sloppy or fraudulent. It is honesty of purpose as against catering to cheap or sensational sentiment. It does not allow compromise with the second-rate.   —Barbara Tuchman, "The Decline of Quality"

5 Division or analysis

With division or analysis, you separate something into its elements—for instance, you might divide a newspaper into its sections. You may also approach the elements critically, interpreting their meaning and significance (see also **2** pp. 81–83):

> The surface realism of the soap opera conjures up an illusion of "liveness." The domestic settings and easygoing rhythms encourage the viewer to believe that the drama, however ridiculous, is simply an extension of daily life. The conversation is so slow that some have called it "radio with pictures." (Advertisers have always assumed that busy housewives would listen, rather than watch.) Conversation is casual and colloquial, as though one were eavesdropping on neighbors. There is plenty of time to "read" the character's face; close-ups establish intimacy. The sets are comfortably familiar: well-lit interiors of living rooms, restaurants, offices, and hospitals. Daytime soaps have little of the glamour of their prime-time relations. The viewer easily imagines that the conversation is taking place in real time.
>
>   —Ruth Rosen, "Search for Yesterday"

6 Classification

When you classify items, you sort them into groups. The classification allows you to see and explain the relations among the items. The following paragraph identifies three groups, or classes, of parents:

> In my experience, the parents who hire daytime sitters for their school-age children tend to fall into one of three groups. The first group includes parents who work and want someone to be at home when the children return from school. These parents are looking for an extension of themselves, someone who will give the care they would give if they were at home. The second group includes parents who may be home all day themselves but are too disorganized or too frazzled by their children's demands to handle child care alone. They are looking for an organizer and helpmate. The third and final group includes parents who do not want to be bothered by their children, whether they are home all day or not. Unlike the parents in the first two groups, who care for their children however they can, these parents seek a permanent substitute for themselves.   —Nancy Whittle (student), "Modern Parenting"

7 Comparison and contrast

Comparison and contrast may be used separately or together to develop an idea. The following paragraph illustrates one of two common ways of organizing a comparison and contrast: **subject by subject,** first one subject and then the other.

> Consider the differences also in the behavior of rock and classical music audiences. At a rock concert, the audience members yell, whistle, sing along, and stamp their feet. They may even stand during the entire performance. The better the music, the more active they'll be. At a classical concert, in contrast, the better the performance, the more *still* the audience is. Members of the classical audience are so highly disciplined that they refrain from even clearing their throats or coughing. No matter what effect the powerful music has on their intellects and feelings, they sit on their hands.
> —Tony Nahm (student), "Rock and Roll Is Here to Stay"

The next paragraph illustrates the other common organization: **point by point,** with the two subjects discussed side by side and matched feature for feature:

> Arguing is often equated with fighting, but there are key differences between the two. Participants in an argument approach the subject to find common ground, or points on which both sides agree, while people engaged in a fight usually approach the subject with an "us-versus-them" attitude. Participants in an argument are careful to use respectful, polite language, in contrast to the insults and worse that people in a fight use to get the better of their opponents. Finally, participants in an argument commonly have the goal of reaching a new understanding or larger truth about the subject they're debating, while those in a fight have winning as their only goal.
> —Erica Ito (student),"Is an Argument Always a Fight?"

8 Cause-and-effect analysis

When you use analysis to explain why something happened or what did or may happen, then you are determining causes or effects. In the following paragraph the author looks at the cause of an effect—Japanese collectivism:

> The *shinkansen* or "bullet train" speeds across the rural areas of Japan giving a quick view of cluster after cluster of farmhouses surrounded by rice paddies. This particular pattern did not develop purely by chance, but as a consequence of the technology peculiar to the growing of rice, the staple of the Japanese diet. The growing of rice requires the construction and maintenance of an irrigation system, something that takes many hands to build. More importantly, the planting and the harvesting of rice can only be done efficiently with the cooperation of twenty or more people. The "bottom line" is that a single family working alone cannot produce enough rice to survive, but a dozen families working together can produce a surplus. Thus the Japanese have had to develop the capacity to work together in harmony, no matter what the forces of disagreement or social disintegration, in order to survive. —William Ouchi, *Theory Z*

9 Process analysis

When you analyze how to do something or how something works, you explain a process. The following example identifies a process, describes the equipment needed, and details the steps in the process:

> As a car owner, you waste money when you pay a mechanic to change the engine oil. The job is not difficult, even if you know little about cars. All you need is a wrench to remove the drain plug, a large, flat pan to collect the draining oil, plastic bottles to dispose of the used oil, and fresh oil. First, warm up the car's engine so that the oil will flow more easily. When the engine is warm, shut it off and remove its oil-filler cap (the owner's manual shows where this cap is). Then locate the drain plug under the engine (again consulting the owner's manual for its location) and place the flat pan under the plug. Remove the plug with the wrench, letting the oil flow into the pan. When the oil stops flowing, replace the plug and, at the engine's filler hole, add the amount and kind of fresh oil specified by the owner's manual. Pour the used oil into the plastic bottles and take it to a waste-oil collector, which any garage mechanic can recommend.
> —Anthony Andreas (student), "Do-It-Yourself Car Care"

6d Writing introductory and concluding paragraphs

1 Introductions

An introduction draws readers from their world into yours.

- It focuses readers' attention on the topic and arouses their curiosity about what you have to say.
- It specifies your subject and implies your attitude.
- Often it includes your thesis statement.
- It is concise and sincere.

The box below gives options for focusing readers' attention.

Some strategies for introductions

- Ask a question.
- Relate an incident.
- Use a vivid quotation.
- Create a visual image that represents your subject.
- Offer a surprising statistic or other fact.
- Provide background.
- State an opinion related to your thesis.

- Outline the argument your thesis refutes.
- Make a historical comparison or contrast.
- Outline a problem or dilemma.
- Define a word central to your subject.
- In some business or technical writing, simply state your main idea.

(CULTURE LANGUAGE) These options for an introduction may not be what you are used to if your native language is not English. In other cultures readers may seek familiarity or reassurance from an author's introduction, or they may prefer an indirect approach to the subject. In academic and business English, however, writers and readers prefer concise, direct expression.

Effective openings

A very common introduction opens with a statement of the essay's general subject, clarifies or limits the subject in one or more sentences, and then asserts the point of the essay in the thesis statement (underlined in the following examples):

> Can your home or office computer make you sterile? Can it strike you blind or dumb? The answer is: probably not. Nevertheless, reports of side effects relating to computer use should be examined, especially in the area of birth defects, eye complaints, and postural difficulties. Although little conclusive evidence exists to establish a causal link between computer use and problems of this sort, the circumstantial evidence can be disturbing. —Thomas Hartmann,
> "How Dangerous Is Your Computer?"

> The Declaration of Independence is so widely regarded as a statement of American ideals that its origins in practical politics tend to be forgotten. Thomas Jefferson's draft was intensely debated and then revised in the Continental Congress. Jefferson was disappointed with the result. However, a close reading of both the historical context and the revisions themselves indicates that the Congress improved the document for its intended purpose. —Ann Weiss (student), "The Editing of the Declaration of Independence"

In much public writing, it's more important to tell readers immediately what your point is than to try to engage them. This introduction to a brief memo quickly outlines a problem and (in the thesis statement) suggests a way to solve it:

> Starting next month, the holiday rush and staff vacations will leave our department short-handed. We need to hire two or perhaps three temporary keyboarders to maintain our schedules for the month.

Additional effective introductions appear in sample papers elsewhere in this book: p. 34, **2** p. 112, **8** p. 446 and **MLA** p. 510.

Openings to avoid

When writing and revising your introduction, avoid approaches that are likely to bore or confuse readers:

- **A vague generality or truth.** Don't extend your reach too wide with a line such as *Throughout human history . . .* or *In today's world. . . .* You may have needed a warm-up paragraph to start drafting, but your readers can do without it.

- **A flat announcement.** Don't start with *The purpose of this essay is . . .* , *In this essay I will . . .* , or any similar presentation of your intention or topic.
- **A reference to the essay's title.** Don't refer to the title of the essay in the first sentence—for example, *This is a big problem* or *This book is about the history of the guitar.*
- **According to Webster. . . .** Don't start by citing a dictionary definition. A definition can be an effective springboard to an essay, but this kind of lead-in has become dull with overuse.
- **An apology.** Don't fault your opinion or your knowledge with *I'm not sure if I'm right, but I think . . .* , *I don't know much about this, but . . .* , or a similar line.

2 Conclusions

Your conclusion finishes off your essay and tells readers where you think you have brought them. It answers the question "So what?"

Effective conclusions

Usually set off in its own paragraph, the conclusion may consist of a single sentence or a group of sentences. It may take one or more of the approaches listed in the box below.

Some strategies for conclusions

- Recommend a course of action.
- Summarize the paper.
- Echo the approach of the introduction.
- Restate your thesis and reflect on its implications.
- Strike a note of hope or despair.
- Give a symbolic or powerful fact or other detail.
- Give an especially compelling example.
- Create an image that represents your subject.
- Use a quotation.

The following paragraph concludes the essay on the Declaration of Independence whose introduction appears on the previous page. The writer both summarizes her essay and echoes her introduction.

> The Declaration of Independence has come to be a statement of this nation's political philosophy, but that was not its purpose in 1776. Jefferson's passionate expression had to bow to the goals of the Congress as a whole to forge unity among the colonies and to win the support of foreign nations. —Ann Weiss (student), "The Editing of the Declaration of Independence"

In the next paragraph the author concludes an essay on environmental protection with a call for action:

> Until we get the answers, I think we had better keep on building power plants and growing food with the help of fertilizers and such insect-controlling chemicals as we now have. The risks are well known, thanks to the environmentalists. If they had not created a widespread public awareness of the ecological crisis, we wouldn't stand a chance. But such awareness by itself is not enough. Flaming manifestos and prophecies of doom are no longer much help, and a search for scapegoats can only make matters worse. The time for sensations and manifestos is about over. Now we need rigorous analysis, united effort and very hard work.
>
> —Peter F. Drucker,
> "How Best to Protect the Environment"

Conclusions to avoid

Several kinds of conclusions rarely work well:

- **A repeat of the introduction.** Don't simply replay your introduction. The conclusion should capture what the paragraphs of the body have added to the introduction.
- **A new direction.** Don't introduce a subject different from the one your essay has been about.
- **A sweeping generalization.** Don't conclude more than you reasonably can from the evidence you have presented. If your essay is about your frustrating experience trying to clear a parking ticket, you cannot reasonably conclude that *all* local police forces are too tied up in red tape to be of service to the people.
- **An apology.** Don't cast doubt on your essay. Don't say, *Even though I'm no expert* or *This may not be convincing, but I believe it's true* or anything similar. Rather, to win your readers' confidence, display confidence.

7 Document Design

Imaginehowharditwouldbetoreadandwriteiftextlookedlikethis. To make reading and writing easier, we place spaces between words. This convention and many others—such as page margins, paragraph breaks, and headings—have evolved over time to help writers communicate clearly with readers.

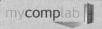

my**comp**lab

Visit *mycomplab.com* for more resources as well as exercises on document design.

7a Designing academic papers and other documents

The design guidelines offered in this chapter apply to all types of documents, including academic papers, Web sites, business reports, flyers, and newsletters. Each type has specific requirements as well, covered elsewhere in this book.

1 Designing academic papers

Many academic disciplines prefer specific formats for students' papers. This book details two such formats:

- **Modern Language Association,** used in English, foreign languages, and other humanities (**MLA** pp. 506–08).
- **American Psychological Association,** used in the social sciences and some natural and applied sciences (**APA** pp. 539–42).

Other academic formats can be found in the discipline style guides listed in **8** pp. 451, 455, and 459.

The design guidelines in this chapter extend the range of elements and options covered by most academic styles. Your instructors may want you to adhere strictly to a particular style or may allow some latitude in design. Ask them for their preferences.

2 Writing online

In and out of school, you are likely to do a lot of online writing—certainly e-mail and possibly blogs and other Web sites. The purposes and audiences for online writing vary widely, and so do readers' expectations for its design. See **2** pp. 116–25 for the approaches you can take in different online writing situations.

3 Designing business documents and other public writing

When you write outside your college courses, your audience will have certain expectations for how your documents should look and read. Guidelines for such writing appear later in this book:

- **Public writing,** including letters, job applications, reports, proposals, flyers, newsletters, and brochures (**2** pp. 129–40).
- **Oral presentations,** including *PowerPoint* slides and other visual aids (**2** pp. 125–29).

7b Considering principles of design

Most of the principles of design respond to the ways we read. White space, for instance, relieves our eyes and helps to lead us through a document. Groupings or lists help to show relationships.

Type sizes, images, and color add variety and help to emphasize important elements.

The sample documents shown on pp. 56–57 illustrate quite different ways of presenting a report for a marketing course. Even at a glance, the second document is easier to scan and read. It makes better use of white space, groups similar elements, uses bullets and fonts for emphasis, and more successfully integrates the visual data of the chart.

As you design your own documents, think about your purpose, the expectations of your readers, and how readers will move through your document. Also consider the following general principles, noting that they overlap and support one another:

- **Conduct readers through the document.** Establish flow, a pattern for the eye to follow, with headings, lists, and other elements.

- **Use white space to ease crowding and focus readers' attention.** Provide ample margins, and give breathing room to headings, lists, and other elements. Even the space indicating new paragraphs (indentions or blank lines) gives readers a break and reassures them that ideas are divided into manageable chunks.

- **Group information to show relationships.** Use headings (like those in this chapter) and lists (like the one you're reading) to convey the similarities and differences among parts of a document.

- **Emphasize important elements.** Establish hierarchies of information with type fonts and sizes, headings, indentions, color, boxes, and white space. In this book, for example, the importance of headings is clear from their size and color and from the presence of decorative elements, such as the box around 7c in the heading below.

- **Standardize to create and fulfill expectations.** Help direct readers through a document by, for instance, using the same size and color for all headings at the same level of importance. Standardizing also reduces clutter, making it easier for readers to determine the significance of the parts.

7c Using the elements of design

Applying the preceding principles involves margins, text, lists, headings, color, and illustrations. You won't use all these elements for every project, and in many writing situations you will be required to follow a prescribed format (see opposite on formats in academic writing). If you are addressing readers who have vision loss, consider the additional guidelines discussed on pp. 65–66.

Original design

Runs title and subtitle together. Does not distinguish title from text.	Generation Online: College Students and the Internet
Crowds the page with minimal margins.	College life once meant classrooms of students listening to teachers or groups of students talking over lunch in the union. But the reality today is more complex: students interact with their peers and professors by computer as much as face to face. As these students graduate and enter the workforce, all of society will be affected by their experience.
Downplays paragraph breaks with small indentions.	According to the Pew Internet Research Center (2008), today's college students are practiced computer and Internet users. The Pew Center reports that 24 percent of students in college today started using computers between ages five and eight. By age eighteen all students were using computers. Almost all college students, 92 percent, rely on the Internet, with 66 percent of students using more than one e-mail address. Computer ownership among this group is also very high: 85 percent have purchased or have been given at least one computer.
Buries statistics in a paragraph. Obscures relationships with non-parallel wording.	Students are eager to tap into the Internet's benefits and convenience.

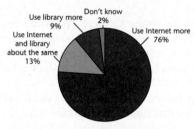

Use library more 9%
Use Internet and library about the same 13%
Don't know 2%
Use Internet more 76%

Does not introduce the figure, leaving readers to infer its meaning and purpose.	
Overemphasizes the figure with large size and excessive white space.	Figure 1
Presents the figure undynamically, flat on.	
Does not caption the figure to explain what it shows, offering only a figure number and a partial text explanation.	The Internet has eclipsed the library as the site of college students' research, as shown in Figure 1 from the Pew Report. In fact, a mere 9 percent of students

Note Your word processor may provide wizards or templates for many kinds of documents, such as letters, memos, reports, agendas, résumés, and brochures. **Wizards** guide you through setting up and writing complicated documents. **Templates** are preset forms to which you add your own text, headings, and other elements. Wizards and templates can be helpful, but not if they lead you to create cookie-cutter documents no matter what the writing situation. Always keep in mind that a document should be appropriate for your subject, audience, and purpose.

1 Setting margins

Margins at the top, bottom, and sides of a page help to prevent the page from overwhelming readers with unpleasant crowding. Most academic and business documents use a minimum one-inch margin on all sides. Publicity documents, such as flyers and bro-

Revised design

**Generation Online:
College Students and the Internet**

College life once meant classrooms of students listening to teachers or groups of students talking over lunch in the union. But the reality today is more complex: students interact with their peers and professors by computer as much as face to face. As these students graduate and enter the workforce, all of society will be affected by their experience.

According to the Pew Internet Research Center (2008), today's college students are practiced computer users and Internet users.

- They started young: 24 percent were using computers between ages five and eight, and all were using them by age eighteen.
- They rely on the Internet: 92 percent have used the network, and 66 percent use more than one e-mail address.
- They own computers: 85 percent have purchased or have been given at least one computer.

Students are eager to tap into the Internet's benefits and convenience. Figure 1, from the Pew Report, shows that the Internet has eclipsed the library as the site of college students' research. In fact, a mere 9 percent of students reported using the library more than the Internet as a starting point for research.

■9% ■2% ■76%
■13%

■ Use Internet more
■ Use Internet and library about the same
■ Use library more
■ Don't know

Figure 1. College students' use of the Internet and the library for research

Distinguishes title from subtitle and both from text.

Provides adequate margins.

Emphasizes paragraph breaks with white space.

Groups statistics in a bulleted list set off with white space. Uses parallel wording for parallel information.

Introduces the figure to indicate its meaning and purpose.

Reduces white space around the figure.

Presents the figure to emphasize the most significant segment.

Captions the figure so that it can be read independently from the text.

chures, often use narrower margins, compensating with white space between elements. (See **2** pp. 139–40.)

2 Creating readable text

A document must be readable. You can make text readable by attending to line spacing, type fonts and sizes, highlighting, word spacing, and line breaks.

Line spacing

Most academic documents are double-spaced, with an initial indention for paragraphs, while most business documents are single-spaced, with an extra line of space between paragraphs. Double or triple spacing sets off headings in both types. Web sites and publicity documents, such as flyers and brochures, tend to use more line spacing to separate and group distinct parts of the content.

Type fonts and sizes

The readability of text also derives from the type fonts (or faces) and their sizes. For academic and business documents, generally choose a type size of 10 or 12 points, as in these samples:

```
10-point Courier        10-point Times New Roman
12-point Courier        12-point Times New Roman
```

These fonts and the one you're reading have **serifs**—the small lines that finish the letters. Serif fonts are suitable for formal writing and are often easier to read on paper. **Sans serif** fonts (*sans* means "without" in French) include this one found on many word processors:

10-point Arial   **12-point Arial**

Sans serif fonts can be easier to read on a computer screen and are clearer on paper for readers with some vision loss (see p. 66).

Your word processor probably offers many decorative fonts:

10-point Bodega Sans   **10-POINT COMIC**
10-POINT STENCIL   *10-point Park Avenue*

Decorative fonts are generally inappropriate for academic and business writing, where letter forms should be conventional and regular. But on some Web sites and in publicity documents, decorative fonts can attract attention, create motion, and reinforce a theme.

Note The point size of a type font is often an unreliable guide to its actual size, as the decorative fonts above illustrate. Before you use a font, print out a sample to be sure it is the size you want.

Highlighting

Within a document's text, <u>underlined</u>, *italic*, **boldface,** or even color type can emphasize key words or sentences. Underlining is rarest these days, having been replaced by italics. Both academic and business writing sometimes use boldface for strong emphasis—as with a term being defined—and publicity documents often rely extensively on boldface to draw the reader's eye. Neither academic nor business writing generally uses color within passages of text. In Web and publicity documents, however, color may be effective if it is dark enough to be readable. (See p. 60 for more on color.)

No matter what your writing situation, use highlighting selectively to complement your meaning, not merely for decoration.

Word spacing

In most writing situations, follow these guidelines for spacing within and between words:

- Leave one space between words.
- Leave one space after all punctuation, with these exceptions:

Dash (two hyphens or the so-called em dash on a computer)	book--its	book—its
Hyphen	one-half	
Apostrophe within a word	book's	
Two or more adjacent marks	book.")	
Opening quotation mark, parenthesis, or bracket	("book	[book

■ **Leave one space before and after an ellipsis mark.** In the examples below, ellipsis marks indicate omissions within a sentence and at the end of a sentence. See **5** pp. 341–42 for additional examples.

book . . . in   book. . . . The

Line breaks

Your word processor will generally insert appropriate breaks between lines of continuous text: it will not, for instance, automatically begin a line with a comma or period, and it will not end a line with an opening parenthesis or bracket. However, you will have to prevent it from breaking a two-hyphen dash or a three-dot ellipsis mark by spacing to push the beginning of each mark to the next line.

When you instruct it to do so (usually under the Tools menu), your word processor will also automatically hyphenate words to prevent very short lines. If you must decide yourself where to break words, see **6** pp. 353–54.

3 Using lists

Lists give visual reinforcement to the relations between like items—for example, the steps in a process or the elements of a proposal. A list is easier to read than a paragraph and adds white space to the page.

When wording a list, work for parallelism among items—for instance, all complete sentences or all phrases (see also **3** p. 156). Set the list with space above and below and with numbering or bullets (centered dots or other devices, such as the blue squares used in this book). On most word processors you can format a numbered or bulleted list automatically using the Format menu.

4 Using headings

Headings are signposts: they direct the reader's attention by focusing the eye on a document's most significant content. Most Web and publicity documents use headings both decoratively and functionally, to capture and then direct readers' attention. In contrast, most academic and business documents use headings only functionally, to divide text, orient readers, and create emphasis.

When you use headings in academic and business documents, follow these guidelines:

- **Use one, two, or three levels of headings** depending on the needs of your material and the length of your document. Some level of heading every two or so pages will help keep readers on track.

- **Create an outline of your document** to plan where headings should go. Use the first level of heading for the main points (and sections) of your document. Use a second and perhaps a third level of heading to mark subsections of supporting information.

- **Keep headings as short as possible** while making them specific about the material that follows.

- **Word headings consistently**—for instance, all questions (*What Is the Scientific Method?*), all phrases with *-ing* words (*Understanding the Scientific Method*), or all phrases with nouns (*The Scientific Method*).

- **Indicate the relative importance of headings** with type size, positioning, and highlighting, such as capital letters, underlining, or boldface.

First-Level Heading

Second-Level Heading

Third-Level Heading

Generally, you can use the same type font and size for headings as for the text.

- **Don't break a page immediately after a heading.** Push the heading to the next page.

Note Document format in psychology and some other social sciences requires a particular treatment of headings. See **APA** pp. 539–41.

5 Using color

With a computer and a color printer, most writers can produce documents that use color for bullets, headings, borders, boxes, illustrations, and other elements. Web and publicity documents almost always use color, whereas academic and business documents consisting only of headings and text may not need color at all. (Ask your instructor or supervisor for his or her preferences.) If you do use color in an academic document, follow these guidelines:

- **Print text in black,** not red, blue, or another color.
- **Make sure that color headings are dark enough to be readable.**

- Stick to the same color for all headings at the same level—for instance, red for main headings, black for secondary headings.
- Use color for bullets, lines, and other nontext elements. But use no more than a few colors to keep pages clean.
- Use color to distinguish the parts of illustrations—the segments of charts, the lines of graphs, and the parts of diagrams. Use only as many colors as you need to make your illustration clear.

See also p. 66 on the use of color for readers who have vision loss.

7d Using illustrations

An illustration can often make a point for you more efficiently than words can. Tables present data. Figures (such as graphs and charts) usually recast data in visual form. Diagrams, drawings, and photographs can explain processes, represent what something looks like, or add emphasis.

1 Using illustrations appropriately for the writing situation

Academic and many business documents tend to use illustrations differently from publicity documents. In the latter, illustrations generally attract attention, enliven the piece, or emphasize a point, and they may not be linked directly to the document's text. In academic and business writing, however, illustrations directly reinforce and amplify the text. Follow these guidelines for academic and most business writing:

- **Focus on a purpose for each illustration**—a reason for including it and a point you want it to make. Otherwise, readers may find it irrelevant or confusing.
- **Provide a source note for someone else's independent material**—whether data or an entire illustration (see **7** p. 394). Each discipline has a slightly different style for such source notes: those in the illustrations on the next several pages reflect MLA style for English and some other humanities.
- **Number figures, photographs, and other images together:** Figure 1, Figure 2, and so on.
- **Number and label tables separately:** Table 1, Table 2, and so on.
- **Refer to each illustration in your text**—for instance, "See fig. 2." Place the reference at the point(s) in the text where readers will benefit by consulting the illustration.

■ **Determine the placement of illustrations.** The social sciences and some other disciplines require each illustration to fall on a page by itself immediately after the text reference to it (see **APA** p. 542). You may want to follow this rule in other situations as well if you have a large number of illustrations. Otherwise, you can embed them in your text pages just after you refer to them. When embedding illustrations, consider where they will help but not distract readers.

2 Using tables

Tables usually present raw data, making complex information accessible to readers. The data may show how variables relate to one another, how variables change over time, or how two or more groups contrast. The following table emphasizes the last function.

Table

A self-explanatory title falls above the table.	The layout of rows and columns is clear: headings align with their data, and numbers align vertically down columns.
Self-explanatory headings label horizontal rows and vertical columns.	

Table 1

Public- and private-school enrollment of US students age five and older, 2006

	Number of students	Percentage in public school	Percentage in private school
All students	74,220,937	83.2	16.8
Kindergarten	4,012,680	86.0	14.0
Grades 1-4	15,758,734	88.8	11.2
Grades 5-8	16,498,217	89.4	10.6
Grades 9-12	17,500,473	90.5	9.5
College (undergraduate)	17,063,732	77.0	23.0
Graduate and professional school	3,387,101	59.8	40.2

Source: Data from *2006 American Community Survey*; US Census Bureau, n.d.; Web; 10 Oct. 2008; table S1404.

3 Using figures

Figures represent data or show concepts visually. They include charts, graphs, diagrams, and photographs.

Pie charts

Pie charts show the relations among the parts of a whole. The whole totals 100 percent, and each pie slice is proportional in size to its share of the whole. Use a pie chart when shares, not the underlying data, are your focus.

Pie chart

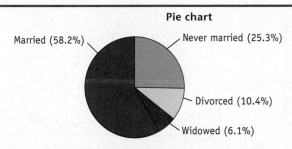

Color distinguishes segments of the chart. Use distinct shades of gray, black, and white if your paper will not be read in color.

Segment percentages total 100.

Every segment is clearly labeled. You can also use a key, as in the chart on p. 57.

Self-explanatory caption falls below the chart.

Fig. 1. Marital status in 2006 of adults age eighteen and over. Data from *Statistical Abstract of the United States: 2008*; US Census Bureau, 27 Mar. 2007; Web; 10 Oct. 2008.

Bar charts

Bar charts compare groups or time periods on a measure such as quantity or frequency. Use a bar chart when relative size is your focus. Be sure to start with a zero point in the lower left corner so that the values on the vertical axis are clear.

Bar chart

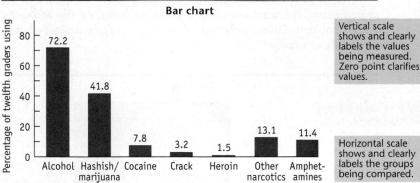

Vertical scale shows and clearly labels the values being measured. Zero point clarifies values.

Horizontal scale shows and clearly labels the groups being compared.

Self-explanatory caption falls below the chart.

Fig. 2. Lifetime prevalence of use of alcohol and other drugs among twelfth graders in 2007. Data from *Monitoring the Future: A Continuing Study of American Youth*; U of Michigan, 11 Dec. 2007; Web; 10 Aug. 2008.

Line graphs

Line graphs show change over time in one or more subjects. They are an economical and highly visual way to compare many points of data. Be sure to start with a zero point in the lower left corner so that the values on the vertical axis are clear.

Line graph

Vertical scale shows and clearly labels the values being measured. Zero point clarifies values.

Color and labels distinguish the subjects being compared. Use dotted and dashed black lines if your paper will not be read in color.

Horizontal scale shows and clearly labels the range of dates.

Self-explanatory caption falls below the graph.

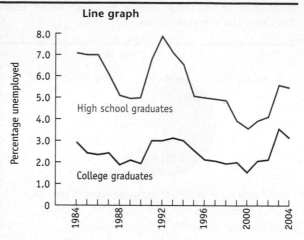

Fig. 3. Unemployment rates of high school graduates and college graduates, 1984-2004. Data from Antony Davies; *The Economics of College Tuition*; Mercatus Center, George Mason U, 3 Mar. 2005; Web; 26 June 2008.

Diagrams

Diagrams show concepts visually, such as the structure of an organization, the way something works or looks, or the relations among subjects. Often, diagrams show what can't be described economically in words.

Diagram

Diagram makes concept comprehensible.

Self-explanatory caption falls below the diagram.

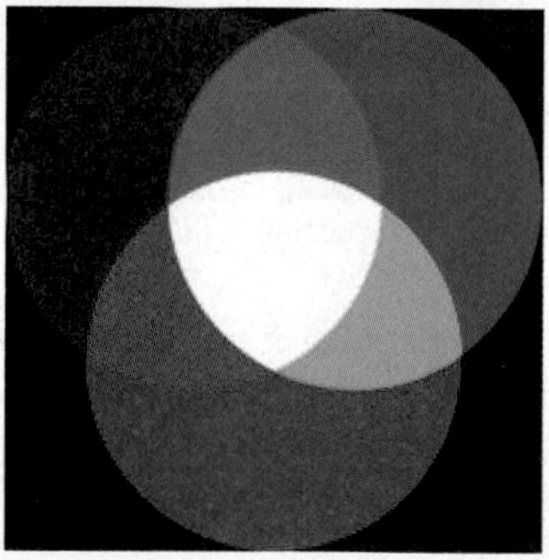

Fig. 4. RGB color theory, applied to televisions and computer monitors, in which all possible colors and white are created from red, green, and blue. From "Color Theory"; *Wikipedia*; Wikimedia, 15 Mar. 2005; Web; 13 May 2008.

Photographs and other images

Sometimes you may focus an entire paper on analyzing an image such as a photograph, painting, or advertisement. But most commonly you'll use images to add substance to ideas or to enliven them. You might clarify a psychology paper with a photograph from a key experiment, add information to an analysis of a novel with a drawing of the author, or capture the theme of a brochure with a cartoon. Images grab readers' attention, so use them carefully to explain, reinforce, or enhance your writing.

Note When using an image prepared by someone else—for instance, a photograph downloaded from the Web—you must verify that the source permits reproduction of the image before you use it. In most documents, but especially in academic papers, you must also fully cite the source of any borrowed image. See **7** pp. 429–30 on copyright issues with Internet sources.

Photograph

Photograph shows subject more economically and dramatically than words could.

Fig. 5. View of Saturn from the *Cassini* spacecraft, showing the planet and its rings. From *Cassini-Huygens: Mission to Saturn and Titan*; US Natl. Atmospheric and Space Administration, Jet Propulsion Laboratory, 24 Feb. 2005; Web; 26 Apr. 2008.

Self-explanatory caption falls below the image.

7e Considering readers with vision loss

Your audience may include readers who have low vision, problems with color perception, or difficulties processing visual information. If so, consider adapting your design to meet these readers' needs. Here are a few pointers:

- **Use large type fonts.** Most guidelines call for 14 points or larger.
- **Use standard type fonts.** Many people with low vision find it easier to read sans serif fonts such as Arial than serif fonts (see

p. 58). Avoid decorative fonts with unusual flourishes, even in headings.

- Avoid words in all-capital letters.
- **Avoid relying on color alone to distinguish elements.** Label elements, and distinguish them by position or size.
- **Use red and green selectively.** To readers who are red-green colorblind, these colors will appear in shades of gray, yellow, or blue.
- **Use contrasting colors.** To make colors distinct, choose them from opposite sides of the color spectrum—violet and yellow, for instance, or orange and blue.
- **Use only light colors for tints behind type.** Make the type itself black or a very dark color.

PART 2

Writing in and out of College

8 Academic Skills *69*

9 Critical Thinking and Reading *77*

10 Academic Writing *90*

11 Argument *97*

12 Online Writing *116*

13 Oral Presentations *125*

14 Public Writing *129*

Writing in and out of College

8 Academic Skills

When you take college courses, you enter an academic discipline—a community of instructors and students whose basic goal is to build knowledge about a subject, whether it is English, history, engineering, or something else. You participate in a discipline community first by studying a subject, acquiring its vocabulary, and learning to express yourself in its ways. As you gain experience and knowledge, you contribute to the community by asking questions and communicating your answers in writing. This active, involved learning is the core of academic work. It may seem beyond you at first, as you try to grasp the content of readings and identify important ideas. But the transition will be easier if you follow this chapter's advice for getting the most from your classes, understanding assigned reading, becoming an academic writer, and preparing for exams.

8a | Listening and taking notes in class

When you begin each class meeting, push aside other concerns so that you can focus and listen. Either on paper or on a computer, record what you hear as completely as possible while sorting out the main ideas from the secondary and supporting ones. (See the box below.) Such active note taking will help you understand the instructor's approach to the course and provide you with complete material for later study.

Tips for taking class notes

- **Use your own words.** You will understand and retain the material better if you rephrase it. But use the speaker's words if necessary to catch everything.
- **Leave space in your notes if you miss something.** Ask someone for the missing information as soon as possible after class.
- **Include any reading content mentioned by your instructor.** Use your notes to integrate all the components of the course—your instructor's views, your own thoughts, and the assigned reading.

(continued)

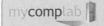

Visit *mycomplab.com* for more resources on academic skills.

Tips for taking class notes
(continued)

■ **Review your notes shortly after class.** Reinforce your new knowledge when it is fresh by underlining key words and ideas, adding headings and comments in the margins, converting your notes to questions, or outlining the lecture based on your notes.

8b Reading for comprehension

The assigned reading you do for college courses—such as textbooks, journal articles, essays, and works of literature—requires a greater focus on understanding and retention than does the reading you do for entertainment or for practical information. The process outlined below may seem time consuming, but with practice you'll become efficient at it.

Note The following process stresses ways of understanding what you read. In critical reading, covered in the next chapter, you extend this process to analyze and evaluate what you read and see.

1 Writing while reading

Reading for comprehension is an *active* process. Students often believe they are reading actively when they roll a highlighter over the important ideas in a text, but truly engaged reading requires more than that. If you take notes while reading, you "translate" the work into your own words and reconstruct it for yourself.

The substance of your reading notes will change as you preview, read, and summarize. At first, you may jot quick, short notes in the margins, on separate pages, or on a computer. (Use the last two for material you don't own or are reading online.) As you delve into the work, the notes should become more detailed, restating important points, asking questions, connecting ideas. (See p. 80 for an example of a text annotated in this way by a student.) For some reading, you may want to keep a reading journal that records both what the work says and what you think about it.

2 Previewing

For most course reading, you should skim before reading word for word. Skimming gives you an overview of the material: its length and difficulty, organization, and principal ideas.

- **Gauge length and level.** Is the material brief and straightforward enough to read in one sitting, or do you need more time?
- **Examine the title and introduction.** The title and first couple of paragraphs will give you a sense of the topic, the author's approach, and the main ideas. As you read them, ask yourself what you already know about the subject so that you can integrate new information with old.
- **Move from heading to heading or paragraph to paragraph.** Viewing the headings as headlines or as the levels of an outline will give you a feeling for which ideas the author sees as primary and which subordinate. In a text without headings, reading the first sentence of each paragraph will give you a sense of the author's important ideas.
- **Note highlighted words.** You will likely need to learn the meanings of terms in **bold**, *italic*, or color.
- **Slow down for pictures, diagrams, tables, graphs, and other illustrations.** They often contain concentrated information.
- **Read the summary or conclusion.** These paragraphs often recap the main ideas.
- **Think over what you've skimmed.** Try to recall the central idea, or thesis, and the sequence of ideas.

3 Reading

After previewing a text, you can settle into it to learn what it has to say.

First reading

The first time through new material, read as steadily and smoothly as possible, trying to get the gist of what the author is saying.

- **Read in a place where you can concentrate.** Choose a quiet environment away from distractions such as music or talking.
- **Give yourself time.** Rushing yourself or worrying about something else you have to do will prevent you from grasping what you read.
- **Try to enjoy the work.** Seek connections between it and what you already know. Appreciate new information, interesting relationships, forceful writing, humor, good examples.
- **Make notes sparingly during this first reading.** Mark major stumbling blocks—such as a paragraph you don't understand—so that you can try to resolve them before rereading.

CULTURE LANGUAGE If English is not your first language and you come across unfamiliar words don't stop and look up every one. You will lose more in concentration than you will gain in understanding. Instead, try to guess the meanings of unfamiliar words from their contexts, circle them, and look them up later.

Rereading

After the first reading, plan on at least one other. This time read *slowly*. Your main concern should be to grasp the content and how it is constructed. That means rereading a paragraph if you didn't get the point or using a dictionary to look up words you don't know.

Use your pen, pencil, or keyboard freely to highlight and distill the text:

- **Distinguish main ideas from supporting ideas.** Look for the central idea, or thesis, for the main idea of each paragraph or section, and for the evidence supporting ideas.
- **Learn key terms.** Understand both their meanings and their applications.
- **Discern the connections among ideas.** Be sure you see why the author moves from point A to point B to point C and how those points work together to support the central idea. It often helps to outline the text or summarize it (see below).
- **Add your own comments.** In the margins or separately, note links to other readings or to class discussions, questions to explore further, possible topics for your writing, points you find especially strong or weak. (This last category will occupy much of your time when you are expected to read critically. See pp. 81–83.)

4 | Summarizing

A good way to master the content of a text is to summarize it: reduce it to its main points, in your own words.

Writing a summary

- **Understand the meaning.** Look up words or concepts you don't know so that you understand the author's sentences and how they relate to one another.
- **Understand the organization.** Work through the text to identify its sections—single paragraphs or groups of paragraphs focused on a single topic. To understand how parts of a work relate to one another, try drawing a tree diagram or creating an outline (1 pp. 18–21).
- **Distill each section.** Write a one- or two-sentence summary of each section you identify. Focus on the main point of the section, omitting examples, facts, and other supporting evidence.

- **State the main idea.** Write a sentence or two capturing the author's central idea.
- **Support the main idea.** Write a full paragraph (or more, if needed) that begins with the central idea and supports it with the sentences that summarize sections of the work. The paragraph should concisely and accurately state the thrust of the entire work.
- *Use your own words.* By writing, you re-create the meaning of the work in a way that makes sense for you.

Summarizing even a passage of text can be tricky. Below is one attempt to summarize the following material from an introductory biology textbook.

Original text

As astronomers study newly discovered planets orbiting distant stars, they hope to find evidence of water on these far-off celestial bodies, for water is the substance that makes possible life as we know it here on Earth. All organisms familiar to us are made mostly of water and live in an environment dominated by water. They require water more than any other substance. Human beings, for example, can survive for quite a few weeks without food, but only a week or so without water. Molecules of water participate in many chemical reactions necessary to sustain life. Most cells are surrounded by water, and cells themselves are about 70–95% water. Three-quarters of Earth's surface is submerged in water. Although most of this water is in liquid form, water is also present on Earth as ice and vapor. Water is the only common substance to exist in the natural environment in all three physical states of matter: solid, liquid, and gas.

—Neil A. Campbell and Jane B. Reece, *Biology*

Draft summary

Astronomers look for water in outer space because life depends on it. It is the most common substance on Earth and in living cells, and it can be a liquid, a solid (ice), or a gas (vapor).

This summary accurately restates ideas in the original, but it does not pare the passage to its essence. The work of astronomers and the three physical states of water add color and texture to the original, but they are asides to the key concept that water sustains life because of its role in life. The following revision narrows the summary to this concept:

Revised summary

Water is the most essential support for life—the dominant substance on Earth and in living cells and a component of life-sustaining chemical processes.

Note Do not count on the AutoSummarize function on your word processor for summarizing texts that you may have copied onto your computer. The summaries are rarely accurate, and you will not gain the experience of interacting with the texts on your own.

8c Becoming an academic writer

As a member of an academic community, you will communicate with other members mainly through writing. Chapter 10 provides a detailed introduction to academic writing, and **8** (Chapters 55–57) treats writing in specific disciplines. The disciplines do differ in their conventions for writing, but in all of them you will be expected to do the following:

- **Know the writing situation posed in each assignment.** Most assignments will at least suggest possible subjects and imply a purpose and an audience. In that context, you refine your subject, your purpose, and your sense of audience as you proceed through the writing process. For a review of assessing the writing situation, see **1** pp. 3–5.
- **Develop and organize your writing.** Most academic papers center on a main point, or thesis, and support the thesis with evidence. For more on developing a thesis and organizing a paper, see **1** pp. 14–21.
- **Synthesize your own and others' ideas.** Academic writing often involves interacting with the works of other writers—responding to them, comparing them, and using them to answer questions. Such interaction requires you to read critically (the subject of the next chapter) and to **synthesize**, or integrate, others' ideas into your own. For more on synthesis, see p. 92.
- **Revise and edit your writing.** Academic writing is careful writing. Allow yourself enough time to revise and edit so that readers can see your main ideas, follow your train of thought, and make sense of your sentences. Consult this book's revision and editing checklists in **1** pp. 27 and 31.
- **Acknowledge your sources.** Academic writers build on the work of others by fully crediting borrowed ideas and information. Always record the publication information of any source you consult so that you can cite it if you decide to use it later in your writing. See **7** pp. 423–30 for a discussion of avoiding plagiarism. For guides to specific documentation styles, see **MLA** pp. 464–505 (English and some other humanities), **APA** pp. 521–39 (social sciences), **Chic** pp. 549–59 (history, philosophy,

and other humanities), and **CSE** pp. 560–66 (natural and applied sciences).

8d Preparing for exams

Studying for an exam involves three main steps, each requiring about a third of the preparation time: reviewing the material, organizing summaries of the material, and testing yourself. Your main goals are to strengthen your understanding of the subject, making both its ideas and its details more memorable, and to increase the flexibility of your new knowledge so that you can apply it in new contexts.

Note Cramming for an exam is about the least effective way of preparing for one. It takes longer to learn under stress, and the learning is shallower, more difficult to apply, and more quickly forgotten. Information learned under stress is even harder to apply in stressful situations such as taking an exam. And the lack of sleep that usually accompanies cramming makes a good performance even more unlikely. If you must cram for a test, face the fact that you can't learn everything. Spend your time reviewing main concepts and facts.

1 Reviewing and memorizing the material

Divide your class notes and reading assignments into manageable units. Reread the material, recite or write out the main ideas and selected supporting ideas and examples, and then skim for an overview. Proceed in this way through all the units of the course, returning to earlier ones as needed to refresh your memory or to relate ideas.

During this stage you should be memorizing what you don't already know by heart. Try these strategies for strengthening your memory:

- **Link new and known information.** For instance, to remember a sequence of four dates in twentieth-century African history, link the dates to simultaneous and more familiar events in the United States.
- **Create groups of ideas or facts that make sense to you.** For instance, memorize French vocabulary words in related groups, such as words for parts of the body or parts of a house. Keep the groups small: research has shown that we can easily memorize about seven items at a time but have trouble with more.
- **Create narratives and visual images.** You may recall a story or a picture more easily than words. For instance, to remember

how the economic laws of supply and demand affect the market for rental housing, you could tie the principles to a narrative about the aftermath of the 1906 San Francisco earthquake, when half the population was suddenly homeless. Or you could visualize a person who has dollar signs for eyes and is converting a spare room into a high-priced rental unit, as many did after the earthquake to meet the new demand for housing.

- Use *mnemonic devices*, or tricks for remembering. Say the history dates you want to remember are separated by five years, then four, then nine. By memorizing the first date and recalling $5 + 4 = 9$, you'll have command of all four dates.

2 Organizing summaries of the material

Allow time to reorganize the material in your own way, creating categories that will help you apply the information in various contexts. For instance, in studying for a biology exam, work to understand a process, such as how a plant develops or how photosynthesis occurs. Or in studying for an American government test, explain the structures of the local, state, and federal levels of government. Other useful categories include advantages/disadvantages and causes/effects. Such analytical thinking will improve your mastery of the course material and may even prepare you directly for specific essay questions.

3 Testing yourself

Convert each heading in your lecture notes and course reading into a question. Answer in writing, going back to the course material to fill in what you don't yet know. Be sure you can define and explain all key terms. For subjects that require solving problems (such as mathematics, statistics, or physics), work out a difficult problem for every type on which you will be tested. For all subjects, focus on the main themes and questions of the course. In a psychology course, for example, be certain you understand principal theories and their implications. In a literature course, test your knowledge of literary movements and genres or the relations among specific works.

When you are satisfied with your preparation, stop studying. If your exam is the next day, get as much sleep as your schedule allows. You will be able to think more clearly on exam day if you are rested.

9 Critical Thinking and Reading

Throughout college and beyond, you will be expected to think, read, and write critically. **Critical** here does not mean "negative" but "skeptical," "exacting," "creative." You already operate critically every day as you figure out why things happen to you or what your experiences mean. This chapter introduces more formal methods for reading texts critically (below), developing a critical response (p. 81), and viewing images critically (p. 83).

Note Critical thinking plays a large role in research writing. See **7** pp. 399–410 on evaluating print and online sources and **7** pp. 410–11 on synthesizing sources.

9a | Using techniques of critical reading

In college and work, much of your critical thinking will focus on written texts (a short story, a journal article, a blog) or on visual objects (a photograph, a chart, a film). Like all subjects worthy of critical consideration, such works operate on at least three levels: (1) what the creator actually says or shows, (2) what the creator does not say or show explicitly but builds into the work (intentionally or not), and (3) what you think. Discovering the first of these levels—reading for comprehension—is discussed in the preceding chapter as part of academic skills (see pp. 70–72). This chapter builds on the earlier material to help you discover the other two levels.

CULTURE LANGUAGE The idea of reading critically may require you to make some adjustments if readers in your native culture tend to seek understanding or agreement more than engagement from what they read. Readers of English use texts for all kinds of reasons, including pleasure, reinforcement, and information. But they also read skeptically, critically, to see the author's motives, test their own ideas, and arrive at new knowledge.

1 Previewing the material

When you're reading a work of literature, such as a short story or a poem, it's often best just to plunge right in. But for critical reading of other works, it's worthwhile to skim before reading word for word, forming expectations and even some preliminary questions. The preview will make your reading more informed and fruitful.

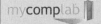

Visit *mycomplab.com* for more resources on critical thinking and reading.

77

- **What is the work's subject and structure?** Following the steps outlined on p. 71, gauge the length and level, read the title and introduction for clues to the topic and main ideas, read the headings, note highlighted words (defined terms), examine illustrations, and read the summary or conclusion.
- **What are the facts of publication?** Does the date of publication suggest currency or datedness? Does the publisher or publication specialize in a particular kind of material—for instance, scholarly articles or popular books? For a Web document, who or what sponsors the site: an individual? a nonprofit organization? an academic institution? a corporation? a government body?
- **What do you know about the author?** Does a biography tell you about the author's publications, interests, biases, and reputation in the field? For an online source, which may be posted by an unfamiliar or anonymous author, what can you gather about the author from his or her words? If possible, trace unfamiliar authors to learn more about them.
- **What is your preliminary response?** What do you already know about the author's subject? What questions do you have about either the subject or the author's approach to it? What biases of your own might influence your reception of the work—for instance, curiosity, boredom, or an outlook similar or opposed to the author's?

Reprinted on these pages is an essay by Thomas Sowell, an economist, newspaper columnist, and author of many books on economics, politics, and education. The essay was first published in the 1990s, but the debate over student loans has never died down. Preview the essay using the preceding guidelines, and then read it once or twice, until you think you understand what the author is saying. Note your questions and reactions in writing.

Student Loans

The first lesson of economics is scarcity: There is never enough of 1 anything to fully satisfy all those who want it.

The first lesson of politics is to disregard the first lesson of econom- 2 ics. When politicians discover some group that is being vocal about not having as much as they want, the "solution" is to give them more. Where do politicians get this "more"? They rob Peter to pay Paul.

After a while, of course, they discover that Peter doesn't have 3 enough. Bursting with compassion, politicians rush to the rescue. Needless to say, they do not admit that robbing Peter to pay Paul was a dumb idea in the first place. On the contrary, they now rob Tom, Dick, and Harry to help Peter.

The latest chapter in this long-running saga is that politicians have 4 now suddenly discovered that many college students graduate heavily in debt. To politicians it follows, as the night follows the day, that the government should come to their rescue with the taxpayers' money.

How big is this crushing burden of college students' debt that we 5 hear so much about from politicians and media deep thinkers? For those students who graduate from public colleges owing money, the debt averages a little under $7000. For those who graduate from private colleges owing money, the average debt is a little under $9000.

Buying a very modestly priced automobile involves more debt than 6 that. And a car loan has to be paid off faster than the ten years that college graduates get to repay their student loans. Moreover, you have to keep buying cars every several years, while one college education lasts a lifetime.

College graduates of course earn higher incomes than other peo- 7 ple. Why, then, should we panic at the thought that they have to repay loans for the education which gave them their opportunities? Even graduates with relatively modest incomes pay less than 10 percent of their annual salary on the first loan the first year—with declining percentages in future years, as their pay increases.

Political hysteria and media hype may focus on the low-income 8 student with a huge debt. That is where you get your heart-rending stories—even if they are not all that typical. In reality, the soaring student loans of the past decade have resulted from allowing high-income people to borrow under government programs.

Before 1978, college loans were available through government pro- 9 grams only to students whose family income was below some cut-off level. That cut-off level was about double the national average income, but at least it kept out the Rockefellers and the Vanderbilts. But, in an era of "compassion," Congress took off even those limits.

That opened the floodgates. No matter how rich you were, it still 10 paid to borrow money through the government at low interest rates. The money you had set aside for your children's education could be invested somewhere else, at higher interest rates. Then, when the student loan became due, parents could pay it off with the money they had set aside—pocketing the difference in interest rates.

To politicians and the media, however, the rapidly growing loans 11 showed what a great "need" there was. The fact that many students welshed when time came to repay their loans showed how "crushing" their burden of debt must be. In reality, those who welsh typically have smaller loans, but have dropped out of college before finishing. People who are irresponsible in one way are often irresponsible in other ways.

No small amount of the deterioration of college standards has been 12 due to the increasingly easy availability of college to people who are not very serious about getting an education. College is not a bad place to hang out for a few years, if you have nothing better to do, and if someone else is paying for it. Its costs are staggering, but the taxpayers carry much of that burden, not only for state universities and city colleges, but also to an increasing extent even for "private" institutions.

Numerous government subsidies and loan programs make it possi- 13 ble for many people to use vast amounts of society's resources at low cost to themselves. Whether in money terms or in real terms, federal aid to higher education has increased several hundred percent since 1970.

That has enabled colleges to raise their tuition by leaps and bounds and enabled professors to be paid more and more for doing less and less teaching.

Naturally all these beneficiaries are going to create hype and hysteria `14` to keep more of the taxpayers' money coming in. But we would be fools to keep on writing blank checks for them.

When you weigh the cost of things, in economics that's called `15` "trade-offs." In politics, it's called "mean-spirited." Apparently, if we just took a different attitude, scarcity would go away.

—Thomas Sowell

2 Reading

Reading is itself more than a one-step process. You want to understand the first level on which the text operates—what the author actually says—and begin to form your impressions.

A procedure for this stage appears in the preceding chapter (pp. 71–72). To recap: Read once through fairly smoothly, trying to appreciate the work and keeping your notes to a minimum. Then read again more carefully, this time making detailed notes, to grasp the ideas and their connections and to pose questions. In the following example, a student, Charlene Robinson, annotates the first four paragraphs of "Student Loans":

> The first lesson of economics is scarcity: There is never enough of anything to fully satisfy all those who want it.
>
> The first lesson of politics is to disregard the first lesson of economics. When politicians discover some group that is being vocal about not having as much as they want, the "solution" is to give them more. Where do politicians get this "more"? They rob Peter to pay Paul.
>
> After a while, of course, they discover that Peter doesn't have enough. Bursting with compassion, politicians rush to the rescue. Needless to say, they do not admit that robbing Peter to pay Paul was a dumb idea in the first place. On the contrary, they now rob Tom, Dick, and Harry to help Peter.
>
> The latest chapter in this long-running saga is that politicians have now suddenly discovered that many college students graduate heavily in debt. To politicians it follows, as the night follows the day, that the government should come to their rescue with the taxpayers' money.

Basic contradiction between economics and politics

← biblical reference?

← ironic and dismissive language

politicians = fools? or irresponsible

3 Summarizing

Summarizing a text—distilling it to its essential ideas, in your own words—is an important step for comprehending it and is discussed in detail in the previous chapter (pp. 72–74). Here, we'll look at how Charlene Robinson summarized paragraphs 1–4 of Thomas Sowell's "Student Loans." She first drafted this sentence:

Draft summary

As much as politicians would like to satisfy voters by giving them everything they ask for, the government cannot afford a student loan program.

Reading the sentence and Sowell's paragraphs, Robinson saw that this draft misread the text by asserting that the government cannot afford student loans. She realized that Sowell's point is more complicated than that and rewrote her summary:

Revised summary

As their support of the government's student loan program illustrates, politicians ignore the economic reality that using resources to benefit one group (students in debt) involves taking the resources from another group (taxpayers).

Note Using your own words when writing a summary not only helps you understand the meaning but also constitutes the first step in avoiding plagiarism. The second step is to cite the source when you use it in something written for others. See **7** pp. 423–30.

9b Developing a critical response

Once you've grasped the content of what you're reading—what the author says—then you can turn to understanding what the author does not say outright but suggests or implies or even lets slip. At this stage you are concerned with the purpose or intention of the author and with how he or she carries it out.

Critical thinking and reading consist of four overlapping operations: analyzing, interpreting, synthesizing, and (often) evaluating.

1 Analyzing

Analysis is the separation of something into its parts or elements, the better to understand it. To see these elements in what you are reading, begin with a question that reflects your purpose in analyzing the text: why you're curious about it or what you're trying to make out of it. This question will serve as a kind of lens that highlights some features and not others.

Analyzing Thomas Sowell's "Student Loans" (pp. 78–80), you might ask one of these questions:

Questions for analysis	Elements
What is Sowell's attitude toward politicians?	References to politicians: content, words, tone
How does Sowell support his assertions about the loan program's costs?	Support: evidence, such as statistics and examples

2 Interpreting

Identifying the elements of something is only a start: you also need to interpret the meaning or significance of the elements and of the whole. Interpretation usually requires you to infer the author's **assumptions**—opinions or beliefs about what is or what could or should be. (*Infer* means to draw a conclusion based on evidence.)

Assumptions are pervasive: we all adhere to certain values, beliefs, and opinions. But assumptions are not always stated outright. Speakers and writers may judge that their audience already understands and accepts their assumptions; they may not even be aware of their assumptions; or they may deliberately refrain from stating their assumptions for fear that the audience will disagree. That is why your job as a critical thinker is to interpret what the assumptions are.

Thomas Sowell's "Student Loans" is based on certain assumptions, some obvious, some not. Analyzing Sowell's attitude toward politicians requires focusing on the statements about them. They "disregard the first lesson of economics" (paragraph 2), which implies that they ignore important principles (knowing that Sowell is an economist himself makes this a reasonable assumption). Politicians also "rob Peter to pay Paul," are "[b]ursting with compassion," "do not admit . . . a dumb idea," are characters in a "long-running saga," and arrive at the solution of spending taxes "as the night follows the day"—that is, inevitably (paragraphs 2–4). From these statements and others, we can infer the following:

> Sowell assumes that politicians become compassionate when a cause is loud and popular, not necessarily just, and they act irresponsibly by trying to solve the problem with other people's (taxpayers') money.

3 Synthesizing

If you stopped at analysis and interpretation, critical thinking and reading might leave you with a pile of elements and possible meanings but no vision of the whole. With **synthesis** you make connections among parts *or* among wholes. You use your perspective—your knowledge and beliefs—to create a new whole by drawing conclusions about relationships and implications.

A key component of academic reading and writing, synthesis receives attention in the next chapter (p. 92) and then in the context of research writing (see **7** pp. 410–11). Sometimes you'll respond directly to a text, as in the following statement about Thomas Sowell's essay "Student Loans," which connects Sowell's assumptions about politicians to a larger idea also implied by the essay:

> Sowell's view that politicians are irresponsible with taxpayers' money reflects his overall opinion that the laws of economics, not politics, should drive government.

Often synthesis will take you outside the text to its surroundings. The following questions can help you investigate the context of a work:

■ **How does the work compare with works by others?** For instance, how have other writers responded to Sowell's views on student loans?

■ **How does the work fit into the context of other works by the same author or group?** How do Sowell's views on student loans typify, or not, the author's other writing on political and economic issues?

■ **What cultural, economic, or political forces influence the work?** What other examples might Sowell have given to illustrate his view that economics, not politics, should determine government spending?

■ **What historical forces influence the work?** How has the indebtedness of college students changed over the past four decades?

4 Evaluating

Critical reading and writing often end at synthesis: you form and explain your understanding of what the work says and doesn't say. If you are also expected to **evaluate** the work, however, you will go further to judge its quality and significance. You may be evaluating a source you've discovered in research (see **7** pp. 399–410), or you may be completing an assignment to state and defend a judgment, such as *Thomas Sowell does not summon the evidence to support his case.* You can read Charlene Robinson's critical response to Thomas Sowell's "Student Loans" by following the links in the e-book version of this handbook at *mycomplab.com.*

Evaluation takes a certain amount of confidence. You may think that you lack the expertise to cast judgment on another's work, especially if the work is difficult or the author well known. True, the more informed you are, the better a critical reader you are. But conscientious reading and analysis will give you the internal authority to judge a work *as it stands* and *as it seems to you*, against your own unique bundle of experiences, observations, and attitudes.

9c Viewing images critically

Every day we are bombarded with images—pictures on billboards, commercials on television, graphs and charts in newspapers and textbooks, to name just a few examples. Most images slide by without our noticing them, or so we think. But images, sometimes even more than text, can influence us covertly. Their creators have purposes, some worthy, some not, and understanding those purposes requires critical reading. The method parallels that in the previous section for reading text critically: preview, read for comprehension, analyze, interpret, synthesize, and (often) evaluate.

1 Previewing an image

Your first step in exploring an image is to form initial impressions of the work's origin and purpose and to note distinctive features. This previewing process is like the one for previewing a text (pp. 77–78):

- **What do you see?** What is most striking about the image? What is its subject? What is the gist of any text or symbols? What is the overall effect of the image?
- **What are the facts of publication?** Where did you first see the image? Do you think the image was created especially for that location or for others as well? What can you tell about when the image was created?
- **What do you know about the person or group that created the image?** For instance, was the creator an artist, scholar, news organization, or corporation? What seems to have been the creator's purpose?
- **What is your preliminary response?** What about the image interests, confuses, or disturbs you? Are the form, style, and subject familiar or unfamiliar? How might your knowledge, experiences, and values influence your reception of the image?

If possible, print a copy of the image or scan it into your reading journal, and write comments in the image margins or separately.

2 Reading an image

Reading an image requires the same level of concentration as reading a text. Try to answer the following questions about the image. If some answers aren't clear at this point, skip the question until later.

- **What is the purpose of the image?** Is it mainly explanatory, conveying information, or is it argumentative, trying to convince readers of something or to persuade them to act? What information or point of view does it seem intended to get across?
- **Who is the intended audience for the image?** What does the source of the image, including its publication facts, tell about the image creator's expectations for readers' knowledge, interests, and attitudes? What do the features of the image itself add to your impression?
- **What do any words or symbols add to the image?** Whether located on the image or outside it (such as in a caption), do words

or symbols add information, focus your attention, or alter your impression of the image?

- ■ **What people, places, things, or action does the image show?** Does the image tell a story? Do its characters or other features tap into your knowledge, or are they unfamiliar?
- ■ **What is the form of the image?** Is it a photograph, advertisement, painting, graph, diagram, cartoon, or something else? How do its content and apparent purpose and audience relate to its form?

The illustration below shows the notes that a student, Matthew Greene, made on an advertisement for *BoostUp.org*.

Annotation of an image

Advertisement for *BoostUp.org*, 2007

3 Analyzing an image

Elements for analysis

As when analyzing a written work, you analyze an image by identifying its elements. The image elements you might consider appear in the box below. Keep in mind that an image is a visual *composition* whose every element likely reflects a deliberate effort to communicate. Still, few images include all the elements, and you can narrow the list further by posing a question about the image you are reading, as illustrated opposite.

Elements of images

- **Emphasis:** Most images pull your eyes to certain features: a graph line moving sharply upward, a provocative figure, bright color, thick lines, and so on. The cropping of a photograph or the date range in a chart will also reflect what the image creator considers important.

- **Narration:** Most images tell stories, whether in a sequence (a TV commercial or a graph showing changes over time) or at a single moment (a photograph, a painting, or a pie chart). Sometimes dialog or a title or caption contributes to the story.

- **Point of view:** The image creator influences responses by taking account of both the viewer's physical relation to the image subject—for instance, whether it is seen head-on or from above—and the viewer's assumed attitude toward the subject.

- **Arrangement:** Patterns among colors or forms, figures in the foreground and background, and elements that are juxtaposed or set apart contribute to the image's meaning and effect.

- **Color:** An image's colors can direct the viewer's attention and convey the creator's attitude toward the subject. Color may also suggest a mood, an era, a cultural connection, or another frame in which to view the image.

- **Characterization:** The figures and objects in an image have certain qualities—sympathetic or not, desirable or not, and so on. Their characteristics reflect the roles they play in the image's story.

- **Context:** The source of an image or the background in an image affects its meaning, whether it is a graph from a scholarly journal or a photo of a car on a sunny beach.

- **Tension:** Images often communicate a problem or seize attention with features that seem wrong, such as misspelled or misaligned words, distorted figures, or controversial relations between characters.

- **Allusions:** An **allusion** is a reference to something the audience is likely to recognize and respond to. Examples include a cultural symbol such as a dollar sign, a mythological figure such as a unicorn, or a familiar movie character such as Darth Vader from *Star Wars*.

Question for analysis

You can focus your analysis of elements by framing your main interest in the image as a question. Matthew Greene posed this question about the *BoostUp.org* ad: *Does the ad move readers to learn more about* BoostUp.org *and how they can help teens to graduate?* The question led Greene to focus on certain elements of the ad:

Image elements	Responses
Emphasis	The ad's grayness and placement of Kody at the far left puts primary emphasis on the boy's isolation. Danny R.'s message, breaking up the gray, receives secondary emphasis.
Narration	The taped-on message suggests a story and connection between Kody and Danny R. Danny R. might be a friend, relative, or mentor. Based on the direct appeal in the word bubble, it appears that Danny R. is trying to help Kody graduate by offering to help him with schoolwork.
Arrangement	The ad places Danny R. and Kody together on the left side of the page, with Danny's message a bright spot on the dull landscape. The appeal to help Kody graduate is subtle and set on its own—the last thing readers look at. It also pulls the elements together so that the ad makes sense.
Color	The lack of color in most of the photo emphasizes Kody's isolation. The whiteness of Danny R.'s message relieves the grayness, like a ray of hope.

Sample Web pages for analysis

The screen shots on the next page are from *AIDS Clock*, an interactive Web site sponsored by the United Nations Population Fund (*www.unfpa.org/aids_clock*). The top image is the home page, displaying a traditional world map. The bottom image appears when viewers click on "Resize the map": now each country's size reflects the number of its people who live with HIV, the virus that causes AIDS. (For example, South Africa grows while the United States shrinks.) The large red number in the upper right changes every fifteen seconds. The "Wake up video" to its left scrolls through photos of people along with text urging viewers to join the World AIDS Campaign. Try to answer the questions in the annotations above the screen shots.

4 Interpreting an image

The strategies for interpreting an image parallel those for interpreting a written text (p. 82). In this process you look more deeply at the elements, considering them in relation to the image creator's

Elements of Web pages

Emphasis and color: What elements on these pages draw your attention? How does color distinguish and emphasize elements?

Narration: What story do the two Web pages tell? What does each map contribute to the story? What does the red number contribute? (Notice that the number changes from the first screen to the second.)

Arrangement: What does the arrangement of elements on the pages contribute to the story being told?

Tension: How do you respond to the distorted map in the second image? What does the distortion contribute to your view of the Web site's effectiveness?

Context: How does knowing the Web site's sponsoring organization, the United Nations Population Fund, affect your response to these images?

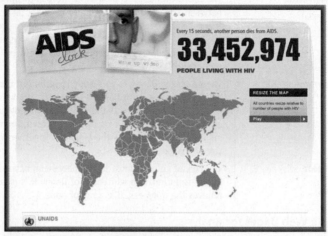

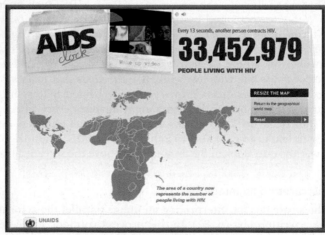

AIDS Clock Web pages, 2008

likely assumptions and intentions. You aim to draw reasonable inferences about *why* the image looks as it does, such as this inference about the *BoostUp.org* advertisement on page 85:

> The creators of the *BoostUp.org* ad assume that readers want students to graduate from high school.

This statement is supported by the ad's text: the word bubble connecting to the *BoostUp.org* logo specifically says, "Help Kody graduate at BoostUp.org."

5 Synthesizing ideas about an image

As discussed on pp. 82–83, with synthesis you take analysis and interpretation a step further to consider how a work's elements and underlying assumptions relate and what the overall message is. You may also expand your synthesis to view the whole image in a larger context: How does the work fit into the context of other works? What cultural, economic, political, or historical forces influence the work?

Placing an image in its context often requires research. For instance, to learn more about the assumptions underlying the *BoostUp.org* advertisement and the goals of the larger ad campaign, Matthew Greene visited the Web sites of *BoostUp.org* and the Ad Council, one of the ad's sponsors. The following entry from his reading journal synthesizes this research and his own ideas about the ad:

> The *BoostUp.org* magazine ad that features Kody is part of a larger campaign designed to raise public awareness about high school dropouts and encourage pubic support to help teens stay in school. Sponsored by the US Army and the nonprofit Ad Council, *BoostUp.org* profiles high school seniors who are at risk of dropping out and asks individuals to write the students personal messages of support. Ads like "Kody" are the first point of contact between the public and the teens, but they don't by themselves actually help the teens. For that, readers need to visit *BoostUp.org*. Thus the ad's elements work together like pieces of a puzzle, with the solution to be found only on the Web site.

6 Evaluating an image

If your critical reading moves on to evaluation, you'll form judgments about the quality and significance of the image: Is the message of the image accurate and fair, or is it distorted and biased? Can you support, refute, or extend the message? Does the image achieve its apparent purpose, and is the purpose worthwhile? How does the image affect you?

You can read Matthew Greene's response to the *BoostUp.org* advertisement by following the links in the e-book version of this handbook at *mycomplab.com*.

10 Academic Writing

The academic disciplines differ widely in their subjects and approaches, but they all share the common goal of building knowledge through questioning, research, and communication. The differences among disciplines lie mainly in the kinds of questions asked, the kinds of research done to find the answers, and the **genres,** or types of writing, used to communicate the answers, such as case studies, research reports, literary analyses, and reviews of others' writings.

Both a discipline's concerns and the kind of writing create an academic writing situation, which in turn shapes a writer's choice of subject, conception of audience, definition of purpose, choice of structure and content, and even choice of language. This chapter introduces academic writing situations in general. See **8** (Chapters 55–57) for the particular goals and expectations of writing about literature and in other humanities, the social sciences, and the natural and applied sciences.

10a Writing in response to texts

Academic knowledge building depends on reading, analyzing, and expanding on the work of others. Thus many academic writing assignments require you to respond to one or more texts—not only to written products such as short stories and journal articles but also to visual communications such as images, charts, films, and advertisements. As you form a response to a text, you will synthesize, or integrate, its ideas and information with yours to come to your own conclusions.

Note A common academic assignment, the research paper, expects you to consult and respond to multiple texts in order to support and extend your ideas. See **7** (Chapters 50–54). This section focuses on responding directly to a single text, but the skills involved apply to research writing as well.

1 Deciding how to respond

When an assignment asks you to respond directly to a text, you might take one of the following approaches. (Note that the word

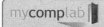

Visit *mycomplab.com* for more resources on academic writing.

author refers to a photographer, painter, or other creator as well as to a writer.)

- **Agree with and extend the author's ideas,** exploring related ideas and providing additional examples.
- **Agree with the author on some points but disagree on others.**
- **Disagree with the author on one or more main points.**
- **Explain how the author achieves a particular effect,** such as evoking a historical period or balancing opposing views.
- **Analyze the overall effectiveness of a text**—for example, how well a writer supports a thesis with convincing evidence or whether an advertisement succeeds in its unstated purpose.

2 | Forming a response

You will likely have an immediate response to at least some of the texts you analyze: you may agree or disagree strongly with what the author is saying. But for some other responses, you may need time and thought to determine what the author is saying and what you think about it.

Whatever your assignment, your first task is to examine the text thoroughly so that you're sure you understand what the author says outright and also assumes or implies. You can use the process of critical reading described in the previous chapter to take notes on the text, summarize it, and develop a critical response. Then, as you write, you can use the tips in the following box to convey your response to readers.

Responding to a text

- **Make sure your writing has a point**—a central idea, or thesis, that focuses your response. (For more on developing a thesis, see 1 pp. 14–16.)
- **Include a very brief summary if readers may be unfamiliar with your subject.** But remember that your job is not just to report what the text says or what an image shows; it is to *respond* to the work from your own critical perspective. (For more on summary, see pp. 72–74.)
- **Center each paragraph on an idea of your own that supports your thesis.** Generally, state the idea outright, in your own voice.
- **Support the paragraph idea with evidence from the text**—quotations, paraphrases, details, and examples.
- **Conclude each paragraph with your interpretation of the evidence.** As a general rule, avoid ending paragraphs with source evidence; instead, end with at least a sentence that explains what the evidence shows.

3 Emphasizing synthesis in your response

Following the suggestions in the preceding box will lead you to show readers the synthesis you achieved by thinking critically about the text. That is, you integrate your perspective with that of the author in order to support a conclusion of your own about the work.

A key to synthesis is deciding how to present evidence from your reading and observation in your writing. Especially when you are writing about a relatively unfamiliar subject, you may be tempted to let a text or other source do the talking for you through extensive summary or quotations. However, readers of your academic writing will expect to see you managing ideas and information to make your points. Thus a typical paragraph of text-based writing should open with your own idea, give evidence from the text, and conclude with your interpretation of the evidence. You can see examples of this paragraph pattern in the research paper in **MLA** pp. 510–16.

Note Effective synthesis requires careful handling of evidence from the text (quotations and paraphrases) so that it meshes smoothly into your sentences yet is clearly distinct from your own ideas. See **7** pp. 418–23 on integrating borrowed material.

10b Determining purpose

For most academic writing, your general purpose will be mainly explanatory or mainly argumentative. That is, you will aim to clarify your subject so that readers understand it as you do, or you will aim to gain readers' agreement with a debatable idea about the subject. (See **1** pp. 6–7 for more on general purposes and pp. 97–116 for more on argument.)

Your specific purpose—including your subject and how you hope readers will respond—depends on the kind of writing you're doing. For instance, in a literature review for a biology class, you want readers to understand the research area you're covering, the recent contributions made by researchers, the issues needing further research, and the sources you consulted. Not coincidentally, these topics correspond to the major sections of a literature review. In following the standard format, you both help to define your purpose and begin to meet the discipline's (and thus your instructor's) expectations.

Your specific purpose will be more complex as well. You take a course to learn about a subject and the ways experts think about it. Your writing, in return, contributes to the discipline through the knowledge you uncover and the lens of your perspective. At the same time, as a student you want to demonstrate your competence with research, evidence, format, and other requirements of the discipline.

10c Analyzing audience

Many academic writing assignments will specify or assume an educated audience or an academic audience. Such readers look for writing that is clear, balanced, well organized, and well reasoned, among other qualities discussed in the next section. Other assignments will specify or assume an audience of experts on your subject, readers who look in addition for writing that meets the subject's requirements for claims and evidence, organization, language, format, and other qualities.

Of course, much of your academic writing will have only one reader besides you: the instructor of the course for which you are writing. Instructors fill two main roles as readers:

- **They represent the audience you are addressing.** They may actually be members of the audience, as when you address academic readers or subject experts. Or they may imagine themselves as members of your audience—reading, for instance, as if they sat on the city council. In either case, they're interested in how effectively you write for the audience.
- **They serve as coaches,** guiding you toward achieving the goals of the course and, more broadly, toward the academic aims of building and communicating knowledge.

Like everyone else, instructors have preferences and peeves, but you'll waste time and energy trying to anticipate them. Do attend to written and spoken directions for assignments, of course. But otherwise view your instructors as representatives of the community you are writing for. Their responses will be guided by the community's aims and expectations and by a desire to teach you about them.

10d Choosing structure and content

Many academic writing assignments will at least imply how you should organize your paper and even how you should develop your ideas. Like the literature review mentioned opposite, the type of paper required will break into discrete parts, each with its own requirements for content.

No matter what type of paper an assignment specifies, the broad academic aims of building and exchanging knowledge determine features that are common across disciplines. Follow these general guidelines for your academic writing, supplementing them as indicated with others elsewhere in this book:

- **Develop a thesis**—a central idea or claim to which everything in the paper clearly relates. Usually, state your thesis near the beginning of the paper. For more on theses, see **1** pp. 14–16.

- **Support the thesis with evidence,** drawn usually from research and sometimes from your own experience. The kinds of evidence will depend on the discipline you're writing in and the type of paper you're doing. For more on evidence in the disciplines, see **8** pp. 440–43 (literature), 448–49 (other humanities), 452 (social sciences), and 455–56 (natural and applied sciences).
- **Synthesize.** Put your sources to work for you by thinking critically about them. Integrate them into your own perspective using your own voice. For more on synthesis, see p. 92 and **7** pp. 410–11 in the discussion of research writing.
- **Acknowledge sources fully, including online sources.** *Not* acknowledging sources undermines the knowledge-sharing foundation of academic writing and opens you to charges of plagiarism, which can be punishable (see **7** pp. 423–30). For lists of disciplines' documentation guides, see **8** pp. 451, 455, and 459. For documentation guidelines and samples, see **MLA** pp. 464–508 (English and some other humanities), **APA** pp. 521–39 (social sciences), **Chic** pp. 549–59 (history, philosophy, and other humanities), and **CSE** pp. 560–66 (natural and applied sciences).
- **Organize clearly within the framework of the type of writing you're doing.** Develop your ideas as simply and directly as your purpose and content allow. Clearly relate sentences, paragraphs, and sections so that readers always know where they are in the paper's development.

CULTURE LANGUAGE These features are far from universal. In other cultures, for instance, academic writers may be indirect or may not have to acknowledge well-known sources. Recognizing such differences between practices in your native culture and in the United States can help you adapt to US academic writing.

10e Using academic language

American academic writing relies on a dialect called standard American English. The dialect is also used in business, the professions, government, the media, and other sites of social and economic power where people of diverse backgrounds must communicate with one another. It is "standard" not because it is better than other forms of English, but because it is accepted as the common language, much as the dollar bill is accepted as the common currency.

Standard American English varies a great deal, from the formal English of a President's State of the Union address through the middle formality of this handbook to the informal chitchat between anchors on morning TV. Even in academic writing, standard American

English allows much room for the writer's own tone and voice, as these passages on the same topic show:

More formal

Using the technique of "color engineering," manufacturers and advertisers can heighten the interest of consumers in a product by adding color that does not contribute to the utility of the product but appeals more to emotions. In one example from the 1920s, manufacturers of fountain pens, which had previously been made of hard black rubber, dramatically increased sales simply by producing the pens in bright colors.

> Two complicated sentences, one explaining the technique and one giving the example
>
> Drawn-out phrasing, such as *interest of consumers* instead of *consumers' interest*
>
> Formal vocabulary, such as *heighten, contribute,* and *utility*

Less formal

A touch of "color engineering" can sharpen the emotional appeal of a product or its ad. New color can boost sales even when the color serves no use. In the 1920s, for example, fountain-pen makers introduced brightly colored pens along with the familiar ones of hard black rubber. Sales shot up.

> Four sentences, two each for explaining the technique and giving the example
>
> More informal phrasing, such as *Sales shot up*
>
> More informal vocabulary, such as *touch, boost,* and *ad*

As different as they are, both examples illustrate several common features of academic language:

- It follows the conventions of standard American English for grammar and usage. These conventions are described in guides to the dialect, such as this handbook. Note that standard American English excludes many forms that are encouraged by rapid communication in e-mail and in text or instant messaging, such as incomplete sentences, no capital letters, and shortened spellings (*u* for *you, b4* for *before, thru* for *through,* and so on). (See **3** pp. 163–64 for more on these forms.)

- It uses a standard vocabulary, not one that only some groups understand, such as slang, an ethnic or regional dialect, or another language. (See **3** pp. 163 and 164–65 for more on specialized vocabularies.)

- It creates some distance between writer and reader with the third person (*he, she, it, they*). The first person (*I, we*) is sometimes appropriate to express personal opinions or invite readers to think along, but not with a strongly explanatory purpose (*I discovered that "color engineering" can heighten . . .*). The second person (*you*) is appropriate only in addressing readers directly (as in this handbook), and even then it may seem condescending or too chummy (*You should know that "color engineering" can heighten . . .*).

- It is authoritative and neutral. In the preceding examples, the writers express themselves confidently, not timidly (as in *One possible example of color engineering that might be considered in this case is . . .*). They also refrain from hostility (*Advertisers will stop at nothing to achieve their goals*) and enthusiasm (*Color engineering is genius at work*).

At first, the diverse demands of academic writing may leave you groping for an appropriate voice. In an effort to sound fresh and confident, you may write too casually:

Too casual

"Color engineering" is a great way to get at consumers' feelings. . . . When the guys jazzed up the color, sales shot through the roof.

In an effort to sound "academic," you may produce wordy and awkward sentences:

Wordy and awkward

The emotions of consumers can be made more engaged by the technique known as "color engineering." . . . A very large increase in the sales of fountain pens was achieved by the manufacturers of the pens as a result of this color enhancement technique. [The passive voice in this example, such as *increase . . . was achieved* instead of *the manufacturers achieved,* adds to its wordiness and indirection. See **4** pp. 236–38 for more on verb voice.]

A cure for writing too informally or too stiffly is to read academic writing so that the language and style become familiar and to edit your writing (see **1** pp. 29–31).

(CULTURE LANGUAGE) If your first language is not English or is an English dialect besides standard American, you know well the power of communicating with others who share your language. Learning to write standard American English in no way requires you to abandon your first language. Like most multilingual people, you are probably already adept at switching between languages as the situation demands—speaking one way with your relatives, say, and another way with an employer. As you practice academic writing, you'll develop the same flexibility with it.

Exercise 10.1 Using academic language

Revise the following paragraph to make the language more academic while keeping the factual information the same.

If you buy into the stereotype of girls chatting away on their cell phones, you should think again. One of the major wireless companies surveyed 1021 cell phone owners for a period of five years and—surprise!—reported that guys talk on cell phones more than girls do. In fact, guys were way ahead of girls, using an average of 571 minutes a month compared to 424 for girls. That's 35 percent more time on the phone! The survey also asked about conversations on home phones, and while girls still beat the field, the guys are catching up.

11 Argument

Argument is writing that attempts to solve a problem, open readers' minds to an opinion, change readers' own opinions, or move readers to action. Using a variety of techniques, you engage readers to find common ground and narrow the distance between your views and theirs.

CULTURE LANGUAGE The ways of conceiving and writing arguments described here may be initially uncomfortable to you if your native culture approaches such writing differently. In some cultures, for example, a writer is expected to begin indirectly, to avoid asserting his or her opinion outright, to rely for evidence on appeals to tradition, or to establish a compromise rather than argue a position. In American academic and business settings, writers aim for a well-articulated opinion, evidence gathered from many sources, and a direct and concise argument for the opinion.

11a Understanding and using the elements of argument

An argument has four main elements: subject, claims, evidence, and assumptions. (The last three are adapted from the work of the British philosopher Stephen Toulmin.)

1 The subject

An argument starts with a subject and often with a view of the subject as well—that is, an idea that makes you want to write about the subject. (If you don't have a subject or you aren't sure what you think, see **1** pp. 9–13 for some invention techniques.) Your subject should meet several requirements:

- **It can be disputed:** reasonable people can disagree over it.
- **It *will* be disputed:** it is controversial.
- **It is narrow enough to research and argue in the space and time available.**

On the flip side of these requirements are several kinds of subjects that will not work as the starting place of argument: indisputable

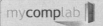

mycomplab

Visit *mycomplab.com* for more resources and exercises on argument.

facts, such as the functions of the human liver; personal preferences or beliefs, such as a moral commitment to vegetarianism; and ideas that few would disagree with, such as the virtues of a secure home.

Exercise 11.1 Testing argument subjects

Analyze each subject below to determine whether it is appropriate for argument. Explain your reasoning in each case.

1 Granting of athletic scholarships
2 Care of automobile tires
3 Censoring the Web sites of hate groups
4 History of the town park
5 Housing for the homeless
6 Billboards in urban residential areas or in rural areas
7 Animal testing for cosmetics research
8 Cats versus dogs as pets
9 Ten steps in recycling wastepaper
10 Benefits of being a parent

---

2 Claims

Claims are statements that require support. In an argument you develop your subject into a central claim or **thesis,** asserted outright in a **thesis statement** (see **1** pp. 14–16). This central claim is what the argument is about.

A thesis statement is always an **opinion**—that is, a judgment based on facts and arguable on the basis of facts. It may be one of the following:

■ **A claim about past or present reality:**

In both its space and its equipment, the college's chemistry laboratory is outdated.

Academic cheating increases with students' economic insecurity.

■ **A claim of value:**

The new room fees are unjustified given the condition of the dormitories.

Computer music pirates undermine the system that encourages the very creation of music.

■ **A recommendation for a course of action,** often a solution to a perceived problem:

The college's outdated chemistry laboratory should be replaced incrementally over the next five years.

Schools and businesses can help to resolve the region's traffic congestion by implementing car pools and rewarding participants.

The backbone of an argument consists of specific claims that support the thesis statement. These may also be statements of opinion, or they may fall into one of two other categories:

- **Statements of** *fact,* including facts that are generally known or are verifiable (such as the cost of tuition at your school) and those that can be inferred from verifiable facts (such as the monetary value of a college education).
- **Statements of** *belief,* or convictions based on personal faith or values, such as *The primary goal of government should be to provide equality of opportunity for all.* Although seemingly arguable, a statement of belief is not based on facts and so cannot be contested on the basis of facts.

3 Evidence

Evidence demonstrates the validity of your claims. The evidence to support the claim that the school needs a new chemistry lab might include the present lab's age, an inventory of facilities and equipment, and the testimony of chemistry professors.

There are several kinds of evidence:

- **Facts,** statements whose truth can be verified or inferred: *Poland is slightly smaller than New Mexico.*
- **Statistics,** facts expressed as numbers: *Of those polled, 22 percent prefer a flat tax.*
- **Examples,** specific instances of the point being made: *Many groups, such as the elderly and people with disabilities, would benefit from this policy.*
- **Expert opinions,** the judgments formed by authorities on the basis of their own examination of the facts: *Affirmative action is necessary to right past injustices, a point argued by Howard Glickstein, a past director of the US Commission on Civil Rights.*
- **Appeals to readers' beliefs or needs,** statements that ask readers to accept a claim in part because it states something they already accept as true without evidence: *The shabby, antiquated chemistry lab shames the school, making it seem a second-rate institution.*

Evidence must be reliable to be convincing. Ask these questions about your evidence:

- **Is it accurate**—trustworthy, exact, and undistorted?
- **Is it relevant**—authoritative, pertinent, and current?
- **Is it representative**—true to its context, neither under- nor overrepresenting any element of the sample it's drawn from?
- **Is it adequate**—plentiful and specific?

4 Assumptions

An **assumption** is an opinion, a principle, or a belief that ties evidence to claims: the assumption explains why a particular piece of evidence is relevant to a particular claim. For instance:

Claim: The college needs a new chemistry laboratory.
Evidence (in part): The testimony of chemistry professors.
Assumption: Chemistry professors are the most capable of evaluating the present lab's quality.

Assumptions are not flaws in arguments but necessities: we all acquire beliefs and opinions that shape our views of the world. Interpreting a work's assumptions is a significant part of critical reading and viewing (see pp. 82 and 87), and discovering your own assumptions is a significant part of argument. If your readers do not share your assumptions or if they perceive that you are not forthright about your biases, they will be less receptive to your argument.

11b Writing reasonably

Reasonableness is essential if an argument is to establish common ground between you and your readers. Readers expect logical thinking, appropriate appeals, fairness toward the opposition, and, combining all of these, writing that is free of fallacies.

1 Logical thinking

The thesis of your argument is a conclusion you reach by reasoning about evidence. Two processes of reasoning, induction and deduction, are familiar to you even if you aren't familiar with their names.

Induction

When you're about to buy a used car, you consult friends, relatives, and consumer guides before deciding what kind of car to buy. Using **induction,** or **inductive reasoning,** you make specific observations about cars (your evidence) and you induce, or infer, a **generalization** that Car X is most reliable. The generalization is a claim supported by your observations.

You might also use inductive reasoning in a term paper on print advertising:

Evidence: Advertisements in newspapers and magazines.
Evidence: Comments by advertisers and publishers.
Evidence: Data on the effectiveness of advertising.
Generalization or claim: Print is the most cost-effective medium for advertising.

Reasoning inductively, you connect your evidence to your generalization by assuming that what is true in one set of circumstances (the evidence you examine) is also true in a similar set of circumstances (evidence you do not examine). With induction you create new knowledge out of old.

The more evidence you accumulate, the more probable it is that your generalization is true. Note, however, that absolute certainty is not possible. At some point you must *assume* that your evidence justifies your generalization, for yourself and your readers. Most errors in inductive reasoning involve oversimplifying either the evidence or the generalization. See pp. 104–05 on fallacies.

Deduction

You use **deduction**, or **deductive reasoning**, when you proceed from your generalization that Car X is the most reliable used car to your own specific circumstances (you want to buy a used car) to the conclusion that you should buy Car X. In deduction your assumption is a generalization, principle, or belief that you think is true. It links the evidence (new information) to the claim (the conclusion you draw). With deduction you apply old information to new.

Say that you want the school administration to postpone new room fees for one dormitory. You can base your argument on a deductive **syllogism**:

> **Premise:** The administration should not raise fees on dorm rooms in poor condition. [A generalization or belief that you assume to be true.]
> **Premise:** The rooms in Polk Hall are in poor condition. [New information: a specific case of the first premise.]
> **Conclusion:** The administration should not raise fees on the rooms in Polk Hall. [Your claim.]

As long as the premises of a syllogism are true, the conclusion derives logically and certainly from them. Errors in constructing syllogisms lie behind many of the fallacies discussed on pp. 103–04.

2 Rational, emotional, and ethical appeals

In most arguments you will combine **rational appeals** to readers' capacities for logical reasoning with **emotional appeals** to readers' beliefs and feelings. The following example illustrates both: the second sentence makes a rational appeal (to the logic of financial gain), and the third sentence makes an emotional appeal (to the sense of fairness and open-mindedness).

> Advertising should show more physically challenged people. The millions of Americans with disabilities have considerable buying power, yet so far advertisers have made no attempt to tap that power. Further, by keeping people with disabilities out of the mainstream depicted in ads,

advertisers encourage widespread prejudice against disability, prejudice that frightens and demeans those who hold it.

For an emotional appeal to be successful, it must be appropriate for the audience and the argument:

- **It must not misjudge readers' actual feelings.**
- **It must not raise emotional issues that are irrelevant to the claims and the evidence.** See the next two pages on specific inappropriate appeals, such as bandwagon and ad hominem.

A third kind of approach to readers, the **ethical appeal,** is the sense you give of being a competent, fair person who is worth heeding. A rational appeal and an appropriate emotional appeal contribute to your ethical appeal, and so does your acknowledging opposing views (see below). An argument that is concisely written and correct in grammar, spelling, and other matters will underscore your competence. In addition, a sincere and even tone will assure readers that you are a balanced person who wants to reason with them.

A sincere and even tone need not exclude language with emotional appeal—words such as *frightens* and *demeans* at the end of the example about advertising. But avoid certain forms of expression that will mark you as unfair:

- **Insulting words,** such as *idiotic* or *fascist.*
- **Biased language,** such as *fags* or *broads* (see **3** pp. 165–68).
- **Sarcasm,** such as the phrase *What a brilliant idea* to indicate contempt for the idea and its originator.
- **Exclamation points!** They'll make you sound shrill!

3 | Acknowledgment of opposing views

A good test of your fairness in argument is how you handle possible objections. Assuming your thesis is indeed arguable, then others can marshal their own evidence to support a different view or views. By dealing squarely with these opposing views, you show yourself to be honest and fair. You strengthen your ethical appeal and thus your entire argument.

Before or while you draft your essay, list for yourself all the opposing views you can think of. You'll find them in your research, by talking to friends and classmates, and by critically thinking about your own ideas. You can also look for a range of views in an online discussion that deals with your subject. Two places to start are the *Yahoo!* archive of discussion groups at *groups.yahoo.com* and the *Google* blog directory at *blogsearch.google.com*.

A common way to handle opposing views is to state them, refute those you can, grant the validity of others, and demonstrate why, despite their validity, the opposing views are less compelling than your own. A somewhat different approach, developed by the psychologist Carl Rogers, emphasizes the search for common ground. In a **Rogerian argument** you start by showing that you understand readers' views and by establishing points on which you and readers agree and disagree. Creating a connection in this way can be especially helpful when you expect readers to resist your argument, as it encourages them to hear you out as you develop your claims.

4 Fallacies

Fallacies—errors in argument—either evade the issue of the argument or treat the argument as if it were much simpler than it is.

Evasions

An effective argument squarely faces the central issue or question it addresses. An ineffective argument may dodge the issue in one of the following ways:

- **Begging the question:** treating an opinion that is open to question as if it were already proved or disproved.

  The college library's expenses should be reduced by cutting subscriptions to useless periodicals. [Begged questions: Are some of the library's periodicals useless? Useless to whom?]

- **Non sequitur** (Latin: "It does not follow"): linking two or more ideas that in fact have no logical connection.

  She uses a wheelchair, so she must be unhappy. [The second clause does not follow from the first.]

- **Red herring:** introducing an irrelevant issue intended to distract readers from the relevant issues.

  A campus speech code is essential to protect students, who already have enough problems coping with rising tuition. [Tuition costs and speech codes are different subjects. What protections do students need that a speech code will provide?]

- **Appeal to readers' fear or pity:** substituting emotions for reasoning.

  She should not have to pay taxes because she is an aged widow with no friends or relatives. [Appeals to people's pity. Should age and loneliness, rather than income, determine a person's tax obligation?]

- **Bandwagon:** inviting readers to accept a claim because everyone else does.

  As everyone knows, marijuana use leads to heroin addiction. [What is the evidence?]

- **Ad hominem** (Latin: "to the man"): attacking the qualities of the people holding an opposing view rather than the substance of the view itself.

  One of the scientists has been treated for emotional problems, so his pessimism about nuclear waste merits no attention. [Do the scientist's previous emotional problems invalidate his current views?]

Oversimplifications

In a vain attempt to create something neatly convincing, an ineffective argument may conceal or ignore complexities in one of the following ways:

- **Hasty generalization:** making a claim on the basis of inadequate evidence.

  It is disturbing that several of the youths who shot up schools were users of violent video games. Obviously, these games can breed violence, and they should be banned. [A few cases do not establish the relation between the games and violent behavior. Most youths who play violent video games do not behave violently.]

- **Sweeping generalization:** making an insupportable statement. Many sweeping generalizations are **absolute statements** involving words such as *all, always, never,* and *no one* that allow no exceptions. Others are **stereotypes,** conventional and oversimplified characterizations of a group of people:

  People who live in cities are unfriendly.
  Californians are fad-crazy.
  Women are emotional.
  Men can't express their feelings.

  (See also **3** pp. 165–68 on sexist and other biased language.)
- **Reductive fallacy:** oversimplifying (reducing) the relation between causes and effects.

  Poverty causes crime. [If so, then why do people who are not poor commit crimes? And why aren't all poor people criminals?]

- **Post hoc fallacy** (from Latin, *post hoc, ergo propter hoc:* "after this, therefore because of this"): assuming that because *A* preceded *B*, then *A* must have caused *B*.

  The town council erred in permitting the adult bookstore to open, for shortly afterward two women were assaulted. [It cannot be assumed without evidence that the women's assailants visited or were influenced by the bookstore.]

- **Either/or fallacy:** assuming that a complicated question has only two answers, one good and one bad, both good, or both bad.

Either we permit mandatory drug testing in the workplace or productivity will continue to decline. [Productivity is not necessarily dependent on drug testing.]

Exercise 11.2 Identifying and revising fallacies

Fallacies tend to appear together, as each of the following sentences illustrates. Identify at least one fallacy in each sentence. Then revise the sentences to make them more reasonable.

1 The American government can sell nuclear technology to nonnuclear nations, so why can't individuals, who after all have a God-given right to earn a living as they see fit?
2 A successful marriage demands a maturity that no one under twenty-five possesses.
3 Students' persistent complaints about the grading system prove that it is unfair.
4 People watch television because they are too lazy to talk or read or because they want mindless escape from their lives.
5 Racial tension is bound to occur when people with different backgrounds are forced to live side by side.

11c Organizing an argument

All arguments include the same parts:

- The *introduction* **establishes the significance of the subject and provides background.** The introduction may run a paragraph or two, and it generally includes the thesis statement. However, if you think your readers may have difficulty accepting your thesis statement before they see at least some support for it, then it may come later in the paper. (See **1** pp. 50–52 for more on introductions.)
- The *body* states and develops the claims supporting the thesis. In one or more paragraphs, the body develops each claim with clearly relevant evidence. See the next page for more on organizing the body.
- The *response to opposing views* details and addresses those views, either demonstrating your argument's greater strengths or conceding the opponents' points. See the next page for more on organizing this response.
- The *conclusion* completes the argument, restating the thesis, summarizing the supporting claims, and making a final appeal to readers. (See **1** pp. 52–53 for more on conclusions.)

The structure of the body and the response to opposing views depends on your subject, purpose, audience, and form of reasoning. Here are several possible arrangements:

A common scheme	A variation
Claim 1 and evidence	Claim 1 and evidence
Claim 2 and evidence	Response to opposing views
Claim X and evidence	Claim 2 and evidence
Response to opposing views	Response to opposing views
	Claim X and evidence
	Response to opposing views

The Rogerian scheme	The problem-solution scheme
Common ground and concession to opposing views	The problem: claims and evidence
Claim 1 and evidence	The solution: claims and evidence
Claim 2 and evidence	Response to opposing views
Claim X and evidence	

11d Using visual arguments

In a **visual argument** you use one or more images to engage and convince readers. Advertisements often provide the most vivid and memorable examples of visual arguments, but writers in almost every field—from medicine to music, from physics to physical education—support their claims with images. The main elements of written arguments discussed on pp. 98–100—claims, evidence, and assumptions—appear also in visual arguments.

1 Claims

The claims in an image may be made by composition as well as by content, with or without accompanying words. For instance:

Image   A photograph framing hundreds of chickens crammed into small cages, resembling familiar images of World War II concentration camps.

Claim   Commercial poultry-raising practices are cruel and unethical.

Image   A chart with dramatically contrasting bars that represent the optimism, stress, and heart disease reported by people before and after they participated in a program of daily walking.

Claim   Daily exercise leads to a healthier and happier life.

The following advertisement is one of a series featuring unnamed but well-known people as milk drinkers. The celebrity here is Serena Williams, a tennis champion. The ad makes several claims both in the photograph and in the text.

Claims in an image

Image claim: Strong, shapely women drink milk.

Image claim: Attractive people drink milk.

Image claim: Athletes drink milk.

Text claim: Milk can help dieters reduce to a healthy weight.

Advertisement by the Milk Processor
Education Program

2 Evidence

The kinds of evidence offered by images parallel those found in written arguments:

- **Facts:** You might provide facts in the form of data, as in a graph showing a five-year rise in oil prices. Or you might draw an inference from data, as the ad above does by stating that milk can help dieters "lose weight and burn more fat."
- **Examples:** Most often, you'll use examples to focus on an instance of your argument's claims, as Serena Williams represents milk drinkers in the ad above.
- **Expert opinions:** You might present a chart from an expert showing a trend in unemployment among high school graduates.
- **Appeals to beliefs or needs:** You might depict how things clearly ought to be (an anti-drug brochure featuring a teenager who is confidently refusing peer pressure) or, in contrast, show how things clearly should not be (a Web site for an anti-hunger campaign featuring images of emaciated children).

To make an image work hard as evidence, be sure it relates directly to a point in your argument, adds to that point, and gives readers something to think about. Always include a caption that provides source information and that explicitly ties the image to your text, so that readers don't have to puzzle out your intentions. Number images in sequence (Fig. 1, Fig. 2, and so on), and refer to them by number at the appropriate points in your text. (See **1** pp. 61–65 for more on captioning and numbering illustrations.)

The images below and opposite supported an argument with this thesis: *Despite proof that the depiction of smoking in movies encourages children and teens to smoke, studios continue to release youth-oriented movies that show stars smoking.*

Image as evidence

Advertisement by a reputable research and advocacy group, reinforcing the thesis and providing data about depictions of smoking in movies

[One in a Series]

Eighty percent of this year's nominated movies feature smoking. And the winner is

the global tobacco industry. It gains at least $4 billion in lifetime sales revenue, in the U.S. alone, from the new teen smokers recruited to smoke by films each year. In 2007, two-thirds of new U.S. releases featured smoking: 39% of G/PG movies, 66% of PG-13 films, 84% of R-rated films. Together, these movies delivered **6.6 billion tobacco impressions** to North American theater audiences. R-rating smoking is reasonable, responsible—and inevitable. You'll still be able to include smoking in any film, just like this year's R-rated nominees for Best Picture. Yet by keeping smoking out of the G/PG/PG-13 films that kids see most, you'll save 60,000 lives a year. So who's trying to stop the "R"? Must be somebody with a lot to lose.

SMOKE FREE MOVIES

SmokeFreeMovies.ucsf.edu

Smoke Free Movie policies—the R-rating, certification of no payoffs, anti-tobacco spots, and an end to brand display—are endorsed by the World Health Organization, American Medical Association, AMA Alliance, American Academy of Pediatrics, American Heart Association, American Legacy Foundation, American Lung Association, Campaign for Tobacco-Free Kids, Society for Adolescent Medicine, Los Angeles County Department of Health Services, New York State PTA, and others. To explore the critical health issue, visit our web site or write: Smoke Free Movies, UCSF School of Medicine, San Francisco, CA 94143-1390.

Caption interpreting the ad and providing source information

Fig. 1. Advertisement by the research and advocacy group Smoke Free Movies, providing data on the depiction of smoking in movies and linking the tobacco industry to the practice. From "Our Ads"; *Smoke Free Movies*; U of California, San Francisco, Cardiovascular Research Inst., 2008; Web; 23 Apr. 2008.

Image as evidence

Photograph of an actress smoking in a PG-13 movie —a visual example of the claim that youth-oriented movies depict smoking

Fig. 2. The actress Kate Hudson in *Raising Helen,* one of many PG-13 movies released each year in which characters smoke. Photograph by Peggy Storm; *gettyimages.com*; Getty Images, 2003; Web; 21 Apr. 2008.

Caption explaining the image, tying it to the text of the paper and providing source information

3 Assumptions

Like a written argument, a visual argument is based on assumptions—your ideas about the relation between evidence and claims (p. 100). Look again at the milk ad featuring Serena Williams (p. 107). The advertiser seems to have assumed that a celebrity endorsement would strengthen the claims and evidence about the benefits of drinking milk. In addition, the photograph of Williams emphasizes qualities that the advertiser presumably thought would appeal to readers: strength, shapeliness, beauty, even glamour.

As in written arguments, the assumptions in visual arguments must be appropriate for your readers if the argument is to succeed with them. The milk ad originally appeared in sports magazines, so the advertiser could assume that readers knew of and admired Williams. But to readers uninterested in sports or tennis, the photograph might actually undermine the ad's effectiveness.

4 Appeals

Images can help to strengthen the rational, emotional, and ethical appeals of your written argument (pp. 101–02):

- **Images can contribute evidence,** as long as they come from reliable sources, present information accurately and fairly, and relate clearly to the argument's claims.

- **Images can appeal to a host of ideas and emotions,** including patriotism, curiosity, moral values, sympathy, and anger. Any such appeal should correctly gauge readers' beliefs and feelings, and it should be clearly relevant to the argument.
- **Images can show that you are a competent, fair, and trustworthy source of information,** largely through their relevance, reliability, and sensitivity to readers' needs and feelings.

To see how appeals can work in images, look at a photograph used in the sample argument paper on p. 113. This image illustrates the writer's claim that television can ease loneliness.

Appeals in an image

Rational appeal: Backs up the writer's claim that TV can ease loneliness: the man appears to live alone (only one chair is visible) and is interacting enthusiastically with the TV

Emotional appeal: Reinforces the benefits of TV watching: the man's isolation may be disturbing, but his excitement is pleasing

Ethical appeal: Conveys the writer's competence through the appropriateness of the image for the point being made

Fig. 1. Television can be a source of companionship for people whose living situations and limited mobility leave them lonely. Photograph by Jean Michel Foujols; *Corbis*; Corbis, 2005; Web; 13 Oct. 2008.

5 Recognizing fallacies

When making a visual argument, you'll need to guard against all the fallacies discussed on pp. 103–06. Here we'll focus on specific visual examples. The first, the milk ad on p. 107, uses Serena Williams for snob appeal, inviting readers to be like someone they admire. If you drink milk, the ad says subtly, you too may become strong, beautiful, and fearless (notice that Williams looks unguardedly into the camera). The ad does have some substance in its specific and verifiable claim that drinking "24 ounces a day of lowfat or fat free milk" could help people reduce to a healthy weight, but Williams herself, with her milk mustache, makes a stronger claim.

Another example of a visual fallacy is the hasty generalization, a claim that is based on too little evidence or that misrepresents the facts. This fallacy appears in the following graph, which is intended to support this claim: *After a steep decline over the preceding five years, the teen birthrate shot up in 2006.* At first glance, the graph seems to demonstrate the claim, but a close look reveals that it badly misrepresents the data. If the graph were not distorted, the line would be nearly flat.

Fallacy in an image

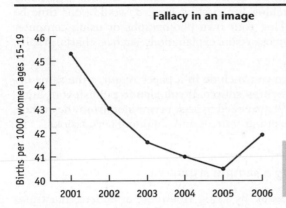

The vertical axis lacks a zero point and covers a small span, thus misrepresenting and exaggerating both the decline and the increase in the birthrate.

Fig. 2. Steep decline and sharp increase in the birthrate among women ages 15 to 19 in the United States, 2001–06. Data from Brady E. Hamilton et al.; *National Vital Statistics Reports*; US Dept. of Health and Human Services, Centers for Disease Control and Prevention, 1 May 2008; Web; 10 July 2008.

6 Choice of images

You can wait until you've drafted an argument before concentrating on what images to include. This approach keeps your focus on the research and writing needed to craft the best argument from sources. But you can also begin thinking visually at the beginning of a project, as you might if your initial interest in the subject was sparked by a compelling image. Either way, ask yourself some basic questions as you consider visual options:

■ **Which parts of your argument require visual evidence or can use visual reinforcement?** Do readers need a visual to understand your argument? Can a claim be explained better visually than verbally? Can a graph or chart present data compactly and interestingly? Can a photograph appeal effectively to readers' beliefs and values?

- **What are the limitations or requirements of your writing situation?** What do the type of writing you're doing and its format allow? Look through examples of similar writing to gauge the kinds of illustrations readers will expect.
- **What kinds of visuals are readily available on your subject?** As you researched your subject, what images seemed especially effective? What sources have you not yet explored? (See **7** pp. 395–96 for tips on locating images.)
- **Should you create original images tailored to your argument?** Instead of searching for existing images, would your time be better spent taking your own photographs or using computer software to compose visual explanations, such as charts, graphs, and diagrams?

Note Any image you include in a paper requires the same detailed citation as a written source. If you plan to publish your argument online, you will also need to seek permission from the author. See **7** pp. 423–31 on citing sources and obtaining permissions.

11e Examining a sample argument

The following essay by Craig Holbrook, a student, illustrates the principles discussed in this chapter. As you read the essay, notice especially the structure, the relation of claims and supporting evidence (including illustrations), the kinds of appeals Holbrook makes, and the ways he addresses opposing views.

TV Can Be Good for You

Introduction

Identification of prevailing view

Disagreement with prevailing view

Thesis statement making three claims for television

Background for claim 1: effects of loneliness

Evidence for effects of loneliness

Television wastes time, pollutes minds, destroys brain cells, and turns some viewers into murderers. Thus runs the prevailing talk about the medium, supported by serious research as well as simple belief. But television has at least one strong virtue, too, which helps to explain its endurance as a cultural force. It provides replacement voices that ease loneliness, spark healthful laughter, and even educate young children.

Most people who have lived alone understand the curse of silence, when the only sound is the buzz of unhappiness or anxiety inside one's own head. Although people of all ages who live alone can experience intense loneliness, the elderly are especially vulnerable to solitude. For example, they may suffer increased confusion or depression when left alone for long periods but then

rebound when they have steady companionship (Bondevik and
Skogstad 329-30).

A study of elderly men and women in New Zealand found that
television can actually serve as a companion by assuming "the role
of social contact with the wider world," reducing "feelings of isolation and loneliness because it directs viewers' attention away from
themselves" ("Television Programming"). (See fig. 1.) Thus television's replacement voices can provide comfort because they distract
from a focus on being alone.

Fig. 1. Television can be a source of companionship for people whose
living situations and limited mobility leave them lonely. Photograph
by Jean Michel Foujols; *Corbis*; Corbis, 2005; Web; 13 Oct. 2008.

The absence of real voices can be most damaging when it
means a lack of laughter. Here, too, research shows that television can have a positive effect on health. Laughter is one of the
most powerful calming forces available to human beings, proven
in many studies to reduce heart rate, lower blood pressure, and
ease other stress-related ailments (Burroughs, Mahoney, and Lippman 172; Griffiths 18). (See fig. 2.) Television offers plenty of
laughter: the recent listings for a single Friday night included
more than twenty comedy programs running on the networks and
on basic cable.

A study reported in a health magazine found that laughter
inspired by television and video is as healthful as the laughter

Evidence for effects of
television on loneliness

Statement of claim 1

Illustration supporting
claim 1

Background for
claim 2: effects of
laughter

Evidence for effects of
laughter

Evidence for comedy
on television

Evidence for effects of
laughter in response
to television

Illustration supporting healthful effects of laughter

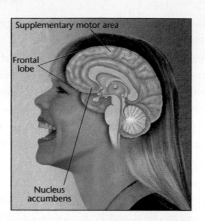

Fig. 2. According to the Society for Neuroscience, the process of understanding and being amused by something funny stimulates at least three main areas of the brain. The society makes no recommendation about TV watching, but other studies show the healthful effects of the activity. Illustration by Lydia Kibiuk from *Brain Briefings*; Soc. for Neuroscience, Dec. 2001; Web; 12 Oct. 2008.

generated by live comedy. Volunteers laughing at a video comedy routine "showed significant improvements in several immune functions, such as natural killer-cell activity" (Laliberte 78). Further, the effects of the comedy were so profound that "merely anticipating watching a funny video improved mood, depression, and anger as much as two days beforehand" (Laliberte 79). Even for people with plenty of companionship, television's replacement voices can have healthful effects by causing laughter.

Statement of claim 2

Television also provides information about the world. This service can be helpful to everyone but especially to children, whose natural curiosity can exhaust the knowledge and patience of their parents and caretakers. While the TV may be baby-sitting children, it can also enrich them. For example, educational programs such as those on the Discovery Channel, the Disney Channel, and PBS offer a steady stream of information at various cognitive levels. (See fig. 3.) Even many cartoons, which are generally dismissed as mindless entertainment or worse, can familiarize children with the material of literature, including strong characters enacting classic narratives.

Background for claim 3: educational effects

Evidence for educational programming on television

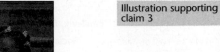

Fig. 3. Educational television programs such as *Sesame Street* are an important source of learning for children. Characters such as Elmo (shown here) promote reading, learning, and healthy behaviors. Photograph from *The State of the World's Children*; United Nations Children's Fund, 2002; Web; 12 Oct. 2008.

Three researchers conducting a review of studies involving children and television found that TV can inspire imaginative play, which psychologists describe as important for children's cognitive development (Thakkar, Garrison, and Christakis 2028). In the studies reviewed, children who watched *Mister Rogers' Neighborhood*, a show that emphasized make-believe, demonstrated significant increases in imaginative play (2029). Thus high-quality educational programming can both inform young viewers and improve their cognitive development.

> Evidence for educational effects of television on children

> Statement of claim 3

The value of these replacement voices should not be oversold. Almost everyone agrees that too much TV does no one any good and may cause much harm. Many studies show that excessive TV watching increases violent behavior, especially in children, and can cause, rather than ease, other antisocial behaviors (Reeks 114; Walsh 34). In addition, human beings require the give and take of actual interaction. Steven Pinker, an expert in children's language acquisition, warns that children cannot develop language properly by watching television. They need to interact with actual speakers who respond directly to their needs (282). Replacement voices are not real voices and in the end can do only limited good.

> Anticipation of objection: harm of television

> Anticipation of objection: need for actual interaction

> Qualification of claims in response to objections

But even limited good is something, especially for those who are lonely or neglected. Television is not an entirely positive force, but neither is it an entirely negative one. Its voices can provide company, laughter, and information whenever they're needed.

> Conclusion

Works Cited

Bondevik, Margareth, and Anders Skogstad. "The Oldest Old, ADL, Social Network, and Loneliness." *Western Journal of Nursing Research* 20.3 (1998): 325-43. Print.

Burroughs, W. Jeffrey, Diana L. Mahoney, and Louis G. Lippman. "Attributes of Health-Promoting Laughter: Cross-Generational Comparison." *Journal of Psychology* 136.2 (2004): 171-81. Print.

Griffiths, Joan. "The Mirthful Brain." *Omni* Aug. 1996: 18-19. Print.

Laliberte, Richard W. "The Benefits of Laughter." *Shape* Sept. 2003: 78-79. Print.

Pinker, Steven. *The Language Instinct: How the Mind Creates Language*. New York: Harper, 1994. Print.

Reeks, Anne. "Kids and TV: A Guide." *Parenting* Apr. 2005: 110-15. Print.

"Television Programming for Older People: Summary Research Report." *NZ on Air*. NZ on Air, 25 July 2004. Web. 15 Oct. 2008.

Thakkar, Rupin R., Michelle M. Garrison, and Dimitri A. Christakis. "A Systematic Review for the Effects of Television Viewing by Infants and Preschoolers." *Pediatrics* 18.5 (2006): 2025-31. Web. 12 Oct. 2008.

Walsh, Teri. "Too Much TV Linked to Depression." *Prevention* Feb. 2001: 34-36. Print.

—Craig Holbrook (student)

12 Online Writing

In and out of college, you will write extensively online. Many forms of online writing expand your options as a writer, but they also present distinctive challenges. This chapter discusses some of the options and challenges of e-mail (facing page), online collaboration (p. 119), and Web composition (p. 120).

mycomplab

Visit *mycomplab.com* for more resources as well as exercises on online writing.

12a Using e-mail

To use e-mail productively for college work, pause to weigh each element of the message. Consider especially your audience and purpose and how your tone will come across to readers. In the message shown below, the writer knows the recipients well and yet has serious information to convey to them, so he writes informally but states his points and concerns carefully. Writing to the corporation mentioned in the message, the writer would be more formal in both tone and approach. Although e-mail is typically more casual than printed correspondence, in academic settings a crafted message is more likely to achieve the intended purpose. Proofread all but the most informal messages for errors in grammar, punctuation, and spelling.

For more on using e-mail to interact with other students in a course, see p. 119. For more on using e-mail as a research tool, see **7** p. 393.

1 Addressing messages

Send a message only to the people who need to read it. As a general rule, avoid sending messages to many recipients at once—all the students in a course, say, or all the participants in a discussion group—unless what you have to say applies to all of them. Occasionally, you may indeed have a worthwhile idea or important

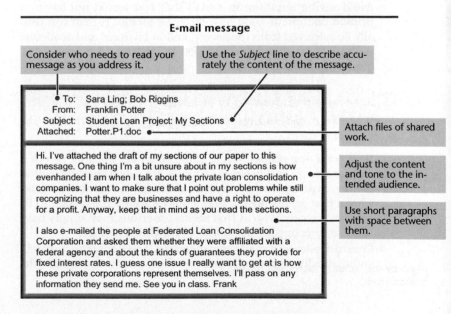

E-mail message

Consider who needs to read your message as you address it.

Use the *Subject* line to describe accurately the content of the message.

> To: Sara Ling; Bob Riggins
> From: Franklin Potter
> Subject: Student Loan Project: My Sections
> Attached: Potter.P1.doc

Attach files of shared work.

Hi. I've attached the draft of my sections of our paper to this message. One thing I'm a bit unsure about in my sections is how evenhanded I am when I talk about the private loan consolidation companies. I want to make sure that I point out problems while still recognizing that they are businesses and have a right to operate for a profit. Anyway, keep that in mind as you read the sections.

Adjust the content and tone to the intended audience.

I also e-mailed the people at Federated Loan Consolidation Corporation and asked them whether they were affiliated with a federal agency and about the kinds of guarantees they provide for fixed interest rates. I guess one issue I really want to get at is how these private corporations represent themselves. I'll pass on any information they send me. See you in class. Frank

Use short paragraphs with space between them.

information that everyone on the list will want to know. But spamming—flooding entire lists with irrelevant messages—is rude and irritating.

Similarly, avoid sending frivolous messages to all the members of a group. Instead of dashing off "I agree" and distributing the two-word message widely, put some time into composing a thoughtful response and send it only to those who will be interested.

2 Composing messages

The messages you send are going to people, not just inboxes, so craft your messages with the recipients in mind.

- **Don't say or do anything you wouldn't say or do face to face.**
- **Use names.** In the body of your message, address your reader(s) by name if possible and sign off with your own name and information on how to contact you. Your own name is especially important if your e-mail address does not spell it out.
- **Pay careful attention to tone.** Refrain from flaming, or attacking, correspondents. Don't use all capital letters, which SHOUT. And use irony or sarcasm only cautiously: in the absence of facial expressions, either one can lead to misunderstanding. To indicate irony and emotions, you can use an emoticon such as the smiley :-). These sideways faces can easily be overused, though, and should not substitute for thoughtfully worded opinions.
- **Avoid saying anything in e-mail that you would not say in a printed document such as a letter or memo.** E-mail can usually be retrieved from the server, and in business and academic settings it may well be retrieved in disputes over contracts, grades, and other matters.

3 Reading and responding to messages

When you read and respond to messages, again consider the people behind them.

- **Be a forgiving reader.** Avoid nitpicking over spelling or other surface errors. And because attitudes are sometimes difficult to convey, give authors an initial benefit of the doubt: a writer who at first seems hostile may simply have tried too hard to be concise; a writer who at first seems unserious may simply have failed at injecting humor into a worthwhile message.
- **Consider who will read your response.** The Reply function will automatically address the person who wrote you, whereas the

Reply All function will address others who may have been sent copies of the original message. Before you send the message, choose the readers who need to see it.

- **Respect others' privacy.** Forward messages only with permission or only if you know that the author of the message won't mind. If you add more recipients to your response, make sure not to pass on previous private messages by mistake.
- **Avoid participating in flame "wars,"** overheated dialogs that contribute little or no information or understanding. If a war breaks out in a discussion, ignore it: don't rush to defend someone who is being attacked, and don't respond even if you are under attack yourself.

12b Collaborating online

Many instructors integrate online collaboration into their courses, encouraging students to work in groups for discussing ideas and exchanging and commenting on drafts of projects.

1 Participating in discussions

Online conversations in your courses will occur either in real-time chat, which occurs immediately, like a telephone conversation, or in a delayed medium such as e-mail, a blog, or a wiki. Chat discussions can be fast-paced and often work better for brain-storming topics and exchanging impressions than for careful articulation of ideas. Delayed conversations allow detailed, thoughtful messages and responses, so they are good places to develop ideas, explore assignments, and respond to others' work. For either type of conversation, observe the guidelines for composing and responding to messages on the preceding pages.

2 Working on drafts

In writing and other courses, you and your fellow students may be invited to exchange and respond to one another's projects by e-mail or over the Web. To guide your reading of others' work, use the revision checklist in **1** p. 27 and the collaboration tips in **1** pp. 36–38. Focus on the deep issues in others' drafts, especially early drafts: thesis, purpose, audience, organization, and support for the thesis. Hold comments on style, grammar, punctuation, and other surface matters until you're reviewing later drafts, if indeed you are expected to comment on them at all.

12c Creating Web compositions

Creating a Web page or site is sometimes as simple as saving a document in a different format, but more often it means thinking in a new way.

The diagrams on the next page show a key difference between traditional printed documents and Web sites. Most traditional documents are meant to be read in sequence from start to finish. In contrast, most Web sites are intended to be examined in whatever order readers choose as they follow links to pages within the site and to other sites. A Web site thus requires careful planning of the links between pages and thoughtful cues to orient readers.

When you create a composition for the Web, it will likely fall into one of two categories: pages such as class papers that resemble printed documents in being linear and text-heavy and that call for familiar ways of writing and reading; or "native" hypertext documents that you build from scratch, which call for screen-oriented writing and reading. These two categories are discussed on pp. 122–26.

Note If you anticipate that some of your readers may have visual, hearing, or reading disabilities, you'll need to consider their needs while designing Web sites. Some of these considerations are covered under document design in **1** pp. 65–66, and others are fundamental to any effective Web design, as discussed in this section. In addition, avoid any content that relies exclusively on images or sound, instead supplementing such elements with text descriptions, and try to provide key concepts both as text and as images and sound. For more on Web design for readers with disabilities, visit the World Wide Web Consortium at *www.w3.org/WAI* or the American Council for the Blind at *acb.org/accessible-formats.html*.

1 Using HTML

Most Web pages are created using hypertext markup language, or HTML, and an HTML editor. The HTML editing program inserts command codes into your document that achieve the effects you want when the material appears on the Web.

From the user's point of view, most HTML editors work much as word processors do, with similar options for sizing, formatting, and highlighting copy and with a display that shows what you will see in the final version. Indeed, you can compose a Web page without bothering at all about the behind-the-scenes HTML coding. As you gain experience with Web building, however, you may want to create more sophisticated pages by editing the codes themselves.

Traditional print document

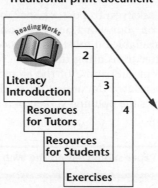

Web site

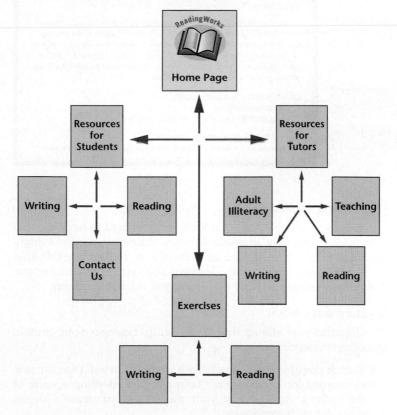

2 Creating online papers

If an instructor asks you to post a paper to a Web site or blog, you can compose it on your word processor and then use the Save As HTML function available on most word processors to translate it into a Web page. After translating the paper, your word processor should allow you to modify some of the elements on the page, or you can open the translated document in an HTML editor. The illustration below shows the opening screen of a student's project for a composition course.

Paper submitted on the Web

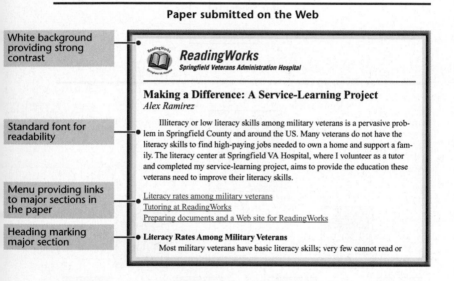

White background providing strong contrast

Standard font for readability

Menu providing links to major sections in the paper

Heading marking major section

ReadingWorks
Springfield Veterans Administration Hospital

Making a Difference: A Service-Learning Project
Alex Ramirez

Illiteracy or low literacy skills among military veterans is a pervasive problem in Springfield County and around the US. Many veterans do not have the literacy skills to find high-paying jobs needed to own a home and support a family. The literacy center at Springfield VA Hospital, where I volunteer as a tutor and completed my service-learning project, aims to provide the education these veterans need to improve their literacy skills.

Literacy rates among military veterans
Tutoring at ReadingWorks
Preparing documents and a Web site for ReadingWorks

Literacy Rates Among Military Veterans
Most military veterans have basic literacy skills; very few cannot read or

3 Creating original sites

When you create an original Web site, you need to be aware that Web readers generally alternate between skimming pages for highlights and focusing intently on sections of text. To facilitate this kind of reading, you'll want to consider your site's structure and content, flow, ease of navigation, and use of images, video, and sound.

Structure and content

Organize your site so that it efficiently arranges your content and orients readers:

- **Sketch possible site plans before getting started.** (See the previous page for an example.) Your aim is to develop a sense of the major components of your project and to create a logical space for each component.

- Consider how menus on the site's pages can provide overviews of the organization as well as direct access to the pages. The Web page below includes a menu on the left.
- Treat the first few sentences of any page as a get-acquainted space for you and your readers. On the page below, the text hooks readers with questions and then orients them with general information.
- Distill your text so that it includes only essential information. Concise prose is essential in any writing situation, of course. But Web readers expect to scan text quickly and, in any event, have difficulty following long text passages on a computer screen.

Original Web site

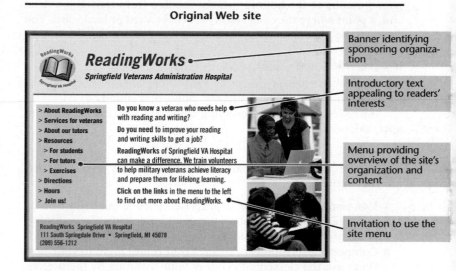

Banner identifying sponsoring organization

Introductory text appealing to readers' interests

Menu providing overview of the site's organization and content

Invitation to use the site menu

Flow

Beginning Web authors sometimes start at the top of the page and then add element upon element until information proceeds down the screen much as it would in a printed document. However, by thinking about how information will flow on a page, you can take better advantage of the Web's visual nature. Follow these guidelines:

- Standardize elements of your design to create expectations in readers and to fulfill those expectations. For instance, develop a uniform style for the main headings of pages, for headings within pages, and for menus.
- Make scanning easy for readers. Focus readers on crucial text by adding space around it or enlarging it. Add headings to break

up text and to highlight content. Use lists to reinforce the parallel importance of items. (See **1** pp. 59–60 for more on headings and lists.)

Easy navigation

A Web site of more than a few pages requires a menu on every page that lists the features of the site, giving its plan at a glance. By clicking on any item in the menu, readers can go directly to a page that interests them.

You can embed a menu at the top, side, or bottom of a page. Menus at the top or side are best on short pages because they will not scroll off the screen as readers move down the page. On longer pages, menus at the bottom prevent readers from reaching a dead end, a point where they can't easily move forward or backward. You can also use a combination of menus.

Images, video, and sound

Most Web readers expect at least some enhancement of text with multimedia elements—images, video, and sound.

Note See **7** p. 430 on observing copyright restrictions with images, video, and sound.

Images

To use photographs, charts, and other images effectively, follow these guidelines:

- **Use visual elements for a purpose.** They should supplement text, highlight important features, and direct the flow of information. Don't use them as mere decoration.
- **Compose descriptions of images that relate them to your text.** Don't ask the elements to convey your meaning by themselves.
- **Provide alternative descriptions of images** for readers with vision loss or readers whose Web browsers can't display the images.

Video and sound

Video and sound files can provide information that is simply unavailable in printed documents. For instance, as part of a film review you might show and analyze a short clip from the film. Or as part of a project on a controversial issue you might provide links to sound files containing political speeches.

Video and sound files can be difficult to work with and can be slow to download at the reader's end. Make sure they're worth the time: they should provide essential information and should be well integrated with the rest of your composition.

Sources of multimedia elements

You can use your own multimedia elements or obtain them from other sources:

- **Create your own graphs, diagrams, and other illustrations using a graphics program.** Any graphics program requires learning and practice to be used efficiently but can produce professional-looking illustrations.
- **Incorporate your own artwork, photographs, video clips, and sound recordings.** You may be able to find the needed equipment and software at your campus computer lab.
- **Obtain icons, video, and other multimedia elements from other electronic sources.** Be sure to acknowledge your sources and to obtain reprint permission if needed (see **7** pp. 429–30).

---

13 Oral Presentations

Effective speakers use organization, voice, and other techniques to help their audiences follow and appreciate their presentations.

13a Organizing the presentation

Give your oral presentation a recognizable shape so that listeners can see how ideas and details relate to each other.

The introduction

The beginning of an oral presentation should try to accomplish three goals:

- **Gain the audience's attention and interest.** Begin with a question, an unusual example or statistic, or a short, relevant story.
- **Put yourself in the speech.** Demonstrate your expertise, experience, or concern to gain the interest and trust of your audience.
- **Introduce and preview your topic and purpose.** By the time your introduction is over, listeners should know what your subject is and the direction you'll take to develop your ideas.

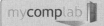

mycomplab

Visit *mycomplab.com* for more resources as well as exercises on oral presentations.

Your introduction should prepare your audience for your main points but not give them away. Think of it as a sneak preview of your speech, not the place for an apology such as *I wish I'd had more time to prepare . . .* or a dull statement such as *My speech is about. . . .*

Supporting material

Just as you do when writing, you should use facts, statistics, examples, and expert opinions to support the main points of your oral presentation. In addition, you can make your points more memorable with vivid description, well-chosen quotations, true or fictional stories, and analogies.

The conclusion

You want your conclusion to be clear, of course, but you also want it to be memorable. Remind listeners of how your topic and main idea connect to their needs and interests. If your speech was motivational, tap an emotion that matches your message. If your speech was informational, give some tips on how to remember important details.

13b Delivering the presentation

Methods of delivery

You can deliver an oral presentation in several ways:

- **Impromptu, without preparation:** Make a presentation without planning what you will say. Impromptu speaking requires confidence and excellent general preparation.
- **Extemporaneously:** Prepare notes to glance at but not read from. This method allows you to look and sound natural while ensuring that you don't forget anything.
- **Speaking from a text:** Read aloud from a written presentation. You won't lose your way, but you may lose your audience. Avoid reading for an entire presentation.
- **Speaking from memory:** Deliver a prepared presentation without notes. You can look at your audience every minute, but the stress of retrieving the next words may make you seem tense and unresponsive.

Vocal delivery

The sound of your voice will influence how listeners receive you. Rehearse your presentation several times until you are confident that you are speaking loudly, slowly, and clearly enough for your audience to understand you.

Physical delivery

You are more than your spoken words when you make an oral presentation. If you are able, stand up to deliver your presentation, turning your body toward one side of the room and then the other, stepping out from behind any lectern or desk, and gesturing as appropriate. Above all, make eye contact with your audience as you speak. Looking directly in your listeners' eyes conveys your honesty, your confidence, and your control of the material.

Visual aids

You can supplement an oral presentation with visual aids such as posters, models, slides, or videos.

- **Use visual aids to underscore your points.** Short lists of key ideas, illustrations such as graphs or photographs, or objects such as models can make your presentation more interesting and memorable. But use visual aids judiciously: a battery of illustrations or objects will bury your message rather than amplify it.
- **Coordinate visual aids with your message.** Time each visual to reinforce a point you're making. Tell listeners what they're looking at. Give them enough viewing time so they don't mind turning their attention back to you.
- **Show visual aids only while they're needed.** To regain your audience's attention, remove or turn off any aid as soon as you have finished with it.

Many speakers use *PowerPoint* or other software to present visual aids. Screens of brief points supported by data, images, or video can help listeners follow your main points. (See the next page for examples.) To use *PowerPoint* or other software effectively, follow the guidelines above and also the following:

- **Don't put your whole presentation on screen.** Select your key points, and distill them to as few words as possible. Think of the slides as quick, easy-to-remember summaries.
- **Use a simple design.** Avoid turning your presentation into a show about the software's many capabilities.
- **Use a consistent design.** For optimal flow through the presentation, each slide should be formatted similarly.
- **Add only relevant illustrations.** Avoid loading the presentation with mere decoration.

Practice

Take time to rehearse your presentation out loud, with the notes you will be using. Gauge your performance by making an audio- or videotape of yourself or by practicing in front of a mirror.

PowerPoint **slides**

First slide, introducing the project and presentation

Making a Difference?

A Service-Learning Project at ReadingWorks

Springfield Veterans
Administration Hospital

Jessica Cho
Nathan Hall
Alex Ramirez

FALL 2008

Simple, consistent slide design focusing viewers' attention on information, not *PowerPoint* features

Semester goals

Later slide, using brief, bulleted points to be explained by the speaker

Photographs reinforcing the project's activities

- Tutor military veterans
- Research adult literacy
- Keep a journal
- Collaborate on documents for ReadingWorks
- Report experiences and findings

Practicing out loud will also tell you if your presentation is running too long or too short.

If you plan to use visual aids, you'll need to practice with them, too. Your goal is to eliminate hitches (upside-down slides, missing charts) and to weave the visuals seamlessly into your presentation.

Stage fright

Many people report that speaking in front of an audience is their number-one fear. Even many experienced and polished speakers have some anxiety about delivering an oral presentation, but they use this nervous energy to their advantage, letting it propel them into working hard on each presentation. Several techniques can help you reduce anxiety:

- **Use simple relaxation exercises.** Deep breathing or tensing and relaxing your stomach muscles can ease some of the physical symptoms of speech anxiety—stomachache, rapid heartbeat, and shaky hands, legs, and voice.
- **Think positively.** Instead of worrying about the mistakes you might make, concentrate on how well you've prepared and practiced your presentation and how significant your ideas are.
- **Don't avoid opportunities to speak in public.** Practice and experience build speaking skills and offer the best insurance for success.

 14 Public Writing

Writing outside of school, such as for business or for community work, resembles academic writing in many ways. It usually involves the same basic writing process, discussed in **1** pp. 3–34: assessing the writing situation, developing what you want to say, freely working out your meaning in a draft, and revising and editing so that your writing will achieve your purpose with readers. It often involves research, as discussed in **7** pp. 371–431. And it involves the standards of conciseness, appropriate and exact language, and correct grammar and usage discussed in **3** through **6**.

But public writing has its own conventions, too. They vary widely, depending on what you're writing and why, whether it's a proposal for your job or a flyer for a community group. This chapter covers several types of public writing: business letters and résumés (next page); memos, reports, and proposals (p. 135); and flyers, newsletters, and brochures for community work (p. 137).

CULTURE LANGUAGE Public writing in the United States, especially business writing, favors efficiency and may seem abrupt or impolite compared with such writing in your native culture. For instance, a business letter elsewhere may be expected to begin with polite questions about the addressee or with compliments for the addressee's company, whereas US business letters are expected to get right to the point.

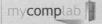

mycomplab

Visit *mycomplab.com* for more resources as well as exercises on public writing.

14a Writing business letters and résumés

When you write for business, you are addressing busy people who want to see quickly why you are writing and how they should respond to you. Follow these general guidelines:

- **State your purpose right at the start.**
- **Be straightforward, clear, concise, objective, and courteous.**
- **Observe conventions of grammar and usage,** which make your writing clear and impress your reader with your care.

1 Business letter format

For any business letter, use either unlined white paper measuring 8½″ × 11″ or what is called letterhead stationery with your address printed at the top of the sheet. Type the letter single-spaced (with double spacing between elements) on only one side of a sheet. A common business-letter form is illustrated on the next page:

- **The *return-address heading* gives your address and the date.** Do not include your name. If you are using stationery with a printed heading, you need only give the date.
- **The *inside address* shows the name, title, and complete address of the person you are writing to.**
- **The *salutation* greets the addressee.** Whenever possible, address your letter to a specific person. (Call the company or department to ask whom to address.) If you can't find a person's name, then use a job title (*Dear Human Resources Manager, Dear Customer Service Manager*) or use a general salutation (*Dear Smythe Shoes*). Use *Ms.* as the title for a woman when she has no other title, when you don't know how she prefers to be addressed, or when you know that she prefers *Ms.*
- **The *body* contains the substance.** Instead of indenting the first line of each paragraph, double-space between paragraphs.
- **The *close* should reflect the level of formality in the salutation:** *Respectfully, Cordially, Yours truly,* and *Sincerely* are more formal closes; *Regards* and *Best wishes* are less formal.
- **The *signature* has two parts:** your name typed four lines below the close, and your handwritten signature in the space between. Give your name as you sign checks and other documents.
- **Include any additional information below the signature,** such as *Enc.* (indicating an enclosure with the letter) or *cc: Margaret Zusky* (indicating that a copy is being sent to the person named).

Use an envelope that will accommodate the letter once it is folded horizontally in thirds. The envelope should show your name and address in the upper left corner and the addressee's name, title,

Business letter (job application)

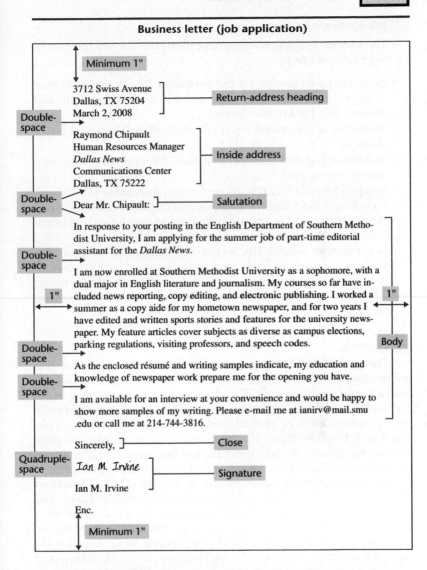

and address in the center. For easy machine reading, the United States Postal Service recommends all capital letters and no punctuation (spaces separate the elements on a line), as in this address:

RAYMOND CHIPAULT
HUMAN RESOURCES MANAGER
DALLAS NEWS
COMMUNICATIONS CENTER
DALLAS TX 75222-0188

2 Job-application letter

The sample on the preceding page illustrates the key features of a job-application letter:

■ **Interpret your résumé for the particular job.** Don't detail your entire résumé, reciting your job history. Instead, highlight and reshape only the relevant parts.

■ **Announce at the outset what job you seek and how you heard about it.**

■ **Include any special reason you have for applying,** such as a specific career goal.

■ **Summarize your qualifications for this particular job,** including relevant facts about education and employment history and emphasizing notable accomplishments. Mention that additional information appears in an accompanying résumé.

■ **Describe your availability.** At the end of the letter, mention that you are free for an interview at the convenience of the addressee, or specify when you will be available (for instance, when your current job or classes leave you free, or when you could travel to the employer's city).

3 Résumé

The résumé that accompanies a job application should provide information in table format that allows a potential employer to evaluate your qualifications. The résumé should include your name and address, a career objective, your education and employment history, special skills or awards, and information about how to obtain your references. Fit all the information on one uncrowded page unless your education and experience are extensive. The sample opposite gives guidelines for a résumé that you submit in print.

Employers may ask for an electronic version of your résumé so that they can add it to a computerized database of applicants. The employers may scan your printed résumé to convert it to an electronic file, which they can then store in an appropriate database, or they may request that you embed your résumé in an e-mail message. To produce a scannable or electronic résumé, follow the guidelines below and consult the sample on p. 134.

■ **Keep the design simple for accurate scanning or electronic transmittal.** Avoid images, unusual type, more than one column, vertical or horizontal lines, italics, and underlining.

■ **Use concise, specific words to describe your skills and experience.** The employer's computer may use keywords (often nouns) to identify the résumés of suitable job candidates, and you want to ensure that your résumé includes the appropriate

Résumé (print)

Ian M. Irvine	3712 Swiss Avenue Dallas, TX 75204 214-744-3816 ianirv@mail.smu.edu	Name and contact information

Position desired	Part-time editorial assistant.	Career objective stated simply and clearly
Education	*Southern Methodist University*, 2006 to present. Current standing: sophomore. Major: English literature and journalism. Journalism courses: news reporting, copy editing, electronic publishing, communication arts, broadcast journalism. *Abilene (Texas) Senior High School*, 2002-06. Graduated with academic, college-preparatory degree.	Education before work experience for most college students
Employment history	2006 to present. Reporter, *Daily Campus*, student newspaper of Southern Methodist University. Write regular coverage of baseball, track, and soccer teams. Write feature stories on campus policies and events. Edit sports news, campus listings, features. Summer 2007. Copy aide, *Abilene Reporter-News*. Assisted reporters with copy routing and research. Summer 2006. Painter, Longhorn Painters, Abilene. Prepared and painted exteriors and interiors of houses.	Headings marking sections, set off with space and highlighting Conventional use of capital letters: yes for proper nouns and after periods; no for job titles, course names, department names, and so on
Special skills	Fluent in Spanish. Proficient in Internet research and word processing.	
References	Available on request: Placement Office Southern Methodist University Dallas, TX 75275	Standard, consistent type font

keywords. Name your specific skills—for example, the computer programs you can operate—and write concretely with words like *manager* (not *person with responsibility for*) and *reporter* (not *staff member who reports*). Look for likely keywords in the employer's description of the job you seek.

4 Electronic communication

Electronic communication—mainly e-mail and faxes—adds a few twists to business writing. E-mail now plays such a prominent

Résumé (scannable or electronic)

Ian M. Irvine
3712 Swiss Avenue
Dallas, TX 75204
214-744-3816
ianirv@mail.smu.edu

KEYWORDS: Editor, editorial assistant, publishing, electronic publishing.

OBJECTIVE
Part-time editorial assistant.

EDUCATION
Southern Methodist University, 2006 to present.
Major: English literature and journalism.
Journalism courses: news reporting, copy editing, electronic publishing,
communication arts, broadcast journalism.

Abilene (Texas) Senior High School, 2002-06.
Academic, college preparatory degree.

EMPLOYMENT HISTORY
Reporter, Daily Campus, Southern Methodist University, 2006 to present.
Writer of articles for student newspaper on sports teams, campus policies,
and local events. Editor of sports news, campus listings, and features.

Copy aide, Abilene Reporter-News, Abilene, summer 2007.
Assistant to reporters, routing copy and doing research.

Painter, Longhorn Painters, Abilene, summer 2006.
Preparation and painting of exteriors and interiors of houses.

SPECIAL SKILLS
Fluent in Spanish.
Proficient in Internet research and word processing.

REFERENCES
Available on request:
Placement Office
Southern Methodist University
Dallas, TX 75275

Marginal annotations:

Accurate keywords, allowing the employer to place the résumé into an appropriate database

Simple design, avoiding unusual type, italics, multiple columns, decorative lines, and images

Standard font easily read by scanners

Every line aligning at left margin

---

role in communication of all sorts that it is discussed extensively as part of writing online (see pp. 117–19). Generally, the standards for business e-mail are the same as for other business correspondence.

Faxes follow closely the formats of print documents, but there are unique concerns:

- **Consider legibility.** Small type, photographs, horizontal lines, and other elements that look fine on your copy may not be legible to the addressee.

- **Include a cover sheet.** Most faxes require a cover sheet with the addressee's name, company, and fax number; the date, time, and subject; your own name and fax and telephone numbers; and the total number of pages (including the cover sheet) in the fax.
- **Advise your addressee to expect a fax.** Fax transmissions can go astray. The advice is essential if the fax is confidential, because the machine is often shared.
- **Consider urgency.** Transmission by fax can imply that the correspondence is urgent. If yours isn't, you may want to use the mail instead.

14b Writing memos, reports, and proposals

1 Memos

Business memorandums (memos, for short) address people within the same organization. Most memos deal briefly with a specific topic, such as an answer to a question or an evaluation.

Both the form and the structure of a memo are designed to get to the point and dispose of it quickly (see the sample on the next page). State your reason for writing in the first sentence. Devote the first paragraph to a concise presentation of your answer, conclusion, or evaluation. In the rest of the memo explain your reasoning or evidence. Use headings or lists as appropriate to highlight key information.

2 Reports and proposals

Reports and proposals are text-heavy documents, sometimes lengthy, that convey information such as the results of research, a plan for action, or a recommendation for change. As with other business correspondence, you will prepare a report or proposal for a specific purpose, and you will be addressing interested but busy readers.

Reports and proposals usually divide into sections. The sections vary depending on the purpose of the document, but usually they include an overview or summary, which tells the reader what the document is about; a statement of the problem or need, which justifies the report or proposal; a statement of the plan or solution, which responds to the need or problem; and a recommendation or evaluation. Consider the following guidelines as you prepare a report or proposal:

- **Do your research.** The standard formats of reports and proposals require you to be well informed, so be alert to where you have enough information or where you don't.
- **Focus on the purpose of each section.** Stick to the point of each section, saying only what you need to say, even if you have

Business memo

Bigelow Wax Company

Heading: company's name, addressee's name, writer's name and initials, date, and subject description

TO: Aileen Rosen, Director of Sales
FROM: Patricia Phillips, Territory 12   *PP*
DATE: March 17, 2008
SUBJECT: 2007 sales of Quick Wax in Territory 12

Body: single-spaced with double spacing between paragraphs; paragraphs not indented

Since it was introduced in January 2007, Quick Wax has been unsuccessful in Territory 12 and has not affected the sales of our Easy Shine. Discussions with customers and my own analysis of Quick Wax suggest three reasons for its failure to compete with our product.

1. Quick Wax has not received the promotion necessary for a new product. Advertising—primarily on radio—has been sporadic and has not developed a clear, consistent image for the product. In addition, the Quick Wax sales representative in Territory 12 is new and inexperienced; he is not known to customers, and his sales pitch (which I once overheard) is weak. As far as I can tell, his efforts are not supported by phone calls or mailings from his home office.

2. When Quick Wax does make it to the store shelves, buyers do not choose it over our product. Though priced competitively with our product, Quick Wax is poorly packaged. The container seems smaller than ours, though in fact it holds the same eight ounces. The lettering on the Quick Wax package (red on blue) is difficult to read, in contrast to the white-on-green lettering on the Easy Shine package.

3. Our special purchase offers and my increased efforts to serve existing customers have had the intended effect of keeping customers satisfied with our product and reducing their inclination to stock something new.

People receiving copies

Copies: L. Mendes, Director of Marketing
       J. MacGregor, Customer Service Manager

additional information. Each section should accomplish its purpose and contribute to the whole.

- **Follow an appropriate format.** In many businesses, reports and proposals have specific formatting requirements. If you are unsure about the requirements, ask your supervisor.

A sample report appears on the facing page. For a sample proposal, follow the links in the e-book version of this handbook at *mycomplab.com*.

Report

Canada Geese at ABC Institute:
An Environmental Problem

Summary

The flock of Canada geese on and around ABC Institute's grounds has grown dramatically in recent years to become a nuisance and an environmental problem. This report reviews the problem, considers possible solutions, and proposes that ABC Institute and the US Fish and Wildlife Service cooperate to reduce the flock by humane means.

The Problem

Canada geese began living at Taylor Lake next to ABC Institute when they were relocated there in 1985 by the state game department. As a nonmigratory flock, the geese are present year-round, with the highest population each year occurring in early spring. In recent years the flock has grown dramatically. The Audubon Society's annual Christmas bird census shows a thirty-fold increase from the 37 geese counted in 1986 to the 1125 counted in 2008.

The principal environmental problem caused by the geese is pollution of grass and water by defecation. Geese droppings cover the ABC Institute's grounds as well as the park's picnicking areas. The runoff from these droppings into Taylor Lake has substantially affected the quality of the lake's water, so that local authorities have twice (2007 and 2008) issued warnings against swimming.

Possible Solutions

The goose overpopulation and resulting environmental problems have several possible solutions:

- Harass the geese with dogs and audiovisual effects (light and noise) so that the geese choose to leave. This solution is inhumane to the geese and unpleasant for human neighbors.
- Feed the geese a chemical that will weaken the shells of their eggs and thus reduce growth of the flock. This solution is inhumane to the geese and also impractical, because geese are long-lived.
- Kill adult geese. This solution is, obviously, inhumane to the geese.
- Thin the goose population by trapping and removing many geese (perhaps 600) to areas less populated by humans, such as wildlife preserves.

Though costly (see figures below), the last solution is the most humane. It would be harmless to the geese, provided that sizable netted enclosures are used for traps. [Discussion of solution and "Recommendations" section follow.]

Side annotations:

Descriptive title conveying report's contents

Standard format: summary, statement of the problem, solutions, and (not shown) recommendations

Major sections delineated by headings

Formal tone, appropriate to a business-writing situation

Single spacing with double spacing between paragraphs and around the list

Bulleted list emphasizing alternative solutions

14c Writing for community work

At some point in your life, you're likely to volunteer for a community organization such as a soup kitchen, a daycare center, or a literacy program. Many college courses involve service learning, in which you do such volunteer work, write about the experience for your course, and write *for* the organization you're helping.

The writing you do for a community group may range from flyers to grant proposals. Two guidelines will help you prepare effective projects like the ones here, for a literacy program.

- **Craft each document for its purpose and audience.** You are trying to achieve a specific aim with your readers, and the approach and tone you use will influence their responses. If, for example, you are writing letters to local businesses to raise funds for a homeless shelter, bring to mind the people who will

---

Flyer

FIRST ANNUAL AWARDS DINNER

ReadingWorks
Springfield VA Hospital

Large type and color focusing a distant reader's attention on important information: what's happening, when, where, and who is invited

White space drawing viewers' eyes to main message and creating flow among elements

WHEN

Friday night
May 23
7:30 to 10:30

For information contact ReadingWorks 209-556-1212

Color highlighting only key information

WHERE

Suite 42
Springfield VA Hospital

WHO

Students, tutors, and their families are invited to join us for an evening of food and music as we celebrate their efforts and accomplishments.

Less important information set in smaller type

ReadingWorks of Springfield Veterans Administration Hospital
111 South Springdale Drive
Springfield, MI 45078

read your letter. How can you best persuade those readers to donate money?

- **Expect to work with others.** Much public writing is the work of more than one person. Even if you draft the document on your own, others will review the content, tone, and design. Such collaboration is rewarding, but it sometimes requires patience and goodwill. See **1** pp. 36–38 for advice on collaborating.

Newsletter

ReadingWorks

Springfield Veterans Administration Hospital SUMMER 2008

From the director

Can you help? With more and more learners in the ReadingWorks program, we need more and more tutors. You may know people who would be interested in participating in the program, if only they knew about it.

Those of you who have been tutoring VA patients in reading and writing know both the great need you fulfill and the great benefits you bring to the students. New tutors need no special skills—we'll provide the training—only patience and an interest in helping others.

We've scheduled an orientation meeting for Friday, September 12, at 6:30 PM. Please come and bring a friend who is willing to contribute a couple of hours a week to our work.

Thanks,
Kate Goodman

IN THIS ISSUE

FIRST ANNUAL AWARDS DINNER

A festive night for students and tutors

The first annual ReadingWorks Awards Dinner on May 23rd was a great success. Springfield's own Golden Fork provided tasty food and Amber Allen supplied lively music. The students decorated Suite 42 on the theme of books and reading. In all, 127 people attended.

The highlight of the night was the awards ceremony. Nine students, recommended by their tutors, received certificates recognizing their efforts and special accomplishments in learning to read and write:

Ramon Berva
Edward Byar
David Dunbar
Tony Garnier
Chris Guigni
Akili Haynes
Josh Livingston
Alex Obeld
B. J. Resnansky

In addition, nine tutors received certificates commemorating five years of service to ReadingWorks:

Anita Crumpton
Felix Cruz-Rivera
Bette Elgen
Kayleah Bortoluzzi
Harriotte Henderson
Ben Obiso
Meggie Puente
Max Smith
Sara Villante

Congratulations to all!

PTSD: New Guidelines

Most of us are working with veterans who have been diagnosed with post-traumatic stress disorder. Because this disorder is often complicated by alcoholism, depression, anxiety, and other problems, the National Center for PTSD has issued some guidelines for helping PTSD patients in ways that reduce their stress.

- The hospital must know your tutoring schedule, and you need to sign in and out before and after each tutoring session.
- To protect patients' privacy, meet them only in designated visiting and tutoring areas, never in their rooms.
- Treat patients with dignity and respect, even when (as sometimes happens) they grow frustrated and angry. Seek help from a nurse or orderly if you need it.

Multicolumn format allowing room for headings, articles, and other elements on a single page

Two-column heading emphasizing the main article

Elements helping readers skim for highlights: spacing, varied font sizes, lines, and a bulleted list

Color focusing readers' attention on banner, headlines, and table of contents

Lively but uncluttered overall appearance

Box in the first column highlighting table of contents

Brochure

Do you know a veteran who needs help with reading and writing?

Do you need to improve your reading and writing skills to get a job?

ReadingWorks can make a difference. We organize volunteers to help military veterans achieve literacy and to prepare them for life-long learning.

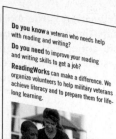

For more information about our services, call Kate Goodman at 209-556-1212 or visit www.readingworks.org.

ReadingWorks
Springfield VA Hospital
111 South Springdale Drive
Springfield, MI 45078

ReadingWorks
Springfield VA Hospital

Helping military veterans achieve literacy

Panel 2: The right page when the cover is opened, the first one readers see, containing key information

Panel 6: The back, usually including the return address and space for a mailing label and postage

Panel 1: The cover, drawing readers' attention to the group's name, purpose, and affiliation

 ReadingWorks
Springfield VA Hospital

OUR MISSION
- We provide workshops and formal lessons for veterans wishing to develop their reading and writing skills
- We train volunteers to tutor veterans one on one.
- We maintain outreach programs to provide access to literacy training for all veterans.
- We create literacy resources and share them with others who promote literacy for veterans.

OUR SERVICES

One-on-one tutoring
One to three hours a week with a trained volunteer tutor.

Workshops and classes
Small-group meetings centered on reading and writing, computer skills, and English as a second language.

Library
Books and other resources for students at various literacy levels.

Computer lab
Five computers with high-speed Internet access and a full range of software.

OUR TUTORS

The goodwill and generosity of our volunteer tutors allows us to reach out to those who have served our country.

If you or someone you know can join our team, contact Kate Goodman at 209-556-1212.

Hours
12:00 to 8:00, Mon., Wed.
9:00 to 5:00, Tues., Thurs., Fri.
Eligibility
Any veteran of the US military is eligible for our services.

How to reach us
Springfield VA Hospital
Room 172, first floor
111 South Springdale Drive
Springfield, MI 45078
209-556-1212
www.readingworks.org

Panel 3: The left page when the cover is opened, reinforcing the message of panel 2

Varied type, color, and photographs, adding visual interest and focusing readers' attention

Panels 4 and 5: The inside panels, containing contact information and other details

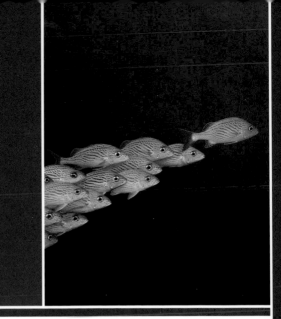

PART 5

Clarity and Style

Clarity and Style

15 Emphasis

Emphatic writing leads readers to see your main ideas both within and among sentences. You can achieve emphasis by attending to your subjects and verbs (below), using sentence beginnings and endings (p. 145), coordinating equally important ideas (p. 148), and subordinating less important ideas (p. 150). In addition, emphatic writing is concise writing, the subject of Chapter 20.

Grammar checkers A grammar checker may spot some problems with emphasis, such as nouns made from verbs, passive voice, wordy phrases, and long sentences that may also be flabby and unemphatic. However, no checker can help you identify the important ideas in your sentences or determine whether those ideas receive appropriate emphasis.

15a Using subjects and verbs effectively

The heart of every sentence is its subject, which usually names the actor, and its predicate verb, which usually specifies the subject's action: *Children* [subject] *grow* [verb]. When these elements do not identify the key actor and action in the sentence, readers must find that information elsewhere and the sentence may be wordy and unemphatic.

In the following sentences, the subjects and verbs are underlined.

Unemphatic   The <u>intention</u> of the company <u>was</u> to expand its workforce. A <u>proposal was</u> also <u>made</u> to diversify the backgrounds and abilities of employees.

These sentences are unemphatic because their key ideas do not appear in their subjects and verbs. In the revision on the next page the sentences are not only clearer but more concise.

Key terms

subject Who or what a sentence is about: *Biologists often study animals.* (See **4** pp. 197–98.)

predicate The part of a sentence containing a verb that asserts something about the subject: *Biologists often study animals.* (See **4** pp. 197–98.)

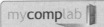

Visit *mycomplab.com* for more resources and exercises on emphasis.

Revised	The company intended to expand its workforce. It also proposed to diversify the backgrounds and abilities of employees.

The constructions discussed below and opposite usually drain meaning from a sentence's subject and verb.

Nouns made from verbs

Nouns made from verbs can obscure the key actions of sentences and add words. These nouns include *intention* (from *intend*), *proposal* (from *propose*), *decision* (from *decide*), *expectation* (from *expect*), and *inclusion* (from *include*).

Unemphatic	After the company made a decision to hire more workers with disabilities, its next step was the construction of wheelchair ramps and other facilities.
Revised	After the company decided to hire more workers with disabilities, it next constructed wheelchair ramps and other facilities.

Weak verbs

Weak verbs, such as *made* and *was* in the unemphatic sentence above, tend to stall sentences just where they should be moving and often bury key actions:

Unemphatic	The company is now the leader among businesses in complying with the 1990 disabilities act. Its officers make frequent speeches on the act to business groups.
Revised	The company now leads other businesses in complying with the 1990 disabilities act. Its officers frequently speak on the act to business groups.

Forms of *be, have,* and *make* are often weak, but don't try to eliminate every use of them: *be* and *have* are essential as helping verbs (*is going, has written*); *be* links subjects and words describing them (*Planes are noisy*); and *have* and *make* have independent meanings (among them "possess" and "force," respectively). But do consider replacing forms of *be, have,* and *make* when one of the words following the verb could be made into a strong verb itself, as in the following examples.

Key terms

noun A word that names a person, thing, quality, place, or idea: *student, desk, happiness, city, democracy.* (See 4 pp. 190–91.)

helping verb A verb used with another verb to convey time, obligation, and other meanings: *was drilling, would have been drilling.* (See 4 p. 193.)

Unemphatic	Emphatic
was influential	influenced
is a glorification	glorifies
have a preference	prefer
had the appearance	appeared, seemed
made a claim	claimed

Passive voice

Verbs in the passive voice state actions received by, not performed by, their subjects. Thus the passive de-emphasizes the true actor of the sentence, sometimes omitting it entirely. Generally, prefer the active voice, in which the subject performs the action. (See also **4** pp. 236–37 for help with editing the passive voice.)

Unemphatic	The 1990 law is seen by most businesses as fair, but the costs of complying have sometimes been objected to.
Revised	Most businesses see the 1990 law as fair, but some have objected to the costs of complying.

Exercise 15.1 Revising: Emphasis of subjects and verbs

Rewrite the sentences in the following paragraph so that their subjects and verbs identify the key actors and actions.

1 Many heroes were helpful in the emancipation of the slaves. 2 However, the work of Harriet Tubman, an escaped slave herself, stands above the rest. 3 Tubman's accomplishments included the guidance of hundreds of slaves to freedom on the Underground Railroad. 4 A return to slavery was risked by Tubman or possibly death. 5 During the Civil War she was also a carrier of information from the South to the North. 6 After the war Tubman was instrumental in helping to raise money for former slaves who were in need of support.

15b Using sentence beginnings and endings

Readers automatically seek a writer's principal meaning in the main clause of a sentence—essentially, in the subject that names the actor and in the verb that usually specifies the action (see p. 143).

Key terms

passive voice The verb form when the subject names the *receiver* of the verb's action: *The house was destroyed by the tornado.*

active voice The verb form when the subject names the *performer* of the verb's action: *The tornado destroyed the house.*

main clause A word group that can stand alone as a sentence, containing a subject and a predicate and not beginning with a subordinating word: *The books were expensive.* (See **4** p. 208.)

Thus you can help readers understand the meaning you intend by controlling the information in your subjects and the relation of the main clause to any modifiers attached to it.

Old and new information

Generally, readers expect the beginning of a sentence to contain information that they already know or that you have already introduced. They then look to the ending for new information. In the unemphatic passage below, the second and third sentences both begin with new topics, while the old topics appear at the ends of the sentences. The pattern of the passage is A→B. C→B. D→A.

> **Unemphatic** _A Education often means _B controversy these days, with rising costs and constant complaints about its inadequacies. But the _C value of schooling should not be obscured by the _B controversy. The single best _D means of economic advancement, despite its shortcomings, remains _A education.

In the more emphatic revision, the old information begins each sentence and new information ends the sentence. The passage follows the pattern A→B. B→C. A→D.

> **Revised** _A Education often means _B controversy these days, with rising costs and constant complaints about its inadequacies. But the _B controversy should not obscure the _C value of schooling. _A Education remains, despite its shortcomings, the single best means of economic _D advancement.

Cumulative and periodic sentences

You can call attention to information by placing it first or last in a sentence, reserving the middle for incidentals:

> **Unemphatic** Education remains the single best means of economic advancement, despite its shortcomings. [Emphasizes shortcomings.]
>
> **Revised** Despite its shortcomings, education remains the single best means of economic advancement. [Emphasizes advancement more than shortcomings.]

Key term

modifier A word or word group that describes another word or word group: *sweet* candy, *running in the park*. (See **4** pp. 194 and 205.)

Revised	Education remains, despite its shortcomings, the single best means of economic advancement. [De-emphasizes shortcomings.]

A sentence that adds modifiers to the main clause is called **cumulative** because it accumulates information as it proceeds:

Cumulative	Education has no equal in opening minds, instilling values, and creating opportunities.
Cumulative	Most of the Great American Desert is made up of bare rock, rugged cliffs, mesas, canyons, mountains, separated from one another by broad flat basins covered with sun-baked mud and alkali, supporting a sparse and measured growth of sagebrush or creosote or saltbush, depending on location and elevation. —Edward Abbey

The opposite kind of sentence, called **periodic**, saves the main clause until just before the end (the period) of the sentence. Everything before the main clause points toward it:

Periodic	In opening minds, instilling values, and creating opportunities, education has no equal.
Periodic	With people from all over the world—Korean doctors, Jamaican cricket players, Vietnamese engineers, Haitian cabdrivers, Chinese grocers, Indian restaurant owners—the American mosaic is continually changing.

The periodic sentence creates suspense by reserving important information for the end. But readers should already have an idea of the sentence's subject—because it was mentioned in the preceding sentence—so that they know what the opening modifiers describe.

Exercise 15.2 Sentence combining: Beginnings and endings

Locate the main idea in each group of sentences below. Then combine each group into a single sentence that emphasizes that idea by placing it at the beginning or the end. For sentences 2–5, determine the position of the main idea by considering its relation to the previous sentences: if the main idea picks up a topic that's already been introduced, place it at the beginning; if it adds new information, place it at the end.

Example:
The storm blew roofs off buildings. It caused extensive damage. It knocked down many trees.

Main idea at beginning: The storm caused extensive damage, blowing roofs off buildings and knocking down many trees.

Main idea at end: Blowing roofs off buildings and knocking down many trees, the storm caused extensive damage.

1 Pat Taylor strode into the room. The room was packed. He greeted students called "Taylor's Kids." He nodded to their parents and teachers.

2 This was a wealthy Louisiana oilman. He had promised his "Kids" free college educations. He was determined to make higher education available to all qualified but disadvantaged students.
3 The students welcomed Taylor. Their voices joined in singing. They sang "You Are the Wind Beneath My Wings." Their faces beamed with hope. Their eyes flashed with self-confidence.
4 The students had thought a college education was beyond their dreams. It seemed too costly. It seemed too demanding.
5 Taylor had to ease the costs and the demands of getting to college. He created a bold plan. The plan consisted of scholarships, tutoring, and counseling.

15c Using coordination

Use **coordination** to show that two or more elements in a sentence are equally important in meaning and thus to clarify the relationship between them:

Ways to coordinate information in sentences

- **Link main clauses with a comma and a coordinating conjunction:** *and, but, or, nor, for, so, yet.*

  Independence Hall in Philadelphia is faithfully restored, but many years ago it was in bad shape.

- **Relate main clauses with a semicolon alone or a semicolon and a conjunctive adverb:** *however, indeed, thus,* etc.

  The building was standing; however, it suffered from neglect.

- **Within clauses, link words and phrases with a coordinating conjunction:** *and, but, or, nor.*

  The people and officials of the nation were indifferent to independence Hall or took it for granted.

- **Link main clauses, words, or phrases with a correlative conjunction:** *both . . . and, not only . . . but also,* etc.

  People not only took the building for granted but also neglected it.

┌─ **Key terms** ───────────────────────────────────
coordinating conjunctions *And, but, or, nor,* and sometimes *for, so, yet.* (See **4** p. 196.)

conjunctive adverbs Modifiers that describe the relation of the ideas in two clauses, such as *hence, however, indeed,* and *thus.* (See **4** p. 288.)

correlative conjunctions Pairs of connecting words, such as *both . . . and, either . . . or, not only . . . but also.* (See **4** p. 196.)
└──

Grammar checkers A grammar checker may spot some errors in punctuating coordinated elements, and it can usually flag long sentences that may contain excessive coordination. But otherwise a checker can provide little help with coordination because it cannot recognize the relations among ideas in sentences.

1 Coordinating to relate equal ideas

Coordination shows the equality between elements, as illustrated by the examples in the box opposite. At the same time that it clarifies meaning, it can also help smooth choppy sentences:

Choppy sentences	We should not rely so heavily on oil. Coal and uranium are also overused. We have a substantial energy resource in the moving waters of our rivers. Smaller streams add to the total volume of water. The resource renews itself. Oil and coal are irreplaceable. Uranium is also irreplaceable. The cost of water does not increase much over time. The costs of coal, oil, and uranium rise dramatically.

The revision groups coal, oil, and uranium and clearly opposes them to water (the connecting words are underlined):

Ideas coordinated	We should not rely so heavily on oil, coal, and uranium, for we have a substantial energy resource in the moving waters of our rivers and streams. Oil, coal, and uranium are irreplaceable and thus subject to dramatic cost increases; water, however, is self-renewing and more stable in cost.

2 Coordinating effectively

Use coordination only to express the *equality* of ideas or details. A string of coordinated elements—especially main clauses—implies that all points are equally important:

Excessive coordination	The weeks leading up to the resignation of President Nixon were eventful, and the Supreme Court and the Congress closed in on him, and the Senate Judiciary Committee voted to begin impeachment proceedings, and finally the President resigned on August 9, 1974.

Such a passage needs editing to stress the important points (underlined below) and to de-emphasize the less important information:

Revised	The weeks leading up to the resignation of President Nixon were eventful, as the Supreme Court and the Congress closed in on him and the Senate Judiciary Committee voted to begin impeachment proceedings. Finally, the President resigned on August 9, 1974.

Even within a single sentence, coordination should express a logical equality between ideas:

Faulty   John Stuart Mill was a nineteenth-century utilitarian, and he believed that actions should be judged by their usefulness or by the happiness they cause. [The two clauses are not separate and equal: the second expands on the first by explaining what a utilitarian such as Mill believed.]

Revised   John Stuart Mill, a nineteenth-century utilitarian, believed that actions should be judged by their usefulness or by the happiness they cause.

Exercise 15.3   **Sentence combining: Coordination**

Combine sentences in the following passages to coordinate related ideas in the ways that seem most effective to you. You will have to supply coordinating conjunctions or conjunctive adverbs and the appropriate punctuation.

1 Many chronic misspellers do not have the time to master spelling rules. They may not have the motivation. They may rely on dictionaries to catch misspellings. Most dictionaries list words under their correct spellings. One kind of dictionary is designed for chronic misspellers. It lists each word under its common *mis*spellings. It then provides the correct spelling. It also provides the definition.

2 Henry Hudson was an English explorer. He captained ships for the Dutch East India Company. On a voyage in 1610 he passed by Greenland. He sailed into a great bay in today's northern Canada. He thought he and his sailors could winter there. The cold was terrible. Food ran out. The sailors mutinied. The sailors cast Hudson adrift in a small boat. Eight others were also in the boat. Hudson and his companions perished.

15d   Using subordination

Use **subordination** to indicate that some elements in a sentence are less important than others for your meaning. Usually, the main idea appears in the main clause, and supporting details appear in subordinate structures:

Ways to subordinate information in sentences

- Use a subordinate clause beginning with a subordinating word: *who (whom), that, which, although, because, if,* etc.

  Although some citizens had tried to rescue independence Hall, they had not gained substantial public support.

  The first strong step was taken by the federal government, which made the building a national monument.

- **Use a phrase.**

    Like most national monuments, Independence Hall is protected by the National Park Service.

    Protecting many popular tourist sites, the service is a highly visible government agency.

- **Use a short modifier.**

    At the red brick Independence Hall, park rangers give guided tours and protect the irreplaceable building from vandalism.

Grammar checkers A grammar checker may spot some errors in punctuating subordinated elements, and it can usually flag long sentences that may contain excessive subordination. But otherwise a checker can provide little help with subordination because it cannot recognize the relations among ideas in sentences.

1 Subordinating to emphasize main ideas

A string of main clauses can make everything in a passage seem equally important:

String of main clauses	Computer prices have dropped, and production costs have dropped more slowly, and computer manufacturers have had to struggle, for their profits have been shrinking.

Emphasis comes from keeping the truly important information in the main clause (underlined) and subordinating the less important details:

Revised	Because production costs have dropped more slowly than prices, computer manufacturers have had to struggle with shrinking profits.

2 Subordinating effectively

Use subordination only for the less important information in a sentence.

Key terms

subordinate clause A word group that contains a subject and verb, begins with a subordinating word such as *because* or *who,* and is not a question: *Words can do damage when they hurt feelings.* (See **4** p. 208.)

phrase A word group that lacks a subject or predicate or both: *Words can do damage by hurting feelings.* (See **4** p. 203.)

Faulty	Ms. Angelo was in her first year of teaching, although she was a better instructor than others with many years of experience.

The preceding sentence suggests that Angelo's inexperience is the main idea, whereas the writer intended to stress her skill *despite* her inexperience. Reducing the inexperience to a subordinate clause and elevating the skill to the main clause (underlined) gives appropriate emphasis:

Revised	Although Ms. Angelo was in her first year of teaching, <u>she was a better instructor than others with many years of experience.</u>

Subordination loses its power to organize and emphasize when too much loosely related detail crowds into one long, meandering sentence:

Overloaded	The boats that were moored at the dock when the hurricane, which was one of the worst in three decades, struck were ripped from their moorings, because the owners had not been adequately prepared, since the weather service had predicted that the storm would blow out to sea, which they do at this time of year.

The revision stresses important information in the main clauses (underlined):

Revised	Struck by one of the worst hurricanes in three decades, <u>the boats at the dock were ripped from their moorings.</u> <u>The owners were unprepared</u> because the weather service had said that hurricanes at this time of year blow out to sea.

Exercise 15.4 Revising: Subordination for emphasis

Emphasize the important information in the following paragraph by giving it in main clauses and subordinating other information.

1 During the Civil War, soldiers often admired their commanding officers, and they gave them nicknames, and these names frequently contained the word *old*, but not all of the commanders were old. 2 Confederate General Thomas "Stonewall" Jackson was also called "Old Jack," and he was not yet forty years old. 3 Another Southern general in the Civil War was called "Old Pete," and his full name was James Longstreet. 4 The Union general Henry W. Halleck had a reputation as a good military strategist, and he was an expert on the work of a French military authority, Henri Jomini, and Halleck was called "Old Brains." 5 Well before the Civil War, General William Henry Harrison won the Battle of Tippecanoe, and he received the nickname "Old Tippecanoe," and he used the name in his presidential campaign slogan, "Tippecanoe and Tyler, Too," and he won the election in 1840, but he died of pneumonia a month after taking office.

Exercise 15.5 Sentence combining: Subordination

Combine each of the following pairs of sentences twice, each time using one of the subordinate structures in parentheses to make a single sentence. You will have to add, delete, change, and rearrange words.

Example:

During the late eighteenth century, workers carried beverages in brightly colored bottles. The bottles had cork stoppers. (*Clause beginning that. Phrase beginning with.*)

During the late eighteenth century, workers carried beverages in brightly colored bottles that had cork stoppers.

During the late eighteenth century, workers carried beverages in brightly colored bottles with cork stoppers.

1 The bombardier beetle sees an enemy. It shoots out a jet of chemicals to protect itself. (*Clause beginning when. Phrase beginning seeing.*)
2 The beetle's spray is very potent. It consists of hot and irritating chemicals. (*Phrase beginning consisting. Phrase beginning of.*)
3 The spray's two chemicals are stored separately in the beetle's body and mixed in the spraying gland. The chemicals resemble a nerve-gas weapon. (*Phrase beginning stored. Clause beginning which.*)
4 The tip of the beetle's abdomen sprays the chemicals. The tip revolves like a turret on a World War II bomber. (*Phrase beginning revolving. Phrase beginning spraying.*)
5 The beetle defeats most of its enemies. It is still eaten by spiders and birds. (*Clause beginning although. Phrase beginning except.*)

Exercise 15.6 Revising: Effective subordination

Revise the following paragraph to eliminate faulty or excessive subordination and thus to emphasize the main ideas. Correct faulty subordination by reversing main and subordinate structures. Correct excessive subordination by coordinating equal ideas or by making separate sentences.

1 Genaro González is a successful writer, which means that his stories and novels have been published to critical acclaim. 2 In interviews, he talks about his love of writing, even though he has also earned a doctorate in psychology because he enjoys teaching. 3 González's first story, which reflects his growing consciousness of his Aztec heritage and place in the world, is titled "Un Hijo del Sol." 4 He wrote the first version of "Un Hijo del Sol" while he was a sophomore at the University of Texas-Pan American, which is in the Rio Grande valley of southern Texas, which Gonzáles called "el Valle" in the story, and where he now teaches psychology. 5 Gonzáles, who writes equally well in English and Spanish, received a large fellowship that enabled him to take a leave of absence from his teaching job at Pan American so that for a year he could write full-time.

Exercise 15.7 Revising: Coordination and subordination

The following paragraph consists entirely of simple sentences. Use coordination and subordination to combine sentences in the ways you think most effective to emphasize main ideas.

Sir Walter Raleigh personified the Elizabethan Age. That was the period of Elizabeth I's rule of England. The period occurred in the last half of the sixteenth century. Raleigh was a courtier and poet. He was also an explorer and entrepreneur. Supposedly, he gained Queen Elizabeth's favor. He did this by throwing his cloak beneath her feet at the right moment. She was just about to step over a puddle. There is no evidence for this story. It does illustrate Raleigh's dramatic and dynamic personality. His energy drew others to him. He was one of Elizabeth's favorites. She supported him. She also dispensed favors to him. However, he lost his queen's goodwill. Without her permission he seduced one of her maids of honor. He eventually married the maid of honor. Elizabeth died. Then her successor imprisoned Raleigh in the Tower of London. Her successor was James I. The king falsely charged Raleigh with treason. Raleigh was released after thirteen years. He was arrested again two years later on the old treason charges. At the age of sixty-six he was beheaded.

16 Parallelism

Parallelism gives similar grammatical form to sentence elements that have similar function and importance.

The air is dirtied by factories belching smoke
and
cars spewing exhaust.

In this example the two underlined phrases have the same function and importance (both specify sources of air pollution), so they also have the same grammatical construction. Parallelism makes form follow meaning.

Grammar checkers A grammar checker cannot recognize faulty parallelism because it cannot recognize the relations among ideas.

16a Using parallelism with *and, but, or, nor, yet*

The coordinating conjunctions *and, or, nor,* and *yet* always signal a need for parallelism.

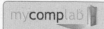

The industrial base was <u>shifting</u> and <u>shrinking</u>. [Parallel words.]

Politicians rarely <u>acknowledged the problem</u> or <u>proposed alternatives</u>. [Parallel phrases.]

Industrial workers were understandably disturbed <u>that they were losing their jobs</u> and <u>that no one seemed to care</u>. [Parallel clauses.]

When sentence elements linked by coordinating conjunctions are not parallel in structure, the sentence is awkward and distracting:

Nonparallel	The reasons steel companies kept losing money were <u>that their plants were inefficient</u>, <u>high labor costs</u>, and <u>foreign competition was increasing</u>.
Revised	The reasons steel companies kept losing money were <u>inefficient plants</u>, <u>high labor costs</u>, and <u>increasing foreign competition</u>.
Nonparallel	Success was difficult even for efficient companies because <u>of the shift away from all manufacturing in the United States</u> and <u>the fact that steel production was shifting toward emerging nations</u>.
Revised	Success was difficult even for efficient companies because <u>of the shift away from all manufacturing in the United States</u> and <u>toward steel production in emerging nations</u>.

All the words required by idiom or grammar must be stated in compound constructions (see also p. 179):

Faulty	Given training, workers can acquire the <u>skills</u> and <u>interest</u> in other jobs. [Idiom dictates different prepositions with *skills* and *interest*.]
Revised	Given training, workers can acquire the skills <u>for</u> and interest in other jobs.

16b Using parallelism with *both . . . and, not . . . but*, or another correlative conjunction

Correlative conjunctions stress equality and balance between elements. Parallelism confirms the equality.

Key terms

coordinating conjunctions Words that connect elements of the same kind and importance: *and, but, or, nor,* and sometimes *for, so, yet.* (See **4** p. 196.)

correlative conjunctions Pairs of words that connect elements of the same kind and importance, such as *but . . . and, either . . . or, neither . . . nor, not . . . but, not only . . . but also.* (See **4** p. 196.)

It is not a tax bill but a tax relief bill, providing relief not for the needy but for the greedy.

—Franklin Delano Roosevelt

With correlative conjunctions, the element after the second connector must match the element after the first connector:

Nonparallel	Huck Finn learns not only that human beings have an enormous capacity for folly but also enormous dignity. [The first element includes *that human beings have;* the second element does not.]
Revised	Huck Finn learns that human beings have not only an enormous capacity for folly but also enormous dignity. [Repositioning *that human beings have* makes the two elements parallel.]

16c Using parallelism in comparisons

Parallelism confirms the likeness or difference between two elements being compared using *than* or *as:*

Nonparallel	Huck Finn proves less a bad boy than to be an independent spirit. In the end he is every bit as determined in rejecting help as he is to leave for "the territory."
Revised	Huck Finn proves less a bad boy than an independent spirit. In the end he is every bit as determined to reject help as he is to leave for "the territory."

(See also **4** pp. 264–65 on making comparisons logical.)

16d Using parallelism with lists, headings, and outlines

The items in a list or outline are coordinate and should be parallel. Parallelism is essential in a formal topic outline and in the headings that divide a paper into sections. (See **1** pp. 20–21 and 59–60 for more on outlines and headings.)

Nonparallel	Revised
Changes in Renaissance England	Changes in Renaissance England
1. Extension of trade routes	1. Extension of trade routes
2. Merchant class became more powerful	2. Increased power of the merchant class
3. The death of feudalism	3. Death of feudalism
4. Upsurging of the arts	4. Upsurge of the arts
5. Religious quarrels began	5. Rise of religious quarrels

Exercise 16.1 Revising: Parallelism

Revise the following paragraph as needed to create parallelism for grammar and coherence. Add or delete words or rephrase as necessary.

1 The ancient Greeks celebrated four athletic contests: the Olympic Games at Olympia, the Isthmian games were held near Corinth, at Delphi the Pythian Games, and the Nemean Games were sponsored by the people of Cleone. 2 Each day the games consisted of either athletic events or holding ceremonies and sacrifices to the gods. 3 Competitors participated in running sprints, spectacular chariot and horse races, and running long distances while wearing full armor. 4 The purpose of such events was developing physical strength, demonstrating skill and endurance, and sharpening the skills needed for war. 5 The athletes competed less to achieve great wealth than for gaining honor both for themselves and their cities. 6 Of course, exceptional athletes received financial support from patrons, poems and statues by admiring artists, and they even got lavish living quarters from their sponsoring cities. 7 With the medal counts and flag ceremonies, today's Olympians sometimes seem to be proving their countries' superiority more than to demonstrate individual talent.

Exercise 16.2 Sentence combining: Parallelism

Combine each group of sentences below into one concise sentence in which parallel elements appear in parallel structures. You will have to add, delete, change, and rearrange words. Each item has more than one possible answer.

Example:
The new process works smoothly. It is efficient, too.
The new process work smoothly and <u>efficiently</u>.

1 People can develop post-traumatic stress disorder (PTSD). They develop it after experiencing a dangerous situation. They will also have felt fear for their survival.

2 The disorder can be triggered by a wide variety of events. Combat is a typical cause. Similarly, natural disasters can result in PTSD. Some people experience PTSD after a hostage situation.

3 PTSD can occur immediately after the stressful incident. Or it may not appear until many years later.

4 Sometimes people with PTSD will act irrationally. Moreover, they often become angry.

5 Other symptoms include dreaming that one is reliving the experience. They include hallucinating that one is back in the terrifying place. In another symptom one imagines that strangers are actually one's former torturers.

17 Variety and Details

Writing that's interesting as well as clear has at least two features: the sentences vary in length and structure, and they are well textured with details.

Grammar checkers Some grammar checkers will flag long sentences, and you can check for appropriate variety in a series of such sentences. But generally these programs cannot help you see where variety may be needed because they cannot recognize the relative importance and complexity of your ideas.

17a Varying sentence length

In most contemporary writing, sentences tend to vary from about ten to about forty words. When sentences are all at one extreme or the other, readers may have difficulty focusing on main ideas and seeing the relations among them.

- **Long sentences.** If most of your sentences contain thirty-five words or more, your main ideas may not stand out from the details that support them. Break some of the long sentences into shorter, simpler ones.
- **Short sentences.** If most of your sentences contain fewer than ten or fifteen words, all your ideas may seem equally important and the links between them may not be clear. Try combining sentences with coordination (p. 148) and subordination (p. 150) to show relationships and stress main ideas over supporting information.

17b Varying sentence structure

A passage will be monotonous if all its sentences follow the same pattern, like soldiers marching in a parade. Try the following techniques for varying structure.

1 Subordination

A string of main clauses in simple or compound sentences can be especially plodding.

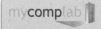

Visit *mycomplab.com* for more resources on variety and details.

Monotonous	The moon is now drifting away from the earth. It moves away at the rate of about one inch a year. This movement is lengthening our days. They increase a thousandth of a second every century. Forty-seven of our present days will someday make up a month. We might eventually lose the moon altogether. Such great planetary movement rightly concerns astronomers, but it need not worry us. It will take 50 million years.

Enliven such writing—and make the main ideas stand out—by expressing the less important information in subordinate clauses and phrases. In the revision below, underlining indicates subordinate structures that used to be main clauses:

Revised	The moon is now drifting away from the earth <u>about one inch a year</u>. <u>At a thousandth of a second every century</u>, this movement is lengthening our days. Forty-seven of our present days will someday make up a month, <u>if we don't eventually lose the moon altogether</u>. Such great planetary movement rightly concerns astronomers, but it need not worry us. It will take 50 million years.

2 Sentence combining

As the preceding example shows, subordinating to achieve variety often involves combining short, choppy sentences into longer units that link related information and stress main ideas. Here is another unvaried passage:

Monotonous	Astronomy may seem a remote science. It may seem to have little to do with people's daily lives. Many astronomers find otherwise. They see their science as soothing. It gives perspective to everyday routines and problems.

Combining five sentences into one, the revision on the next page is both clearer and easier to read. Underlining highlights the changes.

Key terms

main clause A word group that can stand alone as a sentence because it contains a subject and a predicate and does not begin with a subordinating word: *Tourism is an industry. It brings in over $2 billion a year.* (See 4 p. 208.)

subordinate clause A word group that contains a subject and predicate, begins with a subordinating word such as *because* or *who,* and is not a question: *Tourism is an industry <u>that brings in over $2 billion a year</u>.* (See 4 p. 208.)

phrase A word group that lacks a subject or predicate or both: *Tourism is an industry <u>valued at over $2 billion a year</u>.* (See 4 p. 203.)

Revised   Astronomy may seem a remote science <u>having</u> little to do with people's daily lives, <u>but</u> many astronomers <u>find their science soothing</u> <u>because</u> it gives perspective to everyday routines and problems.

3 Varied sentence beginnings

An English sentence often begins with its subject, which generally captures old information from a preceding sentence (see p. 146):

The defendant's <u>lawyer</u> was determined to break the prosecution's witness. <u>He</u> relentlessly cross-examined the stubborn witness for a week.

However, an unbroken sequence of sentences beginning with the subject quickly becomes monotonous:

Monotonous   The defendant's lawyer was determined to break the prosecution's witness. He relentlessly cross-examined the witness for a week. The witness had expected to be dismissed within an hour and was visibly irritated. She did not cooperate. She was reprimanded by the judge.

Beginning some of these sentences with other expressions improves readability and clarity:

Revised   The defendant's lawyer was determined to break the prosecution's witness. <u>For a week</u> he relentlessly cross-examined the witness. <u>Expecting to be dismissed within an hour,</u> the witness was visibly irritated. She did not cooperate. <u>Indeed,</u> she was reprimanded by the judge.

The underlined expressions represent the most common choices for varying sentence beginnings:

- **Adverb modifiers,** such as *For a week* (modifies the verb *cross-examined*).
- **Adjective modifiers,** such as *Expecting to be dismissed within an hour* (modifies *witness*).
- **Transitional expressions,** such as *Indeed*. (See **1** pp. 44–45 for a list.)

 In standard American English, placing certain adverb modifiers at the beginning of a sentence

---

Key terms

adverb A word or word group that describes a verb, an adjective, another adverb, or a whole sentence: *dressed <u>sharply</u>, <u>clearly</u> unhappy, soaring <u>from the mountain</u>*. (See **4** p. 194.)

adjective A word or word group that describes a noun or pronoun: *<u>sweet</u> smile, <u>certain</u> someone*. (See **4** p. 194.)

requires you to alter the normal subject-verb order as well. The most common of these modifiers are negatives, including *seldom, rarely, in no case, not since,* and *not until.*

| | verb |
| adverb | subject | phrase |

Faulty   Seldom <u>a witness</u> <u>has held</u> the stand so long.

| | helping | | main |
| adverb | verb | subject | verb |

Revised   Seldom <u>has</u> <u>a witness</u> <u>held</u> the stand so long.

4   Varied word order

Occasionally you can vary a sentence and emphasize it at the same time by inverting the usual order of parts:

> A dozen witnesses testified for the prosecution, and the defense attorney barely questioned eleven of them. <u>The twelfth, however, he grilled.</u> [Normal word order: *He grilled the twelfth, however.*]

Inverted sentences used without need are artificial. Use them only when emphasis demands.

17c   Adding details

Relevant details such as facts and examples create the texture and life that keep readers awake and help them grasp your meaning. For instance:

Flat   Constructed after World War II, Levittown, New York, consisted of thousands of houses in two basic styles. Over the decades, residents have altered the houses so dramatically that the original styles are often unrecognizable.

Detailed   Constructed <u>on potato fields</u> after World War II, Levittown, New York, consisted of <u>more than seventeen thousand</u> houses in <u>Cape Cod and ranch</u> styles. Over the decades, residents have <u>added expansive front porches, punched dormer windows through roofs, converted garages to sun porches, and otherwise</u> altered the houses so dramatically that the original styles are often unrecognizable.

Exercise 17.1   **Revising: Variety**

The following paragraph consists entirely of simple sentences that begin with their subjects. Use the techniques discussed in this chapter to vary the sentences. Delete, add, change, and rearrange words to make the paragraph more readable and to make important ideas stand out clearly.

The Italian volcano Vesuvius had been dormant for many years. It then exploded on August 24 in the year AD 79. The ash, pumice, and mud from the volcano buried two busy towns. Herculaneum is one. The more famous is Pompeii. Both towns lay undiscovered for many centuries. Herculaneum and Pompeii were discovered in 1709 and 1748, respectively. The excavation of Pompeii was the more systematic. It was the occasion for initiating modern methods of conservation and restoration. Herculaneum was simply looted of its more valuable finds. It was then left to disintegrate. Pompeii appears much as it did before the eruption. A luxurious house opens onto a lush central garden. An election poster decorates a wall. A dining table is set for breakfast.

18 Appropriate and Exact Language

The clarity and effectiveness of your writing will depend greatly on the use of language that is appropriate for your writing situation (below) and that expresses your meaning exactly (p. 170).

18a Choosing appropriate language

Appropriate language suits your writing situation—your subject, purpose, and audience. In most college and career writing you should rely on what's called **standard American English,** the dialect of English normally expected and used in school, business, the professions, government, and the communications media. (For more on its role in academic writing, see **2** pp. 94–96.)

The vocabulary of standard American English is huge, allowing expression of an infinite range of ideas and feelings; but it does exclude words that only some groups of people use, understand, or find inoffensive. Some of these more limited vocabularies should be avoided altogether; others should be used cautiously and in relevant situations, as when aiming for a special effect with an audience you know will appreciate it. Whenever you doubt a word's status, consult a dictionary (see pp. 170–71).

Grammar checkers A grammar checker can often be set to flag potentially inappropriate words, such as nonstandard dialect, slang, colloquialisms, and gender-specific terms (*manmade, mailman*). However, the checker can flag only words listed in its dictionary of questionable words. For example, a checker flagged *businessman* as

Visit *mycomplab.com* for more resources and exercises on appropriate and exact language.

potentially sexist in *A successful businessman puts clients first,* but the checker did not flag *his* in *A successful businessperson listens to his clients.* If you use a checker to review your language, you'll need to determine whether a flagged word is or is not appropriate for your writing situation.

1 Nonstandard dialect ⟨CULTURE LANGUAGE⟩

Like many countries, the United States includes scores of regional, social, and ethnic groups with their own distinct **dialects,** or versions of English. Standard American English is one of those dialects, and so are Black English, Appalachian English, Creole, and the English of coastal Maine. All the dialects of English share many features, but each also has its own vocabulary, pronunciation, and grammar.

If you speak a dialect of English besides standard American English, be careful about using your dialect in situations where standard English is the norm, such as in academic or business writing. Dialects are not wrong in themselves, but forms imported from one dialect into another may still be perceived as unclear or incorrect. When you know standard English is expected in your writing, edit to eliminate expressions in your dialect that you know (or have been told) differ from standard English. These expressions may include *theirselves, hisn, them books,* and others labeled "nonstandard" by a dictionary. They may also include certain verb forms, as discussed in **4** pp. 217–27. For help identifying and editing nonstandard language, see the ⟨CULTURE LANGUAGE⟩ Guide just before the back endpapers of this book.

Your participation in the community of standard English does not require you to abandon your own dialect. You may want to use it in writing you do for yourself, such as journals, notes, and drafts, which should be composed as freely as possible. You may want to quote it in an academic paper, as when analyzing or reporting conversation in dialect. And, of course, you will want to use it with others who speak it.

2 Shortcuts of online communication

Rapid communication by e-mail and text or instant messaging encourages some informalities that are inappropriate for academic writing. If you use these media frequently, you may need to proofread your academic papers especially to identify and revise errors such as the following:

- **Sentence fragments.** Make sure every sentence has a subject and a predicate. Avoid fragments such as *Observing the results* or *After the meeting.* For more on fragments, see **4** pp. 280–83.

- **Missing punctuation.** Between and within sentences, use standard punctuation marks. Check especially for missing commas within sentences and missing apostrophes in possessives and contractions. See **5** pp. 300–14 and 325–31.
- **Missing capital letters.** Use capital letters at the beginnings of sentences, for proper nouns and adjectives, and in titles. See **6** pp. 356–59.
- **Nonstandard abbreviations and spellings.** Avoid forms such as *2* for *to* or *too, b4* for *before, bc* for *because, ur* for *you are* or *you're,* and + or & for *and.* See **6** pp. 349–52 and 363–65.

3 Slang

Slang is the language used by a group, such as musicians or computer programmers, to reflect common experiences and to make technical references efficient. The following example is from an essay on the slang of "skaters" (skateboarders):

> Curtis slashed ultra-punk crunchers on his longboard, while the Rube-man flailed his usual Gumbyness on tweaked frontsides and lofty fakie ollies.
> —Miles Orkin, "Mucho Slingage by the Pool"

Among those who understand it, slang may be vivid and forceful. It often occurs in dialog, and an occasional slang expression can enliven an informal essay. But most slang is too flippant and imprecise for effective communication, and it is generally inappropriate for college or business writing. Notice the gain in seriousness and precision achieved in the following revision:

Slang	Many students start out <u>pretty together</u> but then <u>get weird.</u>
Revised	Many students start out <u>with clear goals</u> but then <u>lose their direction.</u>

4 Colloquial language

Colloquial language is the everyday spoken language, including expressions such as *get together, go crazy, do the dirty work,* and *get along.*

When you write informally, colloquial language may be appropriate to achieve the casual, relaxed effect of conversation. An occasional colloquial word dropped into otherwise more formal writing can also help you achieve a desired emphasis. But most colloquial language is not precise enough for college or career writing. In such writing you should generally avoid any words and expressions labeled "informal" or "colloquial" in your dictionary.

Colloquial	According to a Native American myth, the Great Creator <u>had a dog hanging around with him</u> when he created the earth.

| Revised | According to a Native American myth, the Great Creator was accompanied by a dog when he created the earth. |

5 Technical words

All disciplines and professions rely on specialized language that allows the members to communicate precisely and efficiently with each other. Chemists, for instance, have their *phosphatides*, and literary critics have their *motifs* and *subtexts*. Without explanation, technical words are meaningless to nonspecialists. When you are writing for nonspecialists, avoid unnecessary technical terms and carefully define terms you must use.

6 Indirect and pretentious writing

Small, plain, and direct words are almost always preferable to big, showy, or evasive words. Take special care to avoid euphemisms, double talk, and pretentious writing.

A **euphemism** is a presumably inoffensive word that a writer or speaker substitutes for a word deemed potentially offensive or too blunt, such as *passed away* for *died* or *misspeak* for *lie*. Use euphemisms only when you know that blunt, truthful words would needlessly hurt or offend members of your audience.

A kind of euphemism that deliberately evades the truth is **double talk** (also called **doublespeak** or **weasel words**): language intended to confuse or to be misunderstood. Today double talk is unfortunately common in politics and advertising—the *revenue enhancement* that is really a tax, the *peace-keeping function* that is really war making, the *biodegradable* bags that last decades. Double talk has no place in honest writing.

Euphemism and sometimes double talk seem to keep company with **pretentious writing**, fancy language that is more elaborate than its subject requires. Choose your words for their exactness and economy. The big, ornate word may be tempting, but pass it up. Your readers will be grateful.

| Pretentious | To perpetuate our endeavor of providing funds for our elderly citizens as we do at the present moment, we will face the exigency of enhanced contributions from all our citizens. |
| Revised | We cannot continue to fund Social Security and Medicare for the elderly unless we raise taxes. |

7 Sexist and other biased language

Even when we do not mean it to, our language can reflect and perpetuate hurtful prejudices toward groups of people. Such biased language can be obvious—words such as *nigger, honky, mick, kike, fag, dyke,* and *broad.* But it can also be subtle, generalizing about groups in ways that may be familiar but that are also inaccurate or unfair.

Biased language reflects poorly on the user, not on the person or persons whom it mischaracterizes or insults. Unbiased language does not submit to false generalizations. It treats people respectfully as individuals and labels groups as they wish to be labeled.

Stereotypes of race, ethnicity, religion, age, and other characteristics

A **stereotype** is a generalization based on poor evidence, a kind of formula for understanding and judging people simply because of their membership in a group:

Men are uncommunicative.
Women are emotional.
Liberals want to raise taxes.
Conservatives are affluent.

At best, stereotypes betray a noncritical writer, one who is not thinking beyond notions received from others. In your writing, be alert for statements that characterize whole groups of people:

Stereotype   Elderly drivers should have their licenses limited to daytime driving only. [Asserts that all elderly people are poor night drivers.]

Revised   Drivers with impaired night vision should have their licenses limited to daytime driving only.

Some stereotypes have become part of the language, but they are still potentially offensive:

Stereotype   The administrators are too blind to see the need for a new gymnasium. [Equates vision loss and lack of understanding.]

Revised   The administrators do not understand the need for a new gymnasium.

Sexist language

Among the most subtle and persistent biased language is that expressing narrow ideas about men's and women's roles, position, and value in society. Like other stereotypes, this **sexist language** can wound or irritate readers, and it indicates the writer's thoughtlessness or unfairness. The following box suggests some ways of eliminating sexist language.

Eliminating sexist language

■ **Avoid demeaning and patronizing language:**

Sexist   Dr. Keith Kim and Lydia Hawkins coauthored the article.

Revised   Dr. Keith Kim and Dr. Lydia Hawkins coauthored the article.

Revised   Keith Kim and Lydia Hawkins coauthored the article.

Sexist   Ladies are entering almost every occupation formerly filled by men.

Revised   Women are entering almost every occupation formerly filled by men.

■ **Avoid occupational or social stereotypes:**

Sexist   The considerate doctor commends a nurse when she provides his patients with good care.

Revised   The considerate doctor commends a nurse who provides good care for patients.

Sexist   The grocery shopper should save her coupons.

Revised   Grocery shoppers should save their coupons.

■ **Avoid referring needlessly to gender:**

Sexist   Marie Curie, a woman chemist, discovered radium.

Revised   Marie Curie, a chemist, discovered radium.

Sexist   The patients were tended by a male nurse.

Revised   The patients were tended by a nurse.

■ **Avoid using *man* or words containing *man* to refer to all human beings.** Here are a few alternatives:

businessman	businessperson
chairman	chair, chairperson
congressman	representative in Congress, legislator
craftsman	craftsperson, artisan
layman	layperson
mankind	humankind, humanity, human beings, humans
manmade	handmade, manufactured, synthetic, artificial
manpower	personnel, human resources
policeman	police officer
salesman	salesperson

Sexist   Man has not reached the limits of social justice.

Revised   Humankind [or Humanity] has not reached the limits of social justice.

Sexist   The furniture consists of manmade materials.

Revised   The furniture consists of synthetic materials.

(continued)

Eliminating sexist language
(continued)

- **Avoid the generic *he,*** the male pronoun used to refer to both genders. (See also 4 pp. 254–55.)

  Sexist   The newborn <u>child</u> explores <u>his</u> world.

  Revised   Newborn <u>children</u> explore <u>their</u> world. [Use the plural for the pronoun and the word it refers to.]

  Revised   The newborn child explores the world. [Avoid the pronoun altogether.]

  Revised   The newborn child explores <u>his or her</u> world. [Substitute male and female pronouns.]

  Use the last option sparingly—only once in a group of sentences and only to stress the singular individual.

CULTURE LANGUAGE Forms of address vary widely from culture to culture. In some cultures, for instance, one shows respect by referring to all older women as if they were married, using the equivalent of *Mrs.* Usage in the United States is changing toward making no assumptions about marital status, rank, or other characteristics—for instance, addressing a woman as *Ms.* unless she is known to prefer *Mrs.* or *Miss.*

Appropriate labels

We often need to label groups: *swimmers, politicians, mothers, Christians, Westerners, students.* But labels can be shorthand stereotypes, slighting the person labeled and ignoring the preferences of the group members themselves. Although sometimes dismissed as "political correctness," showing sensitivity about labels hurts no one and helps gain your readers' trust and respect.

- **Avoid labels that (intentionally or not) disparage the person or group you refer to.** A person with emotional problems is not a *mental patient.* A person with cancer is not a *cancer victim.* A person using a wheelchair is not *wheelchair-bound.*
- **Use names for racial, ethnic, and other groups that reflect the preferences of each group's members,** or at least many of them. Examples of current preferences include *African American* or *black, latino/latina* (for Americans and American immigrants of Spanish-speaking descent), and *people with disabilities* (rather than *the disabled* or *the handicapped*). But labels change often. To learn how a group's members wish to be labeled, ask them directly, attend to usage in reputable periodicals, or check a recent dictionary.

■ **Identify a person's group only when it is relevant to the point you're making.** Consider the context of the label: Is it a necessary piece of information? If not, don't use it.

A helpful reference for appropriate labels is *Guidelines for Bias-Free Writing*, by Marilyn Schwartz and the Task Force on Bias-Free Language of the Association of American University Presses.

Exercise 18.1   Revising: Appropriate words

Rewrite the following paragraphs as needed for standard American English, focusing on inappropriate slang, technical or pretentious language, and biased language. Consult a dictionary to determine whether particular words are appropriate and to find suitable substitutes.

1 Acquired immune deficiency syndrome (AIDS) is a major deal all over the world, and those who think the disease is limited to homos, druggies, and foreigners are quite mistaken. 2 Indeed, stats suggest that in the United States one in every five hundred American college kids carries the HIV virus that causes AIDS. 3 If such numbers are to be believed, then doctors and public health officials will continue to have a whole lot of HIV and AIDS victims on their hands in the years to come.
    4 A person with HIV or a full-blown AIDS sufferer deserves to be treated with respect, like someone with any other disease. 5 He should not be dissed or subjected to exclusionary behavior on the part of his fellow citizens. 6 Instead, each victim has the necessity for all the medical care and financial assistance due those who are in the extremity of illness. 7 Many professionals in the medical and social services communities are committed to helping HIV and AIDS patients. 8 For example, a doctor may help his patients by obtaining social services for them as well as by providing medical care. 9 A social worker may visit an HIV or AIDS victim and determine whether he qualifies for public assistance, since many patients don't have the dough for insurance or drugs. 10 Patients who are very ill may require the ministrations of a home-care nurse. 11 She can administer medications and make the sick person as comfy as possible.

Exercise 18.2   Revising: Sexist language

Revise the following paragraph to eliminate sexist language. If you change a singular noun or pronoun to plural, be sure to make any needed changes in verbs or other pronouns.

1 When a student applies for a job, he should prepare the best possible résumé, because the businessman who is scanning a stack of résumés will read them all quickly. 2 The person who wants his résumé to stand out will make sure it highlights his best points. 3 A person applying for a job as a mailman should emphasize his honesty and responsibility. 4 A girl applying for a position as a home-care nurse should also emphasize her honesty and responsibility as well as her background of capable nursing. 5 Someone seeking work as a computer programmer will highlight his experience with computers. 6 Students without extensive job

experience should highlight their volunteer work. **7** For instance, a student may have been chairman of a campus organization or secretary of her church's youth group. **8** If everyone writing a résumé considers what the man who will read it is looking for, the applicant will know better what he should include and how he should format that information.

18b Choosing exact language

To write clearly and effectively, you will want to find the words that fit your meaning exactly and convey your attitude precisely.

Grammar checkers A grammar checker can provide some help with inexact language. For instance, you can set it to flag commonly confused words (such as *continuous/continual*), misused prepositions in idioms (such as *accuse for* instead of *accuse of*), and clichés. But a checker can't help you at all with inappropriate connotation, excessive abstraction, or other problems discussed in this section.

1 Word meanings and synonyms

For writing exactly, a dictionary is essential and a thesaurus can be helpful.

Desk dictionaries

A desk dictionary defines about 150,000 to 200,000 words and provides pronunciation, grammatical functions, etymology (word history), and other information. The sample below is from *Merriam-Webster's Collegiate Dictionary*.

Dictionary entry for *reckon*

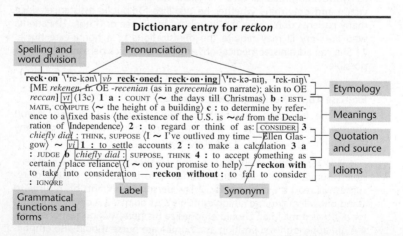

Good desk dictionaries, in addition to *Merriam-Webster's,* include the *American Heritage College Dictionary,* the *Random House Webster's*

College Dictionary, and *Webster's New World Dictionary.* Most of these are available in both print and electronic form (CD-ROM or online). In addition, several Web sites provide online dictionaries or links to online dictionaries.

CULTURE LANGUAGE If English is not your native language, you probably should have a dictionary prepared especially for students using English as a second language (ESL). Such a dictionary contains special information on prepositions, count versus noncount nouns, and many other matters. Reliable ESL dictionaries include *COBUILD English Language Dictionary, Longman Dictionary of Contemporary English,* and *Oxford Advanced Learner's Dictionary.*

Thesauruses

To find a word with the exact shade of meaning you intend, you may want to consult a thesaurus, or book of **synonyms**—words with approximately the same meaning. A thesaurus such as *Roget's International Thesaurus* lists most imaginable synonyms for thousands of words. The word *news,* for instance, has half a page of synonyms in *Roget's International,* including *tidings, gossip,* and *journalism.*

Since a thesaurus aims to open up possibilities, its lists of synonyms include approximate as well as precise matches. The thesaurus does not define synonyms or distinguish among them, however, so you need a dictionary to discover exact meanings. In general, don't use a word from a thesaurus—even one you like the sound of—until you are sure of its appropriateness for your meaning.

Note Your word processor may also include a thesaurus, making it easy to look up synonyms and insert the chosen word into your text. But still you should consult a dictionary unless you are certain of the word's meaning.

Exercise 18.3 **Using a dictionary**

Look up five of the following words in a dictionary. For each word, write down (*a*) the division into syllables, (*b*) the pronunciation, (*c*) the grammatical functions and forms, (*d*) the etymology, (*e*) each meaning, and (*f*) any special uses indicated by labels. Finally, use the word in two sentences of your own.

1 depreciation
2 secretary
3 grammar
4 manifest
5 assassin
6 astrology
7 toxic
8 steal
9 plain (*adjective*)
10 ceremony

---

2 **The right word for your meaning**

All words have one or more basic meanings, called **denotations**—the meanings listed in the dictionary, without reference to emotional associations. If readers are to understand you, you must use words according to their established meanings.

- **Consult a dictionary whenever you are unsure of a word's meaning.**
- **Distinguish between similar-sounding words that have widely different denotations:**

Inexact   Older people often suffer <u>infirmaries</u> [places for the sick].
Exact   Older people often suffer <u>infirmities</u> [disabilities].

Some words, called **homonyms**, sound exactly alike but differ in meaning: for example, *principal/principle* and *rain/reign/rein*. (See **6** pp. 347–48 for a list of commonly confused homonyms.)

- **Distinguish between words with related but distinct meanings:**

Inexact   Television commercials <u>continuously</u> [unceasingly] interrupt programming.
Exact   Television commercials <u>continually</u> [regularly] interrupt programming.

In addition to their emotion-free meanings, many words carry related meanings that evoke specific feelings. These **connotations** can shape readers' responses and are thus a powerful tool for writers. The following word pairs have related denotations but very different connotations:

pride: sense of self-worth
vanity: excessive regard for oneself

firm: steady, unchanging, unyielding
stubborn: unreasonable, bullheaded

enthusiasm: excitement
mania: excessive interest or desire

A dictionary can help you track down words with the exact connotations you want. Besides providing meanings, your dictionary may also list and distinguish synonyms to guide your choices. A thesaurus can also help if you use it carefully, as discussed on the previous page.

Exercise 18.4 **Revising: Denotation**

Revise any underlined word below that is used incorrectly. Consult a dictionary if you are uncertain of a word's precise meaning.

1 The acclaimed writer Maxine Hong Kingston <u>sites</u> her mother's stories about ancestors and ancient Chinese customs as the sources of her first two books, *The Woman Warrior* and *China Men*. **2** One of her mother's tales, about a pregnant aunt who was <u>ostracized</u> by villagers, had a great <u>affect</u> on the young Kingston. **3** The aunt gained <u>avengeance</u> by drowning herself in the village water supply. **4** Kingston made the aunt <u>infamous</u> by giving her <u>immortality</u> in *The Woman Warrior*. **5** Two of

Kingston's <u>progeny</u>, her great-grandfathers, are the focal points of *China Men*. **6** Both men led rebellions against <u>suppressive</u> employers: a sugarcane farmer and a railroad-construction engineer. **7** Kingston's innovative writing <u>infers</u> her opposition to racism and sexism both in the China of the past and in the United States of the present. **8** She was <u>rewarded</u> many prizes for these distinguished books.

Exercise 18.5 Considering the connotations of words

Fill in the blank in each sentence below with the most appropriate word from the list in parentheses. Consult a dictionary to be sure of your choice.

1 Infection with the AIDS virus, HIV, is a serious health _____. (*problem, worry, difficulty, plight*)
2 Once the virus has entered the blood system, it _____ T-cells. (*murders, destroys, slaughters, executes*)
3 The _____ of T-cells is to combat infections. (*ambition, function, aim, goal*)
4 Without enough T-cells, the body is nearly _____ against infections. (*defenseless, hopeless, desperate*)
5 To prevent exposure to the virus, one should be especially _____ in sexual relationships. (*chary, circumspect, cautious, calculating*)

3 Concrete and specific words

Clear, exact writing balances abstract and general words, which outline ideas and objects, with concrete and specific words, which sharpen and solidify.

- **Abstract words** name ideas: *beauty, inflation, management, culture, liberal*. **Concrete words** name qualities and things we can know by our five senses of sight, hearing, touch, taste, and smell: *sleek, humming, rough, salty, musty*.
- **General words** name classes or groups of things, such as *birds, weather,* and *buildings,* and include all the varieties of the class. **Specific words** limit a general class, such as *buildings,* by naming a variety, such as *skyscraper, Victorian courthouse,* or *hut*.

Abstract and general words are useful in the broad statements that set the course for your writing.

The wild horse in America has a <u>romantic</u> history.

Relations between the sexes today are more <u>relaxed</u> than they were in the past.

But such statements need development with concrete and specific detail. Detail can turn a vague sentence into an exact one:

Vague The size of his hands made his smallness real. [How big were his hands? How small was he?]

Exact Not until I saw his delicate, doll-like hands did I realize that he stood a full head shorter than most other men.

Note You can use your computer's Find function to help you find and revise abstract and general words that you tend to overuse. Examples of such words include *nice, interesting, things, very, good, a lot, a little,* and *some.*

Exercise 18.6 **Revising: Concrete and specific words**

Make the following paragraph vivid by expanding the sentences with appropriate details of your own choosing. Substitute concrete and specific words for the abstract and general ones that are underlined.

1 I remember clearly how awful I felt the first time I attended Mrs. Murphy's second-grade class. 2 I had recently moved from a small town in Missouri to a crowded suburb of Chicago. 3 My new school looked big from the outside and seemed dark inside as I walked down the long corridor toward the classroom. 4 The class was noisy as I neared the door; but when I entered, everyone became quiet and looked at me. 5 I felt uncomfortable and wanted a place to hide. 6 However, in a loud voice Mrs. Murphy directed me to the front of the room to introduce myself.

Exercise 18.7 **Using concrete and specific words**

For each abstract or general word below, give at least two other words or phrases that are increasingly specific or concrete. Consult a dictionary as needed. Use the most specific or concrete word from each group in a sentence of your own.

Example:

awake, watchful, vigilant
Vigilant guards patrol the buildings.

1 fabric	6 green	11 teacher
2 delicious	7 walk (*verb*)	12 nice
3 car	8 flower	13 virtue
4 narrow-minded	9 serious	14 angry
5 reach (*verb*)	10 pretty	15 crime

---

4 Idioms

Idioms are expressions in any language that do not fit the rules for meaning or grammar—for instance, *put up with, plug away at, make off with.*

Idioms that involve prepositions can be especially confusing for both native and nonnative speakers of English. Some idioms with prepositions are listed in the following box. (More appear in **4** p. 226–27.)

Idioms with prepositions

abide by a rule
    in a place or state
according to
accords with
accuse of a crime
accustomed to
adapt from a source
    to a situation
afraid of
agree on a plan as a group
    to someone else's plan
    with a person
angry with
aware of
based on
belong in or on a place
    to a group
capable of
certain of
charge for a purchase
    with a crime
concur in an opinion
    with a person
contend for a principle
    with a person
dependent on
differ about or over a question
    from in some quality
    with a person
disappointed by or in a person
    in or with a thing

familiar with
identical with or to
impatient for a raise
    with a person
independent of
infer from
inferior to
involved in a task
    with a person
oblivious of or to one's surroundings
    of something forgotten
occupied by a person
    in study
    with a thing
opposed to
part from a person
    with a possession
prior to
proud of
related to
rewarded by the judge
    for something done
    with a gift
similar to
sorry about an error
    for a person
superior to
wait at a place
    for a train, a person
    in a room
    on a customer

CULTURE LANGUAGE If you are learning standard American English, you are justified in stumbling over its prepositions: their meanings can shift depending on context, and they have many idiomatic uses. In mastering the prepositions of standard English, you probably can't avoid memorization. But you can help yourself by memorizing related groups, such as *at/in/on* and *for/since*.

At, in, or *on* in expressions of time

■ Use *at* before actual clock time: *at 8:30*.

- Use *in* before a month, year, century, or period: *in April, in 2007, in the twenty-first century, in the next month.*
- Use *on* before a day or date: *on Tuesday, on August 3, on Labor Day.*

At, in, or on in expressions of place

- Use *at* before a specific place or address: *at the school, at 511 Iris Street.*
- Use *in* before a place with limits or before a city, state, country, or continent: *in the house, in a box, in Oklahoma City, in China, in Asia.*
- Use *on* to mean "supported by" or "touching the surface of": *on the table, on Iris Street, on page 150.*

For or since in expressions of time

- Use *for* before a period of time: *for an hour, for two years.*
- Use *since* before a specific point in time: *since 1999, since Friday.*

A dictionary of English as a second language is the best source for the meanings of prepositions; see the suggestions on p. 171.

Exercise 18.8 Using prepositions in idioms

In the paragraph below, insert the preposition that correctly completes each idiom. Consult the box on the previous page or a dictionary as needed.

1 Children are waiting longer to become independent _____ their parents. 2 According _____ US Census data for young adults ages eighteen to twenty-four, 57 percent of men and 47 percent of women live full-time with their parents. 3 Some of these adult children are dependent _____ their parents financially. 4 In other cases, the parents charge their children _____ housing, food, and other living expenses. 5 Many adult children are financially capable _____ living independently but prefer to save money rather than contend _____ high housing costs.

Exercise 18.9 Using prepositions in idioms

Complete the following paragraph by filling in the blanks with the appropriate prepositions.

1 The Eighteenth Amendment _____ the US Constitution was ratified _____ 1919. 2 It prohibited the "manufacture, sale, or transportation _____ intoxicating liquors." 3 Temperance groups _____ the United States wanted to prevent drinking, but the more striking effect of Prohibition was the boost it gave to organized crime. 4 According _____ legend, the most smuggling and bootlegging

occurred _____ Chicago. 5 There, _____ February 14, 1929, Al
Capone gained control _____ the Chicago underworld by ordering
the execution _____ his rival Bugsy Moran and his men _____ a
city parking garage. 6 Though Moran escaped unharmed, Capone ruled
Chicago _____ two bloody years before he was convicted of tax
evasion _____ 1931.

5 Figurative language

Figurative language (or a **figure of speech**) departs from the
literal meanings of words, usually by comparing very different ideas
or objects:

Literal	As I try to write, I can think of nothing to say.
Figurative	As I try to write, <u>my mind is a slab of black slate</u>.

Imaginatively and carefully used, figurative language can capture
meaning more precisely and emotionally than literal language. Here
is a figure of speech at work in technical writing (paraphrasing the
physicist Edward Andrade):

> The molecules in a liquid move continuously like couples on an over-
> crowded dance floor, jostling each other.

The two most common figures of speech are the simile and the
metaphor. Both compare two things of different classes, often one
abstract and the other concrete. A **simile** makes the comparison explicit and usually begins with *like* or *as:*

> Whenever we grow, we tend to feel it, <u>as</u> a young seed must feel the
> weight and inertia of the earth when it <u>seeks</u> to break out of its shell on
> its way to becoming a plant. —Alice Walker

A **metaphor** claims that the two things are identical, omitting such
words as *like* and *as:*

> A school is a hopper into which children are heaved while they are
> young and tender; therein they are pressed into certain standard shapes
> and covered from head to heels with official rubber stamps.
> —H. L. Mencken

To be successful, figurative language must be fresh and un-
strained, calling attention not to itself but to the writer's meaning.
Be especially wary of mixed metaphors, which combine two or more
incompatible figures:

Mixed	Various thorny problems that we try to sweep under the rug continue to bob up all the same.
Improved	Various thorny problems that we try to weed out continue to thrive all the same.

Exercise 18.10 Using figurative language

Invent appropriate similes or metaphors of your own to describe each scene or quality below, and use the figure in a sentence.

Example:

The attraction of a lake on a hot day
The small waves like fingers beckoned us irresistibly.

1 The sound of a kindergarten classroom
2 People waiting in line to buy tickets to a rock concert
3 The politeness of strangers meeting for the first time
4 A streetlight seen through dense fog
5 The effect of watching television for ten hours straight

---

6 Trite expressions

Trite expressions, or **clichés,** are phrases so old and so often repeated that they have become stale. They include the following:

add insult to injury	a needle in a haystack
better late than never	point with pride
crushing blow	pride and joy
easier said than done	ripe old age
face the music	rude awakening
few and far between	shoulder the burden
green with envy	shoulder to cry on
hard as a rock	sneaking suspicion
heavy as lead	stand in awe
hit the nail on the head	strong as an ox
hour of need	thin as a rail
ladder of success	tried and true
moving experience	wise as an owl

To edit clichés, listen to your writing for any expressions that you have heard or used before. You can also supplement your efforts with a style checker, which may include a cliché detector. When you find a cliché, substitute fresh words of your own or restate the idea in plain language.

Exercise 18.11 Revising: Trite expressions

Revise the following paragraph to eliminate trite expressions.

1 The disastrous consequences of the war have shaken the small nation to its roots. 2 Prices for food have shot sky high, and citizens have sneaking suspicions that others are making a killing on the black market. 3 Medical supplies are so few and far between that even civilians who are sick as dogs cannot get treatment. 4 With most men fighting or injured or killed, women have had to bite the bullet and shoulder the burden in farming and manufacturing. 5 Last but not least, the war's heavy drain on the nation's pocketbook has left the economy in shambles.

19 Completeness

The most serious kind of incomplete sentence is the grammatical fragment (see **4** pp. 280–83). But sentences are also incomplete when they omit one or more words needed for clarity.

Grammar checkers A grammar checker will not flag most kinds of incomplete sentences discussed in this chapter.

19a Writing complete compounds

You may omit words from a compound construction when the omission will not confuse readers:

> Environmentalists have hopes for alternative fuels and [for] public transportation.

> Some cars will run on electricity, some [will run] on ethanol, and some [will run] on hydrogen.

Such omissions are possible only when the words omitted are common to all the parts of a compound construction. When the parts differ in any way, all words must be included in all parts.

> One new car gets eighty miles per gallon; some old cars get as little as five miles per gallon. [One verb is singular, the other plural.]

> Environmentalists believe in and work for fuel conservation. [Idiom requires different prepositions with *believe* and *work*.]

19b Adding needed words

In haste or carelessness, do not omit small words that are needed for clarity:

> **Incomplete**   Regular payroll deductions are a type painless savings. You hardly notice missing amounts, and after period of years the contributions can add a large total.

┌─ **Key term** ───

compound construction Two or more elements (words, phrases, clauses) that are equal in importance and that function as a unit: *Rain fell, and streams overflowed* (clauses); *dogs and cats* (words).

└──

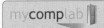

Visit *mycomplab.com* for more resources on complete sentences.

Revised   Regular payroll deductions are a type of painless savings. You hardly notice the missing amounts, and after a period of years the contributions can add up to a large total.

Attentive proofreading is the only insurance against this kind of omission. *Proofread all your papers carefully.* See **1** p. 34 for tips.

 If your native language or dialect is not standard American English, you may have difficulty knowing when to use the English articles *a, an,* and *the.* For guidelines see **4** pp. 268–70.

Exercise 19.1   Revising: Completeness

Add words to the following paragraph so that the sentences are complete and clear.

1 The first ice cream, eaten China in about 2000 BC, was lumpier than modern ice cream. **2** The Chinese made their ice cream of milk, spices, and overcooked rice and packed in snow to solidify. **3** Ice milk and fruit ices became popular among wealthy in fourteenth-century Italy. **4** At her wedding in 1533 to king of France, Catherine de Médicis offered several flavors of fruit ices. **5** Modern sherbets resemble her ices; modern ice cream her soft dessert of thick, sweetened cream.

---

20 Conciseness

Concise writing makes every word count. Conciseness is not the same as mere brevity: detail and originality should not be cut with needless words. Rather, the length of an expression should be appropriate to the thought.

You may find yourself writing wordily when you are unsure of your subject or when your thoughts are tangled. It's fine, even necessary, to grope while drafting. But you should straighten out your ideas and eliminate wordiness during revision and editing.

Grammar checkers A grammar checker will identify at least some wordy structures, such as repeated words, weak verbs, passive voice, and *there is* and *it is* constructions. But a checker can't identify all potentially wordy structures, nor can it tell you whether a structure is appropriate for your ideas.

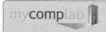

Visit *mycomplab.com* for more resources and exercises on writing concisely.

Ways to achieve conciseness

Wordy (87 words)

The highly pressured <u>nature of</u> critical-care nursing is <u>due to the fact that</u> the patients have life-threatening illnesses. Critical-care	Focus on subject and verb, and cut or shorten empty words and phrases.
nurses must <u>have possession of</u> steady nerves	Avoid nouns made from verbs.
to care for patients who are critically ill and	Cut unneeded repetition.
very sick. The nurses must also have possession of interpersonal skills. They must also	Combine sentences.
have medical skills. It is considered by most health-care professionals that these nurses	Change passive voice to active voice.
are essential if there is to be improvement of	Revise *there is* constructions.
patients who are now in critical care from that status to the status of intermediate care.	Cut unneeded repetition, and reduce clauses and phrases.

Concise (37 words)

Critical-care nursing is highly pressured because the patients have life-threatening illnesses. Critical-care nurses must possess steady nerves and interpersonal and medical skills. Most health-care professionals consider these nurses essential if patients are to improve to intermediate care.

CULTURE LANGUAGE As you'll see in the examples that follow, wordiness is not a problem of incorrect grammar. A sentence may be perfectly grammatical but still contain unneeded words that interfere with the clarity and force of your idea.

20a Focusing on the subject and verb

Using the subjects and verbs of your sentences for the key actors and actions will reduce words and emphasize important ideas. (See pp. 143–45 for more on this topic.)

Wordy The <u>reason</u> why most of the country shifts to daylight time <u>is</u> that winter days are much shorter than summer days.

Concise Most of the <u>country shifts</u> to daylight time because winter days are much shorter than summer days.

Focusing on subjects and verbs will also help you avoid several other causes of wordiness discussed further on pp. 144–45:

Nouns made from verbs

Wordy The <u>occurrence</u> of the winter solstice, the shortest day of the year, <u>is</u> an event occurring about December 22.

Concise	The winter <u>solstice</u>, the shortest day of the year, <u>occurs</u> about December 22.

Weak verbs

Wordy	The earth's axis <u>has</u> a tilt as the planet <u>is</u> in orbit around the sun so that the northern and southern hemispheres <u>are</u> alternately in alignment toward the sun.
Concise	The earth's axis <u>tilts</u> as the planet <u>orbits</u> the sun so that the northern and southern hemispheres alternately <u>align</u> toward the sun.

Passive voice

Wordy	During its winter the northern hemisphere <u>is tilted</u> farthest away from the sun, so the nights <u>are made</u> longer and the days <u>are made</u> shorter.
Concise	During its winter the northern hemisphere <u>tilts</u> away from the sun, <u>making</u> the nights longer and the days shorter.

See also **4** p. 236–37 on changing the passive voice to the active voice, as in the example above.

20b Cutting empty words

Empty words walk in place, gaining little or nothing in meaning. Many can be cut entirely. The following are just a few examples:

all things considered	in a manner of speaking
as far as I'm concerned	in my opinion
for all intents and purposes	last but not least
for the most part	more or less

Other empty words can also be cut, usually along with some of the words around them.

area	element	kind	situation
aspect	factor	manner	thing
case	field	nature	type

Still others can be reduced from several words to a single word:

For	Substitute
at all times	always
at the present time	now, yet
because of the fact that	because

Key terms

passive voice The verb form when the subject names the *receiver* of the verb's action: *The house <u>was destroyed</u> by the tornado.* (See **4** p. 236.)

active voice The verb form when the subject names the *performer* of the verb's action: *The tornado <u>destroyed</u> the house.* (See **4** p. 236.)

due to the fact that	because
for the purpose of	for
in order to	to
in the event that	if
in the final analysis	finally

Cutting or reducing such words and phrases will make your writing move faster and work harder:

Wordy   <u>In my opinion</u>, the council's proposal to improve the city center is inadequate, <u>all things considered</u>.

Revised   The council's proposal to improve the city center is inadequate.

20c Cutting unneeded repetition

Unnecessary repetition weakens sentences:

Wordy   Many <u>unskilled</u> workers <u>without training in a particular job</u> are unemployed <u>and do not have any work</u>.

Concise   Many unskilled workers are unemployed.

Be especially alert to phrases that say the same thing twice. In the examples below, the unneeded words are underlined:

circle <u>around</u>   <u>important</u> [basic] essentials
consensus <u>of opinion</u>   puzzling <u>in nature</u>
cooperate <u>together</u>   repeat <u>again</u>
<u>final</u> completion   return <u>again</u>
<u>frank and</u> honest exchange   square [round] <u>in shape</u>
the future <u>to come</u>   <u>surrounding</u> circumstances

CULTURE LANGUAGE   The preceding phrases are redundant because the main word already implies the underlined word or words. A dictionary will tell you what meanings a word implies. *Assassinate,* for instance, means "murder someone well known," so the following sentence is redundant: *Julius Caesar was <u>assassinated and killed</u>.*

20d Reducing clauses and phrases

Modifiers can be expanded or contracted depending on the emphasis you want to achieve. (Generally, the longer a construction, the more emphatic it is.) When editing sentences, consider whether any modifiers can be reduced without loss of emphasis or clarity.

Key term

modifier A word or word group that limits or qualifies another word: *slippery* road, cars *with tire chains*.

Wordy	The Channel Tunnel, <u>which runs between Britain and France,</u> bores through <u>a bed</u> of solid chalk <u>that is twenty-three miles</u> <u>across.</u>
Concise	The Channel Tunnel <u>between Britain and France</u> bores through twenty-three miles of solid chalk.

20e Revising *there is, here is,* or *it is*

You can postpone the sentence subject with the words *there,* *here,* and *it: There are three points made in the text. Here is the main problem. It was not fair that only seniors could vote.* These **expletive constructions** can be useful to emphasize the subject (as when introducing it for the first time) or to indicate a change in direction. But often they just add words and create limp substitutes for more vigorous sentences:

Wordy	<u>There were</u> delays and cost overruns <u>that</u> plagued construction of the Channel Tunnel. <u>It had been the expectation of investors that</u> they would see earnings soon after <u>there were trains passing through</u> the tunnel, but profits took years to materialize.
Concise	Delays and cost overruns plagued construction of the Channel Tunnel. <u>Investors had expected</u> to see earnings soon after <u>trains began passing</u> through the tunnel, but profits took years to materialize.

CULTURE LANGUAGE When you must use an expletive construction, be careful to include *there, here,* or *it.* Only commands and some questions can begin with verbs.

20f Combining sentences

Often the information in two or more sentences can be combined into one tight sentence:

Wordy	An unexpected problem with the Channel Tunnel is stowaways. The stowaways are mostly illegal immigrants. They are trying to smuggle themselves into England. They cling to train roofs and undercarriages.
Concise	An unexpected problem with the Channel Tunnel is stowaways, <u>mostly</u> illegal immigrants <u>who</u> are trying to smuggle themselves into England <u>by clinging</u> to train roofs and undercarriages.

20g Rewriting jargon

Jargon can refer to the special vocabulary of any discipline or profession (see p. 165). But it has also come to describe vague, inflated language that is overcomplicated, even incomprehensible. When it comes from government or business, we call it **bureaucratese.**

Jargon	The necessity for individuals to become separate entities in their own right may impel children to engage in open rebelliousness against parental authority or against sibling influence, with resultant bewilderment of those being rebelled against.
Translation	Children's natural desire to become themselves may make them rebel against bewildered parents or siblings.

Exercise 20.1 Revising: Writing concisely

Make the following paragraph more concise. Combine sentences when doing so reduces wordiness.

If sore muscles after exercising are a problem for you, there are some measures that can be taken by you to ease the discomfort. It is advisable to avoid heat for the first day of soreness. The application of heat within the first twenty-four hours can cause an increase in muscle soreness and stiffness. In contrast, the immediate application of cold will help to reduce inflammation. Blood vessels are constricted by cold. Blood is kept away from the injured muscles. There are two ways the application of cold can be made: you can take a cold shower or use an ice pack. Inflammation of muscles can also be reduced with aspirin, ibuprofen, or another anti-inflammatory medication. When healing is occurring, you need to take it easy. A day or two after overdoing exercise, it is advisable for you to get some light exercise and gentle massage.

Exercise 20.2 Revising: Conciseness

Make the following paragraph as concise as possible. Be merciless.

At the end of a lengthy line of reasoning, he came to the conclusion that the situation with carcinogens [cancer-causing substances] should be regarded as similar to the situation with the automobile. Instead of giving in to an irrational fear of cancer, we should consider all aspects of the problem in a balanced and dispassionate frame of mind, making a total of the benefits received from potential carcinogens (plastics, pesticides, and other similar products) and measuring said total against the damage done by such products. This is the nature of most discussions about the automobile. Instead of responding irrationally to the visual, aural, and air pollution caused by automobiles, we have decided to live with them (while simultaneously working to improve on them) for the benefits brought to society as a whole.

Sentence Parts and Patterns

Basic Grammar

Grammar describes how language works, and understanding it can help you create clear and accurate sentences. This section explains the kinds of words in sentences (Chapter 21) and how to build basic sentences (22), expand them (23), and classify them (24).

Grammar checkers A grammar checker can both offer assistance and cause problems as you compose sentences. Look for the cautions and tips for using a checker in this and the next part of this book. For more information about grammar checkers, see **1** pp. 32–33.

21 Parts of Speech

All English words fall into eight groups, called **parts of speech:** nouns, pronouns, verbs, adjectives, adverbs, prepositions, conjunctions, and interjections.

Note In different sentences a word may serve as different parts of speech. For example:

The government sent <u>aid</u> to the city. [*Aid* is a noun.]
Governments <u>aid</u> <u>citizens</u>. [*Aid* is a verb.]

The *function* of a word in a sentence always determines its part of speech in that sentence.

21a Recognizing nouns

Nouns name. They may name a person (*Helen Mirren, Jesse Jackson, astronaut*), a thing (*chair, book, Mt. Rainier*), a quality (*pain, mystery, simplicity*), a place (*city, Washington, ocean, Red Sea*), or an idea (*reality, peace, success*).

The forms of nouns depend partly on where they fit in certain groups. As the following examples indicate, the same noun may appear in more than one group.

- A *common noun* names a general class of things and does not begin with a capital letter: *earthquake, citizen, earth, fortitude, army.*

- A *proper noun* names a specific person, place, or thing and begins with a capital letter: *Angelina Jolie, Washington Monument, El Paso, US Congress*.
- A *count noun* names a thing considered countable in English. Most count nouns add *-s* or *-es* to distinguish between singular (one) and plural (more than one): *citizen, citizens; city, cities*. Some count nouns form irregular plurals: *woman, women; child, children*.
- A *noncount noun* names things or qualities that aren't considered countable in English: *earth, sugar, chaos, fortitude*. Noncount nouns do not form plurals.
- A *collective noun* is singular in form but names a group: *army, family, herd, US Congress*.

In addition, most nouns form the **possessive** by adding *-'s* to show ownership (*Nadia's books, citizen's rights*), source (*Auden's poems*), and some other relationships.

21b | Recognizing pronouns

Most **pronouns** substitute for nouns and function in sentences as nouns do: *Susanne Ling enlisted in the Air Force when she graduated.* Pronouns fall into groups depending on their form or function:

- A *personal pronoun* refers to a specific individual or to individuals: *I, you, he, she, it, we,* and *they.*
- An *indefinite pronoun* does not refer to a specific noun: *anyone, everything, no one, somebody,* and so on. *No one came. Nothing moves. Everybody speaks.*
- A *relative pronoun* relates a group of words to a noun or another pronoun: *who, whoever, which, that. Everyone who attended received a prize. The book that won is a novel.*
- An *interrogative pronoun* introduces a question: *who, whom, whose, which, what. What song is that? Who will contribute?*
- A *demonstrative pronoun* identifies or points to a noun: *this, these, that, those,* and so on. *Those berries are ripe. This is the site.*
- An *intensive pronoun* emphasizes a noun or another pronoun: *myself, himself, itself, themselves,* and so on. *I myself asked that question. The price itself is in doubt.*
- A *reflexive pronoun* indicates that the sentence subject also receives the action of the verb: *myself, himself, itself, themselves,* and so on. *He perjured himself. They injured themselves.*

The personal pronouns *I, he, she, we,* and *they* and the relative pronouns *who* and *whoever* change form depending on their function in the sentence. (See Chapter 30.)

21c Recognizing verbs

Verbs express an action (*bring, change, grow, consider*), an occurrence (*become, happen, occur*), or a state of being (*be, seem, remain*).

1 Forms of verbs

Verbs have five distinctive forms. If the form can change as described here, the word is a verb:

- The *plain form* is the dictionary form of the verb. When the subject is a plural noun or the pronoun *I, we, you,* or *they,* the plain form indicates action that occurs in the present, occurs habitually, or is generally true.

  A few artists live in town today.
  They hold classes downtown.

- The *-s form* ends in *-s* or *-es*. When the subject is a singular noun, a pronoun such as *everyone,* or the personal pronoun *he, she,* or *it,* the *-s* form indicates action that occurs in the present, occurs habitually, or is generally true.

  The artist lives in town today.
  She holds classes downtown.

- The *past-tense form* indicates that the action of the verb occurred before now. It usually adds *-d* or *-ed* to the plain form, although most irregular verbs create it in different ways (see pp. 213–16).

  Many artists lived in town before this year.
  They held classes downtown. [Irregular verb.]

- The *past participle* is usually the same as the past-tense form, except in most irregular verbs. It combines with forms of *have* or *be* (*has climbed, was created*), or by itself it modifies nouns and pronouns (*the sliced apples*).

  Artists have lived in town for decades.
  They have held classes downtown. [Irregular verb.]

- The *present participle* adds *-ing* to the verb's plain form. It combines with forms of *be* (*is buying*), modifies nouns and pronouns (*the boiling water*), or functions as a noun (*Running exhausts me*).

  A few artists are living in town today.
  They are holding classes downtown.

The verb *be* has eight forms rather than the five forms of most other verbs:

Plain form	be		
Present participle	being		
Past participle	been		

	I	*he, she, it*	*we, you, they*
Present tense	am	is	are
Past tense	was	was	were

2 Helping verbs

Some verb forms combine with **helping verbs** to indicate time, possibility, obligation, necessity, and other kinds of meaning: *can run, was sleeping, had been working*. In these **verb phrases** *run, sleeping,* and *working* are **main verbs**—they carry the principal meaning.

Verb phrase

Helping   *Main*

Artists <u>can</u>   <u>train</u> others to draw.
The techniques <u>have</u>   <u>changed</u> little.

The most common helping verbs are listed in the box below. See pp. 218–23 for more on helping verbs.

Common helping verbs

Forms of *be:* be, am, is, are, was, were, been, being
Forms of *have:* have, has, had, having
Forms of *do:* do, does, did

be able to	could	may	ought to	used to
be supposed to	had better	might	shall	will
can	have to	must	should	would

Exercise 21.1   Identifying nouns, pronouns, and verbs

Identify the words that function as nouns (N), pronouns (P), and verbs (V) in the following paragraph.

> *Example:*
>
>   N   N   V   N
> <u>Ancestors</u> of the gingko <u>tree</u> <u>lived</u> 175 to 200 million <u>years</u> ago.

1 The ginko tree, which is one of the world's oldest trees, is large and picturesque. **2** Gingko trees may grow to over a hundred feet in height. **3** Their leaves look like fans and are about three inches wide. **4** The leaves turn yellow in the fall. **5** Because it tolerates smoke, low temperatures, and low rainfall, the gingko appears in many cities. **6** A shortcoming, however, is the foul odor of its fruit. **7** Inside the fruit is a large white seed, which some people value as food. **8** The fruit often does not appear until the tree is twenty years old. **9** The tree's name means "apricot" in the Japanese language. **10** Originally, the gingko grew only in China, but it has now spread throughout the world.

21d Recognizing adjectives and adverbs

Adjectives describe or modify nouns and pronouns. They specify which one, what quality, or how many.

old   city   generous   one   two   pears
adjective   noun   adjective   pronoun   adjective   noun

Adverbs describe or modify verbs, adjectives, other adverbs, and whole groups of words. They specify when, where, how, and to what extent.

nearly destroyed   too quickly
adverb   verb   adverb   adverb

very   generous   Unfortunately, taxes will rise.
adverb   adjective   adverb   word group

An -*ly* ending often signals an adverb, but not always: *friendly* is an adjective; *never* and *not* are adverbs. The only way to tell whether a word is an adjective or an adverb is to determine what it modifies.

Adjectives and adverbs appear in three forms: **positive** (*green, angrily*), **comparative** (*greener, more angrily*), and **superlative** (*greenest, most angrily*).

See Chapter 33 for more on adjectives and adverbs.

Exercise 21.2   Identifying adjectives and adverbs

Identify the adjectives (ADJ) and adverbs (ADV) in the following paragraph. Mark *a, an,* and *the* as adjectives.

Example:
                                          ADV
Stress can hit people when they least expect it.

1 You can reduce stress by making a few simple changes. **2** Get up fifteen minutes earlier than you ordinarily do. **3** Eat a healthy breakfast, and eat it slowly so that you enjoy it. **4** Do your more unpleasant tasks early in the day. **5** Carry a book or magazine when you know you'll have to wait in line somewhere. **6** Make promises sparingly and keep them faithfully. **7** Plan ahead to prevent the most stressful situations—for example, carrying spare keys so you won't be locked out of your car or house. **8** See a doctor and dentist regularly. **9** And every day, do at least one thing you really enjoy.

21e Recognizing connecting words: Prepositions and conjunctions

Connecting words are mostly small words that link parts of sentences. They never change form.

1 Prepositions

Prepositions form nouns or pronouns (plus any mo_____
word groups called **prepositional phrases**: _about lov_____
stairs. These phrases usually serve as modifiers in sentences, as __.
The plants trailed down the stairs. (See p. 204.)

Common prepositions

about	before	except for	of	throughout
above	behind	excepting	off	till
according to	below	for	on	to
across	beneath	from	onto	toward
after	beside	in	on top of	under
against	between	in addition to	out	underneath
along	beyond	inside	out of	unlike
along with	by	inside of	outside	until
among	concerning	in spite of	over	up
around	despite	instead of	past	upon
as	down	into	regarding	up to
aside from	due to	like	round	with
at	during	near	since	within
because of	except	next to	through	without

CULTURE LANGUAGE The meanings and uses of English prepositions can be difficult to master. See 3 pp. 174–76 for a discussion of prepositions in idioms. See pp. 226–27 for uses of prepositions in two-word verbs such as _look after_ or _look up_.

2 Subordinating conjunctions

Subordinating conjunctions form sentences into word groups called **subordinate clauses**, such as _when the meeting ended_ or _that she knew_. These clauses serve as parts of sentences: _Everyone was relieved when the meeting ended_. _She said that she knew_. (See pp. 208–09.)

Common subordinating conjunctions

after	even if	rather than	until
although	even though	since	when
as	if	so that	whenever
as if	if only	than	where
as long as	in order that	that	whereas
as though	now that	though	wherever
because	once	till	whether
before	provided	unless	while

> **CULTURE LANGUAGE** Subordinating conjunctions convey meaning without help from other function words, such as the coordinating conjunctions *and, but, for,* or *so:*

Faulty Even though the parents are illiterate, but their children may read well. [*Even though* and *but* have the same meaning, so both are not needed.]

Revised Even though the parents are illiterate, their children may read well.

3 | Coordinating and correlative conjunctions

Coordinating and correlative conjunctions connect words or word groups of the same kind, such as nouns or sentences.

Coordinating conjunctions consist of a single word:

Coordinating conjunctions

and	nor	for	yet
but	or	so	

Biofeedback or simple relaxation can relieve headaches.
Relaxation works well, and it is inexpensive.

Correlative conjunctions are combinations of coordinating conjunctions and other words:

Common correlative conjunctions

both . . . and	neither . . . nor
not only . . . but also	whether . . . or
not . . . but	as . . . as
either . . . or	

Both biofeedback and relaxation can relieve headaches.

The headache sufferer learns not only to recognize the causes of headaches but also to control those causes.

Exercise 21.3 Adding connecting words

Fill each blank in the following paragraph with the appropriate connecting word: a preposition, a subordinating conjunction, or a coordinating conjunction. Consult the lists on p. 195 and above if you need help.

Example:

A Trojan priest warned, "Beware _____ Greeks bearing gifts." (*preposition*)

A Trojan priest warned, "Beware of Greeks bearing gifts."

1 Just about everyone has heard the story _____ the Trojan Horse. (*preposition*) **2** This incident happened at the city of Troy _____ was planned by the Greeks. (*coordinating conjunction*) **3** The Greeks built a huge wooden horse _____ a hollow space big enough to hold many men. (*preposition*) **4** At night, they rolled the horse to the gate of Troy _____ left it there filled with soldiers. (*coordinating conjunction*) **5** _____ the morning, the Trojans were surprised to see the enormous horse. (*preposition*) **6** They were amazed _____ they saw that the Greeks were gone. (*subordinating conjunction*) **7** _____ they were curious to examine this gift from the Greeks, they dragged the horse into the city and left it outside the temple. (*subordinating conjunction*) **8** In the middle of the night, the hidden Greeks emerged _____ the horse and began setting fires all over town. (*preposition*) **9** _____ the Trojan soldiers awoke and came out of their houses, the Greeks killed them one by one. (*subordinating conjunction*) **10** By the next morning, the Trojan men were dead _____ the women were slaves to the Greeks. (*coordinating conjunction*)

21f Recognizing interjections

Interjections express feeling or command attention. They are rarely used in academic or business writing.

Oh, the meeting went fine.
They won seven thousand dollars! Wow!

22 The Sentence

The **sentence** is the basic unit of expression. It is grammatically complete and independent: it does not serve as an adjective, adverb, or other single part of speech.

22a Recognizing subjects and predicates

Most sentences make statements. First the **subject** names something; then the **predicate** makes an assertion about the subject or describes an action by the subject.

Subject	Predicate
Art	thrives.

mycomplab

Visit *mycomplab.com* for more resources and exercises on the sentence.

The **simple subject** consists of one or more nouns or pronouns, whereas the **complete subject** also includes any modifiers. The **simple predicate** consists of one or more verbs, whereas the **complete predicate** adds any words needed to complete the meaning of the verb plus any modifiers.

Sometimes, as in the short example *Art thrives,* the simple and complete subject and predicate are the same. More often, they are different:

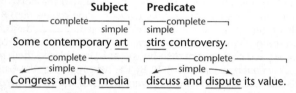

In the second example, the simple subject and simple predicate are both **compound**: in each, two words joined by a coordinating conjunction (*and*) serve the same function.

Note If a sentence contains a word group such as *that makes it into museums* or *because viewers agree about its quality,* you may be tempted to mark the subject and verb in the word group as the subject and verb of the sentence. But these word groups are subordinate clauses, made into modifiers by the words they begin with: *that* and *because.* See pp. 208–09 for more on subordinate clauses.

(CULTURE LANGUAGE) The subject of a sentence in standard American English may be a noun (*art*) or a pronoun that refers to the noun (*it*), but not both. (See p. 293.)

Faulty   Some art it stirs controversy.
Revised Some art stirs controversy.

Tests to find subjects and predicates

The tests below use the following example:

Art that makes it into museums has often survived controversy.

Identify the subject.

■ Ask *who* or *what* is acting or being described in the sentence.

Complete subject   art that makes it into museums

■ **Isolate the simple subject by deleting modifiers**—words or word groups that don't name the actor of the sentence but give information about it. In the example, the word group *that makes it into museums* does not name the actor but modifies it.

Simple subject   art

Identify the predicate.

■ **Ask what the sentence asserts about the subject:** what is its action, or what state is it in? In the example, the assertion about *art* is that it *has often survived controversy.*

Complete predicate has often survived controversy

■ **Isolate the verb, the simple predicate, by changing the time of the subject's action.** The simple predicate is the word or words that change as a result.

Example	Art . . . has often survived controversy.
Present	Art . . . often survives controversy.
Future	Art . . . will often survive controversy.
Simple predicate	has survived

Exercise 22.1 Identifying subjects and predicates

Identify the subject and the predicate of each sentence below. Then use each sentence as a model to create a sentence of your own.

Example:

    subject   predicate
An important scientist / spoke at commencement.

Sample imitation: The hungry family ate at the diner.

1 The leaves fell.
2 October ends soon.
3 The orchard owners made apple cider.
4 They examined each apple carefully for quality.
5 Over a hundred people will buy cider at the roadside stand.

Exercise 22.2 Identifying subjects and predicates

In the following sentences, insert a slash between the complete subject and the complete predicate. Underline each simple subject once and each simple predicate twice.

Example:

The pony, the light horse, and the draft horse / are the three main types of domestic horses.

1 The horse has a long history of service to humanity but today is mainly a show and sport animal. 2 A member of the genus *Equus*, the domestic horse shares its lineage with the ass and the zebra. 3 The domestic horse and its relatives are all plains-dwelling herd animals. 4 The modern horse evolved in North America. 5 It migrated to other parts of the world and then became extinct in the Americas. 6 The Spaniards reintroduced the domestic horse to the Americas. 7 North American wild horses are actually descended from escaped domestic horses. 8 According to records, North Americans hunted and domesticated horses as early as four to five thousand years ago. 9 The earliest ancestor of the modern horse may have been eohippus, approximately 55 million years ago.

22b | Recognizing predicate patterns

All English sentences are based on five patterns, each differing in the complete predicate (the verb and any words following it).

CULTURE LANGUAGE Word order in English sentences may not correspond to word order in the sentences of your native language or dialect. English, for instance, strongly prefers subject first, then verb, whereas some other languages prefer the verb first.

The five basic sentence patterns

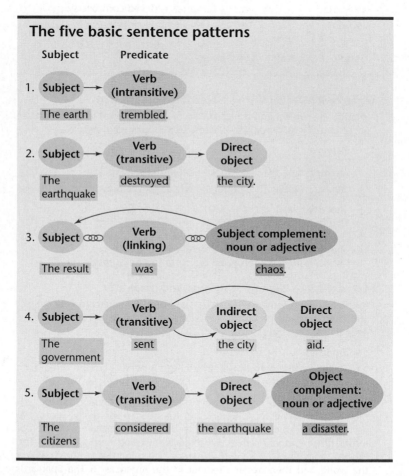

Subject   Predicate

1. Subject → Verb (intransitive)
   The earth   trembled.

2. Subject → Verb (transitive) → Direct object
   The earthquake   destroyed   the city.

3. Subject ∞ Verb (linking) ∞ Subject complement: noun or adjective
   The result   was   chaos.

4. Subject → Verb (transitive)   Indirect object   Direct object
   The government   sent   the city   aid.

5. Subject → Verb (transitive) → Direct object   Object complement: noun or adjective
   The citizens   considered   the earthquake   a disaster.

Pattern 1: The earth trembled.

In the simplest pattern the predicate consists only of an **intransitive verb,** a verb that does not require a following word to complete its meaning.

Subject	Predicate
	Intransitive verb
The earth	trembled.
The hospital	may close.

Pattern 2: The earthquake destroyed the city.

In pattern 2 the verb is followed by a **direct object**, a noun or pronoun that identifies who or what receives the action of the verb. A verb that requires a direct object to complete its meaning is called **transitive**.

Subject	Predicate	
	Transitive verb	*Direct object*
The earthquake	destroyed	the city.
Education	opens	doors.

CULTURE LANGUAGE Only transitive verbs may be used in the passive voice: *The city was destroyed*. Your dictionary will indicate whether a verb is transitive or intransitive. For some verbs (*begin, learn, read, write,* and others), it will indicate both uses.

Pattern 3: The result was chaos.

In pattern 3 the verb is followed by a **subject complement,** a word that renames or describes the subject. A verb in this pattern is called a **linking verb** because it links its subject to the description following. The linking verbs include *be, seem, appear, become, grow, remain, stay, prove, feel, look, smell, sound,* and *taste*. Subject complements are usually nouns or adjectives.

Subject	Predicate	
	Linking verb	*Subject complement*
The result	was	chaos.
The man	became	an accountant.

Pattern 4: The government sent the city aid.

In pattern 4 the verb is followed by a direct object and an **indirect object,** a word identifying to or for whom the action of the verb is performed. The direct object and indirect object refer to different things, people, or places.

> **Key term**
> **passive voice** The verb form when the subject names the receiver of the verb's action: *Bad weather was predicted*. (See p. 236.)

Subject	Predicate		
	Transitive verb	*Indirect object*	*Direct object*
The government	sent	the city	aid.
One company	offered	its employees	bonuses.

A number of verbs can take indirect objects, including *send* and *offer* (preceding examples) and *allow, bring, buy, deny, find, get, give, leave, make, pay, read, sell, show, teach,* and *write.*

CULTURE LANGUAGE Some verbs are never followed by an indirect object—*admit, announce, demonstrate, explain, introduce, mention, prove, recommend, say,* and some others. However, the direct objects of these verbs may be followed by *to* or *for* and a noun or pronoun that specifies to or for whom the action was done: *The manual explains the new procedure <u>to workers</u>. A video demonstrates the procedure <u>for us</u>.*

Pattern 5: The citizens considered the earthquake a disaster.

In pattern 5 the verb is followed by a direct object and an **object complement,** a word that renames or describes the direct object. Object complements may be nouns or adjectives.

Subject	Predicate		
	Transitive verb	*Direct object*	*Object complement*
The citizens	considered	the earthquake	a disaster.
Success	makes	some people	nervous.

Exercise 22.3 Identifying sentence parts

In the following sentences identify the subject (S) and verb (V) as well as any direct object (DO), indirect object (IO), subject complement (SC), or object complement (OC).

Example:

      S   V   V   DO
Crime statistics can cause surprise.

1 The number of serious crimes in the United States decreased.
2 A decline in serious crimes occurred each year.
3 The Crime Index measures serious crime.
4 The FBI invented the index.
5 The four serious violent crimes are murder, robbery, forcible rape, and aggravated assault.
6 The Crime Index calls auto theft, burglary, arson, and larceny-theft the four serious crimes against property.
7 The Crime Index gives the FBI a measure of crime.
8 The index shows trends in crimes and the people who commit them.

9 The nation's largest cities showed the largest decline in crime.
10 However, crime actually increased in smaller cities, proving that the decline in crime is unrepresentative of the nation.

Exercise 22.4 Identifying sentence patterns

In the following sentences, identify each verb as intransitive, transitive, or linking. Then identify each direct object (DO), indirect object (IO), subject complement (SC), and object complement (OC).

Example:

transitive
verb   IO   DO   DO
Children give their parents both headaches and pleasures.

1 Many people find New York City exciting.
2 Tourists flock to New York each year.
3 Often they visit Times Square first.
4 The square's lights are astounding.
5 The flashing signs sell visitors everything from TVs to underwear.

---

23 Phrases and Subordinate Clauses

Most sentences contain word groups that serve as adjectives, adverbs, or nouns and thus cannot stand alone as sentences.

- A *phrase* lacks either a subject or a predicate or both: *fearing an accident; in a panic.*
- A *subordinate clause* contains a subject and a predicate but begins with a subordinating word: <u>when</u> *prices rise;* <u>whoever</u> *laughs.*

23a Recognizing phrases

1 Prepositional phrases

A **prepositional phrase** consists of a preposition plus a noun, a pronoun, or a word group serving as a noun, called the **object of the preposition.** A list of prepositions appears on p. 195.

mycomplab

Visit *mycomplab.com* for more resources and exercises on phrases and subordinate clauses.

Preposition	Object
of	spaghetti
on	the surface
with	great satisfaction
upon	entering the room
from	where you are standing

Prepositional phrases usually function as adjectives or adverbs.

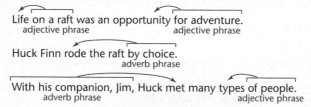

Life on a raft was an opportunity for adventure.
    adjective phrase   adjective phrase

Huck Finn rode the raft by choice.
                  adverb phrase

With his companion, Jim, Huck met many types of people.
    adverb phrase   adjective phrase

Exercise 23.1   Identifying prepositional phrases

Identify the prepositional phrases in the following passage, and underline the word that the phrase modifies.

Example:

After an hour I finally <u>arrived</u> at the <u>home</u> of my professor.

1 On July 3, 1863, at Gettysburg, Pennsylvania, General Robert E. Lee gambled unsuccessfully for a Confederate victory in the American Civil War. **2** The battle of Pickett's Charge was one of the most disastrous conflicts of the war. **3** Confederate and Union forces faced each other on parallel ridges separated by almost a mile of open fields. **4** After an artillery bombardment of the Union position, nearly 12,000 Confederate infantry marched toward the Union ridge. **5** The Union guns had been silent but suddenly roared against the approaching Confederates. **6** Within an hour, perhaps half of the Confederate soldiers lay wounded or dead.

Exercise 23.2   Sentence combining: Prepositional phrases

To practice writing sentences with prepositional phrases, combine each group of sentences below into one sentence that includes one or two prepositional phrases. You will have to add, delete, and rearrange words. Some items have more than one possible answer.

Example:

I will start working. The new job will pay the minimum wage.
I will start working <u>at a new job</u> <u>for the minimum wage</u>.

1 The slow loris protects itself well. Its habitat is Southeast Asia. It possesses a poisonous chemical.
2 The loris frightens predators when it exudes this chemical. The chemical comes from a gland. The gland is on the loris's upper arm.
3 The loris's chemical is highly toxic. The chemical is not like a skunk's spray. Even small quantities of the chemical are toxic.

4 A tiny dose can affect a human. The dose would get in the mouth. The human would be sent into shock.

5 Predators probably can sense the toxin. They detect it at a distance. They use their nasal organs.

2 Verbal phrases

Certain forms of verbs, called **verbals,** can serve as modifiers or nouns. Often these verbals appear with their own modifiers and objects in **verbal phrases.**

Note Verbals cannot serve as verbs in sentences. *The sun rises over the dump* is a sentence; *The sun rising over the dump* is a sentence fragment. (See p. 281.)

Participial phrases

A **participle** is a verb form ending in *-ing* (*walking*) or, often, *-d* or *-ed* (*walked*). Participles and participial phrases serve as adjectives.

Strolling shoppers fill the malls.
adjective

They make selections determined by personal taste.
adjective phrase

Note With irregular verbs, the past participle may have a different ending—for instance, *hidden funds.* (See pp. 213–16.)

CULTURE LANGUAGE For verbs expressing feeling, the present and past participles have different meanings: *It was a boring lecture. The bored students slept.* (See p. 267.)

Gerund phrases

A **gerund** is the *-ing* form of a verb when it serves as a noun. Gerunds and gerund phrases can do whatever nouns can do.

sentence
— subject —
Shopping satisfies personal needs.
noun

object of preposition
Malls are good at creating such needs.
noun phrase

Infinitive phrases

An **infinitive** is the plain form of a verb plus *to: to hide.* Infinitives and infinitive phrases serve as adjectives, adverbs, or nouns.

sentence
—— subject —— ———— subject complement ————
To design a mall is to create an artificial environment.
noun phrase   noun phrase

Malls are designed to make shoppers feel safe.
adverb phrase

The environment supports the impulse to shop.
adjective

CULTURE LANGUAGE Infinitives and gerunds may follow some verbs and not others and may differ in meaning after a verb: *The cowboy stopped to sing. The cowboy stopped singing.* (See pp. 223–25.)

Exercise 23.3   Identifying verbals and verbal phrases

The following sentences contain participles, gerunds, and infinitives as well as participial, gerund, and infinitive phrases. Identify each verbal or verbal phrase.

Example:

Laughing, the talk-show host prodded her guest to talk.

1 Written in 1850 by Nathaniel Hawthorne, *The Scarlet Letter* tells the story of Hester Prynne. **2** Shunned by the community because of her adultery, Hester endures loneliness. **3** She is humble enough to withstand her Puritan neighbors' cutting remarks. **4** Enduring the cruel treatment, the determined young woman refuses to leave her home. **5** By living a life of patience and unselfishness, Hester eventually becomes the community's angel.

Exercise 23.4   Sentence combining: Verbals and verbal phrases

To practice writing sentences with verbals and verbal phrases, combine each of the following pairs of sentences into one sentence. You will have to add, delete, change, and rearrange words. Each item has more than one possible answer.

Example:

My father took pleasure in mean pranks. For instance, he hid the neighbor's cat.

My father took pleasure in mean pranks such as hiding the neighbor's cat.

1 Air pollution is a health problem. It affects millions of Americans.
2 The air has been polluted mainly by industries and automobiles. It contains toxic chemicals.
3 Environmentalists pressure politicians. They think politicians should pass stricter laws.
4 Many politicians waver. They are not necessarily against environmentalism.
5 The problems are too complex. They cannot be solved easily.

---

3 | Absolute phrases

An **absolute phrase** consists of a noun or pronoun and a participle, plus any modifiers. It modifies the entire rest of the sentence it appears in.

┌─────── absolute phrase ───────┐ ┌──────────────→
Their own place established, many ethnic groups are making way for
new arrivals.

Unlike a participial phrase (p. 205), an absolute phrase always
contains a noun that serves as a subject.

┌─── participial
│   phrase ───┐
Learning English, many immigrants discover American culture.

┌─────────── absolute phrase ───────────┐
Immigrants having learned English, their opportunities widen.

Exercise 23.5 **Sentence combining: Absolute phrases**

To practice writing sentences with absolute phrases, combine each pair
of sentences below into one sentence that contains an absolute phrase.
You will have to add, delete, change, and rearrange words.

Example:
The flower's petals wilted. It looked pathetic.
Its petals wilted, the flower looked pathetic.

1 Geraldine Ferraro's face beamed. She enjoyed the crowd's cheers
  after her nomination for Vice President.
2 A vacancy had occurred. Sandra Day O'Connor was appointed the
  first female Supreme Court justice.
3 Her appointment was confirmed. Condoleezza Rice became the first
  female national security adviser.
4 The midterm elections were over. Nancy Pelosi was elected the first
  female minority leader of the House of Representatives.
5 The election was won. Elizabeth Dole was the first woman to become a US senator from North Carolina.

---

4 **Appositive phrases**

An **appositive** is usually a noun that renames another noun. An
appositive phrase includes modifiers as well.

┌─── appositive phrase ┐
Bizen ware, a dark stoneware, is produced in Japan.

Appositives and appositive phrases sometimes begin with *that
is, such as, for example,* or *in other words.*

┌─── appositive phrase ───
Bizen ware is used in the Japanese tea ceremony, that is, the Zen Buddhist
observance that links meditation and art.

Exercise 23.6 **Sentence combining: Appositive phrases**

Combine each pair of sentences into one sentence that contains an appositive phrase. You will have to delete and rearrange words. Some
items have more than one possible answer.

Example:

The largest land animal is the elephant. The elephant is also one of the most intelligent animals.

The largest land animal, the elephant, is also one of the most intelligent animals.

1 Some people perform amazing feats when they are very young. These people are geniuses from birth.
2 John Stuart Mill was a British philosopher. He had written a history of Rome by age seven.
3 Two great artists began their work at age four. They were Paul Klee and Gustav Mahler.
4 Mahler was a Bohemian composer of intensely emotional works. He was also the child of a brutal father.
5 Paul Klee was a Swiss painter. As a child he was frightened by his own drawings of devils.

Exercise 23.7 Identifying phrases

In the paragraphs below, identify every verbal and appositive and every verbal, appositive, prepositional, and absolute phrase. (All the sentences include at least two such words and phrases.)

1 With its many synonyms, or words with similar meanings, English can make choosing the right word a difficult task. 2 Borrowing words from early Germanic languages and from Latin, English acquired an unusual number of synonyms. 3 With so many choices, how does a writer decide between *motherly* and *maternal* or among *womanly, feminine,* and *female?*

4 Some people prefer longer and more ornate words to avoid the flatness of short words. 5 Indeed, during the Renaissance a heated debate occurred between the Latinists, favoring Latin words, and the Saxonists, preferring Anglo-Saxon words derived from Germanic roots. 6 Today, students in writing classes are often told to choose the shorter word, usually an Anglo-Saxon derivative. 7 Better advice, wrote William Hazlitt, is the principle of choosing "the best word in common use." 8 Keeping this principle in mind, a writer would choose either *womanly,* the Anglo-Saxon word, or *feminine,* a French derivative, according to meaning and situation. 9 Of course, synonyms rarely have exactly the same meaning, usage having created subtle but real differences over time. 10 To take another example, the Old English word *handbook* has a slightly different meaning from the French derivative *manual,* a close synonym.

23b Recognizing subordinate clauses

A **clause** is any group of words that contains both a subject and a predicate. There are two kinds of clauses, and the distinction between them is important.

- A *main clause* makes a complete statement and can stand alone as a sentence: *The sky darkened.*
- A *subordinate clause* is just like a main clause *except* that it begins with a subordinating word: <u>when</u> *the sky darkened;* <u>whoever</u> *calls.* The subordinating word reduces the clause from a complete statement to a single part of speech: an adjective, adverb, or noun. Use subordinate clauses to support the ideas in main clauses, as described in **3** pp. 150–52.

Note A subordinate clause punctuated as a sentence is a sentence fragment. (See p. 282.)

Adjective clauses

An **adjective clause** modifies a noun or pronoun. It usually begins with the relative pronoun *who, whom, whose, which,* or *that.* The relative pronoun is the subject or object of the clause it begins. The clause ordinarily falls immediately after the word it modifies.

┌─── adjective clause ──┐
Parents who cannot read may have bad memories of school.

┌──── adjective clause ────┐
One school, which is open year-round, helps parents learn to read.

Adverb clauses

An **adverb clause** modifies a verb, an adjective, another adverb, or a whole word group. It always begins with a subordinating conjunction, such as *although, because, if,* or *when* (see p. 195 for a list).

┌──────────── adverb clause ────────────
The school began teaching parents when adult illiteracy gained national attention.

┌──────── adverb clause ────────┐ ┌─main clause ──
Because it was directed at people who could not read, advertising had to be inventive.

Noun clauses

A **noun clause** replaces a noun in a sentence and serves as a subject, object, or complement. It begins with *that, what, whatever, who, whom, whoever, whomever, when, where, whether, why,* or *how.*

┌──── sentence subject ────┐
Whether the program would succeed depended on door-to-door advertising.
noun clause

┌──── object of verb ────┐
Teachers explained in person how the program would work.
noun clause

Exercise 23.8 Identifying clauses

Underline the subordinate clauses in the following paragraph and identify each one as adjective (ADJ), adverb (ADV), or noun (N) by determining how it functions in its sentence.

1 The Prophet Muhammad, who was the founder of Islam, was born about 570 CE in the city of Mecca. 2 He grew up in the care of his grandfather and an uncle because both of his parents had died when he was very young. 3 His extended family was part of a powerful Arab tribe that lived in western Arabia. 4 When Muhammad was about forty years old, he had a vision while he was in a cave outside Mecca. 5 He believed that God had selected him to be the prophet of a true religion for the Arab people. 6 Viewed as God's messenger, Muhammad attracted many followers before he lost the support of the clans of Mecca. 7 He and his followers moved to Medina, where they established an organized Muslim community that sometimes clashed with the Meccans and with Jewish clans. 8 Throughout his life Muhammad continued as the religious, political, and military leader of Islam as it spread in Asia and Africa. 9 He continued to have revelations, which are recorded in the sacred book of Muslims, the Koran.

Exercise 23.9 Sentence combining: Subordinate clauses

To practice writing sentences with subordinate clauses, combine each pair of main clauses into one sentence. Use either subordinating conjunctions or relative pronouns as appropriate, referring to the lists on pp. 191 and 195 if necessary. You will have to add, delete, and rearrange words. Each item has more than one possible answer.

Example:

She did not have her tire irons with her. She could not change her bicycle tire.

Because she did not have her tire irons with her, she could not change her bicycle tire.

1 Moviegoers expect something. Movie sequels should be as exciting as the original films.
2 A few sequels are good films. Most sequels are poor imitations of the originals.
3 A sequel to a blockbuster film arrives in the theater. Crowds quickly line up to see it.
4 Viewers pay to see the same villains and heroes. They remember these characters fondly.
5 Afterward, viewers often grumble about filmmakers. The filmmakers rehash tired plots and characters.

24 Sentence Types

The four basic sentence structures vary in the number of main and subordinate clauses. Each structure gives different emphasis to the main and supporting information in a sentence.

24a Recognizing simple sentences

A **simple sentence** consists of a single main clause and no subordinate clause.

```
┌──────── main clause ──────────┐
Last summer was unusually hot.
```

```
┌──────────────────────────────── main clause ───────────────────────────────
The summer made many farmers leave the area for good or reduced them
┐
to bare existence.
```

24b Recognizing compound sentences

A **compound sentence** consists of two or more main clauses and no subordinate clause.

```
┌── main clause──┐        ┌────── main clause ───────┐
Last July was hot, but August was even hotter.
```

```
┌──────────── main clause ───────────┐        ┌────────── main clause ──────────┐
The hot sun scorched the earth, and the lack of rain killed many crops.
```

24c Recognizing complex sentences

A **complex sentence** consists of one main clause and one or more subordinate clauses.

```
┌── main clause ──┐┌──────────── subordinate clause ────────────┐
Rain finally came, although many had left the area by then.
```

```
┌──────────────── main clause ─────────────────┐  ┌── subordinate clause ────
Those who remained were able to start anew because the government
        subordinate clause
┐
came to their aid.
```

mycomplab

Visit *mycomplab.com* for more resources and exercises on sentence types.

211

24d | Recognizing compound-complex sentences

A **compound-complex sentence** has the characteristics of both the compound sentence (two or more main clauses) and the complex sentence (at least one subordinate clause).

┌─────── subordinate clause ───────┐┌──────── main clause ────────┐
When government aid finally came, many people had already been reduced

└──────────┐ ┌──── main clause ────┐
to poverty and others had been forced to move.

Exercise 24.1 | Identifying sentence structures

Mark the main clauses and subordinate clauses in the following paragraphs. Then identify each sentence as simple, compound, complex, or compound-complex.

Example:

┌──────── main clause ────────┐ ┌── subordinate clause ──
The human voice is produced in the larynx, which has two bands

└──────────┐
called vocal cords. [Complex.]

1 Our world has many sounds, but they all have one thing in common. **2** They are all produced by vibrations. **3** Vibrations make the air move in waves, and these sound waves travel to the ear. **4** When the waves enter the ear, the auditory nerves convey them to the brain, and the brain interprets them. **5** Some sounds are pleasant, and others, which we call noise, are not. **6** Pleasant sounds, such as music, are produced by regular vibrations at regular intervals. **7** Most noises are produced by irregular vibrations at irregular intervals; an example is the barking of a dog.

8 Sounds, both pleasant and unpleasant, have frequency and pitch. **9** When an object vibrates rapidly, it produces high-frequency, high-pitched sounds. **10** People can hear sounds over a wide range of frequencies, but dogs, cats, and many other animals can hear high frequencies that humans cannot.

───────── Verbs ─────────

Verbs express actions, conditions, and states of being. The basic uses and forms of verbs are described on pp. 192–93. This section explains and solves the most common problems with verbs' forms (Chapter 25), tenses (26), mood (27), and voice (28) and shows how to make verbs match their subjects (29).

25 Verb Forms

25a Use the correct forms of *sing/sang/sung* and other irregular verbs.

Most verbs are **regular:** they form their past tense and past participle by adding *-d* or *-ed* to the plain form.

Plain form	Past tense	Past participle
live	lived	lived
act	acted	acted

About two hundred English verbs are **irregular:** they form their past tense and past participle in some irregular way. Check a dictionary under the verb's plain form if you have any doubt about its other forms. If the verb is irregular, the dictionary will list the plain form, the past tense, and the past participle in that order (*go, went, gone*). If the dictionary gives only two forms (as in *think, thought*), then the past tense and the past participle are the same.

Common irregular verbs

Plain form	Past tense	Past participle
be	was, were	been
become	became	become
begin	began	begun
bid	bid	bid
bite	bit	bitten, bit
blow	blew	blown
break	broke	broken
bring	brought	brought
burst	burst	burst
buy	bought	bought
catch	caught	caught
choose	chose	chosen
come	came	come
cut	cut	cut
dive	dived, dove	dived
do	did	done
dream	dreamed, dreamt	dreamed, dreamt

(continued)

Visit *mycomplab.com* for more resources and exercises on verb forms.

Common irregular verbs

(continued)

Plain form	Past tense	Past participle
drink	drank	drunk
drive	drove	driven
eat	ate	eaten
fall	fell	fallen
find	found	found
flee	fled	fled
fly	flew	flown
forget	forgot	forgotten, forgot
freeze	froze	frozen
get	got	got, gotten
give	gave	given
go	went	gone
grow	grew	grown
hang (suspend)	hung	hung
have	had	had
hear	heard	heard
hide	hid	hidden
hold	held	held
keep	kept	kept
know	knew	known
lead	led	led
leave	left	left
lend	lent	lent
let	let	let
lose	lost	lost
pay	paid	paid
ride	rode	ridden
ring	rang	rung
run	ran	run
say	said	said
see	saw	seen
shake	shook	shaken
shrink	shrank, shrunk	shrunk, shrunken
sing	sang, sung	sung
sink	sank, sunk	sunk
sleep	slept	slept
slide	slid	slid

Key terms

plain form The dictionary form of the verb: *I walk. You forget.* (See p. 192.)

past-tense form The verb form indicating action that occurred in the past: *I walked. You forgot.* (See p. 192.)

past participle The verb form used with *have, has,* or *had: I have walked.* It may serve as a modifier: *It is a forgotten book.* (See p. 192.)

Plain form	Past tense	Past participle
speak	spoke	spoken
spring	sprang, sprung	sprung
stand	stood	stood
steal	stole	stolen
swim	swam	swum
swing	swung	swung
take	took	taken
tear	tore	torn
throw	threw	thrown
wear	wore	worn
write	wrote	written

Grammar checkers A grammar checker may not flag incorrect forms of irregular verbs. For example, a checker flagged *The runner stealed second base* (*stole* is correct) but not *The runner had steal second base* (*stolen* is correct). When in doubt about the forms of irregular verbs, refer to the preceding list or consult a dictionary.

~~CULTURE~~ ~~LANGUAGE~~ Some English dialects use distinctive verb forms that differ from those of standard American English: for instance, *drug* for *dragged*, *growed* for *grew*, *come* for *came*, or *went* for *gone*. In situations requiring standard American English, use the forms in the list here or in a dictionary.

Exercise 25.1 Using irregular verbs

For each irregular verb in brackets, supply either the past tense or the past participle, as appropriate, and identify the form you used.

1 The world population had [grow] by two-thirds of a billion people in less than a decade. 2 Recently it [break] the 6 billion mark. 3 Population experts have [draw] pictures of a crowded future, predicting that the world population may have [slide] up to as many 10 billion by the year 2050. 4 The supply of food, clean water, and land is of particular concern. 5 Even though the food supply [rise] in the last decade, the share to each person [fall]. 6 At the same time the water supply, which had actually [become] healthier in the twentieth century, [sink] in size and quality. 7 Changes in land use [run] nomads and subsistence farmers off their fields, while the overall number of species on earth [shrink] by 20 percent.

8 Yet not all the news is bad. 9 Recently some countries have [begin] to heed these and other problems and to explore how technology can be [drive] to help the earth and all its populations. 10 Population control has [find] adherents all over the world. 11 Crop management has [take] some pressure off lands with poor soil, allowing their owners to produce food, while genetic engineering promises to replenish food supplies that have [shrink]. 12 Some new techniques for waste processing have [prove] effective. 13 Land conservation programs have [give] endangered species room to reproduce and thrive.

25b Distinguish between *sit* and *set*, *lie* and *lay*, and *rise* and *raise*.

The forms of *sit* and *set*, *lie* and *lay*, and *rise* and *raise* are easy to confuse.

Plain form	Past tense	Past participle
sit	sat	sat
set	set	set
lie	lay	lain
lay	laid	laid
rise	rose	risen
raise	raised	raised

In each of these confusing pairs, one verb is intransitive (it does not take an object) and one is transitive (it does take an object). (See pp. 200–201 for more on this distinction.)

Intransitive

The patients lie in their beds. [*Lie* means "recline" and takes no object.]

Visitors sit with them. [*Sit* means "be seated" or "be located" and takes no object.]

Patients' temperatures rise. [*Rise* means "increase" or "get up" and takes no object.]

Transitive

Orderlies lay the dinner trays on tables. [*Lay* means "place" and takes an object, here *trays*.]

Orderlies set the trays down. [*Set* means "place" and takes an object, here *trays*.]

Nursing aides raise the shades. [*Raise* means "lift" or "bring up" and takes an object, here *shades*.]

Exercise 25.2 Distinguishing between *sit/set, lie/lay, rise/raise*

Choose the correct verb from the pair given in brackets. Then supply the past tense or past participle, as appropriate.

Example:

After I washed all the windows, I [lie, lay] down the squeegee and then I [sit, set] the table.

After I washed all the windows, I laid down the squeegee and then I set the table.

1 Yesterday afternoon the child [lie, lay] down for a nap.
2 The child has been [rise, raise] by her grandparents.
3 Most days her grandfather has [sit, set] with her, reading her stories.
4 She has [rise, raise] at dawn most mornings.
5 Her toys were [lie, lay] on the floor.

| **25c** | Use the *-s* and *-ed* forms of the verb when they are required. |

Speakers of some English dialects and nonnative speakers of English sometimes omit the *-s* and *-ed* verb endings when they are required in standard American English.

Grammar checkers A grammar checker will flag many omitted *-s* and *-ed* endings from verbs, as in *he ask* and *was ask*. But it will miss many omissions, too.

1 Required *-s* ending

Use the *-s* form of a verb when *both* of these situations hold:

■ **The subject is a singular noun (*boy*), an indefinite pronoun (*everyone*), or *he*, *she*, or *it*.** These subjects are **third person,** used when someone or something is being spoken about.

■ **The verb's action occurs in the present.**

The letter asks [not ask] for a quick response.
Delay costs [not cost] money.

Be especially careful with the *-s* forms of *be* (*is*), *have* (*has*), and *do* (*does, doesn't*). These forms should always be used to indicate present time with third-person singular subjects.

The company is [not be] late in responding.
It has [not have] problems.
It doesn't [not don't] have the needed data.
The contract does [not do] depend on the response.

In addition, *be* has an *-s* form in the past tense with *I* and third-person singular subjects:

The company was [not were] in trouble before.

I, you, and plural subjects do *not* take the *-s* form of verbs:

I am [not is] a student.
You are [not is] also a student.
They are [not is] students, too.

2 Required *-ed* or *-d* ending

The *-ed* or *-d* verb form is required in *any* of these situations:

■ **The verb's action occurred in the past:**

The company asked [not ask] for more time.

■ **The verb form functions as a modifier:**

The data concerned [not concern] should be retrievable.

■ **The verb form combines with a form of *be* or *have*:**

The company is <u>supposed</u> [not <u>suppose</u>] to be the best.
It has <u>developed</u> [not <u>develop</u>] an excellent reputation.

Watch especially for a needed *-ed* or *-d* ending when it isn't pronounced clearly in speech, as in *asked, discussed, mixed, supposed, walked,* and *used.*

Exercise 25.3 Using *-s* and *-ed* verb endings

Supply the correct form of each verb in brackets. Be careful to include *-s* and *-ed* (or *-d*) endings where they are needed for standard English.

Example:
Unfortunately, the roof on our new house already [leak].
Unfortunately, the roof on our new house already <u>leaks</u>.

1 A teacher sometimes [ask] too much of a student. **2** In high school I was once [punish] for being sick. **3** I had [miss] a week of school because of a serious case of the flu. **4** I [realize] that I would fail a test unless I had a chance to make up the class work, so I [discuss] the problem with the teacher. **5** He said I was [suppose] to make up the work while I was sick. **6** At that I [walk] out of the class. **7** I [receive] a failing grade then, but it did not change my attitude. **8** I [work] harder in the courses that have more understanding teachers. **9** Today I still balk when a teacher [make] unreasonable demands or [expect] miracles.

25d **Use helping verbs with main verbs appropriately.**

Helping verbs combine with main verbs in verb phrases: *The line should have been cut. Who was calling?*

Grammar checkers A grammar checker often spots omitted helping verbs and incorrect main verbs with helping verbs, but sometimes it does not. A checker flagged *Many been fortunate* and *She working* but overlooked other errors, such as *The conference will be occurred.*

┌─ **Key terms** ───

helping verb A word such as *can, may, be, have,* or *do* that forms a verb phrase with another verb to show time, permission, and other meanings. (See p. 193.)

main verb The verb that carries the principal meaning in a verb phrase: *has <u>walked</u>, could be <u>happening</u>.* (See p. 193.)

verb phrase A helping verb plus a main verb: *will be singing, would speak.* (See p. 193.)

1 Required helping verbs

Standard American English requires helping verbs in certain situations:

■ **The main verb ends in** *-ing:*

Researchers <u>are</u> conducting fieldwork all over the world. [Not <u>Researchers conducting</u>. . . .]

■ **The main verb is** *been* **or** *be:*

Many <u>have</u> been fortunate in their discoveries. [Not <u>Many been</u>. . . .]
Some <u>could</u> be real-life Indiana Joneses. [Not <u>Some be</u>. . . .]

■ **The main verb is a past participle**, such as *talked, begun,* or *thrown.*

Their discoveries <u>were</u> covered in newspapers and magazines. [Not <u>Their discoveries covered</u>. . . .]
The researchers <u>have</u> given interviews on TV. [Not <u>The researchers given</u>. . . .]

The omission of a helping verb may create an incomplete sentence, or **sentence fragment**, because a present participle (*conducting*), an irregular past participle (*been*), or the infinitive *be* cannot stand alone as the only verb in a sentence (see p. 280). To work as sentence verbs, these verb forms need helping verbs.

2 Combination of helping verb + main verb

Helping verbs and main verbs combine into verb phrases in specific ways.

Note The main verb in a verb phrase (the one carrying the main meaning) does not change to show a change in subject or time: *she has <u>sung</u>, you had <u>sung</u>.* Only the helping verb may change.

Form of *be* + present participle

The **progressive tenses** indicate action in progress. Create them with *be, am, is, are, was, were,* or *been* followed by the main verb's present participle:

She <u>is working</u> on a new book.

> **Key terms**
>
> **present participle** The *-ing* form of a verb: *flying, playing.* (See p. 192.)
> **progressive tenses** Verb tenses expressing action in progress—for instance, *I am flying. I was flying. I will be flying.* (See p. 230.)

Be and *been* always require additional helping verbs to form progressive tenses:

can	might	should
could	must	will
may	shall	would

} be working

have
has
had

} been working

When forming the progressive tenses, be sure to use the *-ing* form of the main verb.

Faulty Her ideas are <u>grow</u> more complex. She is <u>developed</u> a new approach to ethics.

Revised Her ideas are <u>growing</u> more complex. She is <u>developing</u> a new approach to ethics.

Form of *be* + past participle

The **passive voice** of the verb indicates that the subject *receives* the action of the verb. Create the passive voice with a form of *be* (*be, am, is, are, was, were, being,* or *been*) followed by the main verb's past participle:

Her latest book <u>was completed</u> in four months.

Be, being, and *been* always require additional helping verbs to form the passive voice:

have
has
had

} <u>been</u> completed

am	was
is	were
are	

} <u>being</u> completed

will <u>be</u> completed

Be sure to use the main verb's past participle for the passive voice:

Faulty Her next book will be <u>publish</u> soon.
Revised Her next book will be <u>published</u> soon.

Note Only transitive verbs may form the passive voice:

Faulty A philosophy conference <u>will be occurred</u> in the same week. [*Occur* is not a transitive verb.]

Revised A philosophy conference <u>will occur</u> in the same week.

Key terms

past participle The *-d* or *-ed* form of a regular verb: *hedged, walked.* Most irregular verbs have distinctive past participles: *eaten, swum.* (See p. 192.)

passive voice The verb form when the subject names the receiver of the verb's action: *An essay was written by every student.* (See p. 236.)

See p. 236 for advice on when to use and when to avoid the passive voice.

Forms of *have*

Four forms of *have* serve as helping verbs: *have, has, had, having*. One of these forms plus the main verb's past participle creates one of the **perfect tenses**, those expressing action completed before another specific time or action:

> Some students have complained about the laboratory.
> Others had complained before.

Will and other helping verbs sometimes accompany forms of *have* in the perfect tenses:

> Several more students will have complained by the end of the week.

Forms of *do*

Do, does, and *did* have three uses as helping verbs, always with the plain form of the main verb:

- **To pose a question:** *How did the trial end?*
- **To emphasize the main verb:** *It did end eventually.*
- **To negate the main verb, along with *not* or *never*:** *The judge did not withdraw.*

Be sure to use the main verb's plain form with any form of *do:*

> **Faulty** The judge did remained in court.
> **Revised** The judge did remain in court.

Modals

The modal helping verbs include *can, could, may,* and *might*, along with several two- and three-word combinations, such as *have to* and *be able to*. (See p. 193 for a list of helping verbs.) Use the plain form of the main verb with a modal unless the modal combines with another helping verb (usually *have*):

> **Faulty** The equipment can detects small vibrations. It should have detect the change.
> **Revised** The equipment can detect small vibrations. It should have detected the change.

Key terms

transitive verb A verb that requires an object to complete its meaning: *Every student completed an essay* (*essay* is the object of *completed*). (See p. 201.)

perfect tenses Verb tenses expressing an action completed before another specific time or action: *We have eaten. We had eaten. We will have eaten.* (See p. 229.)

Modals convey various meanings, with these being most common:

- **Ability:** *can, could, be able to*

  The equipment <u>can detect</u> small vibrations. [Present.]

  The equipment <u>could detect</u> small vibrations. [Past.]

  The equipment <u>is able to detect</u> small vibrations. [Present. Past: *was able to*. Future: *will be able to*.]

- **Possibility:** *could, may, might; could/may/might have* + past participle

  The equipment <u>could fail</u>. [Present.]
  The equipment <u>may fail</u>. [Present or future.]
  The equipment <u>might fail</u>. [Present or future.]
  The equipment <u>may have failed</u>. [Past.]

- **Necessity or obligation:** *must, have to, be supposed to*

  The lab <u>must purchase</u> a backup. [Present or future.]

  The lab <u>has to purchase</u> a backup. [Present or future. Past: *had to*.]

  The lab <u>will have to purchase</u> a backup. [Future.]

  The lab <u>is supposed to purchase</u> a backup. [Present. Past: *was supposed to*.]

- **Permission:** *may, can, could*

  The lab <u>may spend</u> the money. [Present or future.]
  The lab <u>can spend</u> the money. [Present or future.]
  The lab <u>could spend</u> the money. [Present or future, more tentative.]
  The lab <u>could have spent</u> the money. [Past.]

- **Intention:** *will, shall, would*

  The lab <u>will spend</u> the money. [Future.]

  <u>Shall</u> we <u>offer</u> advice? [Future. Use *shall* for questions requesting opinion or consent.]

  We <u>would have offered</u> advice. [Past.]

- **Request:** *could, can, would*

  <u>Could</u> [or <u>Can</u> or <u>Would</u>] you please <u>obtain</u> a bid? [Present or future.]

- **Advisability:** *should, had better, ought to; should have* + past participle

  You <u>should obtain</u> three bids. [Present or future.]
  You <u>had better obtain</u> three bids. [Present or future.]
  You <u>ought to obtain</u> three bids. [Present or future.]
  You <u>should have obtained</u> three bids. [Past.]

- **Past habit:** *would, used to*

In years past we <u>would obtain</u> five bids.
We <u>used to obtain</u> five bids.

Exercise 25.4 Using helping verbs

Add helping verbs to the following paragraph where they are needed for standard American English. If a sentence is correct as given, mark the number preceding it.

1 Each year thousands of new readers been discovering Agatha Christie's mysteries. **2** Christie, a well-loved writer who worked as a nurse during World War I, wrote more than sixty-five detective novels. **3** Christie never expected that her mysteries become as popular as they did. **4** Nor did she anticipate that her play, *The Mousetrap*, be performed for decades. **5** At her death in 1976, Christie been the best-selling English novelist for some time. **6** Her books still selling well to readers who like being baffled.

Exercise 25.5 Revising: Helping verbs plus main verbs

Revise the following paragraph so that helping verbs and main verbs are used correctly. If a sentence is correct as given, mark the number preceding it.

1 A report from the Bureau of the Census has confirm a widening gap between rich and poor. **2** As suspected, the percentage of people below the poverty level did increased over the last decade. **3** More than 17 percent of the population is make 5 percent of all the income. **4** About 1 percent of the population will keeping an average of $500,000 apiece after taxes. **5** The other 99 percent all together will retain about $300,000.

25e Use a gerund or an infinitive after a verb as appropriate.

Nonnative speakers of English sometimes stumble over whether to use a gerund or an infinitive after a verb. Gerunds and infinitives may follow certain verbs but not others. And sometimes the use of a gerund or infinitive with the same verb changes the meaning.

Grammar checkers A grammar checker will spot some but not all errors in matching gerunds or infinitives with verbs. For example,

> **Key terms**
>
> **gerund** The *-ing* form of the verb used as a noun: *Smoking is unhealthful.* (See p. 205.)
>
> **infinitive** The plain form of the verb usually preceded by *to: to smoke.* An infinitive may serve as an adjective, adverb, or noun. (See p. 205.)

a checker failed to flag *I practice to swim* and *I promise helping out*. Use the lists given here and a dictionary of English as a second language to determine whether an infinitive or a gerund is appropriate. (See **3** p. 171 for a list of ESL dictionaries.)

1 Either gerund or infinitive

A gerund or an infinitive may come after the following verbs with no significant difference in meaning.

begin	continue	intend	prefer
can't bear	hate	like	start
can't stand	hesitate	love	

The pump began working.
The pump began to work.

2 Meaning change with gerund or infinitive

With four verbs, a gerund has quite a different meaning from an infinitive:

forget	stop
remember	try

The engineer stopped eating. [He no longer ate.]
The engineer stopped to eat. [He stopped in order to eat.]

3 Gerund, not infinitive

Do not use an infinitive after these verbs:

admit	discuss	mind	recollect
adore	dislike	miss	resent
appreciate	enjoy	postpone	resist
avoid	escape	practice	risk
consider	finish	put off	suggest
deny	imagine	quit	tolerate
detest	keep	recall	understand

Faulty   He finished to eat lunch.
Revised   He finished eating lunch.

4 Infinitive, not gerund

Do not use a gerund after these verbs:

agree	claim	manage	promise
appear	consent	mean	refuse
arrange	decide	offer	say
ask	expect	plan	wait
assent	have	prepare	want
beg	hope	pretend	wish

Faulty   He decided <u>checking</u> the pump.
Revised   He decided <u>to check</u> the pump.

5 | Noun or pronoun + infinitive

Some verbs may be followed by an infinitive alone or by a noun or pronoun and an infinitive. The presence of a noun or pronoun changes the meaning.

ask	dare	need	wish
beg	expect	promise	would like
choose	help	want	

He expected <u>to watch</u>.
He expected <u>his workers</u> <u>to watch</u>.

Some verbs *must* be followed by a noun or pronoun before an infinitive:

advise	encourage	oblige	require
allow	forbid	order	teach
cause	force	permit	tell
challenge	hire	persuade	train
command	instruct	remind	urge
convince	invite	request	warn

He instructed <u>his workers</u> <u>to watch</u>.

Do not use *to* before the infinitive when it follows one of these verbs and a noun or pronoun:

feel	hear	make ("force")	watch
have	let	see	

He let his workers <u>learn</u> by observation.

Exercise 25.6   Revising: Verbs plus gerunds or infinitives

Revise the following paragraph so that gerunds or infinitives are used correctly with verbs. Mark the number preceding any sentence that is correct as given.

1 Without enough highly trained people to draw on, American businesses risk to lose their competitive edge. **2** In recent years, American business leaders have found that their workers need improving their math and science skills. **3** Some colleges have responded by encouraging more students to choose math or engineering as their major. **4** A program called HELP Wanted challenges students take action on behalf of American competitiveness. **5** Officials who work with this program hope increasing the number of math, science, and engineering majors and providing more job training.

25f Use the appropriate particles with two-word verbs.

Standard American English includes some verbs that consist of two words: the verb itself and a **particle**, a preposition or adverb that affects the meaning of the verb.

> <u>Look up</u> the answer. [Research the answer.]
> <u>Look over</u> the answer. [Examine the answer.]

The meanings of these two-word verbs are often quite different from the meanings of the individual words that make them up. (There are some three-word verbs, too, such as *put up with* and *run out of.*) A dictionary of English as a second language will define two-word verbs and say whether the verbs may be separated in a sentence, as explained below. (See **3** p. 171 for a list of ESL dictionaries.) A grammar checker will recognize few if any misuses of two-word verbs.

Note Many two-word verbs are more common in speech than in more formal academic or business writing. For formal writing, consider using *research* instead of *look up, examine* or *inspect* instead of *look over.*

1 Inseparable two-word verbs

Verbs and particles that may not be separated by any other words include the following:

catch on	go over	play around	stay away
come across	grow up	run into	stay up
get along	keep on	run out of	take care of
give in	look into	speak up	turn up at

Faulty   Children <u>grow</u> quickly <u>up</u>.
Revised   Children <u>grow up</u> quickly.

2 Separable two-word verbs

Most two-word verbs that take direct objects may be separated by the object.

> Parents <u>help out</u> their children.
> Parents <u>help</u> their children <u>out</u>.

Key terms

preposition A word such as *about, for,* or *to* that takes a noun or pronoun as its object: <u>at</u> the house, <u>in</u> the woods. (See p. 195 for a list of prepositions.)

adverb A word that modifies a verb, adjective, other adverb, or whole word group. (See p. 194.)

If the direct object is a pronoun, the pronoun *must* separate the verb from the particle.

Faulty   Parents <u>help out</u> them.
Revised   Parents <u>help</u> them <u>out</u>.

The separable two-word verbs include the following:

bring up	give back	make up	throw out
call off	hand in	point out	try on
call up	hand out	put away	try out
drop off	help out	put back	turn down
fill out	leave out	put off	turn on
fill up	look over	take out	turn up
give away	look up	take over	wrap up

Exercise 25.7 Revising: Verbs plus particles

The two- and three-word verbs in the paragraph below are underlined. Some are correct as given, and some are not because they should or should not be separated by other words. Revise the verbs and other words that are incorrect. Consult the lists on these pages or an ESL dictionary if necessary to determine which verbs are separable.

1 American movies treat everything from <u>going out with</u> someone to <u>making up</u> an ethnic identity. 2 Some filmmakers like to address current topics, such as <u>getting</u> in today's world <u>along</u>. 3 Others, however, <u>stay</u> from serious topics <u>away</u> and choose lighter themes. 4 Whatever the topic, viewers <u>fill</u> theaters <u>up</u> when a movie is controversial. 5 It seems that filmmakers will <u>keep</u> creating controversy <u>on</u>, <u>trying</u> it <u>out</u> whenever they can. 6 They are always eager to make money and <u>point</u> their influence <u>out</u> to the public.

26 Verb Tenses

Tense shows the time of a verb's action. The box on the next page illustrates the tense forms for a regular verb. (Irregular verbs have different past-tense and past-participle forms. See pp. 213–16.)

Grammar checkers A grammar checker can provide little help with incorrect verb tenses and tense sequences because correctness usually depends on meaning.

Visit *mycomplab.com* for more resources and exercises on verb tenses.

Tenses of a regular verb (active voice)

Present Action that is occurring now, occurs habitually, or is generally true

Simple present Plain form or *-s* form

I walk.
You/we/they walk.
He/she/it walks.

Present progressive *Am, is,* or *are* plus *-ing* form

I am walking.
You/we/they are walking.
He/she/it is walking.

Past Action that occurred before now

Simple past Past-tense form (*-d* or *-ed*)

I/he/she/it walked.
You/we/they walked.

Past progressive *Was* or *were* plus *-ing* form

I/he/she/it was walking.
You/we/they were walking.

Future Action that will occur in the future

Simple future Plain form plus *will*

I/you/he/she/it/we/they will walk.

Future progressive *Will be* plus *-ing* form

I/you/he/she/it/we/they will be walking.

Present perfect Action that began in the past and is linked to the present

Present perfect *Have* or *has* plus past participle (*-d* or *-ed*)

I/you/we/they have walked.
He/she/it has walked.

Present perfect progressive *Have been* or *has been* plus *-ing* form

I/you/we/they have been walking.
He/she/it has been walking.

Past perfect Action that was completed before another past action

Past perfect *Had* plus past participle (*-d* or *-ed*)

I/you/he/she/it/we/they had walked.

Past perfect progressive *Had been* plus *-ing* form

I/you/he/she/it/we/they had been walking.

Future perfect Action that will be completed before another future action

Future perfect *Will have* plus past participle (*-d* or *-ed*)

I/you/he/she/it/we/they will have walked.

Future perfect progressive *Will have been* plus *-ing* form

I/you/he/she/it/we/they will have been walking.

CULTURE · LANGUAGE In standard American English, a verb conveys time and sequence through its form. In some other languages and English dialects, various markers besides verb form may indicate the time of a verb. For instance, in African American dialect *I be attending class on Friday* means that the speaker attends class every Friday. To a speaker of standard American English, however, the sentence may be unclear: last Friday? this Friday? every Friday? The intended meaning must be indicated by verb tense. *I attended class on Friday. I will attend class on Friday. I attend class on Friday.*

26a Observe the special uses of the present tense (*sing*).

The present tense has several distinctive uses.

Action occurring now
She understands the problem.
We define the problem differently.

Habitual or recurring action
Banks regularly undergo audits.
The audits monitor the banks' activities.

A general truth
The mills of the gods grind slowly.
The earth is round.

Discussion of literature, film, and so on
Huckleberry Finn has adventures we all envy.
In that article the author examines several causes of crime.

Future time
Next week we draft a new budget.
Funding ends in less than a year.

(The present tense shows future time with expressions like those in the examples above: *next week, in less than a year.*)

26b Observe the uses of the perfect tenses (*have/had/will have sung*).

The **perfect tenses** consist of a form of *have* plus the verb's past participle (*closed, hidden*). They indicate an action completed before another specific time or action. The present perfect tense also indicates action begun in the past and continued into the present.

present perfect
The dancer has performed here only once. [The action is completed at the time of the statement.]

present perfect
Critics **have written** about the performance ever since. [The action began in the past and continues now.]

past perfect
The dancer **had trained** in Asia before his performance. [The action was completed before another past action.]

future perfect
He **will have danced** here again by the end of the year. [The action begins now or in the future and will be completed by a specific time in the future.]

CULTURE LANGUAGE With the present perfect tense, the words *since* and *for* are followed by different information. After *since*, give a specific point in time: *The play has run since 1989*. After *for*, give a span of time: *It has run for decades*.

26c Observe the uses of the progressive tenses (*is/was/will be singing*).

The **progressive tenses** indicate continuing (therefore progressive) action. In standard American English the progressive tenses consist of a form of *be* plus the verb's *-ing* form (present participle). (The words *be* and *been* must be combined with other helping verbs. See pp. 220–21.)

present progressive
The economy **is improving**.

past progressive
Last year the economy **was stagnating**.

future progressive
Economists **will be watching** for signs of growth.

present perfect progressive
The government **has been expecting** an upturn.

past perfect progressive
Various indicators **had been suggesting** improvement.

future perfect progressive
By the end of this year, investors **will have been watching** interest rates nervously for nearly a decade.

Note Verbs that express unchanging states (especially mental states) rather than physical actions do not usually appear in the progressive tenses. These verbs include *adore, appear, believe, belong, care, hate, have, hear, know, like, love, mean, need, own, prefer, remember, see, sound, taste, think, understand,* and *want*.

Faulty She **is wanting** to study ethics.
Revised She **wants** to study ethics.

26d Keep tenses consistent.

Within a sentence, the tenses of verbs and verb forms need not be identical as long as they reflect actual changes in time: *Ramon will graduate from college thirty years after his father arrived in America.* But needless shifts in tense will confuse or distract readers:

Inconsistent	Immediately after Booth shot Lincoln, Major Rathbone threw himself upon the assassin. But Booth pulls a knife and plunges it into the major's arm.
Revised	Immediately after Booth shot Lincoln, Major Rathbone threw himself upon the assassin. But Booth pulled a knife and plunged it into the major's arm.
Inconsistent	The main character in the novel suffers psychologically because he has a clubfoot, but he eventually triumphed over his disability.
Revised	The main character in the novel suffers psychologically because he has a clubfoot, but he eventually triumphs over his disability. [Use the present tense to discuss the content of literature, film, and so on.]

Exercise 26.1 Revising: Consistent past tense

In the paragraph below, change the tenses of the verbs as needed to maintain consistent simple past tense. If a sentence is correct as given, mark the number preceding it.

1 The 1960 presidential race between Richard Nixon and John F. Kennedy was the first to feature a televised debate. 2 Despite his extensive political experience, Nixon perspires heavily and looks haggard and uneasy in front of the camera. 3 By contrast, Kennedy was projecting cool poise and providing crisp answers that made him seem fit for the office of President. 4 The public responded positively to Kennedy's image. 5 His poll ratings shoot up immediately, while Nixon's take a corresponding drop. 6 Kennedy won the election by a close 118,564 votes.

Exercise 26.2 Revising: Consistent present tense

In the paragraph below, change the tenses of the verbs as needed to maintain consistent simple present tense. If a sentence is correct as given, mark the number preceding it.

1 E. B. White's famous children's novel *Charlotte's Web* is a wonderful story of friendship and loyalty. 2 Charlotte, the wise and motherly spider, decided to save her friend Wilbur, the young and childlike pig, from being butchered by his owner. 3 She made a plan to weave words into her web that described Wilbur. 4 She first weaves "Some Pig" and later presented "Terrific," "Radiant," and "Humble." 5 Her plan succeeded beautifully. 6 She fools the humans into believing that Wilbur was a pig unlike any other, and Wilbur lived.

26e Use the appropriate sequence of verb tenses.

The **sequence of tenses** is the relation between the verb tense in a main clause and the verb tense in a subordinate clause. The tenses should change when necessary to reflect changes in actual or relative time. The main difficulties with tense sequence are discussed on these pages.

1 Past or past perfect tense in main clause

When the verb in the main clause is in the past or past perfect tense, the verb in the subordinate clause must also be past or past perfect:

> main clause: subordinate clause:
> past   past
>
> The researchers <u>discovered</u> that people <u>varied</u> widely in their knowledge of public events.

> main clause: subordinate clause:
> past   past perfect
>
> The variation <u>occurred</u> because respondents <u>had been born</u> in different decades.

> main clause: subordinate clause:
> past perfect   past
>
> None of them <u>had been born</u> when Dwight Eisenhower <u>was</u> President.

Exception Always use the present tense for a general truth, such as *The earth is round:*

> main clause: subordinate clause:
> past   present
>
> Most <u>understood</u> that popular Presidents <u>are</u> not necessarily good Presidents.

2 Conditional sentences

A **conditional sentence** states a factual relation between cause and effect, makes a prediction, or speculates about what might happen. Such a sentence usually contains a subordinate clause beginning with *if, when,* or *unless* and a main clause stating the result. The three kinds of conditional sentences use distinctive verbs.

Key terms

main clause A word group that can stand alone as a sentence because it contains a subject and a predicate and does not begin with a subordinating word. *Books are valuable.* (See p. 209.)

subordinate clause A word group that contains a subject and a predicate, begins with a subordinating word such as *because* or *who,* and is not a question: *Books are valuable when they enlighten.* (See p. 209.)

Factual relation

Statements linking factual causes and effects use matched tenses in the subordinate and main clauses:

> subordinate clause: main clause:
>   present   present
> When a voter <u>casts</u> a ballot, he or she <u>has</u> complete privacy.

> subordinate clause: main clause:
>   past   past
> When voters <u>registered</u> in some states, they <u>had</u> to pay a poll tax.

Prediction

Predictions generally use the present tense in the subordinate clause and the future tense in the main clause:

> subordinate clause: main clause:
>   present   future
> Unless citizens <u>regain</u> faith in politics, they <u>will</u> not <u>vote</u>.

Sometimes the verb in the main clause consists of *may, can, should,* or *might* plus the verb's plain form: *If citizens <u>regain</u> faith, they <u>may vote</u>.*

Speculation

The verbs in speculations depend on whether the linked events are possible or impossible. For possible events in the present, use the past tense in the subordinate clause and *would, could,* or *might* plus the verb's plain form in the main clause:

> subordinate clause: main clause:
>   past   *would* + verb
> If voters <u>had</u> more confidence, they <u>would vote</u> more often.

Use *were* instead of *was* in the subordinate clause, even when the subject is *I, he, she, it,* or a singular noun. (See pp. 234–35 for more on this distinctive verb form.)

> subordinate clause: main clause:
>   past   *would* + verb
> If the voter <u>were</u> more confident, he or she <u>would vote</u> more often.

For impossible events in the present—events that are contrary to fact—use the same forms as above (including the distinctive *were* when applicable):

> subordinate clause: main clause:
>   past   *might* + verb
> If Lincoln <u>were</u> alive, he <u>might inspire</u> confidence.

For impossible events in the past, use the past perfect tense in the subordinate clause and *would, could,* or *might* plus the present perfect tense in the main clause:

> subordinate clause: main clause:
>   past perfect   *might* + present perfect
> If Lincoln <u>had lived</u> past the Civil War, he <u>might have helped</u> stabilize the country.

Exercise 26.3 Using correct tense sequence

In the following paragraph, change the tense of each bracketed verb so that it is in correct sequence with other verbs.

1 Diaries that Adolph Hitler [be] supposed to have written surfaced in Germany. **2** Many people believed that the diaries [be] authentic because a well-known historian [have] declared them so. **3** However, the historian's evaluation was questioned by other authorities, who [call] the diaries forgeries. **4** They claimed, among other things, that the paper [be] not old enough to have been used by Hitler. **5** Eventually, the doubters won the debate because they [have] the best evidence.

Exercise 26.4 Revising: Tense sequence with conditional sentences

In the following paragraph, use the forms of *be* that create correct tense sequence for all verbs.

1 If you think you [be] exposed to the flu, you should get a flu shot. **2** You may avoid the illness altogether, and if you contract it your illness [be] milder. **3** Avoid the vaccine only if you [be] allergic to eggs. **4** If every person [be] willing and able to get the shot, there [be] very little serious flu each year. **5** But nearly universal vaccination [be] possible only if public outreach [be] improved and vaccine supplies [be] adequate.

27 Verb Mood

Mood in grammar is a verb form that indicates the writer's or speaker's attitude toward what he or she is saying. The **indicative mood** states a fact or opinion or asks a question: *The theater needs help.* The **imperative mood** expresses a command or gives a direction. It omits the subject of the sentence, *you: Help the theater.*

The **subjunctive mood** is trickier and requires distinctive verb forms described opposite.

Grammar checkers A grammar checker may spot some errors in the subjunctive mood, but it may miss others. For example, a checker flagged *I wish I was home* (should be *were home*) but not *If I were home, I will not leave* (should be *would not leave*).

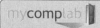

mycomplab

Visit *mycomplab.com* for more resources and exercises on verb mood.

27a Use the subjunctive verb forms appropriately, as in *I wish I were.*

The subjunctive mood expresses a suggestion, requirement, or desire, or it states a condition that is contrary to fact (that is, imaginary or hypothetical).

- Verbs such as *ask, insist, urge, require, recommend,* and *suggest* indicate request or requirement. They often precede a subordinate clause beginning with *that* and containing the substance of the request or requirement. For all subjects, the verb in the *that* clause is the plain form:

  plain form
  Rules require that every donation be mailed.

- Contrary-to-fact clauses state imaginary or hypothetical conditions and usually begin with *if* or *unless* or follow *wish.* For present contrary-to-fact clauses, use the verb's past-tense form (for *be,* use the past-tense form *were*):

  past   past
  If the theater were in better shape and had more money, its future would be assured.

  past
  I wish I were able to donate money.

  For past contrary-to-fact clauses, use the verb's past perfect form (*had* + past participle):

  past perfect
  The theater would be better funded if it had been better managed.

  Note Do not use the helping verb *would* or *could* in a contrary-to-fact clause beginning with *if:*

Not	Many people would have helped if they would have known.
But	Many people would have helped if they had known.

See also p. 233 on verb tenses in sentences like these.

27b Keep mood consistent.

Shifts in mood within a sentence or among related sentences can be confusing. Such shifts occur most frequently in directions.

Inconsistent	Cook the mixture slowly, and you should stir it until the sugar is dissolved. [Mood shifts from imperative to indicative.]

Revised　　　　Cook the mixture slowly, and stir it until the sugar is dissolved. [Consistently imperative.]

Exercise 27.1　Revising: Subjunctive mood

Revise the following paragraph with appropriate subjunctive verb forms. If a sentence is correct as given, mark the number preceding it.

1 If John Hawkins would have known of all the dangerous side effects of smoking tobacco, would he have introduced the plant to England in 1565? **2** In promoting tobacco, Hawkins noted that if a Florida Indian man was to travel for several days, he would have smoked tobacco to satisfy his hunger and thirst. **3** Early tobacco growers in the United States feared that their product would not gain acceptance unless it was perceived as healthful, so they spread Hawkins's story. **4** But local governments, more concerned about public safety and morality than health, passed laws requiring that colonists smoked tobacco only if they were five miles from any town. **5** To prevent decadence, in 1647 Connecticut passed a law mandating that one's smoking of tobacco was limited to once a day in one's own home.

---

28 Verb Voice

The **voice** of a verb tells whether the subject of the sentence performs the action (**active**) or is acted upon (**passive**). The actor in a passive sentence may be named in a prepositional phrase (as in *Rents are controlled by the city*), or the actor may be omitted (as in *Rents are controlled*).

CULTURE LANGUAGE A passive verb always consists of a form of *be* plus the past participle of the main verb: *rents are controlled, people were inspired*. Other helping verbs must also be used with the words *be, being,* and *been: rents have been controlled, people would have been inspired*. Only a transitive verb (one that takes an object) may be used in the passive voice. (See p. 201.)

28a　Generally, prefer the active voice. Use the passive voice when the actor is unknown or unimportant.

The active voice is usually clearer, more concise, and more forthright than the passive voice.

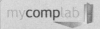

Visit *mycomplab.com* for more resources and exercises on verb voice.

Active and passive voice

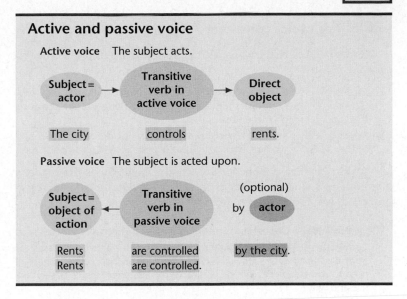

Active voice   The subject acts.

Subject = actor → Transitive verb in active voice → Direct object

The city   controls   rents.

Passive voice   The subject is acted upon.

Subject = object of action ← Transitive verb in passive voice   (optional) by actor

Rents   are controlled   by the city.
Rents   are controlled.

Weak passive	The library is used by both students and teachers for studying and research, and the plan to expand it has been praised by many.
Strong active	Both students and teachers use the library for studying and research, and many have praised the plan to expand it.

The passive voice is useful in two situations: when the actor is unknown and when the actor is unimportant or less important than the object of the action.

The Internet was established in 1969 by the US Department of Defense. The network has been extended internationally to governments, universities, foundations, corporations, and private individuals. [In the first sentence the writer wishes to stress the Internet rather than the Department of Defense. In the second sentence the actor is unknown or too complicated to name.]

After the solution had been cooled to 10°C, the acid was added. [The person who cooled and added, perhaps the writer, is less important than the facts that the solution was cooled and acid was added. Passive sentences are common in scientific writing.]

Grammar checkers Most grammar checkers can be set to spot the passive voice. But they will also flag appropriate uses of the passive voice (such as when the actor is unknown).

28b Keep voice consistent.

Shifts in voice that involve shifts in subject are usually unnecessary and confusing.

| Inconsistent | Internet <u>blogs</u> <u>cover</u> an enormous range of topics. Op-portunities for people to discuss pet issues <u>are provided</u> on these sites. |
| Revised | Internet <u>blogs</u> <u>cover</u> an enormous range of topics <u>and provide</u> opportunities for people to discuss pet issues. |

A shift in voice is appropriate when it helps focus the reader's attention on a single subject, as in *The candidate <u>campaigned</u> vigorously and <u>was nominated</u> on the first ballot.*

Exercise 28.1 **Converting between active and passive voices**

Convert the verbs in the following sentences from active to passive or from passive to active. (In converting from passive to active, you may need to add a subject.) Which version of the sentence seems more effective and why?

Example:

The aspiring actor was discovered in a nightclub.
A talent <u>scout</u> <u>discovered</u> the actor in a nightclub.

1 When the Eiffel Tower was built in 1889, it was thought by the French to be ugly.
2 At the time, many people still resisted industrial technology.
3 The tower's naked steel construction typified this technology.
4 Beautiful ornament was expected to grace fine buildings.
5 Further, a structure without solid walls could not even be called a building.

Exercise 28.2 **Revising: Using the active voice**

In the following paragraph, rewrite passive sentences into the active voice, adding new sentence subjects as needed.

1 Water quality is determined by many factors. 2 Suspended and dissolved substances are contained in all natural waters. 3 The amounts of the substances are controlled by the environment. 4 Some dissolved substances are produced by pesticides. 5 Other substances, such as sediment, are deposited in water by fields, livestock feedlots, and other sources. 6 The bottom life of streams and lakes is affected by sediment. 7 Light penetration is reduced by sediment, and bottom-dwelling organisms may be smothered. 8 The quality of water in city systems is measured frequently. 9 Some contaminants can be removed by treatment plants. 10 If the legal levels are exceeded by pollutants, the citizens must be notified by city officials.

29 Agreement of Subject and Verb

A subject and its verb should agree in number and person.

More <u>Japanese Americans</u> <u>live</u> in Hawaii and California than elsewhere.
        subject   verb

<u>Daniel Inouye</u> <u>was</u> the first Japanese American in Congress.
  subject   verb

Most problems of subject-verb agreement arise when endings are omitted from subjects or verbs or when the relation between sentence parts is uncertain.

Grammar checkers A grammar checker will catch many simple errors in subject-verb agreement, such as *Addie and John is late,* and some more complicated errors, such as *Is Margaret and Tom going with us?* (should be *are* in both cases). But a checker failed to flag *The old group has gone their separate ways* (should be *have*) and offered a wrong correction for *The old group have gone their separate ways,* which is already correct.

29a The -s and -es endings work differently for nouns and verbs.

An *-s* or *-es* ending does opposite things to nouns and verbs: it usually makes a noun *plural,* but it always makes a present-tense verb *singular.* Thus a singular-noun subject will not end in *-s,* but its verb will. A plural-noun subject will end in *-s,* but its verb will not. Between them, subject and verb use only one *-s* ending.

Singular subject	Plural subject
The boy play<u>s</u>.	The boy<u>s</u> play.
The bird soar<u>s</u>.	The bird<u>s</u> soar.

Key terms

	Number	
Person	**Singular**	**Plural**
First	I eat.	We eat.
Second	You eat.	You eat.
Third	He/she/it eats.	They eat.
	The bird eats.	Birds eat.

Visit *mycomplab.com* for more resources and exercises on subject-verb agreement.

The only exceptions to these rules involve the nouns that form ir-regular plurals, such as *child/children, woman/women*. The irregu-lar plural still requires a plural verb: *The children play. The women read.*

CULTURE LANGUAGE If your first language or dialect is not standard American English, subject-verb agreement may be problematic, especially for the following reasons:

- **Some English dialects follow different rules for subject-verb agreement,** such as omitting the *-s* ending for singular verbs or using the *-s* ending for plural verbs.

Nonstandard	The voter resist change.
Standard	The voter resists change.
Standard	The voters resist change.

The verb *be* changes spelling for singular and plural in both present and past tense. (See also pp. 192–93.)

Nonstandard	Taxes is high. They was raised just last year.
Standard	Taxes are high. They were raised just last year.

Have also has a distinctive *-s* form, *has*:

Nonstandard	The new tax have little chance of passing.
Standard	The new tax has little chance of passing.

- **Some other languages change all parts of verb phrases to match their subjects.** In English verb phrases, however, only the helping verbs *be, have,* and *do* change for different subjects. The modal helping verbs—*can, may, should, will,* and others—do not change:

Nonstandard	The tax mays pass next year.
Standard	The tax may pass next year.

The main verb in a verb phrase also does not change for differ-ent subjects:

Nonstandard	The tax may passes next year.
Standard	The tax may pass next year.

29b | **Subject and verb should agree even when other words come between them.**

The catalog of course requirements often baffles [not baffle] students.

The requirements stated in the catalog are [not is] unclear.

Note Phrases beginning with *as well as, together with, along with,* and *in addition to* do not change a singular subject to plural:

The president, as well as the deans, has [not have] agreed.

29c | **Subjects joined by *and* usually take plural verbs.**

Frost and Roethke were contemporaries.

Exceptions When the parts of the subject form a single idea or refer to a single person or thing, they take a singular verb:

Avocado and bean sprouts is a California sandwich.

When a compound subject is preceded by the adjective *each* or *every,* the verb is usually singular:

Each man, woman, and child has a right to be heard.

29d | **When parts of a subject are joined by *or* or *nor,* the verb agrees with the nearer part.**

Either the painter or the carpenter knows the cost.

The cabinets or the bookcases are too costly.

When one part of the subject is singular and the other plural, avoid awkwardness by placing the plural part closer to the verb so that the verb is plural:

Awkward   Neither the owners nor the contractor agrees.

Revised   Neither the contractor nor the owners agree.

29e | **With *everyone* and other indefinite pronouns, use a singular or plural verb as appropriate.**

Most indefinite pronouns are singular in meaning (they refer to a single unspecified person or thing), and they take a singular verb:

Something smells.   Neither is right.

The plural indefinite pronouns refer to more than one unspecified thing, and they take a plural verb:

Both are correct.   Several were invited.

he other indefinite pronouns take a singular or a plural verb nding on whether the word they refer to is singular or plural:

All of the money is reserved for emergencies.

All of the funds are reserved for emergencies.

CULTURE LANGUAGE See p. 272 for the distinction between *few* ("not many") and *a few* ("some").

| **29f** | **Collective nouns such as *team* take singular or plural verbs depending on meaning.** |

Use a singular verb with a collective noun when the group acts as a unit:

The team has won five of the last six meets.

But when the group's members act separately, not together, use a plural verb:

The old team have gone their separate ways.

The collective noun *number* may be singular or plural. Preceded by *a*, it is plural; preceded by *the*, it is singular:

A number of people are in debt.

The number of people in debt is very large.

CULTURE LANGUAGE Some noncount nouns (nouns that don't form plurals) are collective nouns because they name groups: for instance, *furniture, clothing, mail, machinery, equipment, military, police*. These noncount nouns usually take singular verbs: Mail *arrives daily*. But some of these nouns take plural verbs,

---

Key terms

indefinite pronoun A pronoun that does not refer to a specific person or thing:

Singular			*Singular or plural*	*Plural*
anybody	everyone	no one	all	both
anyone	everything	nothing	any	few
anything	much	one	more	many
each	neither	somebody	most	several
either	nobody	someone	some	
everybody	none	something		

collective noun A noun with singular form that names a group of individuals or things—for instance, *army, audience, committee, crowd, family*.

including *clergy, military, people, police,* and any collective noun that comes from an adjective, such as *the poor, the rich, the young, the elderly.* If you mean one representative of the group, use a singular noun such as *police officer* or *poor person.*

29g *Who, which,* and *that* take verbs that agree with their antecedents.

When used as subjects, *who, which,* and *that* refer to another word in the sentence, called the **antecedent.** The verb agrees with the antecedent:

Mayor Garber ought to listen to the people who work for her.

Bardini is the only aide who has her ear.

Agreement problems often occur with *who* and *that* when the sentence includes *one of the* or *the only one of the:*

Bardini is one of the aides who work unpaid. [Of the aides who work unpaid, Bardini is one.]

Bardini is the only one of the aides who knows the community. [Of the aides, only one, Bardini, knows the community.]

CULTURE LANGUAGE In phrases beginning with *one of the,* be sure the noun is plural: *Bardini is one of the aides* [not *aide*] *who work unpaid.*

29h *News* and other singular nouns ending in *-s* take singular verbs.

Singular nouns ending in *-s* include *athletics, economics, mathematics, measles, mumps, news, physics, politics,* and *statistics,* as well as place names such as *Athens, Wales,* and *United States.*

After so long a wait, the news has to be good.

Statistics is required of psychology majors.

A few of these words also take plural verbs, but only when they describe individual items rather than whole bodies of activity or knowledge: *The statistics prove him wrong.*

Measurements and figures ending in *-s* may also be singular when the quantity they refer to is a unit:

Three years is a long time to wait.

Three-fourths of the library consists of reference books.

29i | The verb agrees with the subject even when it precedes the subject.

The verb precedes the subject mainly in questions and in constructions beginning with *there* or *here* and a form of *be:*

Is voting a right or a privilege?

Are a right and a privilege the same thing?

There are differences between them.

29j | *Is, are,* and other linking verbs agree with their subjects, not subject complements.

Make a linking verb agree with its subject, usually the first element in the sentence, not with the noun or pronoun serving as a subject complement.

The child's sole support is her court-appointed guardians.

Her court-appointed guardians are the child's sole support.

29k | Use singular verbs with titles and with words being defined.

Hakada Associates is a new firm.

Dream Days remains a favorite book.

Folks is a down-home word for *people.*

Exercise 29.1 Revising: Subject-verb agreement

Revise the verbs in the following paragraphs as needed to make subjects and verbs agree in number. If a sentence is correct as given, mark the number preceding it.

1 Statistics from recent research suggests that humor in the workplace relieves job-related stress. **2** Reduced stress in the workplace in turn

---

Key terms

linking verb A verb that connects or equates the subject and subject complement: for example, *seem, become, appear,* and forms of *be.* (See p. 201.)

subject complement A word that describes or renames the subject: *They became chemists.* (See p. 201.)

reduce illness and absenteeism. 3 It can also ease friction within an employee group, which then work together more productively.

4 Weinstein Associates is a consulting firm that hold workshops designed to make businesspeople laugh. 5 In sessions held by one consultant, each of the participants practice making others laugh. 6 "Isn't there enough laughs within you to spread the wealth?" the consultant asks the students. 7 She quotes Casey Stengel's rule that the best way to keep your management job is to separate the underlings who hate you from the ones who have not decided how they feel. 8 Such self-deprecating comments in public is uncommon among business managers, the consultant says. 9 Each of the managers in a typical firm takes the work much too seriously. 10 The humorous boss often feels like the only one of the managers who have other things in mind besides profits.

11 Another consultant from Weinstein Associates suggest cultivating office humor with practical jokes and cartoons. 12 When a manager or employees drops a rubber fish in the water cooler or posts cartoons on the bulletin board, office spirit usually picks up. 13 If the job of updating the cartoons is entrusted to an employee who has seemed easily distracted, the employee's concentration often improves. 14 Even the former sourpuss becomes one of those who hides a bad temper. 15 Every one of the consultants caution, however, that humor has no place in life-affecting corporate situations such as employee layoffs.

Exercise 29.2 Adjusting for subject-verb agreement

Rewrite the following paragraphs to change the underlined words from plural to singular. (You will sometimes need to add *a* or *the* for the singular, as in the example below.) Then change verbs as necessary so that they agree with their new subjects.

Example:

Siberian tigers are an endangered subspecies.
The Siberian tiger is an endangered subspecies.

1 Siberian tigers are the largest living cats in the world, much bigger than their relative the Bengal tiger. 2 They grow to a length of nine to twelve feet, including their tails, and to a height of about three and a half feet. 3 They can weigh over six hundred pounds. 4 These carnivorous hunters live in northern China and Korea as well as in Siberia. 5 During the long winter of this Arctic climate, the yellowish striped coats get a little lighter in order to blend with the snow-covered landscape. 6 The coats also grow quite thick, since the tigers have to withstand temperatures as low as −50°F. 7 Siberian tigers sometimes have to travel great distances to find food. 8 They need about twenty pounds of food a day because of their size and the cold climate, but when they have fresh food they may eat as much as a hundred pounds at one time. 9 They hunt mainly deer, boars, and even bears, plus smaller prey such as fish and rabbits. 10 They pounce on their prey and grab them by the back of the neck. 11 Animals that are not killed immediately are thrown to the ground and suffocated with a bite to the throat. 12 Then the tigers feast.

Pronouns

Pronouns—words such as *she* and *who* that refer to nouns—merit special care because all their meaning comes from the other words they refer to. This section discusses pronoun case (Chapter 30), matching pronouns and the words they refer to (31), and making sure pronouns refer to the right nouns (32).

30 Pronoun Case

Case is the form of a noun or pronoun that shows the reader how it functions in a sentence.

- **The subjective case** indicates that the word is a subject or subject complement.
- **The objective case** indicates that the word is an object of a verb or preposition.
- **The possessive case** indicates that the word owns or is the source of a noun in the sentence.

Nouns change form only to show possession: *teacher's* (see **5** pp. 325–27). Most of the pronouns listed on the next page change more frequently.

Key terms

subject Who or what a sentence is about: *Biologists often study animals. They often work in laboratories.* (See pp. 197–98.)

subject complement A word or words that rename or describe the sentence subject: *Biologists are scientists. The best biologists are she and Scoggins.* (See p. 201.)

object of verb The receiver of the verb's action (**direct object**): *Many biologists study animals. The animals teach them.* Or the person or thing the action is performed for (**indirect object**): *Some biologists give animals homes. The animals give them pleasure.* (See pp. 201–02.)

object of preposition The word linked by *with, for,* or another preposition to the rest of the sentence: *Many biologists work in a laboratory. For them the lab often provides a second home.* (See pp. 203–04.)

Visit *mycomplab.com* for more resources and exercises

on pronoun case.

Subjective	Objective	Possessive
I	me	my, mine
you	you	your, yours
he	him	his
she	her	her, hers
it	it	its
we	us	our, ours
you	you	your, yours
they	them	their, theirs
who	whom	whose
whoever	whomever	—

Grammar checkers A grammar checker may flag some problems with pronoun case, but it will also miss a lot. For instance, one checker spotted the error in *We asked whom would come* (should be *who would come*), but it overlooked *We dreaded them coming* (should be *their coming*).

CULTURE LANGUAGE In standard American English, *-self* pronouns do not change form to show function. Their only forms are *myself, yourself, himself, herself, itself, ourselves, yourselves, themselves*. Avoid nonstandard forms such as *hisself, ourself,* and *theirselves*.

30a Distinguish between compound subjects and compound objects: *she and I* vs. *her and me*.

Compound subjects or objects—those consisting of two or more nouns or pronouns—have the same case forms as they would if one noun or pronoun stood alone:

compound
subject
She and Novick discussed the proposal.

compound
object
The proposal disappointed her and him.

If you are in doubt about the correct form, try the test in the following box:

A test for case forms in compound constructions

1. **Identify a compound construction** (one connected by *and, but, or, nor*).

   [He, Him] and [I, me] won the prize.
   The prize went to [he, him] and [I, me].

(continued)

A test for case forms in compound constructions
(continued)

2. **Write a separate sentence for each part of the compound:**

   [He, Him] won the prize. [I, Me] won the prize.
   The prize went to [he, him]. The prize went to [I, me].

3. **Choose the pronouns that sound correct.**

   He won the prize. I won the prize. [Subjective.]
   The prize went to him. The prize went to me. [Objective.]

4. **Put the separate sentences back together.**

   He and I won the prize.
   The prize went to him and me.

30b Use the subjective case for subject complements:
It was she.

After a linking verb, a pronoun renaming the subject (a subject complement) should be in the subjective case:

subject complement
The ones who care most are she and Novick.

subject
complement
It was they whom the mayor appointed.

If this construction sounds stilted to you, use the more natural order: *She and Novick are the ones who care most. The mayor appointed them.*

> **Exercise 30.1** **Choosing between subjective and objective pronouns**
>
> In the following paragraph, select the appropriate subjective or objective pronoun from the pairs in brackets.
>
> **1** Jody and [I, me] had been hunting for jobs. **2** The best employees at our old company were [she, her] and [I, me], so [we, us] expected to find jobs quickly. **3** Between [she, her] and [I, me] the job search had lasted two months, and still it had barely begun. **4** Slowly, [she, her] and [I, me] stopped sharing leads. **5** It was obvious that Jody and [I, me] could not be as friendly as [we, us] had been.

┌─ **Key term** ─────────────────────────────────────
│
│ **linking verb** A verb, such as a form of *be*, that connects a subject and a
│ word that renames or describes the subject (subject complement): *They*
│ *are biologists.* (See p. 201.)
└──

30c The use of *who* vs. *whom* depends on the pronoun's function in its clause.

Use *who* where you would use *he* or *she*—all ending in vowels. Use *whom* where you would use *him* or *her*—all ending in consonants.

1 Questions

At the beginning of a question, use *who* for a subject and *whom* for an object:

subject ⟶
Who wrote the policy?   object ⟵
Whom does it affect?

To find the correct case of *who* in a question, use the following test:

▪ **Pose the question:**

[Who, Whom] makes that decision?
[Who, Whom] does one ask?

▪ **Answer the question, using a personal pronoun.** Choose the pronoun that sounds correct, and note its case:

[She, Her] makes that decision. She makes that decision. [Subjective.]
One asks [she, her]. One asks her. [Objective.]

▪ **Use the same case (*who* or *whom*) in the question:**

Who makes that decision? [Subjective.]
Whom does one ask? [Objective.]

2 Subordinate clauses

In a subordinate clause, use *who* or *whoever* for a subject, *whom* or *whomever* for an object.

subject ⟶
Give old clothes to whoever needs them.

object ⟵
I don't know whom the mayor appointed.

To determine which form to use, try the following test:

▪ **Locate the subordinate clause:**

Few people know [who, whom] they should ask.
They are unsure [who, whom] makes the decision.

─ **Key term** ─────────────────

subordinate clause A word group that contains a subject and a predicate and also begins with a subordinating word, such as *who, whom,* or *because.* (See pp. 208–09.)

- **Rewrite the subordinate clause as a separate sentence, substituting a personal pronoun for *who, whom*.** Choose the pronoun that sounds correct, and note its case:

They should ask [she, her]. They should ask her. [Objective.]
[She, her] makes the decision. She makes the decision. [Subjective.]

- **Use the same case (*who* or *whom*) in the subordinate clause:**

Few people know whom they should ask. [Objective.]
They are unsure who makes the decision. [Subjective.]

Note Don't let expressions such as *I think* and *she says* mislead you into using *whom* rather than *who* for the subject of a clause.

    subject ————⟍
He is the one who I think is best qualified.

To choose between *who* and *whom* in such constructions, delete the interrupting phrase so that you can see the true relation between parts: *He is the one who is best qualified.*

Exercise 30.2 Choosing between *who* and *whom*

In the following paragraph, select the appropriate pronoun from the pairs in brackets.

1 The school administrators suspended Jurgen, [who, whom] they suspected of setting the fire. **2** Jurgen had been complaining to other custodians, [who, whom] reported him. **3** He constantly complained of unfair treatment from [whoever, whomever] happened to be passing in the halls, including pupils. **4** "[Who, Whom] here has heard Mr. Jurgen's complaints?" the police asked. **5** "[Who, Whom] did he complain most about?"

Exercise 30.3 Sentence combining: *Who* versus *whom*

Combine each pair of sentences below into one sentence that contains a clause beginning with *who* or *whom*. Be sure to use the appropriate case form. You will have to add, delete, and rearrange words. Each item may have more than one possible answer.

Example:
James is the candidate. We think James deserves to win.
James is the candidate who we think deserves to win.

1 Some children have undetected hearing problems. These children may do poorly in school.
2 They may not hear important instructions and information from teachers. Teachers may speak softly.
3 Classmates may not be audible. The teacher calls on those classmates.
4 Some hearing-impaired children may work harder to overcome their disability. These children get a lot of encouragement at home.
5 Some hearing-impaired children may take refuge in fantasy friends. They can rely on these friends not to criticize or laugh.

30d Use the appropriate case in other constructions.

1 *We* or *us* with a noun

The choice of *we* or *us* before a noun depends on the use of the noun:

object of
preposition
Freezing weather is welcomed by us skaters.

subject
We skaters welcome freezing weather.

2 Pronoun in an appositive

In an appositive the case of a pronoun depends on the function of the word the appositive describes or identifies:

appositive
identifies object
The class elected two representatives, DeShawn and me.

appositive
identifies subject
Two representatives, DeShawn and I, were elected.

3 Pronoun after *than* or *as*

When a pronoun follows *than* or *as* in a comparison, the case of the pronoun indicates what words may have been omitted. A subjective pronoun must be the subject of the omitted verb:

subject
Some critics like Glass more than he [does].

An objective pronoun must be the object of the omitted verb:

object
Some critics like Glass more than [they like] him.

4 Subject and object of infinitive

Both the object *and* the subject of an infinitive are in the objective case:

subject
of infinitive
The school asked him to speak.

object
of infinitive
Students chose to invite him.

┌─ **Key terms**

appositive A noun or noun substitute that renames another noun immediately before it. (See p. 207.)

infinitive The plain form of the verb plus *to: to run.* (See p. 205.)

5 Case before a gerund

Ordinarily, use the possessive form of a pronoun or noun immediately before a gerund:

The coach disapproved of their lifting weights.

The coach's disapproving was a surprise.

Exercise 30.4 Choosing between subjective and objective pronouns

In the following paragraph, select the appropriate pronoun from the pairs in brackets.

1 Obtaining enough protein is important to [we, us] vegetarians. 2 Instead of obtaining protein from meat, [we, us] vegetarians get our protein from other sources such as eggs, cheese, nuts, and beans. 3 Some of [we, us] vegetarians also eat fish, an excellent source of protein, but vegans avoid all animal products, including eggs and cheese. 4 My friend Jeff claims to know only two vegans, Helena and [he, him]. 5 He believes that [we, us] vegetarians who eat fish and dairy products are not as truly vegetarian as [he, him].

Exercise 30.5 Revising: Pronoun case

Revise all inappropriate case forms in the following paragraph. If a sentence is correct as given, mark the number preceding it.

1 Written four thousand years ago, *The Epic of Gilgamesh* tells the story of Gilgamesh and his friendship with Enkidu. 2 Gilgamesh was a bored king who his people thought was too harsh. 3 Then he met Enkidu, a wild man whom had lived with the animals in the mountains. 4 Immediately, him and Gilgamesh wrestled to see whom was more powerful. 5 After hours of struggle, Enkidu admitted that Gilgamesh was stronger than him. 6 Now the friends needed adventures worthy of them, the two strongest men on earth. 7 Gilgamesh said, "Between you and I, mighty deeds will be accomplished, and our fame will be everlasting." 8 Among their acts, Enkidu and him defeated a giant bull, Humbaba, cut down the bull's cedar forests, and brought back the logs to Gilgamesh's treeless land. 9 Their heroism won them great praise from the people. 10 When Enkidu died, Gilgamesh mourned his death, realizing that no one had been a better friend than him. 11 When Gilgamesh himself died many years later, his people raised a monument praising Enkidu and he for their friendship and their mighty deeds of courage.

Key term

gerund The *-ing* form of a verb used as a noun: *Running is fun.* (See p. 205.)

31 Agreement of Pronoun and Antecedent

The **antecedent** of a pronoun is the noun or other pronoun to which the pronoun refers:

Homeowners fret over their tax bills.
antecedent   pronoun

Its constant increases make the tax bill a dreaded document.
pronoun   antecedent

For clarity, a pronoun should agree with its antecedent in person, number, and gender.

Grammar checkers A grammar checker cannot help you with agreement between pronoun and antecedent because it cannot recognize the intended relation between the two.

CULTURE LANGUAGE The gender of a pronoun should match its antecedent, not a noun that the pronoun may modify: *Sara Young invited her* [not *his*] *son.* Also, English nouns have only neuter gender unless they specifically refer to males or females. Thus nouns such as *book, table, sun,* and *earth* take the pronoun *it.*

31a Antecedents joined by *and* usually take plural pronouns.

Mr. Bartos and I cannot settle our dispute.

The dean and my adviser have offered their help.

Key terms

	Number	
Person	**Singular**	**Plural**
First	*I*	*we*
Second	*you*	*you*
Third	*he, she, it,*	*they,*
	indefinite pronouns,	plural nouns
	singular nouns	
Gender		
Masculine	*he,* nouns naming males	
Feminine	*she,* nouns naming females	
Neuter	*it,* all other nouns	

---

mycomplab

Visit *mycomplab.com* for more resources and exercises on pronoun-antecedent agreement.

Exceptions When the compound antecedent refers to a single idea, person, or thing, then the pronoun is singular:

My friend and adviser offered her help.

When the compound antecedent follows *each* or *every*, the pronoun is singular:

Every girl and woman took her seat.

31b When parts of an antecedent are joined by *or* or *nor*, the pronoun agrees with the nearer part.

Tenants or owners must present their grievances.

Either the tenant or the owner will have her way.

When one subject is plural and the other singular, the sentence will be awkward unless you put the plural subject second:

Awkward   Neither the tenants nor the owner has yet made her case.

Revised   Neither the owner nor the tenants have yet made their case.

31c With *everyone, person,* and other indefinite words, use a singular or plural pronoun as appropriate.

Indefinite words—indefinite pronouns and generic nouns—do not refer to any specific person or thing. Most indefinite pronouns and all generic nouns are singular in meaning. When they serve as antecedents of pronouns, the pronouns should be singular:

Everyone on the women's team now has her own locker.
indefinite
pronoun

Key terms

indefinite pronoun A pronoun that does not refer to a specific person or thing:

Singular			*Singular or plural*	*Plural*
anybody	everyone	no one	all	both
anyone	everything	nothing	any	few
anything	much	one	more	many
each	neither	somebody	most	several
either	nobody	someone	some	
everybody	none	something		

generic noun A singular noun such as *person* and *student* when it refers to a typical member of a group, not to a particular individual.

Every person on the women's team now has her own locker.
generic noun

Five indefinite pronouns—*all, any, more, most, some*—may be singular or plural in meaning depending on what they refer to:

Few women athletes had changing spaces, so most had to change in their rooms.

Most of the changing space was dismal, its color a drab olive green.

Four indefinite pronouns—*both, few, many, several*—are always plural in meaning:

Few realize how their athletic facilities have changed.

Most agreement problems arise with the singular indefinite words. We often use these words to mean "many" or "all" rather than "one" and then refer to them with plural pronouns, as in *Everyone has their own locker.* Often, too, we mean indefinite words to include both masculine and feminine genders and thus resort to *they* instead of the **generic** *he*—the masculine pronoun referring to both genders, as in *Everyone deserves his privacy.* (For more on the generic *he*, which many readers view as sexist, see **3** p. 168.) To achieve agreement in such cases, you have the options listed in the following box.

Ways to correct agreement with indefinite words

■ **Change the indefinite word to a plural, and use a plural pronoun to match:**

Faulty   Every athlete deserves their privacy.
Revised **Athletes** deserve their privacy.

■ **Rewrite the sentence to omit the pronoun:**

Faulty   Everyone is entitled to their own locker.
Revised Everyone is entitled to **a** locker.

■ **Use *he or she* (*him or her, his or her*) to refer to the indefinite word:**

Faulty   Now everyone has their private space.
Revised Now everyone has **his or her** private space.

However, used more than once in several sentences, *he or she* quickly becomes awkward. (Many readers do not accept the alternative *he/she*.) Using the plural or omitting the pronoun will usually correct agreement problems and create more readable sentences.

31d Collective nouns such as *team* take singular or plural pronouns depending on meaning.

Use a singular pronoun with a collective noun when referring to the group as a unit:

The committee voted to disband itself.

When referring to the individual members of the group, use a plural pronoun:

The old team have gone their separate ways.

CULTURE LANGUAGE In standard American English, collective nouns that are noncount nouns (they don't form plurals) usually take singular pronouns: *The mail sits in its own basket.* A few noncount nouns take plural pronouns, including *clergy, military, police, the rich,* and *the poor: The police support their unions.*

Exercise 31.1 Revising: Pronoun-antecedent agreement

Revise the following sentences so that pronouns and their antecedents agree in person and number. Try to avoid the generic *he* (see the previous page). If you change the subject of a sentence, be sure to change the verb as necessary for agreement. Mark the number preceding any sentence that is correct as given.

Example:
Each of the Boudreaus' children brought their laundry home at Thanksgiving.

All of the Boudreaus' children brought their laundry home at Thanksgiving. *Or:* Each of the Boudreaus' children brought his or her laundry home at Thanksgiving.

1 Each girl raised in a Mexican American family in the Rio Grande Valley of Texas hopes that one day they will be given a *quinceañera* party for their fifteenth birthday. 2 Such celebrations are very expensive because it entails a religious service followed by a huge party. 3 A girl's immediate family, unless they are wealthy, cannot afford the party by themselves. 4 The parents will ask each close friend or relative if they can help with the preparations. 5 Surrounded by her family and attended by her friends and their escorts, the *quinceañera* is introduced as a young woman eligible for Mexican American society.

Key term

collective noun A noun with singular form that names a group of individuals or things—for instance, *army, audience, committee, crowd, family, group, team.*

Exercise 31.2 Revising: Pronoun-antecedent agreement

Revise the following sentences so that pronouns and their antecedents agree in person and number. Try to avoid the generic *he* (see p. 255). If you change the subject of a sentence, be sure to change the verb as necessary for agreement. Mark the number preceding any sentence that is correct as given.

1 Despite their extensive research and experience, neither child psychologists nor parents have yet figured out how children become who they are. 2 Of course, the family has a tremendous influence on the development of a child in their midst. 3 Each member of the immediate family exerts their own unique pull on the child. 4 Other relatives, teachers, and friends can also affect the child's view of the world and of themselves. 5 The workings of genetics also strongly influence the child, but it may never be fully understood. 6 The psychology community cannot agree in its views of whether nurture or nature is more important in a child's development. 7 Another debated issue is whether the child's emotional development or their intellectual development is more central. 8 Just about everyone has their strong opinion on these issues, often backed up by evidence. 9 Neither the popular press nor scholarly journals devote much of their space to the wholeness of the child.

32 Reference of Pronoun to Antecedent

A pronoun should refer clearly to its **antecedent,** the noun it substitutes for. Otherwise, readers will have difficulty grasping the pronoun's meaning.

Grammar checkers A grammar checker cannot recognize unclear pronoun reference. For instance, a checker did not flag any of the confusing examples on the next two pages.

CULTURE LANGUAGE In standard American English, a pronoun needs a clear antecedent nearby, but don't use both a pronoun and its antecedent as the subject of the same clause: *Jim* [not *Jim he*] *told Mark to go alone.* (See also p. 293.)

my**comp**lab

Visit *mycomplab.com* for more resources and exercises on pronoun reference.

32a Make a pronoun refer clearly to one antecedent.

When either of two nouns can be a pronoun's antecedent, the reference will not be clear.

Confusing   Emily Dickinson is sometimes compared with Jane Austen, but she was quite different.

Revise such a sentence in one of two ways:

■ **Replace the pronoun with the appropriate noun.**

Clear   Emily Dickinson is sometimes compared with Jane Austen, but Dickinson [or Austen] was quite different.

■ **Avoid repetition by rewriting the sentence.** If you use the pronoun, make sure it has only one possible antecedent.

Clear   Despite occasional comparison, Emily Dickinson and Jane Austen were quite different.

Clear   Though sometimes compared with her, Emily Dickinson was quite different from Jane Austen.

32b Place a pronoun close enough to its antecedent to ensure clarity.

A clause beginning with *who, which,* or *that* should generally fall immediately after the word to which it refers.

Confusing   Jody found a lamp in the attic that her aunt had used.

Clear   In the attic Jody found a lamp that her aunt had used.

32c Make a pronoun refer to a specific antecedent, not an implied one.

A pronoun should refer to a specific noun or other pronoun. A reader can only guess at the meaning of a pronoun when its antecedent is implied by the context, not stated outright.

1 Vague *this, that, which,* or *it*

This, that, which, or *it* should refer to a specific noun, not to a whole word group expressing an idea or situation.

Confusing   The British knew little of the American countryside, and they had no experience with the colonists' guerrilla tactics. This gave the colonists an advantage.

Clear	The British knew little of the American countryside, and they had no experience with the colonists' guerrilla tactics. This <u>ignorance and inexperience</u> gave the colonists an advantage.

2 Indefinite antecedents with *it* and *they*

It and *they* should have definite noun antecedents. Rewrite the sentence if the antecedent is missing.

Confusing	In Chapter 4 of this book it describes the early flights of the Wright brothers.
Clear	<u>Chapter 4</u> of this book describes the early flights of the Wright brothers.

Confusing	Even in reality TV shows, they present a false picture of life.
Clear	Even reality TV <u>shows</u> present a false picture of life.

3 Implied nouns

A noun may be implied in some other word or phrase, as *happiness* is implied in *happy*, *driver* is implied in *drive*, and *mother* is implied in *mother's*. But a pronoun cannot refer clearly to an implied noun, only to a specific, stated one.

Confusing	Cohen's report brought her a lawsuit.
Clear	Cohen was sued over her report.

Confusing	Her reports on psychological development generally go unnoticed outside it.
Clear	Her reports on psychological development generally go unnoticed outside <u>the field</u>.

Exercise 32.1 Revising: Pronoun reference

Rewrite the following paragraph to eliminate unclear pronoun reference. If you use a pronoun in your revision, be sure that it refers to only one antecedent and that it falls close enough to its antecedent to ensure clarity.

1 There is a difference between the heroes of modern times and the heroes of earlier times: they have flaws in their characters. 2 Despite their imperfections, sports fans still admire Pete Rose, Babe Ruth, and Joe Namath. 3 Fans liked Rose for having his young son serve as batboy when he was in Cincinnati. 4. The reputation Rose earned as a gambler and tax evader may overshadow his reputation as a ballplayer, but it will survive. 5 He amassed an unequaled record as a hitter, using his bat to do things no one has ever done, and it remains even though Rose was banned from baseball.

Exercise 32.2 Revising: Pronoun reference

Revise the following paragraph as needed so that pronouns refer to specific, appropriate antecedents. If a sentence is correct as given, mark the number preceding it.

1 In Charlotte Brontë's *Jane Eyre*, she is a shy young woman who takes a job as a governess. 2 Her employer, a rude, brooding man named Rochester, lives in a mysterious mansion on the English moors, which contributes a strange quality to Jane's experience. 3 Stranger still are the fires, eerie noises, and other unexplained happenings in the house; but Rochester refuses to discuss this. 4 Eventually, they fall in love, but the day they are to marry, she learns that he has a wife hidden in the house. 5 She is hopelessly insane and violent and must be guarded at all times, which explains his strange behavior. 6 Heartbroken, Jane leaves the moors, and many years pass before they are reunited.

32d Use *you* only to mean "you, the reader."

You should clearly mean "you, the reader." The context must be appropriate for such a meaning:

Inappropriate	In the fourteenth century you had to struggle simply to survive.
Revised	In the fourteenth century one [or a person] had to struggle simply to survive.

Writers sometimes drift into *you* because *one, a person,* or a similar indefinite word can be difficult to sustain. Sentence after sentence, the indefinite word may sound stuffy, and it requires *he* or *he or she* for pronoun-antecedent agreement (see pp. 254–56). To avoid these problems, try using plural nouns and pronouns:

Original	In the fourteenth century one had to struggle simply to survive.
Revised	In the fourteenth century people had to struggle simply to survive.

32e Keep pronouns consistent.

Within a sentence or a group of related sentences, pronouns should be consistent. Partly, consistency comes from making pronouns and their antecedents agree (see Chapter 31). In addition, the pronouns within a passage should match each other.

Inconsistent	One finds when reading that your concentration improves with practice, so that I now comprehend more in less time.

Revised   I find when reading that <u>my</u> concentration improves with practice, so that <u>I</u> now comprehend more in less time.

Exercise 32.3   Revising: Consistency in pronouns

Revise the following paragraph to make pronouns consistent.

    1 When a taxpayer is waiting to receive a tax refund from the Internal Revenue Service, you begin to notice what time the mail carrier arrives. **2** If the taxpayer does not receive a refund check within six weeks of filing a return, they may not have followed the rules of the IRS. **3** For instance, if a taxpayer does not include a Social Security number on a return, you will have to wait for a refund. **4** If one makes errors on the tax form, they will certainly have to wait and they might be audited, delaying a refund for months or longer. **5** A refund may be held up even if you file on time, because returns received close to the April 15 deadline swamp the IRS.

Exercise 32.4   Revising: Pronoun reference

Revise the following paragraph as needed so that pronouns are consistent and refer to specific, appropriate antecedents.

    1 "Life begins at forty" is a cliché many people live by, and this may or may not be true. **2** Whether one agrees or not with the cliché, you can cite many examples of people whose public lives began at forty. **3** For instance, when she was forty, Pearl Buck's novel *The Good Earth* won the Pulitzer Prize. **4** Kenneth Kanuda, past president of Zambia, was elected to it in 1964, when he was forty. **5** Catherine I became Empress of Russia at age forty, more feared than loved by them. **6** Paul Revere at forty made his famous ride to warn American revolutionary leaders that the British were going to arrest them, which gave the colonists time to prepare for battle. **7** Forty-year-old Nancy Astor joined the British House of Commons in 1919 as its first female member, though they did not welcome her. **8** In 610 CE, Muhammad, age forty, began to have visions that became the foundation of the Muslim faith and still inspire millions of people to become one.

Modifiers

Modifiers describe or limit other words in a sentence. They are adjectives, adverbs, or word groups serving as adjectives or adverbs. This section shows how to solve problems in the forms of modifiers (Chapter 33) and in their relation to the rest of the sentence (34).

33 Adjectives and Adverbs

Adjectives modify nouns (*happy child*) and pronouns (*special someone*). **Adverbs** modify verbs (*almost see*), adjectives (*very happy*), other adverbs (*not very*), and whole word groups (*Otherwise, I'll go*). The only way to tell whether a modifier should be an adjective or an adverb is to determine its function in the sentence.

Grammar checkers A grammar checker will spot some but not all problems with misused adjectives and adverbs. For instance, a checker flagged *Some children suffer bad* and *Jenny did not feel nothing*. But it did not flag *Educating children good should be everyone's focus.*

CULTURE LANGUAGE In standard American English, an adjective does not change along with the noun it modifies to show plural number: *square* [not *squares*] *spaces*. Only nouns form plurals.

33a Use adjectives only to modify nouns and pronouns.

Do not use adjectives instead of adverbs to modify verbs, adverbs, or other adjectives:

Faulty	Educating children good should be everyone's focus.
Revised	Educating children well should be everyone's focus.
Faulty	Some children suffer bad.
Revised	Some children suffer badly.

CULTURE LANGUAGE To negate a verb or an adjective, use the adverb *not*.

Visit *mycomplab.com* for more resources and exercises
262 on adjectives and adverbs.

They are not learning. They are not stupid.

To negate a noun, use the adjective *no*.

No child should fail to read.

33b Use an adjective after a linking verb to modify the subject. Use an adverb to modify a verb.

Some verbs may or may not be linking verbs, depending on their meaning in the sentence. When the word after the verb modifies the subject, the verb is linking and the word should be an adjective: *He looked happy*. When the word modifies the verb, however, it should be an adverb: *He looked carefully*.

Two word pairs are especially tricky. One is *bad* and *badly*:

The weather grew bad.
　　linking　adjective
　　verb

She felt bad.
　　linking　adjective
　　verb

Flowers grow badly in such soil.
　　verb　adverb

The other pair is *good* and *well*. *Good* serves only as an adjective. *Well* may serve as an adverb with a host of meanings or as an adjective meaning only "fit" or "healthy."

Decker trained well.
　　verb　adverb

She felt well.
　　linking　adjective
　　verb

Her health was good.
　　linking　adjective
　　verb

Exercise 33.1　Revising: Adjectives and adverbs

Revise the following paragraph to use adjectives and adverbs appropriately. Mark the number preceding any sentence that is correct as given.

1 The eighteenth-century essayist Samuel Johnson fared bad in his early life. 2 His family was poor, his hearing was weak, and he received little formal education. 3 After failing as a schoolmaster, Johnson moved to London, where he was finally taken serious as a critic and dictionary maker. 4 Johnson was real surprised when he received a pension from King George III. 5 Thinking about his meeting with the king, Johnson felt proudly that he had not behaved badly in the presence of the king. 6 Now, after living cheap for over twenty years, Johnson finally had enough money to eat and dress good. 7 He spent his time writing and living stylish.

┌ **Key term** ─────────────────────────────────

linking verb A verb that connects a subject and a word that describes the subject: *They are golfers.* Linking verbs include *look, sound, feel, appear, seem, become,* and forms of *be.* (See p. 201.)

33c Use the comparative and superlative forms of adjectives and adverbs appropriately.

Adjectives and adverbs can show degrees of quality or amount with the endings *-er* and *-est* or with the words *more* and *most* or *less* and *least*. Most modifiers have three forms:

Positive The basic form listed in the dictionary	**Comparative** A greater or lesser degree of the quality	**Superlative** The greatest or least degree of the quality
Adjectives		
red	redder	reddest
awful	more/less awful	most/least awful
Adverbs		
soon	sooner	soonest
quickly	more/less quickly	most/least quickly

If sound alone does not tell you whether to use *-er/-est* or *more/most,* consult a dictionary. If the endings can be used, the dictionary will list them. Otherwise, use *more* or *most.*

1 Irregular adjectives and adverbs

Irregular modifiers change the spelling of their positive form to show comparative and superlative degrees.

Positive	**Comparative**	**Superlative**
Adjectives		
good	better	best
bad	worse	worst
little	littler, less	littlest, least
many ⎫		
some ⎬	more	most
much ⎭		
Adverbs		
well	better	best
badly	worse	worst

2 Double comparisons

A double comparative or double superlative combines the *-er* or *-est* ending with the word *more* or *most*. It is redundant.

Chang was the wisest [not most wisest] person in town.
He was smarter [not more smarter] than anyone else.

3 Logical comparisons

Absolute modifiers

Some adjectives and adverbs cannot logically be compared—for instance, *perfect, unique, dead, impossible, infinite.* These absolute words can be preceded by adverbs like *nearly* or *almost* that mean "approaching," but they cannot logically be modified by *more* or *most* (as in *most perfect*).

| Not | He was the <u>most unique</u> teacher we had. |
| But | He was a <u>unique</u> teacher. |

Completeness

To be logical, a comparison must also be complete in the following ways:

■ **The comparison must state a relation fully enough for clarity.**

Unclear	Carmakers worry about their industry more than environmentalists.
Clear	Carmakers worry about their industry more than environmentalists <u>do</u>.
Clear	Carmakers worry about their industry more than <u>they worry about</u> environmentalists.

■ **The items being compared should in fact be comparable.**

| Illogical | The cost of a hybrid car can be greater than a gasoline-powered car. [Illogically compares a cost and a car.] |
| Revised | The cost of a hybrid car can be greater than <u>the cost of</u> [or <u>that of</u>] a gasoline-powered car. |

See also **3** p. 156 on parallelism with comparisons.

Any versus *any other*

Use *any other* when comparing something with others in the same group. Use *any* when comparing something with others in a different group.

Illogical	Los Angeles is larger than <u>any</u> city in California. [Since Los Angeles is itself a city in California, the sentence seems to say that Los Angeles is larger than itself.]
Revised	Los Angeles is larger than <u>any other</u> city in California.
Illogical	Los Angeles is larger than <u>any other</u> city in Canada. [The cities in Canada constitute a group to which Los Angeles does not belong.]
Revised	Los Angeles is larger than <u>any</u> city in Canada.

Exercise 33.2 Using comparatives and superlatives

Write the comparative and superlative forms of each adjective or adverb below. Then use all three forms in your own sentences.

Example:
heavy: heavier (comparative), heaviest (superlative)

The barbells were too heavy for me. The trunk was heavier than I expected. Joe Clark was the heaviest person on the team.

1 badly	3 good	5 understanding
2 steady	4 well	

Exercise 33.3 **Revising: Comparisons**

Revise the following paragraph as needed to correct the forms of adjectives and adverbs and to make comparisons logical. Mark the number preceding any sentence that is correct as given.

1 The Brontë sisters—Charlotte, Emily, and Anne—are among the more interesting literary families in English history. 2 Of the three novelists, Charlotte was the older. 3 Critics sometimes dispute whether Charlotte or Emily was more talented. 4 For some readers, Emily's *Wuthering Heights* is among the most saddest stories ever written. 5 For other readers, Charlotte's *Jane Eyre* made more significant contributions to literature than Emily.

33d Watch for double negatives.

In a **double negative** two negative words such as *no, not, none, neither, barely, hardly,* or *scarcely* cancel each other out. Some double negatives are intentional: for instance, *She was not unhappy* indicates with understatement that she was indeed happy. But most double negatives say the opposite of what is intended: *Jenny did not feel nothing* asserts that Jenny felt other than nothing, or something. For the opposite meaning, one of the negatives must be eliminated (*She felt nothing*) or one of them must be changed to a positive (*She did not feel anything*).

Faulty	The IRS cannot hardly audit all tax returns. None of its audits never touch many cheaters.
Revised	The IRS cannot audit all tax returns. Its audits never touch many cheaters.

Exercise 33.4 **Revising: Double negatives**

Identify and revise the double negatives in the following paragraph. Each error may have more than one correct revision. Mark the number preceding any sentence that is correct as given.

1 Interest in books about the founding of the United States is not hardly consistent among Americans: it seems to vary with the national mood. 2 Americans show barely any interest in books about the founders when things are going well in the United States. 3 However, when Americans can't hardly agree on major issues, sales of books about the Revolutionary War era increase. 4 During such periods, one cannot go to no bookstore without seeing several new volumes about John

Adams, Thomas Jefferson, and other founders. 5 When Americans feel they don't have nothing in common, their increased interest in the early leaders may reflect a desire for unity.

33e Distinguish between present and past participles as adjectives.

Both present participles and past participles may serve as adjectives: *a burning building, a burned building*. As in the examples, the two participles usually differ in the time they indicate.

But some present and past participles—those derived from verbs expressing feeling—can have altogether different meanings. The present participle modifies something that causes the feeling: *That was a frightening storm* (the storm frightens). The past participle modifies something that experiences the feeling: *They quieted the frightened horses* (the horses feel fright).

The following participles are among those likely to be confused:

amazing/amazed	fascinating/fascinated
amusing/amused	frightening/frightened
annoying/annoyed	frustrating/frustrated
astonishing/astonished	interesting/interested
boring/bored	pleasing/pleased
confusing/confused	satisfying/satisfied
depressing/depressed	shocking/shocked
embarrassing/embarrassed	surprising/surprised
exciting/excited	tiring/tired
exhausting/exhausted	worrying/worried

Exercise 33.5 Revising: Present and past participles

Revise the adjectives in the following paragraph as needed to distinguish between present and past participles. Mark the number preceding any sentence that is correct as given.

1 Many critics found Alice Walker's novel *The Color Purple* to be a fascinated book, though the reviews were mixed. 2 One otherwise excited critic wished that Walker had deleted the scenes set in Africa. 3 Another critic argued that although the book contained many depressed episodes, the overall effect was pleased. 4 Responding to other readers who had found the book annoyed, this critic pointed out its

---

Key terms

present participle The *-ing* form of a verb: *flying, writing*. (See p. 192.)

past participle The *-d* or *-ed* form of a regular verb: *slipped, walked*. Most irregular verbs have distinctive past participles, such as *eaten* or *swum*. (See p. 192.)

many surprising qualities. 5 In the end most critics agreed that the book was a pleased novel about the struggles of an African American woman. 6 For many, the movie made from the book was less interested. 7 Some viewers found the entire movie irritated, criticizing it for relying on tired feelings. 8 Other viewers thought that Whoopi Goldberg did an amazed job of creating Celie, the central character. 9 Some critics congratulated Steven Spielberg, the director, for creating a fulfilling movie.

33f | Use *a, an, the,* and other determiners appropriately.

Determiners are special kinds of adjectives that mark nouns because they always precede nouns. Some common determiners are *a, an,* and *the* (called **articles**) and *my, their, whose, this, these, those, one, some,* and *any.*

Native speakers of standard American English can rely on their intuition when using determiners, but speakers of other languages and dialects often have difficulty with them. In standard American English, the use of determiners depends on the context they appear in and the kind of noun they precede:

- A *proper noun* names a particular person, place, or thing and begins with a capital letter: *February, Joe Allen, Red River.* Most proper nouns are not preceded by determiners.

- A *count noun* names something that is countable in English and can form a plural: *girl/girls, apple/apples, child/children.* A singular count noun is always preceded by a determiner; a plural count noun sometimes is.

- A *noncount noun* names something not usually considered countable in English, and so it does not form a plural. A noncount noun is sometimes preceded by a determiner. Here is a sample of noncount nouns, sorted into groups by meaning:

Abstractions: confidence, democracy, education, equality, evidence, health, information, intelligence, knowledge, luxury, peace, pollution, research, success, supervision, truth, wealth, work

Food and drink: bread, candy, cereal, flour, meat, milk, salt, water, wine

Emotions: anger, courage, happiness, hate, joy, love, respect, satisfaction

Natural events and substances: air, blood, dirt, gasoline, gold, hair, heat, ice, oil, oxygen, rain, silver, smoke, weather, wood

Groups: clergy, clothing, equipment, furniture, garbage, jewelry, junk, legislation, machinery, mail, military, money, police, vocabulary

Fields of study: architecture, accounting, biology, business, chemistry, engineering, literature, psychology, science

A dictionary of English as a second language will tell you whether a noun is a count noun, a noncount noun, or both. (See 3 p. 171 for recommended dictionaries.)

Note Many nouns are sometimes count nouns and sometimes noncount nouns:

> The library has a room for readers. [*Room* is a count noun meaning "walled area."]
>
> The library has room for reading. [*Room* is a noncount noun meaning "space."]

Grammar checkers Partly because the same noun may fall into different groups, a grammar checker is an unreliable guide to missing or misused articles and other determiners. For instance, a checker flagged the omitted *a* before *Scientist* in *Scientist developed new processes;* it did not flag the omitted *a* before *new* in *A scientist developed new process;* and it mistakenly flagged the correctly omitted article *the* before *Vegetation* in *Vegetation suffers from drought.*

1 *A, an,* and *the*

With singular count nouns

A or *an* precedes a singular count noun when the reader does not already know its identity, usually because you have not mentioned it before:

> A scientist in our chemistry department developed a process to strengthen metals. [*Scientist* and *process* are being introduced for the first time.]

The precedes a singular count noun that has a specific identity for the reader, for one of the following reasons:

■ **You have mentioned the noun before:**

> A scientist in our chemistry department developed a process to strengthen metals. The scientist patented the process. [*Scientist* and *process* were identified in the preceding sentence.]

■ **You identify the noun immediately before or after you state it:**

> The most productive laboratory is the research center in the chemistry department. [*Most productive* identifies *laboratory*. *In the chemistry department* identifies *research center*. And *chemistry department* is a shared facility—see the next page.]

■ **The noun names something unique—the only one in existence:**

> The sun rises in the east. [*Sun* and *east* are unique.]

■ **The noun names an institution or facility that is shared by the community of readers:**

Many men and women aspire to the presidency. [*Presidency* is a shared institution.]

The cell phone has changed business communication. [*Cell phone* is a shared facility.]

The is not used before a singular noun that names a general category:

Wordsworth's poetry shows his love of nature [not the nature].
General Sherman said that war is hell. [*War* names a general category.]
The war in Iraq left many wounded. [*War* names a specific war.]

With plural count nouns

A or *an* never precedes a plural noun. *The* does not precede a plural noun that names a general category. *The* does precede a plural noun that names specific representatives of a category.

Men and women are different. [*Men* and *women* name general categories.]

The women formed a team. [*Women* refers to specific people.]

With noncount nouns

A or *an* never precedes a noncount noun. *The* does precede a noncount noun that names specific representatives of a general category.

Vegetation suffers from drought. [*Vegetation* names a general category.]

The vegetation in the park withered or died. [*Vegetation* refers to specific plants.]

With proper nouns

A or *an* never precedes a proper noun. *The* generally does not precede proper nouns.

Garcia lives in Boulder.

There are exceptions, however. For instance, we generally use *the* before plural proper nouns (*the Murphys, the Boston Celtics*) and before the names of groups and organizations (*the Department of Justice, the Sierra Club*), ships (*the Lusitania*), oceans (*the Pacific*), mountain ranges (*the Alps*), regions (*the Middle East*), rivers (*the Mississippi*), and some countries (*the United States, the Netherlands*).

Exercise 33.6 Revising: *A, an,* and *the*

In the following paragraph, identify and revise errors in the use of *a, an,* and *the* with count, noncount, and proper nouns. Mark the number preceding any sentence that is correct as given.

1 A recent court case has moved some Native Americans to observe that a lot of people want to be the Native Americans now that the tribes have something of the value—namely, gambling casinos. 2 The man named Stephen Jones claimed to be the Native American in order to open casino in the New York's Catskills region. 3 However, the documents Jones provided to support the claim were questioned by a US Bureau of Indian Affairs. 4 On death certificate for Jones's grandfather, the W for *white* had been changed to an I for *Indian* with the ballpoint pen. 5 The ballpoint pens had not been invented until after a grandfather's death. 6 In addition, Jones provided the 1845 census of Indians in New York, and someone had recently added Jones's great-grandfather's name to the list of Indian household heads. 7 Jones, who called himself the Chief Golden Eagle, pled guilty to filing false documents with Bureau of Indian Affairs.

2 | Other determiners

The uses of English determiners besides articles also depend on context and kind of noun. The following determiners may be used as indicated with singular count nouns, plural count nouns, or noncount nouns.

With any kind of noun (singular count, plural count, noncount)

my, our, your, his, her, its, their, possessive nouns (*boy's, boys'*)
whose, which(ever), what(ever)
some, any, the other
no

Their account is overdrawn. [Singular count.]
Their funds are low. [Plural count.]
Their money is running out. [Noncount.]

Only with singular nouns (count and noncount)

this, that

This account has some money. [Count.]
That information may help. [Noncount.]

Only with noncount nouns and plural count nouns

most, enough, other, such, all, all of the, a lot of

Most funds are committed. [Plural count.]
Most money is needed elsewhere. [Noncount.]

Only with singular count nouns

> *one, every, each, either, neither, another*

> <u>One</u> car must be sold. [Singular count.]

Only with plural count nouns

> *these, those*
> *both, many, few, a few, fewer, fewest, several*
> *two, three,* and so forth

> <u>Two</u> cars are unnecessary. [Plural count.]

> **Note** *Few* means "not many" or "not enough." *A few* means "some" or "a small but sufficient quantity."

> <u>Few</u> committee members came to the meeting.
> <u>A few</u> members can keep the committee going.

Do not use *much* with a plural count noun.

> <u>Many</u> [not <u>Much</u>] members want to help.

Only with noncount nouns

> *much, more, little, a little, less, least, a large amount of*

> <u>Less</u> luxury is in order. [Noncount.]

> **Note** *Little* means "not many" or "not enough." *A little* means "some" or "a small but sufficient quantity."

> <u>Little</u> time remains before the conference.
> The members need <u>a little</u> help from their colleagues.

Do not use *many* with a noncount noun.

> <u>Much</u> [not <u>Many</u>] work remains.

Exercise 33.7 Revising: Determiners

In the following paragraph, identify and revise missing or incorrect determiners. Mark the number preceding any sentence that is correct as given.

> 1 Much people love to swim for exercise or just plain fun. 2 Few swimmers, however, are aware of the possible danger of sharing their swimming spot with others. 3 These danger has increased in recent years because of dramatic rise in outbreaks of the parasite cryptosporidium. 4 Swallowing even little water containing cryptosporidium can make anyone sick. 5 Chlorine is used in nearly every public pools to kill parasites, but the chlorine takes six or seven days to kill cryptosporidium. 6 Most health authorities advise people to limit their swimming in public pools and to drink as little of the pool water as possible.

Exercise 33.8 Revising: Adjectives and adverbs

Revise the following paragraph to correct errors in the use of adjectives and adverbs.

1 Americans often argue about which professional sport is better: basketball, football, or baseball. 2 Basketball fans contend that their sport offers more action because the players are constant running and shooting. 3 Because it is played indoors in relative small arenas, basketball allows fans to be more closer to the action than the other sports. 4 Football fanatics say they don't hardly stop yelling once the game begins. 5 They cheer when their team executes a complicated play good. 6 They roar more louder when the defense stops the opponents in a goal-line stand. 7 They yell loudest when a fullback crashes in for a score. 8 In contrast, the supporters of baseball believe that it is the better sport. 9 It combines the one-on-one duel of pitcher and batter struggling valiant with the tight teamwork of double and triple plays. 10 Because the game is played slow and careful, fans can analyze and discuss the manager's strategy.

34 Misplaced and Dangling Modifiers

The arrangement of words in a sentence is an important clue to their relationships. Modifiers will be unclear if readers can't connect them to the words they modify.

Grammar checkers A grammar checker cannot recognize most problems with modifiers. For instance, a checker failed to flag the misplaced modifiers in *Gasoline high prices affect usually car sales* or the dangling modifier in *The vandalism was visible passing the building.*

34a Reposition misplaced modifiers.

A **misplaced modifier** falls in the wrong place in a sentence. It is usually awkward or confusing. It may even be unintentionally funny.

1 Clear placement

Readers tend to link a modifier to the nearest word it could modify. Any other placement can link the modifier to the wrong word.

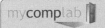

mycomplab

Visit *mycomplab.com* for more resources and exercises on misplaced and dangling modifiers.

Confusing	He served steak to the men on paper plates.
Clear	He served the men steak on paper plates.

Confusing	According to the police, many dogs are killed by automobiles and trucks roaming unleashed.
Clear	According to the police, many dogs roaming unleashed are killed by automobiles and trucks.

2 *Only* and other limiting modifiers

Limiting modifiers include *almost, even, exactly, hardly, just, merely, nearly, only, scarcely,* and *simply*. For clarity place such a modifier immediately before the word or word group you intend it to limit.

Unclear	The archaeologist only found the skull on her last dig.
Clear	The archaeologist found only the skull on her last dig.
Clear	The archaeologist found the skull only on her last dig.

3 Adverbs with grammatical units

Adverbs can often move around in sentences, but some will be awkward if they interrupt certain grammatical units:

■ **A long adverb stops the flow from subject to verb.**

	subject ┌──── adverb ────┐ verb
Awkward	The city, after the hurricane, began massive rebuilding.

	┌──── adverb ────┐ subject verb
Revised	After the hurricane, the city began massive rebuilding.

■ **Any adverb is awkward between a verb and its direct object.**

	┌──── verb ────┐ adverb object
Awkward	The hurricane had damaged badly many homes in the city.

	┌── verb ──┐ object
Revised	The hurricane had badly damaged many homes in the city.
	adverb

Key terms

adverb A word or word group that describes a verb, adjective, other adverb, or whole word group, specifying how, when, where, or to what extent: *quickly see, solid like a boulder.*

direct object The receiver of the verb's action: *The car hit a tree.* (See p. 201.)

- A *split infinitive*—an adverb placed between *to* and the verb—annoys many readers.

ᵧ infinitive ᵧ

Awkward   The weather service expected temperatures to <u>not</u> rise.

infinitive

Revised   The weather service expected temperatures <u>not</u> to rise.

A split infinitive may sometimes be natural and preferable, though it may still bother some readers.

⟋—infinitive—⟍

Several US industries expect to <u>more than</u> triple their use of robots.

Here the split infinitive is more economical than the alternatives, such as *Several US industries expect to increase their use of robots by more than three times.*

- A long adverb is usually awkward inside a verb phrase.

helping
verb ┌————— adverb —————

Awkward   People who have osteoporosis can, by increasing their daily

————————————————————┐ main verb

intake of calcium and vitamin D, improve their bone density.

┌——————————— adverb ———————————————┐

Revised   By increasing their daily intake of calcium and vitamin D,

verb phrase

people who have osteoporosis can improve their bone density.

CULTURE LANGUAGE In a question, place a one-word adverb after the first helping verb and subject:

helping   rest of
verb   subject   adverb   verb phrase
Will spacecraft <u>ever</u> be able to leave the solar system?

4 Other adverb positions

Placements of a few adverbs can be difficult for nonnative speakers of English:

- **Adverbs of frequency** include *always, never, often, rarely, seldom, sometimes,* and *usually.* They generally appear at the beginning of a sentence, before a one-word verb, or after the helping verb in a verb phrase.

┌─ **Key terms** ───────────────────────────

infinitive A verb form consisting of *to* plus the verb's plain (or dictionary) form: *to produce, to enjoy.* (See p. 205.)

verb phrase A verb consisting of a helping verb and a main verb that carries the principal meaning: *will have begun, can see.* (See p. 193.)

helping   main
  verb   adverb   verb
Robots have <u>sometimes</u> put humans out of work.

adverb   verb phrase
<u>Sometimes</u> robots have put humans out of work.

Adverbs of frequency always follow the verb *be*.

  verb adverb
Robots are <u>often</u> helpful to workers.

  verb adverb
Robots are <u>seldom</u> useful around the house.

- **Adverbs of degree** include *absolutely, almost, certainly, completely, definitely, especially, extremely, hardly,* and *only.* They fall just before the word modified (an adjective, another adverb, sometimes a verb).

           adverb   adjective
Robots have been <u>especially</u> useful in making cars.

- **Adverbs of manner** include *badly, beautifully, openly, sweetly, tightly, well,* and others that describe how something is done. They usually fall after the verb.

   verb   adverb
Robots work <u>smoothly</u> on assembly lines.

- **The adverb *not*** changes position depending on what it modifies. When it modifies a verb, place it after the helping verb (or the first helping verb if more than one).

helping   main
  verb   verb
Robots do <u>not</u> think.

When *not* modifies another adverb or an adjective, place it before the other modifier.

          adjective
Robots are <u>not</u> sleek machines.

5 Order of adjectives

English follows distinctive rules for arranging two or three adjectives before a noun. (A string of more than three adjectives before a noun is rare.) The order is shown in the chart on the facing page.

┌ Key term ─────────────────────────────

adjective A word that describes a noun or pronoun, specifying which one, what quality, or how many: *good one, three cars.* (See p. 194.)

└───────────────────────────────────────

Determiner	Opinion	Size or shape	Color	Origin	Material	Noun used as adjective	Noun
many						state	**laws**
	lovely		green	Thai			**birds**
a	fine			German			**camera**
this		square			wooden		**table**
all						business	**reports**
the			blue		litmus		**paper**

See **5** pp. 310–11 on punctuating adjectives before a noun.

Exercise 34.1 **Revising: Misplaced modifiers**

Revise the following paragraph so that modifiers clearly and appropriately describe the intended words.

1 People dominate in our society who are right-handed. **2** Hand tools, machines, and doors even are designed for right-handed people. **3** However, nearly 15 percent may be left-handed of the population. **4** Children when they enter kindergarten generally prefer one hand or the other. **5** Parents and teachers should not try to deliberately change a child's preference for the left hand.

Exercise 34.2 **Revising: Misplaced modifiers**

Revise the following paragraph so that modifiers clearly and appropriately describe the intended words. Mark the number preceding any sentence that is correct as given.

1 Women have contributed much to American culture of significance. **2** For example, during the colonial era Elizabeth Pinckney introduced indigo, the source of a valuable blue dye. **3** Later, Emma Willard founded the Troy Female Seminary, the first institution to provide a college-level education for women in 1821. **4** Mary Lyon founded Mount Holyoke Female Seminary as the first true women's college with directors and a campus who would sustain the college even after Lyon's death. **5** Pauline Wright Davis founded in 1853 *Una*, the first US newspaper that was dedicated to gaining women's rights. **6** Maria Mitchell was the first American woman astronomer who lived from 1818 to 1889. **7** Mitchell's Comet was discovered in 1847, which was named for the astronomer.

Exercise 34.3 **Revising: Placement of adverbs and adjectives**

Revise the following sentences to correct the positions of adverbs or adjectives. Mark the number preceding any sentence that is correct as given.

Example:

~~Gasoline high prices affect usually car sales.~~
High gasoline prices usually affect car sales.

1 Some years ago Detroit cars often were praised.
2 Luxury large cars especially were prized.
3 Then a serious oil shortage led drivers to value small foreign cars that got good mileage.
4 When gasoline ample supplies returned, consumers bought again American large cars and trucks.
5 Consumers not were loyal to the big vehicles when gasoline prices dramatically rose.

34b | Connect dangling modifiers to their sentences.

A **dangling modifier** does not sensibly modify anything in its sentence.

Dangling Passing the building, the vandalism became visible.

Dangling modifiers usually introduce sentences, contain a verb form, and imply but do not name a subject. In the example above, the implied subject is the someone or something passing the building. Readers assume that this implied subject is the same as the subject of the sentence (*vandalism* in the example), but vandalism does not pass buildings. The modifier "dangles" because it does not connect sensibly to the rest of the sentence. Here is another example:

Dangling Although intact, graffiti covered every inch of the walls and windows. [The walls and windows, not the graffiti, were intact.]

Identifying and revising dangling modifiers

■ **Find a subject.** If the modifier lacks a subject of its own (e.g., *when in diapers*), identify what it describes.
■ **Connect the subject and modifier.** Verify that what the modifier describes is in fact the subject of the main clause. If it is not, the modifier is probably dangling:

┌──── modifier ────┐   subject
Dangling   When in diapers, my mother remarried.

■ **Revise as needed.** Revise a dangling modifier (*a*) by recasting it with a subject of its own or (*b*) by changing the subject of the main clause:

Revision *a*   When I was in diapers, my mother remarried.
Revision *b*   When in diapers, I attended my mother's second wedding.

To revise a dangling modifier, you have to recast the sentence it appears in. (Revising just by moving the modifier will leave it dangling: *The vandalism became visible passing the building.*) Choose a revision method depending on what you want to emphasize in the sentence.

- **Rewrite the dangling modifier as a complete clause with its own stated subject and verb.** Readers can accept that the new subject and the sentence subject are different.

  Dangling   Passing the building, the vandalism became visible.

  Revised   As we passed the building, the vandalism became visible.

- **Change the subject of the sentence to a word the modifier properly describes.**

  Dangling   Trying to understand the causes, vandalism has been extensively studied.

  Revised   Trying to understand the causes, researchers have extensively studied vandalism.

Exercise 34.4   Revising: Dangling modifiers

Revise the sentences in the following paragraph to eliminate any dangling modifiers. Each item has more than one possible answer. Mark the number preceding any sentence that is correct as given.

1 Andrew Jackson's career was legendary in his day. 2 Starting with the American Revolution, service as a mounted courier was Jackson's choice. 3 Though not well educated, a successful career as a lawyer and judge proved Jackson's ability. 4 Earning the nicknames "Old Hickory" and "Sharp Knife," Jackson established his military prowess in the War of 1812. 5 Losing only six dead and ten wounded, the triumph of the Battle of New Orleans burnished Jackson's reputation. 6 After putting down raiding parties from Florida, Jackson's victories helped pressure Spain to cede that territory. 7 While Jackson was briefly governor of Florida, the US presidency became his goal. 8 With so many skills and deeds of valor, Jackson's fame led to his election to the presidency in 1828 and 1832.

Exercise 34.5   Revising: Misplaced and dangling modifiers

Revise the following paragraph to eliminate any misplaced or dangling modifiers.

1 Central American tungara frogs silence several nights a week their mating croaks. 2 When not croaking, the chance that the frogs will be eaten by predators is reduced. 3 The frogs seem to fully believe in "safety in numbers." 4 They more than likely will croak along with a large group rather than by themselves. 5 By forgoing croaking on some nights, the frogs' behavior prevents the species from "croaking."

Sentence Faults

A word group punctuated as a sentence will confuse or annoy readers if it lacks needed parts, has too many parts, or has parts that don't fit together.

35 Sentence Fragments

A **sentence fragment** is part of a sentence that is set off as if it were a whole sentence by an initial capital letter and a final period or other end punctuation. Although writers occasionally use fragments deliberately and effectively (see p. 283), readers perceive most fragments as serious errors.

Grammar checkers A grammar checker can spot many but not all sentence fragments, and it may flag sentences that are actually commands, such as *Continue reading*.

35a | Test your sentences for completeness.

A word group that is punctuated as a sentence should pass *all three* of the following tests. If it does not, it is a fragment and needs revision.

Complete sentence versus sentence fragment

A complete sentence or main clause
1. contains a subject and a predicate verb (The wind blows)
2. and is not a subordinate clause (beginning with a word such as *because* or *who*).

A sentence fragment
1. lacks a predicate verb (*The wind blowing*),
2. or lacks a subject (*And blows*),
3. or is a subordinate clause not attached to a complete sentence (*Because the wind blows*).

Visit *mycomplab.com* for more resources and exercises on sentence fragments.

Test 1: Find the predicate verb.

Look for a verb that can serve as the predicate of a sentence. Some fragments lack any verb at all:

Fragment   Uncountable numbers of sites on the Web.

Revised   Uncountable numbers of sites <u>make up</u> the Web.

Other fragments may include a verb form but not a **finite verb**, one that changes form as indicated below. A verbal does not change; it cannot serve as a predicate verb without the aid of a helping verb.

	Finite verbs in complete sentences	Verbals in sentence fragments
Singular	The network <u>grows</u>.	The network <u>growing</u>.
Plural	Networks <u>grow</u>.	Networks <u>growing</u>.
Present	The network <u>grows</u>.	
Past	The network <u>grew</u>.	The network <u>growing</u>.
Future	The network <u>will grow</u>.	

CULTURE LANGUAGE   Some languages allow forms of *be* to be omitted as helping verbs or linking verbs. But English requires stating forms of *be,* as shown in the following revised example.

Fragments   The network growing. It much larger than its developers anticipated.

Revised   The network <u>is</u> growing. It <u>is</u> much larger than its developers anticipated.

Test 2: Find the subject.

The subject of the sentence will usually come before the verb. If there is no subject, the word group is probably a fragment:

Fragment   And has enormous popular appeal.

Revised   And <u>the Web</u> has enormous popular appeal.

┌ Key terms ─────────────────────────────────

predicate The part of a sentence containing a verb that asserts something about the subject: *Ducks <u>swim</u>*. (See pp. 197–98.)

verbal A verb form that can serve as a noun, a modifier, or a part of a sentence verb, but not alone as the only verb of a sentence: *drawing, to draw, drawn*. (See p. 205.)

helping verb A verb such as *is, were, have, might*, and *could* that combines with various verb forms to indicate time and other kinds of meaning: for instance, *<u>were</u> drawing, <u>might</u> draw*. (See p. 193.)

subject The part of a sentence that names who or what performs the action or makes the assertion of the predicate: *<u>Ducks</u> swim*. (See pp. 197–98.)

In one kind of complete sentence, a command, the subject *you* is understood: [*You*] *Experiment with the Web.*

CULTURE LANGUAGE Some languages allow the omission of the sentence subject, especially when it is a pronoun. But in English, except in commands, the subject is always stated:

Fragment Web commerce has expanded dramatically. Has hurt traditional stores.

Revised Web commerce has expanded dramatically. It has hurt traditional stores.

Test 3: Make sure the clause is not subordinate.

A subordinate clause usually begins with a subordinating word, such as one of the following:

Subordinating conjunctions			**Relative pronouns**	
after	once	until	that	who/whom
although	since	when	which	whoever/whomever
as	than	where		whose
because	that	whereas		
if	unless	while		

Subordinate clauses serve as parts of sentences (as nouns or modifiers), not as whole sentences:

Fragment When the government devised the Internet.

Revised The government devised the Internet.

Revised When the government devised the Internet, no expansive computer network existed.

Fragment The reason that the government devised the Internet.

Revised The reason that the government devised the Internet was to link departments and defense contractors.

Note Questions beginning with *how, what, when, where, which, who, whom, whose,* and *why* are not sentence fragments: *Who was responsible? When did it happen?*

35b Revise sentence fragments.

Almost all sentence fragments can be corrected in one of the two ways shown in the box on the facing page. The choice depends

---

Key term

subordinate clause A word group that contains a subject and a predicate, begins with a subordinating word such as *because* or *who,* and is not a question: *Ducks can swim when they are young.* A subordinate clause may serve as a modifier or as a noun. (See pp. 208–09.)

on the importance of the information in the fragment and thus how much you want to stress it.

Revision of sentence fragments

Option 1

Rewrite the fragment as a complete sentence. This revision gives the information in the fragment the same importance as that in other complete sentences.

Fragment	A major improvement in public health occurred with the widespread use of vaccines. Which protected children against life-threatening diseases.
Revised	A major improvement in public health occurred with the widespread use of vaccines. They protected children against life-threatening diseases.

Two main clauses may be separated by a semicolon instead of a period (see 5 p. 318).

Option 2

Combine the fragment with a main clause. This revision subordinates the information in the fragment to the information in the main clause.

Fragment	The polio vaccine eradicated the disease from most of the globe. The first vaccine to be used widely.
Revised	The polio vaccine, the first to be used widely, eradicated the disease from most of the globe.

35c Be aware of the acceptable uses of incomplete sentences.

A few word groups lacking the usual subject-predicate combination are incomplete sentences, but they are not fragments because they conform to the expectations of most readers. They include commands (*Move along. Shut the window.*); exclamations (*Oh no!*); questions and answers (*Where next? To Kansas.*); and descriptions in employment résumés (*Weekly volunteer in soup kitchen.*)

Experienced writers sometimes use sentence fragments when they want to achieve a special effect. Such fragments appear more in informal than in formal writing. Unless you are experienced and thoroughly secure in your own writing, you should avoid all fragments and concentrate on writing clear, well-formed sentences.

Exercise 35.1 Identifying and revising sentence fragments

Apply the tests for completeness to each of the word groups in the following paragraph. If a word group is a complete sentence, mark the number preceding it. If it is a sentence fragment, revise it in two ways: by making it a complete sentence, and by combining it with a main clause written from the information given in other items.

Example:

And could help. [The word group has a verb (*could . . . help*) but no subject.]

Revised into a complete sentence: And <u>he</u> could help.

Combined with a new main clause: <u>He had money</u> and could help.

1 In an interesting magazine article about vandalism against works of art. **2** The focus was on the vandals themselves. **3** The motives of the vandals varying widely. **4** Those who harm artwork are usually angry. **5** But not necessarily at the artist or the owner. **6** For instance, a man who hammered at Michelangelo's *Pietà*. **7** And knocked off the Virgin Mary's nose. **8** Because he was angry with the Roman Catholic Church. **9** Which knew nothing of his grievance. **10** Although many damaged works can be repaired. **11** Usually even the most skillful repairs are forever visible.

Exercise 35.2 Revising: Sentence fragments

Correct any sentence fragment in the following items either by combining it with a complete sentence or by making it a complete sentence. If an item contains no sentence fragment, mark the number preceding it.

Example:

Jujitsu is good for self-protection. Because it enables one to overcome an opponent without the use of weapons.

Jujitsu is good for self-protection because it enables one to overcome an opponent without the use of weapons. *Or:* Jujitsu is good for self-protection. <u>It</u> enables one to overcome an opponent without the use of weapons.

1 Human beings who perfume themselves. They are not much different from other animals.
2 Animals as varied as insects and dogs release pheromones. Chemicals that signal other animals.
3 Human beings have a diminished sense of smell. And do not consciously detect most of their own species' pheromones.
4 The human substitute for pheromones may be perfumes. Most common in ancient times were musk and other fragrances derived from animal oils.
5 Some sources say that people began using perfume to cover up the smell of burning flesh. During sacrifices to the gods.
6 Perfumes became religious offerings in their own right. Being expensive to make, they were highly prized.
7 The earliest historical documents from the Middle East record the use of fragrances. Not only in religious ceremonies but on the body.

8 In the nineteenth century, chemists began synthesizing perfume oils. Which previously could be made only from natural sources.

9 The most popular animal oil for perfume today is musk. Although some people dislike its heavy, sweet odor.

10 Synthetic musk oil would help conserve a certain species of deer. Whose gland is the source of musk.

Exercise 35.3 Revising: Sentence fragments

Revise the following paragraph to eliminate sentence fragments by combining them with main clauses or rewriting them as main clauses.

Baby red-eared slider turtles are brightly colored. With bold patterns on their yellowish undershells. Which serve as a warning to predators. The bright colors of skunks and other animals. They signal that the animals will spray nasty chemicals. In contrast, the turtle's colors warn largemouth bass. That the baby turtle will actively defend itself. When a bass gulps down a turtle. The feisty baby claws and bites. Forcing the bass to spit it out. To avoid a similar painful experience. The bass will avoid other baby red-eared slider turtles. The turtle loses its bright colors as it grows too big. For a bass's afternoon snack.

36 Comma Splices and Fused Sentences

When two main clauses fall in a row, readers need a signal that one main clause is ending and another is beginning. The four ways to provide this signal appear in the box on the next page.

Two problems in punctuating main clauses fail to signal the break between main clauses. One is the **comma splice**, in which the clauses are joined (or spliced) *only* with a comma:

Comma splice The ship was huge, its mast stood eighty feet high.

The other is the **fused sentence** (or **run-on sentence**), in which no punctuation or conjunction appears between the clauses.

Fused sentence The ship was huge its mast stood eighty feet high.

> **Key term**
>
> **main clause** A word group that can stand alone as a sentence because it contains a subject and a predicate and does not begin with a subordinating word: *A dictionary is essential.*

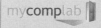

mycomplab

Visit *mycomplab.com* for more resources and exercises on comma splices and fused sentences.

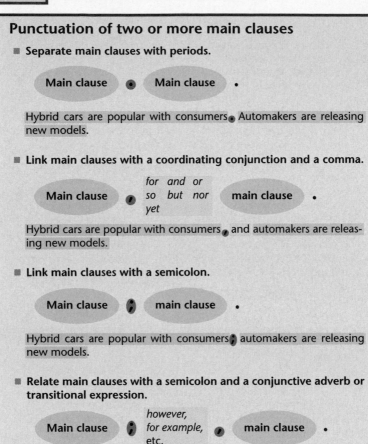

Punctuation of two or more main clauses

■ **Separate main clauses with periods.**

> Main clause **.** Main clause **.**

Hybrid cars are popular with consumers**.** Automakers are releasing new models.

■ **Link main clauses with a coordinating conjunction and a comma.**

> Main clause **,** *for and or*
> *so but nor*
> *yet*
> main clause **.**

Hybrid cars are popular with consumers**,** and automakers are releasing new models.

■ **Link main clauses with a semicolon.**

> Main clause **;** main clause **.**

Hybrid cars are popular with consumers**;** automakers are releasing new models.

■ **Relate main clauses with a semicolon and a conjunctive adverb or transitional expression.**

> Main clause **;** *however,*
> *for example,*
> *etc.*
> **,** main clause **.**

Hybrid cars are popular with consumers**;** as a result**,** automakers are releasing new models.

Grammar checkers A grammar checker can detect many comma splices, but it will miss most fused sentences. For example, a checker flagged *Money is tight, we need to spend carefully* but not *Money is tight we need to spend carefully*. A checker may also question sentences that are actually correct, such as *Money being tighter now than before, we need to spend carefully*.

Key terms

coordinating conjunction *And, but, or, nor, for, so, yet.* (See p. 196.)

conjunctive adverb A modifier that describes the relation of the ideas in two clauses, such as *consequently, however, indeed,* and *therefore.* (See p. 289.)

⸨CULTURE LANGUAGE⸩ In standard American English, a sentence may not include more than one main clause unless the clauses are separated by a comma and a coordinating conjunction or by a semicolon. If your native language does not have such a rule or has accustomed you to writing long sentences, you may need to edit your English writing especially for comma splices and fused sentences.

36a | ## Separate main clauses not joined by *and, but,* or another coordinating conjunction.

If your readers point out comma splices or fused sentences in your writing, you're not creating enough separation between main clauses in your sentences. Punctuate consecutive main clauses in the following ways.

Separate sentences

Make the clauses into separate sentences when the ideas expressed are only loosely related:

| Comma splice | Chemistry has contributed much to our understanding of foods, many foods such as wheat and beans can be produced in the laboratory. |
| Revised | Chemistry has contributed much to our understanding of foods⦁ Many foods such as wheat and beans can be produced in the laboratory. |

Coordinating conjunction

Insert a coordinating conjunction in a comma splice when the ideas in the main clauses are closely related and equally important:

| Comma splice | Some laboratory-grown foods taste good, they are nutritious. |
| Revised | Some laboratory-grown foods taste good, <u>and</u> they are nutritious. |

In a fused sentence insert a comma and a coordinating conjunction:

| Fused sentence | Chemists have made much progress they still have a way to go. |
| Revised | Chemists have made much progress⦁ <u>but</u> they still have a way to go. |

Semicolon

Insert a semicolon between clauses if the relation between the ideas is very close and obvious without a conjunction:

Comma splice	Good taste is rare in laboratory-grown vegetables, they are usually bland.
Revised	Good taste is rare in laboratory-grown vegetables; they are usually bland.

Subordination

When one idea is less important than the other, express the less important idea in a subordinate clause:

Comma splice	The vitamins are adequate, the flavor is deficient.
Revised	Even though the vitamins are adequate, the flavor is deficient.

36b Separate main clauses related by *however, for example*, and so on.

Two groups of words describe how one main clause relates to another: **conjunctive adverbs** and other **transitional expressions**. (See **1** pp. 44–45 for a longer list of transitional expressions.)

Common conjunctive adverbs and transitional expressions

accordingly	for instance	instead	on the contrary
anyway	further	in the meantime	otherwise
as a result	furthermore	in the past	similarly
at last	hence	likewise	still
besides	however	meanwhile	that is
certainly	incidentally	moreover	then
consequently	in contrast	namely	thereafter
even so	indeed	nevertheless	therefore
finally	in fact	nonetheless	thus
for all that	in other words	now	undoubtedly
for example	in short	of course	until now

When two main clauses are related by a conjunctive adverb or another transitional expression, they must be separated by a period or by a semicolon. The adverb or expression is also generally set off by a comma or commas.

> **Key term**
>
> **subordinate clause** A word group that contains a subject and a predicate, begins with a subordinating word such as *because* or *who,* and is not a question: *Ducks can swim when they are young.* A subordinate clause may serve as a modifier or as a noun. (See pp. 208–09.)

Comma splice	Healthcare costs are higher in the United States than in many other countries, <u>consequently</u> health insurance is also more costly.
Revised	Healthcare costs are higher in the United States than in many other countries. <u>Consequently</u>, health insurance is also more costly.
Revised	Healthcare costs are higher in the United States than in many other countries; <u>consequently</u>, health insurance is also more costly.

Conjunctive adverbs and transitional expressions are different from coordinating conjunctions (*and, but,* and so on) and subordinating conjunctions (*although, because,* and so on):

■ **Unlike conjunctions, conjunctive adverbs and transitional expressions do not join two clauses into a grammatical unit.** They merely describe the way two clauses relate in meaning.

■ **Unlike conjunctions, conjunctive adverbs and transitional expressions can be moved within a clause.** No matter where in the clause an adverb or expression falls, though, the clause must be separated from another main clause by a period or semicolon:

Most Americans refuse to give up unhealthful habits; our medical costs, consequently, are higher than those of many other countries.

Exercise 36.1 Identifying and revising comma splices

Correct each comma splice below in *two* of the ways described on pp. 287–88. If a sentence contains no comma splice, mark the number preceding it.

1 Money has a long history, it goes back at least as far as the earliest records. **2** Many of the earliest records concern financial transactions, indeed, early history must often be inferred from commercial activity. **3** Every known society has had a system of money, though the objects serving as money have varied widely. **4** Sometimes the objects had actual value for the society, examples include cattle and fermented beverages. **5** Today, in contrast, money may be made of worthless paper, or it may even consist of a bit of data in a computer's memory. **6** We think of money as valuable, only our common faith in it makes it valuable. **7** That faith is sometimes fragile, consequently, currencies themselves are fragile. **8** Economic crises often shake the belief in money, indeed, such weakened faith helped cause the Great Depression of the 1930s.

Exercise 36.2 Identifying and revising fused sentences

Revise each of the fused sentences in the following paragraph in *two* of the four ways shown on pp. 287–88. If a sentence is correct as given, mark the number preceding it.

1 Throughout history money and religion were closely linked there was little distinction between government and religion. 2 The head of state and the religious leader were often the same person so that all power rested in one ruler. 3 These powerful leaders decided what objects would serve as money their backing encouraged public faith in the money. 4 Coins were minted of precious metals the religious overtones of money were then strengthened. 5 People already believed the precious metals to be divine their use in money intensified its allure.

Exercise 36.3 Sentence combining to avoid comma splices and fused sentences

Using the method suggested in parentheses, combine each pair of sentences below into one sentence without creating a comma splice or fused sentence.

Example:

The sun sank lower in the sky. The colors gradually faded. (*Subordinate one clause to the other.*)

<u>As the sun sank lower in the sky, the colors gradually faded.</u>

1 The exact origin of paper money is unknown. It has not survived as coins, shells, and other durable objects have. (*Subordinate one clause to the other.*)
2 Scholars disagree over where paper money originated. Many believe it was first used in Europe. (*Subordinate one clause to the other.*)
3 Perhaps goldsmiths were also gold bankers. They held the gold of their wealthy customers. (*Supply a semicolon and a conjunctive adverb or transitional expression.*)
4 The goldsmiths probably gave customers receipts for their gold. These receipts were then used in trade. (*Supply a comma and coordinating conjunction.*)
5 The goldsmiths were something like modern-day bankers. Their receipts were something like modern-day money. (*Supply a semicolon.*)

Exercise 36.4 Revising: Comma splices and fused sentences

Revise each comma splice and fused sentence in the following paragraphs using the technique that seems most appropriate for the meaning.

What many call the first genocide of modern times occurred during World War I, the Armenians were deported from their homes in Anatolia, Turkey. The Turkish government assumed that the Armenians were sympathetic to Russia, with whom the Turks were at war. Many Armenians died because of the hardships of the journey many were massacred. The death toll was estimated at between 600,000 and 1 million.

Many of the deported Armenians migrated to Russia, in 1918 they established the Republic of Armenia, they continued to be attacked by Turkey, in 1920 they became the Soviet Republic of Armenia rather than surrender to the Turks. Like other Soviet republics, Armenia became independent in 1991, about 3.4 million Armenians live there now.

A **mixed sentence** contains parts that do not fit together. The misfit may be in meaning or in grammar.

Grammar checkers A grammar checker may recognize a simple mixed construction such as *reason is because*, but it will fail to flag most mixed sentences.

37a Match subjects and predicates in meaning.

In a sentence with mixed meaning, the subject is said to do or be something illogical. Such a mixture is sometimes called **faulty predication** because the predicate conflicts with the subject.

1 Illogical equation with *be*

When a form of *be* connects a subject and a word that describes the subject (a complement), the subject and complement must be logically related:

Mixed   A compromise between the city and the country would be the ideal place to live.

Revised   A community that offered the best qualities of both city and country would be the ideal place to live.

2 *Is when, is where*

Definitions require nouns on both sides of *be*. Clauses that define and begin with *when* or *where* are common in speech but should be avoided in writing:

Mixed   An examination is when you are tested on what you know.

Revised   An examination is a test of what you know.

Key terms

subject The part of a sentence that names who or what performs the action or makes the assertion of the predicate: *Geese fly.* (See pp. 197–98.)

predicate The part of a sentence containing a verb that asserts something about the subject: *Geese fly.* (See pp. 197–98.)

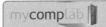

mycomplab

Visit *mycomplab.com* for more resources on mixed sentences.

3 *Reason is because*

The commonly heard construction *reason is because* is redundant since *because* means "for the reason that":

Mixed The <u>reason</u> the temple requests donations <u>is because</u> the school needs expansion.

Revised The <u>reason</u> the temple requests donations <u>is that</u> the school needs expansion.

Revised The temple requests donations <u>because</u> the school needs expansion.

4 Other mixed meanings

Faulty predications are not confined to sentences with *be:*

Mixed The <u>use</u> of emission controls <u>was created</u> to reduce air pollution.

Revised Emission <u>controls were created</u> to reduce air pollution.

37b Untangle sentences that are mixed in grammar.

Many mixed sentences start with one grammatical plan or construction but end with a different one:

Mixed
┌──────── modifier (prepositional phrase) ────────┐ verb
By paying more attention to impressions than facts leads us to misjudge others.

Revised
┌──────── modifier (prepositional phrase) ────────┐ subject
By paying more attention to impressions than facts, <u>we</u>
verb
<u>misjudge</u> others.

Constructions that use *Just because* clauses as subjects are common in speech but should be avoided in writing:

Mixed
┌── modifier (subordinate clause) ──┐┌── verb ──┐
Just because no one is watching doesn't mean we have license to break the law.

Revised
┌── modifier (subordinate clause) ──┐ subject + verb
<u>Even when</u> no one is watching, <u>we don't have</u> license to break the law.

A mixed sentence is especially likely when you are working on a computer and connect parts of two sentences or rewrite half a sentence but not the other half. A mixed sentence may also occur when you don't make the subject and predicate verb carry the principal meaning. (See **3** p. 143.)

Exercise 37.1 Revising: Mixed sentences

Revise the following paragraph so that sentence parts fit together both in grammar and in meaning. Each item has more than one possible answer. If a sentence is correct as given, mark the number preceding it.

1 A hurricane is when the winds in a tropical depression rotate counterclockwise at more than seventy-four miles per hour. 2 People fear hurricanes because they can destroy lives and property. 3 Through storm surge, high winds, floods, and tornadoes is how hurricanes have killed thousands of people. 4 Storm surge is where the hurricane's winds whip up a tide that spills over seawalls and deluges coastal islands. 5 The winds themselves are also destructive, uprooting trees and smashing buildings. 6 By packing winds of 150 to 200 miles per hour is how a hurricane inflicts terrible damage even on inland towns. 7 However, the worst damage to inland areas occurs when tornadoes and floods strike. 8 Many scientists observe that hurricanes in recent years they have become more ferocious and destructive. 9 However, in the last half-century, with improved communication systems and weather satellites have made hurricanes less deadly. 10 The reason is because people have more time to escape. 11 The emphasis on evacuation is in fact the best way for people to avoid a hurricane's force. 12 Simply boarding up a house's windows will not protect a family from wind, water surges, and flying debris.

37c State parts of sentences, such as subjects, only once.

In some languages other than English, certain parts of sentences may be repeated. These include the subject in any kind of clause or an object or adverb in an adjective clause. In English, however, these parts are stated only once in a clause.

1 Repetition of subject

You may be tempted to restate a subject as a pronoun before the verb. But the subject needs stating only once in its clause:

Faulty The <u>liquid</u> <u>it</u> reached a temperature of 180°F.
Revised The <u>liquid</u> reached a temperature of 180°F.

Faulty <u>Gases</u> in the liquid <u>they</u> escaped.
Revised <u>Gases</u> in the liquid escaped.

2 Repetition in an adjective clause

Adjective clauses begin with *who, whom, whose, which, that, where,* and *when* (see also p. 209). The beginning word replaces another word: the subject (*He is the person* <u>*who called*</u>), an object of a verb or preposition (*He is the person whom I mentioned*), or a preposition and pronoun (*He knows the office where [in which] the conference will occur*).

Do not state the word being replaced in an adjective clause:

Faulty The technician <u>whom</u> the test depended on <u>her</u> was burned. [*Whom* should replace *her*.]

Revised The technician <u>whom</u> the test depended on was burned.

Adjective clauses beginning with *where* or *when* do not need an adverb such as *there* or *then*:

Faulty Gases escaped at a moment <u>when</u> the technician was unprepared <u>then</u>.

Revised Gases escaped at a moment <u>when</u> the technician was unprepared.

Note *Whom, which,* and similar words are sometimes omitted but are still understood by the reader. Thus the word being replaced should not be stated.

Faulty Accidents rarely happen to technicians the lab has trained <u>them</u>. [*Whom* is understood: . . . *technicians* <u>whom</u> *the lab has* <u>trained</u>.]

Revised Accidents rarely happen to technicians the lab has trained.

Exercise 37.2 Revising: Repeated subjects and other parts

Revise the sentences in the following paragraph to eliminate any unneeded words. If a sentence is correct as given, mark the number preceding it.

1 Archaeologists and other scientists they can often determine the age of their discoveries by means of radiocarbon dating. **2** This technique is based on the fact that all living organisms contain carbon. **3** The most common isotope is carbon 12, which it contains six protons and six neutrons. **4** A few carbon atoms are classified as the isotope carbon 14, where the nucleus consists of six protons and eight neutrons there. **5** Because of the extra neutrons, the carbon 14 atom it is unstable. **6** What is significant about the carbon 14 atom is its half-life of 5700 years. **7** Scientists they measure the proportion of carbon 14 to carbon 12 and estimate the age of the specimen. **8** Radiocarbon dating it can be used on any material that was once living, but it is most accurate with specimens between 500 and 50,000 years old.

Punctuation

Punctuation

38 End Punctuation

End a sentence with one of three punctuation marks: a period (.), a question mark (?), or an exclamation point (!).

Grammar checkers A grammar checker may flag missing question marks after direct questions or incorrect combinations of marks (such as a question mark and a period at the end of a sentence), but it cannot do much else.

38a Use a period after most sentences and with some abbreviations.

1 Statements, mild commands, and indirect questions

Statement

The airline went bankrupt.   It no longer flies.

Mild command

Think of the possibilities.   Please consider others.

Indirect question

An **indirect question** reports what someone asked but not in the exact form or words of the original question:

The judge asked why I had been driving with my lights off.
No one asked how we got home.

CULTURE LANGUAGE In standard American English, an indirect question uses the wording and subject-verb order of a statement: *The reporter asked why the negotiations failed* [not *why did the negotiations fail*].

2 Abbreviations

Use periods with abbreviations that consist of or end in small letters. Otherwise, omit periods from abbreviations.

Dr.	Mr., Mrs.	e.g.	Feb.	ft.
St.	Ms.	i.e.	p.	a.m., p.m.
PhD	BC, BCE	USA	IBM	AM, PM
BA	AD, CE	US	USMC	AIDS

Visit *mycomplab.com* for more resources and exercises on end punctuation.

Note When a sentence ends in an abbreviation with a period, don't add a second period: *My first class is at 8 a.m.*

Exercise 38. 1 Revising: Periods

Revise the following sentences so that periods are used correctly.

1 The instructor asked when Plato wrote *The Republic*?
2 Give the date within one century
3 The exact date is not known, but it is estimated at 370 BCE
4 Dr Arn will lecture on Plato at 7:30 p.m..
5 The area of the lecture hall is only 1600 sq ft

38b **Use a question mark after a direct question and sometimes to indicate doubt.**

1 Direct questions

Who will follow her?
What is the difference between these two people?

After indirect questions, use a period: *We wondered who would follow her.* (See the preceding page.)

Questions in a series are each followed by a question mark:

The officer asked how many times the suspect had been arrested. Three times? Four times? More than that?

Note Do not combine question marks with other question marks, periods, commas, or other punctuation.

2 Doubt

A question mark within parentheses can indicate doubt about a number or date.

The Greek philosopher Socrates was born in 470 (?) BC and died in 399 BC from drinking poison. [Socrates's birthdate is not known for sure.]

Use sentence structure and words, not a question mark, to express sarcasm or irony.

Not   Stern's friendliness (?) bothered Crane.
But   Stern's <u>insincerity</u> bothered Crane.

Exercise 38.2 Revising: Question marks

Add, delete, or replace question marks as needed in the following sentences.

1 In Homer's *Odyssey*, Odysseus took several years to travel from Troy to Ithaca. Or was it eight years. Or more?

2 Odysseus must have wondered whether he would ever make it home?
3 "What man are you and whence?," asks Odysseus's wife Penelope.
4 Why does Penelope ask, "Where is your city? Your family?"?
5 Penelope does not recognize Odysseus and asks who this stranger is?

38c Use an exclamation point after an emphatic statement, interjection, or command.

No! We must not lose this election!
Come here immediately!

Follow mild interjections and commands with commas or periods, as appropriate: *Oh,* call whenever you can.

Note Do not combine exclamation points with periods, commas, or other punctuation marks. And use exclamation points sparingly, even in informal writing. Overused, they'll fail to impress readers, and they may make you sound overemotional.

Exercise 38.3 Revising: Exclamation points

Add or replace exclamation points as needed in the following sentences.

1 As the firefighters moved their equipment into place, the police shouted, "Move back!".
2 A child's cries could be heard from above: "Help me. Help."
3 When the child was rescued, the crowd called "Hooray."
4 The rescue was the most exciting event of the day!
5 The neighbors talked about it for days!

Exercise 38.4 Revising: End punctuation

Insert appropriate end punctuation (periods, question marks, or exclamation points) where needed in the following paragraph.

When visitors first arrive in Hawaii, they often encounter an unexpected language barrier Standard English is the language of business and government, but many of the people speak Pidgin English Instead of an excited "Aloha" the visitors may be greeted with an excited Pidgin "Howzit" or asked if they know "how fo' find one good hotel" Many Hawaiians question whether Pidgin will hold children back because it prevents communication with *haoles*, or Caucasians, who run businesses Yet many others feel that Pidgin is a last defense of ethnic diversity on the islands To those who want to make standard English the official language of the state, these Hawaiians may respond, "Just 'cause I speak Pidgin no mean I dumb" They may ask, "Why you no listen" or, in standard English, "Why don't you listen"

┌─ **Key term** ───

interjection A word that expresses feeling or commands attention, either alone or within a sentence: *Oh! Hey! Wow!*

39 The Comma

The comma (,) is the most common punctuation mark inside sentences. Its main uses are shown in the box opposite.

Grammar checkers A grammar checker will ignore many comma errors. For example, a checker failed to catch the missing commas in *We cooked lasagna_spinach_and apple pie* and the misused commas in *The trip was short but, the weather was perfect* and *The travelers were tempted by, the many shops.*

39a Use a comma before *and, but,* or another coordinating conjunction linking main clauses.

When a coordinating conjunction links words or phrases, do not use a comma: *Dugain plays and sings Irish and English folk songs.* However, *do* use a comma when a coordinating conjunction joins main clauses, as in the next examples.

> Caffeine can keep coffee drinkers alert, and it may elevate their mood.
>
> Caffeine was once thought to be safe, but now researchers warn of harmful effects.
>
> Coffee drinkers may suffer sleeplessness, for the drug acts as a stimulant to the nervous system.

Note The comma goes *before,* not after, a coordinating conjunction that links main clauses: *Caffeine increases heart rate, and it* [not *and, it*] *constricts blood vessels.*

Exception Some writers omit the comma between main clauses that are very short and closely related in meaning: *Caffeine helps but it also hurts.* If you are in doubt about whether to use the comma in such a sentence, use it. It will always be correct.

Key terms

coordinating conjunctions *And, but, or, nor,* and sometimes *for, so, yet.* (See **4** p. 196.)

main clause A word group that can stand alone as a sentence because it contains a subject and a predicate and does not begin with a subordinating word: *Water freezes at temperatures below 32°F.* (See **4** p. 208.)

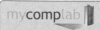

Visit *mycomplab.com* for more resources and exercises on the comma.

Principal uses of the comma

■ **Separate main clauses linked by a coordinating conjunction** (opposite):

| Main clause | **,** | for and or
so but nor
yet | main clause | **.** |

The building is finished**,** but it has no tenants.

■ **Set off most introductory elements** (p. 302):

| Introductory element | **,** | main clause | **.** |

Unfortunately**,** the only tenant pulled out.

■ **Set off nonessential elements** (p. 304):

| Main clause | **,** | nonessential element | **.** |

The empty building symbolizes a weak local economy**,** which affects everyone.

| Beginning of main clause | **,** | nonessential element | **,** | end of main clause | **.** |

The primary cause**,** the decline of local industry**,** is not news.

■ **Separate items in a series** (p. 310):

| . . . | item 1 | **,** | item 2 | **,** | *and*
or | item 3 | . . . |

The city needs healthier businesses**,** new schools**,** and improved housing.

■ **Separate coordinate adjectives** (p. 310):

| . . . | first adjective | **,** | second adjective | word modified | . . . |

A tall**,** sleek skyscraper is not needed.

Other uses of the comma:

Separate parts of dates, addresses, long numbers (p. 312).
Separate quotations and signal phrases (p. 313).

See also p. 314 for when *not* to use the comma.

Exercise 39.1 Revising: Comma with linked main clauses

In the following paragraph, insert a comma before each coordinating conjunction that links main clauses. Do not insert commas between words, phrases, or subordinate clauses. If a sentence is correct as given, mark the number preceding it.

1 Parents once automatically gave their children the father's last name but some no longer do. **2** In fact, parents were once legally required to give their children the father's last name but these laws have been contested in court. **3** Parents may now give their children any last name they choose and some parents opt for the mother's last name. **4** Those parents who choose the mother's last name may do so because they believe the mother's importance should be recognized or because the mother's name is easier to pronounce.

Exercise 39.2 Sentence combining: Linked main clauses

Combine each group of sentences below into one sentence that contains only two main clauses connected by the coordinating conjunction in parentheses. Use commas only to separate the main clauses. You will have to add, delete, and rearrange words.

Example:

The circus had come to town. The children wanted to see it. Their parents wanted to see it. (*and*)

The circus had come to town, and the children and their parents wanted to see it.

1 The arguments for bestowing the mother's surname on children are often strong. They are often convincing. They are not universally accepted. (*but*)

2 Some parents have combined their last names. They have created a new surname. They have given that name to their children. (*and*)

3 Critics sometimes question the effects of unusual surnames on children. They wonder how confusing the new surnames will be. They wonder how fleeting the surnames will be. (*or*)

4 Children with surnames different from their parents' may suffer embarrassment. They may suffer identity problems. Giving children their father's surname is still very much the norm. (*for*)

5 Hyphenated names are awkward. They are also difficult to pass on. Some observers think they will die out in the next generation. Or they may die out before. (*so*)

39b Use a comma to set off most introductory elements.

An **introductory element** begins a sentence and modifies a word or words in the main clause. It is usually followed by a comma.

Subordinate clause

Even when identical twins are raised apart, they grow up very like each other.

Verbal or verbal phrase

Explaining the similarity, some researchers claim that one's genes are one's destiny.

Concerned, other researchers deny the claim.

Prepositional phrase

In a debate that has lasted centuries, scientists use identical twins to argue for or against genetic destiny.

Transitional expression

Of course, scientists can now look directly at the genes themselves to answer questions.

You may omit the comma after a short subordinate clause or prepositional phrase if its omission does not create confusion: *When snow falls the city collapses. By the year 2000 the world population had topped 6 billion.* You may also omit the comma after some transitional expressions when they start sentences: *Thus the debate continues* (see pp. 307–08). However, in both situations the comma is never wrong.

Note Take care to distinguish *-ing* words used as modifiers from *-ing* words used as subjects. The former almost always take a comma; the latter never do.

┌─── modifier ───┐ subject verb
Studying identical twins, geneticists learn about inheritance.

┌─── subject ───┐ verb
Studying identical twins helps geneticists learn about inheritance.

Key terms

subordinate clause A word group that contains a subject and a predicate, begins with a subordinating word such as *because* or *who,* and is not a question: *When water freezes, crystals form.* (See **4** pp. 208–09.)

verbal A verb form used as an adjective, adverb, or noun. A verbal plus any object or modifier is a **verbal phrase**: *frozen water, ready to freeze, rapid freezing.* (See **4** p. 205.)

prepositional phrase A word group consisting of a preposition, such as *for* or *in,* followed by a noun or pronoun plus any modifiers: *in a jar, with a spoon.* (See **4** pp. 203–04.)

transitional expression A word or phrase that shows the relationship between sentences: *for example, however, in fact, of course.* (See **1** pp. 44–45.)

Exercise 39.3 Revising: Comma with introductory elements

In the following paragraph, insert commas wherever they are needed after introductory elements. If a sentence is correct as given, mark the number preceding it.

1 Veering sharply to the right a large flock of birds neatly avoids a high wall. 2 Moving in a fluid mass is typical of flocks of birds and schools of fish. 3 With the help of complex computer simulations zoologists are learning more about this movement. 4 Because it is sudden and apparently well coordinated the movement of flocks and schools has seemed to be directed by a leader. 5 Almost incredibly the group could behave with more intelligence than any individual seemed to possess. 6 However new studies have discovered that flocks and schools are leaderless. 7 As it turns out evading danger is really an individual response. 8 When each bird or fish senses a predator it follows individual rules for fleeing. 9 To keep from colliding with its neighbors each bird or fish uses other rules for dodging. 10 Multiplied over hundreds of individuals these responses look as if they have been choreographed.

Exercise 39.4 Sentence combining: Introductory elements

Combine each pair of sentences below into one sentence that begins with an introductory modifier as specified in parentheses. Follow the introductory element with a comma. You will have to add, delete, change, and rearrange words.

Example:
The girl was humming to herself. She walked upstairs. (*Modifier beginning Humming.*)
Humming to herself, the girl walked upstairs.

1 Scientists have made an effort to explain the mysteries of flocks and schools. They have proposed bizarre magnetic fields and telepathy. (*Modifier beginning In.*)
2 Scientists developed computer models. They have abandoned earlier explanations. (*Modifier beginning Since.*)
3 The movement of a flock or school starts with each individual. It is rapidly and perhaps automatically coordinated among individuals. (*Modifier beginning Starting.*)
4 One zoologist observes that human beings seek coherent patterns. He suggests that investigators saw purpose in the movement of flocks and schools where none existed. (*Modifier beginning Observing.*)
5 One may want to study the movement of flocks or schools. Then one must abandon a search for purpose or design. (*Modifier beginning To.*)

39c **Use a comma or commas to set off nonessential elements.**

Commas around part of a sentence often signal that the element is not necessary to the meaning. This **nonessential element** may modify or rename the word it refers to, but it does not limit the word to a particular individual or group. The meaning of the word would still be clear if the element were deleted:

Nonessential element

The company, which is located in Oklahoma, has a good reputation.

(Because it does not restrict meaning, a nonessential element is also called a **nonrestrictive element**.)

In contrast, an **essential** (or **restrictive**) element *does* limit the word it refers to: the element cannot be omitted without leaving the meaning too general. Because it is essential, such an element is *not* set off with a comma or commas.

Essential element

The company rewards employees who work hard.

Omitting the underlined words would distort the meaning: the company doesn't necessarily reward *all* employees, only the hardworking ones.

The same element in the same sentence may be essential or nonessential depending on your meaning and the context:

Essential

Not all the bands were equally well received, however. The band playing old music held the audience's attention. The other groups created much less excitement. [*Playing old music* identifies a particular band.]

Nonessential

A new band called Fats made its debut on Saturday night. The band, playing old music, held the audience's attention. If this performance is typical, the group has a bright future. [*Playing old music* adds information about a band already named.]

A test for nonessential and essential elements

1. **Identify the element:**

   Hai Nguyen who emigrated from Vietnam lives in Dallas.
   Those who emigrated with him live elsewhere.

2. **Remove the element.** Does the fundamental meaning of the sentence change?

   Hai Nguyen lives in Dallas. *No.*
   Those live elsewhere. *Yes.* [Who are *Those?*]

3. **If *no*,** the element is *nonessential* and *should* be set off with punctuation:

   Hai Nguyen, who emigrated from Vietnam, lives in Dallas.

   If *yes*, the element is *essential* and should *not* be set off with punctuation:

   Those who emigrated with him live elsewhere.

Note When a nonessential element falls in the middle of a sentence, be sure to set it off with a pair of commas, one *before* and one *after* the element.

1 Nonessential phrases and clauses

Most nonessential phrases and subordinate clauses function as adjectives or, less commonly, as adverbs. In each of the following examples, the underlined words could be omitted with no loss of clarity.

> Elizabeth Blackwell was the first woman to graduate from an American medical school, in 1849. [Phrase.]
>
> She was a medical pioneer, helping to found the first medical college for women. [Phrase.]
>
> She taught at the school, which was affiliated with the New York Infirmary. [Clause.]
>
> Blackwell, who published books and papers on medicine, practiced pediatrics and gynecology. [Clause.]

Note Use *that* only in an essential clause, never in a nonessential clause: . . . *school, which* [not *that*] *was affiliated.* . . . Many writers reserve *which* for nonessential clauses.

2 Nonessential appositives

A nonessential appositive merely adds information about the word it refers to.

> Toni Morrison's fifth novel, *Beloved,* won the Pulitzer Prize in 1988. [The word *fifth* identifies the novel, while the title adds a detail.]

In contrast, an essential appositive limits or defines the word it refers to:

> Morrison's novel *The Bluest Eye* is about an African American girl who longs for blue eyes. [Morrison has written more than one novel, so the title is essential to identify the intended one.]

┌ Key terms ─────────────────────

phrase A word group lacking a subject or a verb or both: *in Duluth, carrying water.* (See **4** p. 203.)

subordinate clause A word group that contains a subject and a predicate, begins with a subordinating word such as *who* or *although,* and is not a question: *Samson, who won a gold medal, coaches in Utah.* (See **4** pp. 208–09.)

appositive A noun that renames another noun immediately before it: *His wife, Kyra Sedgwick, is also an actor.* (See **4** p. 207.)

3 Other nonessential elements

Like nonessential modifiers or appositives, many other elements contribute to texture, tone, or overall clarity but are not essential to the meaning. Unlike nonessential modifiers or appositives, these other nonessential elements generally do not refer to any specific word in the sentence.

Note Use a pair of commas—one before, one after—when any of these elements falls in the middle of a sentence.

Absolute phrases

Household recycling having succeeded, the city now wants to extend the program to businesses.

Many businesses, their profits already squeezed, resist recycling.

Parenthetical and transitional expressions

Generally, set off parenthetical and transitional expressions with commas:

The world's most celebrated holiday is, perhaps surprisingly, New Year's Day. [Parenthetical expression.]

Interestingly, Americans have relatively few holidays. [Parenthetical expression.]

US workers, for example, receive fewer holidays than European workers do. [Transitional expression.]

(Dashes and parentheses may also set off parenthetical expressions. See pp. 338–40.)

When a transitional expression links main clauses, precede it with a semicolon and follow it with a comma (see pp. 318–19):

European workers often have long paid vacations; indeed, they may receive a full month after just a few years with a company.

Exception The conjunctions *and* and *but*, sometimes used as transitional expressions, are never followed by commas (see p. 315). Usage varies with some other transitional expressions, depending

---

Key terms

absolute phrase A phrase modifying a whole main clause and consisting of a participle and its subject: *Their homework completed, the children watched TV.* (See 4 p. 206.)

parenthetical expression An explanatory or supplemental word or phrase, such as *all things considered, to be frank,* or a brief example or fact. (See p. 339.)

transitional expression A word or phrase that shows the relationship between sentences: *for example, however, in fact, of course.* (See 1 pp. 44–45.)

on the expression and the writer's judgment. Many writers omit commas with expressions that we read without pauses, such as *also, hence, next, now, then,* and *thus.* The same applies to *therefore* and *instead* when they fall inside or at the ends of clauses.

> US workers, therefore, put in more work days. But the days themselves may be shorter.
>
> Then, the total hours worked would come out roughly the same.

Phrases of contrast
The substance, not the style, is important.
Substance, unlike style, cannot be faked.

Tag questions
They don't stop to consider others, do they?
Jones should be allowed to vote, shouldn't he?

Yes **and** *no*
Yes, the editorial did have a point.
No, that can never be.

Words of direct address
Cody, please bring me the newspaper.
With all due respect, sir, I will not.

Mild interjections
Well, you will never know who did it.
Oh, they forgot all about the baby.

Exercise 39.5 Revising: Punctuation of nonessential and essential elements

Insert commas as needed in the following paragraph to set off nonessential elements, and delete any commas that incorrectly set off essential elements. If a sentence is correct as given, mark the number preceding it.

1 Anesthesia which is commonly used during medical operations once made patients uncomfortable and had serious risks. **2** But new drugs and procedures, that have been developed in recent years, allow patients under anesthesia to be comfortable and much safer. **3** Twenty years ago, any patient, undergoing anesthesia, would have had to stay overnight in a hospital, probably feeling sick and very confused. **4** Today, many patients can have general anesthesia, which renders them com-

---

Key terms

tag question A question at the end of a statement, consisting of a pronoun, a helping verb, and sometimes *not: It isn't wet, is it?*

interjection A word that expresses feeling or commands attention: *Oh, must we?*

pletely unconscious, and still go home the same day. 5 Another form of anesthesia, monitored anesthesia or conscious sedation, allows the patient to be awake while feeling sleepy with no pain. 6 A surgeon may also suggest regional or local anesthesia which numbs only a specific part of the body and leaves the patient completely awake. 7 Sometimes, patients must choose among local, regional, and general anesthesia whether or not they want to make the choice. 8 In that case, patients should ask which type the anesthesiologist would choose if his or her child or spouse were having the surgery.

Exercise 39.6   Revising: Punctuation of nonessential and essential elements

Insert commas as needed in the following paragraphs to set off nonessential elements, and delete any commas that incorrectly set off essential elements. If a sentence is correct as given, mark the number preceding it.

1 Italians insist that Marco Polo the thirteenth-century explorer did not import pasta from China. 2 Pasta which consists of flour and water and often egg existed in Italy long before Marco Polo left for his travels. 3 A historian who studied pasta says that it originated in the Middle East in the fifth century. 4 Most Italians dispute this account although their evidence is shaky. 5 Wherever it originated, the Italians are now the undisputed masters, in making and cooking pasta.

6 Marcella Hazan, who has written several books on Italian cooking, insists that homemade and hand-rolled pasta is the best. 7 However, most cooks buy dried pasta lacking the time to make their own. 8 Homemade or dried, the finest pasta is made from semolina, a flour from hard durum wheat. 9 Pasta manufacturers choose hard durum wheat, because it makes firmer cooked pasta than common wheat does. 10 Pasta, made from common wheat, gets soggy in boiling water.

Exercise 39.7   Sentence combining: Essential and nonessential elements

Combine each pair of sentences below into one sentence that uses the element described in parentheses. Insert commas as appropriate. You will have to add, delete, change, and rearrange words. Some items have more than one possible answer.

Example:

Mr. Ward's oldest sister helped keep him alive. She was a nurse in the hospital. (*Nonessential clause beginning* <u>who</u>.)

Mr. Ward's oldest sister, who was a nurse in the hospital, helped keep him alive.

1 American colonists first imported pasta from the English. The English had discovered it as tourists in Italy. (*Nonessential clause beginning* <u>who</u>.)
2 The English returned from their grand tours of Italy. They were called *macaronis* because of their fancy airs. (*Essential phrase beginning* <u>returning</u>.)

3 A hair style was also called *macaroni.* It had elaborate curls. (*Essential phrase beginning with.*)
4 The song "Yankee Doodle" refers to this hairdo. It reports that Yankee Doodle "stuck a feather in his cap and called it macaroni." (*Essential clause beginning when.*)
5 The song was actually intended to poke fun at unrefined American colonists. It was a creation of the English. (*Nonessential appositive beginning a creation.*)

39d   Use commas between items in a series.

A **series** consists of three or more items of equal importance. The items may be words, phrases, or clauses.

Anna Spingle married at the age of seventeen, had three children by twenty-one, and divorced at twenty-two.

She worked as a cook, a baby-sitter, and a crossing guard.

Some writers omit the comma before the coordinating conjunction in a series (*Breakfast consisted of coffee, eggs, and kippers*). But the final comma is never wrong, and it always helps the reader see the last two items as separate.

Exercise 39.8   Revising: Commas with series items

In the following paragraph, insert commas as needed to punctuate items in series. If a sentence is correct as given, mark the number preceding it.

1 Photographers who take pictures of flowers need to pay special attention to lighting composition and focal point. **2** Many photographers prefer to shoot in the early morning, when the air is calm, the dew is still on the flowers, and the light is soft. **3** Some even like to photograph in light rain because water helps flowers to look fresh colorful and especially lively. **4** In composing a picture, the photographer can choose to show several flowers, just one flower or even a small part of a flower. **5** One effective composition leads the viewer's eye in from an edge of the photo devotes a large amount of the photo to the primary subject and then leads the eye out of the photo. **6** The focus changes as the eye moves away from the subject: the primary subject is in sharp focus, elements near the primary subject are in sharp focus and elements in the background are deliberately out of focus.

39e   Use commas between two or more adjectives that equally modify the same word.

Adjectives that equally modify the same word—**coordinate adjectives**—may be separated either by *and* or by a comma.

Spingle's scratched and dented car is old, but it gets her to work.
She has dreams of a sleek, shiny car.

Adjectives are not coordinate—and should not be separated by commas—when the one nearer the noun is more closely related to the noun in meaning.

Spingle's children work at various part-time jobs.
They all expect to go to a nearby community college.

Tests for commas with adjectives

1. **Identify the adjectives.**

   She was a <u>faithful sincere</u> friend.
   They are <u>dedicated medical</u> students.

2. **Can the adjectives be reversed without changing meaning?**

   She was a <u>sincere faithful</u> friend. *Yes.*
   They are <u>medical dedicated</u> students. *No.*

3. **Can the word *and* be sensibly inserted between the adjectives?**

   She was a <u>faithful and sincere</u> friend. *Yes.*
   They are <u>dedicated and medical</u> students. *No.*

4. **If *yes* to both questions, the adjectives *are* coordinate and *should* be separated by a comma.**

   She was a faithful, sincere friend.

   If *no* to both questions, the adjectives are *not* coordinate and should *not* be separated by a comma.

   They are dedicated medical students.

In the following paragraph, insert commas as needed between adjectives, and delete any unneeded commas. If a sentence is correct as given, mark the number preceding it.

1 Most people have seen a blind person being aided by a patient observant guide dog. **2** What is not commonly known is how normal untrained dogs become these special, highly skilled dogs. **3** An organization called the Seeing Eye breeds dogs to perform this specific, guide job. **4** Enthusiastic affectionate volunteers raise the dogs until they are about seventeen months old. **5** Each dog then undergoes a thorough health examination. **6** Dogs who pass the health exam go through a rigorous, four-month, training program. **7** The trained dog is then matched with a blind person, and the two of them undergo their own intensive communication training before graduating to their life together.

Insert commas as needed in the following paragraph to separate series items or adjectives. If a sentence is correct as given, mark the number preceding it.

1 Shoes with high heels were originally designed to protect the wearer's feet from mud garbage and animal waste in the streets. **2** The first high heels worn strictly for fashion, however, appeared in the sixteenth century. **3** They were made popular when the short powerful King Louis XIV of France began wearing them. **4** At first, high heels were worn by men and were made of colorful silk fabrics soft suedes or smooth leathers. **5** But Louis's influence was so strong that men and women of the court priests and cardinals and even household servants wore high heels. **6** By the seventeenth and eighteenth centuries, only wealthy fashionable French women wore high heels. **7** At that time, French culture represented the one true standard of elegance and refinement. **8** High-heeled shoes for women spread to other courts of Europe among the Europeans of North America and to all social classes. **9** Now high heels are common, though depending on the fashion they range from short squat thick heels to tall skinny spikes. **10** A New York boutique recently showed a pair of purple satin pumps with tiny jeweled bows and four-inch stiletto heels.

39f Use commas in dates, addresses, place names, and long numbers.

Within a sentence, any date, address, or place name that contains a comma should also end with a comma.

Dates

July 4, 1776, is the date the Declaration was signed.

The bombing of Pearl Harbor on Sunday, December 7, 1941, prompted American entry into World War II.

Do not use commas between the parts of a date in inverted order (*15 December 1992*) or in dates consisting of a month or season and a year (*December 1941*).

Addresses and place names

Use the address 220 Cornell Road, Woodside, California 94062, for all correspondence. [Do not use a comma between a state name and a zip code.]

Columbus, Ohio, is the location of Ohio State University.

Long numbers

Use the comma to separate the figures in long numbers into groups of three, counting from the right. With numbers of four digits, the comma is optional.

The new assembly plant cost $7,525,000.

A kilometer is 3,281 feet [*or* 3281 feet].

CULTURE LANGUAGE Usage in standard American English differs from that in some other languages and dialects, which use a period, not a comma, to separate the figures in long numbers.

Exercise 39.11 **Revising: Punctuation of dates, addresses, place names, numbers**

Insert commas as needed in the following paragraph.

1 The festival will hold a benefit dinner and performance on March 10 2009 in Asheville. **2** The organizers hope to raise more than $100000 from donations and ticket sales. **3** Performers are expected from as far away as Milan Italy and Kyoto Japan. **4** All inquiries sent to Mozart Festival PO Box 725 Asheville North Carolina 28803 will receive a quick response. **5** The deadline for ordering tickets by mail is Monday December 3 2008.

39g Use commas with quotations according to standard practice.

The words *she said, he writes,* and so on identify the source of a quotation. These **signal phrases** should be separated from the quotation by punctuation, usually a comma or commas.

"Knowledge is power⬤" writes Francis Bacon.

"The shore has a dual nature⬤" observes Rachel Carson⬤ "changing with the swing of the tides." [The signal phrase interrupts the quotation at a comma and thus ends with a comma.]

Exceptions When a signal phrase interrupts a quotation between main clauses, follow the signal phrase with a semicolon or a period. The choice depends on the punctuation of the original.

Not	"That part of my life was over," she wrote, "his words had sealed it shut."
But	"That part of my life was over," she wrote⬤ "His words had sealed it shut." [*She wrote* interrupts the quotation at a period.]
Or	"That part of my life was over," she wrote⬤ "his words had sealed it shut." [*She wrote* interrupts the quotation at a semicolon.]

Do not use a comma when a signal phrase follows a quotation ending in an exclamation point or a question mark:

"Claude⬤" Mrs. Harrison called.
"Why must I come home⬤" he asked.

Do not use a comma with a quotation that is integrated into your sentence structure, including one introduced by *that:*

James Baldwin insists that⬤"one must never, in one's life, accept . . . injustices as commonplace."

Baldwin thought that the violence of a riot●"had been devised as a corrective" to his own violence.

Do not use a comma with a quoted title unless it is a nonessential appositive:

The Beatles recorded●"She Loves You●" in 1963.
The Beatles' first huge US hit● "She Loves You●," appeared in 1963.

Exercise 39.12 **Revising: Punctuation of quotations**

In the following sentences, insert commas or semicolons as needed to correct punctuation with quotations. If a sentence is correct as given, mark the number preceding it.

1 The writer and writing teacher Peter Elbow proposes an "open-ended writing process" that "can change you, not just your words."

2 "I think of the open-ended writing process as a voyage in two stages" Elbow says.

3 "The sea voyage is a process of divergence, branching, proliferation, and confusion" Elbow continues "the coming to land is a process of convergence, pruning, centralizing, and clarifying."

4 "Keep up one session of writing long enough to get loosened up and tired" advises Elbow "long enough in fact to make a bit of a voyage."

5 "In coming to new land" Elbow says "you develop a new conception of what you are writing about."

39h Delete commas where they are not required.

Commas can make sentences choppy and even confusing if they are used more often than needed.

1 No comma between subject and verb, verb and object, or preposition and object

Not The returning soldiers, received a warm welcome. [Separated subject and verb.]

But The returning soldiers●received a warm welcome.

Not They had chosen, to fight for their country despite, the risks. [Separated verb *chosen* and its object; separated preposition *despite* and its object.]

But They had chosen●to fight for their country despite●the risks.

Key term

nonessential appositive A word or words that rename an immediately preceding noun but do not limit or define the noun: *The author's first story, "Biloxi," won a prize.* (See p. 306.)

2 No comma in most compound constructions

Compound constructions consisting of two elements almost never require a comma. The only exception is the sentence consisting of two main clauses linked by a coordinating conjunction: *The computer failed, but employees kept working* (see p. 300).

Not	┌─────── compound subject ───────┐ Banks, and other financial institutions have helped older people ┌── compound object of preposition ──┐ with money management, and investment.
But	Banks and other financial institutions have helped older people with money management and investment.

Not	┌─────────── compound predicate ───────────┐ One bank created special accounts for older people, and held ┌compound object of verb┐ classes, and workshops.
But	One bank created special accounts for older people and held classes and workshops.

3 No comma after a conjunction

Not	Parents of adolescents notice increased conflict at puberty, and, they complain of bickering.
But	Parents of adolescents notice increased conflict at puberty, and they complain of bickering.

Not	Although, other primates leave the family at adolescence, humans do not.
But	Although other primates leave the family at adolescence, humans do not.

4 No commas around essential elements

Not	Hawthorne's work, *The Scarlet Letter*, was the first major American novel. [The title is essential to distinguish the novel from the rest of Hawthorne's work.]
But	Hawthorne's work *The Scarlet Letter* was the first major American novel.

Key terms

compound construction Two or more words, phrases, or clauses connected by a coordinating conjunction, usually *and, but, or, nor: man and woman, old or young, leaking oil and spewing steam.*

conjunction A connecting word such as a **coordinating conjunction** (*and, but, or,* and so on) or a **subordinating conjunction** (*although, because, when,* and so on). (See **4** pp. 195–96.)

Not The symbols, that Hawthorne uses, have influenced other novelists. [The clause identifies which symbols have been influential.]

But The symbols‿that Hawthorne uses‿have influenced other novelists.

---

5 | No commas around a series

Commas separate the items *within* a series (p. 310) but do not separate the series from the rest of the sentence.

Not The skills of, hunting, herding, and agriculture, sustained the Native Americans.

But The skills of‿hunting herding, and agriculture‿sustained the Native Americans.

---

6 | No comma before an indirect quotation

Not The report concluded, that dieting could be more dangerous than
overeating.

But The report concluded‿that dieting could be more dangerous than
overeating.

Exercise 39.13 Revising: Needless and misused commas

Revise the following paragraph to eliminate needless or misused commas. If a sentence is correct as given, mark the number preceding it.

1 One of the largest aquifers in North America, the Ogallala aquifer, is named after the Ogallala Indian tribe, which once lived in the region and hunted buffalo there. **2** The Ogallala aquifer underlies a region from western Texas through northern Nebraska, and has a huge capacity of fresh water, that is contained in a layer of sand and gravel. **3** But, the water in the Ogallala is being removed faster than it is being replaced. **4** Water is pumped from the aquifer for many purposes, such as, drinking and other household use, industrial use, and, agricultural use. **5** The Great Plains area above the Ogallala, often lacks enough rainfall for the crops, that are grown there. **6** As a consequence, the crops in the Great Plains are watered by irrigation systems, that pump water from the Ogallala, and distribute it from half-mile-long sprinkler arms. **7** Ogallala water is receding between six inches and three feet a year, the amount depending on location. **8** Some areas are experiencing water shortages already, and the pumping continues. **9** A scientific commission recently estimated that, "at the present consumption rate, the Ogallala will be depleted in forty years."

Key term

essential element Limits the word it refers to and thus can't be omitted without leaving the meaning too general. (See pp. 304–05.)

Exercise 39.14 Revising: Commas

Insert commas as needed in the following paragraphs, and delete any misused commas. If a sentence is correct as given, mark the number preceding it.

1 Ellis Island New York reopened for business in 1990 but now the customers are tourists not immigrants. 2 This spot which lies in New York Harbor was the first American soil seen, or touched by many of the nation's immigrants. 3 Though other places also served as ports of entry for foreigners none has the symbolic power of, Ellis Island. 4 Between its opening in 1892 and its closing in 1954, over 20 million people about two-thirds of all immigrants were detained there before taking up their new lives in the United States. 5 Ellis Island processed over 2000 newcomers a day when immigration was at its peak between 1900 and 1920.

6 As the end of a long voyage and the introduction to the New World Ellis Island must have left something to be desired. 7 The "huddled masses" as the Statue of Liberty calls them indeed were huddled. 8 New arrivals were herded about kept standing in lines for hours or days yelled at and abused. 9 Assigned numbers they submitted their bodies to the pokings and proddings of the silent nurses and doctors, who were charged with ferreting out the slightest sign, of sickness disability or insanity. 10 That test having been passed, the immigrants faced interrogation by an official through an interpreter. 11 Those, with names deemed inconveniently long or difficult to pronounce, often found themselves permanently labeled with abbreviations, of their names, or with the names, of their hometowns. 12 But, millions survived the examination humiliation and confusion, to take the last short boat ride to New York City. 13 For many of them and especially for their descendants Ellis Island eventually became not a nightmare but the place where a new life began.

40 The Semicolon

The semicolon (;) separates equal and balanced sentence elements—usually main clauses (next page) and occasionally items in series (p. 320).

Grammar checkers A grammar checker can spot a few errors in the use of semicolons. For example, a checker suggested using a semicolon after *perfect* in *The set was perfect, the director had planned every detail,* thus correcting a comma splice. But it missed

mycomplab

Visit *mycomplab.com* for more resources and exercises on the semicolon.

the incorrect semicolon in *The set was perfect; deserted streets, dark houses, and gloomy mist* (a colon would be correct).

40a Use a semicolon between main clauses not joined by *and*, *but*, or another coordinating conjunction.

When no coordinating conjunction links two main clauses, the clauses should be separated by a semicolon.

A new ulcer drug arrived on the market with a mixed reputation; doctors find that the drug works but worry about its side effects.

The side effects are not minor; some leave the patient quite uncomfortable or even ill.

Note This rule prevents the errors known as comma splices and fused sentences. (See **4** pp. 285–89.)

> **Exercise 40.1   Revising: Punctuation between main clauses**
> In the following paragraph, insert semicolons as needed to separate main clauses. If a sentence is correct as given, mark the number preceding it.
>
> **1** More and more musicians are playing computerized instruments more and more listeners are worrying about the future of acoustic instruments. **2** The computer is not the first technology in music the pipe organ and saxophone were also technological breakthroughs in their day. **3** Musicians have always experimented with new technology while audiences have always resisted the experiments. **4** Most computer musicians are not merely following the latest fad they are discovering new sounds and new ways to manipulate sound. **5** Few musicians have abandoned acoustic instruments most value acoustic sounds as much as electronic sounds.

40b Use a semicolon between main clauses related by *however*, *for example*, and so on.

When a conjunctive adverb or another transitional expression relates two main clauses in a single sentence, the clauses should be separated with a semicolon:

An American immigrant, Levi Strauss, invented blue jeans in the 1860s; eventually, his product clothed working men throughout the West.

> ┌─ **Key terms** ─────────────────────────────
> **main clause** A word group that can stand alone as a sentence because it contains a subject and a predicate and does not begin with a subordinating word: *Parks help cities breathe.* (See **4** p. 208.)
> **coordinating conjunctions** *And, but, or, nor,* and sometimes *for, so, yet.*

The position of the semicolon between main clauses never changes, but the conjunctive adverb or transitional expression may move around within the second clause. Wherever the adverb or expression falls, it is usually set off with a comma or commas. (See p. 307.)

Blue jeans have become fashionable all over the world; however, the American originators still wear more jeans than anyone else.

Blue jeans have become fashionable all over the world; the American originators, however, still wear more jeans than anyone else.

Blue jeans have become fashionable all over the world; the American originators still wear more jeans than anyone else, however.

Note This rule prevents the errors known as comma splices and fused sentences. (See **4** pp. 285–89.)

Exercise 40.2 Revising: Punctuation between main clauses with conjunctive adverbs or transitional expressions

In the following paragraph, insert semicolons as needed to separate main clauses related by a conjunctive adverb or transitional expression. Also insert a comma or commas as needed to set off the adverb or expression.

1 Music is a form of communication like language the basic elements however are not letters but notes. **2** Computers can process any information that can be represented numerically as a result they can process musical information. **3** A computer's ability to process music depends on what software it can run it must moreover be connected to a system that converts electrical vibration into sound. **4** Computers and their sound systems can produce many different sounds indeed the number of possible sounds is infinite. **5** The powerful music computers are very expensive therefore they are used only by professional musicians.

Exercise 40.3 Sentence combining: Related main clauses

Combine each of the following sets of sentences into one sentence containing only two main clauses. As indicated in parentheses, connect the clauses with a semicolon alone or with a semicolon plus a conjunctive adverb or transitional expression followed by a comma. You will have to add, delete, change, and rearrange words. Each item has more than one possible answer.

┌─ **Key terms** ─────────────────────────────────

conjunctive adverb A modifier that describes the relation of the ideas in two clauses, such as *consequently, hence, however, indeed, instead, nonetheless, otherwise, still, then, therefore, thus.* (See **4** p. 288.)

transitional expression A word or phrase that shows the relationship between ideas. Transitional expressions include conjunctive adverbs as well as *for example, in fact, of course,* and many other words and phrases. (See **1** pp. 44–45.)

Example:

The Albanians censored their news. We got little news from them. And what we got was unreliable. (*Therefore and semicolon.*)

The Albanians censored their news⨀ therefore⨀ the little news we got from them was unreliable.

1 Electronic instruments are prevalent in jazz. They are also prevalent in rock music. They are less common in classical music. (*However and semicolon.*)
2 Jazz and rock change rapidly. They nourish experimentation. They nourish improvisation. (*Semicolon alone.*)
3 The notes and instrumentation of traditional classical music were established by a composer. The composer was writing decades or centuries ago. Such music does not change. (*Therefore and semicolon.*)
4 Contemporary classical music not only can draw on tradition. It can also respond to innovations. These are innovations such as jazz rhythms and electronic sounds. (*Semicolon alone.*)
5 Much contemporary electronic music is more than just one type of music. It is more than just jazz, rock, or classical. It is a fusion of all three. (*Semicolon alone.*)

40c Use semicolons between main clauses or series items containing commas.

Normally, commas separate main clauses linked by coordinating conjunctions (*and, but, or, nor*) and separate items in a series. But when the clauses or series items contain commas, a semicolon between them makes the sentence easier to read.

Lewis and Clark led the men of their party with consummate skill, inspiring and encouraging them, doctoring and caring for them⨀ and they kept voluminous journals. —Page Smith

The custody case involved Amy Dalton, the child⨀ Ellen and Mark Dalton, the parents⨀ and Ruth and Hal Blum, the grandparents.

Exercise 40.4 Revising: Punctuation of main clauses and series items containing commas

Substitute semicolons for commas in the following paragraph to separate main clauses or series items that contain commas.

1 The Indian subcontinent is separated from the rest of the world by clear barriers: the Bay of Bengal and the Arabian Sea to the east and west, respectively, the Indian Ocean to the south, and 1600 miles of mountain ranges to the north. 2 In the north of India are the world's highest mountains, the Himalayas, and farther south are fertile farmlands, unpopulated deserts, and rain forests. 3 India is a nation of ethnic and linguistic diversity, with numerous religions, including Hinduism, Islam, and Christianity, with distinct castes and ethnic groups, and with sixteen languages, including the official Hindi and the "associate official" English.

40d Delete or replace unneeded semicolons.

Too many semicolons can make writing choppy. And semicolons are often misused in certain constructions that call for other punctuation or no punctuation.

1 No semicolon between a main clause and a subordinate clause or phrase

The semicolon does not separate unequal parts, such as main clauses and subordinate clauses or phrases.

Not Pygmies are in danger of extinction; because of encroaching development.

But Pygmies are in danger of extinction because of encroaching development.

Not According to African authorities; only about 35,000 Pygmies exist today.

But According to African authorities, only about 35,000 Pygmies exist today.

2 No semicolon before a series or explanation

Colons and dashes, not semicolons, introduce series, explanations, and so forth. (See the next page and p. 338.)

Not Teachers have heard all sorts of reasons why students do poorly; psychological problems, family illness, too much work, too little time.

But Teachers have heard all sorts of reasons why students do poorly: psychological problems, family illness, too much work, too little time.

Exercise 40.5 Revising: Semicolons

In the following paragraph, insert semicolons as needed and eliminate any misused semicolons, substituting other punctuation as appropriate. If a sentence is correct as given, mark the number preceding it.

1 The set, sounds, and actors in the movie captured the essence of horror films. 2 The set was ideal; dark, deserted streets, trees dipping their branches over the sidewalks, mist hugging the ground and creeping up to meet the trees, looming shadows of unlighted, turreted houses. 3 The sounds, too, were appropriate, especially terrifying was the hard, hollow sound of footsteps echoing throughout the film. 4 But the best feature of the movie was its actors; all of them tall, pale, and thin to the point of emaciation. 5 With one exception, they were dressed uniformly in gray and had gray hair. 6 The exception was an actress who dressed only in black as if to set off her pale yellow, nearly white, long hair; the only color in the film. 7 The glinting black eyes of another actor stole almost every scene, indeed, they were the source of the film's mischief.

41 The Colon

The colon (:) is mainly a mark of introduction: it signals that the words following will explain or amplify (below). The colon also has several conventional uses, such as in expressions of time.

Grammar checkers Many grammar checkers cannot recognize missing or misused colons and instead simply ignore them.

41a Use a colon to introduce a concluding explanation, a series, an appositive, and some quotations.

As an introducer, a colon is always preceded by a complete main clause. It may or may not be followed by a main clause. This is one way the colon differs from the semicolon, which generally separates main clauses only. (See pp. 318–19.)

Explanation

Soul food has a deceptively simple definition: the ethnic cooking of African Americans.

Sometimes a concluding explanation is preceded by *the following* or *as follows* and a colon:

A more precise definition might be the following: soul food draws on ingredients, cooking methods, and dishes that originated in Africa, were brought to the New World by slaves, and were modified or supplemented in the Caribbean and the American South.

Note A complete sentence *after* a colon may begin with a capital letter or a small letter (as in the preceding example). Just be consistent throughout an essay.

Series

At least three soul food dishes are familiar to most Americans: fried chicken, barbecued spareribs, and sweet potatoes.

> **Key term**
>
> **main clause** A word group that can stand alone as a sentence because it contains a subject and a predicate and does not begin with a subordinating word: *Soul food is a varied cuisine.* (See **4** p. 208.)

mycomplab

Visit *mycomplab.com* for more resources and exercises on the colon.

Appositive

Soul food has only one disadvantage⬤ fat.

Namely, that is, and other expressions that introduce appositives *follow* the colon: *Soul food has only one disadvantage⬤ namely, fat.*

Quotation

One soul food chef has a solution⬤ "Soul food doesn't have to be greasy to taste good. Instead of using ham hocks to flavor beans, I use smoked turkey wings. The soulful, smoky taste remains, but without all the fat of pork."

Use a colon before a quotation when the introduction is a complete sentence.

41b Use a colon after the salutation of a business letter, between a title and subtitle, and between divisions of time.

Salutation of business letter

Dear Ms. Burak⬤

Title and subtitle

Charles Dickens⬤ An Introduction to His Novels

Time

12⬤26 AM   6⬤00 PM

41c Delete or replace unneeded colons.

Use the colon only at the end of a main clause, not in the following situations:

■ **Delete a colon after a verb.**

Not   The best-known soul food dish i̲s̲: fried chicken.
But   The best-known soul food dish is⬤fried chicken.

■ **Delete a colon after a preposition.**

Not   Soul food recipes can be found i̲n̲: mainstream cookbooks as well as specialized references.

Key terms

appositive A noun or noun substitute that renames another noun immediately before it: *my brother, Jack.* (See **4** p. 207.)

preposition *In, on, outside,* or another word that takes a noun or pronoun as its object: *i̲n̲ the house.* (See **4** p. 195.)

But   Soul food recipes can be found in mainstream cookbooks as well as specialized references.

■ **Delete a colon after** *such as* **or** *including.*

Not   Many Americans have not tasted delicacies <u>such as:</u> chitlins and black-eyed peas.

But   Many Americans have not tasted delicacies <u>such as</u> chitlins and black-eyed peas.

Exercise 41.1   **Revising: Colons**

In the following paragraph, insert colons as needed and delete misused colons. If a sentence is correct as given, mark the number preceding it.

1 In remote areas of many developing countries, simple signs mark human habitation a dirt path, a few huts, smoke from a campfire. 2 However, in the built-up sections of industrialized countries, nature is all but obliterated by signs of human life, such as: houses, factories, skyscrapers, and highways. 3 The spectacle makes many question the words of Ecclesiastes 1.4 "One generation passeth away, and another cometh; but the earth abideth forever." 4 Yet many scientists see the future differently: they hold that human beings have all the technology necessary to clean up the earth and restore the cycles of nature. 5 All that is needed is: a change in the attitudes of those who use technology.

Exercise 41.2   **Revising: Colons and semicolons**

In the following paragraphs, insert colons and semicolons as needed and delete or replace them where they are misused. If a sentence is correct as given, mark the number preceding it.

1 Sunlight is made up of three kinds of radiation: visible rays; infrared rays, which we cannot see; and ultraviolet rays, which are also invisible. 2 Infrared rays are the longest; measuring 700 nanometers and longer; while ultraviolet rays are the shortest; measuring 400 nanometers and shorter. 3 Especially in the ultraviolet range; sunlight is harmful to the eyes. 4 Ultraviolet rays can damage the retina: furthermore, they can cause cataracts on the lens.

5 The lens protects the eye by: absorbing much of the ultraviolet radiation and thus protecting the retina. 6 Protecting the retina, however, the lens becomes a victim; growing cloudy and blocking vision. 7 The best way to protect your eyes is: to wear hats that shade the face and sunglasses that screen out ultraviolet rays. 8 Many sunglass lenses have been designed as ultraviolet screens; many others are extremely ineffective. 9 If sunglass lenses do not screen out ultraviolet rays and if people can see your eyes through them, they will not protect your eyes, and you will be at risk for cataracts later in life. 10 People who spend much time outside in the sun; owe it to themselves to buy and wear sunglasses that shield their eyes.

42 The Apostrophe

The apostrophe (') appears as part of a word to indicate possession (below), the omission of one or more letters (p. 330), or sometimes plural number (p. 331).

Grammar checkers A grammar checker usually has mixed results in recognizing apostrophe errors. For instance, it may flag missing apostrophes in contractions (as in *isnt*) but may not distinguish between *its* and *it's*, *their* and *they're*, *your* and *you're*, *whose* and *who's*. A checker may identify some apostrophe errors in possessives but overlook others, and it may flag correct plurals. Instead of relying on your checker, try using your computer's Search or Find function to hunt for all words you have ended in *-s*. Then check them to ensure that apostrophes are used correctly.

42a Use the apostrophe to show possession.

A noun or indefinite pronoun shows possession with an apostrophe and, usually, an *-s: the dog's hair, everyone's hope*. Only personal pronouns such as *hers* and *its* do not use apostrophes for possession.

Note Apostrophes are easy to misuse. Always check your drafts to be sure that all words ending in *-s* neither omit needed apostrophes nor add unneeded ones. Also, remember that the apostrophe or apostrophe-plus-*s* is an *addition*. Before this addition, always spell the name of the owner or owners without dropping or adding letters.

1 Singular words: Add -'s.

Bill Boughton's skillful card tricks amaze children.
Anyone's eyes would widen.
Most tricks will pique an adult's curiosity, too.

The -'s ending for singular words pertains also to singular words ending in *-s*, as the next examples show.

Henry James's novels reward the patient reader.
The business's customers filed suit.

> **Key term**
>
> **indefinite pronoun** A pronoun that does not refer to a specific person or thing, such as *anyone, each, everybody, no one,* or *something.* (See 4 p. 254.)

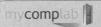

mycomplab

Visit *mycomplab.com* for more resources and exercises on the apostrophe.

Uses and misuses of the apostrophe

Uses of the apostrophe

■ **Use an apostrophe to form the possessives of nouns and indefinite pronouns** (previous and facing pages).

Singular	Plural
Ms. Park's	the Parks'
lawyer's	lawyers'
everyone's	two weeks'

■ **Use an apostrophe to form contractions** (p. 330).

it's a girl	shouldn't
you're	won't

■ **The apostrophe is optional for plurals of abbreviations, dates, and words or characters named as words** (p. 331).

MAs or MA's	Cs or C's
1960s or 1960's	*if*s or *if*'s

Misuses of the apostrophe

■ **Do not use an apostrophe plus -s to form the possessives of plural nouns ending in -s** (opposite). Instead, use an apostrophe alone after the -s that forms the plural.

Not	But
the Kim's car	the Kims' car
boy's fathers	boys' fathers
babie's care	babies' care

■ **Do not use an apostrophe to form plurals of nouns** (p. 328).

Not	But
book's are	books are
the Freed's	the Freeds

■ **Do not use an apostrophe with verbs ending in -s** (p. 328).

Not	But
swim's	swims

■ **Do not use an apostrophe to form the possessives of personal pronouns** (p. 328).

Not	But
it's toes	its toes
your's	yours

Exception An apostrophe alone may be added to a singular word ending in -s when another s would make the word difficult to say: *Moses* mother, Joan Rivers* jokes*. But the added *-s* is never wrong (*Moses's*, *Rivers's*).

2 **Plural words ending in** *-s:* **Add -' only.**

> Workers' incomes have fallen slightly over the past year.
> Many students benefit from several years' work after high school.
> The Jameses' talents are extraordinary.

Note the difference in the possessives of singular and plural words ending in *-s*. The singular form usually takes the apostrophe plus *-s: James's*. The plural takes only the apostrophe: *Jameses'*.

3 **Plural words not ending in** *-s:* **Add -'s.**

> Children's educations are at stake.
> We need to attract the media's attention.

4 **Compound words: Add -'s only to the last word.**

> The brother-in-law's business failed.
> Taxes are always somebody else's fault.

5 **Two or more owners: Add -'s depending on possession.**

Individual possession
> Zimbale's and Mason's comedy techniques are similar. [Each comedian has his own technique.]

Joint possession
> The child recovered despite her mother and father's neglect. [The mother and father were jointly neglectful.]

Exercise 42.1 Forming possessives

Form the possessive of each word or word group in brackets.

> *Example:*
> The [men] blood pressures were higher than the [women].
> The men's blood pressures were higher than the women's.

1 In the myths of ancient Greeks, the [goddesses] roles vary widely. 2 [Demeter] responsibility is the fruitfulness of the earth. 3 [Athena] role is to guard the city of Athens. 4 [Artemis] function is to care for wild animals and small children. 5 [Athena and Artemis] father, Zeus, is the king of the gods.

6 Even a single [goddess] responsibilities are often varied. 7 For instance, over several [centuries] time Athena changes from a [mariner]

goddess to the patron of crafts. 8 She is also concerned with fertility and with [children] well-being, since the strength of Athens depended on a large and healthy population. 9 Athena often changes into [birds] forms, and in [Homer] *Odyssey*, she assumes a [sea eagle] form.

10 In ancient Athens the myths of Athena were part of [everyone] knowledge and life. 11 A cherished myth tells how she fights to retain possession of her [people] land when the god Poseidon wants it. 12 [Athena and Poseidon] skills are different, and each promises a special gift to the Athenians. 13 At the [contest] conclusion, Poseidon has given water and Athena has given an olive tree, for sustenance. 14 The other gods decide that the [Athenians] lives depend more on Athena than on Poseidon.

Exercise 42.2 **Revising: Apostrophes with possessives**

In the following paragraph, insert or reposition apostrophes as needed and delete any needless apostrophes. If a sentence is correct as given, mark the number preceding it.

1 The eastern coast of Belize was once a fishermans paradise, but overfishing caused the fishing industrys sharp decline in this Central American country. 2 The country's government is now showing the world that leaders' foresight can turn a problem into an opportunity. 3 Belize Is capitalizing on something that can capture tourists interest: whale sharks. 4 Huge but harmless to people, whale sharks regularly visit Belizes coast to feed on smaller fishes eggs. 5 The predictable gatherings of the shark's attract large numbers of scuba diver's and snorkeler's, so that the fishs' fascinating beauty has become an economic treasure. 6 A tourists eagerness to spend money for an up-close view of whale sharks is Belizes renewable and reliable resource.

42b **Delete or replace any apostrophe in a plural noun, a singular verb, or a possessive personal pronoun.**

1 Plural nouns

The plurals of nouns are generally formed by adding *-s* or *-es*, never with an apostrophe: *boys, families, Joneses, Murphys*.

Not The Jones' controlled the firm's until 2001.
But The Joneses controlled the firms until 2001.

2 Singular verbs

Verbs ending in *-s* never take an apostrophe:

Not The subway break's down less often now.
But The subway breaks down less often now.

3 Possessives of personal pronouns

His, hers, its, ours, yours, theirs, and *whose* are possessive forms of *he, she, it, we, you, they,* and *who.* They do not take apostrophes:

Not The house is her's. It's roof leaks.

But The house is hers. Its roof leaks.

Don't confuse possessive pronouns with contractions. See the next page.

Exercise 42.3 Distinguishing between plurals and possessives

Supply the appropriate form—possessive or plural—of each word given in brackets. Some words require apostrophes, and some do not.

Example:

A dozen Hawaiian [shirt], each with [it] own loud design, hung in the window.

A dozen Hawaiian shirts, each with its own loud design, hung in the window.

1 Demeter may be the oldest of the ancient Greek [god], older than Zeus. **2** In myth she is the earth mother, which means that the responsibility for the fertility of both [animal] and [plant] is [she]. **3** Many prehistoric [culture] had earth [goddess] like Demeter. **4** In Greek culture the [goddess] festival came at harvest time, with [it] celebration of bounty. **5** The [people] [prayer] to Demeter thanked her for grain and other [gift].

Exercise 42.4 Revising: Misuses of the apostrophe

Revise the following paragraph by deleting or repositioning apostrophes or by repairing incorrect possessive pronouns or contractions. If a sentence is correct as given, mark the number preceding it.

1 Research is proving that athlete's who excel at distance running have physical characteristics that make them faster than most people. **2** For example, they're hearts are larger. **3** An average adult's heart pump's about fifteen liters of blood per minute, but a competitive distance runner's heart circulate's twice as much. **4** Elite runners are also more efficient: they're able to run with less work than less talented runners must exert. **5** In addition, competitive runner's are able to keep running for long time's at high levels of exertion. **6** Although these abilities can be honed in training, they cannot be acquired by a runner: they are his' or her's from birth.

Exercise 42.5 Revising: Contractions and personal pronouns

Revise the following paragraph to correct mistakes in the use of contractions and personal pronouns. If a sentence is correct as given, mark the number preceding it.

1 Roald Dahl's children's novel *James and the Giant Peach* has been enjoyed by each generation of readers since its first publication in 1961. **2** Its a magical story of adventure and friendship. **3** James, a lonely boy whose being raised by his two nasty aunts, accidentally drops some mysterious crystals by an old peach tree in the yard. **4** The peach at the very top grows to an enormous size, and when James crawls inside, he finds friendly, oversized bugs ready to welcome him into there family. 5 As the peach breaks from the tree and rolls into the ocean, their plunged into an adventure that takes them to the top of the Empire State Building.

42c Use the apostrophe to form contractions.

A **contraction** replaces one or more letters, numbers, or words with an apostrophe, as in the following examples:

it is, it has	it's	cannot	can't
they are	they're	does not	doesn't
you are	you're	were not	weren't
who is, who has	who's	class of 2012	class of '12

Note Don't confuse contractions with personal pronouns:

Contractions	**Personal pronouns**
It's a book.	Its cover is green.
They're coming.	Their car broke down.
You're right.	Your idea is good.
Who's coming?	Whose party is it?

Exercise 42.6 Forming contractions

Form contractions from each set of words below. Use each contraction in a complete sentence.

Example:

we are: we're
We're open to ideas.

1	she would	6	she will
2	could not	7	hurricane of 1962
3	they are	8	is not
4	he is	9	it is
5	do not	10	will not

Exercise 42.7 Revising: Contractions and personal pronouns

Revise the following paragraph to correct mistakes in the use of contractions and personal pronouns. If a sentence is correct as given, mark the number preceding it.

1 In Greek myth the goddess Demeter has a special fondness for Eleusis, near Athens, and it's people. 2 She finds rest among the people and is touched by their kindness. 3 As a reward Demeter gives the Eleusians the secret for making they're land fruitful. 4 The Eleusians begin a cult in honor of Demeter, whose worshiped in secret ceremonies.

5 Its unknown what happened in the ceremonies, for no participant ever revealed there rituals.

42d The apostrophe is optional to mark plural abbreviations, dates, and words or characters named as words.

You'll sometimes see apostrophes used to form the plurals of abbreviations (BA's), dates (1900's), and words or characters named as words (*but*'s). However, most current style guides recommend against the apostrophe in these cases.

BAs	PhDs
1990s	2000s

The sentence has too many *buts*.
Two *3*s end the zip code.

Note Italicize or underline a word or character named as a word (see **6** p. 361), but not the added *-s*.

Exercise 42.8 **Revising: Apostrophes**

Revise the following paragraph to correct mistakes in the use of apostrophes or any confusion between contractions and possessive personal pronouns. If a sentence is correct as given, mark the number preceding it.

1 People who's online experiences include blogging, Web cams, and social-networking sites are often used to seeing the details of other peoples private lives. **2** Many are also comfortable sharing they're own opinions, photographs, and videos with family, friend's and even stranger's. **3** However, they need to realize that employers and even the government can see they're information, too. **4** Employers commonly put applicants names through social-networking Web sites such as *MySpace* and *Facebook*. **5** Many companies monitor their employees outbound e-mail. **6** People can take steps to protect their personal information by adjusting the privacy settings on their social-networking pages. **7** They can avoid posting photos of themselves that they wouldnt want an employer to see. **8** They can avoid sending personal e-mail while their at work. **9** Its the individuals responsibility to protect there own private information.

43 Quotation Marks

Quotation marks—either double (" ") or single (' ')—mainly enclose direct quotations from speech or writing, enclose certain titles, and highlight words used in a special sense. These are the uses covered in this chapter, along with placing quotation marks outside or inside other punctuation marks. Additional information on using quotations appears elsewhere in this book:

- **Using commas with signal phrases introducing quotations.** See pp. 313–14.
- **Using the ellipsis mark and brackets to indicate changes in quotations.** See pp. 340–43.
- **Quoting sources versus paraphrasing or summarizing them.** See **7** pp. 414–17.
- **Integrating quotations into your text.** See **7** pp. 418–23.
- **Acknowledging the sources of quotations to avoid plagiarism.** See **7** pp. 427–28.
- **Formatting long prose quotations and poetry quotations.** See **MLA** pp. 507–08 and **APA** p. 541.

Note Always use quotation marks in pairs, one at the beginning of a quotation and one at the end.

Grammar checkers A grammar checker will help you use quotation marks in pairs by flagging a lone mark. It may also look for punctuation inside or outside quotation marks, but it may not detect errors when punctuation should actually fall outside quotation marks.

43a Use double quotation marks to enclose direct quotations.

A **direct quotation** reports what someone said or wrote, in the exact words of the original:

> "Life," said the psychoanalyst Karen Horney, "remains a very efficient therapist."

Note Do not use quotation marks with a direct quotation that is set off from your text. See **MLA** pp. 507–08 and **APA** p. 541. Also

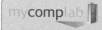

Visit *mycomplab.com* for more resources and exercises on quotation marks.

do not use quotation marks with an **indirect quotation**, which reports what someone said or wrote but not in the exact words.

> The psychoanalyst Karen Horney claimed that ❝life is a good therapist.❞

43b Use single quotation marks to enclose a quotation within a quotation.

> "In formulating any philosophy," Woody Allen writes, "the first consideration must always be: What can we know? Descartes hinted at the problem when he wrote, ❝My mind can never know my body, although it has become quite friendly with my leg.❞"

Notice that two different quotation marks appear at the end of the sentence—one single (to finish the interior quotation) and one double (to finish the main quotation).

Exercise 43.1 Revising: Double and single quotation marks

Insert double and single quotation marks as needed in the following sentences. Mark the number preceding any sentence that is already correct.

1 Why, the lecturer asked, do we say Bless you! or something else when people sneeze but not acknowledge coughs, hiccups, and other eruptions?
2 She said that sneezes have always been regarded differently.
3 Sneezes feel more uncontrollable than some other eruptions, she said.
4 Unlike coughs and hiccups, she explained, sneezes feel as if they come from inside the head.
5 She concluded, People thus wish to recognize a sneeze, if only with a Gosh.

43c Set off quotations of dialog according to standard practice.

When quoting conversations, begin a new paragraph for each speaker.

> ❝What shall I call you? Your name?❞ Andrews whispered rapidly, as with a high squeak the latch of the door rose.
> ❝Elizabeth,❞ she said. ❝Elizabeth.❞
> —Graham Greene, *The Man Within*

When you quote a single speaker for more than one paragraph, put quotation marks at the beginning of each paragraph but at the end of only the last paragraph.

Note Quotation marks are optional for quoting unspoken thoughts or imagined dialog:

I asked myself, "How can we solve this?"
I asked myself, How can we solve this?

43d **Put quotation marks around the titles of works that are parts of other works.**

Use quotation marks to enclose the titles of works that are published or released within larger works. (See the following box.) Use single quotation marks for a quotation within a quoted title, as in the article title and essay title in the box. And enclose all punctuation in the title within the quotation marks, as in the article title.

Titles to be enclosed in quotation marks

Other titles should be italicized or underlined. (See **6** p. 360.)

Song
"The Star-Spangled Banner"

Short poem
"Mending Wall"

Short story
"The Gift of the Magi"

Article in periodical
"Does 'Scaring' Work?"

Essay
"Joey: A 'Mechanical Boy'"

Page or document on a Web site
"Readers' Page" (on the site *Friends of Prufrock*)

Episode of a television or radio program
"The Mexican Connection" (on *60 Minutes*)

Subdivision of a book
"The Mast Head" (Chapter 35 of *Moby-Dick*)

Note Some academic disciplines do not require quotation marks for titles within source citations. See **APA** p. 526 and **CSE** p. 562.

Exercise 43.2 **Revising: Quotation marks for titles**

Insert quotation marks as needed for titles and words in the following sentences. If quotation marks should be used instead of italics, insert them.

1 In Chapter 8, titled *How to Be Interesting*, the author explains the art of conversation.
2 The Beatles' song Let It Be reminds Martin of his uncle.
3 The article that appeared in *Mental Health* was titled *Children of Divorce Ask, "Why?"*

4 In the encyclopedia the discussion under Modern Art fills less than a column.
5 One prizewinning essay, *Cowgirls on Wall Street,* first appeared in *Entrepreneur* magazine.

43e Quotation marks may enclose words being used in a special sense.

On movie sets movable "wild walls" make a one-walled room seem four-walled on film.

Note Use italics or underlining for defined words. (See **6** p. 361.)

43f Delete quotation marks where they are not required.

Title of your paper

Not "The Death Wish in One Poem by Robert Frost"
But The Death Wish in One Poem by Robert Frost
Or The Death Wish in "Stopping by Woods on a Snowy Evening"

Common nickname

Not As President, "Jimmy" Carter preferred to use his nickname.
But As President, Jimmy Carter preferred to use his nickname.

Slang or trite expression

Quotation marks will not excuse slang or a trite expression that is inappropriate to your writing. If slang is appropriate, use it without quotation marks.

Not We should support the President in his "hour of need" rather than "wimp out on him."
But We should give the President the support he needs rather than turn away like cowards.

43g Place other punctuation marks inside or outside quotation marks according to standard practice.

1 Commas and periods: Inside quotation marks

Swift uses irony in his essay "A Modest Proposal."
Many first-time readers are shocked to see infants described as "delicious."

"'A Modest Proposal,'" writes one critic, "is so outrageous that it cannot be believed."

Exception When a parenthetical source citation immediately follows a quotation, place any period or comma *after* the citation:

One critic calls the essay "outrageous" (Olms 26).

Partly because of "the cool calculation of its delivery" (Olms 27), Swift's satire still chills a modern reader.

2 | Colons and semicolons: Outside quotation marks

A few years ago the slogan in elementary education was "learning by playing"; now educators are concerned with basic skills.

We all know what is meant by "inflation": more money buys less.

3 | Dashes, question marks, and exclamation points: Inside quotation marks only if part of the quotation

When a dash, question mark, or exclamation point is part of the quotation, place it *inside* quotation marks. Don't use any other punctuation, such as a period or comma:

"But must you—" Marcia hesitated, afraid of the answer.

"Go away!" I yelled.

Did you say, "Who is she?" [When both your sentence and the quotation would end in a question mark or exclamation point, use only the mark in the quotation.]

When a dash, question mark, or exclamation point applies only to the larger sentence, not to the quotation, place it *outside* quotation marks—again, with no other punctuation:

One evocative line in English poetry—"After many a summer dies the swan"—comes from Alfred, Lord Tennyson.

Who said, "Now cracks a noble heart"?

The woman called me "stupid"!

Exercise 43.3 Revising: Quotation marks

Some of the italicized words in the following paragraph are direct quotations or should be quoted titles. Insert quotation marks where italics should not be used. Be sure that other marks of punctuation are correctly placed inside or outside the quotation marks.

1 In the title essay of her book *The Death of the Moth and Other Essays*, Virginia Woolf describes the last moments of a *frail and diminutive body*. **2** An insect's death may seem insignificant, but the moth is, in Woolf's words, *life, a pure bead*. **3** The moth's struggle against death, *indifferent, impersonal*, is heroic. **4** Where else but in such a bit of life could one see a protest so *superb*? **5** At the end of *The Death of the Moth*, Woolf sees the insect lying *most decently and uncomplainingly composed;* in death it finds dignity.

Revising: Quotation marks

Insert quotation marks as needed in the following paragraph. If a sentence is correct as given, mark the number preceding it.

1 In one class we talked about a passage from I Have a Dream, the speech delivered by Martin Luther King, Jr., on the steps of the Lincoln Memorial on August 28, 1963:

> **2** When the architects of our republic wrote the magnificent words of the Constitution and the Declaration of Independence, they were signing a promissory note to which every American was to fall heir. **3** This note was a promise that all men would be guaranteed the unalienable rights of life, liberty, and the pursuit of happiness.

4 What did Dr. King mean by this statement? the teacher asked. **5** Perhaps we should define promissory note first. **6** Then she explained that a person who signs such a note agrees to pay a specific sum of money on a particular date or on demand by the holder of the note. **7** One student suggested, Maybe Dr. King meant that the writers of the Constitution and Declaration promised that all people in America should be equal. **8** He and over 200,000 people had gathered in Washington, DC, added another student. **9** Maybe their purpose was to demand payment, to demand those rights for African Americans. **10** The whole discussion was an eye-opener for those of us (including me) who had never considered that those documents make promises that we should expect our country to fulfill.

44 Other Marks

The other marks of punctuation are the dash (next page), parentheses (p. 339), the ellipsis mark (p. 340), brackets (p. 343), and the slash (p. 343).

Grammar checkers A grammar checker may flag a lone parenthesis or bracket so that you can match it with another parenthesis or bracket. But most checkers cannot recognize other misuses of the marks covered here and instead simply ignore the marks.

my**comp**lab

Visit *mycomplab.com* for more resources and exercises on the dash, parentheses, the ellipsis mark, brackets, and the slash.

| **44a** | **Use the dash or dashes to indicate shifts and to set off some sentence elements.** |

The dash (—) is mainly a mark of interruption: it signals a shift, insertion, or break. In your papers, form a dash with two hyphens (--) or use the character called an em dash on your word processor. Do not add extra space around or between the hyphens or around the em dash.

Note When an interrupting element starting with a dash falls in the middle of a sentence, be sure to add the closing dash to signal the end of the interruption. See the first example below.

1 Shifts in tone or thought

The novel—if one can call it that—appeared in 2005.
If the book had a plot—but a plot would be conventional.

2 Nonessential elements

Dashes may be used instead of commas to set off and emphasize modifiers, parenthetical expressions, and other nonessential elements, especially when these elements are internally punctuated:

The qualities Monet painted—sunlight, rich shadows, deep colors— abounded near the rivers and gardens he used as subjects.

Though they are close together—separated by only a few blocks—the two neighborhoods could be in different countries.

3 Introductory series and concluding series and explanations

Shortness of breath, skin discoloration or the sudden appearance of moles, persistent indigestion, the presence of small lumps—all these may signify cancer. [Introductory series.]

The patient undergoes a battery of tests—MRI, bronchoscopy, perhaps even biopsy. [Concluding series.]

Many patients are disturbed by the MRI—by the need to keep still for long periods in an exceedingly small space. [Concluding explanation.]

A colon could be used instead of a dash in the last two examples. The dash is more informal.

4 Overuse

Too many dashes can make writing jumpy or breathy.

┌─ **Key term** ───
│ **nonessential element** Gives added information but does not limit the
│ word it refers to. (See pp. 304–06.)
└──

Not	In all his life—eighty-seven years—my great-grandfather never allowed his picture to be taken—not even once. He claimed the "black box"—the camera—would steal his soul.
But	In all his eighty-seven years, my great-grandfather did not allow his picture to be taken even once. He claimed the "black box"—the camera—would steal his soul.

Exercise 44.1 Revising: Dashes

Insert dashes as needed in the following paragraph.

1 The movie-theater business is undergoing dramatic changes changes that may affect what movies are made and shown. 2 The closing of independent theaters, the control of theaters by fewer and fewer owners, and the increasing ownership of theaters by movie studios and distributors these changes may reduce the availability of noncommercial films. 3 Yet at the same time the number of movie screens is increasing primarily in multiscreen complexes so that smaller films may find more outlets. 4 The number of active movie screens that is, screens showing films or booked to do so is higher now than at any time since World War II. 5 The biggest theater complexes seem to be something else as well art galleries, amusement arcades, restaurants, spectacles.

44b Use parentheses to enclose parenthetical expressions and labels for lists within sentences.

Note Parentheses *always* come in pairs, one before and one after the punctuated material.

1 Parenthetical expressions

Parenthetical expressions include explanations, facts, digressions, and examples that may be helpful or interesting but are not essential to meaning. Parentheses de-emphasize parenthetical expressions. (Commas emphasize them more than parentheses do, and dashes emphasize them still more.)

> The population of Philadelphia (now about 1.5 million) has declined since 1950.

Note Don't put a comma before a parenthetical expression enclosed in parentheses. Punctuation after the parenthetical expression should be placed outside the closing parenthesis.

Not	The population of Philadelphia compares with that of Phoenix, (just over 1.6 million.)
But	The population of Philadelphia compares with that of Phoenix (just over 1.6 million).

If you enclose a complete sentence in parentheses, capitalize the sentence and place the closing period *inside* the closing parenthesis:

> In general, coaches will tell you that scouts are just guys who can't coach. (But then, so are brain surgeons.)
> —Roy Blount

2   Labels for lists within sentences

Outside the Middle East, the countries with the largest oil reserves are (1) Venezuela (63 billion barrels), (2) Russia (57 billion barrels), and (3) Mexico (51 billion barrels).

When you set a list off from your text, do not enclose such labels in parentheses.

Exercise 44.2   Revising: Parentheses

Insert parentheses around parenthetical expressions in the following paragraph.

1 Many of those involved in the movie business agree that multi-screen complexes are good for two reasons: 1 they cut the costs of exhibitors, and 2 they offer more choices to audiences. 2 However, those who produce and distribute films and not just the big studios argue that the multiscreen theaters give exhibitors too much power. 3 The major studios are buying movie theaters to gain control over important parts of the distribution process what gets shown and for how much money. 4 For twelve years 1938–50 the federal government forced the studios to sell all their movie theaters. 5 But because they now have more competition television and DVD players, for instance, the studios are permitted to own theaters.

44c   Use the ellipsis mark to indicate omissions from quotations.

The ellipsis mark, consisting of three periods separated by space (. . .), generally indicates an omission from a quotation. All the following examples quote from this passage about environmentalism:

Original quotation

"At the heart of the environmentalist world view is the conviction that human physical and spiritual health depends on sustaining the planet in a relatively unaltered state. Earth is our home in the full, genetic sense, where humanity and its ancestors existed for all the millions of years of their evolution. Natural ecosystems—forests, coral reefs, marine blue waters—maintain the world exactly as we would wish it to be maintained. When we debase the global environment and extinguish the variety of life, we are dismantling a support system that is too complex to understand, let alone replace, in the foreseeable future."

—Edward O. Wilson, "Is Humanity Suicidal?"

1. Omission of the middle of a sentence

"Natural ecosystems ... maintain the world exactly as we would wish it to be maintained."

2. Omission of the end of a sentence, without source citation

"Earth is our home ..." [The sentence period, closed up to the last word, precedes the ellipsis mark.]

3. Omission of the end of a sentence, with source citation

"Earth is our home ..." (Wilson 27). [The sentence period follows the source citation.]

4. Omission of parts of two or more sentences

Wilson writes, "At the heart of the environmentalist world view is the conviction that human physical and spiritual health depends on sustaining the planet ... where humanity and its ancestors existed for all the millions of years of their evolution."

5. Omission of one or more sentences

As Wilson puts it, "At the heart of the environmentalist world view is the conviction that human physical and spiritual health depends on sustaining the planet in a relatively unaltered state ... When we debase the global environment and extinguish the variety of life, we are dismantling a support system that is too complex to understand, let alone replace, in the foreseeable future."

6. Omission from the middle of a sentence through the end of another sentence

"Earth is our home ... When we debase the global environment and extinguish the variety of life, we are dismantling a support system that is too complex to understand, let alone replace, in the foreseeable future."

7. Omission of the beginning of a sentence, leaving a complete sentence

a. Bracketed capital letter

"[H]uman physical and spiritual health," Wilson writes, "depends on sustaining the planet in a relatively unaltered state." [No ellipsis mark is needed because the brackets around the *H* indicate that the letter was not capitalized originally and thus that the beginning of the sentence has been omitted.]

b. Small letter

According to Wilson, "human physical and spiritual health depends on sustaining the planet in a relatively unaltered state." [No ellipsis mark is needed because the small *h* indicates that the beginning of the sentence has been omitted.]

c. Capital letter from the original

Hami comments, "... Wilson argues eloquently for the environmentalist world view." [An ellipsis mark *is* needed because the quoted part of the sentence begins with a capital letter and it is otherwise not clear that the beginning of the original sentence has been omitted.]

8. Use of a word or phrase
Wilson describes the earth as "our home." [No ellipsis mark needed.]

Note these features of the examples:

- ■ **Use an ellipsis mark when it is not otherwise clear that you have left out material from the source,** as when you omit one or more sentences (examples 5 and 6) or when the words you quote form a complete sentence that is different in the original (examples 1–4 and 7c).
- ■ **You don't need an ellipsis mark when it is obvious that you have omitted something,** such as when a bracketed letter or a small letter indicates omission (examples 7a and 7b) or when a phrase clearly comes from a larger sentence (example 8).
- ■ **Place an ellipsis mark after a sentence period** *except* **when a parenthetical source citation follows the quotation,** as in example 3. Then the sentence period falls after the citation.

If you omit one or more lines of poetry or paragraphs of prose from a quotation, use a separate line of ellipsis marks across the full width of the quotation to show the omission.

In "Song: Love Armed" from 1676, Aphra Behn contrasts two lovers' experiences of a romance:

> Love in fantastic triumph sate,
> 　Whilst bleeding hearts around him flowed,
> . . . .
> But my poor heart alone is harmed,
> 　Whilst thine the victor is, and free. (lines 1-2, 15-16)

(See **MLA** pp. 507–08 for the format of displayed quotations like this one.)

Exercise 44.3　Using ellipsis marks
Use ellipsis marks and any other needed punctuation to follow the numbered instructions for quoting from the following paragraph.

　　Women in the sixteenth and seventeenth centuries were educated in the home and, in some cases, in boarding schools. Men were educated at home, in grammar schools, and at the universities. The universities were closed to female students. For women, "learning the Bible," as Elizabeth Joceline puts it, was an impetus to learning to read. To be able to read the Bible in the vernacular was a liberating experience that freed the reader from hearing only the set passages read in the church and interpreted by the church. A Protestant woman was expected to read the scriptures daily, to meditate on them, and to memorize portions of them. In addition, a woman was expected to instruct her entire household in "learning the Bible" by holding instructional and devotional times each day for all household members, including the servants.

—Charlotte F. Otten, *English Women's Voices, 1540–1700*

1 Quote the fifth sentence, but omit everything from *that freed the reader* to the end.
2 Quote the fifth sentence, but omit the words *was a liberating experience that*.
3 Quote the first and sixth sentences.

44d Use brackets to indicate changes in quotations.

Brackets have specialized uses in mathematical equations, but their main use for all kinds of writing is to indicate that you have altered a quotation to explain, clarify, or correct it.

"That Texaco station [just outside Chicago] is one of the busiest in the nation," said a company spokesperson.

The word *sic* (Latin for "in this manner") in brackets indicates that an error in the quotation appeared in the original and was not made by you. Do not underline or italicize *sic* in brackets.

According to the newspaper report, "The car slammed thru [sic] the railing and into oncoming traffic."

Do not use *sic* to make fun of a writer or to note errors in a passage that is clearly nonstandard.

44e Use the slash between options and between lines of poetry run into the text.

Option
Some teachers oppose pass/fail courses.

Poetry
Many readers have sensed a reluctant turn away from death in Frost's lines "The woods are lovely, dark and deep, / But I have promises to keep" (13-14).

When separating lines of poetry in this way, leave a space before and after the slash. (See **MLA** pp. 507–08 for more on quoting poetry.)

Exercise 44.4　Revising: Dashes, parentheses, ellipsis marks, brackets, slashes

Insert dashes, parentheses, ellipsis marks, brackets, or slashes as needed in the following paragraph. In some cases, two or more different marks could be correct.

　　1 "Let all the learned say what they can, 'Tis ready money makes the man." 2 These two lines of poetry by the Englishman William Somerville 1645–1742 may apply to a current American economic problem. 3 Non-American investors with "ready money" pour some of it as much as $1.3 trillion in recent years into the United States. 4 Stocks and bonds, savings deposits, service companies, factories, artworks, political campaigns the investments of foreigners are varied and grow more numerous every day. 5 Proponents of foreign investment argue that it revives industry, strengthens the economy, creates jobs more than 3 million, they say, and encourages free trade among nations. 6 Opponents caution that the risks associated with heavy foreign investment namely decreased profits at home and increased political influence from outside may ultimately weaken the economy. 7 On both sides, it seems, "the learned say, 'Tis ready money makes the man or country." 8 The question is, whose money theirs or ours?

Spelling and Mechanics

PART 6

Spelling and Mechanics

45 Spelling and the Hyphen

You can train yourself to spell better, and this chapter will tell you how. But you can improve instantly by acquiring three habits:

- Carefully proofread your writing.
- Cultivate a healthy suspicion of your spellings.
- Check a dictionary *every time* you doubt a spelling.

Spelling checkers A spelling checker can help you find and track spelling errors in your papers. But its usefulness is limited, mainly because it can't spot the confusion of words with similar spellings, such as *now/not, to/too,* and *their/they're/there.* See **1** pp. 32–33 for more on spelling checkers.

45a Anticipate typical spelling problems.

Certain situations, such as misleading pronunciation, commonly lead to misspelling.

1 Pronunciation

In English, pronunciation of words is an unreliable guide to how they are spelled. Pronunciation is especially misleading with **homonyms,** words pronounced the same but spelled differently. Some homonyms and near-homonyms appear in the following box.

Words commonly confused

accept (to receive)
except (other than)

affect (to have an influence on)
effect (a result)

all ready (prepared)
already (by this time)

allusion (an indirect reference)
illusion (an erroneous belief or
   perception)

ascent (a movement up)
assent (to agree, or an agreement)

bare (unclothed)
bear (to carry, or an animal)

board (a plane of wood)
bored (uninterested)

brake (to stop)
break (to smash)

(continued)

Visit *mycomplab.com* for more resources and exercises on spelling and the hyphen.

Words commonly confused

(continued)

buy (to purchase)
by (next to)

cite (to quote an authority)
sight (the ability to see)
site (a place)

desert (to abandon)
dessert (after-dinner course)

discreet (reserved, respectful)
discrete (individual, distinct)

fair (average, or lovely)
fare (a fee for transportation)

forth (forward)
fourth (after *third*)

hear (to perceive by ear)
here (in this place)

heard (past tense of *hear*)
herd (a group of animals)

hole (an opening)
whole (complete)

its (possessive of *it*)
it's (contraction of *it is* or *it has*)

know (to be certain)
no (the opposite of *yes*)

loose (not attached)
lose (to misplace)

meat (flesh)
meet (to encounter, or a
    competition)

passed (past tense of *pass*)
past (after, or a time gone by)

patience (forbearance)
patients (persons under medical
    care)

peace (the absence of war)
piece (a portion of something)

plain (clear)
plane (a carpenter's tool, or an
    airborne vehicle)

presence (the state of being at
    hand)
presents (gifts)

principal (most important, or
    the head of a school)
principle (a basic truth or law)

rain (precipitation)
reign (to rule)
rein (a strap for an animal)

right (correct)
rite (a religious ceremony)
write (to make letters)

road (a surface for driving)
rode (past tense of *ride*)

scene (where an action occurs)
seen (past participle of *see*)

stationary (unmoving)
stationery (writing paper)

their (possessive of *they*)
there (opposite of *here*)
they're (contraction of *they are*)

to (toward)
too (also)
two (following *one*)

waist (the middle of the body)
waste (discarded material)

weak (not strong)
week (Sunday through Saturday)

weather (climate)
whether (*if*, or introducing a
    choice)

which (one of a group)
witch (a sorcerer)

who's (contraction of *who is* or
    who has)
whose (possessive of *who*)

your (possessive of *you*)
you're (contraction of *you are*)

2 Different forms of the same word

Often, the noun form and the verb form of the same word are spelled differently: for example, *advice* (noun) and *advise* (verb). Sometimes the noun and the adjective forms of the same word differ: *height* and *high*. Similar changes occur in the parts of some irregular verbs (*know, knew, known*) and the plurals of irregular nouns (*man, men*).

3 American vs. British spellings

If you learned English outside the United States, you may be accustomed to British rather than American spellings. Here are the chief differences:

American	British
color, humor	colour, humour
theater, center	theatre, centre
canceled, traveled	cancelled, travelled
judgment	judgement
realize, civilize	realise, civilise
connection	connexion

Your dictionary may list both spellings, but it will specially mark the British one with *chiefly Brit* or a similar label.

45b Follow spelling rules.

1 *ie* vs. *ei*

To distinguish between *ie* and *ei*, use the familiar jingle:

I before *e*, except after *c*, or when pronounced "ay" as in *neighbor* and *weigh*.

i before *e*	believe	thief	hygiene
ei after *c*	ceiling	conceive	perceive
ei sounded as "ay"	sleigh	eight	beige

Exceptions For some exceptions, remember this sentence:

The weird foreigner neither seizes leisure nor forfeits height.

Exercise 45.1 Revising: *ie* and *ei*

In the following paragraph, revise any incorrect spellings of words with *ie* or *ei*. If a sentence is correct as given, mark the number preceding it.

1 Many people perceive donating blood as a rewarding experience. **2** Giving blood is niether painful nor wierd, although many people believe it is both. **3** It takes a leisurely half hour or so, and it gives one a feeling of having acheived something. **4** In truth, there is a slight sting when the needle is inserted into the vien, so the best thing to do then is to focus on something else, like the cieling. **5** After donating blood once, you can expect to receive regular invitations from the blood center to give blood again.

2 Final *e*

When adding an ending to a word with a final *e*, drop the *e* if the ending begins with a vowel:

advise + able = advisable   surprise + ing = surprising

Keep the *e* if the ending begins with a consonant:

care + ful = careful   like + ly = likely

Exceptions Retain the *e* after a soft *c* or *g*, to keep the sound of the consonant soft rather than hard: *courageous, changeable.* And drop the *e* before a consonant when the *e* is preceded by another vowel: *argue + ment = argument, true + ly = truly.*

Exercise 45.2 Revising: Final *e*

In the following paragraph, revise any incorrect changes in words with a final *e*. If a sentence is correct as given, mark the number preceding it.

1 For decades scientists have been secureing metal and plastic bands to the flippers of penguins and useing the numbered bands to observe the birds' behavior. **2** Recently, a five-year study produced truely convinceing evidence that the bands themselves are influenceing the penguins' behavior. **3** For instance, banded penguins are less likly to produce offspring. **4** The researchers recommended replacing the bands with tiny electronic devices implanted under the birds' skin.

---

3 Final *y*

When adding an ending to a word with a final *y*, change the *y* to *i* if it follows a consonant:

beauty, beauties   worry, worried   supply, supplies

But keep the *y* if it follows a vowel, if it ends a proper name, or if the ending is *-ing:*

day, days   Minsky, Minskys   cry, crying

Exercise 45.3 Revising: Final *y*

In the following paragraph, revise any incorrect changes in words with a final *y*. If a sentence is correct as given, mark the number preceding it.

1 My neighbor, Mr. Sorsky, often says he is worryed about his job. **2** However, today's harryed white-collar workers, like Mr. Sorsky, have a much easer situation than did workers of a hundred years ago. 3 Most men used to work in such industrys as farming, mining, and steelworking, in which job loss and injurys were common. 4 Women often worked in low-paying jobs as domestics or millworkers. 5 Many of today's working poor still labor in such triing situations. 6 Perhaps the middle-class Mr. Sorskies of the world should count their blessings instead of complaining about their troubles.

4 Final consonants

When adding an ending to a one-syllable word ending in a consonant, double the final consonant when it follows a single vowel. Otherwise, don't double the consonant.

    slap, slapping   park, parking   pair, paired

In words of more than one syllable, double the final consonant when it follows a single vowel *and* when it ends a stressed syllable once the new ending is added. Otherwise, don't double the consonant.

    refer, referring   refer, reference   relent, relented

Exercise 45.4 Revising: Consonants

In the following paragraph, revise any incorrect changes in words ending in consonants. If a sentence is correct as given, mark the number preceding it.

1 People have always been charmmed by the idea of walking on water. 2 A new device, the W Boat, finaly allows just that. 3 By pairring two connected, buoyant platforms, the inventor of the W Boat created something like long, floatting snowshoes for use on water. 4 Fiting the W Boat technology to everyday use, the inventor also developped a "paddle-skiing" device, which allows a person to paddle while standing. 5 Now strolling on water, as many have dreamed of doing, is an actuality.

5 Prefixes

When adding a prefix, do not drop a letter from or add a letter to the original word:

    unnecessary   disappoint   misspell

Exercise 45.5 Revising: Prefixes

In the following paragraph, revise any incorrect spellings of words with prefixes. If a sentence is correct as given, mark the number preceding it.

1 People often seem to regard bacteria as somehow unatural intruders in human biology. 2 This notion is missinformed, however. 3 Even though it seems ilogical, most bacteria in fact improve health and prolong life. 4 The health benefits of antibacterial soaps and cleaners are overrated. 5 In most situations such products are unecessary to fight

disease, and they can kill bacteria we require. 6 The best yet most underated way to kill harmful bacteria is simple, thorough, and frequent handwashing.

6 Plurals

Most nouns form plurals by adding *s* to the singular form. Add *es* for the plural of nouns ending in *s, sh, ch,* or *x.*

boy, boys	kiss, kisses	church, churches

Nouns ending in *o* preceded by a vowel usually form the plural with *s.* Those ending in *o* preceded by a consonant usually form the plural with *es.*

ratio, ratios   hero, heroes

Some very common nouns form irregular plurals.

child, children	woman, women	mouse, mice

Some English nouns that were originally Italian, Greek, Latin, or French form the plural according to their original language:

analysis, analyses	criterion, criteria	piano, pianos
basis, bases	datum, data	thesis, theses
crisis, crises	medium, media	

A few such nouns may form irregular *or* regular plurals: for instance, *index, indices, indexes; curriculum, curricula, curriculums.* The regular plural is more contemporary.

With compound nouns, add *s* to the main word of the compound. Sometimes this main word is not the last word.

city-states   fathers-in-law   passersby

CULTURE • LANGUAGE Noncount nouns do not form plurals, either regularly (with an added *s*) or irregularly. Examples of noncount nouns include *equipment, intelligence,* and *wealth.* See **4** p. 268.

Exercise 45.6 Revising: Plurals

In the following paragraph, revise any incorrect spellings of plural nouns.

1 Fewer original video games are available these dayes, but sales and production of sequeles to popular games are strong. 2 Mainstream game publishers follow formulaes that have proved profitable, and sequeles are cheaper to produce than original games. 3 What's more, many video game enthusiastes tend to buy new versions of games they already know. 4 Many players crave original games and think of publishers as thiefs because they merely trade on previous successs. 5 But publishers have found that trying to be heros by following their hunchs often results in low profits.

Exercise 45.7   Using correct spellings

In the following paragraph, select the correct spellings from the choices in brackets. Refer as needed to the list of words on pp. 347–48, the preceding rules, or a dictionary.

1 Science [affects, effects] many [important, importent] aspects of our lives, though many people have a [pore, poor] understanding of the [role, roll] of scientific breakthroughs in [their, they're] health. **2** Many people [beleive, believe] that [docters, doctors], more than science, are [responsable, responsible] for [improvements, improvments] in health care. **3** But scientists in the [labratory, laboratory] have made crucial steps in the search for [knowlege, knowledge] about health and [medecine, medicine]. **4** For example, one scientist [who's, whose] discoveries have [affected, effected] many people is Ulf Von Euler. **5** In the 1950s Von Euler's discovery of certain hormones [lead, led] to the invention of the birth control pill. **6** Von Euler's work was used by John Rock, who [developed, developped] the first birth control pill and influenced family [planing, planning]. **7** Von Euler also discovered the [principal, principle] neurotransmitter that controls the heartbeat. **8** Another scientist, Hans Selye, showed what [affect, effect] stress can have on the body. **9** His findings have [lead, led] to methods of [baring, bearing] stress.

Exercise 45.8   Working with a spelling checker

Try your computer's spelling checker on the following paragraph. Type the paragraph and run it through your spelling checker. Then proofread it to correct the errors missed by the checker. (Hint: There are fourteen errors in all.)

1 The whether effects all of us, though it's affects are different for different people. **2** Some people love a fare day with warm temperatures and sunshine. **3** They revel in spending a hole day outside without the threat of rein. **4** Other people prefer dark, rainy daze. **5** They relish the opportunity to slow down and here they're inner thoughts. **6** Most people agree, however, that to much of one kind of whether—reign, sun, snow, or clouds—makes them board.

45c   Use the hyphen to form or divide words.

The hyphen is used either to form compound words or to divide words at the ends of lines.

1 Compound adjectives

When two or more words serve together as a single modifier before a noun, a hyphen forms the modifying words clearly into a unit.

She is a well-known actor.
Some Spanish-speaking students work as translators.

When such a compound adjective follows the noun, the hyphen is unnecessary.

> The actor is well-known.
> Many students are Spanish-speaking.

The hyphen is also unnecessary in a compound modifier containing an -ly adverb, even before the noun: *clearly defined terms*.

When part of a compound adjective appears only once in two or more parallel compound adjectives, hyphens indicate which words the reader should mentally join with the missing part.

> School-age children should have eight- or nine-o'clock bedtimes.

2 Fractions and compound numbers

Hyphens join the numerator and denominator of fractions: *one-half, three-fourths*. Hyphens also join the parts of the whole numbers *twenty-one* to *ninety-nine*.

When a hyphenated number is part of a compound adjective before a noun, join all parts of the modifier with hyphens: *sixty-three-foot wall*.

3 Prefixes and suffixes

Do not use hyphens with prefixes except as follows:

- With the prefixes *self-*, *all-*, and *ex-*: *self-control, all-inclusive, ex-student*.
- With a prefix before a capitalized word: *un-American*.
- With a capital letter before a word: *T-shirt*.
- To prevent misreading: *de-emphasize, re-create a story*.

The only suffix that regularly requires a hyphen is *-elect*, as in *president-elect*.

Exercise 45.9 Revising: Hyphens

Insert hyphens as needed in the following paragraph, and delete them where they are not needed. If a sentence is correct as given, mark the number preceding it.

1 The African elephant is well known for its size. 2 A male elephant weighs five and one half to six tons, and a female weighs up to four tons. 3 Even with the difference in weight, both male and female elephants can grow to a ten-foot height. 4 A newborn elephant calf weighs two to three hundred pounds and stands about thirty three inches high. 5 A two hundred pound, thirty three inch baby is quite a big baby! 6 African elephants reach maturity at the age of fourteen or fifteen and often live for sixty five or seventy years.

4 | Words at the ends of lines

You can avoid occasional short lines in your documents by setting your word processor to divide words automatically at appropriate breaks. (In the Tools menu, select Language and then Hyphenation.) To divide words manually, follow these guidelines:

- **Divide words only between syllables**—for instance, *win-dows*, not *wi-ndows*. Check a dictionary for correct syllable breaks.
- **Never divide a one-syllable word.**
- **Leave at least two letters on the first line and three on the second line.** If a word cannot be divided to follow this rule (for instance, *a-bus-er*), don't divide it.

If you must break an electronic address—for instance, in a source citation—do so only after a slash. Do not hyphenate, because readers may perceive any added hyphen as part of the address.

Not	http://www.library.miami.edu/staff/lmc/soc-race.html
But	http://www.library.miami.edu/staff/lmc/socrace.html

---

46 Capital Letters

Generally, capitalize a word only when a dictionary or conventional use says you must. Consult one of the style guides listed in **8** pp. 455 and 459 for special uses of capitals in the social, natural, and applied sciences.

Grammar checkers A grammar checker will flag overused capital letters and missing capitals at the beginnings of sentences. It will also spot missing capitals at the beginnings of proper nouns and adjectives—*if* the nouns and adjectives are in the checker's dictionary. For example, a checker caught *christianity* and *europe* but not *china* (for the country) or *Stephen king*.

CULTURE LANGUAGE Conventions of capitalization vary from language to language. English, for instance, is the only language to capitalize the first-person singular pronoun (*I*), and its practice of capitalizing proper nouns but not most common nouns also distinguishes it from some other languages.

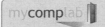

Visit *mycomplab.com* for more resources and exercises on capital letters.

46a Capitalize the first word of every sentence.

No one expected the outcome.

When quoting other writers, you should reproduce the capital letters beginning their sentences or indicate that you have altered the source's capitalization. Whenever possible, integrate the quotation into your own sentence so that its capitalization coincides with yours:

"Psychotherapists often overlook the benefits of self-deception," the author argues.

The author argues that "the benefits of self-deception" are not always recognized by psychotherapists.

If you need to alter the capitalization in the source, indicate the change with brackets:

"[T]he benefits of self-deception" are not always recognized by psychotherapists, the author argues.

The author argues that "[p]sychotherapists often overlook the benefits of self-deception."

Note Capitalization of questions in a series is optional. Both of the following examples are correct:

Is the population a hundred? Two hundred? More?
Is the population a hundred? two hundred? more?

Also optional is capitalization of the first word in a complete sentence after a colon.

46b Capitalize proper nouns, proper adjectives, and words used as essential parts of proper nouns.

1 Proper nouns and proper adjectives

Proper nouns name specific persons, places, and things: *Shakespeare, California, World War I*. **Proper adjectives** are formed from some proper nouns: *Shakespearean, Californian*. Capitalize all proper nouns and proper adjectives but not the articles (*a, an, the*) that precede them:

Proper nouns and adjectives to be capitalized

Specific persons and things

Stephen King
Napoleon Bonaparte

Boulder Dam
the Empire State Building

Specific places and geographical regions

New York City
China

the Mediterranean Sea
the Northeast, the South

But: northeast of the city, going south

Days of the week, months, holidays

Monday
May

Yom Kippur
Christmas

Historical events, documents, periods, movements

the Vietnam War
the Constitution

the Renaissance
the Romantic Movement

Government offices or departments and institutions

House of Representatives
Department of Defense

Polk Municipal Court
Northeast High School

Political, social, athletic, and other organizations and associations and their members

Democratic Party, Democrats
Sierra Club
B'nai B'rith

League of Women Voters
Boston Celtics
Chicago Symphony Orchestra

Races, nationalities, and their languages

Native American
African American
Caucasian

Germans
Swahili
Italian

But: blacks, whites

Religions, their followers, and terms for the sacred

Christianity, Christians
Catholicism, Catholics
Judaism, Orthodox Jews
Islam, Muslims

God
Allah
the Bible [**but** biblical]
the Koran, the Qur'an

---

2 **Common nouns used as essential parts of proper nouns**

Capitalize the common nouns *street, avenue, park, river, ocean, lake, company, college, county,* and *memorial* when they are part of proper nouns naming specific places or institutions:

Main Street
Central Park
Mississippi River
Pacific Ocean

Lake Superior
Ford Motor Company
Madison College
George Washington Memorial

3 | Compass directions

Capitalize compass directions only when they name a specific region instead of a general direction:

Students from the West often melt in eastern humidity.

4 | Relationships

Capitalize the names of relationships only when they precede or replace proper names:

Our aunt scolded us for disrespecting Father and Uncle Jake.

5 | Titles with persons' names

Before a person's name, capitalize his or her title. After or apart from the name, do not capitalize the title.

Professor Otto Osborne	Otto Osborne, a professor
Doctor Jane Covington	Jane Covington, a doctor
Governor Ella Moore	Ella Moore, the governor

Note Many writers capitalize a title denoting very high rank even when it follows a name or is used alone: *Ronald Reagan, past President of the United States.*

46c | Capitalize most words in titles and subtitles of works.

Within your text, capitalize all the words in a title *except* the following: articles (*a, an, the*); *to* in infinitives; and connecting words (prepositions and conjunctions) of fewer than five letters. Capitalize even these short words when they are the first or last word in a title or when they fall after a colon or semicolon.

"Courtship Through the Ages"	*Management: A New Theory*
A Diamond Is Forever	"Once More to the Lake"
"Knowing Whom to Ask"	*An End to Live For*
Learning from Las Vegas	*File Under Architecture*

Note The style guides of the academic disciplines have their own rules for capitals in titles. For instance, MLA style for English and some other humanities capitalizes all subordinating conjunctions but no prepositions. In addition, APA style for the social sciences and CSE style for the sciences capitalize only the first word and proper names in book and article titles within source citations (see **APA** p. 526 and **CSE** p. 562).

46d Use capitals according to convention in online communication.

Online messages written in all-capital letters or with no capital letters are difficult to read. Further, messages in all-capital letters may be taken as rude (see also **2** p. 117). Use capital letters according to rules 46a–46c in all your online communication.

Exercise 46.1 Revising: Capitals

Revise the following paragraph to correct errors in capitalization, consulting a dictionary as needed. If a sentence is correct as given, mark the number preceding it.

1 San Antonio, texas, is a thriving city in the southwest that has always offered much to tourists interested in the roots of spanish settlement in the new world. **2** Most visitors stop at the Alamo, one of five Catholic Missions built by Priests to convert native americans and to maintain spain's claims in the area. **3** The Alamo is famous for being the site of an 1836 battle that helped to create the republic of Texas. **4** San Antonio has grown tremendously in recent years. **5** The Hemisfair plaza and the San Antonio river link tourist and convention facilities. **6** Restaurants, Hotels, and shops line the River. **7** the haunting melodies of "Una paloma blanca" and "malagueña" lure passing tourists into Casa rio and other mexican restaurants. **8** The university of Texas at San Antonio has expanded, and a Medical Center lies in the Northwest part of the city. **9** Sea World, on the west side of San Antonio, entertains grandparents, fathers and mothers, and children with the antics of dolphins and seals. **10** The City has attracted high-tech industry, creating a corridor between san antonio and austin.

---

47 Italics or Underlining

Italic type and <u>underlining</u> indicate the same thing: the word or words are being distinguished or emphasized. Italic type is now used almost universally in academic and business writing, and it has recently become the preferred style of the Modern Language Association (see **MLA** p. 464). Some instructors recommend underlining, so ask your instructor for his or her preference.

Always use either italics or underlining consistently throughout a document in both text and source citations. If you are using italics,

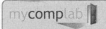

mycomplab

Visit *mycomplab.com* for more resources and exercises on italics or underlining.

make sure that the italic characters are clearly distinct from the regular type. If you are using underlining and you underline two or more words in a row, underline the space between the words, too: <u>Criminal Statistics: Misuses of Numbers</u>.

Grammar checkers A grammar checker cannot recognize problems with italics or underlining. Check your work to ensure that you have used highlighting appropriately.

47a Italicize or underline the titles of works that appear independently.

Within your text, underline or italicize the titles of works that are published, released, or produced separately from other works. (See the box below.) Use quotation marks for all other titles. (See **5** p. 334.)

Titles to be italicized or underlined
Other titles should be placed in quotation marks. (See **5** p. 334.)

Books
War and Peace
And the Band Played On

Plays
Hamlet
The Phantom of the Opera

Computer software
Microsoft Internet Explorer
Acrobat Reader

Web sites
Google
Friends of Prufrock

Pamphlets
The Truth About Alcoholism

Long musical works
Tchaikovsky's *Swan Lake*
But: Symphony in C

Television and radio programs
The Shadow
NBC Sports Hour

Long poems
Beowulf
Paradise Lost

Periodicals
Time
Philadelphia Inquirer

Published speeches
Lincoln's *Gettysburg Address*

Movies, DVDs, and videos
Schindler's List
How to Relax

Works of visual art
Michelangelo's *David*
Picasso's *Guernica*

Exceptions Legal documents, the Bible, the Koran, and their parts are generally not italicized or underlined:

Not We studied the *Book of Revelation* in the *Bible*.
But We studied the Book of Revelation in the Bible.

47b Italicize or underline the names of ships, aircraft, spacecraft, and trains.

Challenger	*Orient Express*	*Queen Mary 2*
Apollo XI	*Montrealer*	*Spirit of St. Louis*

47c Italicize or underline foreign words that are not part of the English language.

Italicize or underline a foreign expression that has not been absorbed into English. A dictionary will say whether a word is still considered foreign to English.

> The scientific name for the brown trout is *Salmo trutta*. [The Latin scientific names for plants and animals are always italicized or underlined.]

> The Latin *De gustibus non est disputandum* translates roughly as "There's no accounting for taste."

47d Italicize or underline words or characters named as words.

Use italics or underlining to indicate that you are citing a character or word as a word rather than using it for its meaning. Words you are defining fall under this convention.

> The word *syzygy* refers to a straight line formed by three celestial bodies, as in the alignment of the earth, sun, and moon.

> Some people say *th*, as in *thought*, with a faint *s* or *f* sound.

47e Occasionally, italics or underlining may be used for emphasis.

Italics or underlining can stress an important word or phrase, especially in reporting how someone said something. But use such emphasis very rarely, or your writing may sound immature or hysterical.

47f In online communication, use alternatives for italics or underlining.

Some forms of online communication do not allow conventional highlighting such as italics or underlining for the purposes described in this chapter. (On Web sites, for instance, underlining often indicates a link to another site.)

To distinguish book titles and other elements that usually require italics or underlining, type an underscore before and after the element: *Measurements coincide with those in _Joule's Handbook_.* You can also emphasize words with asterisks before and after: *I *will not* be able to attend.*

Don't use all-capital letters for emphasis; they yell too loudly. (See also p. 359.)

Exercise 47.1 Revising: Italics or underlining

In the following paragraph, circle (1) the words and phrases that need highlighting with italics or underlining and (2) the words and phrases that are highlighted unnecessarily. If a sentence is correct as given, mark the number preceding it.

1 A number of veterans of the war in Vietnam have become prominent writers. **2** Oliver Stone is perhaps the most famous for writing and directing the films Platoon and Born on the Fourth of July. **3** The fiction writer Tim O'Brien has published short stories about the war in Esquire, GQ, and Massachusetts Review. **4** His dreamlike novel Going After Cacciato is about the horrors of combat. **5** Typically for veterans' writing, the novel uses words and phrases borrowed from Vietnamese, such as *di di mau* ("go quickly") or *dinky dau* ("crazy"). **6** Another writer, Philip Caputo, provides a *gripping* account of his service in Vietnam in the book A Rumor of War. **7** Caputo's book was made into a television movie, also titled *A Rumor of War*. **8** The playwright David Rabe—in such dramas as The Basic Training of Pavlo Hummel, Streamers, and Sticks and Bones— depicts the effects of war *not only* on the soldiers *but also* on their families. **9** Steve Mason, called the *poet laureate of the Vietnam war*, has published two collections of poems on the war: Johnny's Song and Warrior for Peace. **10** And Rod Kane wrote an autobiography about the war, Veterans Day, that received *rave* reviews in the Washington Post.

---

48 Abbreviations

The following guidelines on abbreviations pertain to the text of a nontechnical document. All academic disciplines use abbreviations in source citations, and much technical writing, such as in the sciences and engineering, uses many abbreviations in the document text. For the in-text requirements of the discipline you are writing

Visit *mycomplab.com* for more resources and exercises on abbreviations.

in, consult one of the style guides listed in **8** pp. 451 (humanities), 455 (social sciences), and 459 (natural and applied sciences).

Usage varies, but writers increasingly omit periods from abbreviations that consist of or end in capital letters: *US, BA, USMC, PhD.* See **5** p. 297 on punctuating abbreviations.

Grammar and spelling checkers A grammar checker may flag some abbreviations, such as *ft.* (for *foot*) and *st.* (for *street*). A spelling checker will flag abbreviations it does not recognize. But neither checker can tell you whether an abbreviation is appropriate for your writing situation or will be clear to your readers.

48a Use standard abbreviations for titles immediately before and after proper names.

Before the name	After the name
Dr. James Hsu	James Hsu, MD
Mr., Mrs., Ms., Hon.,	DDS, DVM, PhD,
St., Rev., Msgr., Gen.	EdD, OSB, SJ, Sr., Jr.

Do not use abbreviations such as *Rev., Hon., Prof., Rep., Sen., Dr.,* and *St.* (for *Saint*) unless they appear before a proper name.

48b Familiar abbreviations and acronyms are acceptable in most writing.

An **acronym** is an abbreviation that spells a pronounceable word, such as **WHO, NATO,** and **AIDS.** These and other abbreviations using initials are acceptable in most writing as long as they are familiar to readers.

Institutions	LSU, UCLA, TCU
Organizations	CIA, FBI, YMCA, AFL-CIO
Corporations	IBM, CBS, ITT
People	JFK, LBJ, FDR
Countries	US, USA

Note If a name or term (such as *operating room*) appears often in a piece of writing, then its abbreviation (*OR*) can cut down on extra words. Spell out the full term at its first appearance, indicate its abbreviation in parentheses, and then use the abbreviation.

48c Use *BC, BCE, AD, CE, AM, PM, no.,* and *$* only with specific dates and numbers.

44 BC	AD 1492	11:26 AM (*or* a.m.)	no. 36 (*or* No. 36)
44 BCE	1492 CE	8:05 PM (*or* p.m.)	$7.41

The abbreviations BC ("before Christ"), BCE ("before the common era"), and CE ("common era") always follow a date. In contrast, AD (*anno Domini,* Latin for "in the year of the Lord") precedes a date.

48d Generally reserve Latin abbreviations for source citations and comments in parentheses.

Latin abbreviations are generally not italicized or underlined.

i.e.	*id est:* that is
cf.	*confer:* compare
e.g.	*exempli gratia:* for example
et al.	*et alii:* and others
etc.	*et cetera:* and so forth
NB	*nota bene:* note well

He said he would be gone a fortnight (i.e., two weeks).
Bloom et al., editors, *Anthology of Light Verse*
Trees, too, are susceptible to disease (e.g., Dutch elm disease).

Some writers avoid these abbreviations in formal writing, even within parentheses.

48e Use *Inc., Bros., Co.,* or & (for *and*) only in official names of business firms.

Not	The Santini <u>bros.</u> operate a large moving firm in New York City <u>&</u> environs.
But	The Santini <u>brothers</u> operate a large moving firm in New York City <u>and</u> environs.
Or	Santini <u>Bros.</u> is a large moving firm in New York City <u>and</u> environs.

48f Generally spell out units of measurement and names of places, calendar designations, people, and courses.

In most academic, general, and business writing, the types of words listed below should always be spelled out. (In source citations and technical writing, however, these words are more often abbreviated.)

Units of measurement
The dog is thirty <u>inches</u> [not <u>in.</u>] high.

Geographical names
The publisher is in <u>Massachusetts</u> [not <u>Mass.</u> or <u>MA</u>].

Names of days, months, and holidays

The truce was signed on Tuesday [not Tues.], April [not Apr.] 16.

Names of people

Robert [not Robt.] Frost wrote accessible poems.

Courses of instruction

I'm majoring in political science [not poli. sci.].

Exercise 48.1   Revising: Abbreviations

Revise the following paragraph as needed to correct inappropriate use of abbreviations for nontechnical writing. If a sentence is correct as given, mark the number preceding it.

1 In an issue of *Science* magazine, Dr. Virgil L. Sharpton discusses a theory that could help explain the extinction of dinosaurs. **2** According to the theory, a comet or asteroid crashed into the earth about 65 mill. yrs. ago. **3** The result was a huge crater about 10 km. (6.2 mi.) deep in the Gulf of Mex. **4** Sharpton's measurements suggest that the crater is 50 pct. larger than scientists had previously believed. **5** Indeed, 20-yr.-old drilling cores reveal that the crater is about 186 mi. wide, roughly the size of Conn. **6** The space object was traveling more than 100,000 miles per hour and hit earth with the Impact of 100 to 300 megatons of TNT. **7** On impact, 200,000 cubic km. of rock and soil were vaporized or thrown into the air. **8** That's the equivalent of 2.34 bill. cubic ft. of matter. **9** The impact would have created 400-ft. tidal waves across the Atl. Ocean, temps. higher than 20,000 degs., and powerful earthquakes. **10** Sharpton theorizes that the dust, vapor, and smoke from this impact blocked the sun's rays for mos., cooled the earth, and thus resulted in the death of the dinosaurs.

---

49 Numbers

This chapter addresses the use of numbers (numerals versus words) in the text of a document. All disciplines use many more numerals in source citations.

Grammar checkers A grammar checker will flag numerals beginning sentences and can be customized to ignore or to look for numerals. But it can't tell you whether numerals or spelled-out numbers are appropriate for your writing situation.

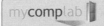

mycomplab

Visit *mycomplab.com* for more resources and exercises on numbers.

<table>
<tr><td>**49a**</td><td>**Use numerals according to standard practice in the field you are writing in.**</td></tr>
</table>

Always use numerals for numbers that require more than two words to spell out:

> The leap year has 366 days.
> The population of Minot, North Dakota, is about 32,800.

In nontechnical academic writing, spell out numbers of one or two words:

> Twelve nations signed the treaty.
> The ball game drew forty-two thousand people. [A hyphenated number may be considered one word.]

In much business writing, use numerals for all numbers over ten: *five reasons, 11 participants.* In technical academic and business writing, such as in science and engineering, use numerals for all numbers over ten, and use numerals for zero through nine when they refer to exact measurements: *2 liters, 1 hour.* (Consult one of the style guides listed in **8** p. 455 and 459 for more details.)

Note Use a combination of numerals and words for round numbers over a million: *26 million, 2.45 billion.* And use either all numerals or all words when several numbers appear together in a passage, even if convention would require a mixture.

CULTURE LANGUAGE In standard American English, a comma separates the numerals in long numbers (26,000), and a period functions as a decimal point (2.06).

<table>
<tr><td>**49b**</td><td>**Use numerals according to convention for dates, addresses, and other information.**</td></tr>
</table>

Days and years
June 18, 1985   AD 12
456 BCE   2010

The time of day
9:00 AM   3:45 PM

Addresses
355 Clinton Avenue
Washington, DC 20036

Exact amounts of money
$3.5 million $4.50

Decimals, percentages, and fractions
22.5   3½
48% (*or* 48 percent)

Scores and statistics
21 to 7   a ratio of 8 to 1
a mean of 26

Pages, chapters, volumes, acts, scenes, lines
Chapter 9, page 123
Hamlet, act 5, scene 3

Exceptions Round dollar or cent amounts of only a few words may be expressed in words: *seventeen dollars; sixty cents.* When the word *o'clock* is used for the time of day, also express the number in words: *two o'clock* (not *2 o'clock*).

49c Spell out numbers that begin sentences.

For clarity, spell out any number that begins a sentence. If the number requires more than two words, reword the sentence so that the number falls later and can be expressed as a numeral.

Not 3.9 billion people live in Asia.
But The population of Asia is 3.9 billion.

Exercise 49.1   Revising: Numbers

Revise the following paragraphs so that numbers are used appropriately for nontechnical writing. If a sentence is correct as given, mark the number preceding it.

1 The planet Saturn is nine hundred million miles, or nearly one billion five hundred million kilometers, from the sun. 2 Saturn orbits the sun only two and four-tenths times during the average human life span. 3 As a result, a year on Saturn equals almost thirty of our years. 4 The planet travels in its orbit at about twenty-one thousand six hundred miles per hour.

5 Saturn is huge: more than seventy-two thousand miles in diameter, compared to Earth's eight-thousand-mile diameter. 6 Saturn is also very cold, with an average temperature of minus two hundred and eighteen degrees Fahrenheit, compared to Earth's fifty-nine degrees Fahrenheit. 7 Saturn is cold because of its great distance from the sun and because its famous rings reflect almost 70 percent of the sunlight that approaches the planet. 8 The ring system is almost forty thousand miles wide, beginning 8800 miles from the planet's visible surface and ending forty-seven thousand miles from that surface.

Research Writing

Research Writing

50 Research Strategy

Research writing gives you a chance to work like a detective solving a case. The mystery is the answer to a question you care about. The search for the answer leads you to consider what others think about your subject, but you do more than simply report their views. You build on them to develop and support your own opinion, and ultimately you become an expert in your own right.

Your investigation will be more productive and enjoyable if you take some steps described in this chapter: plan your work (below), keep a research journal (next page), find an appropriate subject and research question (p. 373), set goals for your sources (p. 374), and keep a working, annotated bibliography (p. 377).

50a | Planning your work

Research writing is a *writing* process:

- You work within a particular situation of subject, purpose, audience, and other factors (see **1** pp. 3–8).
- You gather ideas and information about your subject (**1** pp. 8–13).
- You focus and arrange your ideas (**1** pp. 14–21).
- You draft to explore your meaning (**1** pp. 22–24).
- You revise and edit to develop, shape, and polish (**1** pp. 24–34).

Although the process seems neatly sequential in this list, you know from experience that the stages overlap—that, for instance, you may begin drafting before you've gathered all the information you expect to find, and then while drafting you may discover a source that causes you to rethink your approach. Anticipating the process of research writing can free you to be flexible in your search and open to discoveries.

A thoughtful plan and systematic procedures can help you follow through on the diverse activities of research writing. One step is to make a schedule like the one on the next page that apportions the available time to the necessary work. You can estimate that each segment marked off by a horizontal line will occupy *roughly* one-quarter of the total time—for example, a week in a four-week assignment or two weeks in an eight-week assignment. The most

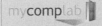

mycomplab

Visit *mycomplab.com* for more resources as well as exercises on research strategy.

unpredictable segments are the first two, so get started early enough to accommodate the unexpected.

Complete
by:

_____ 1. Setting a schedule and beginning a research journal (here and below)

_____ 2. Finding a researchable subject and question (facing page)

_____ 3. Setting goals for sources (p. 374)

_____ 4. Finding print and electronic sources (p. 379), and making a working, annotated bibliography (p. 377)

_____ 5. Evaluating and synthesizing sources (pp. 399, 410)

_____ 6. Gathering information from sources (p. 413), often using summary, paraphrase, and direct quotation (p. 414)

_____ 7. Taking steps to avoid plagiarism (p. 423)

_____ 8. Developing a thesis statement and creating a structure (p. 432)

_____ 9. Drafting the paper (p. 433), integrating summaries, paraphrases, and direct quotations into your ideas (p. 418)

_____ 10. Revising and editing the paper (p. 433)

_____ 11. Citing sources in your text (p. 430)

_____ 12. Preparing the list of works cited or references (p. 430)

_____ 13. Preparing the final manuscript (p. 433)

_____ Final paper due

50b Keeping a research journal

While working on a research project, carry a notebook or a computer with you at all times to use as a **research journal,** a place to record your activities and ideas. (See **1** p. 9 on journal keeping.) In the journal's dated entries, you can write about the sources you consult, the leads you want to pursue, and any difficulties you encounter. Most important, you can record your thoughts about sources, leads, dead ends, new directions, relationships, and anything else that strikes you. The very act of writing in the journal can expand and clarify your thinking.

Note The research journal is the place to track and develop your own ideas. To avoid mixing up your thoughts and those of others, keep separate notes on what your sources actually say, using one of the methods discussed on pp. 413–14.

50c Finding a researchable subject and question

Before reading this section, review the suggestions given in Chapter 1 for finding and narrowing a writing subject (**1** pp. 5–6). Generally, the same procedure applies to writing any kind of research paper. However, selecting and limiting a subject for a research paper can present special opportunities and problems. And before you proceed with your subject, you'll want to transform it into a question that can guide your search for sources.

1 Appropriate subject

Seek a research subject that interests you and that you care about. (It may be a subject you've already written about without the benefit of research.) Starting with your own views will motivate you, and you will be a participant in a dialog when you begin examining sources.

When you settle on a subject, ask the following questions about it. For each requirement, there are corresponding pitfalls.

■ **Are ample sources of information available on the subject?**

Avoid very recent subjects, such as a newly announced medical discovery or a breaking story in today's newspaper.

■ **Does the subject encourage research in the kinds and number of sources required by the assignment?**

Avoid (*a*) subjects that depend entirely on personal opinion and experience, such as the virtues of your hobby, and (*b*) subjects that require research in only one source, such as a straight factual biography.

■ **Will the subject lead you to an objective assessment of sources and to defensible conclusions?**

Avoid subjects that rest entirely on belief or prejudice, such as when human life begins or why women (or men) are superior. Your readers are unlikely to be swayed from their own beliefs.

■ **Does the subject suit the length of paper assigned and the time given for research and writing?**

Avoid broad subjects that have too many sources to survey adequately, such as a major event in history.

2 Research question

Asking a question about your subject can give direction to your research by focusing your thinking on a particular approach. To discover your question, consider what about your subject intrigues or perplexes you, what you'd like to know more about. (See below for suggestions on using your own knowledge.)

Try to narrow your research question so that you can answer it in the time and space you have available. The question *How does human activity affect the environment?* is very broad, encompassing issues as diverse as pollution, distribution of resources, climate change, population growth, land use, biodiversity, and the ozone layer. In contrast, the question *How can buying environmentally friendly products help the environment?* or *How, if at all, should carbon emissions be taxed?* is much narrower. Each question also requires more than a simple *yes* or *no* answer, so that answering, even tentatively, demands thought about pros and cons, causes and effects.

As you read and write, your question will probably evolve to reflect your increasing knowledge of the subject, and eventually its answer will become your main idea, or thesis statement (see p. 432).

50d Setting goals for sources

Before you start looking for sources, consider what you already know about your subject and where you are likely to find information on it.

1 Your own knowledge

Discovering what you already know about your topic will guide you in discovering what you don't know. Take some time to spell out facts you have learned, opinions you have heard or read elsewhere, and of course your own opinions. Use one of the discovery techniques discussed in **1** pp. 9–13 to explore and develop your ideas: keeping a journal, observing your surroundings, freewriting, brainstorming, clustering, and asking questions.

When you've explored your thoughts, make a list of questions for which you don't have answers, whether factual (*How much do Americans spend on green products?*) or more open-ended (*Are green products worth the higher prices?*). These questions will give you clues about the sources you need to look for first.

2 Kinds of sources

For many research projects, you'll want to consult a mix of sources, as described on the next two pages. You may start by seeking the outlines of your topic—the range and depth of opinions about it—in reference works and articles in popular periodicals or through a Web search. Then, as you refine your views and your research question, you'll move on to more specialized sources, such as scholarly books and periodicals and your own interviews or surveys. (See pp. 383–98 for more on each kind of source.)

The mix of sources you choose depends heavily on your subject. For example, a paper on green consumerism would require the use of very recent sources because environmentally friendly products are fairly new to the marketplace. Your mix of sources may also be specified by your instructor or limited by the requirements of your assignment.

Library and Internet sources

The print and electronic sources available through your library—mainly reference works, periodicals, and books—have two big advantages over most of what you'll find on the open Web: they are cataloged and indexed for easy retrieval; and they are generally reliable, having been screened first by their publishers and then by the library's staff. In contrast, the Internet's retrieval systems are more difficult to use effectively, and Internet sources tend to be less reliable because most do not pass through any screening before being posted. (There are many exceptions, such as online scholarly journals and reference works. But these sources are generally available through your library's Web site as well.)

Most instructors expect research writers to consult library sources. But they'll accept Internet sources, too, if you have used them judiciously. Even with its disadvantages, the Internet can be a valuable resource for primary sources, current information, and a diversity of views. For guidelines on evaluating both library and Internet sources, see pp. 399–410.

Primary and secondary sources

Use **primary sources** when they are available or are required by your assignment. These sources are firsthand accounts, such as works of literature, historical documents (letters, speeches, and so on), eyewitness reports (including articles by journalists who are on location), reports on experiments or surveys conducted by the writer, and your own interviews, experiments, observations, or correspondence.

Many assignments will allow you to use **secondary sources**, which report and analyze information drawn from other sources, often primary ones. Examples include a reporter's summary of a controversial issue, a historian's account of a battle, a critic's reading of a poem, and a psychologist's evaluation of several studies. Secondary sources may contain helpful summaries and interpretations that direct, support, and extend your own thinking. However, most research-writing assignments expect your own ideas to go beyond those in such sources.

Scholarly and popular sources

The scholarship of acknowledged experts is essential for depth, authority, and specificity. Most instructors expect students to emphasize scholarly sources in their research. But the general-interest views and information of popular sources can help you apply more scholarly approaches to daily life.

- **Check the title.** Is it technical, or does it use a general vocabulary?
- **Check the publisher.** Is it a scholarly journal (such as *Cultural Geographies*) or a publisher of scholarly books (such as Harvard University Press), or is it a popular magazine (such as *Consumer Reports* or *Newsweek*) or a publisher of popular books (such as Little, Brown)?
- **Check the length of periodical articles.** Scholarly articles are generally much longer than magazine and newspaper articles.
- **Check the author.** Have you seen the name elsewhere, which might suggest that the author is an expert?
- **Check the electronic address.** Addresses, or URLs, for Internet sources include an abbreviation that tells you something about the origin of the source: scholarly sources end in *edu, org,* or *gov,* while popular sources usually end in *com.* (See pp. 389–94 for more on types of online sources.)

Older and newer sources

Check the publication date. For most subjects a combination of older, established sources (such as books) and current sources (such as newspaper articles, interviews, or Web sites) will provide both background and up-to-date information. Only historical subjects or very current subjects require an emphasis on one extreme or another.

Impartial and biased sources

Seek a range of viewpoints. Sources that attempt to be impartial can offer an overview of your subject and trustworthy facts. Sources with clear biases can offer a diversity of opinion. Of course, to discover bias, you may have to read the source carefully (see pp. 399–410); but you can infer quite a bit just from a bibliographical listing.

- **Check the author.** You may have heard of the author as a respected researcher (thus more likely to be objective) or as a leading proponent of a certain view (less likely to be objective).
- **Check the title.** It may reveal something about point of view. (Consider these contrasting titles: "Go for the Green" versus "Green Consumerism and the Struggle for Northern Maine.")

Note Sources you find on the Internet must be approached with particular care. See pp. 401–10.

Sources with helpful features

Depending on your topic and how far along your research is, you may want to look for sources with features such as illustrations (which can clarify important concepts), bibliographies (which can direct you to other sources), and indexes (which can help you develop keywords for electronic searches; see pp. 382–83).

50e Keeping a working, annotated bibliography

To track where sources are, compile a **working bibliography** as you uncover possibilities. When you have a substantial file—say, ten to thirty sources—you can decide which ones seem most promising and look them up first.

1 Source information

When you turn in your paper, you will be expected to attach a list of the sources you have used. So that readers can check or follow up on your sources, your list must include all the information needed to find the sources, in a format readers can understand. (See pp. 430–31.) The box on the next page shows the information you should record for each type of source so that you will not have to retrace your steps later.

Note Whenever possible, record source information in the correct format for the documentation style you will be using. Then you will be less likely to omit needed information or to confuse numbers, dates, and other data when it's time to write your citations. This book describes four styles: MLA (see **MLA** p. 464), APA (see **APA** p. 521), Chicago (see **Chic** p. 549), and CSE (see **CSE** p. 560). For others, consult one of the guides listed in **8** pp. 455 and 459.

2 Annotations

Creating annotations for a working bibliography converts it from a simple list into a tool for assessing sources. When you discover a possible source, record not only its publication information but also the following:

- **What you know about the content of the source.** Periodical databases and book catalogs generally include abstracts, or summaries, of sources that can help with this part of the annotation.
- **How you think the source may be helpful in your research.** Does it offer expert opinion, statistics, an important example, or a range of views? Does it place your subject in a historical, social, or economic context?

Information for a working bibliography

For books

Library call number
Name(s) of author(s), editor(s), translator(s), or others listed
Title and subtitle
Publication data:
  Place of publication
  Publisher's name
  Date of publication
Other important data, such as edition or volume number
Medium (print, Web, etc.)

For periodical articles

Name(s) of author(s)
Title and subtitle of article
Title of periodical
Publication data:
  Volume number and issue number (if any) in which article appears
  Date of issue
  Page numbers on which article appears
Medium (print, Web, etc.)

For electronic sources

Name(s) of author(s)
Title and subtitle of source
Title of Web site, periodical, or other larger work
Publication data, such as data listed above for a book or article; the publisher or sponsor of a Web site; and the date

of release, revision, or online posting
Any publication data for the source in another medium (print, film, etc.)
Format of online source (Web site or page, podcast, e-mail, etc.)
Date you consulted the source
Title of any database used to reach the source
Complete URL (but see the note below)
Digital Object Identifier, if any (for APA style)
Medium (Web, CD-ROM, etc.)

For other sources

Name(s) of author(s), creator(s), or others listed, such as a government department, recording artist, or photographer
Title of work
Format, such as unpublished letter, live performance, or photograph
Publication or production data:
  Publication title
  Publisher's or producer's name
  Date of publication, release, or production
Identifying numbers (if any)
Medium (print, typescript, etc.)

Note MLA documentation style does not require URLs for citations of most electronic sources; other styles do require them. Recording URLs will ensure that you have them if you need them and will make it easy to track down sources if you want to consult them again. For sources you reach through databases, record URLs only if they are usable by others outside your school. Most database URLs are unique to the search or the subscriber.

Taking the time with your annotations can help you discover gaps that may remain in your sources and will later help you decide which sources to pursue in depth. One student annotated a bibliography entry on his computer with a summary and a note on the source features he thought would be most helpful to him:

Entry for an annotated working bibliography

Gore, Al. *An Inconvenient Truth: The Planetary Emergency of Global Warming and What We Can Do about It.* Emmaus: Rodale, 2006. Print.

Book version of the documentary movie supporting Gore's argument that global warming is a serious threat to the planet. Includes summaries of scientific studies, short essays on various subjects, and dozens of images, tables, charts, and graphs. Last chapter offers several suggestions for ways to solve the problem, with an emphasis on changing individual buying habits.

Publication information for source	
Summary of source	
Ideas on use of source	

As you become more familiar with your sources, you can use your initial annotated bibliography to record your evaluations of them as well as more detailed thoughts on how they fit into your research.

51 Finding Sources

This chapter discusses conducting electronic searches (next page) and taking advantage of the range of sources, both print and electronic, that you have access to: reference works (p. 383); books (p. 384); periodicals (p. 385); the Web (p. 389); other online sources (p. 392); government publications (p. 394); images, audio, and video (p. 394); and your own interviews, surveys, and other primary sources (p. 396).

Note As you look for sources, avoid the temptation to seek a "silver bullet"—that is, to locate two or three perfect sources that already say everything you want to say about your subject. Instead of merely repeating others' ideas, read and synthesize many sources so that you develop your own ideas. For more on synthesis, see pp. 410–11.

mycomplab

Visit *mycomplab.com* for more resources as well as exercises on finding sources.

51a Starting with your library's Web site

As you conduct research, the Web will be your gateway to ideas and information. Always start with your library's Web site, not with a public search engine such as *Google*. The library site will lead you to vast resources, including books, periodical articles, and reference works that aren't available on the open Web. More important, unlike many sources on the open Web, every source you find on the library site will have passed through filters to ensure its value. A scholarly journal article, for instance, undergoes at least three successive reviews: subject-matter experts first deem it worth publishing in the journal; then a database vendor deems the journal worth including in the database; and finally your school's librarians deem the database worth subscribing to.

Google and other search engines may seem more user-friendly than the library's Web site and may seem to return plenty of sources for you to work with. Many of the sources may indeed be reliable and relevant to your research, but many more will not be. In the end, a library Web search will be more efficient and more effective than a direct Web search. (For help with evaluating sources from any resource, see pp. 399–410.)

Note Start with the library's Web site, but don't stop there. Many books, periodicals, and other excellent sources are available only on library shelves, not online, and most instructors expect research papers to be built to some extent on these resources. When you spot promising print sources while browsing the library's online databases, make records of them and then look them up at the library.

51b Searching electronically

Searching electronically requires careful planning. Become familiar with the kinds of electronic resources available to you, understand the different search strategies they demand, and take the time to develop **keywords** that name your subject for databases and Web search engines.

1 Kinds of electronic sources

Your school's library, its Web site, and the open Web offer several kinds of electronic resources that are suitable for academic research:

- **The library's catalog of holdings** is a database that lists all the resources that the library owns or subscribes to: books, journals, magazines, newspapers, reference works, and more. The

A tip for researchers

Take advantage of two valuable resources offered by your library:

- **An orientation,** which introduces the library's resources and explains how to reach and use the Web site and the print holdings.
- **Reference librarians,** whose job it is to help you and others navigate the library's resources. Even very experienced researchers often consult reference librarians.

catalog may also include the holdings of other school libraries nearby or in your state.

- **Online databases** include indexes, bibliographies, and other reference works. They are your main route to articles in periodicals, providing publication information, summaries, and often full text. Your library subscribes to the databases and makes them available through its Web site. (You may also discover databases directly on the Web, but, again, the library is a more productive starting place.)
- **Databases on CD-ROM** include the same information as online databases, but they must be read at a library computer terminal. Increasingly, libraries are moving away from CD-ROMs in favor of online databases.
- **Full-text resources** contain the entire contents of articles, book chapters, and even whole books. The library's databases provide access to the full text of many listed sources. In addition, the Web sites of many periodicals and organizations, such as government agencies, offer the full text of articles, reports, and other publications.

2 Databases vs. the open Web

To develop keywords it helps to understand an important difference in how library databases and the open Web work:

- **A database indexes sources by authors, titles, publication years, and its own subject headings.** The subject headings reflect the database's directory of terms and are assigned by people who have read the sources. You can find these subject headings by using your own keywords until you locate a promising source. The information for the source will list the headings under which the database indexes it and other sources like it. (See p. 388 for an illustration.) You can then use those headings for further searches.
- **A Web search engine seeks your keywords in the titles and texts of sites.** The process is entirely electronic, so the results

from a search engine will depend on how well your keywords describe your subject and anticipate the words used in sources. If you describe your subject too broadly or describe it specifically but don't match the vocabulary in relevant sources, your search will turn up few relevant sources and probably many that aren't relevant.

3 Keyword refinement

Every database and search engine provides a system that you can use to refine your keywords for a productive search. The basic operations appear in the following box, but resources do differ. For instance, some assume that *AND* should link keywords, while others provide options specifying "Must contain all the words" and other equivalents for the operations in the box. You can learn a search engine's system by consulting its Advanced Search page.

Ways to refine keywords

Most databases and many search engines work with **Boolean operators,** terms or symbols that allow you to expand or limit your keywords and thus your search.

- **Use *AND* or + to narrow the search** by including only sources that use all the given words. The keywords *green AND products* request only the sources in the shaded area.

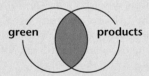

- **Use *NOT* or − ("minus") to narrow the search** by excluding irrelevant words. The keywords *green AND products NOT guide* exclude sources that use the word *guide:*

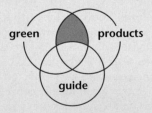

- **Use *OR* to broaden the search** by giving alternate keywords. The keywords *green AND products OR goods* allow for sources that use a synonym for *products:*

- **Use parentheses or quotation marks to form search phrases.** For instance, *(green products)* requests the exact phrase, not the separate words. Only sources using *green products* would turn up.
- **Use wild cards to permit different versions of the same word.** In *consum**, for instance, the wild card * indicates that sources may include *consume, consumer, consumerism,* and *consumption* as well as *consumptive, consumedly,* and *consummate.* The example suggests that you have to consider all the variations allowed by a wild card and whether it opens up your search too much. If you seek only two or three from many variations, you may be better off using *OR: consumption OR consumerism.* (Note that some systems use ?, :, or + for a wild card instead of *.)
- **Be sure to spell your keywords correctly.** Some search tools will look for close matches or approximations, but correct spelling gives you the best chance of finding relevant sources.

Note You will probably have to use trial and error in developing your keywords, sometimes running dry (turning up few or no sources) and sometimes hitting uncontrollable gushers (turning up thousands or millions of mostly irrelevant sources). But the process is not busywork—far from it. Besides leading you eventually to worthwhile sources, it can also teach you a great deal about your subject: how you can or should narrow it, how it is and is not described by others, what others consider interesting or debatable about it, and what the major arguments are. See pp. 391–92 for an example of a student's keyword search of the Web.

51c Finding reference works

Reference works, often available online, include encyclopedias, dictionaries, digests, bibliographies, indexes, atlases, almanacs, and handbooks. Your research *must* go beyond these sources, but they can help you decide whether your topic really interests you and whether it meets the requirements for a research paper (p. 373). Preliminary research in reference works can also help you develop keywords for electronic searches and can direct you to more detailed sources on your topic.

You'll find many reference works through your library and directly on the Web. The following list gives general Web references for all disciplines:

> Internet Public Library (*www.ipl.org*)
> Library of Congress (*lcweb.loc.gov*)
> LSU Libraries Webliography (*www.lib.lsu.edu/weblio.html*)
> World Wide Web Virtual Library (*vlib.org*)

For Web sites in specific academic disciplines, see **8** pp. 444–45 (literature), 450–51 (other humanities), 454–55 (social sciences), and 458–59 (natural and applied sciences).

Note The Web-based encyclopedia *Wikipedia* (found at *wikipedia .org*) is one of the largest reference sites on the Internet. Like any encyclopedia, *Wikipedia* can provide background information for research on a topic; but unlike other encyclopedias, *Wikipedia* is a **wiki,** a kind of Web site that can be contributed to or edited by anyone. Ask your instructor whether *Wikipedia* is an acceptable source before you use it. If you do use it, you must carefully evaluate any information you find, using the guidelines on pp. 401–10.

51d Finding books

Your library's catalog is searchable at a terminal in the library and via the library's Web site. You can search the catalog by author or title, of course, and by your own keywords or the headings found in *Library of Congress Subject Headings* (*LCSH*). The screen shot below shows the complete record for a book, including the *LCSH* headings that can be used to find similar sources.

Book catalog full record

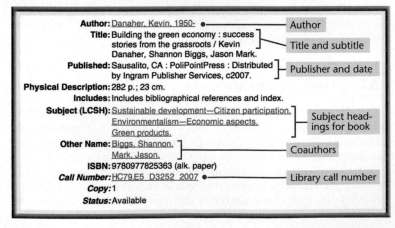

51e Finding periodicals

Periodicals include newspapers, journals, and magazines. Newspapers, the easiest to recognize, are useful for detailed accounts of past and current events. Journals and magazines can be harder to distinguish, but their differences are important. Most college instructors expect students' research to rely more on journals than on magazines.

Journals	Magazines
Examples	
American Anthropologist, Journal of Black Studies, Journal of Chemical Education	*The New Yorker, Time, Rolling Stone, People*
Availability	
Mainly through college and university libraries	Public libraries, newsstands, and bookstores
Purpose	
Advance knowledge in a particular field	Express opinion, inform, or entertain
Authors	
Specialists in the field	May or may not be specialists in their subjects
Readers	
Often specialists in the field	Members of the general public or a subgroup with a particular interest
Source citations	
Source citations always included	Source citations rarely included
Length of articles	
Usually long, ten pages or more	Usually short, fewer than ten pages
Appearance	
Bland, with black-only type, little or no decoration, and only illustrations that directly amplify the text, such as graphs	Generally lively, with color, decoration (headings, sidebars, and other elements), and illustrations (drawings, photographs)
Frequency of publication	
Quarterly or less often	Weekly, biweekly, or monthly
Pagination of issues	
May be paged separately (like a magazine) or may be paged sequentially throughout an annual volume, so that issue number 3 (the third issue of the year) could open on page 373	Paged separately, each beginning on page 1

1 Indexes to periodicals

How indexes work

Periodical databases index the articles in journals, magazines, and newspapers. Often these databases include abstracts, or summaries, of the articles, and they may offer the full text of the articles as well. Your library subscribes to many periodical databases and to services that offer multiple databases. (See p. 389 for a list.) Most databases and services will be searchable through the library's Web site.

Note The search engine *Google* is developing *Google Scholar*, a search engine at *scholar.google.com* that seeks out scholarly articles. It is particularly useful for subjects that range across disciplines, for which discipline-specific databases can be too limited. *Google Scholar* can connect to your library's holdings if you tell it to do so under Scholar Preferences. Keep in mind, however, that *Google Scholar*'s searches are not as yet exhaustive. Your library probably subscribes to most of the periodicals searched by *Google Scholar*, so begin there.

Selection of databases

To decide which databases to consult, you'll need to consider what you're looking for:

- **How broadly and deeply should you search?** Periodical databases vary widely in what they index. Some, such as *ProQuest Research Library*, cover many subjects but don't index the full range of periodicals in each subject. Others, such as *Historical Abstracts*, cover a single subject but then include most of the available periodicals. If your subject ranges across disciplines, then start with a broad database. If your subject focuses on a particular discipline, then start with a narrower database.
- **Which databases most likely include the kinds of resources you need?** The Web sites of most libraries allow you to narrow a database search to a particular kind of periodical (such as newspapers or journals) or to a particular discipline. You can then discover each database's focus by checking the description of the database (sometimes labeled "Help" or "Guide") or the list of indexed resources (sometimes labeled "Publications" or "Index"). The description will also tell you the time period the database covers, so you'll know whether you also need to consult older print indexes at the library.

Database searches

When you first search a database, use your own keywords to locate sources. The procedure is illustrated in the three screen shots shown below and on the next page. Your goal is to find at least one source that seems just right for your subject, so that you can see what subject headings the database itself uses for such sources. Using one or more of those headings will focus and speed your search.

1. Initial keyword search of a periodical database

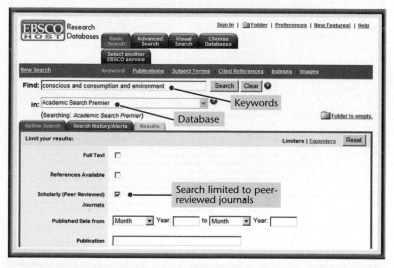

2. Partial keyword search results

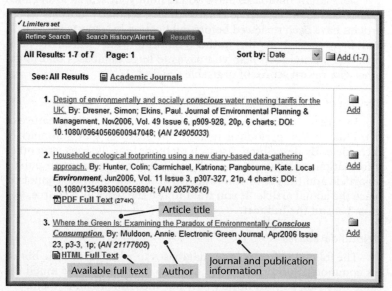

3. Full article record with abstract

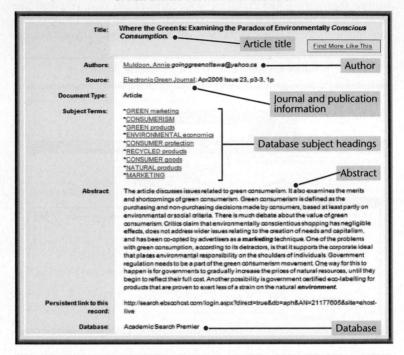

Note Many databases allow you to limit your search to so-called peer-reviewed or refereed journals—that is, scholarly journals whose articles have been reviewed before publication by experts in the field and then revised by the author. Limiting your search to peer-reviewed journals can help you navigate huge databases that might otherwise return scores of unusable articles.

The use of abstracts

In screen 3 above, the full article record shows a key feature of many databases' periodical listings: an **abstract** that summarizes the article. By describing research methods, conclusions, and other information, an abstract can tell you whether you want to pursue an article and thus save you time. However, the abstract cannot replace the actual article. If you want to use the work as a source, you must consult the full text.

Helpful databases

The following list includes databases to which academic libraries commonly subscribe. Some of these databases cover much the same material, so your library may not subscribe to all of them.

EBSCOhost Academic Search. A periodical index covering magazines and journals in the social sciences, sciences, arts, and humanities. Many articles are available full-text.

InfoTrac Expanded Academic. The Gale Group's general periodical index covering the social sciences, sciences, arts, and humanities as well as national news periodicals. It includes full-text articles.

LexisNexis Academic. An index of news and business, legal, and reference information, with full-text articles. *LexisNexis* includes international, national, and regional newspapers, news magazines, legal and business publications, and court cases.

ProQuest Research Library. A periodical index covering the sciences, social sciences, arts, and humanities, including many full-text articles.

2 Locations of periodicals

If an index listing does not include or link directly to the full text of an article, you'll need to consult the periodical itself. Recent issues of periodicals are probably held in the library's periodical room. Back issues are usually stored elsewhere, either in bound volumes or on film that requires a special machine to read. A librarian will show you how to operate the machine.

51f Finding sources on the Web

As an academic researcher, you enter the Web in two ways: through your library's Web site, and through public search engines such as *Yahoo!* and *Google.* The library entrance, covered in the preceding sections, is your main path to the books and periodicals that, for most subjects, should make up most of your sources. The public entrance, discussed here, can lead to a wealth of information and ideas, but it also has a number of disadvantages:

- **The Web is a wide-open network.** Anyone with the right hardware and software can place information on the Internet, and even a carefully conceived search can turn up sources with widely varying reliability: journal articles, government documents, scholarly data, term papers written by high school students, sales pitches masked as objective reports, wild theories. You must be especially diligent about evaluating Internet sources (see pp. 401–10).

- **The Web changes constantly.** No search engine can keep up with the Web's daily additions and deletions, and a source you find today may be different or gone tomorrow. You should not put off consulting an online source that you think you may want to use.

- **The Web provides limited information on the past.** Sources dating from before the 1980s or even more recently probably will not appear on the Web.

■ **The Web is not all-inclusive.** Most books and many periodicals are available only via the library, not directly via the Web.

Clearly, the Web warrants cautious use. It should not be the only resource you work with.

Note Open-source wikis, such as *Wikipedia* and *SourceWatch*, are Web sites that can be contributed to and edited by anyone. Ask your instructor whether wikis are acceptable sources before using one, and evaluate any information you find on a wiki using the guidelines on pp. 401–08.

1 Search engines

To find sources on the Web, you use a **search engine** that catalogs Web sites in a series of directories and conducts keyword searches. Generally, use a directory when you haven't yet refined your topic or you want a general overview. Use keywords when you have refined your topic and you seek specific information.

Current search engines

The box below lists popular search engines. To reach any one of them, enter its address in the Address or Location field of your Web browser.

Web search engines

The features of search engines change often, and new ones appear constantly. For the latest on search engines, see the links collected by *Easy Searcher* at *easysearcher.com*.

Directories that review sites

BUBL Link (*bubl.ac.uk*)
Internet Public Library (*ipl.org/div/subject*)
Internet Scout Project (*scout.wisc.edu/archives*)
Librarians' Internet Index (*lii.org*)

Search engines

AlltheWeb (*alltheweb.com*)
AltaVista (*altavista.com*)
Ask.com (*ask.com*)
Dogpile (*dogpile.com*)
Google (*google.com*)
Livesearch.com (*livesearch.com*)
MetaCrawler (*metacrawler.com*)
Yahoo! (*yahoo.com*)

Note For a good range of reliable sources, try out more than a single search engine, perhaps as many as four or five. No search engine can catalog the entire Web—indeed, even the most powerful engine may not include half the sites available at any given time, and most engines include only a fifth or less. In addition, most search engines accept paid placements, giving higher billing to sites that pay a fee. These so-called sponsored links are usually marked as such, but they can compromise a search engine's method for arranging sites in response to your keywords.

Customized searches

The home page of a search engine includes a field for you to type your keywords into. Generally, it will also include an Advanced Search link that you can use to customize your search. For instance, you may be able to select a range of dates, a language, or a number of results to see. Advanced Search will also explain how to use operators such as *AND* and *NOT* to limit or expand your search.

Search records

Your Web browser includes functions that allow you to keep track of Web sources and your search:

- Use *Favorites* or *Bookmarks* **to save site addresses as links.** Click one of these terms near the top of the browser screen to add a site you want to return to. A favorite or bookmark remains on file until you delete it.
- Use *History* **to locate sites you have visited before.** The browser records visited sites for a certain period, such as a single online session or a week's sessions. (After that period, the history is deleted.) If you forgot to bookmark a site, you can click History or Go to locate your search history and recover the site.

2 A sample search

The following sample Web search illustrates how the refinement of keywords can narrow a search to maximize the relevant hits and minimize the irrelevant ones. Justin Malik, a student researching the environmental effects of green consumer products, first used the keywords *green consumption* on *Google*. But, as shown on screen 1 on the next page, the search produced more than 3.4 *million* hits, an unusably large number and a sure sign that Malik's keywords needed revision.

After several tries, Malik arrived at *"green consumption" "environmental issues"* to describe his subject more precisely. He then added *site:.org* to limit the results to nonprofit organizations. Narrowed in this way, Malik's search still produced 387 hits, but this large number included many potential sources on the first few screens, as shown on screen 2 on the next page.

1. First *Google* search results

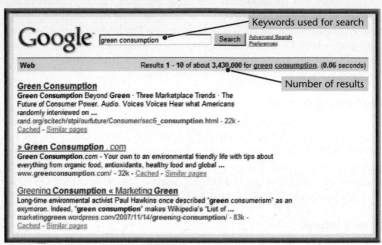

2. *Google* results with refined keywords

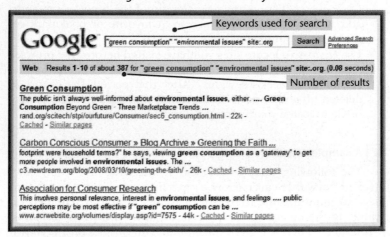

51g Finding other online sources

Several online sources can put you directly in touch with experts and others whose ideas and information may inform your research. Because these sources, like Web sites, are unfiltered, you must always evaluate them carefully. (See pp. 408–10.)

1 E-mail

As a research tool, e-mail allows you to communicate with others who are interested in your topic. You might, for instance, carry on an e-mail conversation with a teacher at your school or interview an expert in another state to follow up on a scholarly article he or she published. (See **2** pp. 117–19 for more on using e-mail.)

2 Blogs

Blogs (Web logs) are personal sites on which an author posts time-stamped comments, generally centering on a common theme, in a format that allows readers to respond to the author or to each other. You can find a directory of blogs at *blogcatalog.com*.

Like all other online media discussed in this section, blogs consulted as potential sources must be evaluated carefully. Some are reliable sources of opinion, news, or evolving scholarship, and many refer to worthy books, articles, Web sites, and other resources. But lots of blogs are little more than outlets for their authors' gripes and prejudices. See pp. 408–10 for tips on telling the good from the bad.

3 Discussion lists

A **discussion list** (sometimes called a **listserv** or just a **list**) uses e-mail to connect individuals who are interested in a common subject, often with a scholarly or technical focus. By sending a question to an appropriate list, you may be able to reach scores of people who know something about your topic. For an index of discussion lists, see *tile.net/lists*.

When conducting research on a discussion list, follow the guidelines for writing e-mail (**2** pp. 117–19) as well as these:

- *Lurk* for a while—read without posting messages. Make sure the discussion is relevant to your topic, and get a sense of how the group interacts.
- **Consult the list's archive.** Your question may already have been answered.
- **Don't ask for information you can find elsewhere.** Most list members are glad to help with legitimate questions but resent messages that rehash familiar debates or that ask them to do someone else's work.
- **Evaluate messages carefully.** Many list subscribers are passionate experts with fair-minded approaches to their topics, but almost anyone with an Internet connection can post a message to a list. See pp. 408–10 on evaluating online sources.

4 Web forums and newsgroups

Web forums and newsgroups are more open and less scholarly than discussion lists, so their messages require even more diligent evaluation. **Web forums** allow participants to join a conversation simply by selecting a link on a Web page. For a directory of forums, see *delphiforums.com*. **Newsgroups** are organized under subject headings such as *soc* for social issues and *biz* for business. For a directory of newsgroups, see *groups.google.com*.

51h Using government publications

Government publications provide a vast array of data, reports, policy statements, public records, and other historical and contemporary information. For US government publications, consult the Government Printing Office's *GPO Access* at *www.gpoaccess.gov*. Also helpful is *Google US Government Search* (*google.com/ig/usgov*) because it returns *.gov* (government) and *.mil* (military) documents and its ranking system emphasizes the most useful documents. Many federal, state, and local government agencies post important publications—legislation, reports, press releases—on their own Web sites. You can find lists of sites for various federal agencies by using the keywords *United States federal government* with a search engine. Use the name of a state, city, or town with *government* for state and local information.

51i Finding images, audio, and video

Images, audio, and video can be used as both primary and secondary sources in a research project. A painting, an advertisement, or a video of a speech might be the subject of a paper and thus a primary source. A podcast of a radio interview with an expert on your subject or a college lecture might serve as a secondary source. Because many of these sources are unfiltered—they can be posted by anyone—you must always evaluate them as carefully as you would any source you find on the open Web.

Note You must also cite every image, audio, and video source fully in your paper, just as you cite text sources, with author, title, and publication information. In addition, some sources will require that you seek permission from the copyright holder, either the source itself or a third party such as a photographer or the creator of video. Permission is especially likely to be required if you are submitting your paper on the public Web. See pp. 429–30 for more about online publication.

1 Images

The use of images to support an argument is discussed in **2** pp. 106–12. To find images, you have a number of options.

- **Scout for images while reading sources.** Your sources may include charts, graphs, photographs, and other images that can support your ideas. When you find an image you may want to use, photocopy or download it so you'll have it available later.
- **Create your own images,** such as photographs or charts. See **1** pp. 62–65 for examples.
- **Use an image search engine.** *Google, Yahoo!, AlltheWeb,* and some other search engines conduct specialized image searches. They can find scores of images, but the results may be inaccurate or incomplete because the sources surveyed often do not include descriptions of the images. (The engines will search file names and any text accompanying the images.)
- **Use a public image database.** The following sites generally conduct accurate searches because their images are filed with information such as a description of the image, the artist's name, and the image's date:

    Adflip (adflip.com): Historical and contemporary print advertisements
    Duke University, *Ad*Access (library.duke.edu/digitalcollections/adaccess)*: Print advertisements spanning 1911–55
    Library of Congress, *American Memory (memory.loc.gov/ammem)*: Maps, photographs, and prints documenting the American experience
    Library of Congress, *Prints and Photographs Online Catalog (loc.gov/rr/print/catalog.html)*: Images from the library's collection, including those available through *American Memory*
    New York Public Library Digital Gallery (digitalgallery.nypl.org/nypldigital): Maps, drawings, photographs, and paintings from the library's collection
    Political Cartoons (politicalcartoons.com): Cartoons on contemporary issues and events

- **Use a public image directory.** The following sites collect links to image sources:

    Art Source (ilpi.com/artsource/general.html): Sources on art and architecture
    Museum Computer Network (mcn.edu/resources/sitesonline.htm): Museum collections
    MuseumLink's Museum of Museums (museumlink.com): Links to museums all over the world
    Washington State University, *Popular Culture: Resources for Critical Analysis (wsu.edu/~amerstu/pop)*: Sources on advertising, fashion, magazines, toys, and other artifacts of popular culture
    Yale University Arts Library, *Image Resources (library.yale.edu/art)*: Sources on the visual and performing arts

■ **Use a subscription database.** Your library may subscribe to the following resources:

ARTstor: Museum collections and a database of images typically used in art history courses

Associated Press, *AccuNet/AP Multimedia Archives*: Historical and contemporary news images

Grove Art Online: Art images and links to museum sites

Many images you find will be available for free, but some sources do charge a fee for use. Before paying for an image, check with a librarian to see if it is available elsewhere for free.

2 Audio and video

Audio and video, widely available on the Web and on CD-ROM, can provide your readers with the experience of "being there." For example, if you are researching the media response to Martin Luther King's famous "I Have a Dream" speech and you are publishing your paper electronically, you might insert links to the speech and to TV and radio coverage of it.

■ **Audio files** such as podcasts, Webcasts, and CDs record radio programs, interviews, speeches, lectures, and music. They are available on the Web and through your library. Online sources of audio include Congress's *American Memory* (see the previous page) and podcasts at *www.podcastdirectory.com.*

■ **Video files** capture performances, public presentations and speeches, news events, and other activities. They are available on the Web and through your library on DVD. Online sources of video include the Library of Congress's *American Memory* (see the previous page); *YouTube*, which includes commercials, historical footage, current events, and much more (*youtube.com*); and search engines such as *Google* (*video.google.com*).

51j Generating your own sources

Academic writing will often require you to conduct primary research for information of your own. For instance, you may need to analyze a poem, conduct an experiment, or interview an expert. Three common forms of primary research are observation, personal interviews, and surveys.

1 Observation

Observation can be an effective way to gather fresh information on your subject. You may observe in a controlled setting—for instance, watching the behavior of children playing in a child-development lab. Or you may observe in a more open setting—for instance, watching the interactions among students at a cafeteria on your campus. Be sure your observation has a well-defined purpose that relates to your research project. Throughout the observation, take careful notes, either on paper or on a handheld computer, and always record the date, time, and location for each session.

2 Personal interviews

An interview can be especially helpful for a research project because it allows you to ask questions precisely geared to your topic. You can conduct an interview in person, over the telephone, or online. A personal interview is preferable if you can arrange it, because you can see the person's expressions and gestures as well as hear his or her tone.

Here are a few guidelines for interviews:

- **Call or write for an appointment.** Tell the person exactly why you are calling, what you want to discuss, and how long you expect the interview to take. Be true to your word on all points.
- **Prepare a list of open-ended questions to ask**—perhaps ten or twelve for a one-hour interview. Plan on doing some research for these questions to discover background on the issues and your subject's published views on the issues.
- **Pay attention to your subject's answers** so that you can ask appropriate follow-up questions. Take care in interpreting answers, especially if you are online and thus can't depend on facial expressions, gestures, and tone of voice to convey the subject's attitudes.
- **Keep thorough notes.** Take notes during an in-person or telephone interview, or record the interview if you have the equipment and your subject agrees. For online interviews, save the discussion in a file of its own.
- **Verify quotations.** Before you quote your subject in your paper, check with him or her to ensure that the quotations are accurate.
- **Send a thank-you note immediately after the interview.** Promise your subject a copy of your finished paper, and send the paper promptly.

3 Surveys

Asking questions of a defined group of people can provide information about respondents' attitudes, behavior, backgrounds, and expectations. Use the following tips to plan and conduct a survey:

- **Decide what you want to find out.** The questions you ask should be dictated by your purpose. Formulating a **hypothesis** about your subject—a generalization that can be tested—will help you refine your purpose.

■ **Define your population.** Think about the kinds of people your hypothesis is about—for instance, college men or preschool children. Plan to sample this population so that your findings will be representative.

■ **Write your questions.** Surveys may contain closed questions that direct the respondent's answers (checklists and multiple-choice, true/false, or yes/no questions) or open-ended questions that allow brief, descriptive answers. Avoid loaded questions that reveal your own biases or make assumptions about subjects' answers.

■ **Test your questions.** Use a few respondents with whom you can discuss the answers. Eliminate or recast questions that respondents find unclear, discomforting, or unanswerable.

■ **Tally the results.** Count the actual numbers of answers, including any nonanswers.

■ **Seek patterns in the raw data.** Such patterns may confirm or contradict your hypothesis. Revise the hypothesis or conduct additional research if necessary.

52 Working with Sources

Research writing is much more than finding sources and reporting their contents. The challenge and interest come from interacting with and synthesizing sources: reading them critically to discover their meanings, judge their relevance and reliability, and create relationships among them; and using them to extend and support your own ideas so that you make your subject your own.

CULTURE LANGUAGE Making a subject your own requires thinking critically about sources and developing independent ideas. These goals may at first be uncomfortable if your native culture emphasizes understanding and respecting established authority more than questioning and enlarging it. The information here will help you work with sources so that you can become an expert in your own right and convincingly convey your expertise to others.

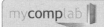

Visit *mycomplab.com* for more resources and exercises on working with sources.

52a Evaluating sources

Before you gather information and ideas from sources, scan them to evaluate what they have to offer and how you might use them.

Note In evaluating sources, you need to consider how they come to you. The sources you find through the library, both in print and on the Web, have been previewed for you by their publishers and by the library's staff. They still require your critical reading, but you can have some confidence in the information they contain. With online sources you reach directly, however, you can't assume similar previewing, so your critical reading must be especially rigorous. Special tips for evaluating Web sites and other online sources begin on p. 401.

1 Relevance and reliability

Not all the sources you find will prove worthwhile: some may be irrelevant to your subject, and others may be unreliable. Gauging the relevance and reliability of sources is the essential task of evaluating them. If you haven't already done so, read this book's chapter on critical thinking and reading (**2** pp. 77–89). It provides a foundation for answering the questions in the following box.

Questions for evaluating sources

For online sources, supplement these questions with those on pp. 401 and 408–09.

Relevance

- **Does the source devote some attention to your subject?** Does it focus on your subject or cover it marginally? How does it compare to other sources you've found?
- **Is the source appropriately specialized for your needs?** Check the source's treatment of a topic you know something about, to ensure that it is neither too superficial nor too technical.
- **Is the source up to date enough for your subject?** When was it published? If your subject is current, your sources should be, too.

Reliability

- **Where does the source come from?** Did you find it through your library or directly through the Internet? (If the latter, see pp. 401 and 404–10.) Is the source popular or scholarly?
- **Is the author an expert in the field?** Check the author's credentials in a biography (if the source includes one), in a biographical reference, or by a keyword search of the Web.

(continued)

> **Questions for evaluating sources**
> *(continued)*
>
> ■ **What is the author's bias?** How do the author's ideas relate to those in other sources? What areas does the author emphasize, ignore, or dismiss?
>
> ■ **Is the source fair, reasonable, and well-written?** Does it provide sound reasoning and a fair picture of opposing views? Is the tone calm and objective? Is the source logically organized and error-free?
>
> ■ **Are the author's claims well supported?** Does the author provide accurate, relevant, representative, and adequate evidence to back up his or her claims? Does the author cite sources, and if so are they reliable?

2 Evaluating library sources

To evaluate sources you find through your library, either in print or on the library's Web site, look at dates, titles, summaries, introductions, headings, author biographies, and any source notes. The following criteria expand on the most important tips in the preceding box. On pp. 402–03 you can see how Justin Malik applied these criteria to two print sources, a magazine article and a journal article, that he consulted while researching green consumerism.

Identify the origin of the source.

Check whether a library source is popular or scholarly. Scholarly sources, such as refereed journals and university press books, are generally deeper and more reliable, though some popular sources, such as first-hand newspaper accounts and books for a general audience, are often appropriate for research projects.

Check the author's expertise.

The authors of scholarly publications tend to be experts whose authority can be verified. Check the source to see whether it contains a biographical note about the author, check a biographical reference, or check the author's name in a keyword search of the Web. Look for other publications by the author and for his or her job and any affiliation, such as teacher at a university, researcher with a nonprofit organization, author of general-interest books, or writer for popular magazines.

Identify the author's bias.

Every author has a point of view that influences the selection and interpretation of evidence. You may be able to learn about an author's bias from biographies, citation indexes, and review indexes. But also look at the source itself. How do the author's ideas relate to those in other sources? What areas does the author empha-

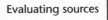

size, ignore, or dismiss? When you're aware of sources' biases, you can attempt to balance them.

Determine whether the source is fair, reasonable, and well written.

Even a strongly biased work should present solid reasoning and give balanced coverage to opposing views—all in an objective tone. Any source should be organized logically and should be written in clear, error-free sentences. The absence of any of these qualities should raise a warning flag.

Analyze support for the author's claims.

Evidence should be accurate, relevant to the argument, representative of its context, and adequate for the point being made (see **2** p. 99). The author's sources should themselves be reliable.

3 | Evaluating Web sites

To a great extent, the same critical reading that helps you evaluate library sources will help you evaluate Web sites that you reach directly. But most Web sites have not undergone prior screening by editors and librarians. On your own, you must distinguish scholarship from corporate promotion, valid data from invented statistics, well-founded opinion from clever propaganda.

The strategy summarized in the box below can help you make such distinctions. On pp. 406–07 you can see how Justin Malik applied this strategy to two Web sites that he consulted while researching green consumerism.

Questions for evaluating Web sites

Supplement these questions with those on pp. 399–400.

- **What type of site are you viewing?** What does the type lead you to expect about the site's purpose and content?
- **Who is the author or sponsor?** How credible is the person or group responsible for the site?
- **What is the purpose of the site?** What does the site's author or sponsor intend to achieve?
- **What does context tell you?** What do you already know about the site's subject that can inform your evaluation? What kinds of support or other information do the site's links provide?
- **What does presentation tell you?** Is the site's design well thought out and effective? Is the writing clear and error-free?
- **How worthwhile is the content?** Are the site's claims well supported by evidence? Is the evidence from reliable sources? When was the site last updated?

(continued on p. 404)

Evaluating library sources

Opposite are sample pages from two library sources that Justin Malik considered for his paper on green consumerism. Malik evaluated the sources using the questions and guidelines on pp. 399–401.

Makower

Jackson

Origin

Interview with Joel Makower published in *Vegetarian Times*, a popular magazine.

Article by Tim Jackson published in *Journal of Industrial Ecology*, a scholarly journal sponsored by two reputable universities: MIT and Yale.

Author

Gives Makower's credentials at the beginning of the interview: the author of a book on green products and of a monthly newsletter on green businesses. Quotes another source that calls Makower the "guru of green business practice."

Includes a biography at the end of the article that describes Jackson as a professor at the University of Surrey (UK) and lists his professional activities related to the environment.

Bias

Describes and promotes green products. Concludes with an endorsement of a for-profit Web site that tracks and sells green products.

Presents multiple views of green consumerism. Argues that a solution to environmental problems will involve green products and less consumption but in different ways than currently proposed.

Reasonableness and writing

Presents Makower's data and perspective on distinguishing good from bad green products, using conversational writing in an informal presentation.

Presents and cites opposing views objectively, using formal academic writing.

Source citations

Lacks source citations for claims and data.

Includes more than three pages of source citations, many of scholarly and government sources and all cited within the article.

Assessment

Probably unreliable: Despite Makower's reputation, the article comes from a nonscholarly source, takes a one-sided approach to consumption, and depends on statistics credited only to Makower.

Probably reliable: The article comes from a scholarly journal, the author is an expert in the field, he discusses many views and concedes some, and his source citations confirm evidence from reliable sources.

First and last pages of an interview with Joel Makower, published in *Vegetarian Times*

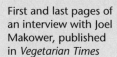

First and last pages of an article by Tim Jackson, published in the *Journal of Industrial Ecology*

(continued from p. 401)

Note To evaluate a Web document, you'll often need to travel to the site's home page to discover the author or sponsor, date of publication, and other relevant information. The page you're reading may include a link to the home page. If it doesn't, you can find it by editing the URL in the Address or Location field of your browser. Working backward, delete the end of the URL up to the last slash and hit Enter. Repeat this step until you reach the home page. There you may also find a menu option, often labeled "About," that will lead you to a description of the site's author or sponsor.

Determine the type of site.

When you search the Web, you're likely to encounter various types of sites. Although they overlap—a primarily informational site may include scholarship as well—the types can usually be identified by their content and purposes. Here are the main types:

- **Scholarly sites:** These sites have a knowledge-building interest and include research reports with supporting data and extensive documentation of scholarly sources. The URLs of the sites generally end in *edu* (originating from an educational institution), *org* (a nonprofit organization), or *gov* (a government department or agency). Such sites are more likely to be reliable than the others described below.

- **Informational sites:** Individuals, nonprofit organizations, corporations, schools, and government bodies all produce sites intended to centralize information on particular subjects. The sites' URLs may end in *edu, org, gov,* or *com* (originating from a commercial organization). Such sites generally do not have the knowledge-building focus of scholarly sites and may omit supporting data and documentation, but they can provide useful information and often include links to scholarly sources.

- **Advocacy sites:** Many sites present the views of individuals or organizations that promote certain policies or actions. Their URLs usually end in *org*, but they may end in *edu* or *com*. Some advocacy sites include serious, well-documented research to support their positions, but others select or distort evidence.

- **Commercial sites:** Corporations and other businesses maintain Web sites to explain or promote themselves or to sell goods and services. The URLs of commercial sites end in *com*. The information on such a site furthers the sponsor's profit-making purpose, but it can include reliable data.

- **Personal sites:** The sites maintained by individuals range from diaries of a family's travels to opinions on political issues to reports on evolving scholarship. The sites' URLs usually end in *com* or *edu*. Personal sites are only as reliable as their authors, but some do provide valuable eyewitness accounts, links to worthy sources, and other usable information. A particular kind of personal site, the blog, is discussed on pp. 393 and 408–10.

Note Informational sites called wikis allow anyone to contribute and edit information on the site. Older entries on reputable wikis, such as *Wikipedia,* tend to be reliable because they have been reviewed and edited by experts, but recent entries may contain errors and even misinformation. Ask your instructor whether wikis are acceptable sources. If so, evaluate them carefully against other, more reliable sources using the following guidelines.

Identify the author and sponsor.

A reputable site will list its authors, will name the group responsible for the site, and will provide information or a link for contacting the author and the sponsor. If none of this information is provided, you should not use the source. If you have only the author's or the sponsor's name, you may be able to discover more in a biographical dictionary, through a keyword search, or in your other sources. Make sure the author and the sponsor have expertise on the subject they're presenting: if an author is a doctor, for instance, what is he or she a doctor of?

Gauge purpose and bias.

A Web site's purpose determines what ideas and information it offers. Inferring that purpose tells you how to interpret what you see on the site. If a site is intended to sell a product or an opinion, it will likely emphasize favorable ideas and information while ignoring or even distorting what is unfavorable. In contrast, if a site is intended to build knowledge—for instance, a scholarly project or journal—it will likely acknowledge diverse views and evidence.

Determining the purpose of a site often requires looking beyond the first page and beneath the surface of words and images. To start, read what the site says about itself, usually found on a page labeled "About." Be suspicious of any site that doesn't provide information about itself and its goals.

Consider context.

Your evaluation of a Web site should be informed by considerations outside the site itself. Chief among these is your own knowledge. What do you already know about the site's subject and the prevailing views of it? Where does this site seem to fit into that picture? What can you learn from this site that you don't already know?

In addition, you can follow some of the site's links to see how they support, or don't support, the site's credibility. For instance,

(continued on p. 408)

Evaluating Web sites

Opposite are screen shots from two Web sites that Justin Malik considered for his paper on green consumerism. Malik evaluated the sources using the questions in the boxes on pp. 399–400 and 401.

We Can Solve the Climate Crisis	*Nature Reports: Climate Change*
Author and sponsor	
Author of article is not listed. Site sponsor is the Alliance for Climate Protection, a nonprofit organization founded by former vice president Al Gore.	Listed authors are scientists, experts on climate change. (Biographies appear at the end of the article.) Site sponsor is the Nature Publishing Group, which also publishes the reputable science journal *Nature*.
Purpose and bias	
Advocacy site with self-stated purpose of "educating people in the US and around the world that the climate crisis is both urgent and solvable." Urges site visitors to register and become active in efforts to stop global warming.	Informational site with the self-stated purpose of providing "authoritative, in-depth reporting on climate change and its wider implications for policy, society and the economy." Article expresses bias toward reducing pollution to stop climate change.
Context	
One of many sites enlisting readers in action against climate change.	One of many sites publishing current research on climate issues.
Presentation	
Inviting, professionally designed site with error-free writing.	Clean, professionally designed site with error-free writing.
Content	
Site looks new, but it and the article are undated. Article clearly explains the science of climate change but without references or links to scholarly research. Other pages on the site feature video clips of individuals making personal appeals to viewers.	Article is current (date above the title) and clearly explains the science of climate change with references and links to scholarly sources. Other links connect to hundreds of articles elsewhere on the site about climate-related topics.
Assessment	
Probably unreliable: Despite the reputation of the site sponsor, the article lacks the source citations needed for credibility about climate change. It's okay that an advocacy site is biased, but it should be more substantial to serve as a source.	**Probably reliable:** The article has an explicit bias toward stopping climate change, but the site sponsor has a scholarly reputation, the authors are climate-change experts, and the references cite many scholarly and government sources.

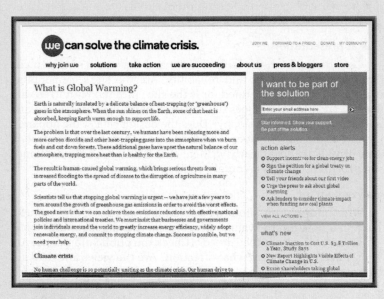

Article published on the Web site *We Can Solve the Climate Crisis*

Article published on the Web site *Nature Reports: Climate Change*

(continued from p. 405)

links to scholarly sources lend authority to a site—but *only* if the scholarly sources actually relate to and back up the site's claims.

Look at presentation.

Considering both the look of a site and the way it's written can illuminate its intentions and reliability. Are the site's elements all functional and well integrated, or is the site cluttered with irrelevant material and graphics? Does the site seem carefully constructed and well maintained, or is it sloppy? Does the design reflect the apparent purpose of the site, or does it undercut or conceal that purpose in some way? Is the text clearly written, or is it difficult to understand? Is it error-free, or does it contain typos and grammatical errors?

Analyze content.

With information about a site's author, purpose, and context, you're in a position to evaluate its content. Are the ideas and information current, or are they dated? (Check the publication date.) Are they slanted and, if so, in what direction? Are the views and data authoritative, or do you need to balance them—or even reject them? Are claims made on the site supported by evidence drawn from reliable sources? These questions require close reading of both the text and its sources.

4 | Evaluating other online sources

Blogs, online discussions, and online images, video, and audio require the same critical scrutiny as Web sites do. Blogs and discussion groups can be sources of reliable data and opinions, but you will also encounter wrong or misleading data and skewed opinions. One podcast may provide an interview with a recognized expert while another claims authority that it doesn't deserve. A *YouTube* search using "I have a dream" brings up videos of Martin Luther King, Jr., delivering his famous speech as well as videos of people speaking hatefully about King and the speech.

Use the following strategy for evaluating blogs, discussion groups, and multimedia sources:

Questions for evaluating blogs, online discussions, images, video, and audio

Supplement these questions with those on pp. 399–401.

- **Who is the author or creator?** How credible is he or she?
- **What is the author's or creator's purpose?** What can you tell about why the author or creator is publishing the work?

- **What does the context reveal?** What do other responses to the work, including responses to a blog posting or the other messages in a discussion thread, indicate about the source's balance and reliability?
- **How worthwhile is the content?** Are the claims made by the author or creator supported by evidence? Is the evidence from reliable sources?
- **How does the source compare with other sources?** Do the claims made by the author or creator seem accurate and fair given what you've seen in sources you know to be reliable?

Identify the author or creator.

Checking out the author or creator of a blog, online posting, video file, or podcast can help you judge its reliability. If the author or creator uses a screen name, write directly to him or her requesting full name and credentials. Do not use the source if you don't get a response. Once you know the person's name, you may be able to obtain background information from a keyword search of the Web or a biographical dictionary.

You can also get a sense of the interests and biases of an author or creator by tracking down his or her other publications. For a blog, check whether the author cites or links to other publications. For a discussion-group posting, look for an archive or other feature that allows you to find additional messages by the same author. For multimedia sources, try to gain an overview of the creator's work.

Analyze the author's or creator's purpose.

What can you tell about *why* the author or creator is publishing the work? Look for claims, the use (or lack) of evidence, and the treatment of opposing views. All these convey the person's stand on the subject and general fairness, and they will help you position the source among your other sources.

Consider the context.

Blogs, discussion-group postings, and multimedia sources are often difficult to evaluate in isolation. Looking beyond a particular contribution to the responses of others will give you a sense of how the author or creator is regarded. On a blog, look at the comments others have posted. Do the same with postings, going back to the initial posting in the discussion thread and reading forward.

Analyze content.

A reliable source will offer evidence for claims and sources for evidence. If you don't see such supporting information, ask the author or creator for it. (If he or she fails to respond, don't use the source.) Then verify the sources with your own research: are they reputable?

The tone of writing can also be a clue to its purpose and reliability. Blogs, online discussions, and some podcasts tend to be more informal and often more heated than other kinds of dialog, but look askance at writing that's contemptuous, dismissive, or shrill.

Compare with other sources.

Always consider blogs, postings, and multimedia sources in comparison to other sources so that you can distinguish singular, untested views from more mainstream views that have been subject to verification. Don't assume that a blog author's information and opinions are mainstream just because you see them on other blogs. The technology allows content to be picked up instantly by other blogs, so widespread distribution indicates only popularity, not reliability.

Be wary of blogs or postings that reproduce periodical articles, reports, or other publications. Try to locate the original version of the publication to be sure it has been reproduced fully and accurately, not quoted selectively or distorted. If you can't locate the original version, don't use the publication as a source.

52b | Synthesizing sources

When you begin to locate the differences and similarities among sources, you move into the most significant part of research writing: forging relationships for your own purpose. This **synthesis** is an essential step in reading sources critically, and it continues through the drafting and revision of a research paper. As you infer connections—say, between one writer's opinions and another's or between two works by the same author—you create new knowledge.

Your synthesis of sources will grow more detailed and sophisticated as you proceed through the process of working with sources described in the balance of this chapter: gathering information from sources (pp. 413–14); deciding whether to summarize, paraphrase, or quote directly from sources (pp. 414–17); and integrating sources into your sentences (pp. 418–23). Unless you are analyzing primary sources such as the works of a poet, at first read your sources quickly and selectively to obtain an overview of your subject and a sense of how the sources approach it. Don't get bogged down in gathering detailed information, but *do* record your ideas about sources in your research journal (p. 372) or your annotated bibliography (p. 377).

Respond to sources.

Write down what your sources make you think. Do you agree or disagree with the author? Do you find his or her views narrow, or do they open up new approaches for you? Is there anything in the source that you need to research further before you can understand it? Does the source prompt questions that you should keep in mind while reading other sources?

Connect sources.

When you notice a link between sources, jot it down. Do two sources differ in their theories or their interpretations of facts? Does one source illuminate another—perhaps commenting or clarifying or supplying additional data? Do two or more sources report studies that support a theory you've read about or an idea of your own?

Heed your insights.

Apart from ideas prompted by your sources, you are sure to come up with independent thoughts: a conviction, a point of confusion that suddenly becomes clear, a question you haven't seen anyone else ask. These insights may occur at unexpected times, so it's good practice to keep a notebook or computer handy to record them.

Draw your own conclusions.

As your research proceeds, the responses, connections, and insights you form through synthesis will lead you to answer your starting research question with a statement of your thesis (see p. 432). They will also lead you to the main ideas supporting your thesis— conclusions you have drawn from your synthesis of sources, forming the main divisions of your paper.

Use sources to support your conclusions.

Effective synthesis requires careful handling of evidence from sources so that it meshes smoothly into your sentences and yet is clearly distinct from your own ideas. When drafting your paper, make sure that each paragraph focuses on an idea of your own, with the support for the idea coming from your sources. Generally, open each paragraph with your idea, provide evidence from a source or sources with appropriate citations, and close with an interpretation of the evidence. (Avoid ending a paragraph with a source citation; instead, end with your own idea.) In this way, your paper will synthesize others' work into something wholly your own. For more on structuring paragraphs in academic writing, see **2** p. 91.

The three passages below address the same issue, the legalization of drugs. What similarities do you see in the authors' ideas? What differences? Write a paragraph of your own in which you use these authors' views as a point of departure for your own view about drug legalization.

Perhaps the most unfortunate victims of drug prohibition laws have been the residents of America's ghettos. These laws have proved largely futile in deterring ghetto-dwellers from becoming drug abusers, but they do account for much of what ghetto residents identify as the drug problem. Aggressive, gun-toting drug dealers often upset law-abiding residents far more than do addicts nodding out in doorways. Meanwhile other residents perceive the drug dealers as heroes and successful role models. They're symbols of success to children who see no other options. At the same time the increasingly harsh criminal penalties imposed on adult drug dealers have led drug traffickers to recruit juveniles. Where once children started dealing drugs only after they had been using them for a few years, today the sequence is often reversed. Many children start using drugs only after working for older drug dealers for a while. Legalization of drugs, like legalization of alcohol in the 1930s, would drive the drug-dealing business off the streets and out of apartment buildings and into government-regulated, tax-paying stores. It also would force many of the gun-toting dealers out of the business and convert others into legitimate businessmen.

—Ethan A. Nadelmann, "Shooting Up"

Statistics argue against legalization. The University of Michigan conducts an annual survey of twelfth graders, asking the students about their drug consumption. In 1980, 56.4 percent of those polled said they had used marijuana in the past twelve months, whereas in 2007 only 41.7 percent had done so. Cocaine use was even more reduced in the same period (22.6 percent to 7.8 percent). At the same time, twelve-month use of legally available drugs—alcohol and nicotine-containing cigarettes—remained constant at about 72 percent and 55 percent, respectively. The numbers of illegal drug users haven't declined nearly enough: those teenaged marijuana and cocaine users are still vulnerable to addiction and even death, and they threaten to infect their impressionable peers. But clearly the prohibition of illegal drugs has helped, while the legal status of alcohol and cigarettes has not made them less popular.

—Sylvia Runkle, "The Case Against Legalization"

I have to laugh at the debate over what to do about the drug problem. Everyone is running around offering solutions—from making drug use a more serious criminal offense to legalizing it. But there isn't a real solution. I know that. I used and abused drugs, and people, and society, for two decades. Nothing worked to get me to stop all that behavior except just plain being sick and tired. Nothing. Not threats, not ten-plus years in prison, not anything that was said to me. I used until I got through. Period. And that's when you'll win the war. When all the dope fiends are done. Not a minute before.

—Michael W. Posey, "I Did Drugs Until They Wore Me Out. Then I Stopped."

52c | Gathering information from sources

You can accomplish a great deal of synthesis while gathering information from your sources. This information gathering is not a mechanical process. Rather, as you read you assess and organize the information in your sources.

Researchers vary in their methods for working with sources, but all methods share the same goals:

- **Keep accurate records of what sources say.** Accuracy helps prevent misrepresentation and plagiarism.
- **Keep accurate records of how to find sources.** These records are essential for retracing steps and for citing sources in the final paper. (See pp. 377–79 on keeping a working bibliography.)
- **Synthesize sources.** Information gathering is a critical process, leading to an understanding of sources, the relationships among them and your own ideas, and their support for your ideas.

To achieve these goals, you can take handwritten notes, type notes into your computer, annotate photocopies or printouts of sources, or annotate downloaded documents. On any given project, you may use all the methods. Each has advantages and disadvantages.

- **Handwritten notes:** Taking notes by hand is especially useful if you come across a source with no computer or photocopier handy. But handwritten notes can be risky. It's easy to introduce errors as you work from source to paper. And it's possible to copy source language and then later mistake and use it as your own, thus plagiarizing the source. Always take care to make accurate notes and to place big quotation marks around any passage you quote.
- **Notes on computer:** Taking notes on a computer can streamline the path of source to note to paper, because you can import the notes into your draft as you write. However, computer notes have the same disadvantages as handwritten notes: the risk of introducing errors and the risk of plagiarizing. As with handwritten notes, be a stickler for accuracy and use quotation marks for quotations.
- **Photocopies and printouts:** Photocopying from print sources or printing out online sources each has the distinct advantages of convenience and reduction in the risks of error and plagiarism during information gathering. But each method has disadvantages, too. The busywork of copying or printing can distract you from the crucial work of synthesizing sources. And you have to make a special effort to annotate copies and printouts with the publication information for sources. If you

don't have this information for your final paper, you can't use the source.

■ **Downloads:** Researching online, you can usually download full-text articles, Web pages, discussion-group messages, and other materials onto your computer. While drafting, you can import source information from one file into another. Like photocopies and printouts, though, downloads can distract you from interacting with sources and can easily become separated from the publication information you must have in order to use the sources. Even more important, directly importing source material creates a high risk of plagiarism. You must keep clear boundaries between your own ideas and words and those of others.

52d Using summary, paraphrase, and quotation

Deciding whether to summarize, paraphrase, or quote directly from sources is an important step in synthesizing the sources' ideas and your own. You engage in synthesis when you use your own words to summarize an author's argument or paraphrase a significant example or when you select a significant passage to quote. Choosing summary, paraphrase, or quotation should depend on why you are using a source.

Note Summaries, paraphrases, and quotations all require source citations. A summary or paraphrase without a source citation or a quotation without quotation marks and a source citation is plagiarism. (See pp. 423–30 for more on plagiarism.)

1 Summary

When you **summarize,** you condense an extended idea or argument into a sentence or more in your own words. (See **2** pp. 80–81 for tips.) **Summary** is most useful when you want to record the gist of an author's idea without the background or supporting evidence. Following is a passage from a scholarly essay about consumption and its impact on the environment. Then a sample computer note shows a summary of the passage.

Original quotation

Such intuition is even making its way, albeit slowly, into scholarly circles, where recognition is mounting that ever-increasing pressures on ecosystems, life-supporting environmental services, and critical natural cycles are driven not only by the sheer number of resource users and the inefficiencies of their resource use, but also by the patterns of resource use themselves. In global environmental policymaking arenas, it is becoming more and more difficult to ignore the fact that the overdeveloped North must restrain its consumption if it expects the underdeveloped South to embrace a more sustainable trajectory.

—Thomas Princen, Michael Maniates, and Ken Conca, "Confronting Consumption," p. 4

Summary of source

Environmental consequences of consumption

Princen, Maniates, and Conca 4

Overconsumption may be a more significant cause of environmental problems than increasing population is.

2 | Paraphrase

When you **paraphrase,** you follow much more closely the author's original presentation, but you restate it using your own words and sentence structures. Paraphrase is most useful when you want to present or examine an author's line of reasoning but you don't feel the original words merit direct quotation. Here is a paraphrase of the quotation from the essay "Confronting Consumption."

Paraphrase of source

Environmental consequences of consumption

Princen, Maniates, and Conca 4

Scholars are coming to believe that consumption is partly to blame for changes in ecosystems, reduction of essential natural resources, and changes in natural cycles. Policy makers increasingly see that wealthy nations have to start consuming less if they want developing nations to adopt practices that reduce pollution and waste. Rising population around the world does cause significant stress on the environment, but consumption is increasing even more rapidly than population.

Notice that the paraphrase follows the original but uses different words and different sentence structures. In contrast, an unsuccessful paraphrase—one that plagiarizes—copies the author's words or sentence structures or both *without quotation marks.* (See p. 428 for examples.)

Paraphrasing a source

- **Read the relevant material several times to be sure you understand it.**
- **Restate the source's ideas in your own words and sentence structures.** You need not put down in new words the whole passage or all the details. Select what is relevant to your topic, and restate only that. If complete sentences seem too detailed or cumbersome, use phrases.
- **Be careful not to distort meaning.** Don't change the source's emphasis or omit connecting words, qualifiers, and other material whose absence will confuse you later or cause you to misrepresent the source.

CULTURE LANGUAGE If English is not your native language and you have difficulty paraphrasing the ideas in sources, try this. Before attempting a paraphrase, read the original passage several times. Then, instead of "translating" line by line, try to state the gist of the passage without looking at it. Check your effort against the original to be sure you have captured the source author's meaning and emphasis without using his or her words and sentence structures. If you need a synonym for a word, look it up in a dictionary.

3 Direct quotation

Your notes from sources may include many quotations, especially if you rely on photocopies, printouts, or downloads. Whether to use a quotation in your draft, instead of a summary or paraphrase, depends on how important the exact words are and on whether the source is primary or secondary (p. 375):

- **Quote extensively when you are analyzing primary sources,** such as literary works and historical documents. The quotations will often be both the target of your analysis and the chief support for your ideas.
- **Quote selectively when you are drawing on secondary sources.** Favor summaries and paraphrases over quotations, and put every quotation to both tests in the box on the next page. Most papers of ten or so pages should not need more than two or three quotations that are longer than a few lines each.

When you quote a source, either in your notes or in your draft, take precautions to avoid plagiarism or misrepresentation of the source:

- **Copy the material carefully.** Take down the author's exact wording, spelling, capitalization, and punctuation.

Tests for direct quotations from secondary sources

The author's original satisfies one of these requirements:

- The language is unusually vivid, bold, or inventive.
- The quotation cannot be paraphrased without distortion or loss of meaning.
- The words themselves are at issue in your interpretation.
- The quotation represents and emphasizes a body of opinion or the view of an important expert.
- The quotation emphatically reinforces your own idea.
- The quotation is an illustration, such as a graph, diagram, or table.

The quotation is as short as possible:

- It includes only material relevant to your point.
- It is edited to eliminate examples and other unneeded material, using ellipsis marks and brackets (**5** pp. 340–43).

- **Proofread every direct quotation at least twice.**
- **Use quotation marks around the quotation** so that later you won't confuse it with a paraphrase or summary. Be sure to transfer the quotation marks into your draft as well, unless the quotation is long and is set off from your text. For advice on handling long quotations, see **MLA** pp. 507–08 and **APA** p. 541.
- **Use brackets** to add words for clarity or to change the capitalization of letters (see **5** p. 343 and **6** p. 356).
- **Use ellipsis marks** to omit irrelevant material (see **5** pp. 340–42).
- **Cite the source of the quotation in your draft.** See pp. 430–31 on documentation.

Exercise 52.2 **Summarizing and paraphrasing**

Prepare two source notes, one summarizing the entire paragraph below and the other paraphrasing the first four sentences (ending with the word *autonomy*). Use the format for a note illustrated on p. 415, omitting only the subject heading.

Federal organization [of the United States] has made it possible for the different states to deal with the same problems in many different ways. One consequence of federalism, then, has been that people are treated differently, by law, from state to state. The great strength of this system is that differences from state to state in cultural preferences, moral standards, and levels of wealth can be accommodated. In contrast to a unitary system in which the central government makes all important decisions (as in France), federalism is a powerful arrangement for maximizing regional freedom and autonomy. The great weakness of our federal system, however, is that people in some states receive less than the best or the most advanced or the least expensive services and policies

that government can offer. The federal dilemma does not invite easy solution, for the costs and benefits of the arrangement have tended to balance out.   —Peter K. Eisinger et al., *American Politics*, p. 44

Exercise 52.3 **Combining summary, paraphrase, and direct quotation**

Prepare a source note containing a combination of paraphrase or summary and direct quotation that states the main idea of the passage below. Use the format for a note illustrated on p. 415, omitting only the
subject heading.

Most speakers unconsciously duel even during seemingly casual
conversations, as can often be observed at social gatherings where they
show less concern for exchanging information with other guests than for
asserting their own dominance. Their verbal dueling often employs very
subtle weapons like mumbling, a hostile act which defeats the listener's
desire to understand what the speaker claims he is trying to say (but is
really not saying because he is mumbling!). Or the verbal dueler may
keep talking after someone has passed out of hearing range—which is
often an aggressive challenge to the listener to return and acknowledge
the dominance of the speaker.   —Peter K. Farb, *Word Play*, p. 107

52e Integrating sources into your text

Integrating sources into your sentences is key to synthesizing
others' ideas and information with your own. Evidence drawn from
sources should *back up* your conclusions, not *be* your conclusions:
you don't want to let your evidence overwhelm your own point of
view. The point of research is to investigate and go beyond sources,
to interpret them and use them to support your own independent
ideas.

Note The examples in this section use the MLA style of source
documentation and also present-tense verbs (such as *disagrees* and
claims). See pp. 421–23 for specific variations in documentation style
and verb tense within the academic disciplines. Several other conventions governing quotations are discussed elsewhere in this book:

- Using commas to punctuate signal phrases (**5** pp. 313–14).
- Placing other punctuation marks with quotation marks (**5** pp. 335–36).
- Using brackets and the ellipsis mark to indicate changes in quotations (**5** pp. 340–42).
- Punctuating and placing parenthetical citations (**MLA** pp. 470–72).
- Formatting long prose quotations and poetry quotations (**MLA** pp. 507–08 and **APA** p. 541).

1 Introduction of borrowed material

Readers will be distracted from your point if borrowed material does not fit into your sentence. In the passage below, the writer has not meshed the structures of her own and her source's sentences:

| Awkward | One editor disagrees with this view and "a good reporter does not fail to separate opinions from facts" (Lyman 52). |

In the following revision the writer adds words to integrate the quotation into her sentence:

| Revised | One editor disagrees with this view, <u>maintaining that</u> "a good reporter does not fail to separate opinions from facts" (Lyman 52). |

To mesh your own and your source's words, you may sometimes need to make a substitution or addition to the quotation, signaling your change with brackets:

Words added	"The tabloids [of England] are a journalistic case study in bad reporting," claims Lyman (52).
Verb form changed	A bad reporter, Lyman implies, is one who "[fails] to separate opinions from facts" (52). [The bracketed verb replaces *fail* in the original.]
Capitalization changed	"[T]o separate opinions from facts" is the work of a good reporter (Lyman 52). [In the original, *to* is not capitalized.]
Noun supplied for pronoun	The reliability of a news organization "depends on [reporters'] trustworthiness," says Lyman (52). [The bracketed noun replaces *their* in the original.]

2 Interpretation of borrowed material

You need to work borrowed material into your sentences so that readers see without effort how it contributes to the points you are making. If you merely dump source material into your paper without explaining how you intend it to be interpreted, readers will have to struggle to understand your sentences and the relationships you are trying to establish. For example, the following passage forces us to figure out for ourselves that the writer's sentence and the quotation state opposite points of view:

| Dumped | Many news editors and reporters maintain that it is impossible to keep personal opinions from influencing the selection and presentation of facts. "True, news reporters, like everyone else, form impressions of what they see and hear. However, a good reporter does not fail to separate opinions from facts" (Lyman 52). |

In the revision, the underlined additions tell us how to interpret the quotation:

> **Revised** Many news editors and reporters maintain that it is impossible to keep personal opinions from influencing the selection and presentation of facts. <u>Yet not all authorities agree with this view. One editor grants that</u> "news reporters, like everyone else, form impressions of what they see and hear." <u>But, he insists,</u> "a good reporter does not fail to separate opinions from facts" (Lyman 52).

Signal phrases

The words *One editor grants* and *he insists* in the revised passage above are **signal phrases:** they tell readers who the source is and what to expect in the quotations that follow. Signal phrases usually contain (1) the source author's name (or a substitute for it, such as *One editor* and *he*) and (2) a verb that indicates the source author's attitude or approach to what he or she says.

Some verbs for signal phrases appear in the following list. These verbs are in the present tense, which is typical of writing in the humanities. In the social and natural sciences, the past tense (*noted*) or present perfect tense (*has noted*) is more common. See pp. 422–23.

Author is neutral	Author infers or suggests	Author argues	Author is uneasy or disparaging
comments	analyzes	claims	belittles
describes	asks	contends	bemoans
explains	assesses	defends	complains
illustrates	concludes	holds	condemns
notes	considers	insists	deplores
observes	finds	maintains	deprecates
points out	predicts		derides
records	proposes	**Author agrees**	disagrees
relates	reveals	admits	laments
reports	shows	agrees	warns
says	speculates	concedes	
sees	suggests	concurs	
thinks	supposes	grants	
writes			

Vary your signal phrases to suit your interpretation of borrowed material and also to keep readers' interest. A signal phrase may precede, interrupt, or follow the borrowed material:

> **Precedes** <u>Lyman insists</u> that "a good reporter does not fail to separate opinions from facts" (52).
>
> **Interrupts** "However," <u>Lyman insists,</u> "a good reporter does not fail to separate opinions from facts" (52).

Follows	"[A] good reporter does not fail to separate opinions from facts," <u>Lyman insists</u> (52).

Background information

You can add information to a quotation to integrate it into your text and to inform readers why you are using it. In most cases, provide the author's name in the text, especially if the author is an expert or if readers will recognize the name:

Author named	Harold Lyman grants that "news reporters, like everyone else, form impressions of what they see and hear." But, Lyman insists, "a good reporter does not fail to separate opinions from facts" (52).

If the source title contributes information about the author or the context of the quotation, you can provide it in the text:

Title given	Harold Lyman, <u>in his book *The Conscience of the Journalist*</u>, grants that "news reporters, like everyone else, form impressions of what they see and hear." But, Lyman insists, "a good reporter does not fail to separate opinions from facts" (52).

If the quoted author's background and experience reinforce or clarify the quotation, you can provide these credentials in the text:

Credentials given	Harold Lyman, <u>a newspaper editor for more than forty years</u>, grants that "news reporters, like everyone else, form impressions of what they see and hear." But, Lyman insists, "a good reporter does not fail to separate opinions from facts" (52).

You need not name the author, source, or credentials in your text when you are simply establishing facts or weaving together facts and opinions from varied sources. In the following passage, the information is more important than the source, so the name of the source is confined to a parenthetical acknowledgment:

> To end the abuses of the British, many colonists were urging three actions: forming a united front, seceding from Britain, and taking control of their own international relations (Wills 325–36).

3 | Discipline styles for integrating sources

The preceding guidelines for introducing and interpreting borrowed material apply generally across academic disciplines, but there are differences in verb tenses and documentation style.

English and some other humanities

Writers in English, foreign languages, and related disciplines use MLA style for documenting sources and generally use the present tense of verbs in signal phrases. In discussing sources other than works of literature, the present perfect tense is also sometimes appropriate:

> Lyman insists . . . [present]
> Lyman has insisted . . . [present perfect]

In discussing works of literature, use only the present tense to describe both the work of the author and the action in the work:

> Kate Chopin builds irony into every turn of "The Story of an Hour." For example, Mrs. Mallard, the central character, finds joy in the death of her husband, whom she loves, because she anticipates "the long procession of years that would belong to her absolutely" (23).

Avoid shifting tenses in writing about literature. You can, for instance, shorten quotations to avoid their past-tense verbs.

> **Shift**   Her freedom elevates her, so that "she carried herself unwittingly like a goddess of victory" (24).
>
> **No shift** Her freedom elevates her, so that she walks "unwittingly like a goddess of victory" (24).

History and other humanities

Writers in history, art history, philosophy, and related disciplines generally use the present perfect tense or present tense of verbs in signal phrases.

> Lincoln persisted, as Haworth has noted, in "feeling that events controlled him."[3]
>
> What Miller calls Lincoln's "severe self-doubt"[6] undermined his effectiveness on at least two occasions.

The raised numbers after the quotations are part of the Chicago documentation style, used in history and other disciplines.

Social and natural sciences

Writers in the sciences generally use a verb's present tense just for reporting the results of a study (*The data suggest* . . .). Otherwise, they use a verb's past tense or present perfect tense in a signal phrase, as when introducing an explanation, interpretation, or other commentary. (Thus when you are writing for the sciences, generally convert the list of signal-phrase verbs on p. 420 from the present to the present perfect tense or past tense.)

> Lin (1999) has suggested that preschooling may significantly affect children's academic performance through high school (pp. 22–23).
>
> In an exhaustive survey of the literature published between 1990 and 2000, Walker (2001) found "no proof, merely a weak correlation, linking place of residence and rate of illness" (p. 121).

These passages conform to APA documentation style. APA style, or one quite similar to it, is also used in sociology, education, nursing, biology, and many other sciences.

Exercise 52.4 Introducing and interpreting borrowed material

Drawing on the ideas in the following paragraph and using examples from your own observations and experiences, write a paragraph about anxiety. Integrate at least one direct quotation and one paraphrase from the following paragraph into your own sentences. In your paragraph, identify the author by name and give his credentials: he is a professor of psychiatry and a practicing psychoanalyst.

> There are so many ways in which human beings are different from all the lower forms of animals, and almost all of them make us uniquely susceptible to feelings of anxiousness. Our imagination and reasoning powers facilitate anxiety; the anxious feeling is precipitated not by an absolute impending threat—such as the worry about an examination, a speech, travel—but rather by the symbolic and often unconscious representations. We do not have to be experiencing a potential danger. We can experience something related to it. We can recall, through our incredible memories, the original symbolic sense of vulnerability in childhood and suffer the feeling attached to that. We can even forget the original memory and be stuck with the emotion—which is then compounded by its seemingly irrational quality at this time. It is not just the fear of death which pains us, but the anticipation of it; or the anniversary of a specific death; or a street, a hospital, a time of day, a color, a flower, a symbol associated with death.
>
> —Willard Gaylin, "Feeling Anxious," p. 23

---

53 Avoiding Plagiarism and Documenting Sources

The knowledge building that is the focus of academic writing rests on the integrity of everyone who participates in using and crediting sources, including students. The work of a writer or creator is his or her intellectual property. You and others may borrow the work's ideas and even its words or an image, but you *must* acknowledge that what you borrowed came from someone else.

When you acknowledge sources in your writing, you are doing more than giving credit to the writer or creator of the work you

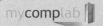

mycomplab

Visit *mycomplab.com* for more resources and exercises on avoiding plagiarism and documenting sources.

consulted. You are also showing what your own writing is based on, which in turn gives you credibility as a researcher and writer. Acknowledging sources creates the trust among scholars, students, writers, and readers that knowledge building requires.

Plagiarism (from a Latin word for "kidnapper") is the presentation of someone else's work as your own. Whether deliberate or accidental, plagiarism is a serious offense. It breaks trust, and it undermines or even destroys your credibility as a researcher and writer. In most colleges, a code of academic honesty calls for severe consequences for plagiarism: a reduced or failing grade, suspension from school, or expulsion.

■ *Deliberate* plagiarism:

> Copying or downloading a phrase, a sentence, or a longer passage from a source and passing it off as your own by omitting quotation marks and a source citation.
>
> Summarizing or paraphrasing someone else's ideas without acknowledging your debt in a source citation.
>
> Handing in as your own work a paper you have bought, copied off the Web, had a friend write, or accepted from another student.

■ *Accidental* plagiarism:

> Reading a wide variety of print or Web sources on a subject without taking notes on them, and then not remembering the difference between what you recently learned and what you already knew.
>
> Forgetting to place quotation marks around another writer's words.
>
> Carelessly omitting a source citation for a paraphrase.
>
> Omitting a source citation for another's idea because you are unaware of the need to acknowledge the idea.

The way to avoid plagiarism is to acknowledge your sources by documenting them. This chapter discusses plagiarism and the Internet, shows how to distinguish what doesn't require acknowledgment from what does, and provides an overview of source documentation.

(CULTURE LANGUAGE) The concept of intellectual property and thus the rules governing plagiarism are not universal. In some other cultures, for instance, students may be encouraged to copy the words of scholars without acknowledgment in order to demonstrate their mastery of or respect for the scholars' work. In the United States, however, using an author's work without a source citation is considered theft. When in doubt about the guidelines in this chapter, ask your instructor for advice.

Checklist for avoiding plagiarism

Type of source

Are you using

- your own independent material,
- common knowledge, or
- someone else's independent material?

You must acknowledge someone else's material.

Quotations

- Do all quotations exactly match their sources? Check them.
- Have you inserted quotation marks around quotations that are run into your text?
- Have you shown omissions with ellipsis marks and additions with brackets?
- Does every quotation have a source citation?

Paraphrases and summaries

- Have you used your own words and sentence structures for every paraphrase and summary? If not, use quotation marks around the original author's words.
- Does every paraphrase and summary have a source citation?

The Web

- Have you obtained any necessary permission to use someone else's material on the Web?

Source citations

- Have you acknowledged every use of someone else's material in each place you used it?
- Does your list of works cited include entries for all the sources you have used?

53a Committing and detecting plagiarism on the Internet

The Internet has made it easier to plagiarize than ever before, but it has also made plagiarism easier to catch.

Even honest students risk accidental plagiarism by downloading sources and importing portions into their drafts. Dishonest students may take advantage of downloading to steal others' work. They may also use the term-paper businesses on the Web, which offer both ready-made research and complete papers, usually for a fee. **Paying for research or a paper does not make it the buyer's work.** Anyone who submits someone else's work as his or her own is a plagiarist.

Students who plagiarize from the Internet both deprive themselves of an education in honest research and expose themselves to detection. Teachers can use search engines to locate specific phrases or sentences anywhere on the Web, including among scholarly publications, all kinds of Web sites, and term-paper collections. They can search the term-paper sites as easily as students can, looking for similarities with papers they've received. They can also use detection programs such as *Turnitin* that compare students' work with other work anywhere on the Internet, seeking matches as short as a few words.

Some instructors suggest that their students use plagiarism-detection programs to verify that their own work does not include accidental plagiarism from the Internet.

53b Knowing what you need not acknowledge

1 Your independent material

Your own observations, thoughts, compilations of facts, or experimental results—expressed in your words and format—do not require acknowledgment. You should describe the basis for your conclusions so that readers can evaluate your thinking, but you need not cite sources for them.

2 Common knowledge

Common knowledge consists of the standard information on a subject as well as folk literature and commonsense observations.

- **Standard information** includes the major facts of history, such as the dates during which Charlemagne ruled as emperor of Rome (800–14). It does *not* include interpretations of facts, such as a historian's opinion that Charlemagne was sometimes needlessly cruel in extending his power.
- **Folk literature,** such as the fairy tale "Snow White," is popularly known and cannot be traced to a particular writer. Literature traceable to a writer is *not* folk literature, even if it is very familiar.
- **Commonsense observations** are things most people know, such as that inflation is most troublesome for people with low and fixed incomes. However, a particular economist's argument about the effects of inflation on Chinese immigrants is *not* a commonsense observation.

If you do not know a subject well enough to determine whether a piece of information is common knowledge, make a record of the source as you would for any other quotation, paraphrase, or summary. As you read more about the subject, the information may come up repeatedly without acknowledgment, in which case it is probably common knowledge. But if you are still in doubt when you finish your research, always acknowledge the source.

53c Knowing what you *must* acknowledge

You must always acknowledge other people's independent material—that is, any facts or ideas that are not common knowledge or your own. The source may be anything, including a book, an article, a movie, an interview, a microfilmed document, a Web page, a newsgroup posting, or an opinion expressed on the radio. You must acknowledge summaries or paraphrases of ideas or facts as well as quotations of the language and format in which ideas or facts appear: wording, sentence structures, arrangement, and special graphics (such as a diagram). You must acknowledge another's material no matter how you use it, how much of it you use, or how often you use it.

1 Copied language: Quotation marks and a source citation

The following example baldly plagiarizes the original quotation from Jessica Mitford's *Kind and Usual Punishment*, p. 9. Without quotation marks or a source citation, the example matches Mitford's wording (underlined) and closely parallels her sentence structure:

Original quotation	"The character and mentality of the keepers may be of more importance in understanding prisons than the character and mentality of the kept."
Plagiarism	But the character of prison officials (the keepers) is of more importance in understanding prisons than the character of prisoners (the kept).

To avoid plagiarism, the writer can paraphrase and cite the source (see the examples on the next page) or use Mitford's actual words *in quotation marks* and *with a source citation* (here, in MLA style):

| Revision (quotation) | According to one critic of the penal system, "The character and mentality of the keepers may be of more importance in understanding prisons than the character and mentality of the kept" (Mitford 9). |

Even with a source citation and with a different sentence structure, the next example is still plagiarism because it uses some of Mitford's words (underlined) without quotation marks:

| Plagiarism | According to one critic of the penal system, the psychology of the kept may say less about prisons than the psychology of the keepers (Mitford 9). |

Revision (quotation)	According to one critic of the penal system, the psychology of ❝the kept❞ may say less about prisons than the psychology of ❝the keepers❞ (Mitford 9).

2 Paraphrase or summary: Your own words and sentence structure and a source citation

The example below changes the sentence structure of the original Mitford quotation on the previous page, but it still uses Mitford's words (underlined) without quotation marks and without a source citation:

Plagiarism	In understanding prisons, we should know more about the character and mentality of the keepers than of the kept.

To avoid plagiarism, the writer can use quotation marks and cite the source (see the previous page and above) or *use his or her own words* and still *cite the source* (because the idea is Mitford's, not the writer's):

Revision (paraphrase)	Mitford holds that we may be able to learn more about prisons from the psychology of the prison officials than from that of the prisoners (9).
Revision (paraphrase)	We may understand prisons better if we focus on the personalities and attitudes of the prison workers rather than those of the inmates (Mitford 9).

In the next example, the writer cites Mitford and does not use her words but still plagiarizes her sentence structure:

Plagiarism	One critic of the penal system maintains that the psychology of prison officials may be more informative about prisons than the psychology of prisoners (Mitford 9).
Revision (paraphrase)	One critic of the penal system maintains that we may be able to learn less from the psychology of prisoners than from the psychology of prison officials (Mitford 9).

Exercise 53.1 Recognizing plagiarism

The following numbered items show various attempts to quote or paraphrase the passage below. Carefully compare each attempt with the original passage. Which attempts are plagiarized, inaccurate, or both, and which are acceptable? Why?

I would agree with the sociologists that psychiatric labeling is dangerous. Society can inflict terrible wounds by discrimination, and by confusing health with disease and disease with badness.
—George E. Vaillant, *Adaptation to Life*, p. 361

1 According to George Vaillant, society often inflicts wounds by using psychiatric labeling, confusing health, disease, and badness (361).

2 According to George Vaillant, "psychiatric labeling [such as 'homo-

sexual' or 'schizophrenic'] is dangerous. Society can inflict terrible wounds by . . . confusing health with disease and disease with badness" (361).

3 According to George Vaillant, when psychiatric labeling discriminates between health and disease or between disease and badness, it can inflict wounds on those labeled (361).

4 Psychiatric labels can badly hurt those labeled, says George Vaillant, because they fail to distinguish among health, illness, and immorality (361).

5 Labels such as "homosexual" and "schizophrenic" can be hurtful when they fail to distinguish among health, illness, and immorality.

6 "I would agree with the sociologists that society can inflict terrible wounds by discrimination, and by confusing health with disease and disease with badness" (Vaillant 361).

53d Using and acknowledging online sources

Online sources are so accessible and so easy to download into your own documents that it may seem they are freely available, exempting you from the obligation to acknowledge them. They are not. Acknowledging online sources is somewhat trickier than acknowledging print sources, but no less essential. Further, if you are publishing your work on the Web, you need to take account of sources' copyright restrictions as well.

1 Online sources in an unpublished project

When you use material from an online source in a print or online document to be distributed just to your class, your obligation to cite sources does not change: you must acknowledge someone else's independent material in whatever form you find it. With online sources, that obligation can present additional challenges:

- **Record complete publication information each time you consult an online source.** Online sources may change or even disappear entirely. See p. 378 for the information to record, such as the electronic address and the publication date. Without the proper information, you *may not* use the source.
- **Acknowledge linked sites.** If you use a Web site and one or more of its linked sites, you must acknowledge the linked sites as well. One person's use of a second person's work does not release you from the responsibility to cite the second work.
- **Seek the author's permission before using an e-mail message, discussion-group posting, or blog contribution.** Obtaining permission advises the author that his or her ideas are about to be distributed more widely and lets the author verify that you have not misrepresented the ideas.

2 Print and online sources in a Web composition

When you use material from print or online sources in a composition for the Web, you must not only acknowledge your sources but also take the additional precaution of observing copyright restrictions.

A Web site is a medium of publication just as a book or magazine is and so involves the same responsibility to obtain reprint permission from copyright holders. The exception is a password-protected site (such as a course site), which many copyright holders regard as private. You can find information about copyright holders and permissions on the copyright page of a print publication (following the title page) and on a page labeled something like "Terms of Use" on a Web site. If you don't see an explicit release for student use or publication on private Web sites, assume you must seek permission.

The legal convention of fair use allows an author to reprint a small portion of copyrighted material without obtaining the copyright holder's permission, as long as the author acknowledges the source. The online standards of fair use differ for print and online sources and are not fixed in either case. The guidelines below are conservative:

- **Print sources:** Quote without permission fewer than fifty words from an article or fewer than three hundred words from a book. You'll need permission to use any longer quotation from an article or book; any quotation at all from a play, poem, or song; and any use of an entire work, such as a photograph, chart, or other illustration.
- **Online sources:** Quote without permission text that represents just a small portion of the whole—say, up to forty words out of three hundred. Follow the print guidelines above for plays, poems, songs, and illustrations, adding multimedia elements (audio or video clips) to the list of works that require reprint permission for any use.
- **Links:** You may need to seek permission to link your site to another one—for instance, if you rely on the linked site to substantiate your claims or to provide a multimedia element.

53e Documenting sources

Every time you borrow the words, facts, or ideas of others, you must **document** the source—that is, supply a reference (or document) telling readers that you borrowed the material and where you borrowed it from.

Editors and teachers in most academic disciplines require special documentation formats (or styles) in their scholarly journals and in students' papers. All the styles use a citation in the text that serves two purposes: it signals that material is borrowed, and it refers readers to detailed information about the source so that they can locate both the source and the place in the source where the borrowed material appears. The detailed source information appears either in footnotes or at the end of the paper.

Aside from these essential similarities, the disciplines' documentation styles differ markedly in citation form, arrangement of source information, and other particulars. Each discipline's style reflects the needs of its practitioners for certain kinds of information presented in certain ways. For instance, the currency of a source is important in the social sciences, where studies build on and correct each other; thus in-text citations in the social sciences include a source's date of publication. In the humanities, however, currency is less important, so in-text citations do not include date of publication.

The disciplines' documentation formats are described in style guides listed in **8** pp. 445 (literature), 451 (other humanities), 455 (social sciences), and 459 (natural and applied sciences). This book also discusses and illustrates four common documentation styles:

- MLA style, used in English, foreign languages, and some other humanities (**MLA** p. 464).
- APA style, used in psychology and some other social sciences (**APA** p. 521).
- Chicago style, used in history, art history, philosophy, religion, and some other humanities (**Chic** p. 549).
- CSE style, used in the biological and some other sciences (**CSE** p. 560).

Always ask your instructor which documentation style you should use. If your instructor does not require a particular style, use the one in this book that's most appropriate for the discipline in which you're writing. Do follow a single system for citing sources so that you provide all the necessary information in a consistent format.

Note Bibliography software—*Zotero, Refworks, Endnote,* and others—can help you format your source citations in the style of your choice. Always ask your instructors if you may use such software for your papers. The programs prompt you for needed information (author's name, book title, and so on) and then arrange, capitalize, underline, and punctuate the information as required by the style. But no program can anticipate all the varieties of source information, nor can it substitute for your own care and attention in giving your sources complete acknowledgment using the required form.

54 Writing the Paper

This chapter complements and extends the detailed discussion of the writing situation and the writing process in Chapters 1–5 (**1** pp. 3–38), which also include many tips for using a word processor. If you haven't already done so, you may want to read those chapters before this one.

54a Focusing and organizing the paper

Before you begin using your source notes in a draft, give some thought to your main idea and your organization.

1 Thesis statement

You began research with a question about your subject (see pp. 373–74). Though that question may have evolved during research, you should be able to answer it once you've consulted most of your sources. Try to state that answer in a **thesis statement**, a claim that narrows your subject to a single idea. Here, for example, are the research question and thesis statement of Justin Malik, whose final paper appears later in this book (**MLA** pp. 510–18):

Research question
How can green consumerism help the environment?

Thesis statement
Although green consumerism can help the environment, consumerism itself is the root of some of the most pressing ecological problems we face. To make a real difference, we must consume less.

A precise thesis statement will give you a focus as you organize and draft your paper. For more on thesis statements, see **1** pp. 14–16.

2 Organization

To structure your paper, you'll need to synthesize, or forge relationships among ideas (see pp. 410–11). Here is one approach:

- **Arrange source information in categories.** Each group should correspond to a main section of your paper: a key idea of your own that supports the thesis.

Visit *mycomplab.com* for more resources as well as exercises on writing and revising a research paper.

- **Review your research journal** for connections between sources and other thoughts that can help you organize your paper.
- **Look objectively at your categories.** If some are skimpy, with little information, consider whether you should drop the categories or conduct more research to fill them out. If most of your information falls into one or two categories, consider whether they are too broad and should be divided. (If any of this rethinking affects your thesis statement, revise it accordingly.)
- **Within each group, distinguish between the main idea and the supporting ideas and evidence.** Only the support should come from your sources. The main idea should be your own.

See **1** pp. 17–21 for more on organizing a paper, including samples of both informal and formal outlines.

54b Drafting, revising, and formatting the paper

1 First draft

In drafting your paper, you do not have to proceed methodically from introduction to conclusion. Instead, draft in sections, beginning with the one you feel most confident about. Each section should center on a principal idea contributing to your thesis, a conclusion you have drawn from reading and responding to sources. Start the section by stating the idea; then support it with information, summaries, paraphrases, and quotations from your notes. Remember to insert source information from your notes as well.

2 Revision and editing

For a complex project like a research paper, you'll certainly want to revise in at least two stages—first for thesis, structure, and other whole-paper issues, and then for clarity, grammar, and other sentence-level issues. Chapter 5 supports this two-stage approach with checklists for revision (**1** p. 27) and editing (**1** p. 31). The box on the next page provides additional steps to take when revising a research paper.

3 Format

The final draft of your paper should conform to the document format recommended by your instructor or by the style guide of the discipline in which you are writing. This book details two common formats: Modern Language Association (**MLA** pp. 506–08) and American Psychological Association (**APA** pp. 539–42).

Checklist for revising a research paper

Assignment

How does the draft satisfy all of the criteria stated in your instructor's assignment?

Thesis statement

How well does your thesis statement describe your subject and your perspective as they emerged during drafting?

Structure

(Outlining your draft can help you see structure at a glance. See **1** p. 26.)

How consistently does borrowed material illuminate and support—not lead and dominate—your own ideas? How well is the importance of ideas reflected in the emphasis they receive? Will the arrangement of ideas be clear to readers?

Evidence

Where might evidence seem weak or irrelevant to readers?

Reasonableness and clarity

How reasonable will readers find your argument? (See **2** pp. 100–05.) Where do you need to define terms or concepts that readers may not know or may dispute?

In any discipline you can use a word processor to present your ideas effectively and attractively with readable typefonts, headings, illustrations, and other elements. See **1** pp. 55–65 for ideas.

Writing in the
Disciplines

Writing in the Disciplines

Chapter 10 (**2** p. 90) outlines the general concerns of subject, purpose, and audience that figure in most academic writing situations. The disciplines have more in common as well: methods of gathering evidence, kinds of assignments, scholarly tools, language conventions, and styles for source citations and document format. This chapter introduces these common goals and requirements. The following chapters then distinguish the disciplines along the same lines, focusing on literature (Chapter 56) and on other humanities, the social sciences, and the natural and applied sciences (Chapter 57).

55a Using methods and evidence

The **methodology** of a discipline is the way its practitioners study their subjects—that is, how they proceed when investigating the answers to questions. Methodology relates to the way practitioners analyze evidence and ideas. For instance, a literary critic and a social historian would probably approach Shakespeare's *Hamlet* quite differently: the literary critic might study the play for a theme among its poetic images; the historian might examine the play's relation to Shakespeare's context—England at the turn of the seventeenth century.

Whatever their approach, academic writers do not compose entirely out of their personal experience. Rather, they combine the evidence of their experience with that appropriate to the discipline, drawing well-supported conclusions about their subjects. The evidence of the discipline comes from research using primary or secondary sources.

- **Primary sources** are firsthand or original accounts, such as historical documents, works of art, and reports on experiments that the writer has conducted. When you use primary sources, you conduct original research and generate your own evidence. You might use your analysis of a painting as evidence for an interpretation of the painting. Or you might use data from your own survey of students to support your conclusions about students' attitudes.
- **Secondary sources** are books and articles written *about* primary sources. Much academic writing requires that you use

Visit *mycomplab.com* for more resources on writing in the disciplines.

437

> ## Guidelines for academic writers
>
> ■ Become familiar with the methodology and the kinds of evidence appropriate for the discipline in which you are writing.
> ■ Analyze the special demands of each assignment. The questions you set out to answer, the assertions you wish to support, will govern how you choose your sources and evidence.
> ■ Become familiar with the discipline's specialized tools and language.
> ■ Use the discipline's style for source citations and document format.

such sources to spark, extend, or support your own ideas, as when you review the published opinions on your subject before contributing conclusions from your original research.

55b Understanding writing assignments

For most academic writing, your primary purpose will be either to explain something to your readers or to persuade them to accept your conclusions. To achieve your purpose, you will adapt your writing process to the writing situation, particularly to your reader's likely expectations for evidence and how you use it. Most assignments will contain keywords that imply some of these expectations—words such as *compare, define, analyze,* and *illustrate* that express customary ways of thinking about and organizing a vast range of subjects. (See **1** p. 13 for more on these so-called patterns of development.) You should be aware of such keywords and alert to them in the wording of assignments.

55c Using tools and language

When you write in an academic discipline, you use the scholarly tools of that discipline, particularly its periodical indexes. In addition, you may use the aids developed by practitioners of the discipline for efficiently and effectively approaching research, conducting it, and recording the findings. Many of these aids, such as a system for recording evidence from sources, are discussed in **7** pp. 371–431 and can be adapted to any discipline. Other aids are discussed in the next two chapters.

Pay close attention to the texts assigned in a course and any materials given out in class, for these items may introduce you to valuable references and other research aids, and they will use the specialized language of the discipline. This specialized language allows practitioners to write to each other both efficiently and precisely. It also furthers certain concerns of the discipline, such as accuracy and objectivity. Scientists, for example, try to interpret their data objectively, so they avoid *undoubtedly, obviously,* and other words that slant conclusions. Some of the language conventions like this one are discussed in the following chapters. As you gain experience in a particular discipline, keep alert for such conventions and train yourself to follow them.

55d Following styles for source citations and document format

Most disciplines publish journals that require authors to use a certain style for source citations and a certain format for documents. In turn, most instructors in a discipline require the same of students writing papers for their courses.

When you cite your sources, you tell readers which ideas and information you borrowed and where they can find your sources. Thus source citations indicate how much knowledge you have and how broad and deep your research was. They also help you avoid **plagiarism,** the serious offense of presenting the words, ideas, and data of others as if they were your own. (See **7** pp. 423–30 on avoiding plagiarism.)

Document format specifies such features as margins and the placement of the title. But it also extends to special elements of the manuscript, such as tables or an abstract, that may be required by the discipline.

The style guides for various disciplines are listed on pp. 451 (humanities), 455 (social sciences), and 459 (natural and applied sciences). If your instructor does not require a particular style, use that of the Modern Language Association, which is described and illustrated at length in **MLA** pp. 464–505.

56 Reading and Writing About Literature

By Sylvan Barnet

Writers of literature—stories, novels, poems, and plays—are concerned with presenting human experience concretely, with *showing* rather than *telling,* with giving a sense of the feel of life. Reading and writing about literature thus require extremely close attention to the feel of the words. For instance, the word *woods* in Robert Frost's "Stopping by Woods on a Snowy Evening" has a rural, folksy quality that *forest* doesn't have, and many such small distinctions contribute to the poem's effect.

When you read literature, you interpret distinctions like these, forming an idea of the work. When you write about literature, you state your idea as your thesis, and you support the thesis with evidence from the work. (See **1** pp. 14–16 for more on thesis statements.)

Note Writing about literature is not merely summarizing literature. Your thesis is a claim about the meaning or effect of the literary work, not a statement of its plot. And your paper is a demonstration of your thesis, not a retelling of the work's changes or events.

56a Using the methods and evidence of literary analysis

1 Reading literature

Reading literature critically involves interacting with a text, not in order to make negative judgments but in order to understand the work and evaluate its significance or quality. Such interaction is not passive, like scanning a newspaper or watching television. Instead, it is a process of engagement, of diving into the words themselves.

You will become more engaged if you write while you read. If you own the book you're reading, don't hesitate to underline or highlight passages that especially interest you. Don't hesitate to annotate the margins, indicating your pleasures, displeasures, and uncertainties with remarks such as *Nice detail* or *Do we need this long description?* or *Not believable.* If you don't own the book, make these notes on separate sheets or on your computer.

An effective way to interact with a text is to keep a **reading journal.** A journal is not a diary in which you record your doings; instead, it is a place to develop and store your reflections on what you read, such as an answer to a question you may have posed in the margin of the text or a response to something said in class. You may, for instance, want to reflect on why your opinion is so different from that of another student. You may even make an entry in the form of a letter to the author or from one character to another. (See **1** pp. 9–10 for more on journal keeping.)

2 Meaning in literature

In analyzing literature, you face right off the question of *meaning.* Readers disagree all the time over the meanings of works of literature, partly because (as noted earlier) literature *shows* rather than *tells:* it gives concrete images of imagined human experiences, but it usually does not say how we ought to understand these images. Further, readers bring different experiences to their reading and thus understand images differently. In writing about literature, then, we can offer only our *interpretation* of the meaning rather than *the* meaning. Still, most people agree that there are limits to interpretation: it must be supported by evidence that a reasonable person finds at least plausible if not totally convincing.

3 Questions for a literary analysis

One reason interpretations of meaning differ is that readers approach literary works differently, focusing on certain elements and interpreting those elements distinctively. For instance, some critics look at a literary work mainly as an artifact of the particular time and culture in which it was created, while other critics stress the work's effect on its readers.

This chapter emphasizes so-called formalist criticism, which sees a literary work primarily as something to be understood in itself. This critical framework engages the reader immediately in the work of literature, without requiring extensive historical or cultural background, and it introduces the conventional elements of literature that all critical approaches discuss, even though they view the elements differently. The following list poses questions for each element that can help you think constructively and imaginatively about what you read.

- *Plot:* **the relationships and patterns of events.** Even a poem has a plot—for instance, a change in mood from grief to resignation.

  What actions happen?
  What conflicts occur?
  How do the events connect to each other and to the whole?

- *Characters:* **the people the author creates,** including the narrator of a story or the speaker of a poem.

  Who are the principal people in the work?
  How do they interact?
  What do their actions, words, and thoughts reveal about their personalities and the personalities of others?
  Do the characters stay the same, or do they change? Why?

- *Point of view:* **the perspective or attitude of the speaker in a poem or the voice who tells a story.** The point of view may be **first person** (a participant, using *I*) or **third person** (an outsider, using *he, she, it, they*). A first-person narrator may be a major or a minor character in the narrative and may be **reliable** or **unreliable** (unable to report events wholly or accurately). A third-person narrator may be **omniscient** (knows what goes on in all characters' minds), **limited** (knows what goes on in the mind of only one or two characters), or **objective** (knows only what is external to the characters).

Who is the narrator (or the speaker of a poem)?
How does the narrator's point of view affect the narrative?

■ *Tone:* **the narrator's or speaker's attitude,** perceived through the words (for instance, joyful, bitter, or confident).

What tone (or tones) do you hear? If there is a change, how do you account for it?
Is there an ironic contrast between the narrator's tone (for instance, confidence) and what you take to be the author's attitude (for instance, pity for human overconfidence)?

■ *Imagery:* **word pictures or details involving the senses of sight, sound, touch, smell, and taste.**

What images does the writer use? What senses do they draw on?
What patterns are evident in the images (for instance, religious or commercial images)?
What is the significance of the imagery?

■ *Symbolism:* **concrete things standing for larger and more abstract ideas.** For instance, the American flag may symbolize freedom, or a dead flower may symbolize mortality.

What symbols does the author use? What do they seem to signify?
How does the symbolism relate to the theme of the work?

■ *Setting:* **the place where the action happens.**

What does the locale contribute to the work?
Are scene shifts significant?

■ *Form:* **the shape or structure of the work.**

What *is* the form? (For example, a story might divide sharply in the middle, moving from happiness to sorrow.)
What parts of the work does the form emphasize, and why?

■ *Themes:* **the main ideas about human experience suggested by the work as a whole.** A theme is neither a plot (what happens) nor a subject (such as mourning or marriage). Rather it is what the author says with that plot about that subject.

Can you state each theme in a sentence? Avoid mentioning specific characters or actions; instead, write an observation applicable to humanity in general. For instance, you might state the following about Gwendolyn Brooks's poem "The Bean

Eaters" (p. 446): *People can live contentedly despite old age and poverty.*

Do certain words, passages of dialog or description, or situations seem to represent a theme most clearly?

How do the work's elements combine to develop a theme?

■ *Appeal:* the degree to which the work pleases you.

What do you especially like or dislike about the work? Why?

Do you think your responses are unique, or would they be common to most readers? Why?

4 Using evidence in writing about literature

The evidence for a literary analysis always comes from at least one primary source (the work or works being discussed) and may come from secondary sources (critical and historical works). For example, in the paper on pp. 446–48 about Gwendolyn Brooks's "The Bean Eaters," the primary material is the poem itself, and the secondary material is the three critical studies of the poem. The bulk of the evidence is usually quotations from the work, although summaries and paraphrases can be useful as well.

Your instructor will probably tell you if you are expected to consult secondary sources for an assignment. They can help you understand a writer's work, but your primary concern should always be the work itself, not what critics A, B, and C say about it. In general, then, quote or summarize secondary material sparingly. And always cite your sources.

56b Understanding writing assignments in literature

A literature instructor may ask you to write one or more of the following types of papers. The first two are the most common.

Key terms

primary source A firsthand account: for instance, a historical document, a work of literature, or your own observations. (See also p. 437.)

secondary source A report on or analysis of other sources, often primary ones: for instance, a historian's account of a battle or a critic's view of a poem. (See also pp. 437–38.)

quotation An exact repetition of an author's words, placed in quotation marks. (See also **7** pp. 416–17.)

paraphrase A restatement of an author's words, closely following the author's line of thought but using different words and sentence structures. (See also **7** pp. 415–16.)

summary A condensation of an extended passage into a sentence or more. (See also **7** pp. 414–15.)

- **A literary analysis paper:** your ideas about a work of literature—your interpretation of its meaning, context, or representations based on specific words, passages, characters, and events.
- **A literary research paper:** analysis of a literary work combined with research about the work and perhaps its author. A literary research paper draws on both primary and secondary sources.
- **A personal response or reaction paper:** your thoughts and feelings about a work of literature.
- **A book review:** a summary of a book and a judgment about the book's value.
- **A theater review:** your reactions to and opinions about a theatrical performance.

56c Using the tools and language of literary analysis

1 Writing tools

The fundamental tool for writing about literature is reading critically. Asking analytical questions such as those on pp. 441–43 can help you focus your ideas. In addition, keeping a reading journal can help you develop your thoughts. Make careful, well-organized notes on any research materials. Finally, discuss the work with others who have read it. They may offer reactions and insights that will help you shape your own ideas.

2 Language considerations

Use the present tense of verbs to describe both the action in a literary work and the writing of an author: *The old people live a meager existence. Brooks emphasizes how isolated the couple is. The critic Harry Shaw reads the lines as perhaps despairing.* Use the past tense to describe events that actually occurred in the past: *Brooks was born in 1917.*

Some instructors discourage students from using the first-person *I* (as in *I felt sorry for the character*) in writing about literature. At least use *I* sparingly to avoid sounding egotistical. Rephrase sentences to avoid using *I* unnecessarily—for instance, *The character evokes the reader's sympathy.*

3 Research sources

In addition to the following resources on literature, you may also want to consult some on other humanities (pp. 450–51).

Specialized encyclopedias, dictionaries, and bibliographies

Cambridge Bibliography of English Literature
Cambridge Encyclopedia of Language

Cambridge Guide to Literature in English
Dictionary of Literary Biography
Handbook to Literature
Literary Criticism Index
McGraw-Hill Encyclopedia of World Drama
New Princeton Encyclopedia of Poetry and Poetics
Oxford Companion to American Literature
Oxford Companion to the Theatre
Schomburg Center Guide to Black Literature from the Eighteenth Century to
the Present

Library databases and indexes

Abstracts of Folklore Studies
Dissertation Abstracts International (doctoral dissertations)
Early English Books Online
Gale Literary Resource Center
Humanities Index
Literary Criticism Index
Literary Index
Literature Online
MLA International Bibliography of Books and Articles on the Modern Languages and Literatures
World Shakespeare Bibliography

Book reviews

Book Review Digest
Book Review Index

Sources on the open Web

Alex Catalog of Electronic Texts (infomotions.com/alex)
EServer (eserver.org)
Internet Public Library: Online Literary Criticism (ipl.org/div/litcrit)
Literary Resources on the Net (andromeda.rutgers.edu/~jlynch/Lit)
Mr. William Shakespeare and the Internet (Shakespeare.palomar.edu)
Online Books Page (onlinebooks.library.upenn.edu/books)
Voice of the Shuttle (vos.ucsb.edu)

56d Documenting sources and formatting papers in literary analysis

Unless your instructor specifies otherwise, use the documentation style of the Modern Language Association, detailed in **MLA** pp. 464–508. In MLA style, parenthetical citations in the text of the paper refer to a list of works cited at the end. Sample papers illustrating this style appear on the following pages, in **2** pp. 112–16, and in **MLA** pp. 510–18.

Use MLA format for headings, margins, long quotations, and other elements, as detailed in **MLA** pp. 506–08.

56e Examining a sample literary analysis

Below and on the next two pages are a poem and a student pa-per on the work. The author develops a thesis about the poem, sup-porting this main idea with quotations, paraphrases, and sum-maries from the work being discussed, a primary source. The author also draws sparingly on secondary sources (other critics' views), which further support his own views.

Note the following features of the student's paper:

- **The writer does not merely summarize the literary work.** He summarizes briefly to make his meaning clear, but his essay con-sists mostly of his own analysis.
- **The writer uses many quotations from the literary work.** The quotations provide evidence for his ideas and let readers hear the voice of the work.
- **The writer integrates quotations smoothly into his own sen-tences.** See **7** pp. 418–23.
- **The writer uses the present tense of verbs** to describe both the author's work and the action in the work.

Poem

Gwendolyn Brooks

The Bean Eaters

They eat beans mostly, this old yellow pair.
Dinner is a casual affair.
Plain chipware on a plain and creaking wood,
Tin flatware.

Two who are Mostly Good.   5
Two who have lived their day,
But keep on putting on their clothes
And putting things away.

And remembering . . .
Remembering, with twinklings and twinges,   10
As they lean over the beans in their rented back room that
        is full of beads and receipts and dolls and cloths,
        tobacco crumbs, vases and fringes.

An essay on poetry with secondary sources

Marking Time Versus Enduring in
Gwendolyn Brooks's "The Bean Eaters"

Gwendolyn Brooks's poem "The Bean Eaters" runs only eleven lines. It is writ-ten in plain language about very plain people. Yet its meaning is ambiguous. One critic, George E. Kent, says the old couple who eat beans "have had their day and exist now as time-markers" (141). However, another critic, D. H. Melhem, perceives not time marking but "endurance" in the old couple (123). The reader must decide if this poem is a despairing picture of old age or a more positive portrait.

"The Bean Eaters" describes an "old yellow pair" who "eat beans mostly" (line 1) off "Plain chipware" (3) with "Tin flatware" (4) in their rented back room" (11). Clearly, they are poor. They live alone, not with friends or relatives—children or grandchildren are not mentioned—but with memories and a few possessions (9-11). They are "Mostly Good" (5), words Brooks capitalizes at the end of a line, perhaps to stress the old people's adherence to traditional values as well as their lack of saintliness. They are unexceptional, whatever message they have for readers.

The isolated routine of the couple's life is something Brooks draws attention to with a separate stanza:

> Two who are Mostly Good.
>
> Two who have lived their day,
>
> But keep on putting on their clothes
>
> And putting things away. (5-8)

Brooks emphasizes how isolated the couple is by repeating "Two who." Then she emphasizes how routine their life is by repeating "putting."

A pessimistic reading of this poem seems justified. The critic Harry B. Shaw reads the lines just quoted as perhaps despairing: "they are putting things away as if winding down an operation and readying for withdrawal from activity" (80). However, Shaw observes, the word "But" also indicates that the couple resist slipping away, that they intend to hold on (80). This dual meaning is at the heart of Brooks's poem: the old people live a meager existence, yes, but their will, their self-control, and their connection with another person—their essential humanity—are unharmed.

The truly positive nature of the poem is revealed in the last stanza. In Brooks's words, the old people remember with some "twinges" perhaps, but also with "twinklings" (10), a cheerful image. As Melhem says, these people are "strong in mutual affection and shared memories" (123). And the final line, which is much longer than all the rest and which catalogs the evidence of the couple's long life together, is almost musically affirmative: "As they lean over the beans in their rented back room that is full of beads and receipts and dolls and cloths, tobacco crumbs, vases and fringes" (11).

What these people have is not much, but it is something.

Works Cited

Brooks, Gwendolyn. "The Bean Eaters." *Literature: Fiction, Poetry, and Drama*. Ed. Sylvan Barnet, William Burto, and William E. Cain. 15th ed. New York: Longman, 2008. 922. Print.

Kent, George E. *A Life of Gwendolyn Brooks*. Lexington: UP of Kentucky, 1990. Print.

Melhem, D. H. *Gwendolyn Brooks: Poetry and the Heroic Voice*. Lexington: UP of Kentucky, 1987. Print.

Shaw, Harry B. *Gwendolyn Brooks*. Boston: Twayne, 1980. Print. Twayne's United States Authors Ser. 395.

—Kenneth Scheff (student)

57 Writing in Other Disciplines

57a Writing in the humanities

The humanities include literature, the visual arts, music, film, dance, history, philosophy, and religion. The preceding chapter discusses the particular requirements of reading and writing about literature. This section concentrates on history. Although the arts, religion, and other humanities have their own concerns, they share many important goals and methods with literature and history.

1 Methods and evidence in the humanities

Writers in the humanities record and speculate about the growth, ideas, and emotions of human beings. Based on the evidence of written words, artworks, and other human traces and creations, humanities writers explain, interpret, analyze, and reconstruct the human experience.

The discipline of history focuses particularly on reconstructing the past. In Greek the word for history means "to inquire": historians inquire into the past to understand the events of the past. Then they report, explain, analyze, and evaluate those events in their context, asking such questions as what happened before or after the events or how the events were related to then existing political and social structures.

Historians' reconstructions of the past—their conclusions about what happened and why—are always supported with reference to the written record. The evidence of history is mainly primary sources, such as eyewitness accounts and contemporary documents, letters, commercial records, and the like. For history papers, you

Visit *mycomplab.com* for more resources as well as exercises on writing in the disciplines.

might also be asked to support your conclusions with those in secondary sources.

In reading historical sources, you need to weigh and evaluate their evidence. If, for example, you find conflicting accounts of the same event, you need to consider the possible biases of the authors. In general, the more a historian's conclusions are supported by public records such as deeds, marriage licenses, and newspaper accounts, the more reliable the conclusions are likely to be.

2 | Writing assignments in the humanities

Papers in the humanities generally perform one or more of the following operations:

- **Explanation:** for instance, showing how a painter developed a particular technique or clarifying a general's role in a historical battle.
- **Analysis:** examining the elements of a philosophical argument or breaking down the causes of a historical event.
- **Interpretation:** inferring the meaning of a film from its images or the significance of a historical event from contemporary accounts of it.
- **Synthesis:** finding a pattern in a historical period or in a composer's works.
- **Evaluation:** judging the quality of an architect's design or a historian's conclusions.

Most likely, you will use these operations in combination—say, interpreting and explaining the meaning of a painting and then evaluating it. (These operations are discussed in more detail in **2** pp. 81–83.)

3 | Tools and language in the humanities

The tools and language of the humanities vary according to the discipline. Major reference works in each field, such as those listed on the next pages, can clarify specific tools you need and language you should use.

Writing tools

A useful tool for the arts is to ask a series of questions to analyze and evaluate a work. (A list of such questions for reading literature appears on pp. 441–43.) In any humanities discipline, a journal—a log of questions, reactions, and insights—can help you discover and record your thoughts.

In history the tools are those of any thorough and efficient researcher: a system for finding and tracking sources; a methodical examination of sources, including evaluating and synthesizing them; a system for gathering source information; and a separate system, such as a research journal, for tracking one's own evolving thoughts.

Language considerations

Historians strive for precision and logic. They do not guess about what happened or speculate about "what if." They avoid trying to influence readers' opinions with words having strongly negative or positive connotations, such as *stupid* or *brilliant*. Instead, historians show the evidence and draw conclusions from that. Generally, they avoid using *I* because it tends to draw attention away from the evidence and toward the writer.

Writing about history demands some attention to the tenses of verbs to maintain consistency. Generally, historians use the past tense to refer to events that occurred in the past. They reserve the present tense only for statements about the present or statements of general truths. For example:

> Franklin Delano Roosevelt died in 1945. Many of Roosevelt's economic reforms persist in programs such as Social Security, unemployment compensation, and farm subsidies.

Research sources on the open Web

The following lists give resources in the humanities. (Resources for literature appear on pp. 444–45.)

General
BUBL LINK (*bubl.ac.uk/link*)
EDSITEment (*edsitement.neh.gov*)
Voice of the Shuttle (*vos.ucsb.edu*)

Art
Artnet (*artnet.com*)
World Wide Arts Resources (*wwar.com/browse.html*)

Dance
Artslynx International Dance Resources (*www.artslynx.org/dance*)
BUBL LINK: Dance (*bubl.ac.uk/link/d/dance.htm*)

Film
Film Studies on the Internet (*www.library.ualberta.ca/subject/film/websites/index.cfm*)
Internet Movie Database (*imdb.com*)

History
Best of History Web Sites (*besthistorysites.net*)
Librarians' Internet Index: History (*lii.org/search/file/history*)
National Women's History Project (*nwhp.org*)

Music
American Music Resource (amrhome.net)
Web Resources Research in Music (music.ucc.ie/wrrm)

Philosophy
Social Science Information Gateway: Philosophy (www.intute.ac.uk/
*   artsandhumanities/philosophy)*
Stanford Encyclopedia of Philosophy (plato.stanford.edu)

Religion
Academic Info: Religion Gateway (academicinfo.net/religindex.html)
Virtual Religion Index (virtualreligion.net/vri)

Theater
McCoy's Brief Guide to Internet Resources in Theatre and Performance
*   Studies (www2.stetson.edu/csata/thr_guid.html)*
Theater Connections (uncc.edu/jvanoate/theater)

4 Documentation and format in the humanities

Writers in the humanities generally rely on one of the following guides for source-citation style:

The Chicago Manual of Style, 15th ed., 2003
A Manual for Writers of Research Papers, Theses, and Dissertations, by Kate
    L. Turabian, 7th ed., rev. Wayne C. Booth, Gregory G. Colomb, and
    Joseph M. Williams, 2007
MLA Handbook for Writers of Research Papers, 6th ed., by Joseph Gibaldi, 2003
MLA Style Manual and Guide to Scholarly Publishing, 3rd ed., 2008

See **MLA** pp. 464–508 for the recommendations of the *MLA Style Manual.* Unless your instructor specifies otherwise, use these recommendations for papers in English and foreign languages. In history, art history, and many other disciplines, however, writers rely on *The Chicago Manual of Style* or the student reference adapted from it, *A Manual for Writers.* Both books detail two documentation styles. One, used mainly by scientists and social scientists, closely resembles the style of the American Psychological Association (see **APA** pp. 521–42). The other style, used more in the humanities, calls for footnotes or endnotes and an optional bibliography. This style is described in **Chic** pp. 549–59.

57b Writing in the social sciences

The social sciences—including anthropology, economics, education, management, political science, psychology, and sociology—focus on the study of human behavior. As the name implies, the social sciences examine the way human beings relate to themselves, to their environment, and to one another.

1 | Methods and evidence in the social sciences

Researchers in the social sciences systematically pose a question, formulate a **hypothesis** (a generalization that can be tested), collect data, analyze those data, and draw conclusions to support, refine, or disprove their hypothesis. This is the scientific method developed in the natural sciences (see p. 456).

Social scientists gather data in several ways:

- **They make firsthand observations of human behavior,** recording the observations in writing or electronically.
- **They interview subjects about their attitudes and behavior,** recording responses in writing or electronically. (See **7** pp. 396–97 for guidelines on conducting an interview.)
- **They conduct broader surveys using questionnaires,** asking people about their attitudes and behavior. (See **7** pp. 397–98 for guidelines on conducting a survey.)
- **They conduct controlled experiments,** structuring an environment in which to encourage and measure a specific behavior.

In their writing, social scientists explain their own research or analyze and evaluate others' research.

The research methods of social science generate two kinds of data:

- *Quantitative data* **are numerical,** such as statistical evidence based on surveys, polls, tests, and experiments. When public-opinion pollsters announce that 47 percent of US citizens polled approve of the President's leadership, they are offering quantitative data gained from a survey. Social science writers present quantitative data in graphs, charts, and other illustrations that accompany their text.
- *Qualitative data* **are not numerical but more subjective:** they are based on interviews, firsthand observations, and inferences, taking into account the subjective nature of human experience. Examples of qualitative data include an anthropologist's description of the initiation ceremonies in a culture she is studying or a psychologist's interpretation of interviews he conducted with a group of adolescents.

2 | Writing assignments in the social sciences

Depending on what social science courses you take, you may be asked to complete a variety of assignments:

- **A summary or review of research** reports on the available research literature on a subject, such as infants' perception of color.

- **A case analysis** explains the components of a phenomenon, such as a factory closing.
- **A problem-solving analysis** explains the elements of a problem, such as unreported child abuse, and suggests ways to solve it.
- **A research paper** interprets and sometimes analyzes and evaluates the writings of other social scientists about a subject, such as the effect of national appeals in advertising.
- **A research report** explains the author's own original research or the author's attempt to replicate someone else's research. (See **APA** pp. 542–45 for an example of a research report.)

Many social science disciplines have special requirements for the content and organization of each kind of paper. The requirements appear in the style guides of the disciplines, listed on p. 455. For instance, the American Psychological Association specifies the outline for research reports that is illustrated in **APA** pp. 539–41. Because of the differences among disciplines and even among different kinds of papers in the same discipline, you should always ask your instructor what he or she requires for an assignment.

3 Tools and language in the social sciences

The following guidelines for tools and language apply to most social sciences. However, the particular discipline you are writing in, or an instructor in a particular course, may have additional requirements.

Writing tools

Many social scientists rely on a **research journal** or **log,** in which they record their ideas throughout the research-writing process. Even if a research journal is not required in your courses, you may want to use one. As you begin formulating a hypothesis, you can record preliminary questions. Then when you are in the field conducting research, you can use the journal to react to the evidence you are collecting, to record changes in your perceptions and ideas, and to assess your progress.

To avoid confusing your reflections on the evidence with the evidence itself, keep records of actual data—notes from interviews, observations, surveys, and experiments—separately from the journal.

Language considerations

Each social science discipline has specialized terminology for concepts basic to the discipline. In sociology, for example, the words *mechanism, identity,* and *deviance* have specific meanings different from those of everyday usage. And *identity* means something different in sociology, where it applies to groups of people, than in psychology, where it applies to the individual. Social scientists also use precise terms to describe or interpret research. For instance, they say *The subject expressed a feeling of* rather than *The subject felt* because human feelings are not knowable for certain; or they say *These studies indicate* rather than *These studies prove* because conclusions are only tentative.

Just as social scientists strive for objectivity in their research, they also strive to demonstrate their objectivity through language in their writing. They avoid expressions such as *I think* in order to focus attention on what the evidence shows rather than on the researcher's opinions. (However, many social scientists prefer *I* to the artificial *the researcher* when they refer to their own actions, as in *I then interviewed the subjects.* Ask your instructor for his or her preferences.) Social scientists also avoid direct or indirect expression of their personal biases or emotions, either in discussions of other researchers' work or in descriptions of research subjects. Thus one social scientist does not call another's work *sloppy* or *immaculate* and does not refer to his or her own subjects as *drunks* or *innocent victims.* Instead, the writer uses neutral language and ties conclusions strictly to the data.

Research sources on the open Web

General
Data on the Net (*3stages.org/idata*)
Social Science Information Gateway (*sosig.ac.uk*)
WWW Virtual Library: Social and Behavorial Sciences (*vlib.org/SocialSciences*)

Anthropology
Anthro.Net (*home1.gte.net/ericjw1/index.html*)
National Anthropological Archives (*www.nmnh.si.edu/naa/index.htm*)

Business and economics
Resources for Economics on the Internet (*rfe.org*)
Virtual International Business and Economic Sources (*library.uncc.edu/ display/?dept=reference&format=open&page=68*)

Education
Educator's Reference Desk (*eduref.org*)
US Department of Education (*ed.gov*)

Ethnic and gender studies
Diversity and Ethnic Studies (*public.iastate.edu/~savega/divweb2.htm*)
Voice of the Shuttle: Gender Studies (*vos.ucsb.edu/browse.asp?id=2711*)

Political science and law
Librarians' Internet Index: Law (*search.lii.org/index.jsp?more=SubTopic3*)
Political Science Resources (*psr.keele.ac.uk*)

Psychology
Psychology: Online Resource Central (*psych-central.com*)
PsychWeb (*psywww.com*)

Sociology
SocioWeb (*socioweb.com*)
WWW Virtual Library: Sociology (*socserv2.mcmaster.ca/w3virtsoclib*)

4 **Documentation and format in the social sciences**

Some of the social sciences publish style guides that advise practitioners how to organize, document, and type papers. The following is a partial list:

American Anthropological Association, *AAA Style Guide,* 2003 (*www.aaanet
.org/publications/guidelines.cfm*)
American Political Science Association, *Style Manual for Political Science,*
2006
American Psychological Association, *Publication Manual of the American
Psychological Association,* 5th ed., 2001, and *APA Style Guide to Elec-
tronic References,* 2007
American Sociological Association, *ASA Style Guide,* 3rd ed., 2007
Linguistic Society of America, "LSA Style Sheet," published every December
in *LSA Bulletin*
A Uniform System of Citation (law), 18th ed., 2005

By far the most widely used style is that of the American Psychological Association, detailed in **APA** pp. 521–42. Always ask your instructor in any discipline what style you should use.

57c   **Writing in the natural and applied sciences**

The natural and applied sciences include biology, chemistry,
physics, mathematics, engineering, computer science, and their
branches. Their purpose is to understand natural and technological
phenomena. (A *phenomenon* is a fact or event that can be known by
the senses.) Scientists conduct experiments and write to explain the
step-by-step processes in their methods of inquiry and discovery.

1 **Methods and evidence in the sciences**

Scientists investigate phenomena by the **scientific method,** a
process of continual testing and refinement. The box on the next
page outlines this method.

Scientific evidence is almost always quantitative—that is, it
consists of numerical data obtained from the measurement of phenomena. These data are called **empirical** (from a Greek word for
"experience"): they result from observation and experience, generally in a controlled laboratory setting but also (as sometimes in

The scientific method

- **Observe carefully.** Accurately note all details of the phenomenon being researched.
- **Ask questions about the observations.**
- **Formulate a** *hypothesis,* or preliminary generalization, that explains the observed facts.
- **Test the hypothesis** with additional observations or controlled experiments.
- **If the hypothesis proves accurate, formulate a** *theory,* or unified model, that explains *why.*
- **If the hypothesis is disproved, revise it or start anew.**

astronomy or biology) in the natural world. Often the empirical evidence for scientific writing comes from library research into other people's reports of their investigations. Surveys of known data or existing literature are common in scientific writing.

2 Writing assignments in the sciences

No matter what your assignment, you will be expected to document and explain your evidence carefully so that anyone reading can check your sources and replicate your research. It is important for your reader to know the context of your research—both the previous experimentation and research on your particular subject (acknowledged in the survey of the literature) and the physical conditions and other variables surrounding your own work.

Assignments in the natural and applied sciences include the following:

- **A summary** distills a research article to its essence in brief, concise form. (Summary is discussed in detail in **2** pp. 72–74.)
- **A critique** summarizes and critically evaluates a scientific report.
- **A laboratory report** explains the procedure and results of an experiment conducted by the writer.
- **A research report** explains the experimental research of other scientists and the writer's own methods, findings, and conclusions.
- **A research proposal** reviews the relevant literature and explains a plan for further research.

A laboratory report has four or five major sections:

1. "**Abstract**": a summary of the report.
2. "**Introduction**" or "**Objective**": a review of why the study was

undertaken, a summary of the background of the study, and a statement of the problem being studied.

3. **"Method"** or **"Procedure"**: a detailed explanation of how the study was conducted, including any statistical analysis.

4. **"Results"**: an explanation of the major findings (including unexpected results) and a summary of the data presented in graphs and tables.

5. **"Discussion"**: an interpretation of the results and an explanation of how they relate to the goals of the experiment. This section also describes new hypotheses that might be tested as a result of the experiment. If the discussion is brief, it may be combined with the results in a single section labeled "Conclusions."

In addition, laboratory or research reports may include a list of references (if other sources were consulted). They almost always include tables and figures (graphs and charts) containing the data from the research.

3 Tools and language in the sciences

Tools and language concerns vary from discipline to discipline in the sciences. Consult your instructor for specifics about the field in which you are writing.

Writing tools

In the sciences a **lab notebook** or **scientific journal** is almost indispensable for accurately recording the empirical data from observations and experiments. Use such a notebook or journal for these purposes:

- **Record observations** from reading, from class, or from the lab.
- **Ask questions and refine hypotheses.**
- **Record procedures.**
- **Record results.**
- **Keep an ongoing record of ideas and findings** and how they change as data accumulate.
- **Sequence and organize your material** as you compile your findings and write your report.

Make sure that your records of data are clearly separate from your reflections on the data so that you don't mistakenly confuse the two in drawing your conclusions.

Language considerations

Science writers use objective language that removes the writer as a character in the situation and events being explained, except as the impersonal agent of change, the experimenter. Although usage is changing, scientists still rarely use *I* in their reports and evaluations, and they often resort to the passive voice of verbs, as in *The mixture was then subjected to centrifugal force*. This conscious objectivity focuses attention (including the writer's) on the empirical data and what they show. It discourages the writer from, say, ascribing motives and will to animals and plants. For instance, instead of asserting that the sea tortoise *evolved* its hard shell *to protect* its body, a scientist would write only what could be observed: that the hard shell *covers and thus protects* the tortoise's body.

Science writers typically change verb tenses to distinguish between established information and their own research. For established information, such as that found in journals and other reliable sources, use the present tense: *Baroreceptors monitor blood pressure*. For your own and others' research, use the past tense: *The bacteria died within three hours. Marti reported some success*.

Each discipline in the natural and applied sciences has a specialized vocabulary that permits precise, accurate, and efficient communication. Some of these terms, such as *pressure* in physics, have different meanings in the common language and must be handled carefully in science writing. Others, such as *enthalpy* in chemistry, have no meanings in the common language and must simply be learned and used correctly.

Research sources on the open Web

General
Google Directory: Science Links (directory.google.com/Top/Science)
Librarians' Internet Index: Science (search.lii.org/index.jsp?more=SubTopic13)
WWW Virtual Library: Natural Sciences and Mathematics (vlib.org/Science
  .html)

Biology
Biology.Arizona.Edu (biology.arizona.edu)
National Biological Information Infrastructure (www.nbii.gov)

Chemistry
Chemistry.org (chemistry.org/portal/a/c/s/1/home.html)
WWW Virtual Library: Links for Chemists (liv.ac.uk/Chemistry/Links/links.html)

Computer science
IEEE Computer Society (computer.org)
University of Texas Virtual Computer Library (utexas.edu/computer/vcl)

Engineering
National Academy of Engineering (nae.edu)
TechXtra: Engineering, Mathematics, and Computing (www.techxtra.ac.uk)

Environmental science
EE-link: Environmental Education on the Internet (eelink.net)
EnviroLink (envirolink.org)

Geology
American Geological Institute (www.agiweb.org)
US Geological Survey Library (library.usgs.gov)

Health sciences
Hardin MD (www.lib.uiowa.edu/hardin/md)
World Health Organization (who.int/en)

Mathematics
Internet Mathematics Library (mathforum.org/library)
Mathematical Atlas (math-atlas.org)

Physics and astronomy
American Institute of Physics (aip.org)
PhysicsWeb (physicsweb.org)

4 | Documentation and format in the sciences

Within the natural and applied sciences, practitioners use one of two styles of documentation, varying slightly from discipline to discipline. Following are some of the style guides most often consulted:

American Chemical Society, *ACS Style Guide: A Manual for Authors and Editors,* 3rd ed., 2006

American Institute of Physics, *Style Manual for Guidance in the Preparation of Papers,* 4th ed., 1997

American Medical Association Manual of Style, 10th ed., 2007

Council of Science Editors, *Scientific Style and Format: The CSE Manual for Authors, Editors, and Publishers,* 7th ed., 2006

The most thorough and widely used of these guides is the last one, *Scientific Style and Format.* See **CSE** pp. 560–66 for a description of the style.

MLA Documentation and Format

MLA Documentation and Format

MLA parenthetical text citations

MLA works-cited models

(continued)

58 MLA Documentation and Format

English, foreign languages, and some other humanities use the documentation style of the Modern Language Association, detailed in the *MLA Handbook for Writers of Research Papers* (6th ed., 2003) and substantially updated in the *MLA Style Manual and Guide to Scholarly Publishing* (3rd ed., 2008). This chapter presents the updated citation formats of the *MLA Style Manual*. In MLA documentation style, you twice acknowledge the sources of borrowed material:

- In your text, a brief parenthetical citation adjacent to the borrowed material directs readers to a complete list of all the works you cite.
- At the end of your paper, the list of works cited includes complete bibliographical information for every source.

Every entry in the list of works cited has at least one corresponding citation in the text, and every in-text citation has a corresponding entry in the list of works cited.

mycomplab

Visit *mycomplab.com* for more resources and exercises
on MLA documentation and format.

This chapter describes MLA documentation: writing text citations (below), placing citations (p. 470), using supplementary notes (p. 472), and preparing the list of works cited (p. 473). A detailed discussion of MLA document format (p. 506) and a sample MLA paper (p. 510) conclude the chapter.

58a Writing parenthetical text citations

1 Citation formats

In-text citations of sources must include just enough information for the reader to locate the following:

- The *source* in your list of works cited.
- The *place* in the source where the borrowed material appears.

For any kind of source, you can usually meet both these requirements by providing the author's last name and (if the source uses them) the page numbers where the material appears. The reader can find the source in your list of works cited and find the borrowed material in the source itself.

The following models illustrate the basic text-citation forms and also forms for more unusual sources, such as those with no named author or no page numbers. See the **MLA** divider for an index to all the models.

Note Models 1 and 2 show the direct relationship between what you include in your text and what you include in a parenthetical citation. If you do *not* name the author in your text, you include the name in parentheses before the page reference (model 1). If you *do* name the author in your text, you do not include the name in parentheses (model 2).

1. Author not named in your text

When you have not already named the author in your sentence, provide the author's last name and the page number(s), with no punctuation between them, in parentheses.

> One researcher concludes that "women impose a distinctive construction on moral problems, seeing moral dilemmas in terms of conflicting responsibilities" (Gilligan 105-06).

See model 6 for the form to use when the source does not have an author. And see models 10 and 11 for the forms to use when the source does not provide page numbers.

2. Author named in your text

When you have already given the author's name with the material you're citing, do not repeat it in the parenthetical citation. Give just the page number(s).

Carol Gilligan concludes that "women impose a distinctive construction on moral problems, seeing moral dilemmas in terms of conflicting responsibilities" (105-06).

See model 6 for the form to use when the source does not list an author. And see models 10 and 11 for the forms to use when the source does not provide page numbers.

3. A work with two or three authors

If the source has two or three authors, give all their last names in the text or in the citation. Separate two authors' names with and.

As Frieden and Sagalyn observe, "The poor and the minorities were the leading victims of highway and renewal programs" (29).

According to one study, "The poor and the minorities were the leading victims of highway and renewal programs" (Frieden and Sagalyn 29).

With three authors, add commas and also and before the final name.

The textbook by Wilcox, Ault, and Agee discusses the "ethical dilemmas in public relations practice" (125).

One textbook discusses the "ethical dilemmas in public relations practice" (Wilcox, Ault, and Agee 125).

4. A work with more than three authors

If the source has more than three authors, you may list all their last names or use only the first author's name followed by et al. (the abbreviation for the Latin *et alii,* "and others"). The choice depends on what you do in your list of works cited (see pp. 474–75).

Increased competition means that employees of public relations firms may find their loyalty stretched in more than one direction (Cameron et al. 417).

Increased competition means that employees of public relations firms may find their loyalty stretched in more than one direction (Cameron, Wilcox, Reber, and Shin 417).

5. A work by an author of two or more cited works

If your list of works cited includes two or more works by the same author, then your citation must tell the reader which of the author's works you are referring to. Give the title either in the text or in a parenthetical citation. In a parenthetical citation, give the full title only if it is brief; otherwise, shorten the title to the first one, two, or three main words (excluding *A, An,* or *The*).

> At about age seven, children begin to use appropriate gestures with their stories (Gardner, *Arts* 144-45).

The full title of Gardner's book is *The Arts and Human Development* (see the works-cited entry on p. 475). This shortened title is italicized because the source is a book.

6. An anonymous work

For a work with no named author or editor (whether an individual or an organization), use a full or shortened version of the title, as explained above. In your list of works cited, you alphabetize an anonymous work by the first main word of the title (see p. 475), so the first word of a shortened title should be the same. The following citations refer to an unsigned source titled "The Right to Die." The title appears in quotation marks because the source is a periodical article.

> One article notes that a death-row inmate may demand his own execution to achieve a fleeting notoriety ("Right" 16).

> "The Right to Die" notes that a death-row inmate may demand execution to achieve a fleeting notoriety (16).

If two or more anonymous works have the same title, distinguish them with additional information in the text citation, such as the publication date.

7. A work with a corporate author

Some works list as author a government body, association, committee, company, or other group. Cite such a work by the organization's name. If the name is long, work it into the text to avoid an intrusive parenthetical citation.

> A 2008 report by the Hawaii Department of Education provides evidence of an increase in graduation rates (12).

8. A nonprint source

Cite a nonprint source such as a Web page or a DVD just as you would any other source. If your works-cited entry lists the source under the name of an author or other contributor, use that name in the text citation. The following example cites an authored source that has page numbers.

> Business forecasts for the fourth quarter tended to be optimistic (White 4).

If your works-cited entry lists the work under its title, cite the work by title in your text, as explained in model 6. The next example cites an entire work (a film on DVD) and gives the title in the text, so it omits a parenthetical citation (see model 10).

Seven decades after its release, *Citizen Kane* is still remarkable for its rich black-and-white photography.

9. A multivolume work

If you consulted only one volume of a multivolume work, your list of works cited will say so (see model 30 on p. 485), and you can treat the volume as you would any book.

If you consulted more than one volume of a multivolume work, give the appropriate volume in your text citation.

After issuing the Emancipation Proclamation, Lincoln said, "What I did, I did after very full deliberations, and under a very heavy and solemn sense of responsibility" (5: 438).

The number 5 indicates the volume from which the quotation was taken; the number 438 indicates the page number in that volume. When the author's name appears in such a citation, place it before the volume number with no punctuation: (Lincoln 5: 438).

If you are referring generally to an entire volume of a multivolume work and are not citing specific page numbers, add the abbreviation vol. before the volume number as in (vol. 5) or (Lincoln, vol. 5) (note the comma after the author's name). Then readers will not misinterpret the volume number as a page number.

10. An entire work or a work with no page or other reference numbers

When you cite an entire work rather than a part of it, you may omit any page or other reference number. If the work you cite has an author, try to work the author's name into your text. You will not need a parenthetical citation then, but the source still must appear in your list of works cited.

Boyd deals with the need to acknowledge and come to terms with our fear of nuclear technology.

Use the same format when you cite a specific passage from a work with no page, paragraph, or other reference numbers, such as a Web source.

If the author's name does not appear in your text, put it in a parenthetical citation.

Almost 20 percent of commercial banks have been audited for the practice (Friis).

11. A work with numbered paragraphs or sections instead of pages

Some electronic sources number each paragraph or section instead of each page. In citing passages in these sources, give the paragraph or section number(s) and distinguish them from page numbers: after the author's name, put a comma, a space, and par. (one paragraph), pars. (more than one paragraph), sec., or secs.

Twins reared apart report similar feelings (Palfrey, pars. 6-7).

12. An indirect source

When you want to use a quotation that is already in quotation marks—indicating that the author you are reading is quoting someone else—try to find the original source and quote directly from it. If you can't find the original source, then your citation must indicate that your quotation of it is indirect. In the following citation, qtd. in ("quoted in") says that Davino was quoted by Boyd.

George Davino maintains that "even small children have vivid ideas about nuclear energy" (qtd. in Boyd 22).

The list of works cited then includes only Boyd (the work consulted), not Davino.

13. A literary work

Novels, plays, and poems are often available in many editions, so your instructor may ask you to provide information that will help readers find the passage you cite no matter what edition they consult.

■ **Novels:** The page number comes first, followed by a semicolon and then information on the appropriate part or chapter of the work.

Toward the end of James's novel, Maggie suddenly feels "the thick breath of the definite—which was the intimate, the immediate, the familiar, as she hadn't had them for so long" (535; pt. 6, ch. 41).

■ **Poems that are not divided into parts:** You may omit the page number and supply the line number(s) for the quotation. To prevent confusion with page numbers, precede the numbers with line or lines in the first citation; then use just the numbers.

In Shakespeare's Sonnet 73 the speaker identifies with the trees of late autumn, "Bare ruined choirs, where late the sweet birds sang" (line 4). "In me," Shakespeare writes, "thou seest the glowing of such fire / That on the ashes of his youth doth lie . . ." (9-10).

(See pp. 446–48 for a sample paper on a poem.)

- **Verse plays and poems that are divided into parts:** Omit a page number and cite the appropriate part—act (and scene, if any), canto, book, and so on—plus the line number(s). Use Arabic numerals for parts, including acts and scenes (3.4), unless your instructor specifies Roman numerals (III.iv).

Later in Shakespeare's *King Lear* the disguised Edgar says, "The prince of darkness is a gentleman" (3.4.147).

- **Prose plays:** Provide the page number followed by the act and scene, if any. For an example, see the reference to *Death of a Salesman* on p. 472.

14. The Bible

When you cite passages of the Bible in parentheses, abbreviate the title of any book longer than four letters—for instance, Gen. (Genesis), 1 Sam. (1 Samuel), Ps. (Psalms), Prov. (Proverbs), Matt. (Matthew), Rom. (Romans). Then give the chapter and verse(s) in Arabic numerals.

According to the Bible, at Babel God "did . . . confound the language of all the earth" (Gen. 11.9).

15. Two or more works in the same citation

When you refer to more than one work in a single parenthetical citation, separate the references with a semicolon.

Two recent articles point out that a computer badly used can be less efficient than no computer at all (Gough and Hall 201; Richards 162).

Since long citations in the text can distract the reader, you may choose to cite several or more works in an endnote or footnote rather than in the text. See pp. 472–73.

2 Placement and punctuation of parenthetical citations

The following guidelines will help you place and punctuate text citations to distinguish between your own and your sources' ideas and to make your own text readable. See also 7 pp. 418–22 on editing quotations and using signal phrases to integrate source material into your sentences.

Where to place citations

Position text citations to accomplish two goals:

- **Make it clear exactly where your borrowing begins and ends.**
- **Keep the citation as unobtrusive as possible.**

You can accomplish both goals by placing the parenthetical citation at the end of the sentence element containing the borrowed material. This sentence element may be a phrase or a clause, and it may begin, interrupt, or conclude the sentence. Usually, as in the following examples, the element ends with a punctuation mark.

> The inflation rate might climb as high as 30 percent (Kim 164), an increase that could threaten the small nation's stability.

> The inflation rate, which might climb as high as 30 percent (Kim 164), could threaten the small nation's stability.

> The small nation's stability could be threatened by its inflation rate, which, one source predicts, might climb as high as 30 percent (Kim 164).

In the last example the addition of one source predicts clarifies that Kim is responsible only for the inflation-rate prediction, not for the statement about stability.

When your paraphrase or summary of a source runs longer than a sentence, clarify the boundaries by using the author's name in the first sentence and placing the parenthetical citation at the end of the last sentence.

> Juliette Kim studied the effects of acutely high inflation in several South American and African countries since World War II. She discovered that a major change in government accompanied or followed the inflationary period in 56 percent of cases (22-23).

When you cite two or more sources in the same paragraph, position authors' names and parenthetical citations so that readers can see who said what. In the following example, the beginnings and ends of sentences clearly mark the different sources.

> Schools use computers extensively for drill-and-practice exercises, in which students repeat specific skills such as spelling words, using the multiplication facts, or, at a higher level, doing chemistry problems. But many education experts criticize such exercises for boring students and failing to engage their critical thinking and creativity. Jane M. Healy, a noted educational psychologist and teacher, takes issue with "interactive" software for children as well as drill-and-practice software, arguing that "some of the most popular 'educational' software . . . may be damaging to independent thinking, attention, and motivation" (20). Another education expert, Harold Wenglinsky of the Educational Testing Service, found in a well-regarded 1998 study that fourth and eighth graders who used computers frequently, including for drill and practice, actually did worse on tests than their peers who used computers less often (*Does It Compute?* 21). In a later article, Wenglinsky concludes that "the quantity

of use matters far less than the quality of use." In schools, he says, high-quality computer work, involving critical thinking, is still rare ("In Search" 17).

How to punctuate citations

Generally place a parenthetical citation *before* any punctuation required by your sentence. If the borrowed material is a quotation, place the citation *between* the closing quotation mark and the punctuation:

> Spelling argues that during the 1970s American automobile manufacturers met consumer needs "as well as could be expected" (26) but not everyone agrees with him.

The exception is a quotation ending in a question mark or exclamation point. Then use the appropriate punctuation inside the closing quotation mark, and follow the quotation with the text citation and a period.

> "Of what use is genius," Emerson asks, "if the organ . . . cannot find a focal distance within the actual horizon of human life?" ("Experience" 60). Mad genius is no genius.

When a citation appears at the end of a quotation set off from the text, place it one space *after* the punctuation ending the quotation. Do not use additional punctuation with the citation or quotation marks around the quotation.

> In Arthur Miller's *Death of a Salesman,* the most poignant defense of Willie Loman comes from his wife, Linda:
>
> > He's not the finest character that ever lived. But he's a human being, and a terrible thing is happening to him. So attention must be paid. He's not to be allowed to fall into his grave like an old dog. Attention, attention must finally be paid to such a person. (56; act 1)

(This citation of a play includes the act number as well as the page number. See p. 470.)

3 | Footnotes or endnotes in special circumstances

Footnotes or endnotes may replace parenthetical citations when you cite several sources at once, when you comment on a source, or when you provide information that does not fit easily in the text. Signal a footnote or endnote in your text with a numeral raised above the appropriate line. Then write a note with the same numeral.

> **Text**   At least five studies have confirmed these results.[1]
>
> **Note**   1. Abbott and Winger 266-68; Casner 27; Hoyenga 78-79; Marino 36; Tripp, Tripp, and Walk 179-83.

In a note, the numeral is not raised, is indented one-half inch, and is followed by a period and a space. If the note appears as a footnote, place it at the bottom of the page on which the citation appears, set it off from the text with quadruple spacing, and single-space the note itself. If the note appears as an endnote, place it in numerical order with the other endnotes on a page between the text and the list of works cited. Double-space all the endnotes.

58b Preparing the MLA list of works cited

At the end of your paper, a list titled Works Cited includes all the sources you quoted, paraphrased, or summarized in your paper. (If your instructor asks you to include sources you examined but did not cite, title the list Works Consulted.)

Follow this format for the list of works cited:

- **Arrange your sources in alphabetical order** by the last name of the author. If an author is not given in the source, alphabetize the source by the first main word of the title (excluding *A*, *An*, or *The*).
- **Type the entire list double-spaced**, both within and between entries.
- **Indent the second and subsequent lines of each entry one-half inch from the left.** Your word processor can format this so-called hanging indent automatically.

For a complete list of works cited, see the paper by Justin Malik (p. 517).

MLA works-cited page

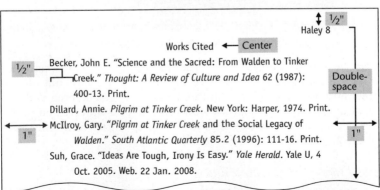

An index to all the following models appears at the **MLA** divider. Use your best judgment in adapting the models to your particular sources. If you can't find a model that exactly matches a source you used, locate and follow the closest possible match. You will certainly need to combine formats—for instance, drawing on model 2 ("Two or three authors") and model 10 ("An article in a national newspaper") for a national newspaper article with two authors.

Note MLA style now requires that you give the medium for every source you cite, such as print, Web, DVD, or television. For example, if you consulted an article in a print magazine, your works-cited entry should list the medium as Print. If you consulted a book on the Web, your works-cited entry should list the medium as Web. The models here all conform to this standard.

1 Listing authors

The following models show how to handle authors' names in citing any kind of source.

1. One author

Ehrenreich, Barbara. *Dancing in the Streets: A History of Collective Joy*. New
    York: Metropolitan-Holt, 2006. Print.

Give the author's full name—last name first, a comma, first name, and any middle name or initial. Omit any title, such as *Dr.* or *PhD*. End the name with a period. If your source lists an editor as author, see model 22, p. 481.

2. Two or three authors

Lifton, Robert Jay, and Greg Mitchell. *Who Owns Death: Capital Punishment,*
    the American Conscience, and the End of Executions. New York: Morrow,
    2000. Print.

Wilcox, Dennis L., Phillip H. Ault, and Warren K. Agee. *Public Relations: Strate-*
    gies and Tactics. 8th ed. New York: Irwin, 2006. Print.

Give the authors' names in the order provided on the title page. Reverse the first and last names of the first author *only*, not of any other authors. Separate two authors' names with a comma and and; separate three authors' names with commas and with and before the third name. If your source lists two or three editors as authors, see model 22, p. 481.

3. More than three authors

Cameron, Glen T., Dennis L. Wilcox, Bryan H. Reber, and Jae-Hwa Shin. *Public*
    Relations Today: Managing Competition and Conflict. New York: Pearson,
    2007. Print.

Cameron, Glen T., et al. *Public Relations Today: Managing Competition and Conflict*. New York: Pearson, 2007. Print.

You may, but need not, give all authors' names if the work has more than three authors. If you choose not to give all names, provide the name of the first author only, and follow the name with a comma and the abbreviation et al. (for the Latin *et alii*, meaning "and others"). If your source lists more than three editors as authors, see model 22, p. 481.

4. The same author(s) for two or more works

Gardner, Howard. *The Arts and Human Development*. New York: Wiley, 1973. Print.

---. *Five Minds for the Future*. Boston: Harvard Business School P, 2007. Print.

Give the author's name only in the first entry. For the second and any subsequent works by the same author, substitute three hyphens for the author's name, followed by a period. Note that the three hyphens stand for *exactly* the same name or names. If the second Gardner source were by Gardner and somebody else, both names would have to be given in full.

Place an entry or entries using three hyphens immediately after the entry that names the author. Within the set of entries by the same author, arrange the sources alphabetically by the first main word of the title, as in the Gardner examples (*Arts*, then *Five*).

If you cite two or more sources that list as author(s) exactly the same editor(s), follow the hyphens with a comma and ed. or eds. as appropriate. (See model 22, p. 481.)

5. A corporate author

Vault Technologies. *Turnkey Parking Solutions*. Salt Lake City: Mills, 2008. Print.

Corporate authors include associations, committees, institutions, government bodies, companies, and other groups. List the name of the group as author when a source gives only that name and not an individual's name.

6. Author not named (anonymous)

The Dorling Kindersley World Reference Atlas. London: Dorling, 2007. Print.

List a work that names no author—neither an individual nor a group—by its full title. If the work is a book, italicize the title. If the work is a periodical article or other short work, enclose the title in quotation marks:

"Let the Horse Race Begin." *Time* 31 Mar. 2008: 22. Print.

Alphabetize the work by the title's first main word, excluding *A, An*, or *The* (*Dorling* in the first example and Let in the second).

2 Listing periodical print sources

Print periodicals include scholarly journals, newspapers, and magazines that are published at regular intervals (quarterly, monthly, weekly, or daily). To cite more than one author, two or more articles by the same author, a corporate author, or an article with no named author, see models 1–6.

Note The treatment of volume and issue numbers and publication dates varies depending on the kind of periodical being cited, as the models indicate. For the distinction between journals and magazines, see **7** p. 385.

Articles in scholarly journals

7. An article in a journal with volume and issue numbers (print)

Bee, Robert. "The Importance of Preserving Paper-Based Artifacts in a Digital
    Age." *Library Quarterly* 78.2 (2008): 174-94. Print.

The facing page shows the basic format for an article in a print journal and the location of the required information in the journal. See p. 479 for parallel information on a newspaper article.

8. An article in a journal with only issue numbers (print)

Rymhs, Deena. "David Collier's *Surviving Saskatoon* and New Comics." *Canadian
    Literature* 194 (2007): 75-92. Print.

If a scholarly journal numbers only issues, not volumes, give the issue number alone after the journal title.

9. An abstract of a journal article or a dissertation (print)

Lever, Janet. "Sex Differences in the Games Children Play." *Social Problems*
    23.2 (1996): 478-87. *Psychological Abstracts* 63.5 (1996): item 1431.
    Print.

For an abstract of an article, first provide the publication information for the article, following model 7. Then give the information for the abstract. If the abstract publisher lists abstracts by item rather than page number, add item before the number.

For an abstract appearing in *Dissertation Abstracts* (*DA*) or *Dissertation Abstracts International* (*DAI*), give the author's name and the title, Diss. (for "Dissertation"), the institution granting the author's degree, the date of the dissertation, and the publication information.

Steciw, Steven K. "Alterations to the Pessac Project of Le Corbusier." Diss.
    U of Cambridge, England, 1986. *DAI* 46.10 (1986): 565C. Print.

Format for a print journal article

① ②
Bee, Robert. "The Importance of Preserving Paper-Based Artifacts in a Digital Age."
 ③ ④ ⑤ ⑥ ⑦
 Library Quarterly 78.2 (2008): 179-94. Print.

Journal cover

⑦ **Medium.** Give the medium of the article, Print, followed by a period.

THE LIBRARY QVARTERLY

③ **Title of periodical,** in italics. Omit any *A, An,* or *The* from the beginning of the title. Do not end with a period.

④ **Volume and issue numbers,** in Arabic numerals, separated by a period. Do not add a period after the issue number.

⑤ **Year of publication,** in parentheses and followed by a colon.

VOLUME 78 · APRIL 2008 · NUMBER 2

② **Title of article,** in quotation marks. Give the full title and any subtitle, separating them with a colon. End the title with a period inside the final quotation mark.

First page of article

THE IMPORTANCE OF PRESERVING PAPER-BASED ARTIFACTS IN A DIGITAL AGE

Robert Bee[1]

The preservation of paper-based artifacts is an essential issue for col agement in academic libraries. In recent years, the library science pr

① **Author.** Give the full name—last name first, a comma, first name, and any middle name or initial. Omit *Dr., PhD,* or any other title. End the name with a period.

[*Library Quarterly,* vol. 78, no. 2, pp. 179–194]
© 2008 by The University of Chicago. All rights reserved.
0024-2519/2008/7802-0002$10.00

179

⑥ **Inclusive page numbers of article,** without "pp." Provide only as many digits in the last number as needed for clarity, usually two.

See also model 40 on p. 488 (entire dissertation), model 63 on p. 499 (abstract on the Web), and model 65 on p. 499 (abstract in an online database).

Note Most instructors expect you to consult and cite full articles, not abstracts. See 7 p. 388.

Articles in newspapers

10. An article in a national newspaper (print)

Stout, David. "Blind Win Court Ruling on US Currency." *New York Times* 21 May
2008, natl. ed.: A23. Print.

See the facing page for an analysis of this entry and the location of the required information in the newspaper.

11. An article in a local newspaper (print)

Arntaenius, Linda. "Merwick Rezoning Pushes Senior Housing Debate." *Town
Topics* [Princeton] 21 May 2008: 1+. Print.

If the city of publication does not appear in the title of a local newspaper, follow the title with the city name, not italicized, in brackets.

Articles in magazines

12. An article in a weekly or biweekly magazine (print)

Fortini, Amanda. "Pomegranate Princess." *New Yorker* 31 Mar. 2008: 92-99. Print.

Give the author, title of the article, and title of the magazine. Follow the magazine title with the day, the month, and the year of publication. (Abbreviate all months except May, June, and July.) Don't place the date in parentheses, and don't provide a volume or issue number. Give the page numbers of the article and the medium, Print.

13. An article in a monthly or bimonthly magazine (print)

Douthat, Ross. "The Return of the Paranoid Style." *Atlantic Monthly* Apr. 2008:
52-59. Print.

Follow the magazine title with the month and the year of publication. (Abbreviate all months except May, June, and July.) Don't place the date in parentheses, and don't provide a volume or issue number. Give the page numbers of the article and the medium, Print.

Reviews, editorials, letters to the editor, interviews

14. A review (print)

Glasswell, Kathryn, and George Kamberelis. "Drawing and Redrawing the Map
of Writing Studies." Rev. of *Handbook of Writing Research,* by Charles A.

Format for a print newspaper article

① ② ③ ④
Stout, David. "Blind Win Court Ruling on US Currency." *New York Times* 21 May 2008,

⑤ ⑥ ⑦
natl. ed.: A23. Print.

⑥ Page number of article, without "pp." Include a section designation before the number when the newspaper does the same, as here. Otherwise, give the section between the edition and the colon. Add a plus sign to the page number when the article continues on a later page.

① Author. Give the full name—last name first, a comma, first name, and any middle name or initial. Omit *Dr., PhD*, or any other title. End with a period.

First page of article

THE NEW YORK TIMES **NATIONAL** WEDNESDAY, MAY 21, 2008
A23

Blind Win Court Ruling on U.S. Currency

By DAVID STOUT

WASHINGTON — In a decision that could radically change the size, the color and even the feel of American money, a federal appeals court ruled on Tuesday that the United States discriminates against the blind and those with limited vision because its paper currency is all the same size regardless of a bill's value.

blind or visually impaired," said Brookly McLaughlin, deputy assistant secretary for public affairs.

Ms. McLaughlin said the Bureau of Engraving and Printing, the Treasury agency that makes paper money, had already contracted with a research firm to study ways to help those who are blind or have poor vision. The re-

in the country could cost $3.5 billion in bill...
Other p...introduce...fected inc...money-di...er machin...makers c...Judge Randolph said.
The suit was brought under the Rehabilitation Act of 1973, which addresses discrimination in fed...

② Title of article, in quotation marks. Give the full title and any subtitle, separating them with a colon. End with a period inside the final quotation mark.

③ Name of newspaper, in italics. Give the title as it appears on the first page, omitting any *A, An,* or *The* from the beginning.

First page of newspaper

"All the News That's Fit to Print" **The New York Times** National Edition
Northern California: Morning... clouds in coastal areas, mostly... ly elsewhere. Cooler, with light... low 50s at coast to low 50s in Central Valley. Weather map, Page A26

VOL. CLVII ... No. 54,317 © 2008 The New York Times WEDNESDAY, MAY 21, 2008 Printed in California $1.25

⑦ Medium. Give the medium of the article, Print, followed by a period.

④ Date of publication. Give the day of the month first, then month, then year. Abbreviate all months except May, June, and July. End the date with a comma if listing the newspaper edition and/or the section designation. Otherwise, end with a colon.

⑤ Edition. If the newspaper lists an edition at the top of the first page, include it after the date. End with a comma if listing the section designation. Otherwise, end with a colon.

MacArthur, Steve Graham, and Jill Fitzgerald. *Reading Research Quarterly* 42.2 (2007): 304-23. Print.

Rev. is an abbreviation for "Review." The names of the authors of the work being reviewed follow the title of the work, a comma, and by. If the review has no title of its own, then Rev. of and the title of the reviewed work immediately follow the name of the reviewer.

15. An editorial (print)

"A Global AIDS Campaign Stalled." Editorial. *New York Times* 21 June 2008, natl. ed.: A18. Print.

For an editorial with no named author, begin with the title and add the word Editorial after the title, as in the example. For an editorial with a named author, start with his or her name and then proceed as in the example.

16. A letter to the editor (print)

McBride, Thad. "Swapping the Suit and Tie." Letter. *Economist* 29 Mar. 2008: 30. Print.

Add the word Letter after the title, if there is one, or after the author's name.

17. An interview (print)

Aloni, Shulamit. Interview. *Palestine-Israel Journal of Politics, Economics, and Culture* 14.4 (2007): 63-68. Print.

Begin with the name of the person interviewed. If the interview does not have a title (as in the example), add Interview after the name. (Replace this description with the title if there is one.) You may also add the name of the interviewer if you know it—for example, Interview by Benson Wright. See model 75 (p. 503) to cite a broadcast interview or an interview you conduct yourself.

Articles in series or in special issues

18. An article in a series (print)

Kleinfeld, N. R. "Living at an Epicenter of Diabetes, Defiance, and Despair." *New York Times* 10 Jan. 2006, natl. ed.: A1+. Print. Pt. 2 of a series, Bad Blood, begun 9 Jan. 2006.

Cite an article in a series following a model on pp. 476–78 (scholarly journal, newspaper, or magazine). If you wish, end the entry with a description to indicate that the article is part of a series.

19. An article in a special issue (print)

Rubini, Monica, and Michela Menegatti. "Linguistic Bias in Personnel Selection." *Celebrating Two Decades of Linguistic Bias Research.* Ed. Robbie M. Sutton and Karen M. Douglas. Spec. issue of *Journal of Language and Social Psychology* 27.2 (2008): 168-81. Print.

Cite an article in a special issue of a periodical by starting with the author and title of the article. Follow with the title of the special issue, Ed., and the names of the issue's editor(s). Add Spec. issue of before the periodical title. Conclude with publication information, using the appropriate model on pp. 476–78 for a journal or magazine.

3 Listing nonperiodical print sources

Nonperiodical print sources are works that are not published at regular intervals, such as books, government publications, and pamphlets. To cite more than one author, two or more articles by the same author, a corporate author, or a source with no named author, see models 1–6.

Books

20. Basic format for a book (print)

Lahiri, Jhumpa. *Unaccustomed Earth*. New York: Knopf, 2008. Print.

The next page shows the basic format for a book and the location of the required information in the book. When other information is required, put it between the author's name and the title or between the title and the publication information, as in the following models.

21. A second or subsequent edition (print)

Bolinger, Dwight L. *Aspects of Language*. 3rd ed. New York: Harcourt, 1981.
    Print.

For any edition after the first, place the edition number after the title. (If an editor's name follows the title, place the edition number after the name. See model 26.) Use the appropriate designation for editions that are named or dated rather than numbered—for instance, Rev. ed. for "Revised edition."

22. A book with an editor (print)

Holland, Merlin, and Rupert Hart-Davis, eds. *The Complete Letters of Oscar*
    Wilde. New York: Holt, 2000. Print.

Handle editors' names like authors' names (models 1–4), but add a comma and the abbreviation ed. (one editor) or eds. (two or more editors) after the last editor's name.

23. A book with an author and an editor (print)

Mumford, Lewis. *The City in History*. Ed. Donald L. Miller. New York: Pantheon,
    1986. Print.

When citing the work of the author, give his or her name first, and give the editor's name after the title, preceded by Ed. (singular only, meaning "Edited by"). When citing the work of the editor, use

Format for a print book

①　　　　　②　　　　③　　④　⑤　⑥
Lahiri, Jhumpa. *Unaccustomed Earth*. New York: Knopf, 2008. Print.

Title page

② Title, in italics. Give the full title and any subtitle, separating them with a colon. End the title with a period.

① Author. Give the full name—last name first, a comma, first name, and any middle name or initial. Omit *Dr., PhD,* or any other title. End the name with a period.

④ Publisher's name. Shorten most publishers' names ("UP" for University Press, "Little" for Little, Brown). Give both imprint and publisher's names when they appear on the title page: e.g., "Vintage-Random" for Vintage Books and Random House.

③ City of publication. Precede the publisher's name with its city, followed by a colon. Use only the first city if the title page lists more than one.

⑥ Medium. Give the medium of the book, Print, followed by a period.

⑤ Date of publication. If the date doesn't appear on the title page, look for it on the next page. End the date with a period.

Unaccustomed Earth

Jhumpa Lahiri

Alfred A. Knopf　　New York • Toronto 2008

model 22 for a book with an editor, adding By and the author's name after the title:

> Miller, Donald L., ed. *The City in History*. By Lewis Mumford. New York:
> Pantheon, 1986. Print.

24. A book with a translator (print)

Alighieri, Dante. *The Inferno*. Trans. John Ciardi. New York: NAL, 1971. Print.

When citing the work of the author, as in the preceding example, give his or her name first, and give the translator's name after the title, preceded by Trans. ("Translated by").

When citing the work of the translator, give his or her name first, followed by a comma and trans. Follow the title with By and the author's name:

Ciardi, John, trans. *The Inferno*. By Dante Alighieri. New York: NAL, 1971. Print.

When a book you cite by author has a translator *and* an editor, give their names in the order used on the book's title page.

25. An anthology (print)

Kennedy, X. J., and Dana Gioia, eds. *Literature: An Introduction to Fiction, Poetry, and Drama*. 10th ed. New York: Longman, 2007. Print.

Cite an entire anthology only when citing the work of the editor or editors or when your instructor permits cross-referencing like that shown in model 27. Give the name of the editor or editors (followed by ed. or eds.) and then the title of the anthology.

26. A selection from an anthology (print)

Mason, Bobbie Ann. "Shiloh." *Literature: An Introduction to Fiction, Poetry, and Drama*. Ed. X. J. Kennedy and Dana Gioia. 10th ed. New York: Longman, 2007. 604-13. Print.

This listing adds the following to the anthology entry in model 25: author of selection, title of selection (in quotation marks), and inclusive page numbers for the selection (without the abbreviation "pp."). If you wish, you may also supply the original date of publication for the work you are citing, after its title. See model 32 on p. 485.

If the work you cite comes from a collection of works by one author that has no editor, use the following form:

Auden, W. H. "Family Ghosts." *The Collected Poetry of W. H. Auden*. New York: Random, 1945. 132-33. Print.

If the work you cite is a scholarly article that was previously printed elsewhere, provide the complete information for the earlier publication of the piece, followed by Rpt. in ("Reprinted in") and the information for the source in which you found the piece:

Molloy, Francis C. "The Suburban Vision in John O'Hara's Short Stories." *Critique: Studies in Modern Fiction* 25.2 (1984): 101-13. Rpt. in *Short Story Criticism: Excerpts from Criticism of the Works of Short Fiction Writers*. Ed. David Segal. Vol. 15. Detroit: Gale, 1989. 287-92. Print.

27. Two or more selections from the same anthology (print)

Erdrich, Louise. "Indian Boarding School: The Runaways." Kennedy and Gioia
1106.

Kennedy, X. J., and Dana Gioia, eds. *Literature: An Introduction to Fiction,
Poetry, and Drama*. 10th ed. New York: Longman, 2007. Print.

Merwin, W. S. "For the Anniversary of My Death." Kennedy and Gioia 877-78.

Stevens, Wallace. "Thirteen Ways of Looking at a Blackbird." Kennedy and
Gioia 880-82.

When you are citing more than one selection from the same source,
your instructor may allow you to avoid repetition by giving the
source in full (the Kennedy and Gioia entry) and then simply cross-
referencing it in entries for the works you used. Thus the Erdrich,
Merwin, and Stevens examples replace full publication information
with Kennedy and Gioia and the appropriate pages in that book. Note
that each entry appears in its proper alphabetical place among
other works cited. Because each entry cross-references the Kennedy
anthology, the medium is not required.

28. An article in a reference work (print)

"Reckon." *Merriam-Webster's Collegiate Dictionary*. 11th ed. 2008. Print.

Wenner, Manfred W. "Arabia." *The New Encyclopaedia Britannica: Macropaedia*.
15th ed. 2007. Print.

List an article in a reference work by its title (first example) unless
the article is signed (second example). For works with entries arranged alphabetically, you need not include volume or page numbers. For well-known works like those above, you may also omit the
editors' names and all publication information except any edition
number and the year of publication. For works that are not well
known, give full publication information:

"Hungarians in America." *The Ethnic Almanac*. Ed. Stephanie Bernardo Johns.
6th ed. New York: Doubleday, 2002. 121-23. Print.

See also models 48 (p. 493) and 68 (p. 501), respectively, to cite reference works appearing on the Web or on a CD-ROM or DVD-ROM.

29. An illustrated book or graphic narrative (print)

Wilson, G. Willow. *Cairo*. Illus. M. K. Perker. New York: Vertigo-DC Comics,
2005. Print.

When citing the work of the writer of a graphic narrative or illustrated book, follow the example above: author's name, title, Illus.
("Illustrated by"), and the illustrator's name. When citing the work

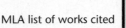

of an illustrator, list his or her name first, followed by a comma and illus. ("illustrator"). After the title and By, list the author's name.

> Garth Williams, illus. *Charlotte's Web*. By E. B. White. 1952. New York: Harper, 1999. Print.

30. A multivolume work (print)

> Lincoln, Abraham. *The Collected Works of Abraham Lincoln*. Ed. Roy P. Basler.
> Vol. 5. New Brunswick: Rutgers UP, 1953. Print. 8 vols.

If you use only one volume of a multivolume work, give that volume number before the publication information (Vol. 5 in the preceding example). You may add the total number of volumes at the end of the entry (8 vols. in the example).

If you use two or more volumes of a multivolume work, give the work's total number of volumes before the publication information (8 vols. in the following example). Your text citation will indicate which volume you are citing (see p. 468).

> Lincoln, Abraham. *The Collected Works of Abraham Lincoln*. Ed. Roy P. Basler.
> 8 vols. New Brunswick: Rutgers UP, 1953. Print.

If you cite a multivolume work published over a period of years, give the inclusive years as the publication date: for instance, Cambridge: Harvard UP, 1978-90.

31. A series (print)

> Bergman, Ingmar. *The Seventh Seal*. New York: Simon, 1995. Print. Mod. Film
> Scripts Ser. 12.

Place the name of the series (not quoted or italicized) at the end of the entry, followed by a period, a series number (if any), and another period. Abbreviate common words such as *modern* and *series*.)

32. A republished book (print)

> James, Henry. *The Bostonians*. 1886. New York: Penguin, 2001. Print.

Republished books include books reissued under new titles and paperbound editions of books originally released in hard covers. Place the original publication date (but not the place of publication or the publisher's name) after the title, and then provide the full publication information for the source you are using. If the book was originally published under a different title, add this title after Rpt. of ("Reprint of") at the end of the entry (after Print) and move the original publication date after the title—for example, Rpt. of *Thomas Hardy: A Life*. 1941.

33. The Bible (print)

The Bible. Print. King James Vers.

The Holy Bible. Trans. Ronald Youngblood et al. Grand Rapids: Zondervan, 1984. Print. New Intl. Vers.

When citing a standard version of the Bible (first example), do not italicize the title or the name of the version at the end. You need not provide publication information. For an edition of the Bible (second example), italicize the title, provide editors' and/or translators' names, give full publication information, and add the version name at the end.

34. A book with a title in its title (print)

Eco, Umberto. *Postscript to* The Name of the Rose. Trans. William Weaver. New York: Harcourt, 1983. Print.

When a book's title contains another book title (here *The Name of the Rose*), do not italicize the second title. When a book's title contains a quotation or the title of a work normally placed in quotation marks, keep the quotation marks and italicize both titles: *Critical Response to Henry James's "The Beast in the Jungle."*

35. Published proceedings of a conference (print)

Stimpson, Bill, ed. *2007 Annual Conference and Exhibition*. Proc. of Amer. Wind Energy Assn. Conf., 3-6 June 2007, New York. Red Hook: Curran, 2008. Print.

To cite the published proceedings of a conference, use a book model—here, an edited book (model 22). Between the title and the publication data, add information about the conference, such as its name, date, and location. You may omit any of this information that already appears in the source title. Treat a particular presentation at the conference like a selection from an anthology (model 26).

36. An introduction, preface, foreword, or afterword (print)

Donaldson, Norman. Introduction. *The Claverings*. By Anthony Trollope. New York: Dover, 1977. vii-xv. Print.

An introduction, foreword, or afterword is often written by someone other than the book's author. When citing such a piece, give its name without quotation marks or italics, as with Introduction above. (If the piece has a title of its own, provide it, in quotation marks, between the name of the author and the name of the book.) Follow the title of the book with By and the book author's name. Give the inclusive page numbers of the part you cite. (In the example above, the small Roman numerals refer to the front matter of the book, before page 1.)

When the author of a preface or introduction is the same as the author of the book, give only the last name after the title:

> Gould, Stephen Jay. Prologue. *The Flamingo's Smile: Reflections in Natural History*. By Gould. New York: Norton, 1985. 13-20. Print.

37. A book lacking publication information or pagination (print)

> Carle, Eric. *The Very Busy Spider*. New York: Philomel, 1984. N. pag. Print.

Some books are not paginated or do not list a publisher or a place of publication. To cite such a book, provide as much information as you can and indicate the missing information with an abbreviation: N.p. if no city of publication, n.p. if no publisher, n.d. if no publication date, and N. pag. if no page numbers.

Other nonperiodical print sources

38. A government publication (print)

> United Nations. Dept. of Economic and Social Affairs. *World Youth Report 2007: Young People's Transition to Adulthood—Progress and Challenges*. New York: United Nations, 2008. Print.
>
> United States. Cong. House. Committee on Agriculture, Nutrition, and Forestry. *Food and Energy Act of 2007*. 110th Cong., 1st sess. Washington: GPO, 2007. Print.
>
> Wisconsin. Dept. of Public Instruction. *Bullying Prevention Program: Grades 6-8*. Madison: Wisconsin Dept. of Public Instruction, 2007. Print.

If a government publication does not list a person as author or editor, give the appropriate agency as author, as in the above examples. Provide information in the order illustrated, separating elements with periods: the name of the government, the name of the agency (which may be abbreviated), and the title and publication information. For a congressional publication (second example), give the house and committee involved before the title, and give the number and session of Congress after the title. In this example, GPO stands for the US Government Printing Office.

If a government publication lists a person as author or editor, treat the source as an authored or edited book:

> Putko, Michelle. *Women in Combat Compendium*. Carlisle: US Army War Coll., Strategic Studies Inst., 2008. Print.

See model 47 (p. 493) to cite a government publication you find on the Web.

39. A pamphlet or brochure (print)

Understanding Childhood Obesity. Tampa: Obesity Action Coalition, 2008. Print.

Most pamphlets and brochures can be treated as books. In this example, the pamphlet has no listed author, so the title comes first. If your source has an author, give his or her name first, followed by the title and publication information.

40. A dissertation (print)

McFaddin, Marie Oliver. *Adaptive Reuse: An Architectural Solution for Poverty and Homelessness.* Diss. U of Maryland, 2007. Ann Arbor: UMI, 2007. Print.

Treat a published dissertation like a book, but after the title insert Diss. ("Dissertation"), the institution granting the degree, and the year.

For an unpublished dissertation, use quotation marks rather than italics for the title and omit publication information.

Wilson, Stuart M. "John Stuart Mill as a Literary Critic." Diss. U of Michigan, 1990. Print.

41. A letter (print)

Buttolph, Mrs. Laura E. Letter to Rev. and Mrs. C. C. Jones. 20 June 1857. *The Children of Pride: A True Story of Georgia and the Civil War.* Ed. Robert Manson Myers. New Haven: Yale UP, 1972. 334-35. Print.

List a published letter under the writer's name. Specify that the source is a letter and to whom it was addressed, and give the date on which it was written. Treat the remaining information like that for a selection from an anthology (model 26, p. 483). (See also model 16, p. 480, for the format of a letter to the editor of a periodical.)

For an unpublished letter in the collection of a library or archive, specify the writer, recipient, and date, as for a published letter. Then provide the medium, either MS ("manuscript") or TS ("typescript"). End with the name and location of the archive.

James, Jonathan E. Letter to his sister. 16 Apr. 1970. MS. Jonathan E. James Papers. South Dakota State Archive, Pierre.

For a letter you received, give the name of the writer, note the fact that the letter was sent to you, provide the date of the letter, and add the medium, MS or TS.

Wynne, Ava. Letter to the author. 6 Apr. 2008. MS.

To cite an e-mail message or a discussion-group posting, see models 70–71 (p. 501).

4 | Listing nonperiodical Web sources

This section shows how to cite nonperiodical sources that you find on the Web. These sources may be published only once or occasionally, or they may be updated frequently but not regularly. (Most online magazines and newspapers fall into the latter category, even if they relate to printed periodicals, because their content changes often and unpredictably. See models 45 and 46.) Some nonperiodical Web sources are available only on the Web (below); others are available in other media as well, such as print or film (pp. 495–97). See models 62–67 (pp. 498–500) to cite a scholarly journal that you find on the Web and any periodical that you find in an on-line database.

The MLA no longer recommends providing a URL (electronic address) in Web source citations because URLs change frequently and because users can search for documents using search engines. However, do include a URL if your source is hard to find without it, if your source could be confused with another one, or if your instructor requires you to include URLs. See model 61 (p. 497) for the form to use when citing a URL.

Note The *MLA Style Manual* does not label its examples of nonperiodical Web sources as particular types. For ease of reference, the following models identify and illustrate the kinds of Web sources you are likely to encounter. If you don't see just what you need, consult the index of models on the **MLA** tabbed divider for a similar source type whose format you can adapt. If your source does not include all of the information needed for a complete citation, find and list what you can.

Nonperiodical sources available only on the Web

Many nonperiodical Web sources are available only online. The following list, adapted from the *MLA Style Manual*, itemizes the possible elements in a nonperiodical Web publication, in order of their appearance in a works-cited entry:

1. **Name of the author or other person responsible for the source,** such as an editor, translator, director, or performer. See models 1–6 (pp. 474–75) for the handling of authors' names. For other kinds of contributors, see models 22–24 (editors and translators) and models 74, 76–77, and 83 (directors, performers, and so on).

2. **Title of the cited work.** Use quotation marks for titles of articles, blog entries, and other sources that are parts of larger works. Use italics for books, plays, and other sources that are published independently.

3. **Title of the Web site,** in italics.

4. **Version or edition cited,** if any, following model 21 (p. 481)—for example, *Index of History Periodicals*. 2nd ed.

5. **Publisher or sponsor of the site,** followed by a comma. If you cannot find a publisher or sponsor, use N.p. ("No publisher") instead.

6. **Date of electronic publication, latest revision, or posting.** If no date is available, use n.d. ("no date") instead.

7. **Medium of publication:** Web.

8. **Date of your access:** day, month, year.

For some Web sources, you may want to include information that is not on this list, such as the names of both the writer and the performers on a television show.

42. A short work with a title (Web)

Molella, Arthur. "Cultures of Innovation." *The Lemelson Center for the Study of Invention and Innovation*. Smithsonian Inst., Natl. Museum of Amer. Hist., Spring 2005. Web. 3 Aug. 2008.

See the facing page for an analysis of this entry and the location of the required information on the Web site. If the short work you are citing lacks an author, follow model 6 (p. 475) for an anonymous source, starting the entry with the title of the work:

"Clean Energy." *Union of Concerned Scientists: Citizens and Scientists for Environmental Solutions*. Union of Concerned Scientists, 5 Feb. 2008. Web. 11 Mar. 2008.

To cite a short Web source that also appears in another medium (such as print), see models 56–60 (pp. 495–97). To cite an article from a Web journal or from an online database, see models 62–67 (pp. 498–500).

43. A short work without a title (Web)

Crane, Gregory, ed. Home page. *The Perseus Digital Library*. Dept. of Classics, Tufts U, n.d. Web. 21 July 2008.

If you are citing an untitled short work from a Web site, such as the home page of a site or a posting to a blog, insert Home page, Online posting, or another descriptive label in place of the title. Do not use quotation marks or italics for this label.

Note that this source lacks a publication date, indicated by n.d. after the sponsor's name.

Format for a short work on the Web

①   ②   ③
Molella, Arthur. "Cultures of Innovation." *The Lemelson Center for the Study of Inven-*
                                              ④   ⑤
tion and Innovation. Smithsonian Inst., Natl. Museum of Amer. Hist., Spring
        ⑥   ⑦
2005. Web. 3 Aug. 2008.

Top of page

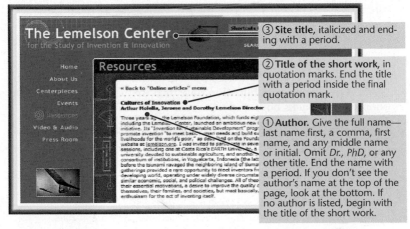

③ **Site title**, italicized and ending with a period.

② **Title of the short work**, in quotation marks. End the title with a period inside the final quotation mark.

① **Author.** Give the full name—last name first, a comma, first name, and any middle name or initial. Omit *Dr., PhD*, or any other title. End the name with a period. If you don't see the author's name at the top of the page, look at the bottom. If no author is listed, begin with the title of the short work.

Bottom of page

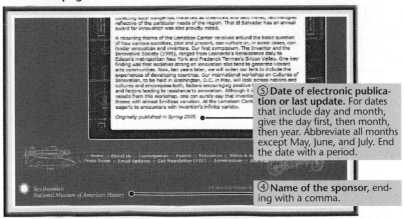

⑤ **Date of electronic publication or last update.** For dates that include day and month, give the day first, then month, then year. Abbreviate all months except May, June, and July. End the date with a period.

④ **Name of the sponsor**, ending with a comma.

⑥ **Medium.** Give the medium of the article, Web, followed by a period.

⑦ **Date of your access.** Give the day first, then month, then year. Abbreviate all months except May, June, and July. End the date with a period. (Since this date does not appear on the site, you'll need to record it separately.)

44. An entire site (Web)

Cheit, Ross E., ed. *The Recovered Memory Project*. Taubman Center for Public
    and Amer. Insts., Brown U, July 2007. Web. 8 Oct. 2008.

When citing an entire Web site—for instance, a scholarly project or a
foundation site—include the name of the editor, author, or compiler
(if available); the title of the site; the sponsor; the date of publication
or most recent update; the medium (Web); and your date of access.

If your source lacks a named author or editor, begin with the
site title:

Union of Concerned Scientists: Citizens and Scientists for Environmental Solutions.
    Union of Concerned Scientists, 5 Feb. 2008. Web. 11 Mar. 2008.

If your source lacks a sponsor, use the abbreviation N.p. ("No publisher"). If it lacks a publication date, use the abbreviation n.d. The
source below lacks both a sponsor and a publication date:

Corbett, John. *STARN: Scots Teaching and Resource Network*. N.p., n.d. Web. 26
    Nov. 2008.

45. An article in a newspaper (Web)

Carvajal, Doreen. "High-Tech Crime Is an Online Bubble That Hasn't Burst."
    New York Times. New York Times, 7 Apr. 2008. Web. 8 Apr. 2008.

List the author, article title, and newspaper title as in model 10 or
11 (p. 478). Then give the publishers's name and the date. End with
the medium of publication (Web) and the date of your access. (See
model 66 to cite a newspaper article in an online database.)

Use the preceding format to adapt the models for print periodicals if you need to cite a Web newspaper review, editorial, letter
to the editor, interview, or article in a series (models 14–18, pp.
478–80).

46. An article in a magazine (Web)

Yabroff, Jennie. "Art Aimed to Shock." *Newsweek*. Newsweek, 26 Apr. 2008.
    Web. 15 May 2008.

List the author, article title, and magazine title as in model 12 or 13
(p. 478). Then give the publisher's name and the date. End with the
medium (Web) and the date of your access. (See model 67 to cite a
magazine article in an online database.)

Use the preceding format to adapt the models for print periodicals if you need to cite a Web magazine review, editorial, letter to
the editor, interview, article in a series, or special issue (models
14–19, pp. 478–80).

47. A government publication (Web)

United States. Dept. of Agriculture. "Inside the Pyramid." *MyPyramid.gov.*
US Dept. of Agriculture, n.d. Web. 1 Mar. 2008.

See model 38 for examples of government publications in print. Provide the same information for online publications along with the facts of Web publication. The example above includes the names of the government and department; the title of the source, in quotation marks; the title of the Web site, in italics; the sponsor; n.d. (because there is no publication date); the medium (Web); and the date of access.

48. An article in a reference work (Web)

"Yi Dynasty." *Encyclopaedia Britannica Online.* Encyclopaedia Britannica, 2008.
Web. 7 Apr. 2008.

This source does not list an author, so the entry begins with the title of the article and then proceeds as for other Web sources. If a reference article has an author, place the name before the article title, as in model 42.

For reference works that you find in print or on CD-ROM or DVD-ROM, see models 28 (p. 484) and 68 (p. 501), respectively.

49. An image (Web)

To cite images that are available only on the Web, give the name of the artist or creator, the title of the work, the date of the work (if any), a word describing the type of image (if not otherwise clear from the image or site title), the title of the Web site, the sponsor, the date of the site, the medium (Web), and your date of access. The following examples show a range of possibilities.

A work of visual art:

Simpson, Rick. *Overload. Museum of Computer Art.* Museum of Computer Art,
2008. Web. 1 Apr. 2008.

A photograph:

Touboul, Jean. *Desert 1.* 2002. Photograph. *Artmuse.net.* Jean Touboul, 2007.
Web. 14 Nov. 2008.

An advertisement:

United States. Dept. of Educ. Federal Student Aid. Advertisement. *Facebook.*
Facebook, 2008. Web. 6 May 2008.

A map, chart, graph, or diagram:

"Greenhouse Effect." Diagram. *Earthguide.* Scripps Inst. of Oceanography,
2008. Web. 17 July 2008.

See also model 60 (p. 497) to cite an image that appears both on the Web and in another medium. And see models 78–82 (pp. 504–05) to cite images that aren't on the Web.

50. A television or radio program (Web)

Seabrook, Andrea, host. *All Things Considered*. Natl. Public Radio, 6 Apr. 2008.

Web. 21 Apr. 2008.

The Web sites of television and radio networks and programs often include both content that was broadcast as part of a show and content that is unique to the site. Cite such material by its title or by the name of the person whose work you cite. Identify the role of anyone but an author (host in the example). Give the site title, the sponsor, the date, the medium (Web), and the date of your access. You may also cite other contributors (and their roles) after the title, as in model 52.

See also model 74 (p. 502) to cite a television or radio program that isn't on the Web.

51. A video recording (Web)

Green Children Foundation, prod. *The Green Children Visit China*. YouTube.

YouTube, 7 Jan. 2008. Web. 28 June 2008.

Cite a video on the Web either by its title or by the name of the person whose work you are citing—in this example, the foundation that produced the video. Identify the role of anyone but an author (prod. in the example). Give the video title, the site title, the sponsor, the date, the medium (Web), and the date of your access. You may also cite other contributors (and their roles) after the title, as in model 52.

See also model 53 to cite a podcast of a video recording; model 59 (p. 496) to cite a video recording or film that appears both on the Web and in another medium (such as DVD); and model 77 (p. 503) to cite a film, DVD, or video recording that isn't on the Web.

52. A sound recording (Web)

Beglarian, Eve. *Five Things*. Perf. Beglarian et al. *Kalvos and Damian*. N.p., 23

Oct. 2001. Web. 8 Mar. 2008.

Cite a musical sound recording by its title or by the name of the person whose work you are citing—in this example, the composer. (If the composer's name comes after the title, precede it with By. See the next example.) This example also gives the work title, the performers of the work, the site title, the sponsor (here unknown, so replaced with N.p.), the date, the medium (Web), and the date of access.

The same format may be used for a spoken-word recording that you find on the Web:

Wasserstein, Wendy, narr. "Afternoon of a Faun." By Wasserstein. *The Borzoi Reader Online*. Knopf, 2001. Web. 14 Feb. 2008.

See also the next model to cite a sound podcast; model 58 to cite a sound recording that appears both on the Web and in another medium (such as CD); and model 76 (p. 503) to cite a sound recording that isn't on the Web.

53. A podcast (Web)

Simon, Bob. "Exonerated." *60 Minutes*. *CBS News*. CBS News, 25 May 2008. Web. 6 June 2008.

This podcast from a news program lists the author of a story on the show, the title of the story (in quotation marks), and the program (italicized) as well as the site title, sponsor, date, medium (Web), and access date. If a podcast does not list an author or other creator, begin with the title.

54. A blog entry (Web)

Marshall, Joshua Micah. "Asking the Tough Questions." *Talking Points Memo*. TPM Media, 15 May 2008. Web. 21 May 2008.

For a blog entry, give the author, the title of the entry, the title of the blog or site, the name of the sponsor (or N.p. if no sponsor is named), the publication date, the medium (Web), and the date of access. See model 43 (p. 490) to cite a blog entry without a title.

55. A wiki (Web)

"Podcast." *Wikipedia*. Wikimedia, n.d. Web. 20 Nov. 2008.

To cite an entry from a wiki, follow the above example: entry title, site title, sponsor, publication date (here n.d. because the wiki entry is undated), medium (Web), and date of access. Begin with the site title if you are citing the entire wiki.

Nonperiodical Web sources also available in print

Some sources you find on the Web may be books, short stories, and other works that have been scanned from print versions. To cite such a source, generally provide the information for both original print publication and Web publication. Begin your entry as if you were citing the print work, consulting models 20–41 for an appropriate format. Then, instead of giving "Print" as the medium, provide the title of the Web site you used, any version or edition number, the medium you used (Web), and the date of your access.

56. A short work with print publication information (Web)

Wheatley, Phillis. "On Virtue." *Poems on Various Subjects, Religious and Moral.*
London, 1773. N. pag. *American Verse Project.* Web. 21 July 2008.

The print information for this poem follows model 26 (p. 483) for a
selection from an anthology, but it omits the publisher's name because the anthology was published before 1900. The print information
ends with N. pag. because the original source has no page numbers.

57. A book with print publication information (Web)

James, Henry. *The Ambassadors.* 1903. New York: Scribner's, 1909. *Oxford Text
Archive.* Web. 5 May 2008.

The print information for this novel follows model 32 (p. 485) for a
republished book, so it includes both the original date of publication (1903) and the publication information for the scanned book.

Nonperiodical Web sources also available in other media

Some images, films, and sound recordings that you find on the
Web may have been published before in other media and then
scanned or digitized for the Web. To cite such a source, generally
provide the information for original publication as well as that for
Web publication. Begin your entry as if you were citing the original,
consulting models 74–84 (pp. 502–05) for an appropriate format.
Then, instead of giving the original medium of publication, provide
the title of the Web site you used, the medium you used (Web), and
your date of access.

58. A sound recording with other publication information (Web)

"Rioting in Pittsburgh." CBS Radio, 1968. *Vincent Voice Library.* Web.
7 Dec. 2008.

For Web sound recordings with original publication information,
base citations on model 76 (p. 503), adding the information for Web
publication.

59. A film or video recording with other publication information (Web)

Coca Cola. Advertisement. Dir. Haskell Wexler. 1971. *American Memory.* Lib. of
Cong. Web. 8 Apr. 2008.

For Web films or videos with original publication information, base
citations on model 77 (p. 503), adding the information for Web publication.

60. An image with other publication information (Web)

Pollock, Jackson. *Lavender Mist: Number 1.* 1950. Natl. Gallery of Art, Washington.

   WebMuseum. Web. 7 Apr. 2008.

Keefe, Mike. "FAA Inspector in a Quandary." Cartoon. *Denver Post* 5 Apr. 2008.

   PoliticalCartoons.com. Web. 7 Apr. 2008.

For Web images with original publication information, base citations on models 78–82 (pp. 504–05), adding the information for Web publication.

Citation of a URL

61. A source requiring citation of the URL

Joss, Rich. "Dispatches from the Ice: The Second Season Begins." *Antarctic*

   Expeditions. Smithsonian Natl. Zoo and Friends of the Natl. Zoo, 26 Oct.

   2007. Web. 26 Sept. 2008. <http://nationalzoo.si.edu/

   ConservationAndScience/AquaticEcosystems/Antarctica/Expedition/

   FieldNew/2-FieldNews.cfm>.

Because a URL does not always provide a convenient or usable route to a source, the MLA no longer recommends including URLs in works-cited entries. However, you should include URLs when your instructor requires them. You should also give a URL when readers may not be able to locate a source without one. For example, using a search engine to find "Dispatches from the Ice" (the title in the example) yields more than ten hits, one of which links to the correct site but the wrong document.

If you need to include a URL, ensure accuracy by using Copy and Paste to duplicate it in a file or an e-mail to yourself. In your list of works cited, give the URL after your date of access and a period. Put angle brackets on both ends of the URL, and end with a period. Break URLs *only* after slashes—do not hyphenate.

5 Listing journals on the Web and periodicals in online databases

This section covers two kinds of periodicals: scholarly journals that you reach directly on the Web (next page) and journals, newspapers, and magazines that you reach in online databases (p. 499). Newspapers and magazines that you reach directly on the Web are typically not periodicals (because their content often changes), so they are covered in models 45 and 46 (p. 492).

Citations for Web journals and for periodicals in online databases resemble those for print periodicals, with some changes for the different medium.

Web journals consulted directly

The journals you find directly on the Web may be published only online or may be published in print versions as well. The citation format is the same in either case: begin with an appropriate print model (pp. 476–78), but replace "Print" with Web and add your access date. Because many Web journals are unpaged, you may have to substitute n. pag. for page numbers.

62. An article in a scholarly journal (Web)

Polletta, Francesca. "Just Talk: Public Deliberation after 9/11." *Journal of Public Deliberation* 4.1 (2008): n. pag. Web. 7 Apr. 2008.

Format for a journal article on the Web

① ② ③
Polletta, Francesca. "Just Talk: Public Deliberation after 9/11." *Journal of Public*
④ ⑤ ⑥ ⑦ ⑧
Deliberation 4.1 (2008): n. pag. Web. 7 Apr. 2008.

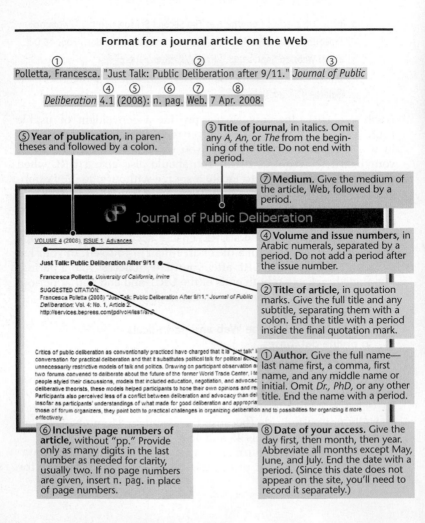

⑤ **Year of publication,** in parentheses and followed by a colon.

③ **Title of journal,** in italics. Omit any *A, An,* or *The* from the beginning of the title. Do not end with a period.

⑦ **Medium.** Give the medium of the article, Web, followed by a period.

④ **Volume and issue numbers,** in Arabic numerals, separated by a period. Do not add a period after the issue number.

② **Title of article,** in quotation marks. Give the full title and any subtitle, separating them with a colon. End the title with a period inside the final quotation mark.

① **Author.** Give the full name—last name first, a comma, first name, and any middle name or initial. Omit *Dr., PhD,* or any other title. End the name with a period.

⑥ **Inclusive page numbers of article,** without "pp." Provide only as many digits in the last number as needed for clarity, usually two. If no page numbers are given, insert n. pag. in place of page numbers.

⑧ **Date of your access.** Give the day first, then month, then year. Abbreviate all months except May, June, and July. End the date with a period. (Since this date does not appear on the site, you'll need to record it separately.)

See the facing page for an analysis of the preceding example and the location of the required information in the Web journal. (For a journal article reached in an online database, see model 64.)

Use the same format to adapt the models for print periodicals if you need to cite a Web journal review, editorial, letter to the editor, interview, article in a series, or special issue (models 14–19, pp. 478–81).

63. An abstract of a journal article (Web)

Polletta, Francesca. "Just Talk: Public Deliberation after 9/11." *Journal of Public Deliberation* 4.1 (2008): n. pag. Abstract. Web. 7 Apr. 2008.

Treat a Web abstract like a Web journal article, but add Abstract between the publication information and the medium. (You may omit this label if the journal title clearly indicates that the cited work is an abstract.) See model 65 to cite an abstract in an online database.

Web periodicals consulted in online databases

Many articles in journals, newspapers, and magazines are available in online databases that you reach through your library's Web site, such as *Academic Search Premier, ProQuest,* and *Project Muse.* Follow models 7–19 (pp. 476–81) for print periodicals, but replace "Print" with the title of the database you consulted, the medium (Web), and the date of your access.

64. An article in a scholarly journal (online database)

Gorski, Paul C. "Privilege and Repression in the Digital Era: Rethinking the Sociopolitics of the Digital Divide." *Race, Gender and Class* 10.4 (2003): 145-76. *Ethnic NewsWatch.* Web. 23 Apr. 2008.

See the next page for an analysis of this entry and the location of the required information in the database.

65. An abstract of a journal article (online database)

Gorski, Paul C. "Privilege and Repression in the Digital Era: Rethinking the Sociopolitics of the Digital Divide." *Race, Gender and Class* 10.4 (2003): 145-76. Abstract. *Ethnic NewsWatch.* Web. 23 Apr. 2008.

Treat an abstract in an online database like a journal article in a database, but add Abstract between the publication information and the database title. (You may omit this label if the journal title clearly indicates that the cited work is an abstract.)

66. An article in a newspaper (online database)

Buckman, Rebecca. "Driver Cell Phone Bans Questioned." *Wall Street Journal* 13 May 2008, eastern ed.: D2+. *ProQuest.* Web. 12 Oct. 2008.

Format for a journal article in an online database

① ②
Gorski, Paul C. "Privilege and Repression in the Digital Era: Rethinking the Socio-
③ ④ ⑤ ⑥
politics of the Digital Divide." *Race, Gender and Class* 10.4 (2003): 145-76.
⑦ ⑧ ⑨
Ethnic NewsWatch. Web. 23 Apr. 2008.

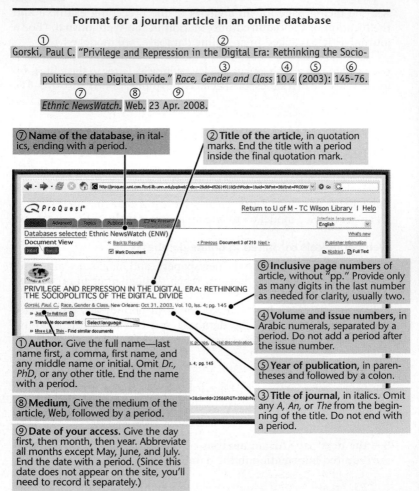

⑦ **Name of the database,** in italics, ending with a period.

② **Title of the article,** in quotation marks. End the title with a period inside the final quotation mark.

⑥ **Inclusive page numbers** of article, without "pp." Provide only as many digits in the last number as needed for clarity, usually two.

④ **Volume and issue numbers,** in Arabic numerals, separated by a period. Do not add a period after the issue number.

① **Author.** Give the full name—last name first, a comma, first name, and any middle name or initial. Omit *Dr.,* *PhD,* or any other title. End the name with a period.

⑤ **Year of publication,** in parentheses and followed by a colon.

⑧ **Medium,** Give the medium of the article, Web, followed by a period.

③ **Title of journal,** in italics. Omit any *A, An,* or *The* from the beginning of the title. Do not end with a period.

⑨ **Date of your access.** Give the day first, then month, then year. Abbreviate all months except May, June, and July. End the date with a period. (Since this date does not appear on the site, you'll need to record it separately.)

Follow model 10 or 11 (p. 478) for citing author, title of article, title of newspaper, publication date, edition (if any), and page numbers. Add the database title, the medium (Web), and your date of access.

67. An article in a magazine (online database)

Brown, Kathryn. "The Skinny on the Environment." *Scientific American* Jan.
2008: 30-37. *Academic Search Premier*. Web. 3 Aug. 2008.

Follow model 12 or 13 (p. 478) for citing author, title of article, title of magazine, publication date, and page numbers. Add the title of the database, the medium (Web), and the date of your access.

6 **Listing other electronic sources**

Publications on CD-ROM or DVD-ROM

68. A nonperiodical CD-ROM or DVD-ROM

Nunberg, Geoffrey. "Usage in the Dictionary." *The American Heritage Dictionary of the English Language.* 4th ed. Boston: Houghton, 2000. CD-ROM.

Single-issue CD-ROMs may be encyclopedias, dictionaries, books, and other resources that are published just once, like print books. Follow models 20–37 for print books (pp. 481–87), but replace "Print" with CD-ROM or DVD-ROM. If the disc has a vendor that differs from the publisher of the work, add the vendor's place of publication, name, and publication date after the medium—for instance, Philadelphia: Soquest, 2006.

See also models 28 (p. 484) and 48 (p. 493) to cite reference works in print and on the Web.

69. A periodical CD-ROM or DVD-ROM

Kolata, Gina. "Gauging Body Mass Index in a Changing Body." *New York Times* 28 June 2005, natl. ed.: D1+. CD-ROM. *New York Times Ondisc.* UMI-ProQuest. Sept. 2005.

Databases on CD-ROM or DVD-ROM are issued periodically—for instance, every six months or every year. The journals, newspapers, and other publications included in such a database are generally available in print as well, so your works-cited entry should give the information for both formats. Start with information for the print version, following models 7–19 (pp. 476–81). Then replace "Print" with the medium (CD-ROM or DVD-ROM), the database title, the vendor's name (UMI-ProQuest in the example), and the database publication date.

E-mail and discussion-group postings

70. An e-mail message

Bailey, Elizabeth. "Re: London." Message to the author. 27 Mar. 2008. E-mail.

For e-mail, give the writer's name; the title, if any, from the e-mail's subject heading, in quotation marks; Message to the author (or the name of a recipient besides you); the date of the message; and the medium, E-mail. You do not need to include the date of your access.

71. A posting to a discussion group

Williams, Frederick. "Circles as Primitive." *The Math Forum @ Drexel.* Drexel U, 28 Feb. 2008. E-mail.

Cite a posting to a discussion group like a blog entry (model 54, p. 495). This example for a discussion-list posting includes author's name, title of the posting, title of the list, name of the sponsor, date of the posting, and medium (E-mail). If the posting is untitled, give Online posting instead. You need not add the date of your access.

Digital files

You may want to cite a digital file that is not on the Web or on a disc, such as a PDF document, a JPEG image, or an MP3 sound recording that you downloaded onto your computer. Use the appropriate model for your kind of source (for instance, model 79 for a personal photograph), but replace the medium with the file format you're using. If you don't know the file format, use Digital file.

72. A text file (digital)

Berg, John K. "Estimates of Persons Driving While Intoxicated." *Law Enforcement Today* 17 Apr. 2008. PDF file.

Fernandez, Carlos. "Summers in Spain." 2008. *Microsoft Word* file.

73. A media file (digital)

Springsteen, Bruce. "Empty Sky." *The Rising*. Columbia, 2002. MP3 file.

Boys playing basketball. Personal photograph by Granger Goetz. 2008. JPEG file.

7 | Listing other sources

The source types covered in this section are not on a computer or, generally, in printed sources. Most of them have parallel citation formats elsewhere in this chapter when you reach them through electronic and print media. See model 17 (p. 480) to cite an interview in print. See models 49–52 (pp. 493–95) to cite images, television and radio programs, video recordings, and sound recordings that are available only on the Web. See models 58–60 (pp. 496–97) to cite such sources when they are available on the Web and in other media. And see model 73 to cite such sources in digital files.

74. A television or radio program

"Piece of My Heart." By Stacy McKee. Dir. Mark Tinker. *Grey's Anatomy*. ABC. KGO, San Francisco, 1 May 2008. Television.

Start with the title unless you are citing the work of a person or persons. The example here cites an episode title (in quotation marks) and the names of the episode's writer and director. By and Dir. identify their roles. Then the entry gives the program title (in italics), the name of the network, the call letters and city of the local station, the date, and the medium (Television). If you list individuals who worked on the entire program, put their names after the program title.

75. A personal or broadcast interview

Paul, William. Personal interview. 6 June 2008.

Diaz, Junot. Interview by Terry Gross. *Fresh Air*. National Public Radio, WGBH, Boston, 18 Oct. 2007. Radio.

Begin with the name of the person interviewed. For an interview you conducted, specify Personal interview or the medium (such as Telephone interview or E-mail interview), and then give the date. For an interview you heard or saw, provide the title if any or Interview if there is no title. Add the name of the interviewer if he or she is identified. Then follow an appropriate model for the kind of source (here, a radio program), and end with the medium (here, Radio).

76. A sound recording

Rubenstein, Artur, perf. Piano Concerto no. 2 in B-flat. By Johannes Brahms. Cond. Eugene Ormandy. Philadelphia Orch. RCA, 1972. LP.

Springsteen, Bruce. "Empty Sky." *The Rising*. Columbia, 2002. CD.

Begin with the name of the individual whose work you are citing. Unless this person is the composer, identify his or her role, as with perf. ("performer") in the first example. If you're citing a work identified by form, number, and key (first example), do not use quotation marks or italics for the title. If you're citing a song or song lyrics (second example), give the title in quotation marks; then provide the title of the recording in italics. Following the title, identify the composer or author if you haven't already, after By, and name and identify other participants you want to mention. Then provide the manufacturer of the recording, the date of release, and the medium: LP in the first example, CD in the second.

77. A film, DVD, or video recording

A Beautiful Mind. Dir. Ron Howard. Universal, 2001. Film.

Start with the title of the work unless you are citing the work of a person (see the next example). Generally, identify and name the director. You may list other participants (writer, lead performers, and so on) as you judge appropriate. For a film, end with the distributor, date, and medium (Film).

For a DVD or videocassette, include the original release date (if any), the distributor's name, and the medium (DVD or Videocassette).

Balanchine, George, chor. *Serenade*. Perf. San Francisco Ballet. Dir. Hilary Bean. 1991. PBS Video, 2006. DVD.

78. A painting, photograph, or other work of visual art

Arnold, Leslie. *Seated Woman*. N.d. Oil on canvas. DeYoung Museum, San Francisco.

Sugimoto, Hiroshi. *Pacific Ocean, Mount Tamalpais*. 1994. Photograph.
Private collection.

To cite an actual work of art, name the artist and give the title (in italics) and the date of creation (or N.d. if the date is unknown). Then provide the medium of the work (such as Oil on canvas or Photograph) and the name and location of the owner, if known. (Use Private collection if not.)

For a work you see only in a reproduction, provide the complete publication information for the source you used. Omit the medium of the work itself, and replace it with the medium of the reproduction (Print in the following example). Omit such information only if you examined the actual work.

Hockney, David. *Place Furstenberg, Paris*. 1985. Coll. Art Gallery, New Paltz.
David Hockney: A Retrospective. Ed. Maurice Tuchman and Stephanie
Barron. Los Angeles: Los Angeles County Museum of Art, 1988. 247. Print.

79. A personal photograph

Common milkweed on Lake Michigan shoreline. Personal photograph by the
author. 22 Aug. 2008.

For a personal photograph by you or by someone else, describe the subject (without quotation marks or italics), say who took the photograph, and add the date.

80. A map, chart, graph, or diagram

"The Sonoran Desert." Map. *Sonoran Desert: An American Deserts Handbook*. By
Rose Houk. Tucson: Western Natl. Parks Assn., 2000. 12. Print.

Unless the creator of an illustration is given on the source, list the illustration by its title. Put the title in quotation marks if it comes from another publication or in italics if it is published independently. Then add a description (Map, Chart, and so on), the publication information, and the medium (here, Print).

81. A cartoon or comic strip

Trudeau, Garry. "Doonesbury." Comic strip. *San Francisco Chronicle* 28 Aug.
2008: E6. Print.

Cite a cartoon or comic strip with the artist's name, the title (in quotation marks), the description Cartoon or Comic strip, the publication information, and the medium (here, Print).

82. An advertisement

Escape Hybrid by Ford. Advertisement. *New Yorker* 10 Dec. 2007: 11. Print.

Cite an advertisement with the name of the product or company advertised, the description Advertisement, the publication information, and the medium (Print, Television, Radio, and so on).

83. A performance

Levine, James, cond. Boston Symphony Orch. Symphony Hall, Boston. 2 May
2008. Performance.

The New Century. By Paul Rudnick. Dir. Nicholas Martin. Mitzi E. Newhouse
Theater, New York. 6 May 2008. Performance.

For a live performance, generally base your citation on film citations (model 77). Place the title first (second example) unless you are citing the work of an individual (first example). After the title, provide relevant information about participants as well as the theater, city, and performance date. Conclude with the medium (Performance).

84. A lecture, speech, address, or reading

Katrib, Ruba. "New Art: South Florida Exhibit." Museum of Contemporary Art.
MOCA at Goldman Warehouse, Miami. 4 Sept. 2007. Address.

Give the speaker's name, the title if any (in quotation marks), the title of the meeting if any, the name of the sponsoring organization, the location of the presentation, and the date. End with a description of the type of presentation (Lecture, Speech, Address, Reading).

Although the MLA does not provide a specific style for citing classroom lectures in your courses, you can adapt the preceding format for this purpose.

Cavanaugh, Carol. Class lecture on teaching mentors. Lesley U. 4 Apr. 2008.
Lecture.

Exercise 58.1 Writing works-cited entries

Prepare works-cited entries from the following information. Follow the MLA models given in this chapter unless your instructor specifies a different style. Arrange the finished entries in alphabetical order, not numbered.

1 An article titled "Use of Third Parties to Collect State and Local Taxes on Internet Sales," appearing in the print periodical *The Pacific Business Journal,* volume 5, issue 2, in 2004. The authors are Malai Zimmerman and Kent Hoover. The article appears on pages 45 through 48 of the journal.

2 A government publication you consulted on November 12, 2008, on the Web. The author is the Advisory Commission on Electronic

Commerce. The commission is an agency of the United States government. The title of the publication is *Report to Congress.* It was published in April 2005.

3 A Web article with no listed author. The title and sponsor of the Web site is Center on Budget and Policy Priorities. The title of the article is "The Internet Tax Freedom Act and the Digital Divide," and the site is dated September 26, 2007. You consulted the site on November 2, 2008.

4 An article in the magazine *Forbes,* published November 28, 2007, on pages 56 through 58. The author is Janet Novack. The title is "Point, Click, Pay Tax." You accessed the source through the *ProQuest* database on November 10, 2008.

5 A print book titled *All's Fair in Internet Commerce, or Is It?* by Sally G. Osborne. The book was published in 2004 by Random House in New York.

6 An e-mail interview you conducted with Nora James on November 1, 2008.

7 An article titled "State and Local Sales/Use Tax Simplification," appearing on pages 67 through 80 of a print anthology, *The Sales Tax in the Twenty-first Century.* The anthology is edited by Matthew N. Murray and William F. Fox. The article is by Wayne G. Eggert. The anthology was published in 2004 by Praeger in Westport, Connecticut.

58c Formatting a paper in MLA style

The MLA's manual for students, the *MLA Handbook,* provides guidelines for a fairly simple document format, with just a few elements. For guidelines on type fonts, headings, lists, illustrations, and other features that MLA style does not specify, see **1** pp. 55–61.

The samples below and on the next page show the formats for the first page and a later page of a paper. For the format of the list of works cited, see p. 473.

First page of MLA paper

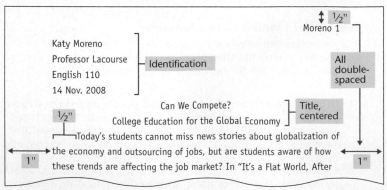

Later page of MLA paper

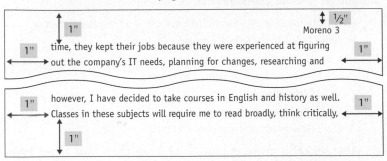

Margins Use minimum one-inch margins on all sides of every page.

Spacing and indentions Double-space throughout. Indent paragraphs one-half inch. (See below for indention of poetry and long prose quotations.)

Paging Begin numbering on the first page, and number consecutively through the end (including the list of works cited). Use Arabic numerals (1, 2, 3) positioned in the upper right, about one-half inch from the top. Place your last name before the page number in case the pages later become separated.

Identification and title MLA style does not require a title page for a paper. Instead, give your name, your instructor's name, the course title, and the date on separate lines in the upper left of the first page—one inch from the top of the paper. (See the sample on the facing page.) Double-space between all lines of this identification.

Double-space again, and center the title. Do not highlight the title with italics, underlining, boldface, larger type, or quotation marks. Capitalize the words in the title according to the guidelines in **6** p. 358. Double-space the lines of the title and between the title and the text.

Poetry and long prose quotations Treat a single line of poetry like any other quotation, running it into your text and enclosing it in quotation marks. You may run in two or three lines of poetry as well, separating the lines with a slash surrounded by space.

> An example of Robert Frost's incisiveness is in two lines from "Death of the Hired Man": "Home is the place where, when you have to go there / They have to take you in" (119-20).

Always set off from your text a poetry quotation of more than three lines. Use double spacing above and below the quotation and for the quotation itself. Indent the quotation one inch from the left margin. *Do not add quotation marks.*

> Emily Dickinson stripped ideas to their essence, as in this description of "A narrow Fellow in the Grass," a snake:
>
> > I more than once at Noon
> > Have passed, I thought, a Whip lash
> > Unbraiding in the Sun
> > When stopping to secure it
> > It wrinkled, and was gone — (12-16)

Also set off a prose quotation of more than four typed lines. (See **7** pp. 416–17 on when to use such long quotations.) Double-space and indent as with the preceding poetry example. *Do not add quotation marks.*

> In the influential *Talley's Corner* from 1967, Elliot Liebow observes that "unskilled" construction work requires more skill than is generally assumed:
>
> > A healthy, sturdy, active man of good intelligence requires from two to four weeks to break in on a construction job. . . . It frequently happens that his foreman or the craftsman he services is not willing to wait that long for him to get into condition or to learn at a glance the difference in size between a rough 2 x 8 and a finished 2 x 10. (62)

Do not use a paragraph indention for a quotation of a single complete paragraph or a part of a paragraph. Use paragraph indentions of one-quarter inch only for a quotation of two or more complete paragraphs.

58d | Examining a sample paper in MLA style

The sample paper beginning on p. 510 follows MLA guidelines for overall format, parenthetical citations, and the list of works cited. Marginal annotations highlight features of the paper.

Note Because the sample paper addresses a current topic, many of its sources come from the Internet and do not use page or other reference numbers. Thus the in-text citations of these sources do not give reference numbers. In a paper relying solely on printed journals, books, and other traditional sources, most if not all in-text citations would include page numbers.

A note on outlines

Some instructors ask students to submit an outline of the final paper. For advice on constructing a formal or topic outline, see **1** pp. 20–21. Below is an outline of the sample paper following, written in complete sentences. Note that the thesis statement precedes either a topic or a sentence outline.

Thesis statement: Although green consumerism can help the environment, consumerism itself is the root of some of the most pressing ecological problems we face. To make a real difference, we must consume less.

I. Green products claiming to help the environment both appeal to and confuse consumers.
   A. The market for ecologically sound products is enormous.
   B. Determining whether or not a product is as green as advertised can be a challenge.

II. Green products don't solve the high rate of consumption that truly threatens the environment.
   A. Overconsumption is a significant cause of three of the most serious environmental problems.
      1. It depletes natural resources.
      2. It contributes to pollution, particularly from the greenhouse gases responsible for global warming.
      3. It produces a huge amount of solid waste.
   B. The availability of greener products has not reduced the environmental effects of consumption.

III. Since buying green products does not reduce consumption, other solutions must be found for environmental problems.
   A. Experts have proposed many far-reaching solutions, but they require concerted government action and could take decades to implement.
   B. For shorter-term solutions, individuals can change their own behavior as consumers.
      1. Precycling may be the greenest behavior that individuals can adopt.
         a. Precycling means avoiding purchase of products that use raw materials and excessive packaging.
         b. More important, precycling means avoiding purchases of new products whenever possible.
      2. For unavoidable purchases, individuals can buy green products and influence businesses to embrace ecological goals.

Justin Malik

Ms. Rossi

English 112-02

18 Mar. 2008

The False Promise of Green Consumerism

They line the aisles of just about any store. They seem
to dominate television and print advertising. Chances are that
at least a few of them belong to you. From organic jeans to
household cleaners to hybrid cars, products advertised as environmentally friendly are readily available and are so popular
they're trendy. It's easy to see why Americans are buying these
things in record numbers. The new wave of "green" consumer
goods makes an almost irresistible promise: we can save the
planet by shopping.

Saving the planet does seem to be urgent. Thanks partly
to former Vice President Al Gore, who sounded the alarm in
1992 with *Earth in the Balance* and again in 2006 with *An Inconvenient Truth,* the threat of global warming has become a
regular feature in the news media and a recurring theme in
popular culture. Unfortunately, as Gore himself points out,
climate change is just one of many environmental problems
competing for our attention: the rainforests are vanishing, our
air and our water are dangerously polluted, an alarming number of species are facing extinction, and landfills are overflowing (*Earth* 23-28). All the bad news can be overwhelming,
and most people feel powerless to halt the damage. Thus it
is reassuring that we may be able to help by making small
changes in what we buy—but it is not entirely true. Although green consumerism can help the environment, consumerism itself is the root of some of the most pressing ecological problems we face. To make a real difference, we must
consume less.

The market for items perceived as ecologically sound is
enormous. Experts estimate that spending on green products already approaches $200 billion a year (Adler et al.). Shoppers re-
spond well to new options, whether the purchase is as minor
as a bottle of chemical-free dish soap or as major as a front-
loading washing machine. Not surprisingly, businesses are

Annotations (left margin):

Identification: writer's name, instructor's name, course title, date.

Title centered.

Double-space throughout.

Introduction: establishes the issue with examples (first paragraph) and back-ground (second paragraph).

Citation form: no paren-thetical citation because author and titles are named in the text and discussion cites entire works.

Citation form: shortened title for one of two works by the same author.

Thesis statement.

Background on green prod-ucts (next two paragraphs).

Citation form: source with more than three authors; no page number because source from an online data-base is unnumbered.

Malik 2

responding by offering as many new eco-products as they can. Sandra Jones of the *Chicago Tribune* reports that "green product introductions [have] skyrocketed" lately. She cites a market research report by the Mintel International Group: in the first five years of this century, new household products labeled as green rose from zero to 153, eco-conscious health and beauty aids increased by more than a thousand percent, and organic food and beverage options nearly tripled (B1). These new products are offered for sale at stores like Wal-Mart, Target, Home Depot, Starbucks, and Pottery Barn. It seems clear that green consumerism has grown into a mainstream interest.

Determining whether or not a product is as green as advertised can be a challenge. Claims vary: a product might be labeled as organic, biodegradable, energy efficient, recycled, carbon neutral, renewable, or just about anything that sounds environmentally positive. However, none of these terms carries a universally accepted meaning, and no enforceable labeling regulations exist ("It's Not Easy"). Some of the new product options offer clear environmental benefits: for instance, compact fluorescent light bulbs last ten times as long as regular bulbs and draw about a third of the electricity (Gore, *Inconvenient* 306), and paper made from recycled fibers saves many trees. But other "green" products just as clearly do little or nothing to help the environment: a disposable razor made with less plastic is still a disposable razor, destined for a landfill after only a few uses.

Distinguishing truly green products from those that are not so green merely scratches the surface of a much larger issue. The products aren't the problem; it's our high rate of consumption that poses the real threat to the environment. We seek what's newer and better—whether cars, clothes, phones, computers, televisions, shoes, or gadgets—and they all require resources to make, ship, and use them. Political scientists Thomas Princen, Michael Maniates, and Ken Conca maintain that overconsumption is a leading force behind several ecological crises, warning that

> ever-increasing pressures on ecosystems, life-
> supporting environmental services, and critical

Brackets signal word added to clarify the quotation.

Source author named in text, so not named in parenthetical citation.

Common-knowledge examples of stores and products do not require source citations.

Citation form: shortened title for anonymous source; page number for a one-page source not required.

Citation form: author not named in the text; shortened title for one of two works by the same author. Position of citation clarifies which example comes from the source.

Environmental effects of consumption (next four paragraphs). Writer synthesizes information from half a dozen sources to develop his own ideas.

Quotation over four lines set off without quotation marks. See pp. 507–08.

Malik 3

natural cycles are driven not only by the sheer number of resource users . . . but also by the patterns of resource use themselves. (4)

Those patterns of resource use are disturbing. In just the second half of the twentieth century, gross world product (the global output of consumer goods) grew at five times the rate of population growth—a difference explained by a huge rise in consumption per person. (See fig. 1.) Such growth might be good for the economy, but it is bad for the environment. As fig. 1 shows, it is accompanied by the depletion of natural resources, increases in the carbon emissions that cause global warming, and increases in the amount of solid waste disposal.

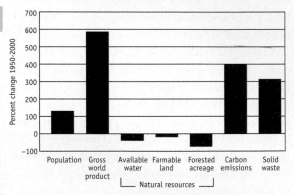

Fig. 1. Global population, consumption, and environmental impacts, 1950-2000. Data from United Nations Development Programme; *Human Development Report: Changing Today's Consumption Patterns—For Tomorrow's Human Development*; New York: Oxford UP; 1998, 4; print; and from Earth Policy Inst.; "Eco-Economy Indicators"; *Earth Policy Institute*; EPI, Feb. 2008; Web; 6 Mar. 2008.

The first negative effect of overconsumption, the depletion of resources, occurs because the manufacture and distribution of any consumer product depends on the use of water, land, and raw materials such as wood, metal, and oil. Paul Hawken, a respected environmentalist, explains that just in the United States "[i]ndustry moves, mines, extracts, shovels, burns, wastes, pumps, and disposes of *4 million pounds of*

Malik 4

material in order to provide one average . . . family's needs for a year" (qtd. in DeGraaf, Wann, and Naylor 85; emphasis added). The United Nations Development Programme's 1998 *Human Development Report* (still the most comprehensive study of the environmental impacts of consumerism) warns that many regions in the world don't have enough water, productive soil, or forests to meet the basic needs of their populations (4). More recent data from the Earth Policy Institute show that as manufacturing and per-person consumption continue to rise, the supply of resources needed for survival continues to decline. Thus heavy consumption poses a threat not only to the environment but also to the well-being of the human race.

In addition to using up scarce natural resources, manufacturing and distributing products harms the earth by spewing pollution into the water, soil, and air. The most worrisome aspect of that pollution may be its link to global warming. As Al Gore explains, the energy needed to power manufacturing and distribution comes primarily from burning fossil fuels, a process that releases carbon dioxide and other greenhouse gases into the air. Those gases build up and trap heat in the earth's atmosphere. The result, most scientists now believe, is increasing global temperatures that will raise sea levels, expand deserts, and cause more frequent floods and hurricanes (*Inconvenient* 26-27, 81, 118-19, 184). As the preceding bar chart shows, carbon emissions, like production of consumer goods in general, are rising at rates out of proportion with population growth. The more we consume, the more we contribute to global warming.

As harmful as they are, gradual global warming and the depletion of resources half a world away can be difficult to comprehend or appreciate. A more immediate environmental effect of our buying habits can be seen in the volumes of trash those habits create. The US Environmental Protection Agency found that in a single year (2006), US residents, corporations, and institutions produced 251 million tons of municipal solid waste, amounting to "4.6 pounds per person per day" (1-2). Nearly a third of that trash came just from the

Citation form: source with three authors; "qtd. in" indicates indirect source (Hawken quoted by DeGraaf, Wann, and Naylor); "emphasis added" indicates italics were not in original quotation.

Citation form: corporate author is named in the text, so page number only.

Citation form: no parenthetical citation because author is named in the text and online source has no page or other reference numbers.

Summary reduces six pages in the source to three sentences. Signal phrase and parenthetical citation mark boundaries of the summary.

Citation form: shortened title for one of two works by the same author; page numbers indicate exact locations of information in source.

Writer's own conclusion from preceding data.

Citation form: author (a US government body) named in text.

Malik 5

wrappers, cans, bottles, and boxes used for shipping consumer goods. Yet the mountains of trash left over from consumption are only a part of the problem. In industrial countries overall, 90 percent of waste comes not from what gets thrown out, but from the manufacturing processes of converting natural resources into consumer products (DeGraaf, Wann, and Naylor 192). Nearly everything we buy creates waste in production, comes in packaging that gets discarded immediately, and ultimately ends up in landfills that are already overflowing.

Unfortunately, the growing popularity of green products has not reduced the environmental effects of consumption. A study conducted by economists Jeff Rubin and Benjamin Tal for the research firm CIBC World Markets found that while eco-friendly and energy-efficient products have become more available, "consumption is growing by ever-increasing amounts." The authors give the example of automobiles: in the last generation, cars have become much more energy efficient, but the average American now drives 2500 more miles a year, for a net gain in energy use (4-5). At the same time, per-person waste production in the United States has risen by more than 20 percent (United States 1). Greener products may reduce our cost of consumption and even reduce our guilt about consumption, but they do not reduce consumption and its effects.

If buying green won't solve the problems caused by overconsumption, what will? Politicians, environmentalists, and economists have proposed an array of far-reaching ideas, including creating a financial market for carbon credits and offsets, aggressively taxing consumption and pollution, offering financial incentives for environmentally positive behaviors, and even abandoning market capitalism altogether (Muldoon). However, all of these are "top-down" solutions that require concerted government action. Gaining support for any one of them, putting it into practice, and getting results could take decades. In the meantime, the environment would continue to deteriorate. Clearly, short-term solutions are also essential.

Citation form: source with three authors; authors not named in text.

Environmental effects of green consumption.

Citation form: authors are named in the text, so page numbers only.

Citation form: US government source not named in text.

Writer's own conclusion from preceding data.

Solutions to problem of consumption (next three paragraphs).

Citation form: author's name only, because scholarly article on the Web has no page or other reference numbers.

Malik 6

The most promising short-term solution is for individuals
to change their own behavior as consumers. The greenest behavior that individuals can adopt may be precycling, the term
widely used for avoiding purchases of products that involve the
use of raw materials. Precycling includes choosing eco-friendly
products made of recycled or nontoxic materials (such as
aluminum-free deodorants and fleece made from soda bottles)
and avoiding items wrapped in excessive packaging (such as
kitchen tools strapped to cardboard and printer cartridges
sealed in plastic clamshells). More important, though, precycling means not buying new things in the first place. Renting
and borrowing, when possible, save money and resources; so
do keeping possessions in good repair and not replacing them
until absolutely necessary. Good-quality used items, from
clothing to furniture to electronics, can be obtained for free,
or very cheaply, through online communities like *Craigslist* and
Freecycle, from thrift stores and yard sales, or by trading with
friends and relatives. When consumers choose used goods over
new, they can help to reduce demand for manufactured products that waste energy and resources, and they can help to
keep unwanted items out of the waste stream.

> Common-knowledge definition and writer's own examples do not require source citations.

Avoiding unnecessary purchases brings personal benefits
as well. Brenda Lin, an environmental activist, explained in an
e-mail interview that frugal living not only saves money but
also provides pleasure:

> Primary source: personal interview by e-mail.

> You'd be amazed at what people throw out or give
> away: perfectly good computers, oriental rugs,
> barely used sports equipment, designer clothes,
> you name it. . . . It's a game for me to find what
> I need in other people's trash or at Goodwill. You
> should see the shock on people's faces when I
> tell them where I got my stuff. I get almost as
> much enjoyment from that as from saving money
> and helping the environment at the same time.

> Quotation of over four lines set off without quotation marks. See pp. 507–08.

> Ellipsis mark signals omission from quotation.

Lin's experience relates to a study of the personal and social
consequences of consumerism by the sociologist Juliet B.
Schor. Schor found that the more people buy, the less happy
they tend to feel because of the stress of working longer

> Citation form: no paren-thetical citation because author is named in the text and interview has no page or other reference numbers.

hours to afford their purchases (11-12). Researching the opposite effect, Schor conducted interviews with hundreds of Americans who had drastically reduced their spending so that they would be less dependent on paid work. For these people, she discovered, a deliberately lower standard of living improved quality of life by leaving more time to spend with family and pursue personal interests (136-42). Reducing consumption, it turns out, does not have to translate into sacrifice.

For unavoidable purchases like food and light bulbs, buying green can make a difference by influencing corporate decisions. Some ecologists and economists believe that as more shoppers choose earth-friendly products over their traditional counterparts—or boycott products that are clearly harmful to the environment—more manufacturers and retailers will look for ways to limit the environmental effects of their industrial practices and the goods they sell (Gore, *Earth* 193; Muldoon). Indeed, as environmental business consultant Gregory C. Unruh points out in an article for *Harvard Business Review*, several major companies, among them Wal-Mart, Coca-Cola, General Electric, and Nike, have already taken up sustainability initiatives in response to market pressure. In the process, the companies have discovered that environmentally minded practices tend to raise profits and strengthen customer loyalty (111-12). By giving industry solid, bottom-line reasons to embrace ecological goals, consumer demand for earth-friendly products can magnify the effects of individual action.

Careful shopping can help the environment, but green doesn't necessarily mean "Go." All consumption depletes resources, increases the likelihood of global warming, and creates waste, so even eco-friendly products must be used in moderation. As individuals, we can each play a small role in helping the environment—and help ourselves at the same time—by not buying anything we don't really need, even if it seems environmentally sound. Reducing our personal impact on the earth is a small price to pay for preserving a livable planet for future generations.

Writer's own conclusion from two sources.

Benefits of green consumerism.

Citation form: two works in the same citation.

Citation form: author is named in the text, so page numbers only.

Conclusion: summary and a call for action.

Works Cited

Adler, Jerry, et al. "The Greening of America." *Newsweek* 14 Aug. 2006: 46-50. *Master File Premier*. Web. 20 Feb. 2008.

DeGraaf, John, David Wann, and Thomas H. Naylor. *Affluenza: The All-Consuming Epidemic*. San Francisco: Berrett-Koehler, 2001. Print.

Earth Policy Inst. "Eco-Economy Indicators." *Earth Policy Institute*. EPI, Feb. 2008. Web. 6 Mar. 2008.

Gore, Al. *Earth in the Balance: Ecology and the Human Spirit*. Boston: Houghton, 1992. Print.

---. *An Inconvenient Truth: The Planetary Emergency of Global Warming and What We Can Do about It*. Emmaus: Rodale, 2006. Print.

"It's Not Easy Buying Green." *Consumer Reports* Sept. 2007: 9. Print.

Jones, Sandra. "Green! It's Easy Being Green When It's in Vogue." *Chicago Tribune* 27 May 2007, final ed.: B1+. Print.

Lin, Brenda. Message to the author. 7 Mar. 2008. E-mail.

Muldoon, Annie. "Where the Green Is: Examining the Paradox of Environmentally Conscious Consumption." *Electronic Green Journal* 23 (2006): n. pag. Web. 28 Feb. 2008.

Princen, Thomas, Michael Maniates, and Ken Conca. Introduction. *Confronting Consumption*. Ed. Princen, Maniates, and Conca. Cambridge: MIT P, 2002. 1-20. Print.

Rubin, Jeff, and Benjamin Tal. "Does Energy Efficiency Save Energy?" *StrategEcon*. CIBC World Markets, 27 Nov. 2007. Web. 13 Mar. 2008.

Schor, Juliet B. *The Overspent American: Upscaling, Downshifting, and the New Consumer*. New York: Basic, 1998. Print.

United Nations Development Programme. *Human Development Report 1998: Changing Today's Consumption Patterns— For Tomorrow's Human Development*. New York: Oxford UP, 1998. Print.

United States. Environmental Protection Agency. Solid Waste and Emergency Response. *Municipal Solid Waste*

New page, double-spaced. Sources alphabetized by authors' last names.

An article with more than three authors, from a weekly magazine in an online database.

A print book with three authors.

A short, titled work on a Web site, with a corporate author.

A print book with one author.

Second source by author of two or more cited works: three hyphens replace author's name.

An anonymous article in a print monthly magazine, listed and alphabetized by title.

A print newspaper article.

A personal interview by e-mail.

An article in a Web scholarly journal that numbers only issues and does not use page numbers.

An introduction to a print anthology.

A short, titled work on a Web site, by two authors.

A print book with one author.

A print book with a corporate author.

A US government source with no named author, so government body given as author.

Generation, Recycling, and Disposal in the United States: Facts and Figures for 2006. US Environmental Protection Agency, Nov. 2007. Web. 4 Feb. 2008.

An article in a scholarly journal that numbers volumes and issues, consulted in an online database.

Unruh, Gregory C. "The Biosphere Rules." *Harvard Business Review* 86.2 (2008): 111-17. *Business Source Premier*. Web. 14 Mar. 2008.

APA Documentation
and Format

APA Documentation and Format

APA parenthetical text citations

APA references

59   APA Documentation and Format

The style guides for psychology and some other social sciences are the *Publication Manual of the American Psychological Association* (5th ed., 2001) and the *APA Style Guide to Electronic References* (2007). In APA documentation style, you acknowledge each of your sources twice:

- In your text, a brief parenthetical citation adjacent to the borrowed material directs readers to a complete list of all the works you refer to.
- At the end of your paper, the list of references includes complete bibliographical information for every source.

Every entry in the list of references has at least one corresponding citation in the text, and every in-text citation has a corresponding entry in the list of references.

This chapter describes APA text citations (next page) and references (p. 525), details APA document format (p. 539), and concludes with a sample APA paper (p. 542).

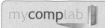

mycomplab

Visit *mycomplab.com* for more resources as well as exercises on APA documentation and format.

59a Writing APA parenthetical text citations

In APA documentation style, parenthetical citations within the text refer the reader to a list of sources at the end of the text. See the **APA** divider for an index to the models for various kinds of sources.

1. Author not named in your text

One critic of Milgram's experiments insisted that the subjects "should have been fully informed of the possible effects on them" (Baumrind, 1988, p. 34).

When you do not name the author in your text, place in parentheses the author's last name and the date of the source. Separate the elements with commas. Position the reference so that it is clear what material is being documented *and* so that the reference fits as smoothly as possible into your sentence structure. (See **MLA** pp. 470–72 for guidelines.) The following would also be correct:

In the view of one critic of Milgram's experiments (Baumrind, 1988), the sub-jects "should have been fully informed of the possible effects on them" (p. 34).

Unless none is available, the APA requires a page or other identifying number for a direct quotation (as in the examples above) and recommends an identifying number for a paraphrase. Use an appropriate abbreviation or symbol before the number—for instance, p. for *page* and ¶ for *paragraph* (or para. if you do not have the symbol). The identifying number may fall with the author and date (first example) or by itself in a separate pair of parentheses (second example). See also model 11, p. 524.

2. Author named in your text

Baumrind (1988) insisted that the subjects in Milgram's study "should have been fully informed of the possible effects on them" (p. 34).

When you use the author's name in the text, do not repeat it in the reference. Place the source date in parentheses after the author's name. Place any page or paragraph reference either after the bor-rowed material (as in the example) or with the date: (1988, p. 34). If you cite the same source again in the paragraph, you need not re-peat the reference as long as it is clear that you are using the same source and the page number (if any) is the same.

3. A work with two authors

Pepinsky and DeStefano (1997) demonstrated that a teacher's language often reveals hidden biases.

One study (Pepinsky & DeStefano, 1997) demonstrated the hidden biases often revealed in a teacher's language.

When given in the text, two authors' names are connected by and. In a parenthetical citation, they are connected by an ampersand, &.

4. A work with three to five authors

Pepinsky, Dunn, Rentl, and Corson (1999) further demonstrated the biases evident in gestures.

In the first citation of a work with three to five authors, name all the authors. In the second and subsequent references to a work with three to five authors, generally give only the first author's name, followed by et al. (Latin abbreviation for "and others"):

In the work of Pepinsky et al. (1999), the loaded gestures included head shakes and eye contact.

However, two or more sources published in the same year could shorten to the same form—for instance, two references shortening to Pepinsky et al., 1999. In that case, cite the last names of as many authors as you need to distinguish the sources, and then give et al.: for instance, (Pepinsky, Dunn, et al., 1999) and (Pepinsky, Bradley, et al., 1999).

5. A work with six or more authors

One study (Rutter et al., 2003) attempted to explain these geographical differences in adolescent experience.

For six or more authors, even in the first citation of the work, give only the first author's name, followed by et al. If two or more sources published in the same year shorten to the same form, give additional names as explained with model 4.

6. A work with a group author

The group's later work improved significantly (Lenschow Research, 2008).

For a work that lists an institution, agency, corporation, or other group as author, treat the name of the group as if it were one person's name. If the name is long and has a familiar abbreviation, you may use the abbreviation in the second and subsequent citations. For example, you might abbreviate American Psychological Association as APA.

7. A work with no author or an anonymous work

One article ("Right to Die," 1996) noted that a death-row inmate may crave notoriety.

For a work with no named author, use the first two or three words of the title in place of an author's name, excluding an initial *The, A,* or *An.* Italicize book and journal titles, place quotation marks around article titles, and capitalize the significant words in all titles cited in the text. (In the reference list, however, do not use quotation marks for article titles, and capitalize only the first word in all but periodical titles. See p. 526.)

For a work that lists "Anonymous" as the author, use that word in the citation: (Anonymous, 2007).

8. One of two or more works by the same author(s)

At about age seven, most children begin to use appropriate gestures to reinforce their stories (Gardner, 1973a).

When you cite one of two or more works by the same author(s), the date will tell readers which source you mean—as long as your reference list includes only one source published by the author(s) in that year. If your reference list includes two or more works published by the same author(s) *in the same year,* the works should be lettered in the reference list (see p. 528). Then your parenthetical citation should include the appropriate letter with the date: 1973a in the example.

9. Two or more works by different authors

Two studies (Marconi & Hamblen, 1999; Torrence, 2007) found that monthly safety meetings can dramatically reduce workplace injuries.

List the sources in alphabetical order by their authors' names. Insert a semicolon between sources.

10. An indirect source

Supporting data appeared in a study by Chang (cited in Torrence, 2007).

The phrase cited in indicates that the reference to Chang's study was found in Torrence. Only Torrence then appears in the list of references.

11. An electronic source

Ferguson and Hawkins (2006) did not anticipate the "evident hostility" of participants (¶ 6).

Electronic sources can be cited like printed sources, usually with the author's last name and the publication date. When quoting or paraphrasing electronic sources that number paragraphs instead of pages, provide the paragraph number preceded by the symbol ¶ if you have it, or by para. Even if the source does not number its paragraphs, you can still direct readers to a specific location by listing the heading under which the quotation appears and then (counting paragraphs yourself) the number of the paragraph in which the quotation appears—for example, (Endter & Decker, 2008, Method section, ¶ 3). When the source does not number pages or paragraphs or provide frequent headings, omit any reference number.

59b Preparing the APA reference list

In APA style, the in-text parenthetical citations refer to the list of sources at the end of the text. This list, titled References, includes full publication information on every source cited in the paper. The list falls at the end of the paper, numbered in sequence with the preceding pages. The sample below shows the elements and their spacing.

APA reference list

Shortened title and page number (see pp. 539–40) → Dating Violence 8 ↕ ½"

References ← Center

½" or 5–7 spaces   Cates, R. L., Rutter, C. H., Karl, J., Linton, M., & Smith, K. (2000). Premarital abuse: A social psychological perspective. *Journal of Family Issues, 13*(1), 79-90.

1½"   Cortes, L. (2005). Beyond date rape: Violence during courtship. *Electronic Journal of Intimate Violence, 5*(2). Retrieved from http://www.acast.nova.edu/health/psy/file-disc /file50.html

Glaser, R., & Rutter, C. H. (Eds.). (1999). Familial violence [Special issue]. *Family Relations, 43*(4).

Double-space   1"

Arrangement Arrange sources alphabetically by the author's last name. If there is no author, alphabetize by the first main word of the title. Do *not* group sources by type (books, journals, and so on).

Spacing Double-space everything in the references, as shown in the sample, unless your instructor requests single spacing. (If you do single-space the entries themselves, always double-space *between* them.)

Indention As illustrated in the sample above, begin each entry at the left margin, and indent the second and subsequent lines five to seven spaces or one-half inch.

Punctuation Separate the parts of the reference (author, date, title, and publication information) with a period and one space. Do not use a final period in references to electronic sources when they conclude with a DOI or a URL (see p. 532).

Authors For works with up to six authors, list all authors with last name first, separating names and parts of names with commas. Use initials for first and middle names. Use an ampersand (&) before the last author's name. See model 3 (opposite) for the treatment of seven or more authors.

Publication date Place the publication date in parentheses after the author's or authors' names, followed by a period. Generally this date is the year only, though for some sources (such as magazine and newspaper articles) it includes month and sometimes day as well.

Titles In titles of books and articles, capitalize only the first word of the title, the first word of the subtitle, and proper nouns; all other words begin with small letters. In titles of journals, capitalize all significant words. Italicize the titles of books and journals. Do not italicize or use quotation marks around the titles of articles.

City of publication For print sources that are not periodicals (such as books or government publications), give the city of publication. The following US cities do not require state names as well: Baltimore, Boston, Chicago, Los Angeles, New York, Philadelphia, and San Francisco. Follow their names with a colon. For most other cities, add a comma after the city name, give the two-letter postal abbreviation of the state, and then add a colon. (You may omit the state if the publisher is a university whose name includes the state name, such as University of Arizona.)

Publisher's name For nonperiodical print sources, give the publisher's name after the place of publication and a colon. Use shortened names for many publishers (such as Morrow for William Morrow), and omit "Co.," "Inc.," and "Publishers." However, give full names for associations, corporations, and university presses (such as Harvard University Press), and do not omit "Books" or "Press" from a publisher's name.

Page numbers Use the abbreviation p. or pp. before page numbers in books and in newspapers. Do *not* use the abbreviation for journals and magazines. For inclusive page numbers, include all figures: 667-668.

An index to the following models appears at the **APA** divider. If you don't see a model listed for the kind of source you used, try to find one that comes close, and provide ample information so that readers can trace the source. Often you will have to combine models to provide the necessary information on a source—for instance, combining "A book with two to six authors" (model 2) and "An article in a journal" (model 12) for a journal article with two or more authors.

1 Listing authors

1. One author

Rodriguez, R. (1982). *A hunger of memory: The education of Richard Rodriguez.* Boston: Godine.

The initial R. appears instead of the author's first name, even though the author's full first name appears on the source. In this book title, only the first words of the title and subtitle and the proper name are capitalized.

2. Two to six authors

Nesselroade, J. R., & Baltes, P. B. (1999). *Longitudinal research in behavioral studies.* New York: Academic Press.

Separate author's names with commas, and use an ampersand (&) before the last author's name.

3. Seven or more authors

Wimple, P. B., Van Eijk, M., Potts, C. A., Hayes, J., Obergau, W. R., Zimmer, S., et al. (2001). *Case studies in moral decision making among adolescents.* San Francisco: Jossey-Bass.

Substitute et al. (Latin abbreviation for "and others") for all authors' names after the first six.

4. A group author

Lenschow Research. (2008). *Trends in secondary curriculum.* Baltimore: Arrow Books.

For a work with a group author—such as a research group, a government agency, or a corporation—begin the entry with the group name. In the reference list, alphabetize the work as if the first main word (excluding *The, A,* and *An*) were an author's last name.

5. Author not named (anonymous)

Merriam-Webster's collegiate dictionary (11th ed.). (2008). Springfield, MA: Merriam-Webster.

Let the horse race begin. (2008, March 31). *Time, 171,* 22.

When no author is named, list the work under its title and alphabetize it by the first main word (excluding *The, A, An*).

For a work whose author is actually given as "Anonymous," use that word in place of the author's name and alphabetize it as if it were a name.

Anonymous. (2006). *Teaching research, researching teaching.* New York: Alpine Press.

6. Two or more works by the same author(s) published in the same year

Gardner, H. (1973a). *The arts and human development.* New York: Wiley.

Gardner, H. (1973b). *The quest for mind: Piaget, Lévi-Strauss, and the struc-*
turalist movement. New York: Knopf.

When citing two or more works by exactly the same author(s), published in the same year, arrange them alphabetically by the first
main word of the title and distinguish the sources by adding a letter
to the date. Both the date and the letter are used in citing the source
in your text (see p. 524).

When citing two or more works by exactly the same author(s)
but *not* published in the same year, arrange the sources in order of
their publication dates, earliest first.

---

2 Listing print periodicals: Journals, newspapers, magazines

7. An article in a journal (print)

Selwyn, N. (2005). The social processes of learning to use computers. *Social*
Science Computer Review, 23(1), 122-135.

The facing page shows the basic format for a print journal article
and the location of the required information in the journal.

Note The APA *Publication Manual* requires a journal's issue number in a reference citation only when the annual volume is not paged
consecutively. However, the 2007 APA update, *APA Style Guide to*
Electronic References, changed the format to require the citation of
both volume and issue numbers if they are available.

8. An abstract of a journal article (print)

Emery, R. E. (2006). Marital turmoil: Interpersonal conflict and the children of
discord and divorce. *Psychological Bulletin, 92*(12), 310-330. Abstract
obtained from *Psychological Abstracts,* 2007, *69*(3), Item 1320.

When you cite the abstract of an article rather than the article itself,
give full publication information for the article, followed by Abstract
obtained from and the information for the collection of abstracts, including title, date, volume and issue numbers, and either page number or other reference number (Item 1320 in the example).

9. An article in a newspaper (print)

Stout, D. (2008, May 28). Blind win court ruling on U.S. currency. *The New*
York Times, p. A23.

Format for a print journal article

① ② ③ ④
Selwyn, N. (2005). The social processes of learning to use computers. *Social Science*
⑤ ⑥
Computer Review, 23(1), 122-135.

Journal cover

⑤ **Volume and issue numbers,** in arabic numerals. Italicize the volume number. Place the issue number (not italicized) in parentheses after the volume number with no space between them. End with a comma.

② **Year of publication,** in parentheses and followed by a period.

④ **Title of periodical,** in italics. Capitalize all significant words and end with a comma.

③ **Title of article.** Give the full article title and any subtitle, separating them with a colon. Capitalize only the first words of the title and subtitle, and do not place the title in quotation marks.

First page of article

The Social Processes of Learning to Use Computers

NEIL SELWYN
Cardiff School of Social Sciences

① **Author.** Give the last name first, a comma, the initial of the first name, and any middle initial, following each initial with a period. Omit *Dr., PhD,* or any other title.

The ability to use a computer is assumed to be a cornerstone of effective ci[...] Age, with a range of initiatives and educational provisions being introdu[...] become competent with information technology (IT). Despite such provi[...] and competence have been found to vary widely throughout the general population, and we know little of how different ways of learning to use computers contribute to people's eventual use of IT. Based on data from in-depth interviews with 100 adults in the United Kingdom, this article examines the range and social stratification of formal and informal learning about computers that is taking place, suggesting that formal computer instruction orientated toward the general public may inadvertently widen the digital knowledge gap. In particular, the data highlight the importance of informal learning about IT and of encouraging such learning, especially in the home.

AUTHOR'S NOTE: This article is based on a project funded by the Economic and Social Research Council (R000239518). I would like to thank the other members of the Adults Learning@Home project (Stephen Gorard and John Furlong) as well as the individuals who took part in the in-depth interviews. Correspondence concerning this article may be addressed to Neil Selwyn, School of Social Sciences, Cardiff University, Glamorgan Building, King Edward VII Avenue, Cardiff CF10 3WT, UK; e-mail: selwynnc@cardiff.ac.uk.

122

⑥ **Inclusive page numbers of article,** without "pp." Do not omit any numerals.

Give month *and* day along with year of publication. Use *The* in the newspaper name if the paper itself does. Precede the page number(s) with p. or pp.

10. An article in a magazine (print)

Wilkinson, A. (2008, June 2). Crime fighting of the future. *The New Yorker*, 26-33.

Give the full date of the issue: year, followed by a comma, month, and day (if any). Give all page numbers even when the article appears on discontinuous pages, without "pp." If a magazine has a volume number, provide it as in model 5.

11. A review (print)

Dinnage, R. (1987, November 29). Against the master and his men [Review of the book *A mind of her own: The life of Karen Horney*]. *The New York Times Book Review*, 10-11.

If the review is not titled, use the bracketed information as the title, keeping the brackets.

3 | Listing print books

12. Basic format for a book (print)

Ehrenreich, B. (2007). *Dancing in the streets: A history of collective joy.* New York: Holt.

Give the author's or authors' names, following models 1–4. Then give the complete title, including any subtitle. Italicize the title, and capitalize only the first words of the title and subtitle. End the entry with the city of publication and the publisher's name. (See p. 526 for how to treat these elements.)

13. A book with an editor (print)

Dohrenwend, B. S., & Dohrenwend, B. P. (Eds.). (1999). *Stressful life events: Their nature and effects.* New York: Wiley.

List the editors' names as if they were authors, but follow the last name with (Eds.).—or (Ed.). with only one editor. Note the periods inside and outside the final parenthesis.

14. A book with a translator (print)

Trajan, P. D. (1927). *Psychology of animals* (H. Simone, Trans.). Washington, DC: Halperin.

The name of the translator appears in parentheses after the title, followed by a comma, Trans. and a closing parenthesis, and a final period. Note also the absence of periods in DC.

15. A later edition (print)

Bolinger, D. L. (1981). *Aspects of language* (3rd ed.). New York: Harcourt Brace
    Jovanovich.

The edition number in parentheses follows the title and is followed
by a period.

16. A work in more than one volume (print)

Lincoln, A. (1953). *The collected works of Abraham Lincoln* (R. P. Basler, Ed.).
    (Vol. 5). New Brunswick, NJ: Rutgers University Press.

Lincoln, A. (1953). *The collected works of Abraham Lincoln* (R. P. Basler, Ed.).
    (Vols. 1-8). New Brunswick, NJ: Rutgers University Press.

The first entry cites a single volume (5) in the eight-volume set. The
second cites all eight volumes. Use the abbreviation Vol. or Vols. in
parentheses and follow the closing parenthesis with a period. In the
absence of an editor's name, the description of volumes would follow
the title directly: *The collected works of Abraham Lincoln* (Vol. 5).

17. An article or a chapter in an edited book (print)

Paykel, E. S. (1999). Life stress and psychiatric disorder: Applications of the
    clinical approach. In B. S. Dohrenwend & B. P. Dohrenwend (Eds.), *Stressful*
    life events: Their nature and effects (pp. 239-264). New York: Wiley.

Give the publication date of the collection (1999 here) as the publication date of the article or chapter. After the article or chapter title
and a period, say In and then provide the editors' names (in normal
order), (Eds.) and a comma, the title of the collection, and the page
numbers of the article in parentheses.

4 Listing Web and other electronic sources

    In 2007 the APA updated its *Publication Manual* with the *APA
Style Guide for Electronic References*. Most electronic references begin as those for print references do: author, date, title. Then you add
information on how to retrieve the source, generally giving either a
DOI (see model 18) or a URL (see model 19). In addition, note the
following:

- APA does not require your access date if the source is unlikely
  to change or if it has a publication date or edition or version
  number. See models 26 and 28 for use of an access date.
- When you need to divide a URL or DOI from one line to the
  next, APA calls for breaking before punctuation such as a period or slash. (But break after the two slashes in http://.) Do not
  hyphenate a URL or a DOI.

If you don't see a model for your particular electronic source, consult the index of models at the **APA** divider for a similar source type whose format you can adapt. If your source does not include all of the information needed for a complete citation, find and list what you can.

18. A journal article with a Digital Object Identifier (DOI) (Web)

Cunningham, J. A., & Selby, P. (2007). Relighting cigarettes: How common is it? *Nicotine and Tobacco Research, 9*(5), 621-623. doi:10.1080 /14622200701239688

The facing page shows the basic format for a periodical article that you access either directly online or through an online database as well as the location of the required information on the source.

Because URLs change often, many publishers now assign a Digital Object Identifier (DOI) to journal articles and other documents. A DOI functions as a unique identifier and a link to the text. When a DOI is available, include it instead of a URL or a database name. (The DOI may be evident on the source, or it may be found by clicking on "Article" or "Cross-Ref.") Do not add a period at the end of the DOI.

19. A journal article without a DOI (Web)

Polletta, F. (2008). Just talk: Public deliberation after 9/11. *Journal of Public Deliberation, 4*(1). Retrieved from http://services.bepress.com/jpd /vol4/iss1/art2

When a journal article does not have a DOI, give its URL instead in a statement beginning Retrieved from. Do not add a period at the end of the URL. If the journal is available only by subscription, give the URL of the journal's home page.

20. A journal article in an online database (Web)

Many reference works and periodicals are available full-text from electronic databases to which your library subscribes, such as ProQuest Direct or LexisNexis. If a database article has a DOI, use model 18. You need not give the database name, as the DOI will lead readers directly to the source.

The APA does not show how to cite an online-database article that lacks a DOI and lacks a URL that others can use. (Many database URLs are not usable because they are unique to the search and/or to the subscribing institution.) Unless your instructor suggests otherwise, give the database name in the retrieval statement, after Retrieved from. Omit any URL.

Format for a journal article on the Web

Cunningham, J. A., & Selby, P. (2007). Relighting cigarettes: How common is it? *Nicotine and Tobacco Research, 9*(5), 621-623. doi:10.1080 /14622200701239688

④ **Title of periodical,** in italics. Capitalize all significant words and end with a comma.

⑤ **Volume and Issue numbers,** in arabic numerals. Italicize the volume number. Enclose the issue number (not italicized) in parentheses after the volume number with no space between them. End with a comma.

Top of page

② **Year of publication,** in parentheses and followed by a period.

⑥ **Inclusive page numbers of article,** without "pp." Do not omit any numerals.

Nicotine & Tobacco Research Volume 9, Number 5 (May 2007) 621-623

Brief report

Relighting cigarettes: How common is it?

John A. Cunningham, Peter Selby

Received 4 April 2005; accepted 26 May 2006

In a representative sample of 434 daily smokers, half reported that they relight cigarettes at least... Relighting cigarettes was positively associated with severity of smoking addiction, as well as with markers of lower socioeconomic status (income, employment status), and with having less... contemplating change were less likely to relight cigarettes. Given that previous research...

③ **Title of article.** Give the full article title and any subtitle, separating them with a colon. Capitalize only the first words of the title and subtitle, and do not place the title in quotation marks.

① **Authors.** Give each author's last name, first initial, and any middle initial. Separate names from initials with commas, and use & before the last author's name. Omit *Dr., PhD,* or any other title. See models 1–4 (pp. 522–23) to cite single and multiple authors.

Bottom of page

more or less harmful (but never safe; Cunningham, Faulkner, Selby, & Cordingley, 2006; Kozlowski et al., 1999).

What other behaviors make a cigarette more harmful? Some evidence indicates that relighting a cigarette might make it more harmful. Two studies have found that smokers who reported relighting cigarettes were more likely to develop some types of

John A. Cunningham, Ph.D., Peter Selby, MBBS, Centre for Addiction and Mental Health and University of Toronto, Ontario, Canada.
Correspondence: John Cunningham, Centre for Addiction and Mental Health, 33 Russell Street, Toronto, Ontario, M5S 2S1, Canada. Tel: +1 (416) 535-8501; Fax: +1 (416) 595-6899; E-mail: john_cunningham@camh.net

ISSN 1462-2203 print/ISSN 1469-994X online © 2007 Society for Research on Nicotine and Tobacco
DOI: 10.3080/14622200701239688

ettes are smoked per day and how... the first cigarette is usually smo... Kozlowski, Frecker, & Robinson... stage of change algorithm (Prochaska & DiClemente, 1983) also were used. Demographic characteristics were recorded. Results are reported as weighted values to adjust for the number of adults in surveyed households. Sample sizes are presented as unweighted values.

Results

Of daily smokers, 17% reported fre... cigarettes and 36% reported somet...

⑦ **Retrieval information,** either a DOI (shown here) or a URL (model 19). See model 20 for how to cite an article without a DOI that you retrieve from a database.

Rosen, I. M., Maurer, D. M., & Darnall, C. R. (2008). Reducing tobacco use in adolescents. *American Family Physician, 77*(4), 483-490. Retrieved from EBSCOhost Academic Search Premier database.

An interview you conduct yourself should not be included in the list of references. Instead, use an in-text parenthetical citation, as shown in model 35 (p. 536) for a nonretrievable online posting.

40. A motion picture

American Psychological Association (Producer). (2001). *Ethnocultural psychotherapy* [Motion picture]. (Available from the American Psychological Association, 750 First Street, NE, Washington, DC 20002-4242, or online from http://www.apa.org/videos/4310240.html)

Howard, R. (Director). (2001). *A beautiful mind* [Motion picture]. United States: Universal.

A motion picture may be a film, DVD, or video. Depending on whose work you are citing, begin with the name or names of the creator, director, producer, or primary contributor, followed by the function in parentheses. (The second example would begin with the producer's name if you were citing the motion picture as a whole, not specifically the work of the director.) Add [Motion picture] after the title. For a motion picture in wide circulation (second example), give the country of origin and the name of the organization that released the picture. For a motion picture that is not widely circulated (first example), give the distributor's name and address in parentheses.

41. A musical recording

Springsteen, B. (2002). Empty sky. On *The rising* [CD]. New York: Columbia.

Begin with the name of the writer or composer. (If you cite another artist's recording of the work, provide this information after the title of the work—for example, [Recorded by E. Davila].) Give the medium in brackets ([CD], [LP], and so on). Finish with the city and name of the recording label.

42. A television series or episode

Rhimes, S. (Executive Producer). (2008). *Grey's anatomy* [Television series]. San Francisco: CBS.

McKee S. (Writer), & Tinker, M. (Director). (2008). Piece of my heart [Television series episode]. In S. Rhimes (Executive Producer), *Grey's anatomy*. San Francisco: CBS.

For a television series, begin with the producers' names and identify their function in parentheses. Add [Television series] after the series title, and give the city and name of the network. For an episode, begin with the writer and then the director, identifying the function of each in parentheses, and add [Television series episode] after the episode title. Then provide the series information, beginning with In and the producers' names and function, giving the series title, and ending with the city and name of the network.

59c Formatting a paper in APA style

The APA *Publication Manual* distinguishes between documents intended for publication (which will be set in type) and those submitted by students (which are the final copy). The following guidelines apply to most undergraduate papers. Check with your instructor for any modifications to this format.

Note See p. 525 for the APA format of a reference list. And see **1** pp. 55–65 for guidelines on type fonts, lists, tables and figures, and other elements of document design.

Margins Use one-inch margins on the top, bottom, and right side. Add another half-inch on the left to accommodate a binder.

Spacing and indentions Double-space your text and references. (See p. 541 for spacing of displayed quotations.) Indent paragraphs and displayed quotations one-half inch or five to seven spaces.

Paging Begin numbering on the title page, and number consecutively through the end (including the reference list). Type Arabic numerals (1, 2, 3) in the upper right, about one-half inch from the top.

Place a shortened version of your title five spaces to the left of the page number. (See the next page.)

Title page Include the full title, your name, the course title, the instructor's name, and the date. (See the next page.) Type the title on the top half of the page, followed by the identifying information, all centered horizontally and double-spaced. Include a shortened form of the title along with the page number at the top of this and all other pages.

Abstract Summarize (in a maximum of 120 words) your subject, research method, findings, and conclusions. (See the next page.) Put the abstract on a page by itself.

Body Begin with a restatement of the paper's title and then an introduction (not labeled). The introduction concisely presents the problem you researched, your research method, the relevant background (such as related studies), and the purpose of your research.

The next section, labeled Method, provides a detailed discussion of how you conducted your research, including a description of the research subjects, any materials or tools you used (such as questionnaires or surveys), and the procedure you followed. In the illustration on p. 541, the labels Method and *Sample* are first-level and

APA title page

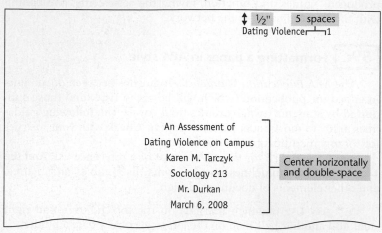

½" · 5 spaces
Dating Violence┌─┐1

An Assessment of
Dating Violence on Campus
Karen M. Tarczyk
Sociology 213
Mr. Durkan
March 6, 2008

Center horizontally
and double-space

APA abstract

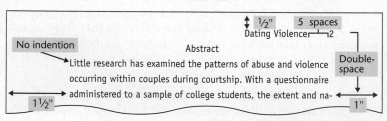

½" · 5 spaces
Dating Violence┌─┐2

No indention

Abstract

Little research has examined the patterns of abuse and violence
occurring within couples during courtship. With a questionnaire
administered to a sample of college students, the extent and na-

1½"

Double-space

1"

First page of APA body

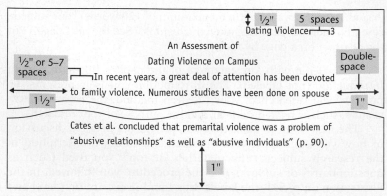

½" · 5 spaces
Dating Violence┌─┐3

An Assessment of
Dating Violence on Campus

½" or 5–7 spaces

In recent years, a great deal of attention has been devoted
to family violence. Numerous studies have been done on spouse

1½"

Double-space

1"

Cates et al. concluded that premarital violence was a problem of
"abusive relationships" as well as "abusive individuals" (p. 90).

1"

Later page of APA body

Dating Violence   4

All the studies indicate a problem that is being neglected. My objective was to gather data on the extent and nature of pre-marital violence and to discuss possible interpretations.

Method   ← Double-space

Sample

I conducted a survey of 200 students (134 females, 66 males) at a large state university in the northeastern United States. The sample consisted of students enrolled in an introductory sociology

---

second-level headings, respectively. When you need one, two, or three levels of headings, use the following formats, always double-spacing above and below:

First-Level Heading

Second-Level Heading

Third-level heading. Run this heading into the text paragraph.

The Results section (labeled with a first-level heading) summarizes the data you collected, explains how you analyzed them, and presents them in detail, often in tables, graphs, or charts.

The Discussion section (labeled with a first-level heading) interprets the data and presents your conclusions. (When the discussion is brief, you may combine it with the previous section under the heading Results and Discussion.)

The References section, beginning a new page, includes all your sources. See pp. 525–26 for an explanation and sample.

Long quotations Run into your text all quotations of forty words or less, enclosed in quotation marks. For quotations of more than forty words, set them off from your text by indenting all lines one-half inch or five to seven spaces, double-spacing above and below. For student papers, the APA allows single-spacing of displayed quotations:

Echoing the opinions of other Europeans at the time, Freud (1961) had a poor view of Americans:

The Americans are really too bad. . . . Competition is much more pungent with them, not succeeding means civil death to every one, and they have no private resources apart from their profession, no hobby, games, love or other interests of a cultured person. And success means money. (p. 86)

Do not use quotation marks around a quotation displayed in this way.

Illustrations Present data in tables and figures (graphs or charts), as appropriate. (See p. 544 and **1** pp. 62–65 for examples.) Begin each illustration on a separate page. Number each kind of illustration consecutively and separately from the other (Table 1, Table 2, etc., and Figure 1, Figure 2, etc.). Refer to all illustrations in your text—for instance, (see Figure 3). Generally, place illustrations immediately after the text references to them.

59d Examining a sample paper in APA style

The following excerpts from a sociology paper illustrate elements of a research paper using the APA style of documentation and format.

[Title page.]

Shortened title and page number.

Dating Violence   1

Double-space all information: title, name, course title, instructor, date.

An Assessment of

Dating Violence on Campus

Karen M. Tarczyk

Sociology 213

Mr. Durkan

March 6, 2008

[New page.]

Dating Violence   2

Abstract: summary of subject, research method, conclusions.

Abstract

Little research has examined the patterns of abuse and violence occurring within couples during courtship. With a questionnaire administered to a sample of college students, the extent and nature of such abuse and violence were investigated. The results, interpretations, and implications for further research are discussed.

Double-space throughout.

[New page.]

Dating Violence   3

Title repeated on first text page.

An Assessment of

Dating Violence on Campus

In recent years, a great deal of attention has been devoted to family violence. Numerous studies have been done on spouse and child abuse.

Dating Violence 4

However, violent behavior occurs in dating relationships as well, yet the problem of dating violence has been relatively ignored by sociological research. It should be examined further since the premarital relationship is one context in which individuals learn and adopt behaviors that surface in marriage.

The sociologist James Makepeace (1989) contended that courtship violence is a "potential mediating link" between violence in one's family of orientation and violence in one's later family of procreation (p. 103). Studying dating behaviors at Bemidji State University in Minnesota, Makepeace reported that one-fifth of the respondents had had at least one encounter with dating violence. He then extended these percentages to students nationwide, suggesting the existence of a major hidden social problem.

More recent research supports Makepeace's. Cates, Rutter, Karl, Linton, and Smith (2000) found that 22.3% of respondents at Oregon State University had been either the victim or the perpetrator of premarital violence. Another study (Cortes, 2005) found that so-called date rape, while much more publicized and discussed, was reported by many fewer woman respondents (2%) than was other violence during courtship (21%).

[The introduction continues.]

All these studies indicate a problem that is being neglected. My objective was to gather data on the extent and nature of premarital violence and to discuss possible interpretations.

Method

Sample

I conducted a survey of 200 students (134 females, 66 males) at a large state university in the northeastern United States. The sample consisted of students enrolled in an introductory sociology course.

[The explanation of method continues.]

The Questionnaire

A questionnaire exploring the personal dynamics of relationships was distributed during regularly scheduled class. Questions were answered anonymously in a 30-minute period. The survey consisted of three sections.

Margin annotations:

Introduction: presentation of the problem researched by the writer.

Citation form: author named in the text.

Citation form: page number given for quotation.

Citation form: source with three to five authors, named in the text.

Citation form: author not named in the text.

First- and second-level headings.

"Method" section: discussion of how research was conducted.

[The explanation of method continues.]

Section 3 required participants to provide information about their current dating relationships. Levels of stress and frustration, communication between partners, and patterns of decision making were examined. These variables were expected to influence the amount of violence in a relationship. The next part of the survey was adopted from Murray Strauss's Conflict Tactics Scales (1992). These scales contain 19 items designed to measure conflict and the means of conflict resolution, including reasoning, verbal aggression, and actual violence. The final page of the questionnaire contained general questions on the couple's use of alcohol, sexual activity, and overall satisfaction with the relationship.

"Results" section: summary and presentation of data.

Results

The questionnaire revealed significant levels of verbal aggression and threatened and actual violence among dating couples. A high number of students, 50% (62 of 123 subjects), reported that they had been the victim of verbal abuse, either being insulted or sworn at. In addition, almost 14% (17 of 123) of respondents admitted being threatened with some type of violence, and more than 14% (18 of 123) reported being pushed, grabbed, or shoved. (See Table 1.)

Reference to table.

[The explanation of results continues.]

[Table on a page by itself.]

Table presents data in clear format.

Table 1

Incidence of Courtship Violence

Type of violence	Number of students reporting	Percentage of sample
Insulted or swore	62	50.4
Threatened to hit or throw something	17	13.8
Threw something	8	6.5
Pushed, grabbed, or shoved	18	14.6
Slapped	8	6.5
Kicked, bit, or hit with fist	7	5.7
Hit or tried to hit with something	2	1.6
Threatened with a knife or gun	1	0.8
Used a knife or gun	1	0.8

Discussion

Violence within premarital relationships has been relatively ignored. The results of the present study indicate that abuse and force do occur in dating relationships. Although the percentages are small, so was the sample. Extending them to the entire campus population of 5,000 would mean significant numbers. For example, if the nearly 6% incidence of being kicked, bitten, or hit with a fist is typical, then 300 students might have experienced this type of violence.

[The discussion continues.]

If the courtship period is characterized by abuse and violence, what accounts for it? The other sections of the survey examined some variables that appear to influence the relationship. Level of stress and frustration, both within the relationship and in the respondent's life, was one such variable. The communication level between partners, both the frequency of discussion and the frequency of agreement, was another.

[The discussion continues.]

The method of analyzing the data in this study, utilizing frequency distributions, provided a clear overview. However, more tests of significance and correlation and a closer look at the social and individual variables affecting the relationship are warranted. The courtship period may set the stage for patterns of married life. It merits more attention.

[New page.]

References

Cates, R. L., Rutter, C. H., Karl, J., Linton, M., & Smith, K. (2000). Premarital abuse: A social psychological perspective. *Journal of Family Issues, 13*(1), 79-90.

Cortes, L. (2005). Beyond date rape: Violence during courtship. *Electronic Journal of Intimate Violence, 5*(2). Retrieved from http://www.acast.nova.edu/health/psy/file-disc/file50.html

Glaser, R., & Rutter, C. H. (Eds.). (1999). Familial violence [Special issue]. *Family Relations, 43*(4).

Makepeace, J. M. (1989). Courtship violence among college students. *Family Relations, 28*(6), 97-103.

Strauss, M. L. (1992). *Conflict Tactics Scales*. New York: Sociological Tests.

Margin notes:

"Discussion" section: interpretation of data and presentation of conclusions.

New page for reference list.

An article in a print journal.

An article in an online journal without a Digital Object Identifier.

A book. ("Tactics Scales" is part of a proper name and so is capitalized.)

Chicago and CSE
Documentation

Chicago and CSE Documentation

60 **Chicago Documentation** *549*

61 **CSE Documentation** *560*

Chicago note and works-cited models

60 Chicago Documentation

History, art history, philosophy, and some other humanities use endnotes or footnotes to document sources, following one style recommended by *The Chicago Manual of Style* (15th ed., 2003) and the student guide adapted from it, Kate L. Turabian's *A Manual for Writers of Research Papers, Theses, and Dissertations* (7th ed., revised by Wayne C. Booth, Gregory G. Colomb, and Joseph M. Williams, 2007).

60a Using Chicago notes and works-cited entries

In the Chicago note style, raised numerals in the text refer to footnotes (bottoms of pages) or endnotes (end of paper). These

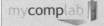

Visit *mycomplab.com* for more resources on Chicago documentation.

notes contain complete source information. A separate list of works cited is optional: ask your instructor for his or her preference.

Whether providing footnotes or endnotes, single-space each note and double-space between notes, as shown in the samples below. Separate footnotes from the text with a short line. Place endnotes directly after the text, beginning on a new page. For the list of sources at the end of the paper, use the format on the facing page. Arrange the sources alphabetically by the authors' last names.

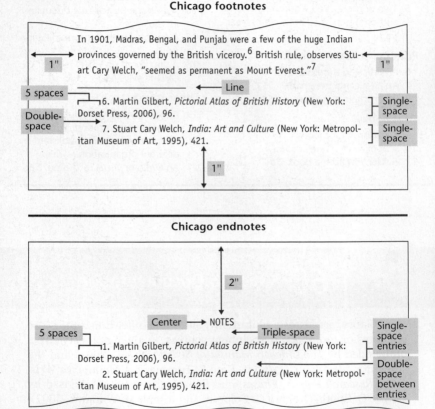

Chicago footnotes

In 1901, Madras, Bengal, and Punjab were a few of the huge Indian provinces governed by the British viceroy.[6] British rule, observes Stuart Cary Welch, "seemed as permanent as Mount Everest."[7]

1" ← → 1"

5 spaces ——— Line

Double-space →

6. Martin Gilbert, *Pictorial Atlas of British History* (New York: Dorset Press, 2006), 96.] Single-space

7. Stuart Cary Welch, *India: Art and Culture* (New York: Metropolitan Museum of Art, 1995), 421.] Single-space

1"

Chicago endnotes

2"

Center → NOTES

5 spaces ← Triple-space

1. Martin Gilbert, *Pictorial Atlas of British History* (New York: Dorset Press, 2006), 96.] Single-space entries

2. Stuart Cary Welch, *India: Art and Culture* (New York: Metropolitan Museum of Art, 1995), 421. Double-space between entries

9. Mohandas Gandhi, *Young India, 1919-1922* (New York: Huebsch), 1923, 101.

Center → 8

¾"

The note and works-cited entry on the facing page illustrate the essentials of each type of reference.

Chicago list of works cited

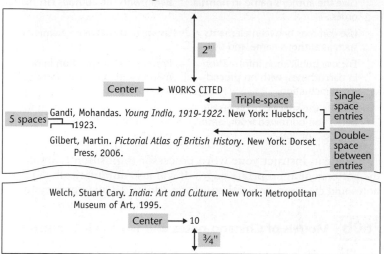

Note

     6. Martin Gilbert, *Pictorial Atlas of British History* (New York: Dorset Press, 2006), 96.

Works-cited entry

Gilbert, Martin. *Pictorial Atlas of British History*. New York: Dorset Press, 2006.

Treat some features of notes and works-cited entries the same:

- Single-space each note or entry, and double-space between the notes.
- Italicize or underline the titles of books and periodicals. Ask your instructor for his or her preference.
- Enclose in quotation marks the titles of parts of books or articles in periodicals.
- Do not abbreviate publishers' names, but omit "Inc.," "Co.," and similar abbreviations.
- Do not use "p." or "pp." before page numbers.

Treat other features of notes and works-cited entries differently:

Note	Works-cited entry
Start with a number that corresponds to the note number in the text.	Do not begin with a number.
Indent the first line five spaces.	Indent the second and subsequent lines five spaces.

Note	Works-cited entry
Give the author's name in normal order.	Begin with the author's last name.
Use commas between elements such as author's name and title.	Use periods between elements.
Enclose publication information in parentheses, with no preceding punctuation.	Precede the publication information with a period, and don't use parentheses.
Include the specific page number(s) you borrowed from, omitting "p." or "pp."	Omit page numbers except for parts of books or articles in periodicals.

You can instruct your word processor to position footnotes at the bottoms of appropriate pages. It will also automatically number notes and even renumber them if you add or delete one or more.

60b Models of Chicago notes and works-cited entries

The models below show notes and works-cited entries together for easy reference. An index to the models appears at the **Chicago** divider. Be sure to use the numbered note form for notes and the unnumbered works-cited form for works-cited entries.

1 Listing authors

1. One, two, or three authors

1. Carol Gilligan, *In a Different Voice: Psychological Theory and Women's Development* (Cambridge: Harvard University Press, 1982), 27.

Gilligan, Carol. *In a Different Voice: Psychological Theory and Women's Development.* Cambridge: Harvard University Press, 1982.

1. Dennis L. Wilcox, Phillip H. Ault, and Warren K. Agee, *Public Relations: Strategies and Tactics,* 6th ed. (New York: Irwin, 2005), 182.

Wilcox, Dennis L., Phillip H. Ault, and Warren K. Agee. *Public Relations: Strategies and Tactics.* 6th ed. New York: Irwin, 2005.

2. More than three authors

2. Geraldo Lopez and others, *China and the West* (Boston: Little, Brown, 2004), 461.

Lopez, Geraldo, Judith P. Salt, Anne Ming, and Henry Reisen. *China and the West.* Boston: Little, Brown, 2004.

3. Author not named (anonymous)

3. *The Dorling Kindersley World Reference Atlas* (London: Dorling Kindersley 2005), 150-51.

The Dorling Kindersley World Reference Atlas. London: Dorling Kindersley, 2005.

2 Listing print periodicals: Journals, newspapers, magazines

4. An article in a journal (print)

4. Janet Lever, "Sex Differences in the Games Children Play," *Social Problems* 23 (1996): 482.

Lever, Janet. "Sex Differences in the Games Children Play." *Social Problems* 23 (1996): 478-87.

Provide the issue number if the journal numbers issues, as shown below. Note that the issue number is required for any journal that pages each issue separately or that numbers only issues, not volumes.

4. Robert Bee, "The Importance of Preserving Paper-Based Artifacts in a Digital Age," *The Library Quarterly* 78, no. 2 (2008): 176.

Bee, Robert. "The Importance of Preserving Paper-Based Artifacts in a Digital Age." *The Library Quarterly* 78, no. 2 (2008): 174-94.

5. An article in a newspaper (print)

5. David Stout, "Blind Win Court Ruling on US Currency," *New York Times*, May 21, 2008, national edition, A23.

Stout, David. "Blind Win Court Ruling on US Currency." *New York Times*, May 21, 2008, national edition, A23.

Chicago style does not require page numbers for newspaper articles, whether in notes or in works-cited entries. Thus A23 could be omitted from the preceding examples.

6. An article in a magazine (print)

6. Amanda Fortini, "Pomegranate Princess," *New Yorker*, March 31, 2008, 94.

Fortini, Amanda. "Pomegranate Princess." *New Yorker*, March 31, 2008, 92-99.

Chicago works-cited style does not require inclusive page numbers for magazine articles, so 92-99 could be omitted from the preceding example.

7. A review (print)

7. John Gregory Dunne, "The Secret of Danny Santiago," review of *Famous All over Town,* by Danny Santiago, *New York Review of Books,* August 16, 1994, 25.

Dunne, John Gregory. "The Secret of Danny Santiago." Review of *Famous All over Town,* by Danny Santiago. *New York Review of Books,* August 16, 1994, 17-27.

3 Listing print books

8. Basic format for a book (print)

8. Barbara Ehrenreich, *Dancing in the Streets: A History of Collective Joy* (New York: Henry Holt, 2006), 97-117.

Ehrenreich, Barbara. *Dancing in the Streets: A History of Collective Joy.* New York: Henry Holt, 2006.

9. A book with an editor (print)

9. Hendrick Ruitenbeek, ed., *Freud as We Knew Him* (Detroit: Wayne State University Press, 1973), 64.

Ruitenbeek, Hendrick, ed. *Freud as We Knew Him.* Detroit: Wayne State University Press, 1973.

10. A book with an author and an editor (print)

10. Lewis Mumford, *The City in History,* ed. Donald L. Miller (New York: Pantheon, 1986), 216-17.

Mumford, Lewis. *The City in History.* Edited by Donald L. Miller. New York: Pantheon, 1986.

11. A translation (print)

11. Dante Alighieri, *The Inferno,* trans. John Ciardi (New York: New American Library, 1971), 51.

Alighieri, Dante. *The Inferno.* Translated by John Ciardi. New York: New American Library, 1971.

12. A later edition (print)

12. Dwight L. Bolinger, *Aspects of Language,* 3rd ed. (New York: Harcourt Brace Jovanovich, 1981), 20.

Bolinger, Dwight L. *Aspects of Language.* 3rd ed. New York: Harcourt Brace Jovanovich, 1981.

13. A work in more than one volume (print)

Citation of one volume without a title:

13. Abraham Lincoln, *The Collected Works of Abraham Lincoln,* ed. Roy P. Basler (New Brunswick: Rutgers University Press, 1953), 5:426-28.

Lincoln, Abraham. *The Collected Works of Abraham Lincoln.* Edited by Roy P. Basler. Vol. 5. New Brunswick: Rutgers University Press, 1953.

Citation of one volume with a title:

13. Linda B. Welkin, *The Age of Balanchine,* vol. 3 of *The History of Ballet* (New York: Columbia University Press, 1999), 56.

Welkin, Linda B. *The Age of Balanchine.* Vol. 3 of *The History of Ballet.* New York: Columbia University Press, 1999.

14. A selection from an anthology (print)

14. Rosetta Brooks, "Streetwise," in *The New Urban Landscape,* ed. Richard Martin (New York: Rizzoli, 2005), 38-39.

Brooks, Rosetta. "Streetwise." In *The New Urban Landscape,* ed. Richard Martin, 37-60. New York: Rizzoli, 2005.

15. A work in a series (print)

15. Ingmar Bergman, *The Seventh Seal,* Modern Film Scripts 12 (New York: Simon and Schuster, 1995), 27.

Bergman, Ingmar. *The Seventh Seal.* Modern Film Scripts 12. New York: Simon and Schuster, 1995.

16. An article in a reference work (print)

16. *Merriam-Webster's Collegiate Dictionary,* 11th ed., s.v. "reckon."

Merriam-Webster's Collegiate Dictionary. 11th ed. S.v. "reckon."

As in the example, use the abbreviation s.v. (Latin *sub verbo,* "under the word") for reference works that are alphabetically arranged. Well-known works like the one listed here do not need publication information except for edition number. Chicago style generally recommends notes only, not works-cited entries, for reference works; however, your instructor may require works-cited entries.

4 | Web and other electronic sources

The Chicago Manual's models for documenting electronic sources derive mainly from those for print sources, with the addition of an electronic address (URL) or other indication of the medium along with any other information that may help readers locate the source. Chicago requires the date of your access to an online source only if the source could change significantly (for instance, a blog). However, your instructor may require access dates for a broader range of online sources, so they are included in the following models (in parentheses at the end).

Note Chicago style allows many ways to break URLs between the end of one line and the beginning of the next: after slashes, before most punctuation marks (periods, commas, question marks, and so on), and before or after equal signs and ampersands (&). *Do not* break after a hyphen or add any hyphens.

17. An article in a journal (Web)

17. Andrew Palfrey, "Choice of Mates in Identical Twins," *Modern Psychology* 4, no. 1 (2003): 28, http://www.liasu/edu/modpsy/palfrey4(1).htm (accessed February 25, 2008).

Palfrey, Andrew. "Choice of Mates in Identical Twins." *Modern Psychology* 4, no. 1 (2003): 26-40. http://www.liasu/edu/modpsy/palfrey4(1).htm (accessed February 25, 2008).

18. An article in a magazine (Web)

18. Nina Shen Rastogi, "Peacekeepers on Trial," *Slate,* May 28, 2008, http://www.slate.com/id/2192272 (accessed June 20, 2008).

Rastogi, Nina Shen. "Peacekeepers on Trial." *Slate,* May 28, 2008. http://www.slate.com/id/2192272 (accessed June 20, 2008).

19. An article in a newspaper (Web)

19. Elissa Gootman, "Gifted Programs in the City Are Less Diverse," *New York Times,* June 19, 2008, http://www.nytimes.com/2008/06/19/nyregion/ 19gifted.html (accessed August 17, 2008).

Gootman, Elissa. "Gifted Programs in the City Are Less Diverse." *New York Times,* June 19, 2008. http://www.nytimes.com/2008/06/19/nyregion/ 19gifted.html (accessed August 17, 2008).

20. An article in an online database (Web)

20. Irina Netchaeva, "E-Government and E-Democracy," *International Journal for Communication Studies* 64 (2002): 470-71, http://www.epnet.com (accessed June 20, 2008).

Netchaeva, Irina. "E-Government and E-Democracy." *International Journal for Communication Studies* 64 (2002): 467-78. http://www.epnet.com (accessed June 20, 2008).

For news and journal databases, including those to which your library subscribes, you may omit the name of the database. Give its main URL (as in the examples) unless the work has a usable URL of its own.

21. A book (Web)

21. Jane Austen, *Emma,* ed. R. W. Chapman (1816; Oxford: Clarendon, 1926; Oxford Text Archive, 2004), chap. 1, http://ota.ahds.ac.uk/Austen/ Emma.1519 (accessed July 15, 2008).

Austen, Jane. *Emma.* Edited by R. W. Chapman. 1816. Oxford: Clarendon, 1926. Oxford Text Archive, 2004. http://ota.ahds.ac.uk/Austen/Emma.1519 (accessed July 15, 2008).

Provide print publication information, if any.

22. An article in a reference work (Web)

22. *Encyclopaedia Britannica Online,* s.v. "Wu-ti," http://www.eb.com:80 (accessed September 23, 2008).

Encyclopaedia Britannica Online. S.v. "Wu-ti." http://www.eb.com:80 (accessed September 23, 2008).

23. An audio or visual source (Web)

A work of art:

23. Jackson Pollock, *Shimmering Substance,* 1946, Museum of Modern Art, New York, http://moma.org/collection/conservation/pollock/ shimmering_substance.html (accessed March 12, 2008).

Pollock, Jackson. *Shimmering Substance.* 1946. Museum of Modern Art, New York. http://moma.org/collection/conservation/pollock/ shimmering_substance.html (accessed March 12, 2008).

See also model 30 to cite a work of art that you view in person.

A sound recording:

23. Ronald W. Reagan, State of the Union Address, January 26, 1982, Vincent Voice Library, Digital and Multimedia Center, University of Michigan, http://www.lib.msu.edu/vincent/presidents/reagan.html (accessed May 6, 2008).

Reagan, Ronald W. State of the Union Address. January 26, 1982. Vincent Voice Library. Digital and Multimedia Center, University of Michigan. http://www .lib.msu.edu/vincent/presidents/reagan.html (accessed May 6, 2008).

A film or film clip:

23. Leslie J. Stewart, *96 Ranch Rodeo and Barbecue* (1951); 16mm; from Library of Congress, *Buckaroos in Paradise: Ranching Culture in Northern Nevada, 1945-1982,* MPEG, http://memory.loc.gov/cgi-bin/query (accessed January 7, 2008).

Stewart, Leslie J. 96 *Ranch Rodeo and Barbecue*. 1951; 16 mm. From Library of Congress, *Buckaroos in Paradise: Ranching Culture in Northern Nevada, 1945-1982.* MPEG, http://memory.loc.gov/cgi-bin/query (accessed January 7, 2008).

24. A message posted to a blog or discussion group (Web)

24. Chris Horner, "EU Emissions," Cooler Heads Blog, June 18, 2008, http://www.globalwarming.org/node/2362 (accessed July 2, 2008).

Horner, Chris. "EU Emissions." Cooler Heads Blog. June 18, 2008. http://www .globalwarming.org/node/2362 (accessed July 2, 2008).

24. Michael Tourville, "European Currency Reform," e-mail to International Finance discussion list, January 6, 2008, http://www.weg.isu .edu/finance-dl/archive/46732 (accessed January 12, 2008).

Tourville, Michael. "European Currency Reform." E-mail to International Finance discussion list. January 6, 2008. http://www.weg.isu.edu/ finance-dl/archive/46732 (accessed January 12, 2008).

25. Electronic mail

25. Elizabeth Bailey, "Re: London," e-mail message to author, May 4, 2008.

Bailey, Elizabeth. "Re: London." E-mail message to author. May 4, 2008.

26. A work on CD-ROM or DVD-ROM

26. *The American Heritage Dictionary of the English Language,* 4th ed. (Boston: Houghton Mifflin, 2000), CD-ROM.

The American Heritage Dictionary of the English Language. 4th ed. Boston: Houghton Mifflin, 2000. CD-ROM.

5 | Listing other sources

27. A government publication (print)

27. House Committee on Ways and Means, *Medicare Payment for Outpatient Physical and Occupational Therapy Services,* 110th Cong., 1st sess., 2007, H. Doc. 772, 18-19.

U.S. Congress. House. Committee on Ways and Means. *Medicare Payment for Outpatient Physical and Occupational Therapy Services.* 110th Cong., 1st sess., 2007. H. Doc. 772.

27. Hawaii Department of Education, *Kauai District Schools, Profile 2007-08* (Honolulu, 2008), 38.

Hawaii. Department of Education. *Kauai District Schools, Profile 2007-08.* Honolulu, 2008.

28. A published letter (print)

28. Mrs. Laura E. Buttolph to Rev. and Mrs. C. C. Jones, June 20, 1857, in *The Children of Pride: A True Story of Georgia and the Civil War,* ed. Robert Manson Myers (New Haven, CT: Yale University Press, 1972), 334.

Buttolph, Laura E. Mrs. Laura E. Buttolph to Rev. and Mrs. C. C. Jones, June 20, 1857. In *The Children of Pride: A True Story of Georgia and the Civil War,* edited by Robert Manson Myers. New Haven, CT: Yale University Press, 1972.

29. A published or broadcast interview

29. Junot Diaz, interview by Terry Gross, *Fresh Air,* NPR, October 18, 2007.

Diaz, Junot. Interview by Terry Gross. *Fresh Air.* NPR. October 18, 2007.

30. A personal letter or interview

30. Ann E. Packer, letter to author, June 15, 2008.

Packer, Ann E. Letter to author. June 15, 2008.

30. William Paul, interview by author, December 19, 2005.

Paul, William. Interview by author. December 19, 2005.

31. A work of art

31. John Singer Sargent, *In Switzerland,* 1908, Metropolitan Museum of Art, New York.

Sargent, John Singer. *In Switzerland.* 1908. Metropolitan Museum of Art, New York.

32. A film, DVD, or video recording

32. George Balanchine, *Serenade,* DVD, San Francisco Ballet (New York: PBS Video, 2006).

Balanchine, George. *Serenade.* DVD. San Francisco Ballet. New York: PBS Video, 2006.

33. A sound recording

33. Johannes Brahms, *Piano Concerto no. 2 in B-flat,* Artur Rubinstein, Philadelphia Orchestra, Eugene Ormandy, compact disc, RCA BRC4-6731.

Brahms, Johannes. *Piano Concerto no. 2 in B-flat.* Artur Rubinstein. Philadelphia Orchestra. Eugene Ormandy. Compact disc. RCA BRC4-6731.

6 | Using shortened notes

To streamline documentation, Chicago style recommends shortened notes for sources that are fully cited elsewhere, either in a complete list of works cited or in previous notes. Ask your instructor whether your paper should include a list of works cited and, if so, whether you may use shortened notes for first references to sources as well as for subsequent references.

A shortened note contains the author's last name, the work's title (minus any initial *A*, *An*, or *The*), and the page number. Reduce long titles to four or fewer key words.

Complete note

4. Janet Lever, "Sex Differences in the Games Children Play," *Social Problems* 23 (1996): 482.

Complete works-cited entry

Lever, Janet. "Sex Differences in the Games Children Play." *Social Problems* 23 (1996): 478-87.

Shortened note

12. Lever, "Sex Differences," 483.

You may use the Latin abbreviation ibid. (meaning "in the same place") to refer to the same source cited in the preceding note. Give a page number if it differs from that in the preceding note.

12. Lever, "Sex Differences," 483.

13. Gilligan, *In a Different Voice,* 92.

14. Ibid., 93.

15. Lever, "Sex Differences," 483.

Chicago style allows for in-text parenthetical citations when you cite one or more works repeatedly. In the following example, the raised number 2 refers to the source information in a note; the number in parentheses is a page number in the same source.

British rule, observes Stuart Cary Welch, "seemed as permanent as Mount Everest."[2] Most Indians submitted, willingly or not, to British influence in every facet of life (42).

61 CSE Documentation

Writers in the life sciences, physical sciences, and mathematics rely for documentation style on *Scientific Style and Format: The CSE Manual for Authors, Editors, and Publishers* (7th ed., 2006), published by the Council of Science Editors.

Scientific Style and Format details both styles of scientific documentation: one using author and date and one using numbers. Both types of text citation refer to a list of references at the end of the paper. Ask your instructor which style you should use.

61a Writing CSE name-year text citations

In the CSE name-year style, parenthetical text citations provide the last name of the author being cited and the source's year of publication. At the end of the paper, a list of references, arranged alphabetically by authors' last names, provides complete information on each source. (See opposite.)

The CSE name-year style closely resembles the APA name-year style detailed in **APA** pp. 522–25. You can follow the APA examples for in-text citations, making several notable changes for CSE:

- **Do not use a comma to separate the author's name and the date:** (Baumrind 1968, p. 34).
- **Separate two authors' names with and (not "&"):** (Pepinsky and DeStefano 1997).
- **For sources with three or more authors, use et al. (Latin abbreviation for "and others") after the first author's name:** (Rutter et al. 1996).

61b Writing CSE numbered text citations

In the CSE number style, raised numbers in the text refer to a numbered list of references at the end of the paper.

Two standard references[1,2] use this term.

These forms of immunity have been extensively researched.[3]

Hepburn and Tatin[2] do not discuss this project.

mycomplab

Visit *mycomplab.com* for more resources on CSE

documentation.

Assignment of numbers The number for each source is based on the order in which you cite the source in the text: the first cited source is 1, the second is 2, and so on.

Reuse of numbers When you cite a source you have already cited and numbered, use the original number again (see the last example on the previous page, which reuses the number 2 from the first example).

This reuse is the key difference between the CSE numbered citations and numbered references to footnotes or endnotes. In the CSE style, each source has only one number, determined by the order in which the source is cited. With notes, in contrast, the numbering proceeds in sequence, so that each source has as many numbers as it has citations in the text.

Citation of two or more sources When you cite two or more sources at once, arrange their numbers in sequence and separate them with a comma and no space, as in the first example on the previous page.

61c Preparing the CSE reference list

For both the name-year and the number styles of in-text citation, provide a list, titled References, of all sources you have cited. Format the page as shown for APA references in **APA** p. 525, except that CSE entries are single-spaced.

The following examples show the differences and similarities between the name-year and number styles:

Name-year style

Hepburn PX, Tatin JM. 2005. Human physiology. New York (NY): Columbia University Press.

Number style

2. Hepburn PX, Tatin JM. Human physiology. New York (NY): Columbia University Press; 2005.

Spacing In both styles, single-space each entry and double-space between entries.

Arrangement In the name-year style, arrange entries alphabetically by authors' last names. In the number style, arrange entries in numerical order—that is, in order of their citation in the text.

Format In both styles, begin the first line of each entry at the left margin and indent subsequent lines.

Authors In both styles, list each author's name with the last name first, followed by initials for first and middle names. Do not use a comma between an author's last name and initials, and do not use periods or space with the initials. Do use a comma to separate authors' names.

Placement of dates In the name-year style, the date follows the author's or authors' names. In the number style, the date follows the publication information (for a book) or the periodical title (for a journal, magazine, or newspaper).

Journal titles In both styles, do not italicize or underline journal titles. For titles of two or more words, abbreviate words of six or more letters (without periods) and omit most prepositions, articles, and conjunctions. Capitalize each word. For example, *Journal of Chemical and Biochemical Studies* becomes J Chem Biochem Stud.

Book and article titles In both styles, do not italicize, underline, or use quotation marks around a book or an article title. Capitalize only the first word and any proper nouns.

Publication information for journal articles The name-year and number styles differ in the placement of the publication date (see the previous page). However, both styles end with the journal's volume number, any issue number in parentheses, a colon, and the article's page numbers, run together without space: 28:329-30 or 62(2):26-40.

The following examples show both a name-year reference and a number reference for each type of source. An index to all the models appears opposite the **CSE** divider (p. 549).

1 Listing authors

1. One author

Gould SJ. 1987. Time's arrow, time's cycle. Cambridge (MA): Harvard University Press.

1. Gould SJ. Time's arrow, time's cycle. Cambridge (MA): Harvard University Press; 1987.

2. Two to ten authors

Hepburn PX, Tatin JM, Tatin JP. 2008. Human physiology. New York (NY): Columbia University Press.

2. Hepburn PX, Tatin JM, Tatin JP. Human physiology. New York (NY): Columbia University Press; 2008.

3. More than ten authors

Evans RW, Bowditch L, Dana KL, Drumond A, Wildovitch WP, Young SL, Mills P, Mills RR, Livak SR, Lisi OL, et al. 2004. Organ transplants: ethical issues. Ann Arbor (MI): University of Michigan Press.

3. Evans RW, Bowditch L, Dana KL, Drummond A, Wildovitch WP, Young SL, Mills P, Mills RR, Livak SR, Lisi OL, et al. Organ transplants: ethical issues. Ann Arbor (MI): University of Michigan Press; 2004.

4. Author not named

Health care for children with diabetes. 2008. New York (NY): US Health Care.

4. Health care for children with diabetes. New York (NY): US Health Care; 2008.

5. Two or more cited works by the same author(s) published in the same year

Gardner H. 1973a. The arts and human development. New York (NY): Wiley.

Gardner H. 1973b. The quest for mind: Piaget, Lévi-Strauss, and the structuralist movement. New York (NY): Knopf.

(The number style does not require such forms.)

2 Listing print periodicals: Journals, newspapers, magazines

6. An article in a journal (print)

Kim P. 2006. Medical decision making for the dying. Milbank Quar. 64(2):26-40.

6. Kim P. Medical decision making for the dying. Milbank Quar. 2006;64(2):26-40.

If a journal article has a Digital Object Identifier (DOI), you may include the number at the end of the entry for readers' convenience. (See **APA** p. 532 for more on DOIs.)

7. An article in a newspaper (print)

Stout D. 2008 May 28. Blind win court ruling on US currency. New York Times (National Ed.). Sect. A:23 (col. 3).

7. Stout D. Blind win court ruling on US currency. New York Times (National Ed.). 2008 May 28;Sect. A:23 (col. 3).

8. An article in a magazine (print)

Wilkinson A. 2008 June 2. Crime fighting of the future. New Yorker. 26-33.

8. Wilkinson A. Crime fighting of the future. New Yorker. 2008 June 2:26-33.

3 Listing print books

9. Basic format for a book (print)

Wilson EO. 2004. On human nature. Cambridge (MA): Harvard University Press.

9. Wilson EO. On human nature. Cambridge (MA): Harvard University Press; 2004.

10. A book with an editor (print)

Jonson P, editor. 2008. Anatomy yearbook 2008. Los Angeles (CA): Anatco.

10. Jonson P, editor. Anatomy yearbook 2008. Los Angeles (CA): Anatco; 2008.

11. A selection from a book (print)

Krigel R, Laubenstein L, Muggia F. 2005. Kaposi's sarcoma. In: Ebbeson P, Biggar RS, Melbye M, editors. AIDS: a basic guide for clinicians. 2nd ed. Philadelphia (PA): Saunders. p. 100-26.

11. Kriegel R, Laubenstein L, Muggia F. Kaposi's sarcoma. In: Ebbeson P, Biggar RS, Melbye M, editors. AIDS: a basic guide for clinicians. 2nd ed. Philadelphia (PA): Saunders; 2005. p. 100-26.

4 Listing Web and other electronic sources

Do not add a period after a URL at the end of an entry. If you must break a URL from one line to the next, do so only after a slash, and do not hyphenate.

12. An article in a journal (Web)

Grady GF. 2007. The here and now of hepatitis B immunization. Today's Med [Internet]. [cited 2007 Dec 7]; 6(2):39-41. Available from: http://www.fmrt.org/todayamedicine/Grady050293.pdf6

12. Grady GF. The here and now of hepatitis B immunization. Today's Med [Internet]. 2007 [cited 2007 Dec 7]; 6(2):39-41. Available from: http://www.fmrt.org/todaysmedicine/Grady050293.pdf6

Give the date of your access, preceded by "cited," in brackets: [cited 2007 Dec 7] in the examples. If the article has no reference numbers (pages, paragraphs, and so on), give your calculation of its length in brackets—for instance, [about 15 p.] or [20 paragraphs]. If the article has a Digital Object Identifier (DOI), you may include the number for readers' convenience. Add it to the end of the entry after a space. (See **APA** p. 532 for more on DOIs.)

13. An article in a database (Web)

McAskill MR, Anderson TJ, Jones RD. 2005. Saccadic adaptation in neurological disorders. Prog Brain Res. 140:417-431. PubMed [database on the Internet]. Bethesda (MD): National Library of Medicine; [cited 2007 Mar 6]. Available from: http://www.ncbi.nlm.nih.gov/PubMed

13. McAskill MR, Anderson TJ, Jones RD. Saccadic adaptation in neurological disorders. Prog Brain Res. 2005;140:417-431. PubMed [database on the Internet]. Bethesda (MD): National Library of Medicine; [cited 2007 Mar 6]. Available from: http://www.ncbi.nlm.nih.gov/PubMed

Provide information on the database: title, [database on the Internet], place of publication, and publisher. (If the database author is different from the publisher, give the author's name before the title.) If you see a date of publication or a copyright date for the database, give it after the publisher's name. Add the date of your access, preceded by cited, in brackets. If the article has a Digital Object Identifier (DOI), you may include the number for readers' convenience. Add it to the end of the entry after a space. (See **APA** p. 532 for more on DOIs.)

14. A book (Web)

Ruch BJ, Ruch DB. 2007. Homeopathy and medicine: resolving the conflict [Internet]. New York (NY): Albert Einstein College of Medicine [cited 2008 Jan 28]. Available from: http://www.einstein.edu/medicine/books/ruch.html

14. Ruch BJ, Ruch DB. Homeopathy and medicine: resolving the conflict [Internet]. New York (NY): Albert Einstein College of Medicine; 2007 [cited 2008 Jan 28]. Available from: http://www.einstein.edu/medicine/books/ruch.html

As with an online journal article, give the date of your access, preceded by cited, in brackets.

15. A Web site

American Medical Association [Internet]. 2008. Chicago (IL): American Medical Association; [cited 2008 Nov 26]. Available from: http://ama-assn.org

15. American Medical Association [Internet]. Chicago (IL): American Medical Association; 2008 [cited 2008 Nov 26]. Available from: http://ama-assn.org

16. A message posted to a discussion list

Stalinsky Q. 2007 Aug 16. Reconsidering the hormone-replacement study. Woman Physicians Congress [discussion list on the Internet]. Chicago (IL): American Medical Association; [cited 2008 Aug 17]. Available from: ama-wpc@ama-assn.org

16. Stalinsky Q. Reconsidering the hormone-replacement study. Woman Physicians Congress [discussion list on the Internet]. Chicago (IL): American Medical Association; 2007 Aug 16 [cited 2008 Aug 17]. Available from: ama-wpc@ama-assn.org

17. A personal online communication (text citation)

At least one member of the research team has expressed reservation about the design of the study (personal communication from L. Kogod, 2008 Feb 6; unreferenced).

A personal letter or e-mail message should be cited in your text, not in your reference list. The format is the same for both the name-year and the number styles.

18. A document on CD-ROM or DVD-ROM

Reich WT, editor. 2008. Encyclopedia of bioethics [DVD-ROM]. New York (NY): Co-Health.

18. Reich WT editor. Encyclopedia of bioethics [DVD-ROM]. New York (NY): Co-Health; 2008.

5 Listing other sources

19. A report written and published by the same organization

Warnock M. 2006. Report of the Committee on Fertilization and Embryology. Waco (TX): Baylor University Department of Embryology. Report No.: BU/DE.4261.

19. Warnock M. Report of the Committee on Fertilization and Embryology. Waco (TX): Baylor University Department of Embryology; 2006. Report No.: BU/DE.4261.

20. A report written and published by different organizations

Hackney, JD (Rancho Los Amigos Hospital, Downey, CA). 2007. Effect of atmospheric pollutants on human physiologic function. Washington (DC): Environmental Protection Agency (US). Report No.: R-801396.

20. Hackney, JD (Rancho Los Amigos Hospital, Downey, CA). Effect of atmospheric pollutants on human physiologic function. Washington (DC): Environmental Protection Agency (US); 2007. Report No.: R-801396.

21. An audio or visual recording

Cell mitosis [DVD-ROM]. 2008. White Plains (NY): Teaching Media.

21. Cell mitosis [DVD-ROM]. White Plains (NY): Teaching Media; 2008.

Glossary of Usage

This glossary provides notes on words or phrases that often cause problems for writers. The recommendations for standard American English are based on current dictionaries and usage guides. Items labeled **nonstandard** should be avoided in academic and business settings. Those labeled **colloquial** and **slang** occur in speech and in some informal writing but are best avoided in formal college and business writing. (Words and phrases labeled *colloquial* include those labeled by many dictionaries with the equivalent term *informal*.)

a, an Use *a* before words beginning with consonant sounds, including those spelled with an initial pronounced *h* and those spelled with vowels that are sounded as consonants: *a historian, a one-o'clock class, a university.* Use *an* before words that begin with vowel sounds, including those spelled with an initial silent *h: an organism, an L, an honor.*

The article before an abbreviation depends on how the abbreviation is to be read: *She was once an AEC undersecretary* (*AEC* is to be read as three separate letters). *Many Americans opposed a SALT treaty* (*SALT* is to be read as one word, *salt*).

See also **4** pp. 269–70 on the uses of *a/an* versus *the.*

accept, except *Accept* is a verb meaning "receive." *Except* is usually a preposition or conjunction meaning "but for" or "other than"; when it is used as a verb, it means "leave out." *I can accept all your suggestions except the last one. I'm sorry you excepted my last suggestion from your list.*

advice, advise *Advice* is a noun, and *advise* is a verb: *Take my advice; do as I advise you.*

affect, effect Usually *affect* is a verb, meaning "to influence," and *effect* is a noun, meaning "result": *The drug did not affect his driving; in fact, it seemed to have no effect at all.* But *effect* occasionally is used as a verb meaning "to bring about": *Her efforts effected a change.* And *affect* is used in psychology as a noun meaning "feeling or emotion": *One can infer much about affect from behavior.*

agree to, agree with *Agree to* means "consent to," and *agree with* means "be in accord with": *How can they agree to a treaty when they don't agree with each other about the terms?*

all ready, already *All ready* means "completely prepared," and *already* means "by now" or "before now": *We were all ready to go to the movie, but it had already started.*

all right *All right* is always two words. *Alright* is a common error.

all together, altogether *All together* means "in unison" or "gathered in one place." *Altogether* means "entirely." *It's not altogether true that our family never spends vacations all together.*

allusion, illusion An *allusion* is an indirect reference, and an *illusion* is a deceptive appearance: *Paul's constant allusions to Shakespeare created the illusion that he was an intellectual.*

almost, most *Almost* means "nearly"; *most* means "the greater number (or part) of." In formal writing, *most* should not be used as a substitute for *almost: We see each other almost [not most] every day.*

a lot *A lot* is always two words, used informally to mean "many." *Alot* is a common misspelling.

among, between In general, use *among* for relationships involving more than two people or for comparing one thing to a group to which it belongs. *The four of them agreed among themselves that the choice was between New York and Los Angeles.*

amount, number Use *amount* with a singular noun that names something not countable (a noncount noun): *The amount of food varies.* Use *number* with a plural noun that names more than one of something countable (a plural count noun): *The number of calories must stay the same.*

and/or *And/or* indicates three options: one or the other or both (*The decision is made by the mayor and/or the council*). If you mean all three options, *and/or* is appropriate. Otherwise, use *and* if you mean both, *or* if you mean either.

ante-, anti- The prefix *ante-* means "before" (*antedate, antebellum*); *anti-* means "against" (*antiwar, antinuclear*). Before a capital letter or *i*, *anti-* takes a hyphen: *anti-Freudian, anti-isolationist.*

anxious, eager *Anxious* means "nervous" or "worried" and is usually followed by *about*. *Eager* means "looking forward" and is usually followed by *to. I've been anxious about getting blisters. I'm eager [not anxious] to get new running shoes.*

anybody, any body; anyone, any one *Anybody* and *anyone* are indefinite pronouns; *any body* is a noun modified by *any; any one* is a pronoun or adjective modified by *any. How can anybody communicate with any body of government? Can anyone help Amy? She has more work than any one person can handle.*

any more, anymore *Any more* means "no more"; *anymore* means "now." Both are used in negative constructions. *He doesn't want any more. She doesn't live here anymore.*

apt, liable, likely *Apt* and *likely* are interchangeable. Strictly speaking, though, *apt* means "having a tendency to": *Horace is apt to forget his lunch in the morning. Likely means "probably going to": Horace is leaving so early today that he's likely to catch the first bus.*

    Liable normally means "in danger of" and should be confined to situations with undesirable consequences: *Horace is liable to trip over that hose.* Strictly, *liable* means "responsible" or "exposed to": *The owner will be liable for Horace's injuries.*

are, is Use *are* with a plural subject (*books are*), *is* with a singular subject (*a book is*).

as   *As* may be vague or ambiguous when it substitutes for *because, since,* or *while: As the researchers asked more questions, their money ran out.* (Does *as* mean "while" or "because"?) *As* should never be used as a substitute for *whether* or *who. I'm not sure whether* [not *as*] *we can make it. That's the man who* [not *as*] *gave me directions.*

as, like   In formal speech and writing, *like* should not introduce a full clause (with a subject and a verb) because it is a preposition. The preferred choice is *as* or *as if: The plan succeeded as* [not *like*] *we hoped. It seemed as if* [not *like*] *it might fail. Other plans like it have failed.*

as, than   In comparisons, *as* and *than* precede a subjective-case pronoun when the pronoun is a subject: *I love you more than he* [*loves you*]. *As* and *than* precede an objective-case pronoun when the pronoun is an object: *I love you as much as* [*I love*] *him.* (See also **4** p. 251.)

assure, ensure, insure   *Assure* means "to promise": *He assured us that we would miss the traffic. Ensure* and *insure* often are used interchangeably to mean "make certain," but some reserve *insure* for matters of legal and financial protection and use *ensure* for more general meanings: *We left early to ensure that we would miss the traffic. It's expensive to insure yourself against floods.*

at   The use of *at* after *where* is wordy and should be avoided: *Where are you meeting him?* is preferable to *Where are you meeting him at?*

awful, awfully   Strictly speaking, *awful* means "awe-inspiring." As intensifiers meaning "very" or "extremely" (*He tried awfully hard*), *awful* and *awfully* should be avoided in formal speech or writing.

a while, awhile   *Awhile* is an adverb; *a while* is an article and a noun. *I will be gone awhile* [not *a while*]. *I will be gone for a while* [not *awhile*].

bad, badly   In formal speech and writing, *bad* should be used only as an adjective; the adverb is *badly. He felt bad because his tooth ached badly.* In *He felt bad,* the verb *felt* is a linking verb and the adjective *bad* describes the subject. See also **4** p. 263.

being as, being that   Colloquial for *because,* the preferable word in formal speech or writing: *Because* [not *Being as*] *the world is round, Columbus never did fall off the edge.*

beside, besides   *Beside* is a preposition meaning "next to." *Besides* is a preposition meaning "except" or "in addition to" as well as an adverb meaning "in addition." *Besides, several other people besides you want to sit beside Dr. Christensen.*

better, had better   *Had better* (meaning "ought to") is a verb modified by an adverb. The verb is necessary and should not be omitted: *You had better* [not just *better*] *go.*

between, among   See *among, between.*

bring, take   Use *bring* only for movement from a farther place to a nearer one and *take* for any other movement. *First take these books to the library for renewal; then take them to Mr. Daniels. Bring them back to me when he's finished.*

but, hardly, scarcely   These words are negative in their own right; using *not* with any of them produces a double negative (see **4** p. 266). *We have but* [not *haven't got but*] *an hour before our plane leaves. I could hardly* [not *couldn't hardly*] *make out her face.*

but, however, yet   Each of these words is adequate to express contrast. Don't combine them. *He had finished, yet* [not *but yet*] *he continued.*

can, may   Strictly, *can* indicates capacity or ability, and *may* indicates permission or possibility: *If I may talk with you a moment, I believe I can solve your problem.*

censor, censure   To *censor* is to edit or remove from public view on moral or some other grounds; to *censure* is to give a formal scolding. *The lieutenant was censured by Major Taylor for censoring the letters her soldiers wrote home from boot camp.*

center around   *Center on* is more logical than, and preferable to, *center around.*

cite, sight, site   *Cite* is a verb usually meaning "quote," "commend," or "acknowledge": *You must cite your sources. Sight* is both a noun meaning "the ability to see" or "a view" and a verb meaning "perceive" or "observe": *What a sight you see when you sight Venus through a strong telescope. Site* is a noun meaning "place" or "location" or a verb meaning "situate": *The builder sited the house on an unlikely site.*

climatic, climactic   *Climatic* comes from *climate* and refers to the weather: *Recent droughts may indicate a climatic change. Climactic* comes from *climax* and refers to a dramatic high point: *During the climactic duel between Hamlet and Laertes, Gertrude drinks poisoned wine.*

complement, compliment   To *complement* something is to add to, complete, or reinforce it: *Her yellow blouse complemented her black hair.* To *compliment* something is to make a flattering remark about it: *He complimented her on her hair. Complimentary* can also mean "free": *complimentary tickets.*

conscience, conscious   *Conscience* is a noun meaning "a sense of right and wrong"; *conscious* is an adjective meaning "aware" or "awake." *Though I was barely conscious, my conscience nagged me.*

contact   Often used imprecisely as a verb instead of a more exact word such as *consult, talk with, telephone,* or *write to.*

continual, continuous   *Continual* means "constantly recurring": *Most movies on television are continually interrupted by commercials. Continuous* means "unceasing": *Some cable channels present movies continuously without commercials.*

could of   See *have, of.*

credible, creditable, credulous   *Credible* means "believable": *It's a strange story, but it seems credible to me. Creditable* means "deserving of credit" or "worthy": *Steve gave a creditable performance. Credulous* means "gullible": *The credulous Claire believed Tim's lies.* See also *incredible, incredulous.*

criteria The plural of *criterion* (meaning "standard for judgment"): *Our criteria are strict. The most important criterion is a sense of humor.*

data The plural of *datum* (meaning "fact"). Though *data* is often used as a singular noun, most careful writers still treat it as plural: *The data fail* [not *fails*] *to support the hypothesis.*

device, devise *Device* is the noun, and *devise* is the verb: *Can you devise some device for getting his attention?*

different from, different than *Different from* is preferred: *His purpose is different from mine.* But *different than* is widely accepted when a construction using *from* would be wordy: *I'm a different person now than I used to be* is preferable to *I'm a different person now from the person I used to be.*

differ from, differ with To *differ from* is to be unlike: *The twins differ from each other only in their hairstyles.* To *differ with* is to disagree with: *I have to differ with you on that point.*

discreet, discrete *Discreet* (noun form *discretion*) means "tactful": *What's a discreet way of telling Maud to be quiet? Discrete* (noun form *discreteness*) means "separate and distinct": *Within a computer's memory are millions of discrete bits of information.*

disinterested, uninterested *Disinterested* means "impartial": *We chose Pete, as a disinterested third party, to decide who was right. Uninterested* means "bored" or "lacking interest": *Unfortunately, Pete was completely uninterested in the question.*

don't *Don't* is the contraction for *do not,* not for *does not: I don't care, you don't care,* and *he doesn't* [not *don't*] *care.*

due to the fact that Wordy for *because.*

eager, anxious See *anxious, eager.*

effect See *affect, effect.*

elicit, illicit *Elicit* is a verb meaning "bring out" or "call forth." *Illicit* is an adjective meaning "unlawful." *The crime elicited an outcry against illicit drugs.*

emigrate, immigrate *Emigrate* means "to leave one place and move to another": *The Chus emigrated from Korea. Immigrate* means "to move into a place where one was not born": *They immigrated to the United States.*

ensure See *assure, ensure, insure.*

enthused Used colloquially as an adjective meaning "showing enthusiasm." The preferred adjective is *enthusiastic: The coach was enthusiastic* [not *enthused*] *about the team's victory.*

et al., etc. Use *et al.,* the Latin abbreviation for "and other people," only in source citations: *Jones et al.* Avoid *etc.,* the Latin abbreviation for "and other things," in formal writing, and do not use it to refer to people or to substitute for precision, as in *The government provides health care, etc.*

everybody, every body; everyone, every one *Everybody* and *everyone* are indefinite pronouns: *Everybody* [*everyone*] *knows Tom steals*. *Every one* is a pronoun modified by *every*, and *every body* a noun modified by *every*. Both refer to each thing or person of a specific group and are typically followed by *of*: *The game commissioner has stocked every body of fresh water in the state with fish, and now every one of our rivers is a potential trout stream.*

everyday, every day *Everyday* is an adjective meaning "used daily" or "common"; *every day* is a noun modified by *every*: *Everyday problems tend to arise every day*.

everywheres Nonstandard for *everywhere*.

except See *accept, except*.

except for the fact that Wordy for *except that*.

explicit, implicit *Explicit* means "stated outright": *I left explicit instructions*. *Implicit* means "implied, unstated": *We had an implicit understanding*.

farther, further *Farther* refers to additional distance (*How much farther is it to the beach?*), and *further* refers to additional time, amount, or other abstract matters (*I don't want to discuss this any further*).

fewer, less *Fewer* refers to individual countable items (a plural count noun), *less* to general amounts (a noncount noun, always singular). *Skim milk has fewer calories than whole milk. We have less milk left than I thought.*

flaunt, flout *Flaunt* means "show off": *If you have style, flaunt it*. *Flout* means "scorn" or "defy": *Hester Prynne flouted convention and paid the price.*

flunk A colloquial substitute for *fail*.

fun As an adjective, *fun* is colloquial and should be avoided in most writing: *It was a pleasurable* [not *fun*] *evening.*

further See *farther, further*.

get This common verb is used in many slang and colloquial expressions: *get lost, that really gets me, getting on. Get* is easy to overuse: watch out for it in expressions such as *it's getting better* (substitute *improving*) and *we got done* (substitute *finished*).

good, well *Good* is an adjective, and *well* is nearly always an adverb: *Larry's a good dancer. He and Linda dance well together. Well* is properly used as an adjective only to refer to health: *You look well*. (*You look good*, in contrast, means "Your appearance is pleasing.")

good and Colloquial for "very": *I was very* [not *good and*] *tired.*

had better See *better, had better*.

had ought The *had* is unnecessary and should be omitted: *He ought* [not *had ought*] *to listen to his mother.*

hanged, hung Though both are past-tense forms of *hang*, *hanged* is used to refer to executions and *hung* is used for all other meanings: *Tom*

Dooley was hanged [not *hung*] *from a white oak tree. I hung* [not *hanged*] *the picture you gave me.*

hardly See *but, hardly, scarcely.*

have, of Use *have,* not *of,* after helping verbs such as *could, should, would, may,* and *might: You should have* [not *should of*] *told me.*

he, she; he/she Convention has allowed the use of *he* to mean "he or she": *After the infant learns to creep, he progresses to crawling.* However, many writers today consider this usage inaccurate and unfair because it seems to exclude females. The construction *he/she,* one substitute for *he,* is awkward and objectionable to most readers. The better choice is to make the pronoun plural, to rephrase, or, sparingly, to use *he or she.* For instance: *After infants learn to creep, they progress to crawling. After learning to creep, the infant progresses to crawling. After the infant learns to creep, he or she progresses to crawling.* See also **3** p. 166 and **4** p. 255.

herself, himself See *myself, herself, himself, yourself.*

hisself Nonstandard for *himself.*

hopefully *Hopefully* means "with hope": *Freddy waited hopefully for a glimpse of Eliza.* The use of *hopefully* to mean "it is to be hoped," "I hope," or "let's hope" is now very common; but since many readers continue to object strongly to the usage, try to avoid it. *I hope* [not *Hopefully*] *the law will pass.*

idea, ideal An *idea* is a thought or conception. An *ideal* (noun) is a model of perfection or a goal. *Ideal* should not be used in place of *idea: The idea* [not *ideal*] *of the play is that our ideals often sustain us.*

if, whether For clarity, use *whether* rather than *if* when you are expressing an alternative: *If I laugh hard, people can't tell whether I'm crying.*

illicit See *elicit, illicit.*

illusion See *allusion, illusion.*

immigrate, emigrate See *emigrate, immigrate.*

implicit See *explicit, implicit.*

imply, infer Writers or speakers *imply,* meaning "suggest": *Jim's letter implies he's having a good time.* Readers or listeners *infer,* meaning "conclude": *From Jim's letter I infer he's having a good time.*

incredible, incredulous *Incredible* means "unbelievable"; *incredulous* means "unbelieving": *When Nancy heard Dennis's incredible story, she was frankly incredulous.* See also *credible, creditable, credulous.*

individual, person, party *Individual* should refer to a single human being in contrast to a group or should stress uniqueness: *The US Constitution places strong emphasis on the rights of the individual.* For other meanings *person* is preferable: *What person* [not *individual*] *wouldn't want the security promised in that advertisement? Party* means "group" (*Can you seat a party of four for dinner?*) and should not be used to refer to an individual except in legal documents. See also *people, persons.*

infer See *imply, infer.*

in regards to Nonstandard for *in regard to, as regards,* or *regarding.*

inside of, outside of The *of* is unnecessary when *inside* and *outside* are used as prepositions: *Stay inside* [not *inside of*] *the house. The decision is outside* [not *outside of*] *my authority. Inside of* may refer colloquially to time, though in formal English *within* is preferred: *The law was passed within* [not *inside of*] *a year.*

insure See *assure, ensure, insure.*

irregardless Nonstandard for *regardless.*

is, are See *are, is.*

is because See *reason is because.*

is when, is where These are faulty constructions in sentences that define: *Adolescence is a stage* [not *is when a person is*] *between childhood and adulthood. Socialism is a system in which* [not *is where*] *government owns the means of production.* See also **4** p. 291.

its, it's *Its* is the pronoun *it* in the possessive case: *That plant is losing its leaves. It's* is a contraction for *it is* or *it has: It's* [*It is*] *likely to die. It's* [*It has*] *got a fungus.* Many people confuse *it's* and *its* because possessives are most often formed with -*'s;* but the possessive *its,* like *his* and *hers,* never takes an apostrophe.

-ize, -wise The suffix -*ize* changes a noun or adjective into a verb: *revolutionize, immunize.* The suffix -*wise* changes a noun or adjective into an adverb: *clockwise, otherwise, likewise.* Avoid the two suffixes except in established words: *I'm highly sensitive* [not *sensitized*] *to that kind of criticism. Financially* [not *Moneywise*], *it's a good time to buy real estate.*

kind of, sort of, type of In formal speech and writing, avoid using *kind of* or *sort of* to mean "somewhat": *He was rather* [not *kind of*] *tall.*

Kind, *sort,* and *type* are singular and take singular modifiers and verbs: *This kind of dog is easily trained.* Agreement errors often occur when these singular nouns are combined with the plural adjectives *these* and *those: These kinds* [not *kind*] *of dogs are easily trained. Kind, sort,* and *type* should be followed by *of* but not by *a: I don't know what type of* [not *type* or *type of a*] *dog that is.*

Use *kind of, sort of,* or *type of* only when the word *kind, sort,* or *type* is important: *That was a strange* [not *strange sort of*] *statement.*

lay, lie *Lay* means "put" or "place" and takes a direct object: *We could lay the tablecloth in the sun.* Its main forms are *lay, laid, laid. Lie* means "recline" or "be situated" and does not take an object: *I lie awake at night. The town lies east of the river.* Its main forms are *lie, lay, lain.* (See also **4** p. 216.)

leave, let *Leave* and *let* are interchangeable only when followed by *alone; leave me alone* is the same as *let me alone.* Otherwise, *leave* means "depart" and *let* means "allow": *Jill would not let Sue leave.*

less See *fewer, less.*

liable See *apt, liable, likely.*

lie, lay See *lay, lie.*

like, as See *as, like.*

like, such as Strictly, *such as* precedes an example that represents a larger subject, whereas *like* indicates that two subjects are comparable. *Steve has recordings of many great saxophonists such as Ben Webster and Lee Konitz. Steve wants to be a great jazz saxophonist like Ben Webster and Lee Konitz.*

likely See *apt, liable, likely.*

literally This word means "actually" or "just as the words say," and it should not be used to qualify or intensify expressions whose words are not to be taken at face value. The sentence *He was literally climbing the walls* describes a person behaving like an insect, not a person who is restless or anxious. For the latter meaning, *literally* should be omitted.

lose, loose *Lose* means "mislay": *Did you lose a brown glove? Loose* means "unrestrained" or "not tight": *Ann's canary got loose. Loose* also can function as a verb meaning "let loose": *They loose the dogs as soon as they spot the bear.*

lots, lots of Colloquial substitutes for *very many, a great many,* or *much.* Avoid *lots* and *lots of* in college or business writing.

may, can See *can, may.*

may be, maybe *May be* is a verb, and *maybe* is an adverb meaning "perhaps": *Tuesday may be a legal holiday. Maybe we won't have classes.*

may of See *have, of.*

media *Media* is the plural of *medium* and takes a plural verb: *All the news media are increasingly visual.* The singular verb is common, even in the media, but many readers prefer the plural verb and it is always correct.

might of See *have, of.*

moral, morale As a noun, *moral* means "ethical conclusion" or "lesson": *The moral of the story escapes me. Morale* means "spirit" or "state of mind": *Victory improved the team's morale.*

most, almost See *almost, most.*

must of See *have, of.*

myself, herself, himself, yourself The *-self* pronouns refer to or intensify another word or words: *Paul helped himself; Jill herself said so.* The *-self* pronouns are often used colloquially in place of personal pronouns, but that use should be avoided in formal speech and writing: *No one except me* [not *myself*] *saw the accident. Our delegates will be Susan and you* [not *yourself*]. See also **4** p. 247 on the unchanging forms of the *-self* pronouns in standard American English.

nowheres Nonstandard for *nowhere.*

number See *amount, number.*

of, have See *have, of.*

off of *Of* is unnecessary. Use *off* or *from* rather than *off of: He jumped off* [or *from*, not *off of*] *the roof.*

OK, O.K., okay All three spellings are acceptable, but avoid this colloquial term in formal speech and writing.

on account of Wordy for *because of.*

on the other hand This transitional expression of contrast should be preceded by its mate, *on the one hand: On the one hand, we hoped for snow. On the other hand, we feared that it would harm the animals.* However, the two combined can be unwieldy, and a simple *but, however, yet,* or *in contrast* often suffices: *We hoped for snow. Yet we feared that it would harm the animals.*

outside of See *inside of, outside of.*

owing to the fact that Wordy for *because.*

party See *individual, person, party.*

people, persons In formal usage, *people* refers to a general group: *We the people of the United States. . . . Persons* refers to a collection of individuals: *Will the person or persons who saw the accident please notify. . . .* Except when emphasizing individuals, prefer *people* to *persons.* See also *individual, person, party.*

per Except in technical writing, an English equivalent is usually preferable to the Latin *per: $10 an* [not *per*] *hour; sent by* [not *per*] *parcel post; requested in* [not *per* or *as per*] *your letter.*

percent (per cent), percentage Both these terms refer to fractions of one hundred. *Percent* always follows a number (*40 percent of the voters*), and the word should be used instead of the symbol (%) in general writing. *Percentage* stands alone (*the percentage of voters*) or follows an adjective (*a high percentage*).

person See *individual, person, party.*

persons See *people, persons.*

phenomena The plural of *phenomenon* (meaning "perceivable fact" or "unusual occurrence"): *Many phenomena are not recorded. One phenomenon is attracting attention.*

plenty A colloquial substitute for *very: The reaction occurred very* [not *plenty*] *fast.*

plus *Plus* is standard as a preposition meaning "in addition to": *His income plus mine is sufficient.* But *plus* is colloquial as a conjunctive adverb: *Our organization is larger than theirs; moreover* [not *plus*], *we have more money.*

precede, proceed The verb *precede* means "come before": *My name precedes yours in the alphabet.* The verb *proceed* means "move on": *We were told to proceed to the waiting room.*

prejudice, prejudiced *Prejudice* is a noun; *prejudiced* is an adjective. Do not drop the *-d* from *prejudiced: I was fortunate that my parents were not prejudiced* [not *prejudice*].

pretty Overworked as an adverb meaning "rather" or "somewhat": *He was somewhat* [not *pretty*] *irked at the suggestion.*

previous to, prior to Wordy for *before.*

principal, principle *Principal* is an adjective meaning "foremost" or "major," a noun meaning "chief official," or, in finance, a noun meaning "capital sum." *Principle* is a noun only, meaning "rule" or "axiom." *Her principal reasons for confessing were her principles of right and wrong.*

proceed, precede See *precede, proceed.*

question of whether, question as to whether Wordy substitutes for *whether.*

raise, rise *Raise* means "lift" or "bring up" and takes a direct object: *The Kirks raise cattle.* Its main forms are *raise, raised, raised. Rise* means "get up" and does not take an object: *They must rise at dawn.* Its main forms are *rise, rose, risen.* (See also **4** p. 216.)

real, really In formal speech and writing, *real* should not be used as an adverb; *really* is the adverb and *real* an adjective. *Popular reaction to the announcement was really* [not *real*] *enthusiastic.*

reason is because Although colloquially common, this expression should be avoided in formal speech and writing. Use a *that* clause after *reason is: The reason he is absent is that* [not *is because*] *he is sick.* Or: *He is absent because he is sick.* (See also **4** p. 292.)

respectful, respective *Respectful* means "full of (or showing) respect": *Be respectful of other people. Respective* means "separate": *The French and the Germans occupied their respective trenches.*

rise, raise See *raise, rise.*

scarcely See *but, hardly, scarcely.*

sensual, sensuous *Sensual* suggests sexuality; *sensuous* means "pleasing to the senses." *Stirred by the sensuous scent of meadow grass and flowers, Cheryl and Paul found their thoughts growing increasingly sensual.*

set, sit *Set* means "put" or "place" and takes a direct object: *He sets the pitcher down.* Its main forms are *set, set, set. Sit* means "be seated" and does not take an object: *She sits on the sofa.* Its main forms are *sit, sat, sat.* (See also **4** p. 216.)

shall, will *Will* is the future-tense helping verb for all persons: *I will go, you will go, they will go.* The main use of *shall* is for first-person questions requesting an opinion or consent: *Shall I order a pizza? Shall we dance? Shall* can also be used for the first person when a formal effect is desired (*I shall expect you around three*), and it is occasionally used with the second or third person to express the speaker's determination (*You shall do as I say*).

should of See *have, of.*

sight, site, cite See *cite, sight, site.*

since *Since* mainly relates to time: *I've been waiting since noon.* But *since* is also often used to mean "because": *Since you ask, I'll tell you.* Revise sentences in which the word could have either meaning, such as *Since I studied physics, I have been planning to major in engineering.*

sit, set See *set, sit.*

site, cite, sight See *cite, sight, site.*

so Avoid using *so* alone or as a vague intensifier: *He was so late. So* needs to be followed by *that* and a clause that states a result: *He was so late that I left without him.*

somebody, some body; someone, some one *Somebody* and *someone* are indefinite pronouns; *some body* is a noun modified by *some;* and *some one* is a pronoun or an adjective modified by *some. Somebody ought to invent a shampoo that will give hair some body. Someone told Janine she should choose some one plan and stick with it.*

sometime, sometimes, some time *Sometime* means "at an indefinite time in the future": *Why don't you come up and see me sometime? Sometimes* means "now and then": *I still see my old friend Joe sometimes. Some time* means "a span of time": *I need some time to make the payments.*

somewheres Nonstandard for *somewhere.*

sort of, sort of a See *kind of, sort of, type of.*

such Avoid using *such* as a vague intensifier: *It was such a cold winter. Such* should be followed by *that* and a clause that states a result: *It was such a cold winter that Napoleon's troops had to turn back.*

such as See *like, such as.*

supposed to, used to In both these expressions, the *-d* is essential: *I used to* [not *use to*] *think so. He's supposed to* [not *suppose to*] *meet us.*

sure Colloquial when used as an adverb meaning *surely: James Madison sure was right about the need for the Bill of Rights.* If you merely want to be emphatic, use *certainly: Madison certainly was right.* If your goal is to convince a possibly reluctant reader, use *surely: Madison surely was right.*

sure and, sure to; try and, try to *Sure to* and *try to* are the correct forms: *Be sure to* [not *sure and*] *buy milk. Try to* [not *Try and*] *find some decent tomatoes.*

take, bring See *bring, take.*

than, as See *as, than.*

than, then *Than* is a conjunction used in comparisons, *then* an adverb indicating time: *Holmes knew then that Moriarty was wilier than he had thought.*

that, which *That* introduces an essential clause: *We should use the lettuce that Susan bought* (*that Susan bought* limits the lettuce to a particular lettuce). *Which* can introduce both essential and nonessential clauses, but many writers reserve *which* only for nonessential clauses:

The leftover lettuce, which is in the refrigerator, would make a good salad (*which is in the refrigerator* simply provides more information about the lettuce we already know of). Essential clauses (with *that* or *which*) are not set off by commas; nonessential clauses (with *which*) are. See also **5** pp. 304–06.

that, which, who   Use *that* for animals, things, and sometimes collective or anonymous people: *The rocket that failed cost millions. Infants that walk need constant tending.* Use *which* only for animals and things: *The river, which flows south, divides two countries.* Use *who* only for people and for animals with names: *Dorothy is the girl who visits Oz. Her dog, Toto, who accompanies her, gives her courage.*

their, there, they're   *Their* is the possessive form of *they: Give them their money. There* indicates place (*I saw her standing there*) or functions as an expletive (*There is a hole behind you*). *They're* is a contraction for *they are: They're going fast.*

theirselves   Nonstandard for *themselves.*

them   In standard American English, *them* does not serve as an adjective: *Those* [not *them*] *people want to know.*

then, than   See *than, then.*

these kind, these sort, these type, those kind   See *kind of, sort of, type of.*

this, these   *This* is singular: *this car* or *This is the reason I left. These* is plural: *these cars* or *These are not valid reasons.*

thru   A colloquial spelling of *through* that should be avoided in all academic and business writing.

to, too, two   *To* is a preposition; *too* is an adverb meaning "also" or "excessively"; and *two* is a number. *I too have been to Europe two times.*

too   Avoid using *too* as a vague intensifier: *Monkeys are too mean.* If you do use *too*, explain the consequences of the excessive quality: *Monkeys are too mean to make good pets.*

toward, towards   Both are acceptable, though *toward* is preferred. Use one or the other consistently.

try and, try to   See *sure and, sure to; try and, try to.*

type of   See *kind of, sort of, type of.* Don't use *type* without *of: It was a family type of* [not *type*] *restaurant.* Or better: *It was a family restaurant.*

uninterested   See *disinterested, uninterested.*

unique   *Unique* means "the only one of its kind" and so cannot sensibly be modified with words such as *very* or *most: That was a unique* [not *a very unique* or *the most unique*] *movie.*

usage, use   *Usage* refers to conventions, most often those of a language: *Is "hadn't ought" proper usage? Usage* is often misused in place of the noun *use: Wise use* [not *usage*] *of insulation can save fuel.*

use, utilize   *Utilize* can be used to mean "make good use of": *Many teachers utilize computers for instruction.* But for all other senses of "place in service" or "employ," prefer *use.*

used to   See *supposed to, used to.*

ProQuest. From "Privilege and Repression in the Digital Era: Rethinking the Sociopolitics of the Digital Divide," *www.proquest.com*. Used by permission.

Rosen, Ruth. "Search for Yesterday" by Ruth Rosen from *Watching Television* edited by Todd Gitlin. New York: Pantheon Books, 1986.

Selwyn, Neil. "The Social Processes of Learning to Use Computers" by Neil Selwyn, *Social Science Computer Review*, 23.1, 122. Copyright © 2005 by Sage Publications Inc. Journals. Reproduced with permission of Sage Publications Inc. Journals in the format Textbook via Copyright Clearance Center.

Sowell, Thomas. "Student Loans" from *Is Reality Optional? and Other Essays* by Thomas Sowell, 1993. Reprinted by permission of Thomas Sowell and Creators Syndicate, Inc.

Stout, David. From "Blind Win Court Ruling on U.S. Currency" by David Stout, *New York Times*, May 21, 2008. All rights reserved. Used by permission and protected by the Copyright Laws of the United States. The printing, copying, redistribution, or retransmission of the Material without express written permission is prohibited.

Tuchman, Barbara. "The Decline of Quality" by Barbara Tuchman, *New York Times*, November 2, 1980. Reprinted by the permission of Russell & Volkening as agents for the author. Copyright © 1980 by Barbara Tuchman.

UNFPA. "AIDS Clock" from the UNFPA.org website, *www.unfpa.org*, 2008. Reprinted with permission.

Woolf, Virginia. *The Waves*. New York: Harcourt, 1931.

Photos

Title page, clockwise from top left: Jamie Grill/Iconica/Getty; The Image Bank/Getty; Stone/Getty; Andersen Ross/Blend Images/Getty; David Fischer/Digital Vision/Getty; **1:** Image Source/Getty; **65:** NASA; **67:** Blend Images/Getty; **85:** *Boostup.org*; **109:** Getty; **110 and 113:** Michael Foujols/Corbis; **114:** Lydia Kibiuk/Society for Neuroscience December 2001; **115:** UNICEF; **141:** Photographer's Choice/Getty; **187:** Sabah Arar/AFP/Getty; **295:** Stone/Getty; **345:** Neo Vision/Getty; **369:** Digital Vision/Getty; **435, 461, 519, and 547:** Stone/Getty; **567:** The Image Bank/Getty.

Index

Throughout this handbook, the symbol ⟨CULTURE LANGUAGE⟩ signals topics for students whose first language or dialect is not standard American English. These topics can be tricky because they arise from rules in standard English that are quite different in other languages and dialects. Many of the topics involve significant cultural assumptions as well.

No matter what your language background, as a college student you are learning the culture of US higher education and the language that is used and shaped by that culture. The process is challenging, even for native speakers of standard American English. It requires not just writing clearly and correctly but also mastering conventions of developing, presenting, and supporting ideas. The challenge is greater if, in addition, you are trying to learn standard American English and are accustomed to other conventions. Several habits can help you succeed:

- **Read.** Besides course assignments, read newspapers, magazines, and books in English. The more you read, the more fluently and accurately you'll write.
- **Write.** Keep a journal in which you practice writing in English every day.
- **Talk and listen.** Take advantage of opportunities to hear and use English.
- **Ask questions.** Your instructors, tutors in the writing lab, and fellow students can clarify assignments and help you identify and solve writing problems.
- **Don't try for perfection.** No one writes perfectly, and the effort to do so can prevent you from expressing yourself fluently. View mistakes not as failures but as opportunities to learn.
- **Revise first; then edit.** Focus on each essay's ideas, support, and organization before attending to grammar and vocabulary. See the revision and editing checklists in **1** pp. 27 and 31.
- **Set editing priorities.** Concentrate first on any errors that interfere with clarity, such as problems with word order or subject-verb agreement.

The following index leads you to text discussions of topics that you may need help with. The pages marked * include exercises for self-testing.

Contents

CULTURE LANGUAGE **Guide on reverse**